MARYLAND

A New Guide to the

Old Line State

STUDIES IN MARYLAND HISTORY AND CULTURE
SPONSORED BY THE HALL OF RECORDS COMMISSION
OF THE DEPARTMENT OF GENERAL SERVICES,
GEORGE R. LEWIS, SECRETARY

SERIES EDITOR
EDWARD C. PAPENFUSE, STATE ARCHIVIST

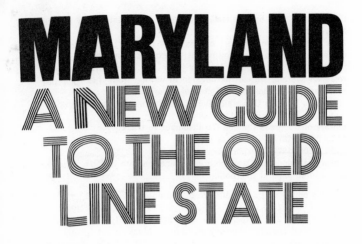

MARYLAND
A NEW GUIDE TO THE OLD LINE STATE

COMPILED AND EDITED BY

EDWARD C. PAPENFUSE · GREGORY A. STIVERSON
SUSAN A. COLLINS · LOIS GREEN CARR

THE JOHNS HOPKINS UNIVERSITY PRESS
Baltimore and London

Manufactured in the United States of America

The Johns Hopkins University Press, Baltimore, Maryland 21218

The Johns Hopkins Press Ltd., London

Library of Congress Catalog Card Number 76-17224

ISBN 0-8018-1874-5 (hardcover)

ISBN 0-8018-1871-0 (paperback)

Library of Congress Cataloging in Publication data will be found on the last printed page of this book.

Photo credits. M. E. Warren: pp. 5, 35, 49, 53, 55, 59, 65, 73, 103, 113, 135, 141, 151, 157, 165, 177, 183, 197, 205, 211, 215, 223, 225, 241, 243, 249, 257, 277, 279, 291, 309, 331, 337, 345, 375, 391, 405, 409, 415, 426, 439. Richard Linfield, courtesy of Charles Mock: p. 11. Baltimore Promotion Council, Inc.: pp. 21, 31 (Jack Engeman), 227. State of Maryland, Department of Economic and Community Development, Division of Tourist Development: pp. 23 (Leet-Melbrook, Inc.), 67 (B. L. Braun), 79, 81, 91, 127, 129, 147, 167, 203, 271 (Richard Weeks), 287, 295, 447 (Bob Willis). Deep Creek Lake–Garrett County Promotion Council: p. 107. *Kent County News*: p. 117. *Marylander and Herald*, Somerset County: p. 191. Special Services Department, Baltimore County Public Library: pp. 299, 305. Maryland Jockey Club: p. 399.

CONTENTS

PREFACE

Until the advent of the railroad in the 1830s, there was little reason to consider travel in the United States a form of recreation or a leisurely pastime. Public transportation was no better than private, and both were hard on the traveler. If you were en route by stage from Philadelphia to Baltimore in 1797 you might spend your first night on the road at Elkton in Cecil County after a harrowing forty-seven-mile journey. The next day you would rise at 3 A.M. and travel fifteen miles to the Susquehanna, have a quick breakfast at an inn, ferry across the river, and continue for thirty-seven miles to Baltimore, arriving about 5 P.M., dirty, tired, and hardly up to sightseeing. Isaac Weld, who went this way in 1795, wrote that the road was so bad on the jaunt before breakfast that "the driver frequently had to call the passengers in the stage to lean out of the carriage first at one side then at the other, to prevent it from oversetting in the deep ruts with which the road abound[ed]." Travel by water could be more comfortable, if weather permitted, but in most cases took longer than travel by land. The journey from Elkton to Baltimore by boat took approximately sixteen hours, while the uncomfortable stage ride took about fourteen and a half.

If public transportation was arduous at best, travel by horseback was not any better. The roads, if they existed, were not clearly marked, and the accommodations often left much to be desired. The average distance traveled in a day was under thirty miles, and the journey was invariably grueling. In 1765 William Gregory rode thirty miles from New Castle, Delaware, to Maryland on his way to the Rock Hall Ferry and points south. By the time he reached his first night's lodging—having once lost his way for lack of signposts—his horse was exhausted, his own "posteriors gelded, and the side of his head swelled up like a pumpkin occasioned by a cold" he had caught in Philadelphia. To make matters worse, the inn was crowded and a noisy party kept him awake most of the night.

What few travel guides existed before the railroads were built were largely limited to functional works such as Christopher Colles's *A Survey of the Roads of the United States of America* (1789) and Moore and Jones's *Traveller's Directory; or, A Pocket Companion* (1802). Both contained "trip tickets" that showed the courses of the main road, "with descriptions of the places through which it passes, and intersections of the cross roads." Moore and Jones also included "an account of such remarkable objects as are generally interesting to travellers," making it clear that if the traveler had any time to spare to see the sights it would be in the major cities, and even then the tour could only be cursory. En route between cities, stops were expected to be made for food and lodging only, and little detail about the surrounding area was thought to be necessary or of interest. For example, Moore and Jones describe Elkton as being "forty-seven miles and a quarter from Philadelphia, a post and considerable trading town, at the head of navigation on the forks of the two branches of Elk River, about three miles above French

Town, where the packets from Baltimore land and embark passengers etc. to and from Philadelphia. Elkton consists of one principal street; it has a courthouse, a jail and an academy."

In the second half of the nineteenth century, as the rail system in the United States expanded, innumerable travelers' guides appeared. The most detailed were those to the major cities, such as *Taintor's Route and City Guides—New York to Philadelphia, Baltimore, and Washington.* This particular guide, in addition to providing city tours, briefly described what was to be seen at train stations in between cities. The entry for Elkton in the 1876 edition of Taintor's guide consists of the following:

ELKTON—Cecil County, Md. 46 m. fr. Phila. fr. Baltimore, 52. This is the county seat of Cecil County and is located a little above the junction of Great and little Elk Creeks. It was settled in 1694 by Swedish fishermen, and was called Head of Elk till 1787, when it received its present name. The prominent buildings, besides the venerable courthouse, are the Elkton Academy, and the Methodist, Episcopal, Presbyterian, and Catholic churches.

With the Centennial Exhibition in Philadelphia in 1876 sightseeing came into its own, and people began to think of traveling great distances purely for amusement. In that year J. B. Lippincott published a "Visitors' Guide" to the exhibition, the only one "sold on the exhibition grounds" and one which, over a six-month period, one in every five Americans had the opportunity to purchase in person.

By 1893, the year of the Columbian exhibition, the leading publisher of European travel guides, the Leipzig firm of Karl Baedeker, decided it was time to publish a comprehensive handbook for travelers in the United States. By then Baedeker guides had become famous in Europe not only for telling the traveler how to get from place to place but also for interpreting, often in great detail, what travelers would see along the way and at their destinations. The prefaces for Baedeker handbooks were all essentially the same.

The chief objects of the Handbook . . . are to supply the traveller with a few remarks on the progress of civilization and art in these interesting countries; to render him as far as possible independent of the embarrassing and expensive services of commissionaires, guides and other of the same Fraternity; to place him in a position to employ his time, his money, and his energy to the best advantage; and thus to enable him to derive the greatest possible amount of pleasure and instruction from his tour.

The Baedeker guide to the United States was written more for the English visitor than for the traveling American. Under the heading "General Hints" could be found such observations as: "The average Englishman will probably find the chief physical discomforts in the dirt of the city streets, the roughness of the country roads, the winter overheating of hotels and railway cars (70–75 degrees Fahrenheit by no means unusual) and in many places the habit of spitting on the floor."

This guide was revised for the last time in 1909, and nothing comparable was undertaken to aid travelers in the United States until 1935. In that year the Works Progress Administration (WPA) launched the Writers' Project to provide relief for unemployed writers by assigning them the primary task of compiling comprehensive travel guides for each of the states. According to the principal architect and editor of the American Guide Series, Katherine Kellock, the inspiration was the Baedeker guide to Russia, which had kept her from getting hopelessly lost and taught her much on a journey to Tashkent during World War I.

Whatever the inspiration for launching the project, by 1935 there was undoubtedly a need both for employment for writers hard hit by the depression and for travel guides to each of the states. Since the appearance of the 1909 American Baedeker, a revolution in transportation had occurred. The automobile, especially with the introduction of relatively cheap models like the Model T Ford, enabled the average American family to tour the countryside at their leisure, unhindered by train or bus schedules. In 1901 the first automobile *Blue Book* appeared, and by 1920 it had grown to thirteen volumes covering the entire United States and southern Canada. These books were advertised in 1920 as telling "you where to go, and how to get there, giving complete maps of every motor road, running directions at every fork and turn, with mileages, all points of local or historical interest, state motor laws, hotel and garage accommodations, ferry and steamship schedules and rates. A veritable motorist's encyclopedia." In fact, these volumes made little mention of what was to be seen along the way. Historical information was sparse, sandwiched in as footnotes between maps and advertisements. Most of the text was given over to dry-as-dust driving instructions, as in this fifty-six-mile tour from Baltimore to Elkton in a 1922 Maryland version of the *Blue Book*, written by the Automobile Club of Maryland.

BALTIMORE TO PHILADELPHIA, PA. 104.7 M
Route 20
Baltimore to Elkton 56.1 M

0.0	From Automobile Club of Maryland Building, **Baltimore,** east on Mt. Royal ave.
0.1	**Left** at trolley on Charles st., over R. R. viaduct and across North ave., leaving trolley 0.5.
1.4	**Right** on E. 33rd st.; into Boulevard.
3.1	**Left** on Harford road, next **right** on Erdman ave.
3.9	**Half**-left with trolley on Belair road; keep **left** 11.4.
15.9	**Left** fork at **Kingsville.**
23.2	**Left** at Inn, **Bel Air,** next **right** 23.3.
28.9	**Right** fork, **Churchville; left** at end 30.4.
35.0	**Left** at stone church beyond R. R.'s, **Aberdeen.**
39.5	**Left** on Union ave., **Havre de Grace.**
39.9	Curve **right** across long toll bridge, Susquehanna River, thru **Perryville** 41; **Charlestown** 47; **Northeast** 50, into **Elkton** 56.1.

To many, especially to those involved in the creation of the Writers' Project, what was needed was a Baedeker for the motorist, what one relief agency employee called "a sort of public Baedeker, which would point out to the curious traveler the points of real travel value in each state and county." Mrs. Kellock and the Washington staff supplied comprehensive instructions to each state project on how to go about writing their guide, and by December, 1935, a staff of twenty-five people were at work on a guide for Maryland.

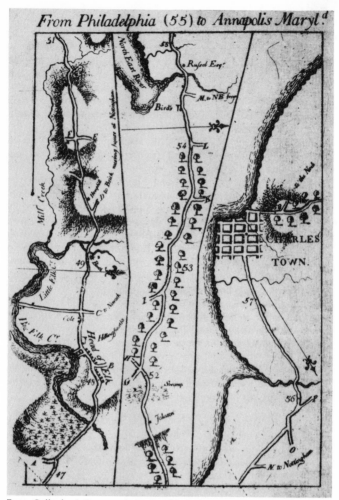

From Colles's *A Survey of the Roads of the United States of America* (1789)

It took four difficult and often controversial years to compile, write, and edit the 543-page *Maryland: A Guide to the Old Line State,* which Oxford University Press published in the summer of 1940. The first third of the book was devoted to interpretive essays which, in terms of staff time, took about three times as long to complete as the tours that composed the rest of the book. Serious field work on the tours did not begin until January, 1938, by which time the Maryland staff had been cut from a record high of seventy-five people in September, 1936, to sixty-two. By December, 1938, the staff had been reduced still further, to forty-seven. During the life of the project the average pay per worker fluctuated between $78.00 and $88.00 per month. In an article in the *Evening Sun* for February 13, 1939, the total cost of the project to that date was put at $165,000, a figure not far from the truth, and the continuing payroll necessary to complete the guide was estimated at $3,200 a month. By February, 1939, the tours were still in a rudimentary state. Just over a week prior to the appearance of the *Sun* article a conference had been held with the Baltimore staff which, in the words of two recently hired editors, H. Bowen Smith and Frank J. Reall, placed "on our shoulders the onus of the sorry results of three years of trying to 'muddle through.' " They warned that the work thus far boded a "badly written, inaccurate" guide.

Katherine Kellock would recall seventeen years later that, although her name did not appear in the guide, she had had

final responsibility for it, within the limits under which the WPA project was operated. I had been one of the promoters of the national project and ultimately became "Tour and Special Volume Editor" for the whole series. I planned the tour coverage for all books, directed collection of the material, edited or supervised the editing of all tour copy, and saw it through the press in most cases. It happens that the Maryland project suffered under heavy disadvantages and it became necessary, at a time when the national project was broken up [1939], for me to take over preparation of the whole book for press, in close cooperation with Mr. Bowen Smith and Mr. Frank Reall. Among us we met the [press] deadline [of January 30, 1940], but all of us were aware of shortcomings and in some cases probable inaccuracies. I myself re-wrote at least a third of the copy, adding material and so on.

In two years time, with staff equivalent to forty full-time employees and at an approximate cost of $77,000, the Maryland Writers' Project produced 348 printed pages of tours of the state. They were well received, and the book sold some 15,000 copies before it went out of print in the late 1950s. Whether or not it was worth the cost is a matter for historians to debate; the project did employ "writers" who might otherwise have gone hungry, and it did, after much pain and travail, produce a volume that reflected well on the whole series.

By 1953, however, the guide was badly outdated and in need of revision, and the Maryland Hall of Records was assigned the task of bringing out a new edition which, because of staff limitations, would be devoted exclusively to tours. A controversy over the terms of the original publishing contract held up work on the revisions until 1957, when with some fanfare, James H. Bready announced in his Baltimore *Sun* column, "Books and Authors," that Lois Green Clark (under the direction of Dr. Morris L. Radoff, the State Archivist, and with the special assistance of Wilbur Hunter, director of the Peale Museum) had begun work on the new guide. As Bready pointed out, "the two biggest changes since 1940 are roads and houses. The 40 tours that filled half [*sic*] the original edition utilize roads that in many stretches have been or soon will be superseded by no-town, no-pause superhighways. . . . Since 1940, again, several scores of old Maryland houses have been bought by persons of means. . . . Undirected, the visitor soon gets lost. He is also uninvited, most of the year, and Mrs. Clark is unpleasantly aware that some manorial millionaires are eager to have their homes deliberately omitted."

In 1957 Bready estimated that it would take at least two years for the revised Maryland guide to be completed and made commercially available. It has taken considerably longer. Mrs. Clark, now Dr. Lois Green Carr, Historian of the St. Mary's City Commission, found it to be an enormous task for one person working part-time to revise, correct, and edit such a large manuscript. When she left the Hall of Records in 1964, the task had not yet been accomplished. Not until June, 1975, was a rough draft ready for reworking and extensive editing by the editor-authors now listed on the title page (Dr. Carr graciously gave of her own time to redo and update some of her earlier work). With the completion of the first rough draft of the tours, prepared by Dr. Carr and to a lesser extent by her successor on the project, Sarah Salter, work commenced in earnest on checking, rewriting, and editing. Sue Collins was on the road for two months, covering every mile of every tour and making corrections wherever necessary; in all, she logged over 6,500 miles. Dr. Papenfuse and Dr. Stiverson, with the aid of Dr. Carr, rewrote and edited all the tours. Nine months after they had begun, on October 23, 1975, an 800-page, 175,000-word manuscript containing less than 20 percent of the text of the original guide was ready for delivery to The Johns Hopkins University Press. On November 2, 1975, James Bready could at last confidently headline his "Books and Authors" column in the *Sun:* "A New Guide Soon to Arrive."

Many people, too many to mention everyone by name, have worked long and hard over the past twenty-three years to make this new guide a reality. Dr. Morris L. Radoff, archivist and records administrator for the State of Maryland for thirty-five years and now archivist emeritus, deserves immeasurable credit for keeping alive the idea of revising the old guide. Without his perseverance the project would have been forgotten long ago. Since the Hall of Records Commission was incorporated into his department in 1968, George Lewis, secretary of General Services, has made certain that the new guide received the funding it deserved. The staff of the Hall of Records, including the summer interns, contributed in many ways to our keeping pace with what proved to be a hectic production schedule. Leslie Newman did a superb job of typing the final manuscript. J. G. Goellner and the staff of The Johns Hopkins University Press have done outstanding work at all stages of publication from design to marketing, and to them we are especially grateful.

We are indebted to M. E. Warren, of Annapolis, who permitted us to feature his splendid photographs in this volume. We also thank John J. Nelson, of the Maryland Department of Economic and Community Development, who allowed us free access to the photographic files of the Division of Tourist Development and who gave us permission to reproduce whatever we chose. Dave Willis and Mianna Jopp of his staff were especially helpful. Particular mention must also be made of the cooperation of the State Highway Administration, on whose excellent county maps the tour maps in this volume are based, and of the help that William H. Jabine, II, of the Department of Natural Resources, gave us in the preparation of the "Maryland at a Glance" section. Our production schedule could never have been met without the assistance of Mary Donaldson, who did much more than compile the index. Mary's experience as an editor and proofreader proved invaluable, and her patience and good humor helped us immeasurably at various critical stages in the preparation of this book.

Every effort has been made to make the manuscript as accurate and readable as possible, but in a book of this type factual errors inevitably occur. We accept full responsibility for them, of course, but would greatly appreciate readers bringing them to our attention along with any suggestions they might have for improving future editions. Any correspondence about the new guide should be addressed to: *Maryland: A New Guide to the Old Line State*, P.O. Box 828, Annapolis, Maryland 21404.

EDITORS' NOTE: Main tours are set in text type. Subtours and town tours are set in reduced type. A bullet ● appears whenever the traveler begins a subtour or backtracks along a subtour. Italic type has been used to designate places that are singled out in boldface type elsewhere in the same tour.

Tour maps and town maps are intended to supplement, not take the place of, ordinary highway maps. Town tours are meant to be walking tours unless stated otherwise.

All buildings and properties are **private** unless specifically designated as being open to the public.

MARYLAND AT A GLANCE

Population. 3,922,399 in 1970 census; ranked 18th among the states.

Area. In square miles: land, 9,874; inland water, 703; Chesapeake Bay, 1,726; total, 12,303. Ranks 42nd among the states.

Physiography. Divided into three provinces with progressively higher altitudes from east to west; Coastal Plain province extends from Atlantic Ocean to Fall Line; Piedmont, or "Foothill," province from Fall Line to crest of the Catoctin Mountains; Appalachian province, from crest of Catoctin Mountains to western boundary of state. Mean elevation, 350 feet; maximum elevation, 3,360 feet on Backbone Mountain.

Distances. Longest east-west, 198.6 miles, from Fairfax Stone to Delaware Line. North-south, 125.5 miles, from Pennsylvania Line to Virginia Line at Smith Point on south-shore mouth of the Potomac River. Shortest north-south, 1.9 miles, from Pennsylvania Line to south bank of Potomac River, near Hancock. Farthest points northwest corner to southeast corner at Atlantic Ocean, 254.7 miles.

Climate. Generally moderate, the climate varies from mild to hot in summer and in winter from moderate in the east and south to very cold in the mountainous region. Average annual rainfall, 41.65"; average annual snowfall, 26.70"; temperature average 64.4° F. maximum, 43.7° F. minimum, and 54° F. mean.

Chesapeake Bay. 195 miles long, with 1,726 square miles in Maryland and 1,511 square miles in Virginia. Varies in width from 3 to 20 miles. Navigable for ocean-going ships and has two outlets to the Atlantic Ocean, one through the Chesapeake and Delaware Canal, one through the mouth of the Bay between the Virginia capes.

Chief Rivers. Potomac, Wye, Patuxent, Susquehanna, Choptank, Nanticoke, Elk, Magothy, Patapsco, Sassafras, South, Severn, Gunpowder, Tred Avon, Bush, Miles, Chester, Northeast, Wicomico, Pocomoke, and Great Bohemia.

Boating Waters. Twenty-three rivers and bays with more than 400 miles of water tributary to the Chesapeake Bay; Chincoteague Bay with 35 miles of water accessible to and from the Atlantic Ocean.

Water Frontage. Sixteen of the 23 counties and Baltimore City border on tidal water. Length of tidal shoreline, including islands, 3,190 miles.

Forest Area. More than 2,970,000 acres, or approximately 47 percent of the land surface. Chief forest products are lumber, pulpwood, and piling. Nine state forests and one state forest nursery cover 118,362 acres.

State Parks and Recreation Areas. Thirty-four operational state parks covering 63,525 acres; 66 lakes and ponds open to public fishing; 9 state forests and portions of nine state parks open to public hunting; 31 wildlife management areas covering 64,799 acres open to public hunting; 3 natural environment areas containing approximately 5,700 acres.

Manufactures, 1975. Number of establishments, 2,471; total employees, 252,000; total payroll, $2,521,456,380; total value added by manufactures, $4,686,400,000. Most important manufactures: food and kindred products, primary metal products, electric and electronic products, transportation equipment, chemical and allied products, machinery (except electrical).

Agriculture, 1974. 17,600 farms covering 2,940,000 acres. Total farm receipts, $621,919,000; most valuable farm products: poultry and poultry products, $167,395,000; field crops, $198,163,000; dairy products, $130,-

816,000; value of crops: corn, $85,844,000; soybeans, $54,830,000; vegetables, $24,872,000; tobacco, $28,556,000; fruits, nuts, and berries, $8,665,000; value of livestock products: cattle, $29,265,000; hogs, $19,-189,000; eggs, $18,746,000; workers employed on farms, 31,000.

Mineral Production, 1974. Stone, 15,853,000 short tons, value, $45,183,000; sand and gravel, 11,946,000 short tons, value, $26,595,000; bituminous coal, 2,174,000 short tons, value, $26,100,000; clays, 867,000 short tons, value, $2,023,000; natural gas, 80,000,000 cubic feet, value, $26,000; peat, 3,000 tons; value of mineral production which cannot be itemized separately, $44,019,000; total value of all mineral production, $145,386,-000.

Seafood Production, 1975. Fish, 14,915,770 pounds, with dockside value of $2,127,551; crabs, 25,901,758 pounds, with dockside value of $5,145,514; oysters, 2,359,749 bushels, with a dockside value of $12,-947,149; clams, including soft-shell, hard-shell, and surf, 6,465,711 pounds, with a dockside value of $2,070,981. Maryland leads the nation in oyster production and ranks second in blue crab production.

Port of Baltimore, 1975. One of the leading ports in the United States, handling in excess of 55,000,000 tons of cargo in 1975, 60 percent of which was foreign commerce and 40 percent coastal trade. Baltimore is the second ranked container cargo port on the East Coast of the United States, with more than 3,000,000 tons moved during 1975. Baltimore also is the largest port of entry for the importation of automobiles in the world, with 135,000 units arriving during the year. Other chief imports are ore, chemicals, petroleum products, gypsum rock, lumber, rolled and finished steel products, fertilizer and materials, unrefined copper, inedible molasses, sugar, and general cargo. Chief exports are grains, machinery, coal and coke, iron and steel scrap, iron and steel semifinished products, earth moving equipment, fertilizers, and general cargo.

Incorporated Cities with Population over 10,000, 1970. Baltimore, 905,759; Rockville, 41,564; Hagerstown, 35,862; Bowie, 35,028; Cumberland, 29,724; Annapolis, 29,592; College Park, 26,156; Frederick, 23,641; Takoma Park, 18,433; Greenbelt, 18,199; Salisbury, 15,252; Hyattsville, 14,998; New Carrollton, 13,395; Aberdeen, 12,375; Cambridge, 11,595; Laurel, 10,525.

STATE SYMBOLS

Great Seal of Maryland. The Great Seal of Maryland is used by the governor and the secretary of state to authenticate the acts of the legislature and for other official purposes. The first Great Seal was brought over during the early days of the colony. It remained in use, although slightly altered, until the Revolution. The State of Maryland adopted a new seal similar in form and spirit to those of the other states. After the passage of a hundred years, Maryland readopted its old seal. Only the reverse of this seal has ever been cut. The obverse is, however, still considered as part of the seal and is used, among other things, for decorating public buildings.

The reverse consists of an escutcheon, or shield, bearing the Calvert and Crossland arms quartered. Above is an earl's coronet and a full-faced helmet. The escutcheon is supported on one side by a farmer and on the other by a fisherman, symbolizing Lord Baltimore's two estates of Maryland and Avalon. The Calvert motto on the scroll is *Fatti maschii parole femine.* The Latin legend on the border is translated "with favor wilt thou compass us as with a shield," the last verse of Psalm 5 as it appears in the Vulgate. The date, 1632, refers to the year the charter was granted to Lord Baltimore for the colony of Maryland.

The obverse of the seal shows Lord Baltimore as a knight in full armor mounted on a charger. The inscription translated is "Cecillus, Absolute Lord of Maryland and Avalon, Baron of Baltimore." Avalon was the name of Lord Baltimore's grant in Newfoundland.

State Flag. Maryland's flag bears the arms of the Calvert and Crossland families. Calvert was the family name of the Lords Baltimore, who founded Maryland. Crossland was the family of the mother of the first Lord Baltimore. The escutcheon, or shield, in the Maryland seal bears the same arms. The flag in its present form was first flown on October 25, 1888, on the Gettysburg Battlefield during ceremonies dedicating monuments to the Maryland regiments of the Army of the Potomac. It was officially adopted as the state flag in 1904. The cross botonny affixed to the top of the flagstaff was made the official ornament in 1945.

State Song. The Maryland State song, "Maryland, My Maryland," was written by a Marylander who was living in the South during the War between the States. Its words reflect the bitter feelings of the composer concerning the riots that occurred in Baltimore in 1861.

State Fish. In 1965, the striped bass or rockfish (*Roccus saxatilis*) was designated as the official fish of the State of Maryland.

State Tree. Maryland has chosen for its tree the white oak (*Quercus alba*). The magnificent specimen shown among the illustrations in this volume is known as the Wye Oak and is located at Wye Mills on the Eastern Shore (*see* Tour 12b).

State Bird. The Baltimore oriole *(Icterus galbula)* is the official Maryland bird. Special provisions have been made for its protection in the state.

State Dog. In 1964, the Chesapeake Bay retriever was declared the official dog of Maryland.

State Flower. The black-eyed Susan *(Rudbeckia hirta)* is the official Maryland flower, designated by the General Assembly in 1918. A yellow daisy, or coneflower, it blooms in late summer.

Maryland Sport. In 1962, the age-old equestrian sport of jousting was proclaimed as the official sport of the State of Maryland.

State Insect. The Baltimore Checkerspot butterfly *(Euphydryas phaeton)* was declared to be the official arthropodic emblem of the State of Maryland in 1973.

Maryland's Nicknames. Although Maryland's nicknames are not official state symbols, the state is known both as the Old Line State and the Free State.

According to some historians, Gen. George Washington bestowed the appellation Old Line State on Maryland because of the magnificent performance of regular troops of the line in several of the more important engagements in the Revolutionary War. The troops of the Maryland Line ranked among the finest in the Continental Army.

The nickname "Free State" is of twentieth-century origin. It was created by Hamilton Owens, editor of the Baltimore *Sun.* Sometime in 1923, Congressman William D. Upshaw of Georgia, a firm supporter of Prohibition, denounced Maryland as a traitor to the Union because it had refused to pass a state enforcement act. Mr. Owens thereupon wrote a mock-serious editorial entitled "The Maryland Free State," arguing that Maryland should secede from the Union. The irony in the editorial was subtle, and on second thought Mr. Owens decided not to print it. The idea stuck in his mind, however, and he later used it in other editorials. The nickname caught on quickly, and the term "Free State" is heard almost as frequently as "Old Line State."

MARYLAND
A New Guide to the
Old Line State

1

(Philadelphia)–PENNSYLVANIA LINE–BEL AIR–BALTIMORE–HYATTSVILLE–DISTRICT OF COLUMBIA LINE; 83.2 m.
U.S. 1

U.S. 1, once the lifeline of the seaboard states from Maine to Florida, has been superseded by a system of limited-access and toll highways. Nevertheless, automobile and truck traffic has increased so much that the route is still heavily traveled. North of Baltimore, the highway passes through open countryside. The roadside itself is heavily developed with commercial establishments, however, so the beautiful farmlands just beyond are often obscured.

The unappealing character of much of U.S. 1 is not peculiar to Maryland. From Maine to Florida, U.S. 1 began as Indian trails that in time became wagon and cattle roads between settlements. As motor transportation was introduced and expanded, the roads were paved and repaved. By the time of World War II, the worst of the curves had been eliminated and the roadway had been widened, but it still remained a relic of horse-and-buggy days. After the war, attempts to improve the road were abandoned in favor of completely new and modern parallel superhighways.

1a. PENNSYLVANIA LINE–BEL AIR–BALTIMORE CITY LINE; 42.6 m.
U.S. 1

This section of U.S. 1 does not appear on any pre-Revolutionary map, but from Baltimore to the Susquehanna River the route is approximately the same as that shown on maps drawn in the 1790s, except that the river crossing was then located north of Conowingo at *Bald Friar*. In colonial times, a road from Bald Friar to New Castle, Delaware, followed the present Md. 273 across Cecil County just south of the Pennsylvania line, with a branch turning north towards Philadelphia at *Calvert*. Present-day U.S. 1 follows this old route (a few miles west of Rising Sun) for a short distance.

U.S. 1 crosses the **Maryland-Pennsylvania Line,** 0.0 m., in **SYLMAR,** about fifty-three miles southwest of Philadelphia.

At 3.8 m. turn left at the junction with Md. 273, the main route of the side tour.

● Md. 273, the old road to New Castle, crosses land that was a source of contention between the Penns and the Calverts from 1681, when Charles II granted Pennsylvania to William Penn, until the Mason-Dixon Line was completed in 1768. The area was sparsely settled in 1680, the year in which Lord Baltimore granted a 32,000-acre tract known as Susquehanna Manor to his kinsman, George Talbot. The northern boundary of Talbot's grant reached five miles into what is now Pennsylvania, and Baltimore probably hoped that by issuing the grant he could better assert his right to all of the land in the area. As a member of the council and a colonel of the rangers in this area, Talbot was one of the most important residents of Cecil County. Talbot's Maryland career came to an end in 1684, however, when he murdered Christopher

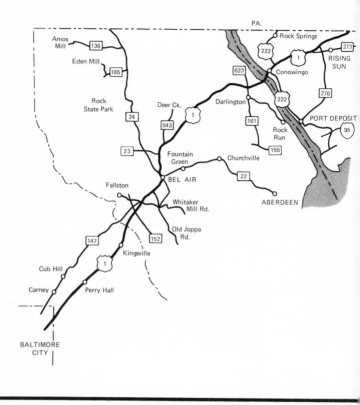

TOUR 1a

Rousby, the King's Collector (*see below*, Mount Ararat). In the meantime, the proprietor of Pennsylvania, William Penn, claimed much of Cecil County, countering Lord Baltimore's grant to Talbot by issuing grants in his own name for the *Nottingham Lots* and a tract on Iron Hill (*see* Tour 2a). Beginning about 1700, Quaker settlers from Pennsylvania and Scotch-Irish Presbyterians from New Castle began to arrive in the area in numbers. Thomas Cresap (*see* Tour 8), who later pioneered in the west, was active in the border difficulties that ensued. In 1738 a temporary dividing line between the two provinces was accepted by both sides.

At 1.4 m. on Md. 273 is the junction with Md. 276.

Go right on this to a junction with Md. 269, 0.8 m. To the right, Md. 269 provides a scenic route through hilly countryside to the steep gorge of Octoraro Creek and the northern tip of *Port Deposit*, 6.6 m. at the junction with U.S. 222 at *Rock Run Mill* (R).

● Continuing south, Md. 276 comes to **West Nottingham Presbyterian Church** and **West Nottingham Academy**, 1.4 m. The founding of this school was one of the few consequences of the Great Revival (1739–40) in Maryland, where the religious upheaval experienced in most of the other colonies was hardly felt. The early Scotch-Irish settlers of the area had established a Presbyterian congregation by 1724, but the evangelist George Whitefield's visit to Cecil County in 1739 split the congregation into New Light (revivalist) and Old Light groups. In 1744, the New Lights built their own church near *Rising Sun* and called Rev. Samuel Finley to be their minister. Finley immediately established what is now the West Nottingham Academy, attracting pupils from a wide area. Among them were Richard Stockton and Benjamin Rush, signers of the Declaration of Independence from New Jersey and Pennsylvania respectively.

Finley left Cecil County in 1761 to become president of the College of New Jersey (now Princeton University), and the New Light Church soon declined. In 1792, members of the church finally joined forces with the other congregation (the Presbyterian leadership of the colonies had declared the split mended as early as 1758), and in 1804 the reunited group finished the present brick church, which evidently underwent Gothic remodeling later in the century. The school was revitalized by the reunion, receiving a charter from the legislature in 1812. The academy was moved to its present location by the church in 1821. The oldest academy building still standing is the low, multigabled brick structure with a small carpenter-Gothic frame bell tower, which was erected in 1865. Today, West Nottingham is a Presbyterian coeducational boarding and day school, well known for its innovative teaching methods.

At 3.7 m. Md. 276 turns right. Here is the **Cummings Tavern** (R), an old 2½-story stone house, now part of a gasoline service station. Nearby, the Comte de Rochambeau's heavy artillery camped on September 9, 1781, before fording the Susquehanna at *Bald Friar.*

At 4.8 m. is an entrance to the former *Bainbridge Naval Training Center* (L), and at 6.1 m. (R) is the entrance lane to **Anchor and Hope Farm.** The old stone house, believed to have been built in the late seventeenth century, stands on a great bluff above *Port Deposit* and the Susquehanna River. During the eighteenth and early nineteenth centuries, the Creswell family owned the estate, including what is now the upper portion of Port Deposit, and operated Creswell's Ferry across the river. The ferry ticket office, with its wicket window, remains in a corner of the living room, which evidently was once the main room of a 1½-story house (a second story has been added). The room still retains two great fireplaces, a box stair behind the chimney, and exposed beaded beams. George Washington took Creswell's Ferry on May 8, 1775, on his way to Philadelphia for the session of the Continental Congress that chose him commander in chief of the American forces.

Md. 276 continues to *Port Deposit* and a junction with U.S. 222 at 6.7 m.

● Md. 273, the main route of the side tour, continues east to **RISING SUN,** 1.9 m., a banking and trading center for grain and dairy farmers. In 1807, the town contained only seven or eight houses and was known as Summer Hill, but by 1817 the name of the town had been changed to Rising Sun, perhaps after a tavern of that name.

CALVERT, 6.9 m. at the junction with Md. 272, is on the **Nottingham Lots,** a township of 18,000 acres laid out in thirty-seven lots of about 500 acres each. In 1702 these lots were granted by William Penn to eighteen Quaker families who had migrated from New Castle the preceding year. The lots were part of the land held in dispute by the Penns and the Calverts (*see above*). According to tradition, Penn himself selected the site for the **East Nottingham Friends Meeting House** (R), donating forty acres of land for its use. By 1724, the 2½-story brick end of the meeting house had been built to replace a log house erected about 1709. The stone end of the structure was added in 1752, and after a fire in 1810 the interior was remodeled. For about three months in 1778, Gen. William Smallwood used the meeting house as a hospital, and some of his soldiers who were taken there are buried in the graveyard. Lafayette's men camped nearby on April 11, 1781, on their march to Yorktown. To reach the church, turn right on Md. 272; then take the first right to the meeting house.

The meeting house has been restored, and a collection of artifacts and documents that illustrate the establishment of the Nottingham Lots, the boundary disputes that followed, and the Mason-Dixon Survey is on display. The brick meeting house area was the home of Benjamin Chandlee (1728–94), an inventor and manufacturer of scientific, mathematical, and chemical instruments. Chandlee's brass dial clocks are collectors' items today.

North of Calvert, Md. 272 leads to the **Pennsylvania Line,** 1.5 m.

● South of Calvert, Md. 272 passes through the village of **ZION,** 1.9 m., and crosses Northeast Creek at 4.0 m. On the old road just to the left is the **Gilpin's Covered Bridge,** which at 119 feet is the longest covered wooden bridge still standing in Maryland. The bridge is of the bowstring type, with great arches made of single timbers that stretch from bank to bank providing support for the structure. The timbers were warped to the required shape by balancing them on stumps and gradually pulling each one down with chains.

Md. 272 intersects the Kennedy Expressway and Tour 33 at 5.3 m., and joins U.S. 40 and Tour 2a at 7.0 m. From here Md. 272 becomes a side tour of Tour 2a.

● On Md. 273 at the crossroads of **BLUEBALL,** 9.5 m., the **Blueball Tavern** (L) (private, but visible from the road) is a long, 2½-story stone building painted white. At one time, the main roads from Lancaster County, Pennsylvania, and New Castle, Delaware, met at this junction. In 1710, Andrew Job established a tavern near this spot on the edge of the Nottingham Lots. In 1718, he supposedly bought an indentured servant named Elizabeth Maxwell. A niece of Daniel Defoe, Elizabeth had run away to America at eighteen years of age. After seven years of servitude, she married Job's son, Thomas. When Elizabeth finally wrote home she found that her mother had died and that she had inherited her mother's furniture and other personal property, which were later sent to her by Defoe.

Three roads intersect Md. 273 where it crosses Little Elk Creek at 12.0 m. A short distance along Rock Church Road (the second road on the left) and delightfully situated on the creek under a rocky hill-

Fox hunt

side is **Rock Presbyterian Church,** a stone structure believed to have been built in 1761. In 1844 the interior was renovated in an attractive Gothic-Revival style. Beside it is a small stone Session House, which for many years doubled as a schoolhouse.

● At 12.2 m. on Md. 273 turn right on Fairhill Drive to **FAIR HILL,** 0.8 m., a small town at the junction of Md. 273 and 213. On the northeast corner of the junction stands the **Mitchell House** (private), a 2½-story stone dwelling believed to have been built in 1764 (date on fireback) but considerably altered at a later date.

Md. 213 continues through several small towns to Elkton, 7.2 m., and a junction with U.S. 40 and Tour 2a at 7.8 m.

To the north, Md. 213, called Lewisville Road, crosses the **Pennsylvania Line,** 1.6 m. This part of northern Maryland and the adjacent area in southern Pennsylvania is a mushroom-raising center.

From Fair Hill, Md. 273 passes through the 7,000-acre Du Pont estate. In the three miles between Fair Hill and Appleton, there are three overpasses constructed by the Fox Catcher Hound Hunt Club to enable fox hunters to cross the highway. Each September, the Fox Catcher National Hunt Steeplechase is run on a three-mile course maintained on the Du Pont estate as one event of the Cecil County Breeders' Fair.

Along Big Elk Creek, 15.2 m., New Munster, a strip five miles long and two miles wide, was laid out in 1683 by George Talbot (*see above*) for Edwin O'Dwire and fifteen other Irishmen. Although they were probably squatters, the Irishmen were welcome settlers in the border area. Md. 273 passes through the crossroads of **APPLETON,** 15.9 m., to the **Delaware Line,** 17.3 m., about two miles from Newark, Delaware.

Richards Oak (R), 5.1 m., stands immediately at the side of U.S. 1, its great branches hanging over the road. According to a plaque put up by the Hytheham Club of Port Deposit in 1922, the Marquis de Lafayette and his troops camped under this tree on April 12, 1781, just before crossing the Susquehanna at Bald Friar. The tree, believed to be over 400 years old, has a trunk circumference of over 22 feet and a spread of over 125 feet.

At 7.8 m. U.S. 222 temporarily joins U.S. 1. At the same junction, Md. 338 branches south.

● Go right on U.S. 222 to a junction with Connoly Road at the crossroads of **ROCK SPRINGS**, 3.2 m. A left turn on Connoly Road leads to a dirt track (closed), 0.7 m., that branches right. Some distance along this track are the **Line Pits,** one of several chrome mines along either side of the Pennsylvania border east of the Susquehanna River that were mined between 1828 and 1880. Isaac Tyson of Baltimore developed most of these mines, and until 1850 they produced most of the world's chrome ore. Hauled by wagon to *Port Deposit,* the ore was then shipped by water to Baltimore. After the Philadelphia, Wilmington, and Baltimore Railroad built a branch through Rising Sun just before the Civil War, the ore was shipped to Baltimore by rail. Operations ended at the mines after richer chrome ores were discovered in Asia Minor. In 1890, prospectors believed they had found gold in the serpentine formations containing the chromite deposit. A gold rush followed, but no commercial deposits of the mineral were found.

U.S. 222 crosses the **Pennsylvania Line,** 3.7 m., at a point about twenty-five miles south of Lancaster, Pennsylvania.

● Go left (south) from U.S. 1 on Md. 338 to the tree-bordered entrance lane (L) of **Octorara** (private), 0.3 m., a well-known Cecil County house that overlooks Octoraro Creek and the Susquehanna River. The small stone wing is believed to have been built in the seventeenth century on the Mount Welcome tract patented by Richard Hall. In 1807, trustees of the bankrupt Elihu Hall sold the property to Henry White Physick (1768–1837), who retired here after a brilliant career as a surgeon and teacher in Philadelphia. Dr. Physick built the large brick wing, and his son, who moved to Cecil County from Charleston, South Carolina, added the two-story gallery porch along the side.

Md. 338 descends a steep hill to Octoraro Creek at **ROWLANDS-VILLE,** 1.3 m. Though there hardly seems room in the narrow gorge, this is an old factory site. An iron-rolling mill operated here from 1828 to 1893, and it was followed by a paper mill. Any of the three roads that climb the opposite side of the gorge will take the traveler to Md. 269 and from there south to Port Deposit.

In **CONOWINGO**, 8.8 m., U.S. 222 branches south along the banks of the wide Susquehanna between the river and a high bluff.

● On U.S. 222 at 4.2 m. the **Port Deposit Quarries** extend two hundred feet up the face of the cliff. Quarrying began here with the building in 1816–17 of a bridge across the river (it was rebuilt in 1829 after a fire and destroyed by a drove of crossing cattle in 1854), which used stone for abutments. Extensive quarrying operations began in 1829 and lasted until recent years.

Opposite the quarries are **Smith's Falls,** named in 1606 by Capt. John Smith, who ascended the Susquehanna River to this point, at which the rocks blocked further passage. On the map he drew, Smith called the place "Smith's Fales," marking it with a cross to symbolize the farthest extent of his exploration. Smith noticed the great abundance of fish in the Susquehanna. Beginning in the 1820s the use of floats, or large anchored rafts, in midstream allowed the setting of long seine nets, making possible huge catches of fish. In 1827, near the Pennsylvania line, Thomas Stump caught about fifteen million shad in a single haul, which amounted to one hundred wagon loads! The fish catches in the river and throughout the Bay area began to decline after the Civil War, and in spite of various attempts to control overfishing, the fish population has not increased significantly.

At 4.7 m. is the junction (L) with Md. 269 (*see above*) at the old stone **Rock Run Mill** (open Sat.–Sun. afternoons, Memorial Day–Labor

Day). It is believed that this structure is "the merchant's mill" mentioned in a petition for a road to this point in 1731.

The mill is on the northern edge of **PORT DEPOSIT** (16' alt., 906 pop.), a town interesting both for its dramatic setting and its history. Here the cliff above the majestic Susquehanna rises more than two hundred feet, leaving space along the shore for only a single street and the railroad track. One other small street has been quarried out of the rock near the southern end of the town.

As early as 1729, Thomas Cresap (*see Tour 8*) operated a ferry near here. By the early nineteenth century, the place was known as Creswell's Ferry (*see above,* Anchor and Hope Farm). The town came into existence with the completion of the Susquehanna, or Maryland, Canal in 1808. The canal ran from the highest point of navigation just below Smith's Falls to the Pennsylvania line and was constructed in an attempt to tap the grain and other products of the rich Pennsylvania hinterland. South from Creswell's Ferry the river was navigable, and in 1812 Philip Thomas, who owned most of the site, laid out the town. In 1813, the legislature named it Port Deposit, but it was still too insignificant to attract the attention of the British, who entered the Susquehanna in 1813 and burned a warehouse across the river. Soon, however, the canal made the town a port of deposit indeed. Great wooden arks and rafts carrying flour and wheat, whiskey, iron, pork, slate, and other products floated down the river and the canal to this point. Their cargo was then transferred to ships, and the rafts and arks themselves were broken up and sold as lumber. In 1822, the town handled $1,337,925 worth of commodities. Nearly 1,000 arks and rafts came down the river and canal, and 128 vessels entered and cleared the port. Herring and shad fisheries also added to the town's economy, and beginning in the 1830s the stone quarries provided another important industry. An iron foundry was established in the town in 1849, which produced the popular Armstrong stove in the 1870s. The canal was unable to compete with the railroad, however, and it finally closed in the 1890s. In 1910, a dam was built across the Susquehanna to the north, ending all rafting and adversely affecting the fisheries. Only quarrying remained an important industry in the town until 1942, when the navy established the nearby *Bainbridge Naval Training Center.* Today, a barge and scow construction yard, which employs over 300 people, is Port Deposit's major industry.

Despite Port Deposit's economic decline, the town retains its dramatic visual appeal. Beginning at the old *Rock Run Mill,* a row of houses and churches, some built of stone, hugs the cliff. At the junction with Md. 276, 5.5 m., a hollow in the cliff has been laid out as a public square, in which several early dwellings still stand. The **Gerry House** (L), four houses south of the intersection, is a three-story stone building with a three-story wooden gallery across the front, the bottom section of which has been enclosed for small shops. The house is believed to have been built in 1813, and Lafayette is supposed to have stopped here in 1824. Nearby is another large stone house believed to have been built before 1818. South of the square, the cliff has been terraced to accommodate a second row of houses, which perches above the first.

Near the end of Main Street is **Washington Hall** (R), a large brick building with brownstone trim built in 1894 to house the **Tome Institute,** a free school for children of the area, founded by Jacob Tome (1819–98). Tome, born in York County, Pennsylvania, arrived in Port Deposit in 1833 on a raft and, though practically penniless, found a partner with capital and entered the lumber business. Tome prospered, becoming one of the leading financiers of Maryland, even extending his investments to include timberlands in Michigan. The Tome Institute was the most important of his many philanthropic ventures. Before his death, Tome had given over $1,500,000 to the institute, and he bequeathed his residuary estate, which came to nearly the same amount, to the town's school system. Incorporated in 1889, the town schools in Port Deposit were opened in 1894. By 1898, 600 children were attending these schools, which still functioned in place of a public education in the community, although enrollment eventually dropped with the development of the county school system. The trustees of the institute used Tome's additional endowment to found a boarding school for boys, and the **Tome School,** situated on the bluff behind Port Deposit, was opened in 1902. Income from the boarding school helped support the free town schools for a generation, but the school never recovered from financial reverses suffered in the depression, and it finally closed in 1941.

Opposite Washington Hall is one of the visual highlights of Port Deposit. A great brick and stone staircase climbs vertically to the Tome School at the top of the bluff; beside the steps a waterfall cascades down. A short distance south of Washington Hall, **88 Main Street** (L), is a handsome two-story stone house built about 1816. Across the street is a marina, where boats may be hired for sport fishing in the still fish-filled waters of the river. At this point, U.S. 222 turns abruptly left and climbs the bluff to the entrance of the **Bainbridge Naval Training Center** (L) (closed March, 1976), 6.7 m., which includes the buildings and grounds of the former Tome School. Bainbridge opened in 1942, and nearly 350,000 navy members were trained there before it closed in 1947. The center was partially reopened in 1951, and by 1964 about one-third of the facility was in use. Bainbridge was the training center for the WAVES and the location of the Service School Command, a complex of specialized technical schools. The Navy Bureau of Personnel operated the facility, maintaining much of its record-keeping equipment here.

At 7.3 m. on U.S. 222 is the road (R) (unmarked) to **Mount Ararat Farms,** a large dairy farm. On this road stands the **Physick House** (L) (private, but visible from the road), 0.4 m., a 2½-story stone building (ca. 1830) with a hipped roof. Nearby is the brow of the crest above the river. The cave in which George Talbot (*see above*) is said to have hidden for months after he murdered Christopher Rousby, the King's Collector, in 1684, is located at the foot of the cliff. Talbot supposedly got food by sending his falcons to hunt for him. Eventually Talbot turned himself in for trial and was sentenced to death by a Virginia court, but he received a pardon from King James II. After Talbot returned to England, his vast landed estate in Maryland reverted to the lord proprietor.

U.S. 222 continues south to an interchange with the Kennedy Expressway and Tour S 1 at 9.1 m. and to a junction with U.S. 40 at 11.0 m.

The Susquehanna River and its tributaries form the largest river system on the Atlantic coast of the United States.

U.S. 1 crosses the river along the top of the **Conowingo Dam** (4,648 feet long, 105 feet high), which was completed in 1927. To the north, the river is dammed for more than fourteen miles to form Conowingo Lake; the water impounded amounts to 150 billion gallons. The old crossing at **BALD FRIAR,** about four miles north of Conowingo, has disappeared. Bald Friar was on the main route to Philadelphia during the eighteenth century, and Lafayette's troops and the Comte de Rochambeau's heavy baggage and artillery both used the crossing on their way to Yorktown in 1781.

Rochambeau's aide-de-camp, Baron Von Closen, described the ford as *diabolique* because of the slippery rocks and potholes that crippled his horses and wrecked his wagons. About half a mile below Bald Friar, but now covered by the lake, is the **Site of Mile's Island,** where Indian carvings of fish, crabs, and other animals could be found on the rocks. Some of the carvings are preserved at the Maryland Academy of Science in Baltimore.

Beside the dam in Harford County is the electric power plant of the Philadelphia Electric Company. When it opened in 1928, the plant was one of the largest in the world.

At 11.3 m. U.S. 1 makes a junction with Md. 623 (R).

● At 0.7 m. on Md. 623 a historic marker indicates a turn (R) into the **Nathan Rigbie House** (private, but visible from the road). The 1½-story stone wing is believed to have been standing before 1732. A box stair rises beside the great open fireplace, and the ceiling beams are exposed and beaded. The living room of the frame addition, believed to have been added about 1750, is paneled on all four walls, and handsome corner cupboards flank the fireplace. On April 13, 1781, Lafayette stopped here to visit Col. James Rigbie, sheriff of Harford County, after fording the Susquehanna at *Bald Friar.* Threatened with the mutiny of part of his troops, Lafayette chose to try Walter Pigot at this spot for treason. Some weeks before, Pigot had been caught attempting to sell flour to the British. He was found guilty and immediately hanged; the speedy trial and the severity of the sentence effectively quelled the mutiny.

At 11.4 m. Md. 161 branches left at an acute angle.

● **Deer Creek Friends Meeting,** 0.2 m. on Md. 161 (closed except for services), is a traditional one-and-a-half-story stone meeting house with two sections divided by a paneled wall separating the men's side on the right from the women's side on the left. The meeting house is believed to have been built in 1784. One of the stones in the cemetery marks the grave of Sarah Rumsey Rigbie, wife of Col. Nathan Rigbie, who died early in the eighteenth century.

Md. 161 continues to **DARLINGTON.** Take a left turn on Shuresville Road at 0.8 m. At the fork of Shuresville Road and Stafford Road, 0.4 m., bear right onto Stafford Road. Continue on Stafford Road to **Susquehanna State Park,** over 600 acres of land along Deer Creek, Rock Run, and the Susquehanna River. The **Rock Run Mill,** 4.3 m., now restored, is believed to have been built near the end of the eighteenth century by John Stump. One wing of the great stone house, located a short distance up Rock Run, was built in 1804 by Stump's partner, John Carter. From the road, which continues south of the mill along the river, are visible remains of the **Tidewater Canal** that was opened in 1839 to connect Columbia, Pennsylvania, with Havre de Grace. Beyond the canal, railroad tracks run beside the river, which is full of boulders and rapids.

● From Darlington, Md. 161 descends to Deer Creek, 2.4 m. Just before the bridge crosses the creek is the entrance (R) to **Wilson Mill,** now on private property. The stone mill was built on land deeded to Nathan Rigbie in 1743, and it now houses an electric generator.

On the opposite side of Deer Creek, a graveled road turns right and for more than half a mile follows the exceptionally beautiful stream. The road then turns abruptly to the left, climbing up the steep hill to a junction with the Glenville Road. The Glenville Road winds through the hilly countryside to a junction with Md. 155 just south of *Churchville,* some five miles away.

● Md. 161 continues to a junction with Green Spring Road (R), 4.1 m.; to the right on this road a grassy lane leads to the **Prospect Schoolhouse** (visible from the road), a small hexagonal stone building built about 1850. The structure was the work of Joshua Stephen, a stonemason who built it to disprove a claim that he did not have the skill required for such construction.

Md. 161 continues to the junction with Md. 155, 5.4 m., a side tour of Tour 2a, at a point 3.8 m. from Churchville and 5.3 m. from Havre de Grace.

At 12.1 m., U.S. 1 passes **Wildsfell** (L) (private, but visible from the road), an octagonal white frame house believed to have been built in the 1840s by a ship's carpenter who used beams from an old clipper ship in its construction.

Between here and Bel Air, U.S. 1 intersects Md. 440 at 13.0 m., Md. 136 at 15.1 m., and Md. 543 at 21.2 m. All of these roads or the side roads that branch off from them pass through fertile hilly countryside.

● To the right, Md. 543 crosses Deer Creek. Here, the water-powered **Walter's Mill,** 3.1 m., began operation about 1803. The present frame building, erected about 1890, stands on the stone foundation of the original mill.

U.S. 1 makes a junction with Md. 23 at 22.2 m. and with Md. 24 in *Bel Air,* 23.3 m.

At the intersection of U.S. 1 and U.S. Business 1, continue on U.S. Business 1. This route enters Bel Air as Broadway Street. At the junction with South Hickory Street, turn right. At the junction of Broadway and E. Main streets, 25.5 m., turn left. At the fork of Main and Bond streets, 25.6 m., bear right on Bond Street. At the intersection of Baltimore Pike and Bond Street, 26.1 m., turn right. This route travels through **BEL AIR** (396′ alt., 6,307 pop.), the county seat of Harford County, which serves as the trading and banking center of the surrounding countryside.

When Harford County was erected from Baltimore County in 1773, the county seat was established at Old Harfordtown on Bush River (*see* Tour 2a). In 1782, the county seat was moved to Aquila Scott's Old Field, which was eventually renamed Bel Air, although the town was not incorporated until 1874.

Immediately after turning onto Baltimore Pike is the **Hays-Jacobs House** (L) (open regularly), on Kenmore Avenue. This simple gambrel-roofed frame house is believed to have been built about 1711 by William Jones, whose name is on a fireback in the north parlor. The house stood on Main Street until 1960, when it was removed to make way for a supermarket. The Harford County Historical Society has restored the dwelling, converting it into a small museum. Lafayette stayed here in 1784, later sending a silvered-copper medallion with a relief of his head to the owner. The medallion is one of the exhibits in the museum.

● Md. 24 travels north of Bel Air through the rolling Piedmont to the Pennsylvania line. From the junction of Business U.S. 1 and Md. 24 in Bel Air, Md. 24 crosses Md. 23 at 3.1 m. and passes through the village of **FOREST HILL** (700 pop.), 3.7 m., to **Rock State Park,** which lies along the banks of Deer Creek. At 8.6 m. the rocks for which the park was named can be seen. The creek has cut straight through the rocks, creating a gorge 250 feet deep. Picnic areas are located on the ridge near the rocks as well as along the creek.

To reach **King and Queen Seats** (the rock formation), turn left off Md. 24 before the bridge. At the next left along this road, turn left to the **Rock Ridge Picnic Area.** At the first picnic area is the trail to the rock formation.

Amos Mill

● At the upper end of the park where Md. 24 crosses the creek there is an iron mill (R), which operated from 1836 to 1874.

At 10.8 m. Md. 24 intersects Md. 165. Turn left on Md. 165 to a junction with Fawn Grove Road to **Eden Mill,** 3.1 m., built sometime before 1850 by Elijah Stansbury. Although formerly known as Stansbury's Mill, the name Eden was attached to the area because Father Eden, a Catholic priest, established a mission nearby. In 1965, the county commissioners purchased Eden Mill and fifty-six acres of land for a county park. Today, various activities are offered, including skating, fishing, skiing, canoeing, hiking, and picnicking.

● At 12.7 m., Md. 24 joins Md. 136. To the left on Md. 136 at 4.0 m. is a junction with Amoss Mill Road. Turn left, crossing Carea Road, to **Amos Mill** (on the corner of Amoss Mill Road and Amos Road), 0.9 m., one of the oldest surviving grist mills in Maryland. The building, a three-story stone and log structure, and most of the machinery in it are over two hundred years old. The wooden mill wheel was replaced with a steel wheel in 1926.

Md. 24 continues to the **Pennsylvania Line,** 15.2 m., at Fawn Grove, Pennsylvania.

Md. 24 going south from Bel Air is a side tour of Tour 2a.

Md. 22 branches off U.S. 1 (Bond Street)-Md. 24 (Main Street) in Bel Air, traveling east to *Churchville* and then south to the junction with U.S. 40 and Tour 2a in Aberdeen.

● At 2.0 m. on Md. 22 is the village of **FOUNTAIN GREEN** and the junction with Md. 543, and at 2.7 m. Tudor Lane turns left through a housing development to **Tudor Hall** (private), 2.9 m. The property on which the house stands was purchased by Junius Brutus Booth, an Englishman who emigrated to America in 1821. The present multigabled brick house with casement windows and other Tudor details was built in 1846 following an English design. An earlier house on this site was the birthplace of Junius Booth's two sons, Edwin and John Wilkes, who were born in 1833 and 1839 respectively. Edwin Booth was a leading Shakespearean actor; his brother, also an actor, shot and killed Abraham Lincoln at Ford's Theatre in Washington, D.C., on April 14, 1865. Eleven days later, John Wilkes Booth died in a burning barn surrounded by his pursuers (*see* Tour 26b, Bel Alton).

● At the crossroads of **FULFORD**, 3.8 m., Thomas Run Road branches left. Take this route to the junction with Medical Hall Road (R), 0.7 m. Turn right. At the junction with Greer Road, 1.4 m., turn left and at 1.8 m. turn again to **Medical Hall** (private), a 2½-story stuccoed brick house built about 1799 by Dr. John Archer (1741–1810). Archer, who was born nearby, obtained his diploma, the first medical degree granted by an American school, from the Philadelphia Medical College in 1768. In 1775, Archer signed the Bush Declaration of Independence, a document registering the willingness of the men of Harford County to fight to preserve their constitutional rights, and he later raised a militia company when war actually broke out with England. Archer and his son, Dr. Thomas Archer, founded the Medical and Chirurgical Faculty of Maryland in 1799, and after his retirement from two terms in Congress (1800–1804), he conducted a medical school at his house. Another son, Stevenson Archer (1786–1848), served in Congress (1811–17; 1819–21), was chief judge of the Circuit Court (1823–44) and chief judge of the Court of Appeals (1844–48). Stevenson was born and died at Medical Hall. The beautifully carved woodwork of the mantel in the house is from Belvedere, ancestral home of the present owner. The delicate reeding and other details of the doorways are typical of woodwork popular about 1800. The wallpaper in the front hall, which depicts scenes from the period after the French Revolution, is over a century old.

● At the crossroads in **CHURCHVILLE**, 5.7 m., stands the **Churchville Presbyterian Church** (L), built in 1820 and remodeled in 1870. During the remodeling, an Italian-Gothic bell tower was added and the interior was greatly changed. The congregation was founded about 1739 after George Whitefield preached several revival sermons in this area.

In Churchville is a junction with Md. 136 (*see above*) and Md. 155, a side tour of Tour 2a.

Md. 22 continues to a junction with the John F. Kennedy Expressway at 9.8 m. and thence to a junction with U.S. 40 and Tour 2a in Aberdeen, 11.8 m.

At 26.9 m. U.S. 1 makes a junction with Toll Gate Road.

● Go right on Toll Gate Road to **Joshua Meadows** (L) (private), 0.3 m., a 1½-story stuccoed brick house believed to have been standing when Thomas Bond gave the land to his son Joshua in 1753; the stone wing is a modern addition. The living room, which once served as the kitchen, has exposed beaded beams and a box stair that rises behind the chimney—features common to early Maryland houses. A beautiful reeded mantel with recessed carving highlights the study. The owners possess a Charles Willson Peale portrait of Capt. Thomas Sprigg.

Continue on Toll Gate Road to a junction with Red Pump Road, 1.9 m. Turn right. At 2.1 m. turn left on Graftons Shop Road. On the right at 2.7 m. stands a brown barn. Opposite the barn, a steep hill leads to **Solomon's Choice** (L) (private), a hall-and-parlor, 1½-story stone building believed to have been built in 1785 by an Episcopal clergyman, John Coleman. The fireplace wall of the living room retains its original pine paneling and roundheaded cupboards with butterfly shelves.

Old Joppa Road branches left off U.S. 1 at 28.5 m.

● Turn left on Old Joppa Road past **Country Life Farm,** a breeding farm for race horses, where the offspring of such winners as Dark Ruler and Occupy may be seen at pasture. At 0.7 m. Whitaker Mill Road branches left. The **Baltimore Fresh Air Farm** (L), 0.3 m., on Whitaker Mill Road is a camp occupying approximately forty acres, operated by the Children's Fresh Air Society of Baltimore City. Since 1891, the society has provided ten-day summer vacations for under-privileged boys and girls between five and twelve years of age. At 1.4 m. Whitaker Mill Road crosses Winter's Run. Here is **Whitaker's (Duncale)** Mill (private, but visible from the road), a picturesque stone structure built in 1851. At 1.5 m. Whitaker Mill Road becomes Ring Factory Road. A left turn on Ring Factory Road leads to a junction with Md. 24 about two miles south of Bel Air.

● Returning to Old Joppa Road, continue past the junction with Hollingsworth Road to the gate (L) to **Olney** (private), 2.3 m. The modest 2½-story brick house, built in 1810 by the Quaker John Saurin Norris, was doubled in size about 1850. In 1930, the imposing marble Doric portico from the Baltimore Athenaeum, which was designed in 1829 by William Small, a Baltimore architect, was added to the garden front. The elaborately carved arches with Corinthian columns and the other woodwork in the living room came from an old house on Fells Point. Olney is a working farm known for its award-winning ponies.

Old Joppa Road crosses Md. 152 at 2.7 m. and makes a junction with Jerusalem Road at 3.4 m. Go right on Jerusalem Road to **Jerusalem Mill,** 3.9 m., on the Little Gunpowder River. Built partly by David Lee in 1772, the mill is unusual in that the first story is of stone, the second of frame, surmounted by two half-stories under a steep gabled roof. Two tiers of alternating dormer windows light the third story and the loft. Although Lee was a Quaker, he supposedly manufactured guns in the stone building behind the mill during the Revolution. The mill has been purchased as part of *Gunpowder State Park* and is to be restored for park use.

At the mill, turn left on Jericho Road. This road crosses the Little Gunpowder Falls on the **Jericho Covered Bridge.** Of bowstring con-struction (*see above,* Gilpin's Covered Bridge), the bridge is said to have been built about 1800, making it one of the oldest such bridges now standing in Maryland.

Jerusalem Road continues to a junction with U.S. 1 at 5.6 m.

At 29.0 m., U.S. 1 makes a junction with Md. 147, the Harford Road, an alternate route to Baltimore that is only two lanes wide and has many curves.

● Go right on Md. 147 to a junction with Md. 152, 1.1 m. Go right on Md. 152. Make a left on Connolly Road to **FALLSTON** (442′ alt., 820 pop.), 0.6 m. Take Old Fallston Road to **Little Falls Meeting House** (R), 1.0 m., a 1½-story stone structure built in 1843 with the tradi-tional door at each end of one side and the partition in the middle of the room to separate men from women. In 1758, this meeting was established as a branch of the Gunpowder Meeting, but in 1815, Little Falls formed its own meeting. In the decades before the Civil War, Fallston was a station in the Underground Railroad.

At 1.1 m., turn left on Laurel Brook Road. At 0.4 m. is the private track into **Bonair,** about a quarter mile in from the road. This lovely stuccoed house with high hipped roof and kicked eaves resembles a small chateau on the Loire. The dwelling was built in 1794 (date on house) by Francis de la Porte, a French officer in Rochambeau's army. Near the house is the tomb in which he, his wife, and his mother are buried. Open by appointment: Margery D. Kelly, Fallston.

● Md. 147 crosses the Little Gunpowder Falls, 3.0 m. Land on either side of the road has been acquired for the *Gunpowder State Park.*

At 8.6 m. the highway skirts the Gunpowder Falls. At 9.1 m. is a marker for a copper works. In 1815, Levi Hollingsworth invested over $100,000 in a copper-rolling mill modeled on those he had studied in England. The mill was one of the earliest in the United States, a forerunner of the copper smelting, rolling, and refining industries that later developed in the Baltimore area. At 9.5 m., the highway crosses the falls and makes a junction in **CUB HILL,** 10.6 m., with Cub Hill Road.

Go right on Cub Hill Road, 0.9 m. Turn right on Old Harford Road to the **Maryland Training School for Boys** (R), 1.4 m. Established in 1850 as the House of Refuge for delinquent boys, the institution was purchased by the state in 1918.

● Near **CARNEY** at 11.8 m. on Md. 147, the outer suburbs of Baltimore begin. At 12.3 m. is the intersection with the Baltimore Beltway West and Tour S 2; at 12.5 m. is the intersection with the Baltimore Beltway East. At 14.5 m., Md. 147 crosses the **Baltimore City Line,** rejoining U.S. 1 in Baltimore at North Avenue.

On U.S. 1 Whitaker Mill Road branches left to the **Baltimore Fresh Air Farm** and **Whitaker's (Duncale) Mill** (*see above*), and at 30.3 m. is the junction with Md. 152.

To the left (west), Md. 152 makes a junction with Old Joppa Road. A right turn (south) on Old Joppa Road leads to a junction with Jerusalem Road; a right on Jerusalem Road leads to *Jerusalem Mill.*

U.S. 1 crosses the Little Gunpowder Falls at 31.6 m., passing through land acquired for **Gunpowder State Park.** More than 10,000 acres along the streams of the Little Gunpowder Falls and the Great Gunpowder Falls have now been acquired as part of the program to save open space and parkland near the Baltimore metropolitan area.

At the crossroads of **KINGSVILLE** (325 pop.), 33.7 m., is the junction with Jerusalem Road (L), which leads to *Jerusalem Mill.* Just beyond the junction is the three-story **Kingsville Inn** (R), which encompasses a small house believed to have been built before 1740. An addition, which still has its original interior paneling, was constructed before the death of its occupant, Rev. Hugh Dean of St. John's Parish. The house was subsequently owned by Dean's son-in-law, John Paul, a Quaker suspected of being sympathetic toward British troops during the American Revolution. Paul was arrested in April, 1781, for supplying flour to the British (*see* Tour 2a, Joppa), but he later escaped.

Nearby is the **Site of Ishmael Day's House,** burned on July 28, 1864, after Day shot and killed a Confederate sergeant, William Fields (of Baltimore), who was trying to pull down the Union flag flying on Day's yard gate. Sergeant Fields was a member of a cavalry detachment commanded by Harry Gilmor. The detachment burned the railroad bridge over the mouth of the Gunpowder River as part of Gens. Jubal Early and Bradley T. Johnson's plan to capture Washington, D.C. (*see* Tour 2a, Carter Area). On August 23, 1864, the Union general Lew Wallace ordered that an estimate be made of Day's loss and that all disloyal and disaffected persons within five miles of his farm be assessed to compensate him.

At 35.7 m., U.S. 1 crosses Great Gunpowder Falls, and at 36.4 m. a historical marker stands at the junction with Perry Hall Road (R).

● This leads to **Perry Hall Mansion** (R) (private, but visible from the road), 0.2 m., a two-part stuccoed stone house. Before a fire in

1824, Perry Hall was twice its present size. Two wings and hyphens led to square pavilions at each end, one containing a bath and the other a Methodist chapel. The main block of the house was built about 1773 and sold to Harry Dorsey Gough (1745–1808) in 1774. Gough added the wings and pavilions after the Revolution. A convert to Methodism, Gough had backslid enough by 1787 to allow his daughter Sophia to marry James Carroll of Mount Clare (*see* West Baltimore) in the Episcopal Church, but he was reconverted during the Great Revival of 1800. For a long time, Gough's home was a center of hospitality for itinerant Methodist preachers, especially Francis Asbury and Thomas Coke. In December, 1784, a number of Methodist preachers and their followers assembled at this house. They rode to Baltimore for the conference at the Lovely Lane Church, the result of which was the organization of the Methodist Church in America (*see* Downtown Baltimore).

In 1786, Gough was elected first president of the Society for Improvement of Agriculture in Maryland. With the marriages of the Carrolls, the Ridgelys, and the Goughs, Mount Clare (*see* West Baltimore), Hampton (*see* Tour 32), and Perry Hall became closely connected, and until the fire, Perry Hall was as fine a mansion as the other two.

At 41.1 m. on U.S. 1 is the junction with the Baltimore Beltway West and Tour S 2. At 41.3 m. is the junction with the Baltimore Beltway East and Tour S 2. The traveler who wishes to by-pass Baltimore should turn south on the beltway (east) to the Harbor Tunnel Thruway and Tour S 1; he can rejoin the tour from the end of the Harbor Tunnel Thruway at Elkridge.

At 42.6 m. U.S. 1 crosses the **Baltimore City Line.**

U.S. 1 passes through Baltimore on Belair Avenue and North Avenue (the city line from 1816 to 1888), turning south on Monroe Street and then west on Wilkens Avenue to Southwestern Boulevard, by which it leaves the city. The route passes hundreds of brick row houses with white marble steps, built mostly between 1880 and 1920. Baltimore and Washington were the last major cities on the heavily traveled north-south route along the Atlantic coast to have by-pass roads constructed around them.

Baltimore is at a junction with U.S. 40 (*see* Tour 2a), Md. 45 (*see* Tour 32), U.S. 140 (*see* Tour 33), Md. 2 (*see* Tour 25), and Md. 3 (*see* Tour 26). The distance on U.S. 1 through the city is 12.1 miles.

1b. BALTIMORE CITY LINE–HYATTSVILLE–DISTRICT OF COLUMBIA LINE; 28.5 m.

U.S. 1

Until 1954, when the Baltimore-Washington Parkway (*see* Tour S 1) opened, this section of U.S. 1 was one of the busiest roads in the nation and one of the most dangerous. Signboards and neon displays competed for the attention of the driver, and traffic in and out of service stations, restaurants, hot dog stands, and tourist cabins created constant hazards. The construction of the parkway and Interstate 95 has reduced through traffic, but motorists must still travel U.S. 1 for tourist services, and the route remains heavily commercialized. Natives often express the belief that their fellow Marylander, Ogden Nash, had this section of U.S. 1 in mind when he wrote:

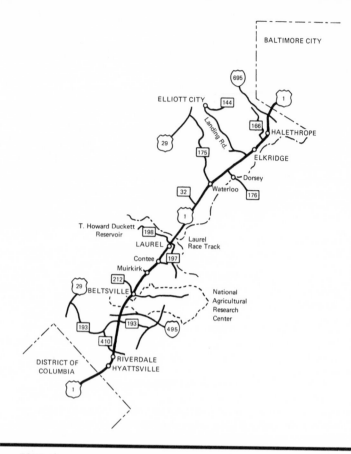

TOUR 1b

> I think that I shall never see
> A billboard lovely as a tree;
> Perhaps unless the billboards fall,
> I'll never see a tree at all.

U.S. 1 crosses the **Baltimore City Line** on Southwestern Boulevard at 0.0 m. and intersects the Baltimore Beltway, Interstate 695.

HALETHORPE, 1.9 m., is inhabited mainly by commuters who work in Baltimore. On a large field (L), 2.1 m., the Fair of the Iron Horse, the centennial celebration of the Baltimore & Ohio Railroad, was held in 1927. Many of the exhibits, which attracted 1,250,000 people, are now at the Baltimore & Ohio Transportation Museum (*see* West Baltimore). In 1910, the first major airplane meet in the United States was held on this same field. Hubert Latham piloted a fifty-horsepower monoplane over Baltimore in the first successful flight over a large American city.

At 3.2 m. is the exit to Md. 166, the Rolling Road, so called because it was laid out during the colonial period as a thoroughfare over which huge hogsheads of tobacco were rolled to the shipping point at *Elkridge Landing.* "Rolling" today could refer to lateral movement, because the rolling road curved back and forth to avoid as much uphill slope as possible on the way to the landing. Tobacco had to be moved by way of the rolling roads to authorized ports for export under government inspection and control.

● Go right on Md. 166 to **RELAY.** To the left a short distance the Baltimore & Ohio Railroad tracks cross the *Thomas Viaduct.* In the brief period before the introduction of steam, B & O Railroad trains stopped for a change of horses at the Relay House, which stood about here. As a combination hotel, ticket office, and waiting room it was the first "mealing station" erected by a railroad for the comfort of its patrons. On May 4, 1861, Gen. Benjamin Butler's troops—among them the Sixth Massachusetts Regiment that on April 19 had been attacked along Pratt Street in Baltimore (*see* Downtown Baltimore)—took possession of the Relay House and fortified the heights above the Thomas Viaduct with two cannon. On May 13 they boarded a train at Relay for Baltimore, where that same night they captured Federal Hill (*see* South Baltimore).

Beyond Relay, at the intersection of Md. 166 and Gun Road (L), turn left on Gun Road to the *Avalon-Orange Grove* area of the *Patapsco State Park.*

● Continuing along Md. 166, the **University of Maryland, Baltimore County** (UMBC) is on the right. On the left is **Catonsville Community College.**

At the intersection of Md. 166 and Hilton Avenue (L), turn left to the **Hilton** area of the **Patapsco State Park.** Maps and exhibits at the Patapsco Valley History Center describe the Patapsco story.

At 3.7 m. the Harbor Tunnel Thruway joins U.S. 1 (*see* Tour S 1).

At 3.8 m. is a stoplight in **ELKRIDGE** (3,444 pop.). In colonial times, this site was called Elkridge Landing, a shipping point for tobacco grown in the watershed of the Patapsco River. In 1763, more than half the crop grown in Anne Arundel County was inspected at the warehouse here, and the river was still deep enough for ocean-going vessels. In 1771, Stephen West and John Dorsey both advertised for sale at Elkridge Landing goods that had been imported from London, including "Silks of the newest Patterns." A few years later the Elkridge iron furnace and forge was producing arms for the Continental Army. In 1781, Lafayette's troops camped at the landing for two days on their way to Yorktown. Today, several manufacturing establishments employ about 300 people.

At the stoplight is the junction with Levering Avenue (River Road).

● Turn right on Levering Avenue (R), 0.4 m., to an old brick house (private, but visible from the road), nearly surrounded by the buildings and equipment of a trucking firm. Immediately after passing the house is the **Thomas Viaduct.** This great stone bridge designed by Benjamin H. Latrobe, son of the architect Benjamin H. Latrobe (*see* Baltimore), was built in 1835 to carry the tiny locomotives and wooden coaches of the Baltimore & Ohio Railroad over the Patapsco River. It was named for Philip Thomas, first president of the railroad. Sixty feet high and supported on eight elliptical granite arches, the structure forms a sweeping curve 612 feet long and carries the heavy freight trains of modern times with ease. In 1964, the secretary of the interior declared the bridge a National Historic Landmark.

At the viaduct, Levering Road becomes River Road. Before Hurricane Agnes (1972), River Road continued along the wooded gorge of the Patapsco through **Patapsco State Park.**

During the eighteenth and early nineteenth centuries, the Patapsco, which falls 300 feet in the fifteen miles from Woodstock to the Chesa-peake Bay, was the source of water power for a number of mills and iron forges. In July, 1868, however, a cloudburst caused a great flood that swept away dams, mills, and houses, a disaster from which most of the valley has never recovered. The state began to acquire land along the lower Patapsco in 1912, and the park in this area was devel-oped by the Civilian Conservation Corps during the 1930s. In 1972, another devastating flood swept the valley in the wake of Hurricane Agnes. In September, 1975, heavy rains caused the river to overflow again, resulting in severe damage along the river.

In the section of the park called **Avalon** (closed), the Avalon Furnace operated from about 1800 until the flood of 1868. Originally, it made bar iron and, after 1840, merchant iron for various uses. In 1848, the furnace supplied rails for the Baltimore & Ohio Railroad. **Orange Grove** (closed) is the **Site of the Gambrill Grist Mill.** The **Cascade Trail** (L), which follows a brook along its steep rocky course, is also within this area.

At 5.0 m. on U.S. 1 is an intersection with Old Montgomery Road.

● Turn right. At 1.3 m. is a junction with Landing Road. Turn right to **Trinity Preparatory School,** 2.5 m., a Catholic school.

At 3.5 m. on Landing Road turn right on Ilchester Road to the en-trance to **St. Mary's College,** a Redemptorist novitiate and mission house founded in 1867. At 4.6 m. Ilchester Road becomes River Road. Here one can see the remains of a Baltimore & Ohio Railroad bridge built in 1830. Proceeding west on River Road at 5.1 m. is **THISTLE.** By the north bank of the Patapsco is a fiberboard mill, the stone portion of which is the **Thistle Factory** (L), erected in 1821 by George and William Morris for the manufacture of cotton prints. Many of the work-ers in the factory were Welsh. They lived in the picturesque stone houses, most now abandoned, that perch on ledges of the cliff across the road.

Farther along the rocky wooded bank of the river—still beautiful although no longer parkland—is a long stone building (R), 6.4 m., that was once part of the **Patapsco Factory** built in 1820 by Edward Gray and severely damaged in the flood of 1868. John Pendleton Kennedy married one of Gray's daughters and lived for many summers in a house that stood next to the mill. After a visit to Kennedy here in 1854, Washington Irving described the countryside as "Mahomet's Paradise" and commented that he would have liked to destroy the mill and the railroad and build chateaus along the river. At the junction of River Road and Md. 144 just outside of Ellicott City, 6.6 m., a large stone building with gables that rise above the roof in stepped parapets is also believed to have been part of the mill.

To the left on Md. 144 is Ellicott City and Tour 2b.

At 7.3 m. on U.S. 1 is a junction with Md. 176.

● To the left on Md. 176 is the **Dorsey Speedway,** 0.4 m., where stock cars are raced every Friday evening from May through September.

At **Waterloo,** 9.1 m., is the junction with Md. 175.

To the left, Md. 175 is a side route of Tour S 1.

To the right, Md. 175 travels to a junction with Md. 103 (Mont-gomery Road), 5.2 m., which joins U.S. 29 and Tour 2b, 7.0 m., just outside Ellicott City.

U.S. 1 makes a junction with Md. 32 at 11.4 m., and at 13.0 m. is the right turn into the **Laurel Raceway,** where harness races are held during part of every June and July. This is the site of an early experiment in monorails. On a banked circular track about two miles in circumference, David J. Weems built an overhead T-rail to serve both for support and as a power feed. A six-ton electric locomotive (now at the Smithsonian in Washington, D.C.) was equipped with three sets of forty-inch drivers, run by a powerful motor without the intervention of gears. At its trial the engine reached a speed of 118 m.p.h., which it maintained for twenty-two minutes, but the superstructure collapsed under the tremendous strain.

At 14.1 m., U.S. 1 enters **LAUREL** (150′ alt., 10,525 pop.), a comfortable suburban town that was once a small industrial center. It stands on land patented in the seventeenth century to Richard Snowden (*see below,* Montpelier), and the Snowdens were long prominent in the town's development. In 1811 Nicholas Snowden built a grist mill that operated until 1824, when it was converted to a factory for spinning yarn. In 1835 Snowden's son-in-law, Horace Capron, was a founder of the Patuxent Company, a cotton mill said to have employed four hundred people, and by the end of the 1840s the community supported three churches. In 1900, Laurel, with its cotton mill, shirt factory, grist mill, and foundry, and with a population of about 3,000, was advertising itself as "destined to become an important center." Instead, the textile mills had closed by 1911 and the town's population failed to increase until nearby Fort Meade expanded during World War II.

On the corner of U.S. 1 and Main Street is **Old Frost's Store,** now a brick-veneered building but in 1810 a frame blacksmith's shop that served the stages.

● One block east of Main Street is the **Laurel Railroad Station** of the Baltimore & Ohio Railroad. Built in 1884 (by E. Francis Baldwin), it is a one-story brick Queen Anne–style structure. One of the few remaining stations, it became a National Landmark in 1973.

● A right turn off U.S. 1 on Montgomery Street, two blocks south of Main Street, leads out of Laurel via Brooklyn Bridge Road to an intersection with West Bond Mill Road (unmarked), 2.0 m.; right on this to the **T. Howard Duckett Reservoir,** built in 1954 to increase the contribution of the upper Patuxent River to the water supply system of the Washington area. Formerly known as Rocky Gorge Reservoir, it contains a lake nine miles long surrounded by woodland. The reservoir and other properties owned by the Washington Suburban Sanitary Commission are part of a system of parks along the valley streams of the Patuxent that are being acquired and developed as nature preserves and for recreation in the Washington metropolitan area.

Md. 198 intersects U.S. 1 in Laurel at 14.4 m.

● Go left on Md. 198 to a junction with Laurel Racetrack Road, 1.0 m.; left here to **Laurel Race Track,** one of three one-mile-tracks in Maryland. Thoroughbred racing started here in 1911. One of the best-known races, begun in 1952, is the Washington, D.C., International, to which horses from many countries of the world are invited, their expenses paid by the track. In 1954, Queen Elizabeth sent her three-year-old, Landau, the first royal British entry ever raced outside the United Kingdom.

● At 0.4 m. on Md. 198 is an intersection with Md. 197 (Bowie Road).

Turn right on Md. 197 past numerous garden-apartment developments, which feature landscaping, outdoor swimming pools, and other amenities. At 1.6 m., opposite the junction with Contee Road, is **Snow Hill** (private, but visible from the apartment development immediately adjacent), a late eighteenth-century Snowden homestead with a great gambrel roof.

Montpelier (L), 2.0 m. immediately after turning on Montpelier Drive (for tourist schedule call [301] 277–9200, Ext. 347), is one of the famous five-part mansions of Maryland. It was begun, probably in mid-eighteenth century, by Thomas Snowden (1722–70), son of Richard Snowden ("Iron Master") and finished by his son, Maj. Thomas Snowden (1751–1803). Firebacks dated 1783 suggest that the house was completed about then. On both the approach and garden fronts of the hip-roofed main house, a three-bay pedimented pavilion accents the entrance. Hyphens lead to flankers, which are gabled on the approach front but semioctagonal facing the garden. The garlanded plaster cornice in the hall is similar to one at Mount Vernon. In the southeast parlor, a corner cupboard framed by fluted pilasters with mixed capitals flanks an elaborately carved mantel. The house is now owned by the Maryland–National Capital Park and Planning Commission.

Richard Snowden, the immigrant, was a Welshman—believed to have served in Cromwell's army—who possessed among his large holdings an iron mine at the head of the South River in 1669. His son Richard was an owner-undertaker of the Patuxent Furnace, established before 1734 at the site of an older Snowden iron works on the Little Patuxent River, now located in the center of Fort Meade. This furnace operated until 1856 and was owned by the Snowdens until 1831. The family acquired thousands of acres in the area from the South River to Sandy Spring.

At 16.4 m., U.S. 1 intersects Contee Road.

● Go left on Contee Road across the B & O Railroad tracks to **Oaklands** (private, but on a high hill), 0.2 m., built about 1798 by Richard Snowden, son of Maj. Thomas Snowden. A nineteenth-century remodeling added a mansard roof.

In **MUIRKIRK,** 17.9 m., a right turn onto Muirkirk Road followed by a right turn onto the highway overpass leads to the **Mineral Pigments Corporation** (R), standing beside the highway. In 1847, William and Elias Ellicott, then owners of the Patuxent Iron Works, built the iron furnace that was the forerunner of the present pigment works. Because Muirkirk iron had great tensile strength, the plant outlasted most of the others that utilized Maryland ore. It allegedly supplied cannon and cannonballs to the Federal army during the Civil War and later produced gun carriages and car wheels. Razed by an explosion in 1880, the plant was immediately rebuilt. About the time of World War I, these works converted to the production of ocher from local ores, but since 1924 they have produced dry pigments from higher-grade foreign ores.

Ammendale Normal Institute (R) (private), 18.8 m., is the provincial house and novitiate of the Brothers of the Christian Schools for the District of Baltimore. Established in 1880, it prepares young men for the teaching brotherhood and is a retreat for aged and invalid members.

At 20.1 m., U.S. 1 intersects Md. 212 (Powder Mill Road).

● Go left 0.5 m. to the **Agricultural Research Center** (visitors' services, tours by appointment only, Mon.–Fri., 8–4:30; closed Sat., Sun., and holidays. Call [301] 344–2483), more than 10,000 acres of experimental farmland of the U.S. Department of Agriculture. The land is divided into experimental pastures, ranges, orchards, gardens, fields for cultivated crops, timber stands, and soil-treatment plots. There are more than 1,000 buildings, some imposing Georgian-style brick struc-

Agricultural Research Center

tures, others utilitarian barns, greenhouses, and poultry houses. Of the 2,000 employees, half are scientists specializing in agricultural research. The center has nearly 4,000 experimental farm animals, 6,000 mature laying and breeding fowls, and about 3,000 small animals used in laboratory tests.

The **Plant Industry Station** is the headquarters of research in field and horticultural crops, soil and water conservation, agricultural engineering, and entomology. The most extensive activities include plant breeding, plant disease, and plant growth studies. Here work is done to develop better field crops and new varieties of vegetables and fruits and to control weeds. New varieties of lima beans, lettuce, potatoes, and onions developed here have won wide popularity with both farmers and consumers. Plant breeders at the station also do research on ornamental crops, such as lilies, snapdragons, azaleas, carnations, and daffodils. More than 200 species and varieties of drug and savory herb plants are maintained in a cultivated garden at the station. Labeled with both their scientific and common names, the plants are in their prime in summer and early fall.

On the south side of the Research Center, the **Farm and Land Management Research Branch** is developing new conservation farming methods. Tests are made in contour cultivation, ridge rows, rotations, mulching, and cover crops. Using facilities provided by the Atomic Energy Commission, the Soil and Water Conservation Research Branch has experimental laboratories for the study of radioactive techniques in soil research. Because of the hazards from radioactive materials, these laboratories are not open to the public.

The **Livestock Research Division** conducts experiments in animal diseases. The Animal Disease Station covers an area of 350 acres with 200 structures, including laboratories, hospital houses, breeding houses, barns, and pens. Another section of this division is devoted to the investigation of animal parasites.

The **Dairy Husbandry Research Branch** concerns itself with problems that affect the efficiency and profitability of dairy farming. A herd of registered Holsteins was established at the center in 1918 and a herd of Jerseys in 1919. The herds are maintained for experimental purposes, chief of which is determining the value of using proved sires. Proved sires brought in for service at the center are usually past seven years of age, beyond the prime for the majority of dairy bulls. Daily exercise has long been recognized as a means of prolonging the usefulness of bulls. However, few older bulls will exercise voluntarily, so an exerciser was designed that enabled many a herd sire to walk himself into a useful old age.

The **Animal and Poultry Husbandry Research Branch** aims to develop new and improved methods of livestock production, including more efficient breeding, feeding, and management of farm livestock and poultry. The popular Beltsville small turkey, with its compact body, short legs, and ample breast meat, was developed at the center.

At 21.3 m. are the buildings of the **Plant Industry Station** of the *Agricultural Research Center.*

Across U.S. 1 just north of the Plant Industry Station, the **Beltsville Industrial Center** is one of a number of areas in the suburbs zoned for the industry necessary to increase the tax base.

At 21.9 m. and 22.1 m., U.S. 1 intersects the Washington Beltway and Tour S 3 and at 23.2 m. is the junction with Md. 193.

To the left Md. 193 travels to a junction with the Baltimore-Washington Parkway and Tour S 1 in Greenbelt, 2.8 m.

● To the right Md. 193 crosses **Paint Branch Park,** a county park, and the campus of the *University of Maryland* to a junction with Md. 212 (Old Riggs Road), 3.3 m.; turn right here to **Adelphi Mill** (L), 0.8 m., by the Northwest Branch of the Anacostia River. This stone structure is believed to have been built about 1796 as a grist mill, although by 1811 it was a wool-carding mill. On the right side of the road the old stone miller's cottage still stands. The buildings are now a recreation center for the county park system.

Md. 193 continues through an area heavily developed in shopping centers and residential subdivisions to a junction with U.S. 29 and Tour 2b at 6.9 m., crossing Md. 650, 4.1 m., Md. 320, 5.0 m., and the Washington Beltway (Tour S 3), 6.3 m.

COLLEGE PARK, 24.1 m. at the Regents Drive entrance to the university, is the seat of the **University of Maryland**. The university campus encompasses 500 acres, with additional acreage being devoted to the research and teaching of agricultural subjects. The university has seventy principal structures built in the Georgian-Colonial style with an additional seventy supplementary buildings. Here are located the Colleges of Agriculture, Business and Management, Engineering, Education, Human Ecology, Journalism, Physical Education, Recreation and Health, the schools of Architecture and Library and Information Services, and the Graduate and Summer Schools. Also located on the campus are the Maryland Agricultural Experiment Station, the Cooperative Extension Service, and the U.S. Bureau of Mines and U.S. Bureau of Commercial Fisheries. In Baltimore (*see* Downtown Baltimore), the university has schools of Medicine, Law, Dentistry, Nursing, Pharmacy, Social Work, and Community Planning.

The **Administration Building** and **Symons Hall** form the center of the various colleges. Of particular interest are the **Armory; Cole Field House,** used for indoor sports; **Byrd Stadium** on the northwest corner of the campus, seating 50,000; and the interdenominational **Chapel,** a memorial to former Maryland students who died in World Wars I and II and in Korea. Facing U.S. 1 is the **Rossborough Inn,** a brick tavern built in 1799 and completely

Adelphi Mill

renovated in 1954 and now used as a faculty club. An attractive boxwood garden is located to the south of the inn.

The present University of Maryland was formed in 1920 by the union of Maryland State College, founded at College Park in 1856, with the old privately owned and operated University of Maryland in Baltimore (*see* Downtown Baltimore), which developed from the College of Medicine of Maryland chartered in 1807. Since 1946, the enrollment of the university has increased enormously to its current level of more than 33,800 students. During the presidency of Dr. H. C. Byrd, the university achieved a national reputation for excellence in football.

At 24.8 m. is the junction (L) with Calvert Road.

● Go left across the railroad tracks to Railroad Avenue, then left again to the **College Park Airport,** 0.5 m., site of the U.S. Army Flying School, opened in 1911. Here Gen. Henry Harley "Hap" Arnold and other Air Force officers received their air training. Closed in 1913, this airport was the Washington, D.C., terminus for the first scheduled airmail service between Washington, Philadelphia, and New York.

At 25.8 m. is the junction with Md. 410.

● Md. 410, the East-West Highway, is a heavily traveled circumferential route around northwest Washington. At 0.5 m. is the intersection with Adelphi Road. From here to Northwest Branch Park, a distance of nearly a mile, the highway passes the southern border of **Prince George's Plaza,** a development of nearly 400 acres, on the former estate of the beer-baron Christian Heurich. A comprehensive plan originally called for office and retail enterprises (to employ about 15,000 people), a variety of housing (from town houses to luxury tower apartments), and community facilities, including park and recreation areas. The land was acquired as a single tract by a developer who foresaw the need for creating high-density communities in the suburbs that would still preserve ample open space for the enjoyment of the residents. He sold parcels of the land with the understanding that each developer would participate in his comprehensive development plan, a necessarily flexible program that was a joint product of public planning agencies and a private firm. Part of the envisioned shopping center, some apartments, and a federal office building designed by Edward Durrell Stone have been constructed. This major experiment in community development has attracted the interest of European as well as American planners.

U.S. 1 intersects with Md. 412 in **RIVERDALE,** 25.9 m., a residential suburb of Washington, D.C.

● To the left on Md. 412 (Riverdale Road) is **Riversdale,** a Calvert mansion that is now used as the headquarters of the Prince George's County Delegation. The building is owned by the Maryland–National Capital Park and Planning Commission. The main block—minus portico— of this elegant five-part mansion is a modified replica of the Chateau du Mick, a Belgian home of Henri Joseph, Baron de Stier, who fled the French Revolution in 1794 and built this house between 1801 and 1802. His daughter Rosalie Eugenia married George Calvert, great-grandson of Benedict Calvert IV, and the couple moved to Riversdale when Baron de Stier returned to Belgium in 1803. The wings had probably been added by the time George Calvert died in 1838. Much of the interior ornamentation, presumably adapted from that of the Chateau du Mick by the English artist William Russell Birch, is elaborate, with highly decorated plaster friezes and cornices. The central salon has three arched panels in each wall, framed by decorated pilasters with Corinthian capitals. Windows and doors fill some panels; others were reserved for paintings. In the west salon, spaces between openings were designed for the great gilt mirrors that are still in place. The ornamentation in the great rooms in the later wings, which have ceilings eighteen feet high, is much more restrained; here no European model was followed.

On the lawn at the back of the house is an old seventeenth-century cannon that may be one of several dredged from the St. Mary's River at St. Inigoes (*see* Tour 29) in 1824; it is a duplicate of the one on the State House grounds at Annapolis that came from this group. The guns are believed to have come with the first colonists on the *Ark* in 1634 and to have been mounted at Fort Inigoes, which guarded the approach to St. Mary's City.

Charles Benedict Calvert (1808–64), who succeeded his father at Riversdale, was famous for his contributions to agriculture. He was one of the founders in 1856 of the Maryland Agricultural College (which formed the nucleus of the present College Park Campus of the University of Maryland). The college was established on part of his holdings, the Ross Borough Farm (*see above,* University of Maryland). The school was only the second agricultural college established in the Western Hemisphere. Calvert also vigorously supported Samuel Finley Breese Morse's efforts to get federal funds for the construction of the first telegraph. On April 9, 1844, Morse made the first successful test of his line from the capital to Riversdale. Charles Calvert was a close friend of Henry Clay, who visited Riversdale frequently. Clay supposedly drafted the Compromise of 1850 here.

U.S. 1 continues through the heavily populated suburbs of **HYATTSVILLE** (14,998 pop.) and **MT. RAINIER** (8,180 pop.), crosses the **District of Columbia Line** at 28.5 m., and continues into downtown Washington via Rhode Island Avenue.

**DELAWARE LINE–BALTIMORE–FREDERICK–HAGERSTOWN–
CUMBERLAND–KEYSER'S RIDGE–PENNSYLVANIA LINE; 210.4 m.**
U.S. 40, Alt. U.S. 40, I-70, and Md. 144

U.S. 40, which begins in Atlantic City and ends at San Francisco, follows one of the oldest routes through Maryland. East of Baltimore, the highway roughly parallels the post road used by colonial travelers. West of Baltimore, it follows the old pioneer route to the Ohio Valley. The section between Cumberland and Wheeling, West Virginia, completed in 1818, was the first road financed by the federal government, and it remained the travel artery across the Allegheny Mountains until 1852. Many of the taverns and blacksmith shops along this route were the nuclei around which present-day villages and towns have risen.

From the Delaware line to Baltimore, U.S. 40 is a dual highway that coincides with the old road for about half its length. East of Baltimore, sections of the old road are incorporated into Md. 7, and west of the city they form part of Md. 144.

2a. DELAWARE LINE–BALTIMORE CITY LINE; 57.4 m.
U.S. 40

From the Delaware line to Baltimore, U.S. 40 is a general-access dual-lane highway. Considered modern and safe when it was completed just before World War II, the route became very dangerous because of dense high-speed traffic within a decade of the war. Although superseded as a through route by the Kennedy Expressway (*see* Tour S 1), the highway is still heavily traveled. Traffic on the old road, Md. 7, which passes through more towns than does U.S. 40, is slower, but in many respects the route is more attractive. Although much of Cecil, Harford, and Baltimore counties is fertile grain and dairying country, the primary area served by U.S. 40 is a rapidly growing industrial corridor, especially south of the Susquehanna River. Even in the eighteenth and nineteenth centuries, ore furnaces and rolling mills, paper and textile mills, were among the small industrial enterprises that flourished sporadically along this route.

U.S. 40 crosses the **Maryland-Delaware Line,** 0.0 m., 16.1 m. west of the Delaware Memorial Bridge.

At 1.1 m. is the junction with Md. 7.

● Go right on Md. 7 to **ELKTON** (29' alt., 5,362 pop.), 1.2 m. at the junction of Main Street and Md. 7, the seat of Cecil County since 1786 and the Gretna Green of the East until 1938. As the closest Maryland county seat south of New York, New Jersey, and Pennsylvania, the town made a lucrative business of marrying couples unwilling to wait the time required in other states to receive a marriage license. Taxicab drivers met the trains and, for a set fee, took couples to the courthouse for the license and then to a parson for the ceremony. Legal marriages could only be performed by a minister, so signs advertising "marrying parsons" lined Main Street. In 1938, Maryland finally adopted the forty-eight-hour waiting period, but under special circumstances, such as the imminent transfer of a soldier overseas, the

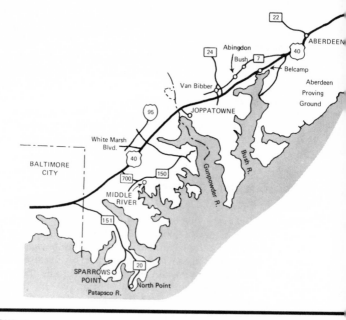

TOUR 2a

courts can waive the restrictions. Elkton still has its "wedding chapels" and remains a popular place for elopements.

During the eighteenth century, Elkton was called Head of Elk because of its location near the source of the Elk River. A post office was located at Head of Elk in 1776, and the town was an early shipping point for the wheat raised in the rich Piedmont. In 1807, Bay craft at Head of Elk loaded 250,000 bushels of flour grown in Lancaster County, Pennsylvania, which had been milled at grist mills on Big and Little Elk creeks. These creeks also supplied the water power for small paper and textile factories that were built in the area in the early nineteenth century. The Chrysler automobile plant at Newark, Delaware, about seven miles away, is the largest employer of area residents today, although over 2,000 people work in Elkton factories producing solid propellants, men's apparel, cable, mobile homes, electric motors, and rubber products.

Elkton was the scene of much activity during the American Revolution. In August of 1777, the British general Robert Howe decided to approach Philadelphia via Head of Elk, apparently because the area was believed to be sympathetic to the British. In March, 1781, Lafayette's troops embarked from Elkton for Annapolis on their way to Yorktown, returning early in April because the Bay was controlled by British ships. On April 11, Lafayette and his men departed again, this time by

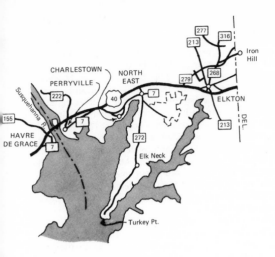

land rather than by water (*see* Tour 1a). They were followed in September by troops under the command of Washington and Rochambeau. In the War of 1812, a force from Adm. George Cockburn's British fleet attacked the town in April, 1813, but was repulsed.

Main Street in Elkton runs east to west and a number of old brick houses can still be seen along it, especially at the eastern end.

At the junction of Md. 7 and Main Street (to the left, through Elkton, Main Street is Md. 7), make a right onto Md. 281 (E. Main Street).

Hermitage Drive turns left off E. Main Street to the **Hermitage** (private, but visible from the road), a brick house, now converted into apartments, covered with yellow stucco. The central section of the house is said to have been built before 1732, when William and Arminta Alexander moved to the property. Their son Robert was a Tory during the American Revolution, who chose exile in England in 1777. According to legend, when Howe landed on Elk Neck in August, 1777, Alexander prepared a dinner, but while he was away delivering his invitation to Howe, the supper was consumed by American soldiers who were spying on the house. E. Main Street crosses **Gray's Hill**, just beyond the town limits; from here George Washington watched the British movements on Elk Neck in August, 1777.

● At 135 E. Main Street is the **Cecil County Public Library** (R) (open Mon., 9–9; Tues.–Fri., 9–5:30; Sat., 9–5; museum open by request), which houses a small, second-floor museum that illustrates the history of Elkton. Among the exhibits are a variety of old maps, including some showing British positions near the town in August, 1777.

Just beyond, continuing west along Main Street, is the **Mitchell House** (R) (private, but visible from the road), of stuccoed brick with the heavy modillioned cornice crossing the gables that is characteristic of old houses in this area. According to tradition, Dr. Abraham Mitchell from Lancaster County, Pennsylvania, built the house in 1769 and during the Revolution treated wounded Continental soldiers here. The Maryland Alcove in the chapel at Valley Forge is dedicated to Mitchell. The house later belonged to his son, Dr. George Mitchell (1785–1832) of Fair Hill (*see* Tour 1a), who was a prominent member of the Pike Expedition to Canada in 1813 and who, as a member of Congress (1822–26, 1829–32), introduced the resolution that led to Lafayette's tour of the United States in 1824.

The **Courthouse** (R), on Main Street east of North Street, was constructed in 1938 on the site of the eighteenth-century Fountain Inn.

Col. Henry Hollingsworth, who played a major role in the Revolution by serving as Commissary for the Eastern Shore, lived in the handsome brick house **Partridge Hill** (L) (private) at 129 Main Street (corner of Bow Street). The house, with its heavy keystone lintels and cornice that cross both gable ends, was standing in 1803 and is believed to have been built before the Revolution. From this corner, four old brick houses can be seen a block up Bow Street. For a block or two east of this point along Main Street the commercial section of Elkton resembles that of most other towns of its size in America.

At the intersection of Md. 7 and U.S. 213 (Main and Bridge streets), go west on Md. 7, then turn left onto Landing Lane, 0.3 m. Continue to U.S. 40, 0.5 m. Continue across U.S. 40 on Landing Lane. At 0.8 m. to the left at a fork is **ELK LANDING,** once the port at Head of Elk, and the **Site of Fort Hollingsworth,** 1.0 m., now on private property. The fort was a small redoubt constructed by local citizens during the War of 1812. After the British burned Frenchtown in late April, 1813, they attempted to reach Elkton by water, but guns at Fort Defiance about a mile further south on Elk Neck drove them back. The British then attempted to approach by land from the other side of the river, but their guide led them to Cedar Point opposite Fort Hollingsworth, and when the militia stationed there opened fire, the British retreated.

Property at Elk Landing came into the possession of Zebulon Hollingsworth, Sr., grandson of the first Hollingsworth in this area, in 1735 and is still in the possession of his descendants. Family account books from the early nineteenth century show that boats carrying flour, nails, bar iron, lumber, pork, and other supplies departed from Elk Landing for Baltimore and returned with coal, coffee, molasses, whiskey, and other supplies. In addition to these commercial activities, the Hollingsworths owned flour mills on both branches of the Elk River, and Henry Hollingsworth was one of the founders of a paper mill erected on Big Elk Creek in 1794.

● Md. 268 leaves Elkton on North Street. At 0.9 m. is the junction with Md. 279. Turn right. At 1.0 m. is the junction with Md. 316; go left to **Gilpin Manor** (L) (private, but visible from the road), 0.1 m., a white-painted stuccoed brick dwelling, the oldest part of which resembles Partridge Hall and other late-eighteenth-century houses in Elkton. Believed to have been built about 1760 by Joseph Gilpin, the house was greatly expanded about a century later. On Md. 316 at 2.7 m., turn left on Md. 277, which crosses Big Elk Creek at 3.2 m. **Elk Forge,** a long low stone building, is thought to have been constructed by a group of Philadelphia businessmen in 1761 to manufacture bar iron from pig iron produced in Lancaster County, Pennsylvania. In August, 1777, the British raided Elk Forge on their march to Philadelphia. Nevertheless, the property was confiscated during the Revolution because one of the principal owners, John Roberts of Philadelphia, was a Loyalist. The building, abandoned at present, was most recently used as a yarn spinning house.

Where Md. 277 crosses the creek is the site of a grist mill that was standing when the Elk Forge property was confiscated. Tradition has it that when the British raided the mill, they compelled the miller to grind flour for them. He mixed some ground glass in with the flour and was hanged when his deed was discovered.

A large four-story stone factory (L), built in 1846 by Daniel Lord of Litchfield, Connecticut, to make cotton damask, once stood at the foot of the hill that rises beyond the creek. The stone houses on either side of the road above were built about the same time to house the factory hands. Lord's brother-in-law, Col. William S. Baldwin of Litchfield, took over the factory and ran the company town with a benevolent, if feudal, hand. The **Baldwin House** (R) (private, but visible from the road), 3.3 m., is said to have been built before the Revolution, although the appearance of the structure suggests construction at the time of the damask factory. At the top of the hill is **Elk Mills**, 3.4 m. The **Baldwin Manufacturing Company,** no longer owned by the Baldwin family, made velours.

At 2.9 m. and 3.2 m. on Md. 279 are junctions with the Kennedy Expressway. At 4.0 m., in Delaware, is the junction with Iron Hill Road.

● Go right on Iron Hill Road to the Pennsylvania Railroad tracks at **IRON HILL, DELAWARE,** 0.4 m. A dirt road along the tracks leads left about a quarter of a mile to where the **Mason-Dixon Tangent Stone** can be seen in a pasture in back of a farmhouse. Beside the weathered marker set by Mason and Dixon in 1765, which still bears the Calvert and Penn coats of arms, is a stone inscribed "Tangent," placed there in 1849 by the Graham Resurvey. Both stones mark the point at which the boundary between Maryland and Delaware is tangent to an arc with a twelve-mile radius centered at New Castle. The tangent line was a boundary mentioned in one of the original deeds of enrollment whereby the Duke of York granted his Delaware territory to William Penn in 1682. Until 1732, however, the contesting Penn and Calvert heirs could not agree whether the twelve miles referred to the circumference or radius of the circle. The line was not finally settled until Mason and Dixon made their survey between 1763 and 1768.

Iron Hill is on the Welsh Tract, 30,000 acres of land William Penn granted to a group of Welsh Baptist miners in 1701 as part of his effort to claim some of what is now within the boundary of Maryland. The name of the tract refers to the iron that was mined here beginning in the early decades of the eighteenth century.

Md. 279 crosses the **Delaware Line,** 4.3 m., at a point about three miles southwest of Newark, Delaware.

Going west out of Elkton, U.S. 40 crosses **Beacon Hill** (L), 5.6 m., believed to have been used in the 1680s by George Talbot (*see* Tour 1a, Susquehanna Manor) as a site for beacon fires to alert settlers of hostile Indian movements.

At 9.1 m., U.S. 40 intersects Md. 272.

To the right, Md. 272 is a side tour of Tour 1a.
● Go left on Md. 272 to **NORTH EAST** (20′ alt., 1,818 pop.), 0.6 m. at the junction with Md. 7. A flour mill and an early bloomery—perhaps the first in Maryland—were erected on this site by 1716, and in 1735 the Principio Company (*see below*) established a forge here that remained in operation until 1780, with a brief revival of activity after the Revolution. From 1829 to 1893, another forge, and later a rolling mill, were constructed on the same site. The buildings in North East today date largely from the late nineteenth and early twentieth centuries. Md. 272 is Main Street and Md. 7, the old U.S. 40, crosses it in the center of town. North East has several small establishments that em-

ploy some 200 people in the production of baskets, fireworks, silica refractories, lumber, and ship repair and marine products. On S. Main Street (R) in a brick-walled churchyard shaded by a variety of trees stands **St. Mary Anne's Protestant Episcopal Church,** a quaint gambrel-roofed structure with clipped gables and wide roundheaded windows built in 1742. The brick is laid in Flemish bond with glazed headers on the main entrance wall and a Tudor-style crenellated stringcourse over the doorways. The Georgian bell tower was added in 1904 by Robert Brookings, founder of the Brookings Institution, in memory of his parents, who are buried in the churchyard.

Md. 272 continues south along the Northeast River, where fishing during the eighteenth and nineteenth centuries was unexcelled. During one twenty-six-day period in 1819, 2,700 barrels of herring were caught at one place on the river with only one haul of the seine each day. At 1.3 m., Irishtown Road branches left and in several places skirts **Elk Neck State Forest,** more than 2,700 acres of state-protected woodland, where hunting and fishing are permitted in season.

● Md. 272 continues to an intersection with Elk Neck Road (unmarked), 6.9 m.; bear right. This continues south to **Elk Neck State Park,** 8.8 m. (camping and picnicking year-round; rowboat rentals, boat launching, swimming, May 30–Labor Day; cabins available June–Sept., by reservation only, through the Annapolis office), part of which was presented to the state in 1936 by the naturalist Dr. William L. Abbott, who had established a game preserve here. From the shores of Elk River near the camping sites, a splendid view of the freighters proceeding up the river to the Chesapeake and Delaware Canal (*see* Tour 12a) can be had. On the other side of the park, a great white clay bank of the Bay shore can be seen, a landmark for mariners since the time of Capt. John Smith. In **ELK NECK,** Elk Neck Road becomes Turkey Point Road. The road ends near **Turkey Point Lighthouse** (1834), 12.2 m., a 35-foot tower on a 100-foot bluff, which is in a second section of the state park.

● From North East, Md. 7 proceeds south to a junction with Md. 267, 2.4 m.; a left turn on this leads through **CHARLESTOWN** (721 pop.), 3.2 m. at the firehouse. Md. 267 turns right at the firehouse on Market Street. Laid out along the shore of the Northeast River in 1742, the town was the residence of Peacock Bigger in 1752, who advertised that he had "just Imported from the West Indies . . . a choice parcel of Rum and Malasses." Eighteenth-century accounts of the town are hardly flattering—in 1762, Benjamin Mifflin described it as "a miserable forlorn place" with a landing too shallow for fifty-ton vessels —and an attempt to make Charlestown the county seat (1782–86) failed when construction of the courthouse was delayed for more than four years. Nevertheless, Charlestown prospered as a fishing town. A traveler in 1793 reported that 2,000 wagons of salted herring were transported from here to the back country each spring, though he described the town as bearing "every aspect of poverty and ruin." By contrast, Charlestown today is a pleasant village with a quiet waterfront, where an abandoned hotel attests to busier days. Three old houses still stand near the firehouse. The **Indian Queen** (private, but visible from the road), supposedly built in the mid-eighteenth century, is a small frame house with a central chimney—unusual in Maryland's hot climate—which allowed corner fireplaces in four rooms. The gambrel-roofed frame house next door is thought to have been the tavern where, according to his diary, George Washington stopped in 1795. On the other side of the road is a well-maintained brick house with inside end chimneys that appears to date from the early nineteenth century. Md. 267 (Market Street) turns right on Baltimore Street.

Md. 267 rejoins Md. 7 at 4.4 m. and Md. 7 rejoins U.S. 40 at 5.6 m.

Md. 7 branches off U.S. 40 again at 13.5 m.

Rural scene

● Go left on Md. 7; along this section of the old post road there are occasional glimpses of the Chesapeake Bay across the fields. The road crosses Principio Creek at 0.6 m. To the left in the beautiful little valley of this creek is the **Site of the Principio Iron Works** (no tres-passing) begun by English capitalists in 1719. Joseph Farmer, who selected the site and began construction of a furnace, was joined in 1722 by Stephen Onion and Thomas Russell, Sr., who bought nearly 12,000 acres to supply iron ore and timber for charcoal. The success of the enterprise, however, must be attributed to John England, an ironmaster of great practical skill and organizing ability, who arrived in 1723 to find that "ye furnis which, according to thy Information when at London, was verey near Ready to blow, is but 18 inch above ye Second Cuplings" and that no iron deposits of value had been purchased. He finished the furnace, located iron deposits on the Patapsco River, and in 1728 arranged an alliance with Augustine Wash-ington (father of George) to acquire his iron ore lands in Stafford County, Virginia. By the time of his death in 1734, England had made the Principio Furnace one of the most successful in the colonies, ca-pable of producing high-quality iron that would sell on the London market. In the 1740s, the Principio properties here, at *North East,* and at Accokeek in Virginia supplied almost half of all the pig iron ex-ported to England. Skilled supervision was a necessity for maintain-ing good quality, however, and in the 1760s and again shortly before the Revolution, Thomas Russell, Jr., came from England to run the furnace. During the Revolution, Russell made bar iron and cannonballs for the Americans, and when the furnace was confiscated as British property in 1780, the forge at North East was given to him as compensa-tion. New owners built another furnace after the Revolution, which was destroyed by the British in 1813. In 1837, the Whitaker Iron Com-pany built a third furnace, which produced pig iron until 1889. Produc-tion of iron coke furnaces from ore mined in Alabama and the Lake Superior region eventually made the Maryland charcoal iron industry obsolete, although a forge here continued to make high-quality iron for steam boiler tubes until 1925. Today, near the breastworks of a dam, part of the nineteenth-century stone furnace and remains of other buildings can be seen covered with honeysuckle and poison ivy.

At 0.8 m. is a stone building (L). The sign on the building indicates that this belonged to the Whitaker Iron Company.

Md. 7 continues to **PERRYVILLE** (20′ alt., 2,091 pop.), 3.1 m. at the junction with U.S. 222 on the Susquehanna River close to its mouth. The Pennsylvania Railroad maintains a division repair shop here, and this was once the **Site of the Susquehanna Lower Ferry,** a crossing used by eighteenth-century travelers who took the coastal route, which is mentioned in many diaries and letters. Washington and Rochambeau and their troops crossed here on their land journey to Yorktown in 1781. **Rodgers Tavern** (R) (under restoration), 3.6 m., by the river at the Pennsylvania Railroad bridge, is an old stone building believed to have been standing in 1745 and to have been a tavern operated by William Stephenson before John Rodgers, father of Com. John Rodgers (*see below,* Iron Hill), took it over in 1780. This appears to be the tavern in which Benjamin Mifflin in 1762 ate "a Fine dish of the Largest Oldwives that Ever I Eat"; George Washington mentions stopping here many times, especially during the 1780s and 1790s. A local group is now restoring the building. A railroad had been built between Philadelphia and Baltimore by 1837, with a steam ferry transferring railroad cars across the river. During the winter of 1852–53, the river froze so hard and so long that the tracks were laid on ice for several weeks. In 1866, a railroad bridge was finally built; it was used as the first highway bridge when the present railroad bridge was built in 1906.

Just beyond the railroad bridge, the road becomes the entrance road to **Perry Point Hospital** (get pass at sentry box), 3.8 m., a Veterans Administration hospital for the mentally ill. **Perry Point Mansion** (private), formerly occupied by the superintendent, is a hip-roofed, stuccoed brick building. The property was patented in 1658 by John Bateman and later named Perry Point. From 1710 to 1729 Richard Perry and his two sons owned the land. In 1729, the Thomas family purchased the property. During the time of the family's ownership (1729–1800), the mill and the house are believed to have been built. In 1800, John Stump bought the manor and the farm of about 1,800 acres. The family turned the farm over to the Union army during the Civil War, and the troops inflicted considerable damage to the house during their stay. In 1918, the U.S. government bought the farm of 516 acres from the Stump family. After the armistice, Perry Point became a rehabilitation center, supply depot, and psychiatric hospital. In 1930, the VA hospital was established. In 1974, the Veterans Administration began restoring the deteriorating house.

U.S. 40 makes a junction with U.S. 222 at 16.3 m. (*see* Tour 1a).

The highway bridge across the Susquehanna River (toll) crosses **GARRETT ISLAND,** named for John W. Garrett (1820–84), president of the Baltimore & Ohio Railroad during the Civil War. In the eighteenth century the island was named for Edward Palmer, an Englishman who is believed to have established the first trading post in the area here in the 1670s.

The Susquehanna River, one of the longest rivers on the Atlantic seaboard, is navigable for the five miles from the Bay to Port Deposit for boats of no more than twelve-foot draft (*see* Tour 1a). Canals that enabled rafts and barges to bring grain, timber, and other products to the mouth of the river were completed on the eastern shore by 1808 and on the western shore by 1839, but railroads supplanted the rafts by the end of the nineteenth century.

At 18.4 m., on the other side of the Susquehanna River, is the junction with Md. 155 and Md. 7.

● Go right on Md. 155. At 1.9 m. a private lane (L) turns into **Sion Hill** (private), which is named for the estate of the Dukes of Northumberland on the Thames River in England. Rev. John Ireland, rector of St. George's Parish (*see below*) from 1787 to 1792, owned Sion Hill from 1789 to 1795 and opened Sion Hill Seminary, a boys' school that did not prosper. In 1795, Gabriel Dennison of Philadelphia bought the property. His daughter married Com. John Rodgers (1771–1838), naval hero of the War of 1812, who was in charge of the naval forces at the Battle of Baltimore (*see* East and Northeast Baltimore, Patterson Park). The Rodgerses made their home at Sion Hill, and their descendants still live here.

At 2.2 m. and 2.6 m. Md. 155 makes junctions with the Kennedy Expressway and Tour S 1. It continues to Churchville, 9.1 m. (*see* Tour 1a).

● To the left, Md. 7 leads to the river and a junction with Union and Washington streets in **HAVRE DE GRACE** (35′ alt., 9,791 pop.), 0.6 m. This site at the mouth of the Susquehanna was probably first settled by William Claiborne's men early in the 1630s. During the eighteenth century it was known as Susquehanna Lower Ferry, and a traveler in 1777 spoke of the taverns here and on the east shore as the "two best [public] houses between Philadelphia and Edenton." The tavern on the west shore at this time was operated by Col. John Rodgers, father of Com. John Rodgers of *Sion Hill*, who later moved his enterprise across the river (*see above*, Rodgers Tavern).

The town of Havre de Grace was established in 1785—the name is said to have been suggested by Lafayette—and it made an unsuccessful bid to become the county seat in 1786. A map printed in 1790 shows sites for a courthouse, jail, almshouse, hospital, and college. There were about fifty dwellings in the town in 1795, described as "decent two-story brick houses," but on May 3, 1813, Adm. George Cockburn's fleet shelled and burned the town, damaging or destroying nearly every building. During the nineteenth century, herring fishing was an important business in the town, especially after 1820, when a local fisherman, Asabel Bailey, devised the float—a platform anchored in the river from which huge seine nets were set and hauled. Today, Havre de Grace, with its magnificent transportation facilities provided by railroads, express highways, and the Bay, and its beautiful location at the mouth of the river, is at the northern end of an industrial corridor that begins in Baltimore. The town has hopes of becoming a major industrial center, and at present there are chemical and plastic companies, a boat yard, bottling plants, a tin-can factory, a soap and wax products company, and a cyanamid company located in the area.

By the river beside the railroad bridge is a large 2½-story stuccoed brick house with great double end chimneys, locally called the **Ferry House** (L), which was built to replace the one destroyed by the British. The building now serves as an American Legion Post. Just beyond, Union and Washington streets fork. For a block or two, Washington Street (L) is the main commercial area. Union Street (R), Md. 7, is an attractive tree-lined residential section. At the corner of Union Street and Congress Avenue is **St. John's Protestant Episcopal Church** (L), part of which was built in 1809. The British wrecked the interior in 1813; the walls survived. In 1831 and again in the 1860s the building was expanded, but it remains a simple brick structure with narrow roundheaded windows.

At the end of Union Street, past the **Harford Memorial Hospital**, is the **City Park** (picnicking and fishing), which fronts on the Bay and includes a yacht anchorage. To the east of the park on Concord Point at the end of Lafayette Street (two streets before the park) is the **Havre de Grace Lighthouse**, built in 1829 on the site of the small fort from which a local hero, Lt. John O'Neill, fired a single cannon at the British during the attack in 1813. O'Neill was captured and held prisoner for three days before being released. Until his death in 1838, O'Neill was the lighthouse keeper, and his descendants continued to hold the post until the 1920s. The light is now automatic.

● Md. 7 turns right off Union Street onto Revolution Street just before the hospital and travels 1.2 m. to the edge of town. Just before the road crosses the railroad track to rejoin U.S. 40, a paved road branches left and a historic marker records that the Comte de Rochambeau camped here on September 9, 1781, after crossing the Susquehanna River. The road once led to the Havre de Grace Race Track, a mile course that opened in 1912. Until the track was closed in 1950, special trains ran from Philadelphia, Baltimore, and Washington to Havre de Grace for the brief period of the races each year.

At 21.2 m. on U.S. 40 is a junction with Md. 132.

● Turn left on Md. 132, which immediately turns right. Go straight ahead on Oakington Road to **Oakington** (private), 1.5 m., the 555-acre estate of Millard D. Tydings (1890–1961), U.S. senator from Maryland from 1927 to 1951. Tydings's son Joseph, who served in the U.S. Senate from 1964 to 1970, now lives here. The central section of the great stone house is said to have been built in 1810 by John Wilson Stump, son of John Stump of Stafford (*see* Tour 1a, Susquehanna State Park). In 1900, two frame wings were added, one of which has been replaced by a large stone addition. In a beautiful box garden at the side of the house are many old-fashioned flowers.

ABERDEEN (80′ alt., 7,403 pop.), 22.3 m., is the home of many of the civilian employees of the nearby proving ground. Along U.S. 40 are numerous restaurants and service stations.

Right from Aberdeen on Md. 22 to the intersection with the Kennedy Expressway and Tour S 1, 2.0 m., and to Churchville, 6.3 m., the road becomes a side route of Tour 1a.

Left on Md. 22 leads to the *Aberdeen Proving Ground.*

At 24.6 m. is the junction with Md. 715.

● Go right on Md. 715, which is the main access road to the **Aberdeen Proving Ground** (visitor information available at the main gate), established in 1917 to develop and test ordnance; it is now a 80,000-acre reservation, nearly one-half of it water, employing both military and civilian personnel. Near the entrance, a display of U.S. tanks (R) illustrates their development beginning with 1918 models. On the Ground are outdoor displays of foreign artillery, foreign tanks, and U.S. artillery. To the right, at the end of Aberdeen Road, signs point the way to Building #5, the **Ordnance Museum.** Here is perhaps the most complete collection of ordnance in the world, including German V-1 and V-2 rockets.

At 25.3 m. is a junction with Md. 7.

● Go left 0.3 m. to Perryman Road, then right at an acute angle to **Old Spesutie Church** (R), 1.5 m. Built in 1851 from plans drawn by John Rudolph Niernsee and J. Crawford Neilson, a team who designed many of the churches and houses in and about Mount Vernon Place in Baltimore, it replaced a church raised in 1760, and bricks from the original structure were used in its construction. The rectangular structure of the church was dictated by its placement on the old foundations, but the architects added a pentagonal apse and a bell tower at one corner, square at the base but tapering to an octagonal spire. The church serves St. George's Parish, laid out in 1693 as one of the original Anglican parishes in Maryland. The small brick **Vestry House,** which was built in 1766 and doubled as a schoolhouse, still stands in the churchyard. Among those buried under the old trees is Col. Thomas White (1704–79), father of the first bishop of the Protestant Episcopal

Lighthouse, Havre de Grace

Church in the United States, William White. The name Spesutie means Utie's Hope and is the name given by Col. Nathaniel Utie to the island, now part of the Aberdeen Proving Ground, that he owned and lived on in the 1660s when he was commander of the northern frontier.

● Go right on Md. 7 to **BUSH** (150′ alt.), 4.0 m., the first county seat of Harford County (1744–82); the town was originally called Harford Town for Henry Harford, the last lord proprietor. Here, on March 22, 1775, the thirty-four members of the Committee of Observation for Harford County signed what is known as the Bush Declaration, a statement in which they pledged their support to the Continental Congress "at the risque of our lives and fortunes."

John Paca, father of William Paca, laid out **ABINGDON** (150′ alt.), 4.8 m., in 1779, and in June, 1785, **Cokesbury College** (L) (historical marker at 5.3 m.), first Methodist college in the Western Hemisphere, was established here by Bishops Thomas Coke and Francis Asbury. Discipline was stern, with one rule stating that "students shall be indulged with nothing which the world calls play. Let this rule be observed with the strictest nicety: for those who play when they are young will play when they are old." The curriculum included seven hours of study daily, a manual training course, and gardening. The college building burned in 1795.

At 6.1 m. Md. 7 crosses a small stream called Ha Ha Branch, which derives its name from the nearby "Ah Ah tracts"—Ah Ah, Indeed; Ah Ah, the Cow Pasture; and others. For generations a laughing ghost kept night walkers at bay in the vicinity of Ha Ha Branch.

At 6.7 m. is an historical marker (L) that commemorates the **Site of the Birthplace of William Paca** (1740–1800), a signer of the Declaration of Independence (*see* Annapolis Tour). The actual site of the Paca homestead is believed to be about a mile and a half closer to the Bay on the south side of U.S. 40.

In **VAN BIBBER**, 6.8 m., is the junction with Md. 24. To the left Md.

24 crosses U.S. 40, 0.7 m., to *Edgewood Arsenal;* to the right it intersects with the Kennedy Expressway, 0.8 m., continues past **St. Mary's Protestant Episcopal Church** (R) (open), a picturesque stone building (1851), and joins Tour 1a in Bel Air, 6.8 m.

At 27.5 m. on U.S. 40, a small dirt lane (R) crosses the railroad tracks to **Sophia's Dairy** (private), a large 2½-story brick house built in 1768 by Capt. Aquila Hall, sheriff, county justice, and signer of the Bush Declaration (*see above*). The house is well known for its beautiful double stairway in the wide central hall.

At **BELCAMP** (640 pop.), 27.7 m., is the Bata Shoe Company's factory and housing estate. The entire community has been erected since 1939 by a Czechoslovakian firm that left Zlin, Czechoslovakia, after the Nazi occupation. It comprises a model factory turning out 170,000 pairs of shoes weekly, a five-story hotel and community center, and nearly a hundred brick and frame houses, all occupied by company employees at low rentals.

At 29.9 m. is the junction with Emmorton Road.

Right on Emmorton Road to Md. 24, 1.3 m., and left on Md. 24 leads to I-95, 1.6 m., and Bel Air, 7.6 m. (*see* Tour 1a).

● Go right on Md. 24 to **Edgewood Arsenal** (admission on pass at sentry box), 2.0 m., the U.S. Army chemical warfare station that was merged with Aberdeen Proving Ground in 1971. The entire section of land at Gunpowder Neck, which housed portions of Edgewood Arsenal and Aberdeen Proving Ground, is referred to as the Edgewood Area of the Proving Ground.

At 35.9 m. is the junction (L) with Joppa Farm Road at the Joppa Town Shopping Center just north of Gunpowder Falls.

● Turn left on Joppa Farm Road to Townewood Road, 0.3 m. Turn right on Townewood Road to Town Center Drive, 0.8 m. Turn left to Bridge Drive, 1.2 m. Turn right on Bridge Drive to the **Site of Joppa Town**, which is located on the Gunpowder River. This town was the seat of Baltimore County from 1712 to 1768. The town was laid out in 1724 and became a major tobacco exporting point, but as the harbor silted up and Baltimore grew, Joppa suffered from the competition. In 1768, Baltimore became the county seat and from then on Joppa declined. In old Joppa Town, only the **Rumsey House** (private) (straight ahead on Bridge Drive), an interesting 2½-story brick structure with a gambrel roof, is left. The house is believed to have been built about 1720 by James Maxwell, one of the early justices of the county, and to have been enlarged about 1771 when it was acquired by Col. Benjamin Rumsey, a member of the Continental Congress who died here in 1808.

It was here at Joppa Town that John Paul, Walter Pigot, and two others were arrested in April, 1781, for furnishing the British with flour. Pigot had mistaken Lafayette's men for the British as the French were returning by ship from Annapolis to Elkton and had offered them the flour, which was on a boat hidden in the Gunpowder River. John Paul escaped, allegedly by hiding under the hoop skirts of one of the Joppa ladies, but Pigot was imprisoned at the home of Sheriff James Rigbie and was tried by court-martial and hanged (*see* Tour 1a, Nathan Rigbie House).

Ebenezer Road branches left off U.S. 40 at 40.2 m.

● Go left 3.8 m. to a junction with Md. 150 (Eastern Boulevard); continue straight ahead to the **Dundee Beach** area of **Gunpowder State Park**, 1.9 m., where a beach marina and other public facilities have been constructed. Gunpowder State Park, encompassing about 10,000 acres of land, lies along the Gunpowder River and Big and Little Gunpowder falls, all streams of great natural beauty.

A left turn off Eastern Boulevard and another left on Greenbank Road leads to the Pennsylvania Railroad Bridge (visible from the road) across the Gunpowder River.

On July 11, 1864, Confederate cavalry commanded by Harry Gilmor captured the morning express from the North at Magnolia across the river, emptied it of passengers, set it afire, and pushed it onto the railroad bridge, partly burning the structure. A Federal gunboat, which was supposed to be protecting the bridge, failed to get up steam in time to do more than rescue the passengers. Gilmor's mission was to cut Federal communications with the North after the Battle of the Monocacy. At the same time, Gen. Bradley Johnson was to cut the railroad connections between Baltimore and Washington at Beltsville and then dash to the prisoner-of-war camp at Point Lookout in St. Mary's County (see Tour 29), release its ten to twelve thousand prisoners, and march them to Washington, D.C. In the meantime, Gen. Jubal Early was to have reached and taken the capital, and the prisoners were to be armed from the arsenal there. In fact, Early found Washington so well defended that he called off Johnson's trip to Point Lookout. If the plan had been successful the course of the war might have been dramatically altered. Gilmor later claimed, perhaps correctly, that with a few more men he could have taken Baltimore with ease, for he met almost no resistance.

At 40.4 m. is the White Marsh access road to I-95 (R), 1.0 m., and at 43.7 m., Md. 700 (Martin Boulevard) turns left.

● Take Md. 700 to the **Martin Company**, 2.0 m. (no admittance), formerly the Glenn L. Martin Company, now a division of Martin Marietta Corp. More than 1,000 employees work here on aerospace production and aircraft modification. The Vanguard satellite was made at the plant.

At 44.7 m. and 44.9 m. are the connections with the Baltimore Beltway and Tour S 2 and at 45.1 m. U.S. 40 crosses the **Baltimore City Line.** At 47.4 m. is a connection to the Harbor Tunnel Thruway and Tour S 1. This route by-passes downtown Baltimore via the Harbor Tunnel (toll) and I-695, the Baltimore Beltway (Tour S 2).

At 48.5 m. is a junction with Md. 151 (Erdman Avenue) going east.

● Erdman Avenue joins the North Point Road at 1.0 m. and becomes a dual highway that travels the peninsula between the Back and Patapsco rivers to Sparrows Point. The shore of the Patapsco is heavily industrialized, and the area behind has developed rapidly. At 5.0 m. is a junction (marked) with Md. 20, the old North Point Road, on the right, and a junction with an unmarked road on the left.

Go left on the unmarked road to the **Aquila Randall Monument,** 0.3 m., raised in 1817 to the memory of a member of the Mechanical Volunteers, Fifth Regiment of Maryland Militia, who died in the Battle of North Point, September 12, 1814. At about this place, where the head of Bear Creek is little more than half a mile from the Back River, the main engagement between the British and Americans took place. About 4,000 British troops had landed at the tip of the peninsula early on the morning of September 12. Gen. John Stricker and about 3,185 Americans had taken positions at the head of Bear Creek the preceding night. Around noon, a British advance party led by Maj. Gen. Robert Ross encountered a volunteer American detachment sent to attack it, and close to this spot Ross was killed by an unknown American rifleman (see East and Northeast Baltimore, Wells-McComas Monument). Six hundred of the American troops were held in reserve and over 900 fled when attacked by the main force of the British, but the remaining 1,500 stood firm. After an hour of fighting, by Stricker's account, he ordered a retreat to the line held by the reserves. According to the British account, the Americans "fled as every man best could from the field." In any case, the British did not pursue. Stricker regrouped his men a mile and a half away, awaited further attack, and then withdrew to Worthington's Mill near the well-defended eastern defense line of Baltimore (*see* East and Northeast Baltimore, Patterson Park). This tenacious defense by 1,500 Americans facing 4,000 trained British regulars was sufficient to deter further British efforts to take the city once the naval bombardment of Fort McHenry had failed (*see* South Baltimore, Fort McHenry).

At 1.4 m., the unmarked road joins Md. 151.

Continuing down Md. 151, in a large field on the right, is the **Site of the Gorsuch Farmhouse,** 6.7 m., where General Ross breakfasted on September 12, 1814, and is supposed to have boasted that he would "eat dinner in Baltimore or in Hell."

Md. 151 crosses the narrow neck created by Humphrey Creek, where General Stricker started an entrenchment on the night of September 11–12 that was not yet completed when the British reached it early in the morning. Here an overpass leads to Md. 20, 7.1 m., which continues to **Fort Howard,** 4.0 m. (obtain pass at sentry box). From 1896 to 1924, a Coast Guard artillery station here protected Baltimore. A marker on North Point marks the place where the British landed. Since 1944, the fort has been a Veterans Administration hospital.

● At 7.8 m. on Md. 151 is **SPARROWS POINT** (7,550 pop.), best known for the steel mill and shipyard of the **Bethlehem Steel Company.** The Pennsylvania Steel Company built blast furnaces here in 1889 to make pig iron from Cuban ores, which was then shipped to its Harrisburg steel mill. Two years later the Maryland Steel Company, organized under the same ownership, took over the Sparrows Point plants and began to manufacture Bessemer steel. In 1916, Bethlehem bought the plant and developed it into the largest Tidewater steel mill in the United States, capable of producing 1,000 tons of steel per hour. When fully operational, the steel mill and shipyard here employ over 25,000 men. Md. 151 ends at Sparrows Point.

U.S. 40 crosses Baltimore via Orleans Street, Franklin Street, and Edmondson Avenue. On its way this route passes the Johns Hopkins Hospital, the Gay Street Firehouse, the First Unitarian Church, the Minor Basilica of the Assumption of the Blessed Virgin Mary, the Enoch Pratt Free Library, and the Franklin Street Presbyterian Church. The western city line is crossed at 57.4 m.

2b. BALTIMORE CITY LINE–FREDERICK; 39.9 m.
Md. 144 and I-70

Before 1765 a road—not much more than a trail—had been cut from Baltimore to Frederick Town. About 1774 the Ellicotts, at their own expense, opened a superior wagon road from their mills to Baltimore, a distance of twelve miles; they then extended it to join the older road toward Frederick Town at a point four miles north of their mills. This then became the main route between the two towns.

Generations ago, the road was kept in repair by "wheelbarrow men," bands of prisoners directed by armed overseers. At night the road workers were housed and fed in widely dispersed log cabins built every few miles along the road.

The first section of U.S. 40, 9.1 miles long, was opened to

traffic in 1939. This concrete extension of Edmondson Avenue in Baltimore by-passed Catonsville and Ellicott City and rejoined Md. 144, which was old U.S. 40, 3.7 miles west of Ellicott City. U.S. 40–I-70 now extends across Maryland and runs parallel to Md. 144 from Baltimore to Frederick.

Between Baltimore and Catonsville is a suburban area of small homes, with a few larger houses that were built late in the nine-teenth century, when this section was a fashionable summer settlement. West of Ellicott City is farming country, now dotted with patches of new housing.

West of Baltimore, Md. 144 follows Frederick Avenue. At 0.0 m. is the **National Cemetery** (L), and the **Baltimore City Line.** Just beyond the city line is a junction with Nunnery Lane (R).

● Turn right at Nunnery Lane, 0.3 m. At the end of Nunnery Lane turn right. Go straight on Edmondson Avenue. Turn left onto Academy Road. At the corner of Academy Road and Whitfield Avenue is **Mount De Sales Academy,** a Roman Catholic secondary and college prepara-tory school for girls which was established in 1852. The library con-tains 142 plates of Audubon's *Quadrupeds of North America* and some 50 plates of Rex Brasher's *Birds and Trees of North America.*

CATONSVILLE (500′ alt., 54,812 pop.), 1.2 m. at the intersection with Ingleside Avenue, is a suburb of comfortable homes and modern stores. It is older than Baltimore and was first called Johnnycake, after an inn here that was famed for its cornbread. About 1800 the town was renamed in honor of Richard Caton, a son-in-law of Charles Carroll of Carrollton. An estate that in-cluded the site was Carroll's gift to the Catons.

Today Catonsville is liberally supplied with colleges. The larg-est is the University of Maryland, Baltimore County Campus, which is south of Md. 144 and is most easily reached by the Baltimore Beltway exit for Wilkens Avenue. Other schools in-clude St. Mary's Seminary, a Roman Catholic institution, and Catonsville Community College. Spring Grove State Hospital is also located here between the beltway and the grounds of the German Orphans' Home on Bloomsbury Avenue.

On Md. 144, make a right on Ingleside Avenue, 1.3 m.

● **St. Timothy's Protestant Episcopal Church** (R), 0.2 m., is a rectangular stone building of Gothic design erected in 1844. It is next to the **Site of the old Catonsville Military Academy,** founded in 1845 and believed to be the first religiously affiliated military school in the United States. John Wilkes Booth, assassin of Abraham Lincoln, was a student here (1851–52). The academy burned in 1862.

On Md. 144, the business section of **ELLICOTT CITY** (144′ alt., 9,506 pop.), 4.4 m., county seat and principal banking and trading center of Howard County, lies along narrow congested Main Street. The houses, built of dark local granite, appear to be wedged in the rocky hillside. Some of the buildings on the south side of Main Street straddle the narrow Tiber Creek, which flows into the Patapsco at this point. The town developed around the Ellicotts' grist and flour mills established in 1774 on the east bank of the river. Following the building of the Cum-berland Road westward and the coming of the railroad in 1830, the town grew rapidly. In 1864, many men, wounded in the

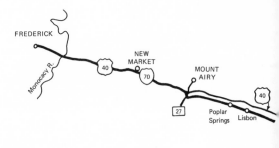

Battle of the Monocacy, received care here until they could be sent to Baltimore.

To the left is the **Site of Ellicotts' Mills,** founded by John, Joseph, and Andrew Ellicott, sons of Andrew Ellicott, a Quaker who emigrated in 1730 from England to Bucks County, Pennsylvania. They bought land and water rights here in 1774 and brought machinery of their own invention by boat from Philadelphia to Elkridge Landing and thence overland to the mill site, where they built comfortable dwellings for themselves and their workers. Two of Joseph Ellicott's sons, who grew up here, became noted surveyors. Andrew (1754–1820) redrew L'Enfant's plan of Washington, D.C., for Thomas Jefferson and surveyed several state boundaries and, in 1796, the frontier between the United States and Florida, which at that time belonged to Spain. Andrew's protégé, Benjamin Banneker, the noted black scientist, assisted him in the Washington project. Joseph (1760–1826) was the surveyor and the western land agent for the Holland Land Company. He founded Buffalo, New York, and advocated construction of the Erie Canal, later correcting the early surveys made for the project. He spent his last years in an asylum suffering from melancholia. For sixty years Ellicotts successfully operated the mill here, and Patapsco flour became widely known. During the Panic of 1837, however, the plant was turned over to Charles Gambrill and Charles Carroll, son of Charles Carroll of Carrollton. Thirty-one years later the mill, bridge, dam, and several houses were washed away in a flood, and forty-two persons were drowned. In 1972 and again in 1975 severe damage was caused by hurricanes Agnes and Eloise respectively.

On the road in front of the mill is the site of the **Jonathan Ellicott House** (1782), a 2½-story stone structure with dormers. The building was destroyed by the flood of Hurricane Agnes in 1972. About 200 yards west is the **George Ellicott Residence,** a three-story stone building erected before 1790 and much altered since then.

The first building (R) on Main Street, west of the railroad

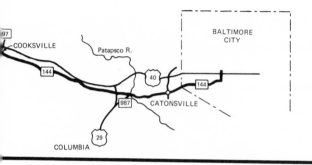

bridge over the street, is the old **Patapsco Hotel,** a granite structure. Tradition has it that on a Sunday morning during his presidential campaign Henry Clay appeared on the balcony that extended across the front of this building. A crowd quickly gathered and shouted for a speech. Clay held up his arms for silence. But before he could begin, the sound of a church bell was heard, whereupon Clay called out: "My friends and fellow citizens, the notes of yonder church bell remind me that this is a day for prayer and not for public speaking." Once more he raised his hands, this time in benediction, and retired to his room.

The exterior of the stone **Baltimore & Ohio Railroad Depot,** directly opposite, is little changed since the first horsecars were hauled here from Baltimore over strap-iron rails on May 24, 1830. The rounded stone wall, extending south from the station and now part of the platform, was the foundation of a turntable. The depot is now registered as a National Historic Landmark and is undergoing restoration.

The old **Colonial Inn and Opera House** (R), two doors west of the hotel, is a five-story building with a series of cellars dug out of the rocky hillside behind each of the first four stories. It is reported to be the site where John Wilkes Booth made his theatrical debut.

In the **Ellicott Burial Ground,** a few hundred yards (L) on steep Columbia Pike, are the graves of Andrew and John Ellicott and some of their descendants. Beyond the cemetery a private lane leads to the **Friends Meeting House** (private), a plain rectangular brick building with low gables, built in 1800; it has served as a meeting house, a war hospital, and a school.

Left on Merryman Street (opposite Court House Road) is a **Log Cabin** (L) (not open) built by a settler in 1780. It was a meeting site for the St. Luke A.M.E. Church.

Facing Court House Road (R) is the **Howard County Courthouse** (L) (open Mon.–Fri., 10–3; Sat.–Sun., 10–4) on Capitoline Hill. Like most buildings in Ellicott City it is a Classic-

Revival structure of local granite. The battered old British cannon on the lawn, captured at the Battle of Bladensburg in the War of 1812 by "Bachelor" John Dorsey, was one of the few souvenirs the Americans got out of that encounter.

Next to the Court House is the **First Presbyterian Church,** home of the **Howard County Historical Society** (open first and third Tues. of every month, 1–3:30). The church was built in 1844.

On Church Road is the **Old Manse** (L). This building served as the parsonage, or manse, for the Presbyterian Church.

Further up Church Road on the left is **Mount Ida.** It was built by an Ellicott in 1828.

The **Angelo Cottage** (R) (private), also on Church Road, is a Gothic-Revival house built in 1831 by Samuel Vaughn, a French artist. The octagonal-turreted structure, overlooking a ravine from the rim of Tarpeian Rock, aroused such curiosity that the B & O Railroad ran excursion trains to the site from Baltimore in 1831.

On Institute Road, at the top of the hill, are the gutted, roofless walls of the **Patapsco Female Institute** (L), a large granite Greek-Revival structure overlooking the Patapsco River valley. Established on seven acres of land donated in 1829 by the Ellicott family, the school was supported by private contributions and annual grants by the state. For fifteen years before the Civil War, the headmistress was Mrs. Almira Hart Lincoln Phelps, a pioneer in education for women. Winnie Davis, daughter of Jefferson Davis, and Alice Montague, mother of the Duchess of Windsor, were pupils here. After the war the fortunes of the school declined, and it finally closed its doors in 1890.

● Md. 987, the Old Columbia Pike, turns left from Main Street in Ellicott City to wind steeply up Tongue Row, flanked by picturesque old stone houses. This area was once owned by a Mrs. Tongue. It is now occupied by shops and businesses. At 1.6 m. on Md. 987, turn south on U.S. 29.

COLUMBIA (420' alt., 8,815 pop.), a new town built up around the intersection of Md. 108 and U.S. 29 since 1966, has followed a carefully planned development balanced between residential housing, shops, and industry to sustain the community. It has proved to be a successful venture in the "New Town" concept.

At 6.9 m. on Md. 144 is **St. John's Protestant Episcopal Church** (R). Originally a chapel of ease of Queen Caroline Parish in 1728, it was incorporated in 1822 by the General Assembly of Maryland.

At 8.7 m. Md. 144 is intersected by Centennial Lane.

● Turn left. At 1.2 m. is a side road (Burnside Drive) on the right. Take this road to the white pillars on the left. This is the entrance to **Burleigh Manor** (private), a yellow brick house built around 1805 by Col. Rezin Hammond, a Revolutionary War leader who participated in the burning of the *Peggy Stewart* at Annapolis. The house remained in the Hammond family for almost 150 years. The main 2½-story structure is connected with a two-story wing by a short gallery. An unusual feature is the wide L-shaped hall. During World War II, Burleigh Manor was owned by Mrs. Anthony J. Drexel Biddle, Jr., of Philadelphia, who bought it for her daughter and son-in-law, Prince Alexandre Hohenlohe of Poland.

Md. 144 joins U.S. 40 at 8.9 m. by the Font Hill Golf Club. At 9.4 m. Md. 144 branches left.

An old house (L), 10.3 m., formerly the gatehouse of Doughoregan Manor and a good example of Gothic-Revival architecture, marks the junction with Manor Lane.

● Left on Manor Lane to the tree-lined entrance (R) to **Doughoregan Manor** (private; St. Mary's Chapel open for Mass Sun. only), the home of Charles Carroll of Carrollton, who survived all other signers of the Declaration of Independence. The two-story manor house, built between 1735 and 1745, is 300 feet long with two ells; the whole exemplifies the eighteenth-century passion for axial symmetry. The south ell contains servants' quarters; the north ell is a richly furnished Roman Catholic chapel, a reminder of the days when Roman Catholic services were conducted privately. The chapel has been remodeled several times but still retains the same general lines as the manor house. The central section of the roof is surmounted by a railed platform and an octagonal cupola. From the roof promenade can be seen a great part of the original estate of more than 13,000 acres with beautiful lawns shaded by great elms and more farm buildings and quarters that housed almost a thousand slaves. A Doric portico with chamber above has been added to the front. The interior is paneled with oak and decorated with hunting scenes and family portraits by Kuhn, Sully, and other early American painters.

Charles Carroll of Carrollton, of the third generation of this illustrious family, was born in Annapolis, September 19, 1737. His grandfather, land agent for Lord Baltimore, had acquired thousands of desirable acres in the colony, including the manor of Carrollton near Frederick. Young Carroll spent several years in France and completed his education with the study of law in London. Returning to America when he was twenty-eight, he found himself barred from practicing his profession because of the restrictions placed on Roman Catholics. In 1768 he married his cousin Mary Darnall.

With the growth of unrest in the colonies, Carroll began to play an increasingly important role in politics. A delegate to the Maryland Convention in June, 1776, Carroll was instrumental in securing passage of the resolution permitting the colony's delegation in the Continental Congress to vote for independence. Although not present when the vote for independence was taken on July 4, he was one of the Marylanders who signed the parchment copy (on display at the National Archives, Washington, D.C.) on August 2. After the Revolution he was senator from Maryland in the first U.S. Congress.

A shrewd businessman, Carroll was involved in many of the major commercial and industrial enterprises of the young nation. He was a member of the Potomac Company and of its successor, the Chesapeake & Ohio Canal Company, and a director of the Baltimore & Ohio Railroad. With his vast land holdings and the fortune he had accumulated, Carroll was thought to be one of the wealthiest men in America at the time of his death in 1832. He was buried in the chapel here.

A subsequent occupant of the manor, John Lee Carroll, was governor of Maryland (1876–80).

At 10.6 m. on Md. 144 is the junction with Folly Quarter Road, leading through the University of Maryland Central Farm.

● Left on Folly Quarter Road 3.3 m. to an intersection.
Straight ahead on Sheppard Lane from the intersection 1.8 m. is **Walnut Grove** (private), a 2½-story gray stone house with gables and dormers built about 1740 on a knoll some distance from the road. It was the home of Capt. Gassaway Watkins, commander of the Fifth Maryland Regiment at the Battle of Cowpens during the Revolution and of troops at Annapolis during the War of 1812.

● Turn right onto Folly Quarter Road at the intersection with Sheppard Lane; at 3.7 m. is the **Novitiate of the Franciscan Fathers,** a large marble structure with two ells facing an open court. It was erected in 1930 and patterned after the Convent of St. Francis at Assisi, Italy. The **Folly Quarter Mansion,** a 2½-story house built in 1832 with matching front and rear porticoes, is used now as a recreation hall. Large granite blocks laid in coursed ashlar and portico columns carved from single granite blocks give the house solid dignity.

The house was planned by Charles Carroll of Carrollton for his granddaughter at a cost, it is said, of more than $100,000. Long neglected, it was finally bought by Van Lear Black (1875–1930), Baltimore newspaper publisher, who staged rodeos and other spectacular entertainments for guests prominent in journalistic, governmental, and diplomatic circles.

At 5.2 m. is the entrance lane (L) to **Glenelg Manor,** now housing the **Glenelg Country School.** The large ivy-covered Gothic-Revival house is surrounded by giant hemlock and locust trees and overlooks rolling farmlands. The main two-story U-shaped house has a three-story crenelated tower on the left wing. There are several gray stone outbuildings, one of which is a Gothic-Revival "prospect tower."

At 12.0 m. on Md. 144 is the junction with Triadelphia Road.

At 17.7 m. is the junction with Md. 97 at **COOKSVILLE.** In 1825, Lafayette and his party were entertained at Joshua Roberts Tavern. During the Civil War, the Maryland militia fought a skirmish with the Confederate cavalry, commanded by Gen. J. E. B. Stuart near here. The Confederates defeated the militia and moved north on Md. 97 to Hood's Mill and Westminster.

At 20.1 m. is the junction with Daisy Road.

At 20.8 m. is the town of **LISBON.**

At 22.2 m. is **POPLAR SPRINGS.**

At 27.0 m., Md. 144 junctions with Md. 27 in **MOUNT AIRY.** From Md. 27, take I-70–U.S. 40 west to Frederick. As the expressway crosses the Monocacy River, a glimpse to the right may be rewarded with a fleeting view of the old bridge. **Jug Bridge,** 38.8 m., spanning the Monocacy River, was so named because of a huge stone jug (R) at the eastern end. This is said to contain a demijohn of whiskey sealed up with loving care by the trowel master. The bridge was constructed in 1807 for the turnpike company building the Frederick Road. Lafayette was met here in 1824 by a delegation from Frederick and escorted into the city. The jug is now at the exit of Patrick Street from Md. 40 at 39.9 m.

Proceeding west on I-70–U.S. 40, bear right at the interchange with U.S. 15. At the interchange of U.S. 15 and U.S. 40, take the second exit, which leads to the junction of U.S. 40 and Alt. U.S. 40, which leads to Tour 2c.

2c. FREDERICK–HAGERSTOWN; 21.8 m.
Alt. U.S. 40

The tour from Frederick northwest to Hagerstown is paralleled by I-70 and an improved U.S. 40. The older road, Alt. U.S. 40, is the route of the tour. It crosses farmlands in rolling valleys, interrupted by the long ridges of Catoctin and South mountains. Wheat was the basic crop of the small farmers who settled here, and it remained the staple produce until this century, when

dairying and other kinds of animal husbandry began to predominate. Many of the early settlers were of German descent; some
farm buildings have been protected from evil spirits by
"hex" signs since they were built. Braddock's troops and later
the armies of the Civil War marched along this route. The
peaceful fields saw many skirmishes.

The western city limit of **Frederick,** where Alt. U.S. 40
branches left from U.S. 40, 0.0 m., was formerly a separate settlement known as **Braddock,** or **Old Braddock,** to distinguish it
from Braddock Heights. It was a stop on the eastern extension
of the Old Cumberland Road to Baltimore, where teamsters
stopped for rest and uproarious drinking bouts. In 1830, according to neighborhood legend, a guest buried a chest of jewels
on a nearby mountainside. Two years later he returned and while
attempting to recover his cache was fatally injured in a mountain storm. As he was dying the stranger confessed the jewels
had been stolen from a grand duchess in France. The landlord
dug fruitlessly, but residents of the vicinity insist the treasure
awaits the persistent or lucky prospector.

During the Antietam campaign in September, 1862, a detachment of Confederate cavalry stopped at a tavern here for refreshments and was captured by Federal troops.

Alt. U.S. 40 crosses Catoctin Mountain at **BRADDOCK
HEIGHTS,** 2.4 m. A summer resort was founded here in 1896 on
the ridge of the mountain (950′ alt.). The ridge is only 250 feet
wide here. As winter sports became more popular, a ski center
was set up at this slope, which is located close to Baltimore and
Washington.

MIDDLETOWN (575′ alt., 1,262 pop.), 4.1 m., settled in the
eighteenth century by people of English and German stock, was ·
incorporated in 1833. The town has an air of old-fashioned comfort, founded chiefly on the prosperity of the agricultural region
it serves. It is immaculately clean and has solidly built and
well-appointed houses. The *Valley Register,* a weekly newspaper,
has been published here since 1844.

Several Civil War skirmishes took place in the vicinity, and
Middletown homes and churches were crowded with wounded
after the battles of South Mountain and Antietam. Col. Ruther-
ford B. Hayes, commander of the Twenty-third Ohio Volunteers
and later president of the United States, was among those injured at South Mountain.

In front of her house on Main Street, according to Middletown historians, seventeen-year-old Nancy Crouse stood with the
Union flag wrapped around her when Confederate cavalrymen
galloped into town. Nancy, unfortunately, overestimated Southern
gallantry, for the flag was wrested from her and destroyed.

In the Lutheran Cemetery is a twelve-foot marble shaft marking the **Grave of Sergeant Everhart,** a local hero credited with
having saved the lives of General Lafayette and Col. William
Augustine Washington. Lafayette was wounded at the Battle of
the Brandywine on September 11, 1777, and was carried to safety
by Everhart. On July 17, 1781, at the Battle of Cowpens, Everhart came to the aid of his commander, Colonel Washington,
who was engaged in a personal encounter with a British officer.
The cemetery is on the **Site of the Martenbox Church,** where

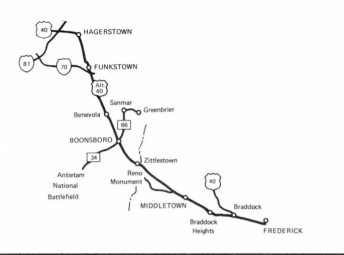

TOUR 2c

Everhart, a Methodist minister, preached after the Revolutionary War.

Alt. U.S. 40 crosses Catoctin Creek, 6.2 m. At the western end of the bridge is Marker Road.

● Left on this road to **Fox's Tavern** (L) (private), 1.8 m., a stone building erected shortly after the Revolutionary War. During the War of 1812, it is said, soldiers came to the tavern seeking shelter from the rain, and "all got Galory and engaged in a free fight, laying aside Captain Smith's commission, while King Whiskey took command."

At 2.6 m. is the junction of Marker and Bolivar roads. Bear right on Bolivar Road. At 2.9 m. is the junction of Bolivar and Reno Monument roads. Bear left onto Reno Monument Road. At the junction of Reno Monument and Reno School roads, 3.8 m., bear left on Reno Monument Road.

The **Reno Monument** (L), 3.8 m., marks the spot where Maj. Gen. Jesse Lee Reno, commander of the Ninth Army Corps, U.S. Volunteers, was killed during the Battle of South Mountain in the late summer of 1862. A few yards from the monument are foundation stones and part of the fences of **Old Wise's Cabin.** The federal government paid "Old Wise" five dollars for each soldier he buried after the Battle of South Mountain. He is said to have tossed fifty bodies unceremoniously into a nearby well, which caused their disgruntled ghosts to haunt the mountain demanding decent burial. Supposedly one threatened to haunt him forever unless its body was turned over. After dark the old man decently reburied the body and the ghost disappeared.

The route continues across South Mountain (1,100′ alt.).

Returning to Alt. U.S. 40, the **Little Stone Church** (R) was built in 1881 by Mrs. Madeleine Dahlgren, widow of Adm. John A. B. Dahlgren, expert on naval ordnance. The admiral's grave is inside the church.

The Battle of South Mountain was fought here and at Fox's Gap, one mile south, on September 14, 1862, during Lee's first invasion of Maryland. Opposed to Lee's forces were Federal troops under Gen. George B. McClellan. The battle began at Fox's Gap and continued there and along South Mountain throughout the day. Gens. Robert E. Lee and J. Longstreet were at Hagerstown when they received word of the desperate straits of the Confederates on South Mountain. Longstreet's men reached the scene about four in the afternoon, but the Confederates were outflanked and at nightfall were forced to retire toward Sharpsburg. Federal losses in killed, wounded, and missing totaled 1,831, and Confederate losses were approximately the same; however, the heroic defense of their position by Gen. D. H. Hill's forces probably saved the Confederate army from destruction as it gave Lee time to concentrate his forces at Sharpsburg.

South Mountain has been the subject of many legends and superstitions. As late as 1859 many residents of the section believed that bands of Indians still passed over the mountain secretly. Lights moving at night along the mountainside long were known in the vicinity as "the Saxon's fire." According to the tale, a youthful Saxon who was marching with troops on his way to the Seminole War stopped at the Mountain House Tavern and fell in love with the innkeeper's daughter. He deserted and hid on the mountain until the troops moved on so that he could marry the girl.

At 10.3 m. is the T-junction with Washington Monument Road (R).

● Turn onto this road, 0.1 m., to **Washington Monument State Park.** A monument erected here on July 4, 1827, was completed in one day by citizens of Boonsboro. During the Antietam and Gettysburg campaigns in the Civil War this mound, which had almost fallen to pieces, was patched with logs and used as a Union signal station. In 1934 ten acres of land, including the monument, were deeded to the State of Maryland, and additional land was subsequently acquired for a state park. A copy of the earlier monument was built of local stone by the Civilian Conservation Corps and rededicated July 4, 1936. From the tower, reached by an interior stairway, the Hagerstown, Potomac, Cumberland, and Middletown valleys and parts of neighboring states are visible.

On Washington Monument Road is a junction with Zittlestown Road. Make a left on this road to **ZITTLESTOWN.** The town received its name from the large Zittle family here. Zittlestown Road joins with Alt. U.S. 40 outside Zittlestown.

BOONSBORO (530' alt., 1,410 pop.), 12.6 m., is a closely built residential town. Solid brick and stone houses have low front porches close to the sidewalks. Boonsboro has not always been a quiet town. It was settled in 1774 by George and William Boone, whom legend has related to the more famous Daniel. The town was prosperous in the 1830s when the National Pike was alive with westward-moving traffic; its blacksmith shops and stores were busy, and its inns and taverns were filled with travelers and teamsters.

Thomas J. "Stonewall" Jackson narrowly escaped capture near Boonsboro on September 11, 1862. Col. Henry Kyd Douglas, one of his staff officers, was advancing into town with a few cavalrymen when a detachment of Federal cavalry dashed out of the Sharpsburg Road and drove the Confederates back toward their main column. On the way back they met General Jackson, unmounted and leading his horse, far ahead of his troops. The Confederate detail wheeled about, called to imaginary reinforcements, and charged the Federals. The ruse succeeded and the Federal cavalry withdrew before what they believed to be a superior force.

Four days after the Battle of South Mountain, Fitzhugh Lee's cavalry, while protecting the rear of General Lee's army as it moved toward Sharpsburg, had a skirmish in the streets of Boonsboro with advancing Federal troops. After the Battle of Antietam, Boonsboro's churches and many of its private homes were used for the care of the wounded.

On July 8, 1863, Federal cavalry holding Boonsboro had an all-day engagement here with Gen. J. E. B. Stuart's cavalry.

Church Street near Main Street is the **Site of the Salem Union Church,** in which Lutheran and Reformed congregations jointly worshiped from 1810 to 1870, when a new building was erected. The earlier church served as a military hospital during the Civil War. The Salem Church became the center of a town controversy. The Lutherans advocated roundheaded windows, while the Reformed members of the congregation insisted on square windows, contending that the other type was "sinful." A compromise resulted in square windows on one side of the building and round windows on the other. Toleration was again necessary when a dispute arose concerning heat in the church. Some brethren demanded comfort, others felt heat would be "sacrilege and gross impiety." In order that both body and spirit might be satisfied, the elders installed a stove on one side of the church. It is said that the body won out in the conflict; even the most pious were finally forced by the cold to the warmer side of the building.

In the adjoining graveyard a monument to William Boone, one of the town's founders, was erected in 1935 to replace the simple stone that had marked the grave for 137 years.

On Main Street near Church Street is an old cannon (R) that was cast in a local furnace for use in the War of 1812. For many years it was a focal point for political celebrations here.

Md. 66 and Md. 34 intersect Alt. U.S. 40 in Boonsboro. At 13.2 m. Md. 34 (L) goes southwesterly to the Antietam National Battlefield, 6.3 m. (*see* Tour 6). At 13.7 m. Md. 66 (R) goes north to **SANMAR,** 2.9 m., where a right turn leads to the entrance of **Greenbrier State Park.** A forty-two-acre lake within the park is open for swimming, in season. Its refreshing water, supplied by mountain springs, has been stocked for fishing.

A few hundred yards north of U.S. 40, on the outskirts of **BENEVOLA,** 16.7 m., beside Beaver Creek, is the **Site of an Army of the Potomac Headquarters,** where on July 9–14, 1863, General Meade held several councils of war with his corps commanders, deliberating over President Lincoln's orders to attack Lee before the latter could retire south of the Potomac.

FUNKSTOWN (524' alt., 1,051 pop.), 21.1 m., is named for Jacob Funk, to whom in 1754 Frederick Calvert granted a tract of land on which this town was laid out. First called Jerusalem, Funkstown missed its opportunity to grow when in 1776 shrewd Jonathan Hager, proprietor of Hagers Town, rode to Annapolis and had his settlement named the county seat. Hardly more than a suburb of Hagerstown, Funkstown now has an appearance of modest prosperity, and its sturdy old brick and stone houses are tidy and well kept.

Near the center of town is the **Site of South's Hotel** built during the days of the turnpike era. John Brown stopped here in

Washington Monument

June, 1859, when he was transporting pikes to arm the slaves in preparation for the great projected uprising (*see* Tour 5).

Between Funkstown and Hagerstown Confederate cavalry and troops held back Federal forces from July 7 to 10, 1863, then withdrew to Hagerstown.

Alt. U.S. 40 crosses Antietam Creek at 21.5 m. The bridges with limestone arches, constructed in 1823, were scenes of conflict during the Civil War and withstood frequent efforts to destroy them.

Alt. U.S. 40 crosses the line of battle of General Meade's Army of the Potomac at 21.8 m., just outside of Hagerstown, where on July 10–14, 1863, the Confederates held the heights while awaiting recession of the flooded waters of the Potomac before crossing into Virginia. Both armies threw up breastworks; the Confederates hoped to avenge their Gettysburg defeat, and the Union command hoped to hold the advantages already gained. By July 14 the Potomac had receded enough to permit Lee's army to withdraw.

Alternate U.S. 40 enters Hagerstown via Frederick Street. At the junction with Locust Street, turn right and at the intersection of Locust and Franklin streets, turn right. Franklin continues to an interchange with Interstate 81. Take I-81 south to the interchange with I-70, a superhighway, the beginning of Tour 2d.

2d. HAGERSTOWN–CUMBERLAND; 56.0 m.
I-70 and U.S. 40

The route followed is that of the Bank Road, a turnpike built between 1816 and 1821 to connect Baltimore to the National Road at Cumberland. The banks of Baltimore and the western towns were required by the state to finance the turnpike. The wagon road that the turnpike replaced had passed over the Potomac River into Virginia and back, following a roundabout route to avoid steep mountain grades. The Bank Road was

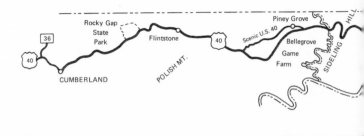

shorter and relatively well built; it also avoided the river cross-ings, which were dangerous and sometimes impassable during spring floods, and it kept within Maryland the profits from the trade that was thriving on traffic with the west. The road was a profitable investment for the banks. It generated substantial toll revenue and stimulated the economic development of the towns and countryside along its way.

The fertile valley of Conococheague Creek, seven miles west of Hagerstown, was the westernmost limit of settlement in Maryland during the third quarter of the eighteenth century. While hunters and traders ventured into the mountains, farmers stopped short of the inhospitable slopes. Not until the plateau land west of Cumberland was released for settlement after 1774 did many farmers cross the Allegheny barrier.

During the French and Indian War (1754–63), Fort Cumber-land was too distant to protect the Conococheague settlers. *Fort Frederick,* a magnificent stone stronghold, and a series of small wood-stockaded forts were erected in the western part of what is now Washington County to provide refuge during Indian raids and to safeguard supplies. The steepening contours of the land along this frontier defense line proved suitable for orchard development. Peaches and apples are still produced here in commercial orchards, although the roadside fruit and cider stands that catered to travelers in the past have generally dis-appeared with the advent of the limited-access highway.

The long grade of Sideling Hill, culminating in a 300-degree curve at its summit, marks the entry into the mountain barrier. The densely wooded ridges have been tamed only to the extent of yielding lumber and maple products. The **Green Ridge State Forest,** on both sides of the road, is open for hunting in season. **Rocky Gap State Park,** near Cumberland in the heart of the mountains, provides facilities for general outdoor recreation.

● **Old Conococheague Bridge,** a limestone masonry span built in 1819, carried traffic of the Bank Road and its successors over Conococheague Creek for more than one hundred years. It was finally replaced by a concrete structure now used by U.S. 40. To reach it from I-70, turn north on Md. 63 at the first interchange, 1.7 m., then turn left on U.S. 40 at Huyett's Crossroads, 1.8 m. from the inter-change; Conococheague Creek is 2.6 m. west of Huyett's Cross-roads on U.S. 40, and the old bridge is to the right of the present highway.

At the interchange of I-70 with Md. 68, 7.9 m., turn north on Md. 68 to **CLEAR SPRING** (566′ alt., 488 pop.), 0.7 m., a trading village named for a spring so large that at one time it turned a mill wheel. The Federal-style brick buildings of Clear Spring line both sides of U.S. 40 for about half a mile. Now overshadowed by Hagerstown and by-passed by the new highway, Clear Spring has declined since its prosperous nineteenth-century years, when its stores and banks dominated the commercial life of western Washington County. Among the locally prominent nineteenth-century residents were John Thompson Mason, a native of Virginia whom Thomas Jefferson asked to be his attorney general in 1800, and his son, Judge John Thompson Mason, who served on the Maryland Court of Appeals in the 1850s.

● From the junction of Md. 40 and Md. 68, make a left (west) to an intersection at 0.2 m. Turn right to Broadfording Road at 0.3 m. which leads off to the northeast from U.S. 40, behind the elementary school. **Montpelier** (private), the family home of the Masons, is 2.5 m. from Clear Spring on Broadfording Road. A two-story brick and stone manor house in the Georgian style, Montpelier was built around 1770 by Richard Barnes, a wealthy St. Mary's County planter whose sister married the first John Thompson Mason. Judge John Thompson Mason and his older brother, Abram Barnes, were born here. Richard Barnes had agreed to leave Montpelier to Mason's son, provided that the son assume the name of his mother's family.

● **Stafford Hall** (private), the mansion built by Judge John Thompson Mason around 1835, is on Cohill Road, 0.5 m. north of U.S. 40. The intersection of U.S. 40 and Cohill Road is 1.4 m. east of Clear Spring. The large two-story brick and stone structure has nine double chimneys. It is said that the complex structure of eclectic design contains a secret room, protected by a curse that strikes down anyone who tries to find it. Two persons have died suddenly after searching for the room. One, a nine-year-old child, confessed on her deathbed that she had spent many afternoons looking for the room, and begged her family never to attempt to locate it.

The Mason family, like many in Clear Spring, tended to sympathize with the Confederacy during the Civil War. Judge Mason was one of the prominent leaders imprisoned in Fort McHenry during the war. After his release, he resumed the practice of law, and died in 1873 while arguing a case in court.

At the interchange of I-70 with Md. 56, 13.0 m., turn south on Md. 56 to **BIG POOL,** a popular fishing spot formed by water backed up for the C & O Canal. For years Big Pool was the western terminus of the Western Maryland Railroad. Around the turn of the century, however, when a syndicate headed by Jay Gould acquired the company, it found that the stretch between Big Pool and Cumberland was a crucial gap in its efforts to compete with railroads that already had east-west connections. Although Gould's interest in the venture ceased in 1907 because of personal financial difficulties, the line was soon extended, closing the gap.

● Md. 56 continues through Big Pool to the entrance of **Fort Frederick State Park** (R), 1.6 m. from the interchange. **Fort Frederick,** partially restored, was erected in 1756 for defense against the French and Indians and was named for Frederick Calvert, sixth Lord Baltimore. It is square with large bastions at its corners. The walls, seventeen feet high, were made of stone because Horatio Sharpe, governor of the province at that time, was convinced of the vulnerability to attack by fire of the more typical frontier forts made of wood. The fort was garrisoned during both the Revolution and the Civil War but was never seriously attacked. British and Hessian prisoners were confined in it during the Revolution. It was abandoned after 1783 until the Civil War, when a cannon was installed, pointing through a hole made in the south wall, to command the canal and river below. Possibly the strength of the position chosen by Governor Sharpe, who had a military background, deterred attack. The only action in the area was a skirmish on Christmas Day, 1861, following hostilities at Dams 4 and 5 and Point of Rocks farther down the Potomac River.

A museum in the park contains artifacts and other objects of interest. The arboretum area includes a variety of trees, including species from Europe and Japan, which were planted in the 1930s when the fort was restored by the Civilian Conservation Corps (open to the public May 1–Oct. 14, 8–9:30; Oct. 15–Apr. 30, 9–6).

The state's official bicentennial troops, the **First Maryland Regiment,** perform here on the last full weekend of June, July, August, and September.

Continuing beyond Fort Frederick, Md. 56 crosses Green Spring Run, 3.2 m. from the interchange. The **Site of the Green Spring Furnace,** about 100 yards upstream from Md. 56, can be discerned from here, but only a few ruins remain. The land was granted in 1768 for a "Forge Mill" and an "Iron Work for running of Pigg Iron" to Lancelot Jacques and Thomas Johnson; Johnson was a partner in the enterprise until 1776 when he became the first governor of the State of Maryland. Jacques manufactured cannons for the Continental Army during the Revolution. A later furnace on the site, built in 1848, was the focus of a Civil War skirmish in 1862.

Just past Green Spring Run, turn right on McCoy's Ferry Road, 3.3 m., to the **Site of McCoy's Ferry,** 1.2 m. (bear right onto the gravel road at 1.0 m.), where the first Civil War action in Maryland occurred in May, 1861, when a party of Confederates attempted to seize the ferryboat.

The village of **INDIAN SPRINGS** is 1.5 m. north of the interchange with I-70 on Md. 56. **Indian Springs Wildlife Management Area** lies about four miles north and northeast of the village on the Pennsylvania line.

● The **Parkhead Evangelical Church** (R), 2.5 m. west of Indian Springs on U.S. 40 (make a left onto U.S. 40 at the junction of U.S. 40 and Md. 56), was built in 1833 but has been extensively remodeled. Before the congregation was integrated, the choir loft was the gallery reserved for blacks. At an unknown site north of the highway around Parkhead, a small log outpost, named **Fort Mills,** was erected in 1756. It was one of the several wooden forts that were constructed for the protection of settlers during the French and Indian War. U.S. 40 merges with I-70 just west of the Parkhead Evangelical Church.

Near Hancock, 23.6 m., I-70 runs into Pennsylvania while the tour continues westward on U.S. 40. To reach the center of

Fort Frederick

Hancock, turn south on U.S. 522. Maryland is less than two miles wide from north to south here, its narrowest point. **HANCOCK** (450′ alt., 1,832 pop.) was chiefly a trading center for the fruit-growing region and a stopover point for travelers on the turnpike and later on the C & O Canal. Now it produces dresses, raincoats, and travel trailers.

St. Thomas Episcopal Church, Church and High streets, a brick building with a square belfry, was founded in 1835. In 1861 and 1862 it was used as a hospital to shelter Federal wounded. Artillery was placed near it as a defense against Stonewall Jackson's guns across the river.

● Canal Road, south of Main Street down Pennsylvania Avenue, runs along the C & O Canal in the **Tonoloway** area of the **C & O Canal Historical Park. Fort Tonoloway State Park,** southwest of Hancock, may be reached either by this route or from Md. 144 west of the town. The original fort was a stockaded blockhouse built in 1755 after the defeat of General Braddock. It was abandoned after the completion of *Fort Frederick.*

● Woodmont Road (Md. 522), to the left from Md. 144, 3.7 m. west of Hancock, runs down between Tonoloway Ridge and Sideling Hill to the Potomac River, where a sharp turn to the right at 6.4 m. takes one along the Pearre Road by the C & O Canal into the **Sideling Hill Wildlife Management Area,** 8.6 m. from Md. 144 (hunting permitted under state regulations). The **Woodmont Rod and Gun Club** (private) has a stone clubhouse (1930) overlooking the Potomac near the intersection of Woodmont and Pearre roads. Several presidents have been members or guests of the club during the hundred years since it was founded by Grover Cleveland (president of the United States for two terms, 1885–89 and 1893–97) and Adm. Robley D. "Fighting Bob" Evans. At the climax of a distinguished naval career spanning both the Civil War and the Spanish-American War, Admiral Evans was made commander of the Asiatic Fleet in 1902.

U.S. 40 climbs **Sideling Hill** (1,595′ alt.), 28.2 m., which offers an excellent view of the surrounding countryside. In the valley

west of the hill, U.S. 40 enters Allegany County as it crosses
Sideling Hill Creek, 38.5 m. Shortly thereafter U.S. 40 splits,
the older, more scenic route taking the right fork through **Piney
Grove** and the **Bill Meyer Wildlife Management Area.** South of
the fork, the **Bellegrove Game Farm** raises indigenous game to
stock the forests of the thinly populated area. **Green Ridge
State Forest** lies on both sides of U.S. 40 through eastern
Allegany County to **Polish Mountain** (1,340′ alt.), 47.9 m., although most of the forest is south of the highway, extending
to the Potomac River.

In **FLINTSTONE** (828′ alt., est. 350 pop.), 50.7 m., the **Flintstone Hotel,** also called the Piper Hotel, still stands much as
it was when it was built around 1807 as an inn on the road to
Cumberland. The twenty-two-room brick building, with fireplaces in almost every room, still displays hand-hewn log beams
and the original shutters. Some of the outbuildings also remain.
Small factories in Flintstone produce maple sugar candies and
rough lumber.

Beyond Flintstone, at 56.0 m., **Rocky Gap State Park** (R) has
public facilities for outdoor recreation. As the road approaches Cumberland, the Colonial Manor Motel still caters to
travelers, just as it did when it was built around 1800 as Turkey
Flight Manor. A minor engagement was fought here during the
Civil War, in which the Union general B. F. Kelley successfully
prevented units under Generals McCausland and B. T. Johnson
from attacking Cumberland. During the action, known as the
Battle of Folck's Mill, a corner of the inn was struck by cannon
fire.

At the interchange of U.S. 40 and 48, turn right onto Baltimore Avenue. At the intersection with Henderson Avenue,
which becames U.S. 40, turn right for Tour 2e.

2e. CUMBERLAND–KEYSER'S RIDGE–PENNSYLVANIA LINE;
33.3 m.
U.S. 40

This picturesque route along U.S. 40 westward from Cumberland generally follows the route of an Indian footpath that
developed into the Cumberland Road, which carried thousands
of pioneers over the Alleghenies to the rich lands beyond. In
1755 Gen. Edward Braddock led his ill-fated army of British regulars and reluctantly supplied colonial militia out of Cumberland to
attack the French at Fort Duquesne, now Pittsburgh. To accommodate the wagons considered essential to support such a
military operation, his men cut through dense forests, built
bridges, and attempted to level a road through the formidable
terrain. In particularly rough places alternative routing around
obstacles was necessary. Delays occasioned by this ambitious
and only partly successful effort gave the French and their Indian
allies ample opportunity to stage the ambush that turned back
the expedition.

In 1806 the U.S. Congress authorized federal funds to construct a road from Cumberland to the Ohio River basin to connect the East Coast and the Mississippi River, three years after
the Louisiana Purchase peacefully terminated foreign claims to

Cumberland Narrows

the mid-continent. Officially designated the Cumberland Road, it was also known as the National Road or the National Pike, being the first federally funded highway. The twenty-foot-wide graveled road, with stone bridges, reached Wheeling, West Virginia, in 1821, and was continued on through Indiana and Illinois to link St. Louis and Baltimore in the 1830s.

As U.S. 40 crosses the west limit of the city of Cumberland, **Will's Creek** flows beside it in a concrete floodway (L). At 0.0 m. U.S. 40 goes over Will's Creek; a small park at the bridge marks the location where the creek, the road, and two railway roadbeds enter the **Narrows** to squeeze between the craggy bluffs of **Will's Mountain** (R) and **Haystack Mountain** (L). "Will" was the European name given to a Shawnee (Shawanese) chief whose tribe lived in a town to the west of the Narrows before 1750.

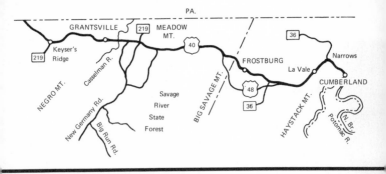

TOUR 2e

The discovery of the Narrows as an opening to the West is attributed to a naval officer attached to Braddock's army, Lieutenant Spendelowe, who was killed in the ambush of the expedition. Braddock's vanguard unit had cut and hauled its way directly over the mountain, "entirely demolishing three wagons and shattering several," before Spendelowe's intelligence showed the feasibility of the gap.

Md. 36 intersects U.S. 40 at 0.9 m. (*see* Tour 10). Looking east from this point, one can see the white-scarred open face of the mountain. To the north more terraced scarring is visible on a far slope. Native limestone supports a cement and concrete products industry. Steep slopes denuded of natural cover complicate the flooding that has always plagued the valley of Will's Creek.

The interchanges with U.S. 48, the National Freeway, are at 4.1 m. and 4.6 m.

A **Tollhouse** (L), 5.3 m. at La Vale, has been preserved from the days of the National Road and still displays the rates of toll collected from travelers in the second quarter of the nineteenth century. The gate posts that enforced the toll stop now stand on either side of U.S. 40. The tollhouse itself is an unusual seven-sided brick two-story tower, with one-story single rooms added on the two long sides of the tower. Completed in 1836, it was one of the two tollhouses built in Maryland pursuant to the act of Congress in 1831 that instituted the collection of tolls in preparation for extensive improvements of the road, including its macadamization, begun in 1832. It became known as the Six-Mile House, that being its distance from the entrance to the toll road in downtown Cumberland. Furnished with period objects, the interior of the Tollhouse is open to the public (May–Oct., Wed., Fri., and Sun., 1–4, and by request).

The **Clarysville Inn** (L), 7.3 m., was also known as the Eight-Mile House. Built in 1807, the 2½-story structure of brick and stone has been enlarged, but the original style has been maintained. It still serves travelers as a restaurant. During the Civil War it was the headquarters of a Federal hospital camp.

From the Clarysville Inn an interesting conjunction of the three bridges that have spanned Braddock's Run over the years can be observed. A stone arch bridge that carried the National Road for a century has now been abandoned and is deteriorating. Beside it is the present U.S. 40 bridge. About a quarter of a mile to the south, soaring high above the valley floor, the freeway bridge now carries the heavy volume of traffic on U.S. 48. The acceleration in highway improvement is not merely attributable to the increased pace of technological development; rather, the coming of the railway made the National Road obsolete in the second half of the nineteenth century. An observer in 1882 commented that the dust of the heavy traffic of its early years had settled, giving root to grass and shrubbery, and the snakes of the mountains sunned themselves in the center of the highway. Not until the internal combustion engine became the dominant mode of transport, supplanting the horse and the iron horse, did the road receive more than local traffic.

ECKHART (1,720' alt.), 7.8 m., formerly **Eckhart Mines,** was the center of the early coal mining industry in the region. Prospering because of its position on the National Road, it declined in the 1840s when the railroad was completed to Cumberland and horse-drawn tramlines were constructed to bring coal from other mines down out of the mountains. The coal at Eckhart Mines was first mined around 1804. When the road went through, wagons hauled the coal down to the banks of the Potomac in Cumberland, where it accumulated until the spring floods raised the level of the water in the river. Flatboats knocked together from the abundant mountain timber and some permanent keelboats were then loaded with coal and sent rushing down the flooded valleys to market. Wrecks were frequent. In high water the treacherous currents could hurl the clumsy boats against the banks or into the many obstructions swept along with the floods; if the water level dropped too low, the boats crashed on the rocks that prevented regular navigation. At the end of the journey, the flatboats were sold along with the coal, and the surviving crewmen walked back to Cumberland.

FROSTBURG (1,929' alt., 7,327 pop.), 9.1 m. at the junction of Md. 36 and U.S. 40 (*see* Tour 10), was described in 1860 by a distinguished visitor, William Cullen Bryant, as a little town "flying high among the mountain ridges, where the winter comes early and lingers late." Its name is not derived from its climate, however, but from a prominent early citizen, Meshach Frost, around whose tavern on the National Road the settlement grew. After several decades as tavern keeper and postmaster, Frost became active in the coal mining industry in the 1840s. Coal dominated the economy of the George's Creek basin between Frostburg and Westernport for the succeeding century. Today the principal products of Frostburg are clothing, lumber, and fire brick, the latter made from the rich clay strata that interleave the coal deposits of Maryland and Pennsylvania.

Frostburg State College is an accredited four-year liberal arts college. It first opened in 1902 as a state normal school, offering a two-year course of study to prepare high school graduates to teach school. From its original enrollment of fifty-seven, the college had expanded to 3,200 full-time students in 1976. Summer masters' programs and other part-time studies are also offered.

Ascending toward the crest of **Big Savage Mountain** (2,850' alt.), 12.3 m., U.S. 40 enters Garrett County, erected in 1872 as the westernmost county in Maryland. **Little Savage Mountain** (2,816′ alt.) rises just beyond Big Savage Mountain, with the upper waters of the Little Savage River flowing under the road between the two crests. The Savage River system, draining the eastern slopes of Garrett County and largely contained in the Savage River State Forest, joins the Potomac at Bloomington. Streams rising to the west of Savage Mountain and Backbone Mountain, the continuation of the ridge along the Potomac below Bloomington, are part of the Ohio-Mississippi system.

Before the Civil War the road at this point went through a black forest of dense, tall virgin pine. While some travelers were pleasantly impressed by the cathedrallike atmosphere of the still, dim passage through the stately trees, most were apprehensive of ambush by hostile Indians and, later, by highwaymen who preyed on the traffic of the National Road. Reflecting such fears the stretch of road was called the "Shades of Death."

The western forests supplied settlers with building material, fuel, and much of their household equipment and furnishings. One of the first commercial uses made of the pines was the manufacture of tar. Yellow pine, which contains a large proportion of pitch, was fired in kilns, to extract the tar. It was sold to wagoners on the National Road, who used it in place of axle grease. It was also used for medicinal potions.

Lumbering is still important in the economy of Garrett County. Over 70 percent of the surface of the county is forested, mostly with second- and third-growth hardwoods. The towering pines of the virgin forest were nearly all cut down when major logging operations began in the area after the Civil War. The logs were transported by water to sawmills located downstream. In most cases the water level of the creeks had to be raised artificially with "splash dams." The logs were slid into the pond behind the dam, then sent booming downstream when the dam was intentionally breached. Programs to replant a mixed evergreen-hardwood forest and to sustain the wildlife habitat with clearings supporting berries, grasses, and edible shrubbery have been underway since the 1930s, when the Civilian Conservation Corps established camps in the forests. Under such programs, now administered by the state, lumbering is fostered and controlled, while deer, ruffed grouse, wild turkeys, rabbits, raccoons, and squirrels delight the observant visitor and attract a growing number of hunters.

At 14.1 m. U.S. 40 and U.S. 48 join together (U.S. 48 is under construction).

The **Savage River State Forest,** mostly south of U.S. 40, may be entered by the Lower New Germany Road, left at 19.4 m. The forest contains 52,770 acres of mountainous woodlands and swift, clear trout streams. Two state parks within it, New Germany and Big Run, provide campsites, boating, and other outdoor activities. Many miles of roads and trails in the forest and parks are open to the public.

After crossing **Meadow Mountain** (2,900′ alt.), 20.1 m., U.S. 40 descends to a pleasant glade known as **Little Meadows** (private), where Braddock's expedition camped in 1755. The

Casselman River Bridge

Red House Tavern, serving Braddock's Road, was established at the edge of the meadow in 1760. The log structure was replaced by the present **Stone House Inn** (R), 20.9 m., built near it around 1818 on the side of the National Road. Many glades such as this spread over the central plateau of Garrett County. Covered with tall grasses, they were welcome oases in the heavily forested land and drew many settlers to their rich soil. They are the silted-in lake beds of an earlier geological age.

At a crossroads, 21.1 m., U.S. 219 (*see* Tour 11) joins U.S. 40 from the north.

● To the left, on Chestnut Ridge Road, go 3.0 m. to New Germany Road, then left on New Germany Road 2.0 m. to **New Germany State Park.**

Fairview Road, branching southeast from New Germany Road beyond New Germany, leads into the headwaters of **Silver Bell Run.** The Silver Bell Mining Company attempted a mining venture here in 1891 during a brief silver "rush" in the Savage River valley.

● Farther down New Germany Road, take the left fork, Big Run Road (gravel), 8.0 m., to **Big Run State Park.**

On the east bank of the Casselman River, 23.4 m., **Penn Alps, Inc.** (R), a nonprofit center for mountain crafts and traditions, maintains a showroom, restaurant, and some guest rooms. A restored log cabin, dated about 1820, has been moved to its grounds, and the largest pottery kiln in Maryland is used by its craftsmen. Nearby is the **Stanton Mill** (private), a 2½-story white frame structure built in 1856 on the foundations of a 1797 grist mill.

As U.S. 40 crosses the Casselman River, 23.5 m., the old **Casselman River Bridge** can be seen at the right. Its eighty-foot span made it the largest stone arch bridge in the country when it was built for the National Road in 1813. It has been named a National Historic Landmark. In the early days of the automobile, a daring activity of many young people was hitting the "hump" in the bridge with sufficient speed to launch their Model T's into a brief stomach-bending flight, ending in a spine-jolting landing. The fine old bridge easily withstood that stress, although even its builder, David Shriver, had expressed some anxiety over whether it would be able to support even its own weight during its construction. A small state park at the bridge has picnicking facilities.

GRANTSVILLE (2,351′ alt., 480 pop.), 24.0 m., was settled primarily by German-speaking Amish and Mennonites who moved down from Pennsylvania to the excellent farmlands of the area. The distinctive dress of each of those groups may still be seen on its streets. Maple syrup and sugar have been produced in its New-England-like climate since its earliest days. An Amish food cooperative and country market just south of town offers country-smoked pork and other fresh farm products for sale. Other local industries manufacture shirts and make fire clay products. The **Casselman Hotel** (R), a 2½-story white-painted brick inn, still offers food and shelter to travelers. It was built in 1824 as the Drover's Inn and, despite minor alterations, is one of Garrett County's few remaining true Federal-style buildings.

The **Fuller-Baker Log House** (R), 25.1 m., is a structurally well-preserved inn dating from the heyday of the National Road. Not merely a cabin, the two-story house with its end chimneys was probably built around 1814. From it can be seen two of the stone arch bridges for the National Road, now abandoned.

Negro Mountain (3,075′ alt.), 27.4 m., is in the northern portion of the Savage River State Forest. It was named to honor Nemesis, a black member of an expedition headed by Capt. Michael Cresap, one of Maryland's leading pioneers (*see* Tour 8, Oldtown). The expedition was attacked on the mountain by a party of Indians, avenging the Ohio massacre of the family of their chief, Logan, an act that had been erroneously attributed to Cresap. The massacre led to a general border uprising in 1774, known as Lord Dunmore's War, after the governor of Virginia at the time. Nemesis, a giant of a man, was killed during the attack and is buried on the mountain.

At the summit of **Keyser's Ridge**, 29.9 m., U.S. 219 goes left from U.S. 40 south toward Oakland (*see* Tour 11). U.S. 40 continues along the approximate route of the National Road to the Pennsylvania line, 33.3 m., which it crosses at a point about twenty-nine miles southeast of Uniontown, Pennsylvania.

(Gettysburg)–PENNSYLVANIA LINE–THURMONT–FREDERICK–POINT OF ROCKS–VIRGINIA LINE–(Leesburg); 37.4 m.
U.S. 15

The tour route runs along the base of the eastern slope of Catoctin Mountain, the easternmost of the Blue Ridge range in Maryland. Side roads to the west go up into the mountain forests, frequently by tumbling streams that have been stocked with trout. To the east lie the farms of the Monocacy River basin, where grain, apples, vegetables, and livestock are still produced in the same agricultural pattern that was established by the first English, Scotch-Irish, and German settlers in the mid-eighteenth century. Some of the less productive land has been allowed to revert to forest; with the expansion of a natural habitat, the deer, raccoons, and other small animals have increased their numbers. Festivals in the spring and fall mark the changing seasons, bringing visitors to see the delicate apple blossoms against the pale greens of new crops and then the strong autumn colors of the mountain foliage.

U.S. 15 crosses the **Maryland-Pennsylvania Line** at 0.0 m., about nine miles southwest of Gettysburg. At the intersection of U.S. 15 and U.S. 15 Business area, continue straight on U.S. 15.

EMMITSBURG (400' alt., 1,532 pop.) (R), 1.3 m., was first known as Poplar Fields or Silver Fancy, changing its name to Emmitsburg around 1786, after William Emmit, or Emmitt, a prominent local landholder. At the time of the name change it was a village of seven families, with a merchant, a tavern-keeper, a hatter, a blacksmith, a carpenter, and two brothers who were merchants and architects. Today the largest factory in the town makes shoes.

● Turn left on Md. 97 from Emmitsburg to the Monocacy River, 4.6 m. Dinosaur tracks preserved in limestone were discovered just north of the bridge over the river here in the late nineteenth century. The slabs were moved to *Mount St. Mary's College* and the Maryland Academy of Sciences in Baltimore.

TANEYTOWN (493' alt., 1,731 pop.), 7.5 m., was laid out around 1740 by Frederick Taney, a member of an influential Calvert County family. Roger B. Taney, chief justice of the United States (1836–64), was also a member of the family (*see* Frederick Tour). By the end of the eighteenth century Taneytown was a well-established trading center for the agricultural region of northwest Frederick County, and it had at least one industry. Muskets were manufactured here for the government in an operation that, while relying heavily on hand labor, also used a grindstone powered by a horse. After a fire early in the nineteenth century, the government factory was transferred to Harpers Ferry. Now the principal manufacture of the town is rubber footware.

To the east of U.S. 15 as it passes Emmitsburg are the buildings of the former **St. Joseph's College,** which, when it closed in 1973, was an accredited college for women. St. Joseph's was founded in 1809 as a girls' school by Elizabeth Seton (1774–1821). Mother Seton, a widow with five children and a convert to Catholicism, also founded a religious community at Emmitsburg that adopted the rule of the Sisters of Charity. She was named Mother Superior of the order by Bishop John Carroll (*see* Downtown Baltimore and Tour 4). The sisterhood is active in schools, orphanages, and hospitals. The cabin where Mother Seton lived and taught has been preserved. Her tomb nearby is next to that of her nephew, James Roosevelt Bayley, archbishop of Baltimore from 1872 to 1877. She was beatified in 1963; ceremonies at Mount St. Mary's College in September, 1975, marked her canonization.

Mount St. Mary's College (R), on U.S. 15 at 3.8 m., is a private four-year Roman Catholic college for men and a seminary. It was founded in 1808 by Father Dubois, later bishop of New York. The first American cardinal, Msgr. John McCloskey (1810–

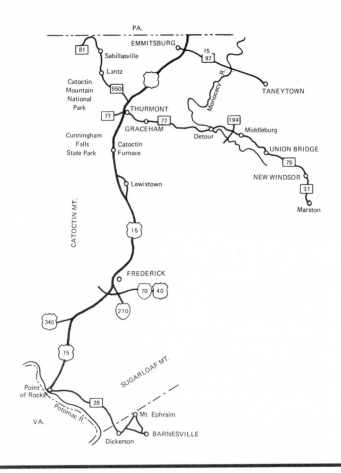

TOUR 3

85) studied here, as did Edward Douglass White (1845–1921), who in 1910 became the first Southerner to be named chief justice of the United States after the Civil War. Although the enrollment at Mount St. Mary's is less than one thousand students, its basketball teams have frequently been ranked among the best in the nation.

A replica of the **Grotto of Lourdes,** on the mountain above the college, was the first Catholic shrine in the United States. The grounds are marked by a towering column surmounted by a gilded representation of the Virgin Mary.

THURMONT (519′ alt., 2,359 pop.), 8.5 m., was first settled around 1751 when Jacob Weller and his family stopped here, dropping out of a group moving westward from Pennsylvania. According to legend, one of the Weller children had fallen ill, and the family stopped at a large spring here to nurse him. The village grew slowly until after the turn of the century. In 1800 a hotel was built, and a store opened in 1806. In 1810 the first tannery opened, beginning an industry that was to thrive in the region. The hides, from cattle fattened on the lush fields, were processed with acids from the bark of thousands of trees. In 1811 Jacob Weller, a son of the original settlers, opened a forge that manufactured edge-tools—augers, chisels, axes, etc.— with power supplied by the waters of Fishing Creek. It was the first such plant south of New York, and it supplied iron tools to a large market in the Southern states and the West Indies. A woolen mill and more tanneries completed the early industrial picture. The town was then called Mechanicstown, probably because the majority of its residents were employed as mechanics rather than in trade or services for the agricultural region. Another Weller, Joseph, is credited with the first manufacture of friction matches, or lucifers, in the United States. In 1825 he purchased some French matches and investigated their composition successfully. He was able to set up a plant to dip the wooden shafts into a mixture of his secret formula in the **Old Match House,** on W. Main Street. Luckily the success of his enterprise enabled him to expand and set up in a larger plant elsewhere, because it appears that his factory burned down twice.

The Western Maryland Railroad was completed into Mechanicstown in 1872, bringing with it influences that led to many changes. Its altitude and mountain scenery made the town a popular resort once it had become accessible by rail. Its old name, a bit long for the railway timetables, was changed to Thurmont, meaning "gateway to the mountains." Rail transportation made possible market expansion. Thurmont's local industry was, in some cases, unable to compete with goods brought in by the expansion of other markets (especially those that had long been on rail routes and were well established), while materials and distribution made new opportunities for other endeavors. A cannery was among the first new plants built after the railroad came through. Today Thurmont has a diverse base of small manufacturers. Among its products are clothing, furniture and other wood products, business forms, and shoes.

As U.S. 15 enters Thurmont at 8.5 m., there is an interchange with Md. 550.

● Turn right on Md. 550 (formerly Md. 81), which follows the northern edge of the *Catoctin Mountain National Park* through **LANTZ** (not marked), 4.2 m., and **SABILLASVILLE,** 5.6 m. This is the path of the old Gap Road over the Blue Ridge, built to connect the *Catoctin Furnace* with the forges of Franklin County, Pennsylvania.

At 6.9 m. on Md. 550 are the grounds of the **Victor Cullen School** (R), a training school for boys who have been alleged or adjudicated to be in need of supervision. The facilities were formerly used as a sanatorium for tubercular patients. The hospital was established in 1908 and accommodated as many as 500 victims of the disease in the 1930s. The virtual elimination of tuberculosis as a public health problem allowed the state to convert the property to its present use.

Just beyond, Md. 550 (which becomes Md. 81) passes through **BLUE RIDGE SUMMIT,** 7.2 m. This old resort area on the Maryland-Pennsylvania line was a particularly popular mountain retreat for the diplomatic community in Washington, D.C., before air conditioning made summer life more tolerable in the metropolitan centers.

About a mile beyond Blue Ridge Summit, turn right at the T-junction. Continue on Md. 81, on the northern boundary of Fort Ritchie, then turn left under the railroad bridge, 0.9 m., to **PEN MAR** and the **Pen Mar**

State Park. Pen Mar was developed as a mountain resort and amusement park by the Western Maryland Railway. The Appalachian Trail crosses the road here. Excellent views are afforded by **High Rock** (1,822' alt.), 1.9 m., left from the park, and **Quirauk** (1,445' alt.), 3.2 m., left from High Rock.

Return to U.S. 15 and proceed south to Md. 77.

● Take Md. 77, the Thurmont-Foxville Road, west out of Thurmont into the Catoctin Mountain National Park and Cunningham Falls State Park. After going under U.S. 15 in the western part of Thurmont, the road ascends Catoctin Mountain beside Hunting Creek. This was once the principal road from Baltimore to Hagerstown.

Catoctin Mountain National Park, to the left, was acquired in 1936 by the federal government. At that time, it was primarily marginal farmland. Many trees had been cut for charcoal and lumber to fire the furnaces of local industry, and the remaining oaks and chestnuts had been killed when their bark was stripped for use in the tanning process. The steep contours, combined with unscientific farming practices, eroded and depleted the soil of the farms located in the area. Of the fifty families that were relocated in the federal purchase, only eight had been able to make a living entirely from their land. The government project involved an experiment in creating parks from such lands. Almost 6,000 acres have been permitted to develop into an Eastern hardwood climax forest, populated with deer, a few foxes, many raccoons, squirrels and other small animals, and a variety of birds. Campgrounds, hiking trails, and marked nature trails are provided for park visitors.

The presidential retreat, **Camp David,** is in the middle of the park. It is closed to the public, but its entrance and some of the maximum security fencing can be seen to the right on Park Central Road, north of the visitor center on Md. 77.

Cunningham Falls State Park (L), on the south side of Md. 77, was created in 1954 when the federal government gave the state 4,446 acres from the **Catoctin Recreation Demonstration Area.** The state park includes the upper reaches of Big Hunting Creek and, on one of its tributaries, Cunningham Falls. Bear left on Catoctin Hollow Road just past the National Park Service Visitor Center, then continue about one mile, following the signs to the **West Picnic Area** of the state park. Trails from the picnic area lead to the falls. Alternatively, continue past the turnoff to a parking area (L) off Md. 77. The falls are fairly close to this area by foot. The state park offers picnicking, camping, and other recreational facilities at the West Picnic Area and at the **Manor House Day Area,** just off U.S. 15 in the southeast quadrant of the park.

Return again to the intersection with U.S. 15.

● Take Md. 77 east out of Thurmont (Rocky Ridge Road). Just before the city limits is **Apple's Church** (R), mother church to both the Lutheran and Reformed denominations in this section. German services for the two groups were held in a log structure on this site from about 1770. A stone building replaced the log church in 1826, and shortly thereafter some of the services were conducted in English. In 1857 the Lutherans moved to a separate church in Thurmont, but the Reformed congregation continued to meet here till 1879.

GRACEHAM, 1.8 m., is a town in which tree-lined streets, old houses with gardens in the rear, and the old Moravian church mark the tempo of life. The Moravian Congregation of Monocacy, an offshoot of Apple's Church, purchased thirty acres here in 1782, and divided twelve of them into half-acre building lots that were leased to members of the church for an average of eighty-eight cents a year. The first house in the village was erected in 1782, and in 1792 a man named Moeller received permission to bake gingerbread and brew small beer, dis-

Mother Seton's tomb

pensing the latter "under strict regulation." In 1822 the stuccoed brick church replaced a log structure.

DETOUR, 8.1 m., was so called because the former name of Double Pipe Creek was too long for Western Maryland Railway timetables. A sawmill was recorded in 1770 near this site, but the village developed around another sawmill and a woolen mill built in 1794 by Joshua Delaplane, a French settler. The woolen mill was in operation until 1849.

From Detour, immediately after crossing the bridge, turn left onto Keysville Road (unmarked). At 2.3 m. Keysville Road intersects Keysville-Bruceville Road. Go right onto Keysville-Bruceville Road 0.8 m. to **Terra Rubra** (private), birthplace on August 1, 1779, of Francis Scott Key, author of "The Star-Spangled Banner" (*see* West Baltimore). The tract, patented to Francis's English grandfather, Philip Key, was named for the color of the soil. The first house, completed in 1770, was destroyed by a storm in 1850 and replaced by the present brick building. Half of the land was confiscated from Francis's Tory uncle, who joined the British army during the Revolution. The other half, including the mansion, was inherited by John Ross Key, father of Francis and an officer in the Continental Army.

After Francis Scott Key was graduated from St. John's College in Annapolis in 1796, he studied law there under Judge J. T. Chase. In 1801 Key and Roger B. Taney (*see* Frederick Tour), later chief justice of the United States, practiced in Frederick. Taney married Key's sister. Key moved to Georgetown, where he practiced law with his uncle, Philip Barton Key. From 1833 to 1841 he was district attorney for the District of Columbia.

Although himself a slaveholder, Key in 1816 became a director of the American Colonization Society, whose purpose was to promote "a plan for colonizing [with their consent] the Free People of Colour residing in our country, in Africa or such other place as Congress shall deem most expedient."

● The main side route continues on Md. 77 through Detour. At 10.0 m. Md. 77 joins Md. 194 (Francis Scott Key Highway) and Mt. Union Road.

Go straight on Mt. Union Road through **MIDDLEBURG**, 11.0 m. At 12.9 m. turn right onto Union Bridge Road. At 14.2 m. Union Bridge Road curves to the right. Continue on Union Bridge Road. At 14.4 m. Union Bridge Road runs into Md. 75. Continue straight on Md. 75 to Union Bridge.

UNION BRIDGE (402' alt., 904 pop.), 14.5 m., on Little Pipe Creek, was settled in the 1730s by William Farquhar, who became prosperous making buckskin breeches. The village received its present name when the settlers, many of them Quakers, built a bridge here uniting the hitherto scattered Pipe Creek settlements. From its early days Union Bridge showed industrial initiative. A linseed oil mill and the first nail factory in the state were operating here about 1800, and a resident, Jacob R. Thomas, invented a mechanical reaper that was unsuccessful in its trial in 1811 but was later perfected by Thomas's cousin, Obed Hussey.

At the junction of Union Bridge Road and Md. 75, 14.4 m., turn left onto Md. 75. Continue to **NEW WINDSOR** (450' alt., 788 pop.), 4.3 m., which was settled in the early nineteenth century. First called Sulphur Springs, it was renamed in 1844. An international gift shop here supports missionary efforts of the Brethren Church.

South of New Windsor, on Md. 31, make a left onto Wakefield Valley Road, 1.0 m. At the fork make a right onto Wilt Road, then another right onto Strawbridge Lane. The much altered **Strawbridge House,** near New Windsor, is one of the twelve designated National Methodist Shrines.

● At 4.7 m. on Md. 31 from New Windsor, make a left onto Marston Road. A marker on a lane (R) at 0.4 m. is on the **Site of Sam's Creek Meeting House,** probably the first Methodist meeting house in America, built in 1764 by a congregation organized by Robert Strawbridge, who had been converted to Methodism in his native Ireland and who came to Maryland some time after 1759. After the little square log building was razed in 1844, the congregation started using the present **Bethel Chapel,** built in 1821 and remodeled in 1860. Strawbridge, who preached in various parts of the province, died in 1781 at Towson and is buried in Mount Olivet Cemetery, Baltimore.

Catoctin Furnace, 11.9 m., still displays the ruins of an iron furnace that may have been opened in 1774. It is said that the Catoctin Furnace supplied cannonballs for the siege of Yorktown during the Revolution.

LEWISTOWN, 14.6 m., was first settled around 1745, and after the Revolution became the home of several Hessian soldiers captured during the war. The Lewistown State Fish Hatchery is west of the town toward the Frederick Municipal Forest and Gambrill State Park.

Richfields (private), 20.3 m., was the home of Thomas Johnson, member of the Continental Congress from Maryland, who nominated George Washington for commander in chief of the colonial armies on June 15, 1775. Johnson later became Maryland's first governor.

Winfield Scott Schley, born at Richfields in 1839, was graduated from the U.S. Naval Academy in 1860 and twenty-four years later won national acclaim when an expedition under his command rescued a party of explorers. In 1898, during the Spanish-American War, while temporarily in command of the American

Catoctin Furnace

fleet, he bottled up the Spanish fleet under Cervera in the harbor of Santiago, then destroyed it when Cervera attempted to escape.

Schley was hailed by the press of the nation as the hero of Santiago, but he was officially reproved for having failed to obey an order of Com. William T. Sampson. The Sampson-Schley controversy continued for some time, but both officers were made rear admirals in 1899. Schley died in New York in 1911.

Further on, U.S. 15 joins with U.S. 340. At 25.3 m. U.S. 15 bears left with U.S. 340. At 30.2 m. U.S. 15 and U.S. 340 split. Bear left, continuing on U.S. 15. At 37.0 m. is the junction with Md. 28.

● Left on Md. 28 is **POINT OF ROCKS** (230' alt., 325 pop.), well known to fishermen. The town was not laid out until 1835, but it achieved national recognition in 1830 when the Baltimore & Ohio Railway and the Chesapeake & Ohio Canal fought over the right of way on the narrow strip of land here between the base of Catoctin Mountain and the Potomac. After a long legal battle a compromise was reached that lasted until 1867, when the railroad tunneled through the mountain.

Point of Rocks was a strategic site during the Civil War. Although no major engagements took place here, there was much skirmishing and raiding, and it was here that Gen. Joseph Hooker received telegraphed orders to turn over the Army of the Potomac to General Meade just before the Battle of Gettysburg.

Near Point of Rocks is a quarry of the unusual calico marble from which were made several columns for the Capitol in Washington.

At 4.7 m. on Md. 28 is a T-junction. Make a right, continuing on Md. 28.

At 6.5 m. is the Frederick-Montgomery County Line.

At 8.2 m. is **DICKERSON.** Turn left onto Mt. Ephraim Road. At the fork, go left (straight) continuing on Mt. Ephraim Road. **Sugar Loaf Mountain** (1,300' alt.), isolated to the north, is largely covered with brown sandstone and heavily wooded slopes. Lookouts were placed on it during the Civil War. The entire area is now a park, open to the public without charge.

At the fork make a right onto Harriss Road (the first 1.9 m. is gravel). At 2.2 m. is the intersection with Barnesville Road, which leads to **BARNESVILLE.** The **Arabian Horse Museum** is at Ridge and Barnesville roads near Barnesville.

On U.S. 15, just before crossing the Potomac River, the site of the Indian town of Canarest, on a Potomac island, can be seen. Now called Heater's Island, it was occupied by the Tuscarora during their flight from South Carolina to join the Five Nations in New York. The tribe stayed here for two years (1711–13).

At 37.4 m., after crossing the Potomac River Bridge, U.S. 15 crosses the **Virginia Line.**

FREDERICK–ROCKVILLE–DISTRICT OF COLUMBIA LINE; 37.4 m.
Md. 355

Maryland Route 355 roughly follows an Indian path, later a colonial road, that was used by General Braddock on his way West in 1755. It is now paralleled by Interstate 270, a high-speed limited-access highway. From the city of Frederick, Md. 355 rolls southeasterly through rich farmland that is gradually being converted to residential and commercial use. As the highway enters Montgomery County and approaches the District of Columbia, more and more intensive residential and commercial development may be observed. Newly established along the route are many industries in the aerospace, computer, health, and nuclear energy fields, together with related agencies of the federal government. The Md. 355–I-270 corridor has become the "Main Street" of clusters of bedroom communities whose breadwinners commute daily into Washington, D.C. The lavish scale of building in the area is tangible evidence of the burgeoning population of the Washington metropolitan area and reflects the fact that in terms of per capita income, Montgomery County is one of the richest counties in the United States.

Md. 355, designated Market Street in **FREDERICK,** crosses I-70 N at a limited-access interchange on the southern limit of the city (*see* Frederick Tour), 0.0 m. The northern boundary of the **Monocacy Battlefield** is at 1.1 m.

On July 7, 1864, Gen. Lew Wallace, with 2,650 men under Gen. E. B. Tyler, took up a position at the railroad junction on the Monocacy River, planning to check the advance of Gen. Jubal Early and a force of approximately 17,500 Confederate troops. On July 8, Wallace was joined by 3,350 men from Gen. James B. Ricketts's division. The bloody battle fought the next day ended in a decisive Union defeat, but the delay it caused Early probably prevented the capital from falling into the hands of the Confederates. The Federal casualties totaled 1,294, over 668 of whom were missing; the Confederates lost between 1,300 and 1,500 men.

In **Best's Grove** (R), 1.3 m., Confederate troops under Jackson and Longstreet camped September 5 and 6, 1862, when they crossed the Potomac River into Maryland ten days before the Antietam campaign. Here on September 8, Lee drafted his proclamation assuring Marylanders that they would not be molested by his troops and urging them to support the Confederacy.

At 1.9 m. is a **Confederate Monument** (R).

To the left at 2.2 m. is **Frederick Junction,** where a spur into Frederick joins the main line of the B & O Railroad by the Monocacy River. When Union forces fled across the old iron railroad bridge here after the Battle of the Monocacy, some fell between the ties to the river forty feet below, but the Confederates held their artillery fire and many crossed in safety. On the bank of the river (L) is the **Site of the Old Fort Furnace.** Here in 1755, Maj. Gen. Edward Braddock held a conference with provincial officers to plan his ill-fated Fort Duquesne campaign. Before the coming of steam engines, the water of the Monocacy at Frederick Junction was used to power the grindstones of the Araby Flour Mills, founded in 1830.

● Just beyond the Monocacy River Bridge on Md. 355, 2.7 m., bear right along Araby Road, then turn right again at 0.5 m. on the Baker Valley Road to **Thomas House** (R) (private, but visible from the road). The 2½-story brick house was built about 1780 by James Marshall. When the house was bombarded during the Battle of the Monocacy, the Thomas family and neighbors took refuge in the cellar. Gens. U. S. Grant, David A. Hunter, and Philip Sheridan conferred here on August 5, 1864, and decided on the Virginia campaign against Gen. Jubal Early.

After passing through the village of **URBANA**, 5.9 m., Md. 355 enters Montgomery County, 10.1 m. Acting upon a longstanding local grievance against the lord proprietor, one of the first acts of the Maryland Convention of 1776 was the division of Frederick County into three parts. Two new counties were erected, Montgomery to the south and Washington to the west of the present Frederick County. Although a rapidly expanding population had long justified such a division, political considerations of representation and patronage influenced the proprietary government against the change. Befitting their origin in the Revolution, the new counties were named for military leaders in the fight against Great Britain. Washington County was named for the commander in chief of the Continental Army, and Montgomery County was named to honor Gen. Richard Montgomery (1736–75), a native of Ireland who had emigrated to New York in 1772 after years of service in the British army. Montgomery was commissioned in the Continental Army sent to invade Canada upon the outbreak of the Revolution, and he succeeded to its command. After taking Montreal, he was killed during the attempt to capture Quebec on New Year's Eve, 1775.

West of **HYATTSTOWN** (450′ alt.), 10.2 m., founded in 1809 by Jesse Hyatt, are quarries that supplied roofing slate for the first Capitol in Washington. In 1862, Gen. Stonewall Jackson engaged in an artillery skirmish here with Gen. N. P. Banks.

To the left of Md. 355 between Hyattstown and Clarksburg, the **Little Bennett Regional Park** offers limited public facilities in an unspoiled setting on Little Bennett Creek. **CLARKSBURG** (700′ alt.), 14.3 m. at the junction of Md. 355 and Md. 121, is thought to be on the site of an early Indian trading post. It is

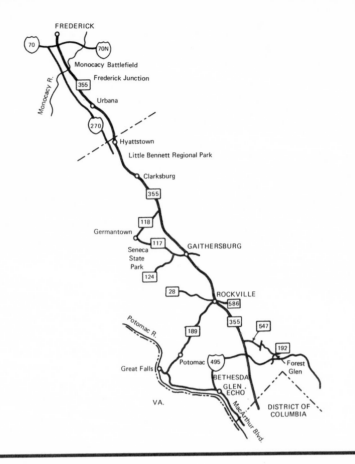

now the home of COMSAT, a communications satellite laboratory.

On the **Site of Dowden's Ordinary** (L), Michael Dowden built a seventeen-room log tavern in 1754 where Maryland troops sent by Governor Sharpe to assist General Braddock encamped in 1755. The tavern was razed in 1920. A stone marks its site.

● Turn right at Md. 118, 18.1 m., off Md. 355 to **GERMANTOWN**, 2.0 m. (past the I-270 interchange), where Energy Research Development and Application is located directly across from a large division of Fairchild Industries, Inc., which produces spacecraft, space subsystems, and communications systems.

GAITHERSBURG (512' alt., 8,344 pop.), 21.7 m. at the junction of Md. 355 and Md. 124 was named for Benjamin Gaither, who built a house here in 1802 on farmland that was part of the Deer Park tract surveyed in 1722. The settlement grew slowly until the metropolitan branch of the B & O Railroad came through in 1873. In the burst of growth that followed, the town became a milling and trade center in what was predominantly a farming area until the mid-twentieth century, when the growth of Washington's metropolitan area began to encompass it.

In 1899, Gaithersburg was selected as one of six sites around the world on the 30°8' north latitude where observatories were set up to study the wobble of the earth on its axis that changes the latitudes of the earth with respect to fixed stars. Other observatories were in Ohio, California, Japan, Turkey, and Italy. Industries that have been established here specialize in engineering, communications systems, and computer applications.

● To the west from Gaithersburg on Md. 124, the **National Bureau of Standards** complex lies to the left, 0.9 m. on Quince Orchard Road. The bureau is charged with insuring a consistent system of physical measurements throughout the country (the "standard yardstick"). It also publishes a consumer information series and provides technical notes on materials and test methodologies (open for tours, Tues. at 1:30, Fri. at 9:30).

At the National Bureau of Standards, Clopper Road (Md. 117) branches off to the right. **Seneca State Park,** 2.4 m. along the road, features an extensive peony collection, with thousands of plants and hundreds of varieties. The collection was begun in 1913 by Edward Schwartz; an early annual visitor to his display was President Woodrow Wilson. Mr. Schwartz's family continued the collection until 1963, when the land was acquired as part of the proposed state park. The peonies were neglected for years for lack of funds, but the state has now reclaimed the hardy plants. The peak of the season is usually in late May.

ROCKVILLE (421' alt., 41,564 pop.), 27.3 m. at the junction of Md. 355 and Washington Street, has been the seat of Montgomery County since 1777. County officers first met at Hungerford's tavern here, then in a house owned by Thomas O. Williams that was improved with public funds to function as a courthouse. Williams laid out lots for a town around the courthouse in 1784, naming it Williamsburg. The boundaries of the lots were disputed, so in 1801 an act was passed by the Maryland Assembly requiring a new survey and changing the town's name to Rockville.

In the Civil War, Rockville was frequently raided by Confederate troops seeking horses. After the defeat of Gen. Lew Wallace at the Battle of the Monocacy, Confederate forces under Gen. Jubal Early passed through on their way to and from the attack on Washington.

Today, Rockville is a thriving suburban center in the Washington metropolitan area. In addition to extensive commercial development that serves residents of the area, Rockville has developed into a center of research and technology for the aerospace, computer, communications, and nuclear energy industries. Both private concerns and government agencies conduct biological research here. The U.S. Department of Health, Education, and Welfare employs thousands; its Food and Drug Administration and Health Services Center are both located in Rockville.

To the right of Md. 355 is the Rockville Campus of **Montgomery College.** The Takoma Park Campus was founded in 1945 as the first junior college in the nation. Northeast of the city, **Rock Creek Park** and **Lake Norbeck** are open for public recreation. Md. 355 passes through Rockville, where in 1774 Charles Hungerford operated the tavern where the freemen of the area gathered in response to the blockade of Boston, resolving to break off trade with Great Britain. The same tavern, operated by Hungerford's successor, was the county meeting place and temporary courthouse after Montgomery County was erected in 1776.

The **Beall-Dawson House,** 103 West Montgomery Avenue, was completed around 1815 as a city residence for Upton Beall, an attorney and landowner of the prominent Beall family. Only the front and street side of the two-story brick house are laid in Flemish bond, giving some credence to the story that construction of the house was interrupted by the War of 1812. Rich interior detail is set off by the eleven-foot ceilings of the first floor. The house, which is owned jointly by the Montgomery County Historical Society and the City of Rockville, is open Tues.–Sat., 12–4, and the first Sun. of each month, 2–5.

Bear right onto Washington Street. At 0.7 m. is the intersection of Washington Street and Montgomery Avenue. To the left, at the intersection of Md. 355 and Md. 586 (Viers Mill Rd.), is the old painted brick parish church of St. Mary's, now **Our Lady's Chapel** (L) (1817), which stands beside the modern circular St. Mary's Roman Catholic Church (1967). Eight stained-glass windows are set into arches projecting through its domed roof.

● Straight ahead on Washington Street is the limestone **Montgomery County Courthouse** (R), built in 1931 in the Classical tradition. The old courthouse, built in 1891, was retained and is used by the county. Turn left at the intersection. At 0.9 m. is the intersection of Md. 28 and Md. 189 (Falls Road).

Md. 28 goes northwesterly out of Rockville past the village of Hunting Hill; chromium ore was pit-mined nearby in the nineteenth century.

● Return to the junction and bear left on Falls Road to **POTOMAC,** one of the centers of gracious residential life in Montgomery County. The Potomac Polo Club, the only polo club in Maryland, plays teams throughout the country during the summer months.

Continuing on Falls Road past Potomac, turn right on MacArthur Boulevard, 7.6 m., to the **Great Falls of the Potomac,** 1.2 m. Here the Potomac River descends from the plateau down to tidewater in a spectacular series of rapids and cataracts. The falls are part of a park that includes restored portions of the C & O Canal and the Great Falls Tavern (now a museum). Numerous ruins and artifacts date from the period when water power was harnessed for industrial purposes before it was replaced by steam and eventually electricity. The museum is open 9–5:30 in the winter and 9–8 in the summer.

● To the left from its intersection with Falls Road, toward Washington, MacArthur Boulevard passes abandoned gold mines. California soldiers stationed on the Potomac during the Civil War discovered the precious metal in 1864. One of them, John Clear, returned after the war and organized a company that mined small quantities of gold between 1869 and 1880. The mines were briefly reopened in 1935 after revaluation increased the price of gold.

About three miles down MacArthur Boulevard from the intersection, the long hangarlike buildings of the **Naval Ship Research and Development Center** may be seen on the right between the road and the Potomac River. The installation was begun in 1936 as a model basin in which the design and operation of ships could be studied. It includes a long towing tank, the aquatic equivalent of a wind tunnel, in which scale models are tested under controlled conditions.

The old **Cabin John Bridge** (R) on MacArthur Boulevard is a single masonry arch 220 feet long built in 1857–63 to carry the water con-

Great Falls of the Potomac

duit supplying Washington, D.C., from the Potomac at Great Falls. The span also served as a bridge for the old Conduit Road, now Mac-Arthur Boulevard. Jefferson Davis, as secretary of war under President Franklin Pierce, directed the Army Engineers, who undertook the construction of the bridge. When the Civil War began and Davis became president of the Confederate States, his name was cut ~ut of the stone at the entrance of the bridge; it was restored under Theodore Roosevelt's administration.

As MacArthur Boulevard enters **GLEN ECHO,** a marker on the highway (L) is opposite the entrance drive to the **Clara Barton House** (R). Its two steeple-roofed towers are visible through the trees. Clara Barton (1821–1912), founder of the American Red Cross, was given this house in 1897 by the city of Johnstown, Pennsylvania, in appreciation for her humanitarian work in the aftermath of the great Johnstown Flood of 1889. Much of the lumber used in this construction was salvaged from emergency buildings put up after the flood. The exterior and interior wooden galleries are designed to resemble an elegant riverboat. The house, which was the headquarters of the American Red Cross until 1904, is open to the public in the afternoons from 1–5, except Mondays and holidays.

Glen Echo Park (R) is an old amusement park constructed at the terminus of a mass transit line from Washington. Its rides and pavilions delighted generations of city residents out for a day in the country. The merry-go-round is open Apr.–Oct., Sat.–Sun.

South from Rockville, Md. 355 is heavily developed as it approaches Washington. Josiah Henson, whose life was the basis for Harriet Beecher Stowe's *Uncle Tom's Cabin,* grew to manhood as a slave on a plantation near the intersection of Md. 355 and Old Georgetown Road, 28.1 m. An oak log cabin in the area has been restored and may have been his home.

Henson (1789–1883) was born in Charles County, Maryland. During his childhood his parents were sold separately, his father to a Southerner and his mother to a Montgomery County planter. In his book, *Truth Stranger Than Fiction,* Henson described people he had known in Montgomery County, and they were later fictionalized by Stowe. Henson escaped slavery by fleeing to Canada in 1830. A Methodist preacher, he was active in the abolitionist movement, speaking and traveling in England to raise money for the cause. One of his Maryland descendants, Matthew Henson, accompanied Adm. Robert E. Peary on the expedition to the North Pole in 1909.

Georgetown Preparatory School (R), 29.2 m. on Md. 355, was established by Archbishop John Carroll at Georgetown in 1789 and transferred to this site in 1919. It was the nucleus from which Georgetown University developed.

● Turn left on Md. 547 (Strathmore Road) opposite the school. Strathmore Road becomes Knowles Avenue at the intersection with Beach Drive, 1.3 m. At 1.8 m. turn left on Md. 185. At 1.9 m. turn right on Md. 192. Take Md. 192 to **FOREST GLEN**, 3.5 m., once a trading post on an Indian path. The land is part of a grant made in 1680 to the Carroll family. At 3.8 m. turn left on Forest Glen Road. Turn left on Rosensteel Avenue, 4.0 m., to **St. John's Cemetery** (L). A small frame building in St. John's Cemetery is a reproduction of the original St. John the Evangelist Mission Church of 1774, where Archbishop Carroll was serving when he was appointed official head of the Roman Catholic Church in America in 1784.

John Carroll (1735–1815), first American archbishop, was an outstanding figure in the history of the Roman Catholic Church in the United States. He was born in Maryland but educated in Europe because of the restrictions on Catholic education in the province. After joining the Society of Jesus in 1753, he continued his studies and taught in Europe. Following suppression of the Jesuits by the Pope in 1773, Carroll returned to the United States, where he founded a mission on his mother's land at Forest Glen. He supported the American cause in the War for Independence and was active in diplomatic affairs during the war. One of his chief aims was the separation of the church hierarchy in the United States from supervision by church officials in London. In response to an American petition, Pope Pius VI granted Carroll some episcopal powers and made him head of the missions in the new country in 1784. Carroll immediately began planning a college, which he considered to be an essential part of the work of the church. The Georgetown Preparatory School, and eventually Georgetown University, were the result. At his insistence, the school was open to students of every religious persuasion from the beginning.

In 1790, Carroll was made bishop of Baltimore, and in 1808 he became archbishop, with suffragans in Boston, New York, and Kentucky. When the Society of Jesus was reactivated in 1814, Archbishop Carroll wished to return to Georgetown as a simple teaching Jesuit. Age overtook him, however, in his archiepiscopal role. After his death in 1815 he was interred in the Baltimore Cathedral (*see* Downtown Baltimore).

● Returning to the intersection of Knowles Avenue and Beach Drive, turn left. Rising above the gorge of Rock Creek at Stoneybrook Road above Beach Drive and the beltway is the striking **Washington Temple of the Church of Jesus Christ of Latter Day Saints** (1974) (not open to the public). The nine-level marble sheathed structure is surmounted by six towers; a gleaming golden representation of the Angel Moroni caps the east spire, 288 feet above the ground (585 feet above sea level). Joseph Smith, founder of the religious body, related that the angel appeared to him and directed him to the gold plates from which he translated the Book of Mormon.

Inside the Washington Beltway (I-495), Md. 355 (Wisconsin Avenue) passes by the main entrance to the **National Institutes of Health (NIH)** (R), 34.2 m. NIH conducts and supports research in human diseases and disorders and administers programs to meet health manpower needs. It also oversees the collection and dissemination of research findings and other information on medicine and health. The **Naval Medical Center** (L) is directly across Wisconsin Avenue.

BETHESDA (340' alt., 71,621 pop.), 35.1 m., south of the Washington Beltway on Md. 355, is an unincorporated suburb of Washington that has shared in the overall growth of the metropolitan area, expanding to its present size from a population of 200 in 1940. Although many Bethesdans work in Washington, Bethesda's stores, banks, and other commercial establishments, together with a large biological supplies producer and the Armed Forces Radiobiology Laboratory, employ many local residents. The Topographic Center of the Defense Mapping Agency is also located here.

Md. 355 crosses the **District of Columbia Line** at 37.4 m., south of the Washington Beltway and about five miles northwest of the Zero Milestone of the United States on the Ellipse behind the White House.

FREDERICK–WEST VIRGINIA LINE–(Harpers Ferry); 13.9 m.
Md. 180

Md. 180 parallels U.S. 340, a new road (Md. 180 was formerly U.S. 340). It branches from U.S. 340 at a cloverleaf in southwestern Frederick, just before U.S. 340 goes under I-70. Jefferson Street, from downtown Frederick, leads out to the intersection.

The cloverleaf is on a tract originally patented as Dickson's Struggle. **Prospect Hall** (now Prospect Hall School), the country home of Benjamin Tasker Dulany, son of Daniel, stands on this tract also. This Dulany, unlike his father, espoused the American cause and became one of Washington's aides. Washington's favorite horse, Blueskin, was a present from Dulany. After the Revolution, Washington returned the horse to Mrs. Dulany and in writing of the incident said: ". . . Marks of antiquity have supplanted the place of those beauties with which the horse abounded in his better days, nothing but the recollections of which and of his having been the favorite of Mr. Dulany in the days of his courtship, can reconcile her to the meager appearance he now makes." There is a legend that Blueskin is buried somewhere on the grounds.

The first settlers of **JEFFERSON,** 6.0 m., arrived in 1779. In the days when highway robbers had headquarters here it became known as The Trap. The present name was adopted in 1832, six years after Thomas Jefferson's death.

In **PETERSVILLE,** from the junction with Md. 79, 10.7 m., go right 0.2 m. on Catholic Church Road, to **St. Mary's Church,** built in 1826 with money contributed by Gov. Thomas Sim Lee. For nearly seventy years this was the only Roman Catholic Church between Frederick and Harpers Ferry, West Virginia. The brick church has a portico with four Doric columns. A house north of here became Lee's home after the Revolution. Lee was

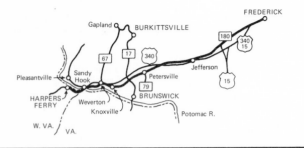

governor of Maryland from 1779 to 1782 and from 1792 to 1794 and had earlier served as a member of the Continental Congress. He also attended the Maryland Convention that ratified the Constitution of the United States in 1788. Elected U.S. senator in 1794 and governor of Maryland for a third term in 1798, he declined both honors.

At 12.4 m. Md. 17 intersects Md. 180.

● Right on Md. 17 to the **Site of the Horsey Distillery** (R) (private), 2.8 m., established in 1850. At first, whiskey manufactured at this plant was loaded on slow-sailing vessels, shipped around Cape Horn to California, and then shipped back to the plant, because the rocking of the ship was believed to age the whiskey more rapidly. The plant continued in operation until the prohibition amendment went into force.

BURKITTSVILLE (550' alt.), 4.3 m. at Main Street, at the foot of South Mountain, was called Harley's Post Office until it was laid out as a town and named for a settler, Henry Burkitt, in 1829.

Left 1.1 m. from Burkittsville on Gapland Road to the **War Correspondents Memorial,** erected by George Alfred Townsend (Gath), Civil War correspondent and novelist, in honor of his fellow newspapermen who covered the Civil War. This strange structure, designed by Townsend to include the most bizarre features of a Moorish arch at a railroad station and a tower on a firehouse—both of which had aroused his admiration—was dedicated on October 16, 1896, with much publicity. The arch is of local stone trimmed with brown sandstone, blue limestone, and brick. The front is decorated with red brick panels into which the words *War Correspondents* have been cut. In a niche near the top of the arch is a six-foot figure of Orpheus sheathing a sword and playing a pipe. Tablets on one side of the arch bear the names of 147 correspondents and artists of the war, and other tablets include a description of the engagement that occurred in the area. The grounds and memorial were given to the State of Maryland by Townsend in 1904.

Born in Delaware in 1841, Townsend spent most of his life in Maryland. After the Civil War, when royalties from *Katy of Catoctin* and *The Entailed Hat* began to pour in, he built his retreat in this area. In all he built five houses here, one for his own use, one for his wife, and the others for his children, their nurses, and his servants. He entertained extravagantly, and invitations to parties at Gapland were welcomed by outstanding people of the period. Each of the five houses was a fantastic architectural conception, with entrances and exits placed at the whim of the owner, and numerous spires, arches, and turrets jutting from the roofs. Set in marble in the walls were quotations from the Classics. One of the buildings has been restored.

When Gath's fortunes began to decline, he had to move from his elaborate establishment, on which he had spent half a million dollars, to simpler quarters in Washington, D.C. He died in 1914, and in 1922 his heirs sold this estate for $9,500. An effort was made to convert it into a summer hotel, but the plan was abandoned and Gapland was left to the mercy of vandals and the elements. In 1938 it was sold at auction for $750. It eventually came into the hands of the state, which administers the area as **Gathland State Park.**

● Left on Md. 17 to **BRUNSWICK** (248' alt., 3,566 pop.), 1.2 m., a community that grew up around the repair shops established here in 1890 by the Baltimore & Ohio Railroad. The town is on part of the large tract patented as Hawkins' Merry Peep o'Day by John Hawkins in 1753. In 1787 the tract was laid out as the town of Berlin, but the name was changed in 1890 to avoid confusion with the Berlin on Maryland's Eastern Shore.

The **Potomac River Bridge** was built in 1894 on the piers of a covered wooden span burned by the Confederates. The old bridge had been used by the Confederate troops for frequent dashes into Maryland to cut the B & O Railroad tracks and telegraph lines. Following the battles of Antietam and Gettysburg, the Federal armies under General Mc-Clellan and General Meade, respectively, crossed the Potomac here for their advances into Virginia.

KNOXVILLE, 13.9 m., like Brunswick, relied on B & O Railroad repair shops. Laid out in 1772 on several lots of the Merryland Tract, the town prospered in the days of the Chesapeake & Ohio Canal. Small industries developed, including iron smelting, which continued until about 1890.

Just west of Knoxville, in 1835, Casper W. Wever, a civil engineer who built the first bridge at Harpers Ferry, tried to establish a manufacturing town to be called Weverton. Wever drew plans for factory and home sites here, constructed a power dam across the river, and built several mills that were never used. One factory, which manufactured files, operated from 1846 until the beginning of the Civil War, and a marble works also did business for a brief period. The entire plan collapsed after Wever's death, and the town today is marked only by the crumbling walls of stone houses.

At modern **WEVERTON** is the junction with Md. 67. To reach it from Knoxville, follow Md. 180 into its merger with U.S. 340, then take the first exit (Md. 67 to Boonsboro). At the stop sign, make a left and pick up U.S. 340 E. Make a right on Md. 180. Follow Md. 180 to Sandy Hook Road, which is outside **SANDY HOOK,** a village that was established around 1832 to serve traffic on the Chesapeake & Ohio Canal. First known as Keep Tryst, its present name is said to refer to a nearby quicksand pool in which a teamster lost his horses.

● Make a left onto Sandy Hook Road, 0.0 m., which hugs the Maryland bank of the Potomac across from Harpers Ferry, West Virginia. The **Harpers Ferry National Historical Park** stretches up the heights to the right. The craggy slopes on both sides of the river were occupied by Union and Confederate troops several times during the Civil War as each side sought to control the strategic railroad crossing.

Continue on Sandy Hook Road to **PLEASANTVILLE,** then straight ahead on Harpers Ferry Road to the first crossroads, 5.7 m. Straight across the intersection Chestnut Grove Road begins (Harpers Ferry Road bends left). The **John Brown House** (L) (private) is located 0.7 m. from the crossroads. Early in June, 1859, Brown, under an assumed name, with two of his sons and a follower, Jerry Anderson, rented this farmhouse and 160 acres, allegedly for farming purposes. Brown's daughter and daughter-in-law soon joined him. For about three months the group received from Northern abolitionists packages of

arms and ammunition, which were stored in a log cabin; in the attic
of the farmhouse Brown gathered about a thousand pikes that had been
sent to him from Connecticut. On the night of October 16, after attending services at a Dunkard church, Brown, with less than a score of
followers, surprised the little garrison at Harpers Ferry and captured
the arsenal. The anticipated uprising of slaves throughout the South
failed to materialize, and a day later the arsenal was recaptured by
troops under the command of Robert E. Lee. Another detachment
under J. E. B. Stuart seized the house in which Brown had been living,
confiscated the firearms and pikes, and found among his papers the
constitution of the revolutionary government Brown had intended to set
up. Brown was tried, sentenced, and hanged on December 2, 1859, at
Charles Town, West Virginia. Though many of the abolitionists had disapproved of Brown's action, his dignified conduct at his trial and his
execution made him a martyr in their eyes, and the incident widened
the breach between the North and the South.

Md. 180 joins U.S. 340 outside Sandy Hook and crosses the
Potomac River into West Virginia. U.S. 340 continues to Harpers
Ferry.

HAGERSTOWN–ANTIETAM BATTLEFIELD–SHARPSBURG–
BOONSBORO; 17.0 m.
Md. 65 and 34

Maryland Route 65 leaves Hagerstown via Potomac Street and
intersects Interstate 70 at 0.0 m., just south of Hagerstown.
The route followed by the tour goes through rolling farmland to
Antietam National Battlefield, scene of a major battle in the Civil
War. In Sharpsburg, the village just beyond the battlefield, the
tour turns on Md. 34, going through Keedysville to Boonsboro.

The **Maryland Correctional Institution** (L), 2.8 m., is a medium-
security prison that also incorporates the **Maryland Correctional
Training Center.** Approximately a thousand prisoners at the
Training Center receive educational and vocational training.
Those "less amenable to treatment programs" are housed in the
Correctional Institution proper, which has a capacity of six hundred inmates. The prisoners work in a cannery and in metal-
working, wood-working, and brush shops. A work release program is also conducted at the center.

● At the junction with Md. 68, 3.8 m., turn right to College Road,
1.9 m. Make a right onto College Road to the **St. James' School,** 2.4 m.,
an Episcopal preparatory school. When it opened in 1842, it was housed
in **Fountain Rock,** a home built here in 1792 by Gen. Samuel Ringgold on his 17,000-acre estate. Henry Clay and Presidents Madison and
Monroe were among the noted guests at Fountain Rock. St. James
was founded as the diocesan school of the Episcopal Church in Maryland. The Civil War, however, depleted its student body, most of which
joined the Southern armies and failed to return. It has continued as a
secondary school. Like so many Washington County residents in the
area, the staff of the school gave food, water, and medical assistance
to the wounded and exhausted soldiers of both sides after the Battle
of Antietam.

● To the left on Md. 68 from its junction with Md. 65, the **Devil's**

John Brown House

Backbone County Park on Antietam Creek, 1.7 m., has been carefully designed to preserve the natural beauty of the environment while providing facilities for picnicking and recreation. A picturesque waterfall in the creek may best be seen from a nature trail that climbs the steep bank.

Continuing down Md. 65, **Rockland** (L) (private, but is visible from the road), 4.4 m., a rambling twenty-four-room brick mansion erected around 1808 by Frisby Tilghman. Tilghman, a planter who was active in local politics, served as a colonel in the War of 1812. In the rear wing of the mansion, several rooms are said to be haunted by slaves who met violent deaths while quartered in them.

TILGHMANTON, 4.6 m., a crossroad settlement named for Colonel Tilghman, was on his 10,000-acre Rockland estate.

On the **Antietam National Battlefield** (L), an engagement between the Southern Army of Northern Virginia, commanded by Gen. Robert E. Lee, and the Union Army of the Potomac, commanded by Gen. George B. McClellan, took place on September 17, 1862. The battle ended in a draw, and the next night Lee withdrew his army across the Potomac. This battle is said to have been the "bloodiest one-day battle" of the Civil War.

The **Park Administration Building** (L), 9.7 m., has a collection of weapons and other artifacts found on the battlefield and presents a slide show illustrating the main lines of the battle. Here information can be obtained on the automobile or bicycle tours of the battlefield that have been laid out by the Park Service.

SHARPSBURG (425' alt., 833 pop.), 10.6 m., is at the intersection of Md. 65 and Md. 34. The main tour continues to the left on Md. 34 toward Boonsboro. The Chesapeake & Ohio Canal National Historical Park maintains a center in Sharpsburg for the administration of the northern stretches of the canal.

● To the right on Md. 34 through the village of Sharpsburg, the **Site of Lee's Headquarters** (R), 0.8 m., is now commemorated by a historical marker.

TOUR 6

Beyond the village, the plain brick mansion of **Mount Airy** (L) (private, but visible from the road), 1.6 m., was erected around 1800. Two weeks after the Battle of Antietam, President Lincoln visited the wounded who were being cared for in the building.

Ferry Hill (R), 3.2 m., was also used as a hospital after the battle. General Lee's son was among the wounded who were treated here. The substantial brick house was built around 1813 on a rise commanding a view of the Potomac.

Md. 34 crosses the West Virginia line, 3.7 m., at the far end of the bridge over the Potomac River to Shepherdstown, West Virginia.

● Returning east along Md. 34 into Sharpsburg, make a left on Potomac Street; then a left on Chapline Street to Snyder's Landing Road. This road leads northwest out of the village of Sharpsburg down to the **C & O Canal** beside the river, 1.3 m.

● Continuing east on Md. 34, make a right on Mechanic Street, which becomes Harpers Ferry Road. Harpers Ferry Road leads south from Sharpsburg to the village of **Antietam** on the Potomac, 3.2 m. Cannon and cannonballs for the Revolution were cast in the Antietam Iron Works, which operated here from 1765 to 1880. In 1785, James Rumsey built some of the machinery here for what is considered by many to have been the first steam-propelled boat successfully to navigate upstream.

● Continuing east on Md. 34, turn right on Church Street. **Burnside Bridge,** one of the key strategic positions during the Battle of Antietam, is 0.9 m. south of Sharpsburg along Burnside Bridge Road (a continuation of Md. 65, beyond the intersection with Md. 34). As the road crosses Antietam Creek, one can see the original Burnside Bridge to the right. To reach the bridge turn right on Rodman Avenue, 0.6 m. from Sharpsburg, and left again at 0.5 m. on the Old Bridge Road. This takes one through part of the Antietam Battlefield.

From the junction with Md. 68, Md. 34 goes easterly through the battlefield area across Antietam Creek to the village of **KEEDYSVILLE** (350' alt., 431 pop.), 13.4 m. The town was first called Centerville, until its residents requested a new name be-

Antietam National Battlefield

cause of confusion with the Queen Anne's County seat on the Eastern Shore. The petition had so many Keedy signatures on it that the name of Keedysville was decided upon.

BOONSBORO (530' alt., 1,410 pop.), 17.0 m., is on Alt. U.S. 40, the former main highway to the west (*see* Tour 2c).

PENNSYLVANIA LINE–HAGERSTOWN–WILLIAMSPORT–WEST VIRGINIA LINE; 13.5 m.
U.S. 11

U.S. 11, 0.0 m. at the **Maryland-Pennsylvania Line,** crosses the farmlands of the Hagerstown valley and goes through Hagerstown, emerging on the south side of the city into an agricultural area. It has been superseded as a principal traffic artery by Interstate 81, a limited-access highway that runs parallel to U.S. 11 and by-passes Hagerstown.

The **Hagerstown Municipal Airport** (R), 0.4 m., has been used for test flights of aircraft manufactured by Fairchild Industries, established in Hagerstown in 1929.

Rest Haven Cemetery (R), 3.7 m., on the northern limit of Hagerstown, was formerly Bellevue, an estate of Maj. Charles Carroll. Major Carroll, a cousin of Charles Carroll of Carrollton, moved to New York State around 1810 and became one of the developers of the city of Rochester.

HAGERSTOWN (552' alt., 35,862 pop.), 5.5 m. (*see* Hagerstown Tour), is at the junction of U.S. 40 and I-70 (*see* Tour 2d), Md. 65 (*see* Tour 6), Md. 64 and Md. 60.

● Northern Avenue (L), 3.7 m., goes along the northern limits of Hagerstown, past the **Western Maryland State Hospital** (R), a 282-bed center for rehabilitation services and the care of the chronically ill. At 1.2 m. Northern Avenue intersects Md. 60.

FIDDLERSBURG, 0.6 m. beyond that intersection on Fiddlersburg Road, a continuation of Northern Avenue, is one of the older settlements in the county. It is said to have been named for a group of musicians who lived here and traveled through the region playing at social affairs.

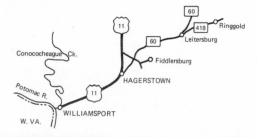

● Returning to the intersection, go left on Md. 60, northeast toward Leitersburg. At 2.8 m. is the **Downing House** (L) (private, but visible from the road), a 2½-story stone structure with a gable roof. It has been dated as early as 1750, which would make it one of the oldest houses in Western Maryland.

LEITERSBURG (596′ alt., 2,260 pop.), 6.1 m., was named for Jacob Leiter, a German immigrant who purchased land here in 1762 and whose grandson, Andrew Leiter, laid out the town site in 1815. The **Leiter Burying Ground** (L), to the northwest of Leitersburg on the Leitersburg State Line Road, is next to **Strite's Mill** (R) at its far end. The mill, erected in 1792 on Leiter land, is named for Christian Strite, who purchased it in 1843; he and his descendants ground wheat and corn at the mill for more than one hundred years.

From Leitersburg, take Ringgold Street to Md. 418. Make a right onto Md. 418 to **RINGGOLD,** 2.9 m., settled in 1825 as Ridgeville. It was renamed in 1850 for Maj. Samuel Ringgold, a son of Washington County's Gen. Samuel Ringgold (see Tour 6, Fountain Rock). Major Ringgold was mortally wounded in 1846 in the Battle of Palo Alto at the beginning of the Mexican War. He is credited with major innovations in the use of artillery and with the invention of the McClellan saddle, which became a standard in the army until World War I. The McClellan saddle is a durable unpadded design particularly distinguished by an elongated opening through the center of the seat which allows ventilation for the rider and prevents pressure on the horse's backbone.

The brick **Franzite Church** in Ringgold was built by the New Mennonite congregation.

Tammany (R) (private, but visible from the road), 10.1 m., at the junction of Tammany Lane and U.S. 11, south of Hagerstown, was built around 1789 by Matthew Van Lear, a Pennsylvanian of Dutch Calvinist descent who had made his fortune in the Indian trade. The 2½-story building is constructed of square brick fired on the premises. The wing has a T-shaped end chimney typical of the period. Some of the original flooring and woodwork is intact.

Springfield (L) (private), 11.4 m. at the junction of Springfield Lane and Md. 11, was purchased by Revolutionary War general Otho Holland Williams, founder of *Williamsport.* The central part of the house, of stone and brick now covered with clapboard, was probably built before the Revolution. Its two-story pedimented porch and small-paned windows, together with the batten double doors at either end of the entrance hall, link it to Tidewater Maryland architecture of the mid-eighteenth century. The brick right wing and many of the outbuildings are thought to have been added under the direction of General Williams. The large square brick left wing, now a separate residence, was built around 1878.

Otho Holland Williams was born in 1749 in Prince George's County, Maryland. Orphaned at the age of thirteen, he soon went to work in the clerk's office of Frederick County and then in Baltimore County. When the Revolutionary War broke out, he secured a commission as lieutenant in a rifle company sent by Maryland to join the Continental Army under George Washington, then camped outside Boston. Williams served with distinction during Washington's campaigns in New York until he was captured at the fall of Fort Washington, when his company was holding the rear while the main body of Washington's army retreated across the Hudson to New Jersey. He spent fifteen months as a prisoner, at first confined in a crude warehouse and then in one of the damp, rotting hulls in New York Harbor, where his health was permanently impaired. After being exchanged in 1778, the young officer returned to field command. His brilliant performance led eventually to his promotion to the rank of brigadier general. At the close of the war he received a political appointment as collector of the Port of Baltimore, an office of honor and profit. The responsibilities were not onerous, so General Williams was able to direct improvements on the lands he had purchased at Springfield and plan the development of Williamsport nearby. He died in 1794 at the age of forty-five and is buried at Williamsport.

WILLIAMSPORT (380′ alt., 2,270 pop.), 11.5 m., was laid out in 1787 on the high ground at the confluence of Conococheague Creek and the Potomac River, under the sponsorship of Gen. Otho Holland Williams. Early hopes for its development were based upon the ample supply of water power for mills and proposed transport routes up the Potomac into the West and up the valleys of Antietam and Conococheague creeks into Pennsylvania. Shipping from Williamsport down the Potomac to tidal waters had already been established; although the Great Falls of the Potomac limited the trade, improvements were anticipated.

President George Washington inspected Williamsport in 1791, after it had petitioned Congress to be selected as the site of the proposed federal city. The barrier of the Great Falls was cited as one cause for the denial of the petition, and the site selected, present-day Washington, is located well below that point.

The little city did prosper on a modest scale; mills, taverns, and some shipping trade were established. Later proposals for extensive development of Williamsport were thwarted when it was by-passed by the B & O Railroad in the 1830s and when its petition to be the site of a national foundry in 1858 was finally denied. Its location on the C & O Canal and I-81 have stimulated some industry in the town. The town's present manufacturing base includes a long-established tannery, brick kilns, and limestone quarrying enterprises. Newer plants make pipe, travel trailers, and labels.

U.S. 11 crosses the **West Virginia Line,** 13.5 m., on the other side of the Potomac River about thirteen miles northeast of Martinsburg, West Virginia.

CUMBERLAND–OLDTOWN–WEST VIRGINIA LINE; 25.9 m.
Md. 51

This tour begins on Industrial Boulevard, Md. 51, from an interchange with U.S. 48 in downtown Cumberland (*see* Cumberland Tour), 0.0 m. After passing through extensive railroad yards, Md. 51 emerges from the city and runs toward the southeast through the narrow, wooded Potomac valley. The abandoned C & O Canal bed lies between the road and the river and has been restored for recreational use along much of its course as the C & O Canal Historical Park.

EVITTS CREEK, 2.8 m., and Evitts Mountain, to the north, were named for the first European known to have settled in the mountains of Allegany County. James Evitt, or Evart, built a solitary cabin on the mountain by the creek about seven miles north of here, where he lived off the land as a hermit until his lonely and unnoticed death sometime before 1749. His withdrawal into the wilderness was attributed to an unhappy love affair. Reservoirs on the upper reaches of the creek now supply water to the city of Cumberland.

Near the highway at 3.0 m. (L) is the place where in 1755 Jane Frazier, an early settler, was captured by Indians as she was going to Will's Creek for supplies, accompanied by a single manservant, who was killed and scalped in the struggle. According to a narrative thought to have been written by Jane Frazier herself, she was taken to her captors' village in the Ohio Territory, where she was adopted into the tribe. Nearly a year later she escaped with two fellow captives. They faced a perilous journey of more than 300 miles through territory controlled by Indian tribes allied with the French, then at war with Britain and its colonists. The wilderness supplied cover to the fugitives but little for them to eat. After a week, "the men shot a turkey and being so very hungry they foundered themselves and next morning neither one of them was able to travel." Jane went on alone, living on bark and herbs and sleeping in trees or hollows to conceal herself at night. Eighteen days after the escape she found a trail that she followed to *Oldtown,* where she was rejoicingly greeted by friends.

Escorted by about fifty neighbors, who were singing, blowing horns, and carrying flags, Jane Frazier rode home to Evitts Creek, where her husband lived with his new wife. "Nearing the house my husband came out very frightened at the parade. . . . Then coming nearer he saw me and grabbed me off the horse shouting with all his power 'The lost is found, the dead alive,' and so would not let me go for some time fearing it was all an apparition. We went into the house and I met his second wife. She seemed a very nice woman but he told her he could not give me up again, that as I was living their marriage had been illegal, but he would support her as he had promised. . . . And she being a woman of good sense took it all in good part, wishing me luck and said she would come some time and hear me tell about my captivity." Having learned the Indian language and their ways, Jane, together with her husband and children, accompanied the 1758 expedition led by Gen. John Forbes that drove the French and Indians from Fort Duquesne. The Fraziers then settled in Pennsylvania.

Where Md. 51 takes a sharp curve to the left, 5.9 m., a road leads off (R) to a large plant opened in 1956 where over a thousand people are employed making plate and float glass. After the curve, the roadbed of Md. 51 is incised into the steep slopes that drop down to the Potomac as it skirts the jutting ends of Irons and Collier mountains.

At the base of **Irons Mountain,** 6.8 m., part of the C & O Canal has been restored. The turn, to the right, is a difficult one. It would be safer to proceed past the turnoff, turn around at the next convenient place, and approach the turn from the opposite direction. This part of the **C & O Canal Historical Park** is located at Lock 72 of the canal. The lock has been restored together with the two-story board and batten house beside it, where the lock tender lived. Each lock tender, who could be responsible for up to three locks, was given a house, an acre of land for a garden, and a salary. In return he or she—there were several women lock tenders—was on duty twenty-four hours a day, ready to operate the cumbersome lock gates upon the summons of passing boatmen.

The **Spring Gap Recreation Area** (R), 8.0 m., also part of the park, offers picnic tables and other conveniences. As an alternative to the awkward procedure described above to reach Lock 72, one could park at Spring Gap and take a pleasant hike along the towpath of the canal upriver to the lock.

Below the village of **SPRING GAP,** Md. 51 diverges northward from the river and canal for several miles.

● Immediately after crossing the bridge over Mill Run, 10.6 m., turn left on the Cresap Mill Road, up the hollow between Martin Mountain (L) and Warrior Mountain (R) to the **Warrior Mountain Wildlife Management Area,** which straddles the crest of that mountain just south of its highest point (2,133′ alt.). Cresap Mill Road follows the route of one of the branches of the Warrior Path, an Indian trail from Iroquois country in upstate New York to the grounds of the southern tribes. The path forded the Potomac at Oldtown.

OLDTOWN, the first colonial settlement in what is now Allegany County, where the trail from Virginia and Maryland to the west forded the Potomac, has been by-passed in the construction of Md. 51. To reach the center of the historic village, turn right cautiously, at 15.0 m., through a one-lane passage under the railway bed, then turn right again on the old road.

Oldtown was established on the site of an Indian town, for the Indians had discovered and used the ford long before the arrival of Europeans in the New World. A branch of the Indian thoroughfare, Athiamiowee, known to the English as the Warrior Path (literally, "path of the armed ones"), crossed the North Branch of the Potomac here, about two miles above the point where the South Branch joins it to double the river's flow. As a principal north-south artery, the path was used by both hunting and war parties. It connected the Six Nations of the Iroquois Confederation to the north with the Catawbas, Cherokees, and

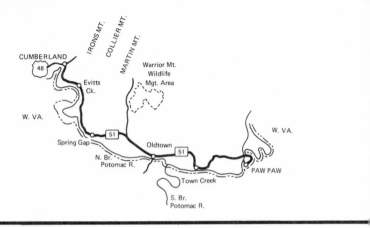

other southern tribes. In the course of their great migrations, the Shawnees temporarily built a village here in the last decade of the seventeenth century. It became known as King Opessa's Town, named after a tribal chieftain around 1711. Sometime before 1732 the village was abandoned when the Indians moved on. The site was then called Shawanese Old Town or, more simply, Old Town by the English explorers, hunters, and traders penetrating into the mountains in ever increasing numbers.

In 1741 Col. Thomas Cresap (ca. 1700–90) built a fortified dwelling here, positioning himself on the Warrior Path to engage in the lucrative fur trade with the Indians of the various tribes passing through the mountains. Cresap called his home Skipton, after his birthplace in Yorkshire, England. During a long and eventful life, Cresap played a prominent part in the frontier development of Maryland.

After his arrival in the colony around 1717, Cresap struggled to make his fortune. His early efforts put him into debt, but by 1729 he had established a farm on the disputed northern border with Pennsylvania under lenient terms offered by Lord Baltimore. Supported by the proprietary government, which made him a local magistrate and captain of militia, Cresap stubbornly asserted Maryland sovereignty in the area. His aggressive defiance of Pennsylvania authority escalated the controversy into armed conflict, the Conojacular War, and earned him the respect of influential Maryland officials. The Pennsylvanians viewed him as the "Maryland Monster." They captured him in 1737, when a party of twenty-four armed men surrounded his house before dawn. After the Pennsylvanians had scorned Cresap's attempt to dissuade them peacefully from their purpose, during which he read to them from a law book, the siege was on. Volleys of shots were exchanged; Cresap was wounded and his wife went into labor. They held out until the house was set afire, when Cresap led his household in a desperate break for the forest. He was captured and taken in irons to Philadelphia, which he promptly declared to be the prettiest city in Maryland. Cresap's confinement on dubious legal grounds soon became an embarrassment to Penn's government, which was seeking to have the border question settled in the English courts (where the dispute was finally decided in favor of Pennsylvania in 1750). After his release, by order of the King, Cresap took his family to the far western part of the colony, building a home on Antietam Creek near Hagerstown. When a cargo of furs he had sent to England was intercepted by a French ship and lost, he deeded his Antietam landholdings to his principal creditor, Daniel Dulany, Sr., and moved westward again, this time beyond the edge of settlement to Oldtown.

At Oldtown Cresap quickly reestablished and extended trading relationships with the tribes using the Warrior Path. In the Treaty of Lancaster, made between the English and the Six Nations in 1744, his cabin on the Potomac was used as a marker. That treaty required, among other provisions, that the colonists furnish food and supplies to Indian parties passing along the western paths, where the settlers had decimated the game on which the Indians had formerly relied for food in their travels. Cresap, both as a trader and as a representative of the Maryland government, handed out food so generously that he was called Big Spoon by the Indians. His hospitality also extended to all others traveling in the West. Indian scouts, missionaries, traders, explorers, and surveyors stopped at Cresap's for rest and refreshment, as well as to buy supplies and horses and to hire scouts. Among his guests in 1748 was young George Washington on his first surveying trip into the West, who commented on the well-stocked trading post and described a "Daunce" performed by some thirty Indians who also had been cheered by the offerings of their "Big Spoon."

Cresap was deeply involved with the efforts of the Ohio Company to settle the land beyond the mountain barrier and divert its Indian trade from the French and the Pennsylvanians. His travels into the West assisted in the establishment of a regular trade route up from the Potomac. He continued to be active in government as well, serving as a magistrate and as a colonel of militia, dealing with the Indians, and surveying the Potomac boundary. When the French moved into the Ohio country in force in 1753, they warned him to retire from his settlement, which they claimed as French territory. As described by a member of Braddock's expedition, Cresap "refused it like a man of Spirit" and proceeded to assist Washington and Braddock in the military operations of the French and Indian War, serving as commissary. The logistics of supply defeated even the best efforts of the "Rattlesnake Colonel" and his son Daniel to satisfy British demands, which were made in ignorance of the rugged conditions of the remote, mountainous region. Some complaints were made accusing the Cresaps of profiteering on the transactions. Although the colonel was apparently a canny businessman, whose expense accounts for public business were frequently questioned by the assembly, it must be remembered that those who issued the complaints were seeking a scapegoat to cover the failures of the poorly planned campaigns.

After Braddock's defeat, Indian raids menaced the settlers at Oldtown for years. The outpost was maintained, although Cresap was forced to remove his family to Williamsport briefly in 1756. He and his sons led counterattacks against the raiding parties, during one of which his son Thomas was killed. As late as 1763 the colonists around Oldtown were driven to seek refuge in the stockade around Cresap's post by an Indian attack. The close of the French and Indian War later that year found the old colonel still in possession of a good estate and prominent in Maryland affairs as a member of the assembly. He and his son Michael pursued his interests in the Ohio lands, although British policy obstructed settlement west of the mountains. They also laid out and sold lots at Oldtown. When he was at least seventy years old, Thomas Cresap undertook the long voyage back to England, where he visited his family and pressed his western land claims. Michael Cresap took a group of settlers into the Ohio Valley and later distinguished himself in the Indian war of 1774 (Lord Dunmore's War). That war has also been called Cresap's War, because a false tale was widely circulated attributing to Michael the massacre of the Indian family that provoked the hostilities. Daniel, the other surviving son, prospered as a frontier trader in the Potomac valley west of Cumberland (*see* Tour 9).

The Cresap family strongly supported the American cause during the Revolutionary War. Michael received a commission to lead a company of riflemen to join Washington outside Boston in 1775. According to a contemporary letter, "he being absent when it [the commission] arrived, his father, the brave old Colonel Cresap, ninety-two years of age, took the command, and determined to join the army at their head, if his son should not arrive in season." (Cresap himself was unsure of his age, but he was probably in his mid-seventies at the time.) Michael did arrive in time to lead the riflemen to Massachusetts, where they were the first unit from the south to arrive in response to Washington's call. The stalwart frontiersmen in their fringed leather jackets astounded the other troops with their feats of marksmanship and were particularly valuable because of their experience in the Indian fighting of the West. Michael's health unfortunately compelled him to yield the command. On his way home he died in New York, where he was buried in the yard of Trinity Church at Wall Street and lower Broadway in October of 1775.

Daniel Cresap was a captain in the Maryland militia during the Revolution; he and other members of the family survived the rigors of the war and, together with the old colonel, shared in the period of western expansion at its close. In 1785 Maj. Andrew Ellicott, who had achieved fame as a Revolutionary soldier before he became a surveyor (*see* Tour 2b), stopped at Oldtown on a trip west and wrote, "This evening I spent with the Celebrated Col. Cressap. . . . Now more than 100 Years Old he lost his Eye sight about 18 months ago; but his other faculties are yet unimpaired his sense Strong and Manly and his Ideas flow with ease." The grand old man of the Maryland frontier died in 1790, leaving a substantial estate and many tales, both true and legendary, of his exploits and adventures during a remarkable career in the midst of events that shaped the destiny of America.

The **Michael Cresap House** (R) in the center of Oldtown, a battered stone building, has been altered extensively since the completion of its original section in 1765. Skipton, the fortified dwelling and trading post built by Thomas Cresap in 1741, stood in a field overlooking the river about one-half mile south of his son's home.

The turnpike across Maryland to the National Road at Cumberland, completed around 1820, passed ten miles to the north of Oldtown and diverted the commerce that had formerly pushed along the wagon roads through the village. The Baltimore & Ohio Railroad also by-passed Oldtown, running along the south side of the river from Harpers Ferry to Cumberland. However, the Chesapeake & Ohio Canal was dug right through the village, bringing first the trade of the construction laborers and then more lasting and unmixed benefits as water transportation linked Oldtown with Cumberland and Georgetown. Construction laborers on the canal enlivened their rough existence with a series of fights and riots. Most of the workers were from Ireland, and antagonism between groups from the different counties of the homeland sometimes erupted into factional strife. Other violence, during which even the local militia—called out to restore order—sympathized with the laborers, occurred when paydays were missed because of the recurring financial crises of the canal company. Fighting also marked the relations between crews working on different sections; the tunnel workers were particularly set apart because of the length and relatively skilled nature of their work. When contractors hired Germans or native-born local workers, the Irish also violently objected, for such measures frequently meant cuts in pay and fewer Irish jobs. The most serious incident at Oldtown happened on New Year's Day, 1838, when a raid by tunnel workers nearly demolished a tavern in the village. The rioters dispersed before a posse led by the county sheriff and the Cumberland militia arrived. The **Oldtown-Battie Mixon** area of the **C & O Canal Historical Park** is located on the canal at the Oldtown lock.

In the early days of the Civil War, Company B of the Second Regiment, Potomac Home Guard, was organized here. Three of its men were wounded in a skirmish with Confederate troops on a march to Springfield, Virginia, and are believed to have been the first Marylanders to shed blood for the Union. Although Oldtown remained in Northern hands during the war, it was raided on several occasions by Confederate units under J. D. Imboden and J. H. McNeill, who seized horses and supplies.

Left from Oldtown 0.3 m. over the canal to the **Old Potomac Ford,** now crossed by a toll bridge, where on August 1, 1864, a Confederate force returning from an attack on Chambersburg, Pennsylvania, fought its way back through the Union line to safety in West Virginia. Chambersburg had been burned by the raiders in retaliation for the destruction being wrought on the South by Federal armies. The Union line along the Potomac was alerted to prevent the return of the Southerners, holding them in Maryland until Federal cavalry under Gen. William W. Averell could catch up to them. The Union forces at Oldtown were drawn up in the woods along the ridge between the canal and the river to guard the ford.

When the Southern advance, under Maj. Harry Gilmor and his Maryland battalion, reached the crossing at dawn, they were forced to pull back by an ambush launched from the ridge under cover of a heavy morning fog. As the mists lifted, Gen. Bradley T. Johnson's cavalry attempted a dash across the canal bridge but were repulsed. Meanwhile, three of Gen. John C. McCausland's regiments had crossed the canal farther up; assaulting the flank of the Union line, they succeeded in driving the Federals across the Potomac, where they crowded into the cars of an ironclad train on the B & O tracks drawn up directly in line with the ford. A gun battery was brought across the canal to shell the train. The gunner, George McElwee, sighted coolly through the thick of the engagement and struck the engine with his first shot, exploding the boiler. The Union defenders stampeded, most taking refuge in a blockhouse beyond the disabled train. After firing a few more shots through the porthole of the armored car, which knocked out its gun, the Confederates crossed the river, destroyed the train, and received the surrender of some eighty men in the blockhouse. By noon the entire Confederate force had completed the crossing, well in advance of General Averell's pursuit.

In the years after the Civil War, Oldtown remained a rural village. Traffic on the canal was minor and erratic compared to that of the thriving B & O Railroad across the river in West Virginia. Even the post office serving Oldtown's residents was in the West Virginia town of Green Spring for years. Construction of the Hancock-Cumberland section of the Western Maryland Railroad in 1905–6 and of the Potomac River Bridge, begun in 1910, improved access to the village. With the dawning age of the automobile and the decline of the canal, which closed down altogether in 1924, the isolation of Oldtown and its Appalachian surroundings from the pressures of economic development in the twentieth century continued.

The South Branch of the Potomac River joins the North at a point known as Potomac Forks, a two-mile hike down the canal towpath from Oldtown. Lord Baltimore's charter had designated the Potomac River as the southern boundary of the grant. When explorers later discovered the forks, it became necessary to determine which was the true river to divide Virginia from Maryland. Lord Fairfax had been granted an enormous tract in northwestern Virginia; the surveyors he sent out claimed the North Branch as the boundary, setting up the Fairfax Stone (*see* Tour 11). Negotiations between Virginia and Maryland lasted for years, continuing through the Revolution. While the North Branch seemed to have a greater flow of water and was therefore assumed to be longer, when Thomas Cresap surveyed the sources of the river in 1754, the southern branch proved to have the westernmost origin. Virginia was adamant in asserting the Fairfax marker, however, and eventually prevailed.

Beyond Oldtown, Md. 51 again diverges from the river, looping back to it at **TOWN CREEK,** 18.2 m. The highway skirts the southern edge of the Green Ridge State Forest (*see* Tour 2d). Several roads (L) lead into the reservation.

Just before coming to the Potomac River Bridge, 25.9 m., park (L) and walk along the towpath of the C & O Canal about one-half mile, past milestone #156, to the **Paw Paw Canal Tunnel.** To avoid a deep double bend in the river, the canal engi-

Paw Paw Canal Tunnel

neers undertook the most ambitious and expensive achievement of the company, driving a 3,117-foot passage through Anthony Ridge. Lee Montgomery, a Methodist parson turned contractor, supervised the project, aided by prayer and a "Little Stick," according to a report of the canal commissioner. Financial difficulties halted construction time and again as estimates proved far too low. Because of its cost, the final arching of the tunnel with an eighteen-inch brick lining was deferred until after the formal opening of the canal to Cumberland. During the most prosperous years of the canal, 1870–75, the one-way tunnel became a bottleneck, adding to the delays at the locks that handicapped the canal in its competition with the railroad.

The tunnel route was over five miles shorter than the river bank alternative. The election to drive the tunnel and the deep cut at its lower end were typical of the long-range view reflected in the engineering decisions of the canal. Construction was generally of the highest quality attainable at that time; the precise and expensive masonry work throughout was deliberately chosen to minimize repairs during operation. However, the time required to complete the stonework and to arrange financing to cover its escalating costs delayed opening of the canal. By then, the railroad and alternative water routes had secured the western trade. In fairness, limitations inherent in canal transport, technical innovations in railway design, and the population patterns that developed in the West would in any case have eventually diverted traffic from the canal. The canal's sturdy construction did keep it operable during seventy-five years of Potomac floods, and much of it has endured as a monument to the ability and ambitious energy of young America.

Md. 51 crosses the **West Virginia Line,** 25.9 m., on the Potomac River Bridge into Paw Paw, West Virginia.

TOUR 9

CUMBERLAND–McCOOLE–WEST VIRGINIA LINE–(Keyser);
18.8 m.
U.S. 220

South of Cumberland, U.S. 220 runs through a long agricultural valley by the Potomac. The relatively broad plain, one of the few in Allegany County, is noted for its fruit and dairy products. The high ridges of Haystack Mountain and, below Cresaptown, Dan's Mountain, wall the western side of the valley; its eastern boundary is the North Branch of the Potomac River, flowing beneath the curiously humped crests of Knobly Mountain on the West Virginia side of the river.

U.S. 220 is easily accessible from an interchange on U.S. 48, the National Freeway, 0.0 m.

North from Cumberland, U.S. 220 was developed as Maryland's link in the **Appalachian Thruway,** running from Cumberland across Pennsylvania to Cortland, New York, where it joins U.S. 81 just south of Syracuse.

POTOMAC PARK is a residential area between Cumberland and Amcelle with lettered street names—Avenue A, Avenue B, etc.—although it is not arranged in the standard grid pattern that such names imply. Turn left on Main Street to the **Cumberland Fairgrounds** on the river bank, where the Allegany County Fair is held each summer.

The **Celanese Fibers Company** at Amcelle, 3.5 m., manufactures acetate fibers and other synthetics and plastics. The company has been operating here since 1924 and is the second-largest single employer in the area, with 2,300 people working for it. In earlier years, the company's work force approached ten thousand.

CRESAPTOWN (780' alt., 1,731 pop.), 4.5 m., is named for Joseph Cresap, a son of Daniel Cresap, who settled here after the Revolution. It is northeast of the peak on Dan's Mountain known as **Dan's Rock** (2,895' alt.), which was named for Joseph's father (*see* Tour 10). On the night of February 21, 1865, a Confederate force of about sixty mounted men in McNeill's Partisan Rangers crossed the Union lines here, surprising a sentry from whom the password was extracted. Using the information, the Rangers rode directly into Cumberland where they captured two Union generals (*see* Cumberland essay).

South of Cresaptown, the road that is now U.S. 220 was the scene of a celebrated local crime. On September 8, 1828, George Swearingen, then sheriff of Washington County, was traveling on horseback with his young wife and their three-year-old child. Stopping at a secluded place on the road, he killed his wife and cut her horse's knee. His story that the horse had stumbled, throwing her to the ground where she struck her head on a stone, was at first accepted because of his prominence. However, within a few days the child's prattling had aroused suspicions, instigating an exhumation of the body and a more careful examination of the horse's knee. Before Swearingen could be arrested, he had disappeared with a beautiful young woman, Rachel Cunningham. It was revealed that her considerable charms and unconventional practices had led to several divorces in the course of her earlier adventures in Pennsylvania. The couple was found months later in New Orleans, and Swearingen was brought back to trial. Thousands witnessed his public hanging in Cumberland. Rachel Cunningham died forty years later, in the almshouse of Baltimore.

At 7.3 m., Md. 9 (L) goes toward the **Allegany Ballistics Laboratory,** where research and development of solid rocket propellants is conducted. The laboratory was established in 1945 by the Hercules Power Company, a large war materials contractor.

RAWLINGS, 9.9 m., was named for Col. Moses Rawlings of Oldtown, who commanded a rifle regiment under George Washington during the Revolution. He and his unit were highly commended for their bravery when they covered Washington's withdrawal from Fort Washington to New Jersey in 1776. The survivors, including the colonel, were captured. Later in the war, Colonel Rawlings commanded Fort Frederick (*see* Tour 2d) when/ it was used to house prisoners of war.

The tour ends at **McCOOLE,** 18.8 m., a suburb of Keyser (formerly New Creek), West Virginia, across the river. Keyser developed as an important point on the B & O Railroad, which crossed the river here to run up the Potomac valley about six miles to Bloomington, where it recrossed to the Maryland side to ascend the Seventeen-Mile Grade over the Continental Divide (*see* Tour 11).

● Right on Md. 135, through the narrow gorge, from McCoole to **WESTERNPORT,** 4.7 m. The slopes above the river are riddled with deserted mine shafts that lead to the coal veins of the region lying north and west of McCoole (*see* Tour 10).

10

PENNSYLVANIA LINE–MOUNT SAVAGE–LONACONING–WESTERNPORT; 30.7 m.

Md. 35 and 36

This tour follows the streams that cut gorges through the Allegheny plateau, exposing coal strata that supported a substantial mining industry for over one hundred years. It passes through miners' villages and mill towns built during the mid-nineteenth century, when the completion of the C & O Canal and the B & O Railroad made coal markets available. The railroad itself, together with the conversion of industry and shipping to steam power, stimulated the demand for coal. Coal production in the region peaked in 1907. Its slow decline thereafter resulted from the development of alternative energy sources, most notably petroleum, and the exhaustion of the more easily mined coal veins.

Md. 35 crosses the **Pennsylvania Line** at **ELLERSLIE** (732′ alt., 1,931 pop.), 0.0 m., about thirty-three miles southwest of Bedford, Pennsylvania, where Maryland railroads sent spurs to join the Pennsylvania system. The road runs parallel to Will's Creek south to **CORRIGANVILLE** (715′ alt.), located near a limestone ridge that has been extensively quarried to produce crushed stone for highway construction and other purposes.

At the intersection with Md. 36, 2.4 m., turn right; Md. 36 runs beside Jennings Run up into the northern part of the Maryland coal region. At 4.9 m. the road and the stream pass through a narrow glen cutting a gap through Piney Mountain.

MOUNT SAVAGE (1,206′ alt., 1,413 pop.), 7.3 m., became an industrial center after a blast furnace was built here in 1839. To secure the natural advantage presented by the conjunction of both coal and iron ore in the surrounding slopes, another blast furnace and a rolling mill were added soon afterwards. In 1844, the rolling mill produced the first solid railroad tracks made in the United States. In 1845 the town's population reached 3,000, and a railroad line was begun to replace the road between Mount Savage and Cumberland. The iron works failed in 1847, however. Overextension, the inferior quality of the iron ore available, and the assistance given to foreign competition by a tariff act adopted in 1846 are variously cited as causes. While the iron industry never fully recovered, a firebrick plant established during the boom period of the town, using the fireclay that interleaves the coal strata, prospered for decades and is still in operation. During the 1880s President Franklin D. Roosevelt's father, James, headed the company that owned the firebrick refractory, which, like most of the enterprises in the coal basin, was controlled by New York investors.

The industries of Mount Savage built company housing for their employees. Some of its street names—Old Row, New Row, Brickyard Row, Foundry Row, Low Row, and Jealous Row—survive as a legacy of that period. Housing operations were undertaken primarily as a profit-making venture by the employers.

Although most units were rented, some of the company-built houses were sold outright to workers in the Maryland mining fields, unlike the true company towns of Pennsylvania and West Virginia. Maryland, however, did not altogether escape the paternalistic control inherent in the company housing system. As landlord, the companies could and did use the threat of eviction to keep workers subservient during labor controversies. On the other hand, rents in company housing were generally lower than those charged by private landlords, encouraging its occupancy. In a typical early industrial combination of the profit motive and paternalism, residents in company housing tended to be the last laid off and the first rehired as operations followed market cycles. It was the practice of the more enlightened employers to reduce rents during hard times, making slightly more acceptable the simultaneous unilateral pay cuts they imposed in order to meet competition. Another factor giving employers leverage in the turbulent labor relations of the preunion era was the company store, where prices tended to be higher but where credit was extended. The widespread practice of deferring payment for over two months for work performed left a running back pay account in the company's control. Company stores never had a monopoly in Maryland's mining towns, again in contrast to the situation in the neighboring states.

A large proportion of the new proletariat created by the industrialization of the valley from Mount Savage south to the Potomac was of immigrant origin. Prominent ethnic groups included the Irish, Germans, Welsh, and Scots. Mount Savage in 1856 was termed the "Limerick of Allegany." **FROSTBURG,** 12.0 m. (*see* Tour 2e), had an annual Welsh festival, an *Eisteddfod.* In 1873 the Frostburg mining journal announced the featured performer at that year's celebration to be Mr. Crwdgimpas Ap Thomas, a native of Moclgwynstrwnstrell, who would appear in ancient Druid costume to play the Llanrhauadrmochant and other selections on the Brownwrw-Cymrongldrwstcwmdathugwestly ("Welsh harp").

At 12.3 m. in Frostburg U.S. 40 unites briefly with Md. 36, which then splits off to the left at 13.2 m. Continuing on Md. 36, the interchanges with U.S. 48 are at 14.7 m. and 14.8 m.

As one approaches Midland, a strip-mining residue (L) marks the site of the former town of Ocean, a community of more than 1,200 residents in 1907. Its name, from the Ocean mine nearby, commemorated the desirability of the Allegany coal for steamships. Tests made by the navy in 1844 confirmed the high ratio of fuel value to bulk and the even-burning qualities of the semibituminous coal of the George's Creek basin.

At **MIDLAND** (1,715′ alt., 665 pop.), 18.6 m., is the intersection with Old Dan's Rock Road.

● Turn left to **Dan's Rock** (2,895′ alt.). The peak offers a scenic overview of the George's Creek valley to the west, with Big Savage Mountain rising on the far side; eastward the broad agricultural valley of the Potomac is bounded by the ridges of West Virginia beyond the river. A heavily wooded wildlife management area runs southwest from the rock along the crests of Dan's Mountain.

The rock and mountain are named for Daniel Cresap, one of the sons

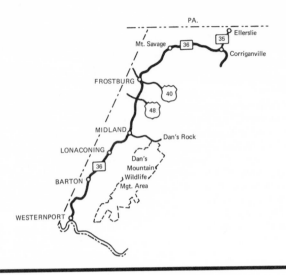

TOUR 10

of Col. Thomas Cresap, the pioneer who settled at Oldtown (*see* Tour 8). In the years before the Revolution, Daniel Cresap hunted the mountain and the George's Creek valley, named for his frequent hunting companion, Indian George. George was a lifelong associate of the Cresap family, who was said to have been left in their care by his father, Nemacolin, the Delaware guide who worked with Thomas Cresap for the Ohio Company. Daniel Cresap is reported to have died on the mountain after being shot during a skirmish with unfriendly Indians.

LONACONING (1,560' alt., 1,572 pop.), 20.9 m., is thought to be the location of George's camp; the Indian name means "where many waters meet," and the several streams that join George's Creek here made it an excellent choice for a campsite. Lonaconing was developed as a company town by the George's Creek Coal and Iron Company, which built a blast furnace, houses, and a company store here in 1835–38. Although the furnace never became industrially significant, the coal mines supported sustained growth for the town. During the economic expansion following the Civil War, the town's population increased from about 880 in 1865 to over 3,000 in 1870; at that time it was reported that "houses [were] being built on the steep hills and far back into the ravines." The population reached 5,000 in 1881, the rate of increase being retarded by the depression of 1877. During the 1870s the miners of Lonaconing were among the first in the United States to establish cooperative stores. The two that were organized operated successfully in competition with the company and independent stores, one of them remaining in business until 1921.

The spirit of cooperation and consciousness of organization in which the miners joined together for the cooperative stores enhanced their political power as well; mining legislation to improve working conditions and provide for safety inspections was enacted during the period 1876–80. At the same time the owners of the mines also continued the process of consolidation and unified activity. In 1877 and 1878, mine owners were able to enforce cuts in pay to bring Maryland rates closer to the level of the developing Pennsylvania bituminous coalfields. In 1880, in order to salvage their safety inspection act, the miners had to accept an act permitting the owners to organize a special iron and coal police force. When a mine strike led by the Knights of Labor in 1879 succeeded in obtaining an increase in the coal pay rate, the miners joined the union in great numbers. Its early successes and growing power set the stage for confrontation.

Early in 1882 mine owners, after a secret meeting in Baltimore, jointly announced new rules, including a pay cut and longer working hours. They had prepared for a strike and had obtained the backing of the railroad. When the miners walked out in response, the owners did nothing to negotiate their differences, blacklisting the members of the miners' committee who had sought arbitration. A barracks was built at Eckhart, enclosed by a stockade. When it was completed six weeks after the strike began, the companies swore in a special police force. The following day strikebreakers were brought in and housed in the barracks under police guard. At the same time eviction notices were issued to the strikers living in company housing. Strikers' demonstrations remained nonviolent, and the community rallied to the support of the miners. No financial assistance could be offered by the national office of the Knights of Labor, and a solidarity strike in the competitive Pennsylvania fields failed. When the owners announced two months later that they were bringing in a second corps of strikebreakers, the strike collapsed. The miners had been convinced that mining could not be economically done by unskilled workers and had held on hoping that the companies would eventually be worn down by the expenses of training replacements working under the stress of the situation. The Knights of Labor never recovered from the subsequent decline in membership, and the Great Strike ended in complete victory for the owners.

Labor tensions erupted in strikes again in 1886 and 1894, when the lower valley struck but the northern valley mines above Lonaconing kept operating. For the first time in Maryland, the militia was called out against the coal miners to protect the northern valley workers against threatened violence. After less than two months the strike was broken when construction of a strikebreakers' compound was begun at Lonaconing and eviction notices were served on strikers in company housing.

The northern valley operators attributed the loyalty of their workers during the strike, in the face of the appeal of solidarity and even threats from the lower valley miners, to their enlightened policies of providing improved facilities, including showers and toilets at some mines, and generally good ventilation. They also attempted to secure a workforce of "carefully selected" intelligent and reliable men. As a reward for remaining on the job, miners of the dominant northern valley company received free rent and free coal for almost a year after the strike.

Unionization in the coalfields was again set back in the next long strike, 1922–23, when the first real violence occurred as strikebreakers were brought in. Mineworkers finally organized the Maryland coal basin during the Great Depression of the 1930s. Cooperating with the operators who were also in dire financial condition, work-sharing was initiated in some mines. After the stimulation of World War II, the decline in Maryland mining continued, and by 1950 most mines had been closed. The little mining activity still going on is predominantly conducted by the strip method. More than 90 percent of the remaining estimated coal reserve in the region is recoverable only with deep mining techniques, which have proved to be too expensive in competition with other energy sources.

At 21.3 m., turn left on Jackson Mountain Road at the sign to **Dan's Mountain Wildlife Management Area,** 2.0 m., a rugged tract along the upper slopes of Dan's Mountain reserved by the state for the support of indigenous wildlife.

BARTON (1,320' alt., 723 pop.), 26.1 m., was laid out in 1853 along the railroad that was being constructed to connect Lonaconing with the main line of the B & O Railroad through the Potomac valley. Barton quickly developed as coal mines were dug into the fourteen-foot "Big Vein" situated several hundred feet above the village. The coal was lowered by coal cars operating on the inclined plane principle down the steep slopes from the mine entrances. As the coal reached the bottom, it was loaded on railcars.

Below Barton, Md. 36 winds through the narrow valley along George's Creek as the road descends to the Potomac. The slopes of the gorge show evidence of strip mining activity along the coal veins which, being nearly horizontal, run higher and higher above the road. At the head of the valley, they are several hundred feet under the surface. The rushing creek, no longer impounded to power mill wheels, runs red with oxidized pyrites as the opened surfaces of the ridges above expose iron compounds to the atmosphere.

At **WESTERNPORT** (922' alt., 3,106 pop.), 30.7 m., George's Creek empties into the Potomac. Standardized frame company housing flanks Md. 36 as it enters the little city. Many of the older houses in Westernport have been swept away in floods or were cleared during highway construction. Of those remaining, the Mullins House, **69–75 Main Street,** is of interest in that its solid construction, with reinforced beams, reflects its earlier use as a bank. Perhaps the oldest structure surviving is the **Welsh Theater,** in the first block of Main Street on the west side. Constructed of logs, now sheathed, its unusual roof line slants abruptly down from the facade. Westernport was considered the height of navigation on the North Branch of the Potomac, hence its name, and flats of coal were sent down from here by water during flood seasons. Logs were also boomed downstream when timber companies stripped the slopes of the upper Potomac and Savage river watersheds in the post–Civil War period. Westernport has continued to enjoy relative prosperity, unlike the other towns of the George's Creek coal region. The large paper and pulp plant upriver in Luke has grown and sustained employment since its establishment in 1888. The plant, which now employs about 2,000 people, has greatly improved pollution abatement procedures in recent years. The fumes generated in its industrial processes have entirely denuded the slope downwind from the plant, and they are responsible for the distinctive aroma of the Westernport-Luke valley.

PENNSYLVANIA LINE–KEYSER'S RIDGE–ACCIDENT–OAKLAND–WEST VIRGINIA LINE–(Fairfax Stone); 55.8 m.
U.S. 219

U.S. 219 runs the length of the central plateau, parallel to the ridges of the Alleghenies, on which much of the arable one-third of the land of Garrett County is located. Settlement of the farmland was deterred by the refusal of the colonial government to issue land warrants west of Cumberland until a survey had been made enabling the proprietor to reserve choice manor lands for himself. After this was done in 1774 the western lands were released, and a number of tracts were surveyed and patented immediately. The pace slowed again during the Revolution. As an inducement to military service, lots were promised during recruiting, and lands were held vacant until a general survey made in 1788 laid off 4,165 fifty-acre lots for the Revolutionary War soldiers. Acknowledgment of the fact that many settlers had already moved to the western lands was necessary even at that time; the surveyor indicated on his plot which lands had been settled and improved, and residents on them were given priority to purchase legal title for their claims.

At a point 2.0 m. south of the Mason-Dixon line, U.S. 219 joins U.S. 40 (*see* Tour 2e) and runs with it through Grantsville to **KEYSER'S RIDGE,** 10.8 m., where U.S. 219 turns south toward Oakland. Also at this point is a future interchange with U.S. 48, the National Freeway.

At 15.7 m., U.S. 219 crosses **Bear Creek.** Native trout and the abundance of game along the creek made it a favorite hunting ground for the Indians and the pioneers. Bears, which were particularly prized for their fat, lived in the caves and dens along the creek. The bears of Garrett County fattened for hibernation on acorns and chestnuts. Chestnut trees were numerous in the county until they were destroyed by blight.

● Immediately after crossing Bear Creek, turn right on an access road toward Friendsville.

At 0.2 m. along the access road, there is an intersection with Accident-Bear Creek Road. Turn right to **Kaese Mill** (R) (private), 0.4 m., a nineteenth-century frame grist mill, originally water powered. Beyond the mill is the **Bear Creek Fish Rearing Station** (open to visitors daily, 9–4), 1.0 m., where trout are raised to stock the icy mountain streams and ponds.

● Turning left at the T-junction, the road, County Route 53, follows the gorge of Bear Creek to **FRIENDSVILLE,** 6.9 m. Along the slopes by the road natural gas wellheads are capped in secured enclosures. Friendsville is at the confluence of Bear Creek and the **Youghiogheny River.** Early spellings of the Indian word indicate some confusion in its pronunciation: it appears variously as Yox-, Yaw-, and Yauyougaine. Now it is usually heard as a quick, slurred Yock-a-ga-ny. An archaeological dig under the future U.S. 48 interchange at Friendsville yielded evidence of the Indian presence. When John Friend brought his family to the Friendsville region in the 1760s, relations with the Shawnee tribe were peaceful. As the settlers started filling up the lands, most of the Indians departed, and the rest were killed or assimilated.

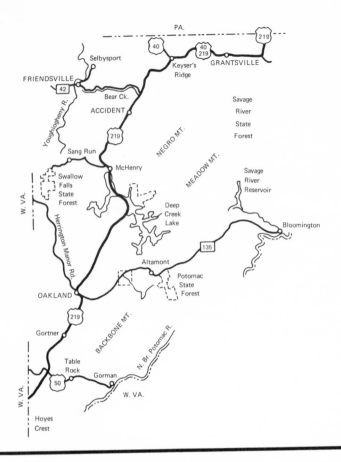

TOUR 11

The Youghiogheny River has been designated a protected scenic river. It is unpolluted for its first twenty-five miles in Maryland, and measures are being taken to preserve its beauty. Some coal and iron ore are present in the basin of the river, but it is not commercially attractive given present technology. An iron furnace operated in Friendsville between 1828 and 1839, using the local coal and ore, but it was not successful. Lumber and wood products are now manufactured here.

North of Friendsville, County Route 53 runs along the east side of the Youghiogheny River Reservoir, through the remains of the village of **SELBYSPORT**, 11.5 m. Selbysport once flourished as the head of navigation on the Youghiogheny River. It was the scene of the only disturbance in Garrett County during the War of 1812. At a gathering of the county militiamen, a faction led by Meshach Browning (*see below*) brawled with a faction of the opposite political party, the Democrats, when the latter refused to serve under Browning, a Federalist officer.

● West of Friendsville, Md. 42 passes **Friends Graveyard,** 0.4 m., where some members of the founding family are interred, and then goes through **Blooming Rose.** The Blooming Rose area was the first to be developed west of Savage Mountain. In 1791 about forty families were living on the lands between Buffalo Run and the Youghiogheny River. To serve them, the first church and first school in the county were established here.

Continuing south along U.S. 219, one comes to **ACCIDENT** (2,400' alt., 237 pop.), 17.3 m.

● Turn left on the Accident-Bittinger Road to the **Drane House** (L) (private, but visible from the road), 0.3 m. This small 1½-story house, of log construction now covered with siding, is considered the oldest building still standing in Garrett County. An unknown settler built the smaller of its two sections prior to 1800. James Drane, a tobacco planter and Revolutionary War veteran from Prince George's County, became the first permanent settler in Accident in 1800. He added the second section to the house shortly thereafter.

Accident is named for the tract near which it is located. In the confusion of the land rush of 1774 that followed the release of the western lands, two separate surveying parties accidently surveyed the same land. The conflict was resolved amiably, and the incident was memorialized in the name given to the tract. From 1875 to 1915, Accident was the home of Melky Miller's Maryland Rye Whiskey. The distillery, including bonded warehouses where the raw product mellowed in barrels for years, succumbed to fire and neglect. Principal employers in the village now produce wood manufactures, peat moss and humus, and machine works.

At 23.4 m. U.S. 219 is intersected by a road that turns right to **McHENRY**, a village on the shore of Deep Creek Lake. Named for James McHenry (*see* Downtown Baltimore), the village is on a tract he purchased in 1810.

● Sang Run Road, going west out of McHenry, passes a ski area on **Marsh Mountain** (3,080' alt.) (L).

Turn left, continuing on Sang Run Road, at the intersection with Hoyes-Sang Run Road, 2.6 m., to **SANG RUN**, 4.4 m. "Sang" is a version of "ginseng," a wild plant once found in profusion on the hillsides. Its root, which is roughly human-shaped, is prized for medicinal purposes in the Orient. The high price it brought made it an object of such intense commercial interest that it is now rarely found. Children could collect it, thereby freeing adults to run the subsistence farms of the pioneer families. Other cash sources for such families were the sale of furs and the collection of bounties. Allegany County, shortly after its erection in 1789, for example, offered a bounty on wolf scalps. Other creatures whose extinction was soon encouraged under the bounty system included foxes, hawks, cats, and owls.

Meshach Browning (1781–1859), the best known of the early farmer-hunters, lived on Sang Run. He estimated his total hunting kill at "1,800 to 2,000 deer, 300 to 400 bears, about 50 panthers and catamounts, with scores of wolves and wildcats." Urged by the friends he had entertained with his tales, he wrote *Forty-Four Years of The Life of a Hunter*, describing his life during the years in which Garrett County was settled. It makes clear that the meat and money he made from hunting were necessary for the survival of himself and his family. In it he notes a serious decline in the game population, criticizing wasteful hunting and land-use practices. Crossing the Youghiogheny at Sang Run, the road becomes gravel as it ascends Piney Mountain to the northern part of Swallow Falls State Forest and *Cranesville Sub-Arctic Swamp*.

Beyond McHenry, U.S. 219 runs above the 3,900-acre **Deep Creek Lake,** the largest freshwater lake in Maryland. It is formed by a dam erected in 1923–25 as part of a hydroelectric project and has become an important recreational area.

At 28.9 m. turn left at the sign to **Deep Creek State Park.**

● The state park offers public lake access, a beach, and many other facilities for outdoor activities. Foot and snowmobile trails have been laid out through the park. A trail up the southern slope of **Meadow Mountain** is a one-mile climb from the lake level (averaging 2,462') to the summit (3,020'), where a panoramic view of the lake and surrounding countryside rewards the hiker. Deep Creek, which was impounded to make the lake, was one of the best trout streams in the county. Meshach Browning wrote: "Mary [his wife] asked me to catch a mess of trout for our breakfast next morning. To gratify her I went to Deep Creek, where success was certain." Fishing and ice fishing are still popular on the lake. The predominant game fish is the small mouth bass; other species include large mouth and rock bass, bluegill, several trout varieties and, in the winter, northern pike.

A secondary road intersecting U.S. 219 from the right at 30.0 m. is an alternate route to *Swallow Falls State Park and Forest* and *Cranesville Sub-Arctic Swamp.*

The Mount Nebo Wildlife Management Area (R), at 33.4 m., supports game and varied wildfowl on its swamps and ponds in the forests.

OAKLAND (2,650' alt., 1,256 pop.), 36.2 m., is the seat of Garrett County and its largest town. It developed here where the Glades Path, a packhorse trail up from Virginia, crossed a shallow ford on the Little Youghiogheny River. The first permanent settler, William Armstrong, built a cabin at the ford in 1806. The crossing became known as Yough Glades. Mills were built along the river as the settlement grew. When the route of the railroad was confirmed in 1849, the town was formally laid out. Several resort hotels flourished in the town after the railroad made the pleasant summer climate accessible to visitors from the coastal cities. The B & O Railroad, which invested in the hotel business, advertised the county as "The Switzerland of America." One of the prominent summer vacationers was Gen. Lew Wallace, who stayed at an Oakland hotel one summer in the course of his eight-year writing project that resulted in the publication of *Ben Hur*. Tourism is still important in the local economy, although, as in most of the Appalachian region, unemployment is a continuing problem. A plant manufacturing ophthalmic lenses opened here in 1971 and has become the largest local employer. Other industries include a chicken processing plant, a computer service center, and several manufacturers of wood products.

The Garrett County Historical Museum, at Center and Second streets, has a well-displayed collection of tools and equipment used in the early economic life of the county, together with household furnishings, Indian artifacts, and other items of interest (open Mon.–Thurs., 9–5; Fri., 9–5 and 6–8; Sat., 9–12; closed Sun).

Crook's Crest (private) is a rambling frame Victorian house, typical of its period, built around 1890 by Gen. George Crook, who achieved military prominence in the western wars against the Apaches and the Sioux after his Civil War service (*see* Cumberland). From downtown, go up (west) Pennington Street and turn right on Crook's Crest to the top of Hoop Pole Ridge. General Crook's funeral shortly after the house was completed brought many of his friends and army acquaintances from around the country to Oakland. Among the mourners was Buffalo Bill Cody, whose Wild West shows had made him such a national figure that he had no difficulty cashing a $100 check in an Oakland store.

Muddy Creek Falls in Swallow Falls State Park

● Make a right on Green Street. Go straight onto Liberty Street. The **B & O Railroad Station** on Liberty Street is a well-preserved two-story brick building in the Queen Anne style, built in 1884. The imaginative corbeling of the brickwork unifies the recesses and projections that relieve the mass. It is set back from the street on the left; the facade on the track side of the building features a round tower. Liberty Street, going west out of Oakland past the B & O Railroad Station, becomes County Route 20, the Herrington Manor Road. The entrance to **Herrington Manor State Park** is on the left at 4.3 m. The park, which has a stocked lake, provides swimming, boating, fishing, cabins, and nature study trails. Hiking trails start near the parking lots. McCulloh's Path, one of the Indian foot trails going between Virginia and the Ohio territory, passes through the park.

At a fork, 6.3 m. on County 20 from Oakland, bear left on the Cranesville Road to the **Cranesville Sub-Arctic Swamp.** The swamp, a nature sanctuary, lies at the head of Muddy Creek on the Maryland-West Virginia border, about five miles from the fork along the left side of the road. A number of the plants found in the swamp are relics of an earlier era, before climate changes pushed back most of the viable habitat for such species toward the Arctic Circle. It is the most southern range of the tamarack and other northern plant forms. The swamp has been designated a National Natural History Landmark.

● The entrance to **Swallow Falls State Park** (L) is on County 20, 7.6 m. north of the Oakland city limit. Within the park, hiking trails lead to **Muddy Creek Falls,** a fifty-one-foot spill over rock ledges in a lovely mountain setting. In 1918, and again in 1921, Henry Ford, Harvey Firestone, and Thomas Edison camped here to enjoy the delights of wilderness living. A photograph now at the Ford Museum in Dearborn, Michigan, shows the father of the assembly line scrubbing his laundry in the creek. Downstream from the falls, Muddy Creek empties into the Youghiogheny River just above the unusual rock formation at Swallow Falls. The falls were named for the birds that nest in the eroded crevices of the rock. Below the Swallow Falls, a trail leads back from the river bank into a virgin stand of pines and hemlocks, the last in Maryland of this size.

Coming south out of Oakland, U.S. 219 makes a right angle turn at 37.5 m.

● Straight ahead, on Md. 135, the small village of **MOUNTAIN LAKE PARK** is all that remains of an extensive complex of hotels, sporting facilities, an auditorium, and a tabernacle that clustered around the village at the turn of the century. Founded in 1881 with a strong religious emphasis, the resort featured both camp meetings and cultural activities at its annual summer "Mountain Chautauqua." College-level instruction in languages, literature, and the sciences was provided by professors from institutions such as Goucher College and Cornell and Boston universities. Addresses were delivered by notable visitors including William Jennings Bryan, Samuel Gompers, and President William Howard Taft. Such elevated pursuits were relieved from time to time with magicians, jugglers, bell ringers, and a full athletic program. A positive description was published in the 1899 issue of the Mountain Chautauqua magazine: "*What Mountain Lake Park Is Not:* It is not a place for expensive dressing and meaningless idling—Not a place given to social frivolities. . . . Not a place where hotel keepers get all your earnings of the year. . . ." In pointed contrast, a *Baltimore Sun* reporter in 1900 wrote of "the comfortable and well-appointed folk who loaf luxuriously and cultivate the delights of an elegant ease and idleness on the porches of the hotel at Deer Park."

At 4.3 m. on Md. 135, turn right on Deer Park Hotel Road to the **Site of the Deer Park Hotel,** 0.4 m. The Deer Park Hotel, built by the B & O Railroad in 1873, became a favorite resort for the wealthy of Baltimore and Washington. Presidents Grant, Harrison, and Cleveland were among its guests, and William McKinley visited it before he became president. Facilities for cricket, baseball, golf, and tennis were built. For the active, carriage rides up the mountain to *Eagle Rock* and through the cool forests were provided.

The Deer Park Spring, which still produces pure mountain water that is sold commercially, supplied the hotel and its swimming pool and Turkish baths. Those who preferred a more stimulating beverage could join the "club" (men only) adjacent to the hotel. The popularity of the hotel declined after 1900, and it finally closed in 1929. The hotel was razed in 1944. Some of the opulent cottages still remain, occupied all year round.

Turn left at the Deer Park Hotel site, and up the hill that rose behind the hotel, where the railroad and some private individuals built summer homes. A marker on the lawn in front of the **Grover Cleveland Cottage** (L) (private) describes the public details of President Cleveland's honeymoon spent here after his White House wedding in 1886. The name "cottage" is seen to be misleading; the grey-shingled frame building is two and one-half stories tall and contains sufficient room to accommodate a considerable presidential entourage.

Up from the Cleveland Cottage near the top of the hill, the **Pennington Cottage** (R) (private) has been restored. It was built in 1892 by Josias Pennington, a Baltimore architect, as his own summer residence. The high ceilings and large rooms of the cottage set off elaborate lighting fixtures, now converted to electricity. Other details of the house include finely worked interior trim in the public rooms, and a twelve-by-seventy-foot wraparound porch designed so that at any time of the day it is partly in the sun and partly in the shade. Much of the original furniture has been kept, and some pieces originally in the Deer Park Hotel have been acquired.

● Returning to Md. 135, turn right at 4.7 m. on Boiling Spring Road. The present village of **DEER PARK,** 0.4 m., like Mountain Lake Park, does not reflect the splendid days of the old hotels. At 3.3 m. on Boiling Spring Road turn left on the dirt Eagle Rock Road to **Eagle Rock.** Unsafe ruins of a wooden observation tower stand on top of the enormous rock, which still affords a fine view of the valleys and the **Potomac State Forest** on Backbone Mountain.

● Md. 135 makes a right angle at 7.3 m. The **Log Church** (L), 7.7 m., was built in 1934 of chestnut logs. Also called Our Father's House, it was first a nondenominational chapel and is now an Episcopal mission. Sunday services are held here in the summers.

Just beyond the Log Church, at 8.0 m., Md. 135 crosses the B & O Railroad tracks near **Altamont,** the highest point in Maryland on the railway (2,628′) where it crosses Backbone Mountain. From here down to the Potomac is the **Seventeen-Mile Grade,** a relatively steep slope of 116 feet to the mile. Although many of the coal and lumber spur tracks into the mountain ravines had even steeper sections, this is considered close to the limit for long, heavy mainline trains. Brakemen, riding outside the cars even on the coldest winter days, controlled the dangerous momentum that could build up on the long steep grade. Md. 135, running roughly parallel to the tracks about one mile to the south down Backbone Mountain to Bloomington, is lined with signs warning truckers to stop frequently in order to maintain control on the downhill pitch of the run. Treacherously, the road narrows to cross the Savage River bridge at the base of the mountain, then makes an abrupt right angle turn at the sheer bluff on the far side. Md. 135 continues to Luke, in Allegany County (*see* Tour 10).

A dam at **BLOOMINGTON,** 21.2 m., will harness the North Branch of the Potomac. Although it is being constructed primarily for flood control, it will also create a beautifully situated lake in the deep valley. Pollution, mainly acid-mine drainage, will limit its recreational development. The slopes on either side of the Potomac are rich in coal seams. Although most mining presently being done here is by the strip method, a much larger reserve of coal lies well beneath the surface where deep-mining techniques must be used for its recovery. Until the price of coal increases or technological innovations reduce cost, it is unlikely that most of the deep reserves will be tapped. Water pollution from coal mines occurs in two general forms. A solid, "yellow boy," stains surface waters. It occurs naturally to some degree and was a clue for prospectors. Killing acids form and run off when the coal veins are opened to the atmosphere, allowing oxygen and air moisture to interact with pyrites and other mineral compounds. Antipollution programs emphasize the sealing or flooding of abandoned mines to cut off air exposure, with treatment of the remainder. Mine drainage pollutes almost one-third of the surface water of Garrett County.

The **Savage River Reservoir,** five miles up the Savage River Road from Bloomington, provides unpolluted mountain water for boating, fishing, and swimming. **Big Run State Park,** at the head of the lake, has public facilities. White water canoe racing has become popular on the wild river; Olympic tryouts held here drew large crowds.

Francis Thomas, a governor of Maryland, had a farm near the remains of the old town of Bond, south of the Savage River Reservoir. He raised Peruvian alpacas there after his return from an ambassadorship to Peru in 1875. Following his term as governor (1842–45), which was marred by a divorce scandal that ended his bid for the presidency, Governor Thomas lived almost as a recluse. He remained a Garrett County resident, intermittently active in state and national politics, until the Civil War period, when he resumed his public career. He died in 1876, after being hit by a train as he was walking along the tracks near his home on the Seventeen-Mile Grade.

South of Oakland, U.S. 219 crosses **McCulloh's Path** at 40.9 m. The path was made by the Indians, who called it the Great Warrior Path, and was followed by early traders and pioneers going between Virginia and the Ohio River. George Washington traveled on it on his journey of 1784 assessing the possibilities of a water route from the Potomac over the Alleghenies.

The countryside to the left at **GORTNER,** 41.7 m., is known as Pleasant Valley. A considerable Amish community settled there. In 1864 Gen. Benjamin F. Kelley bought over one thousand acres in the valley from the Pendleton family, Union sympathizers from Virginia who had temporarily moved to Maryland during the Civil War. General Kelley, a cavalry officer from New Hampshire, commanded the Union troops assigned to protect the strategic and extremely vulnerable railroad tracks through Maryland between Harpers Ferry and Grafton. He shipped ill and injured army horses to his farm, where the chance of their recovery was considered good if they had survived the railroad trip to Oakland and the walk to the farm from the depot. The general lived on the farm after the war until his death in 1891 at the age of eighty-four. His military saddle, found in a box of unclaimed freight at the Oakland railroad station in 1910, is now on display at the Garrett County Historical Museum. In one of the more embarrassing episodes of the Civil War, Generals Kelley and Crook, while sleeping at hotels in Cumberland, were captured by Confederate troops (*see* Cumberland).

U.S. 219 intersects U.S. 50, the **Northwestern Turnpike,** at 45.7 m. The **Red House Tavern** (L) was built when the turnpike came through in about 1840. The turnpike probably received its name because for almost its entire length, except for a nine-mile section that crosses the tip of Maryland, it was in what was then the northwesternmost part of Virginia. Intended as Virginia's route to the west, it was laid out by Col. Claudius Crozet, a military engineer who had served under Napoleon in the Russian campaign. Like the National Road across Maryland that it was built to rival, it became obsolete with the completion of the railroad across the mountains in the early 1850s, reviving only with the development of the automobile. At the right of the highway intersection, the Chimney Corner Restaurant was built in 1932 of solid chestnut logs with an immense double firebox chimney.

● Turning east (L) at the intersection, U.S. 50 climbs Backbone Mountain. At 2.5 m., Table Rock Road goes right, paralleling the crest of the mountain ridge. Near the corner, **Table Rock,** an outcropping that was a favorite picnic spot at the turn of the century, can be reached by an overgrown footpath (L).

U.S. 50 east of the Backbone Mountain crest at Table Rock follows the route of the Northwestern Turnpike to **GORMAN,** 7.0 m., where the turnpike crossed the Potomac on a covered bridge. During the Civil War, **Fort Pendleton** was built on the Maryland hillside overlooking the bridge to protect the crossing. It was rarely garrisoned, the fort being of little strategic importance. The wooden fort burned in 1888, but the marks of its trenches can be discerned in the pasture (private) where it stood. They can best be seen from the West Virginia hillside across the river.

U.S. 219 south of Redhouse crosses the **West Virginia Line** at 48.7 m., about forty-nine miles northeast of Elkins, West Virginia. In the Monongahela National Forest about two miles beyond Silver Lake, a footpath (L) from U.S. 219 leads up Backbone Mountain to **Hoyes Crest,** the highest point in Maryland (3,360').

In West Virginia, at 55.8 m. on U.S. 219, a gravel road goes

Kayak racing on the Savage River

left to the **Fairfax Stone.** The stone is a replica of the one placed to mark the first fountain of the North Branch of the Potomac, which was the description of the southwestern tip of Lord Baltimore's grant. From the stone, the western border of Maryland ran due north to the Mason-Dixon line. It was later discovered that the real "first fountain" rose over a mile to the west, where a "Potomac Stone" was placed in 1897 during a survey made in preparation for litigation in the Supreme Court to settle the boundary issue. Maryland lost its case, just as it had lost its other boundary disputes to the north, south, and east. The state line now runs north on a line with the Fairfax Stone, but it begins about a mile above the stone, on the south bank of the Potomac.

ELKTON–CHESTERTOWN–WYE MILLS–EASTON–CAMBRIDGE–SALISBURY–OCEAN CITY; 146.8 m.
Md. 213 and U.S. 50

Along this route, which traverses all but the southern tip of Maryland's Eastern Shore, agriculture and the seafood industry are the chief sources of income. A series of navigable rivers and bays indents the whole Eastern Shore, so that most farms and towns are near a landing. These waterways were the main arteries of transportation from the earliest days of settlement to the advent of the automobile in the twentieth century. The Upper Shore is rolling country and its rivers are lined by high bluffs of great beauty; the lower peninsula is flat and the line between river and marsh is often indistinct. Field crops, particularly grains and soybeans, and milk are the chief agricultural products of the Upper Shore, with vegetables and broiler chickens important in the flatlands to the south. The marketing of many of these products is dependent on the fast transportation that good highways now provide.

The mild climate, easily worked soil, and abundance and variety of fish have created a pattern of living in this area that has persisted for three centuries despite the nearness of the industrial North and the introduction of a variety of improvements. Tradition is strong throughout the area, most noticeably in farming and fishing methods, and the famed Eastern Shore cooking.

Divided from the rest of Maryland by the Bay, Eastern Shore residents have long felt that they had more in common with Delaware and the Eastern Shore counties of Virginia than with the Western Shore of Maryland. On five occasions between the 1700s and the 1850s, Eastern Shore leaders in the General Assembly attempted to secede from the rest of Maryland, proposing that the Eastern Shore either become a separate province or part of Delaware. The most determined attempt occurred in the 1830s and was only fended off when the assembly appropriated $1,000,000 for the purchase of Eastern Shore Railroad bonds to help finance a railroad between Elkton and Crisfield. The Panic of 1837 put an end to the company, however, and when a railroad was finally built, it was located in Delaware with the Maryland portion of the Eastern Shore connected to it by feeder lines. As a result, the economy of the Eastern Shore, which in the days of water transportation had focused on the Bay, became bound to Wilmington and Philadelphia. Automobile transportation and the construction of the Bay bridges have not yet completely altered the pattern.

The Bay bridges now make Baltimore and Washington more accessible to Eastern Shore residents, and U.S. 301, which connects the Bay bridges with the Delaware River Bridge and the New Jersey Turnpike, has brought even New York City within easy reach of what was formerly an isolated rural area. Nearly every county now has an Economic Development Commission or a Chamber of Commerce trying to attract research facilities and light industry. A less visible but equally important new source of economic growth on the Eastern Shore is the retirement industry, with increasing numbers of people who enjoy hunting, fishing, and boating settling in the area to enjoy their new leisure.

12a. ELKTON–CHESTERTOWN; 36.0 m.
Md. 213

The route from Elkton to Chestertown descends through the rolling land of Cecil County to the fertile farmlands of Kent County. In the early eighteenth century this was tobacco country, but by the time of the Revolution most farmers had converted to cash grain crops. Today, the addition of dairy and beef cattle and hogs has diversified the economy even more, but the once famous fruit orchards that grew here in the early twentieth century are nearly all gone. Along the waterfront, fishing and small boat industries are still important activities. Towns are small, functioning chiefly as county seats and centers of rural trade. The main road passes handsome brick houses built in the late eighteenth or early nineteenth centuries, with the older houses usually being located on side roads nearer the water.

Md. 213 branches south from Main Street at Bridge Street in **ELKTON** (29′ alt., 5,362 pop.), 0.0 m. **Holly Hall** (L), 0.4 m., a very large 2½-story brick mansion with a hip roof, is believed to have been built before 1802 by Maj. James Sewall. During the War of 1812, Sewall commanded a battalion at Fort Defiance, a fortification that was hurriedly constructed a mile below Elkton after the British admiral George Cockburn attacked Elk River points in 1813. The Cecil Center now occupies the building. At 0.5 m. is the junction with U.S. 40 and Tour 2a.

At 1.3 m. is the junction with Frenchtown Road.

● Go right on this road to the **Site of Frenchtown,** 1.0 m., and the remains of the eighteenth-century Frenchtown tavern on the banks of the Elk River. Until 1837, Frenchtown was a busy port and a relay station on the main routes between Baltimore and points north. The land trip of 16.5 m. between Frenchtown and New Castle, Delaware, greatly shortened the water journey to Philadelphia and New York. As a result, freight lines took goods by sloop (later by steamboat) to Frenchtown, and from there they were transported by wagon and stagecoach to New Castle. The British bombarded Frenchtown on April 29, 1813, plundering and burning the wharf, fishery, warehouse, and five vessels in the harbor. A garrison stationed behind a redoubt at the landing place retreated, but a group of stagecoach drivers twice repulsed the enemy before being forced to withdraw. The town itself was spared, and only two months later, on June 21, 1813, the *Chesapeake,* the first steamboat on the Chesapeake Bay, docked at Frenchtown on her maiden voyage from Baltimore.

In 1815, the New Castle and Frenchtown Turnpike Company, chartered in 1809, opened a toll road. In 1827, this company became the New Castle and Frenchtown Turnpike and Railroad Company, one of the earliest in the United States. The railroad line opened on July 4, 1831, but for the first year the cars were pulled by horses. On September 10, 1832, a locomotive named the *Delaware,* pulling two cars, made its initial trip. The *Delaware* had a quaint braking system. When the locomotive approached a stop, the engineer shut off the power and sent up a signal of steam from the safety valve. Several men at the station then grabbed the engine with their hands, while the station agent thrust a fence rail between the spikes of the *Delaware's* wheels! With the completion of a railroad line from Baltimore to Philadelphia through Elkton in 1837, business here declined; the railroad made its last trip in 1854.

At 4.8 m. is the junction with Md. 285.

● Go left on this; Md. 285 joins Md. 284. Bear left at this junction to **CHESAPEAKE CITY NORTH** (1,031 pop.), 0.4 m., on Back Creek. This is the Maryland terminus of the **Chesapeake & Delaware Canal,** a vital link in coastal transportation that shortens the water route between Baltimore and Philadelphia by 296 miles. As early as 1661, Augustine Herman (*see below*) predicted the construction of such a waterway, and during the eighteenth century it was proposed several times. In 1799, Maryland chartered a canal company, and construction began in 1801 under the supervision of Benjamin H. Latrobe. Work was

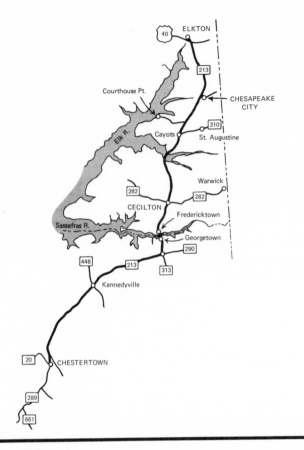

TOUR 12a

suspended in 1803 and not resumed until 1824, but the canal finally opened for navigation in 1829. One of the most difficult tasks faced by the builders of the canal was constructing a lock, made necessary to compensate for a difference of several feet between the level of the Bay and the Delaware River. The original cost was $2,250,000. The federal government purchased the canal in 1919 for $2,500,000, lowering the channel to sea level in 1927 at a cost of more than $10,000,000. During World War II, the canal was of great strategic importance because it enabled shipping to escape submarines in the Atlantic. In 1962, construction began on a project that made the waterway 35 feet deep and 400 feet wide throughout the entire length between the two great bays.

Chesapeake City came into existence because of the canal, and its fortunes have fluctuated with it. When the lock system was changed to the sea-level course, necessitating removal of the bridge from the main street to the western edge of the town, a new main street was established. The chief business of the town, besides maintenance of the canal itself, is servicing the boats that pass through, including thousands of pleasure craft that annually use the waterway for the cruise north to Maine or south to Florida and the islands. The town also services and provisions many small craft that cruise on the Chesapeake Bay.

Md. 213 crosses over the whole of Chesapeake City, as well as the Chesapeake and Delaware Canal, on a great bridge that was opened on September 20, 1949. The height of the bridge is necessary to permit shipping to go through the canal without requiring a draw span. This bridge replaced one that was demolished on July 28, 1942, by the tanker *Franz Klasen*. Fortunately for wartime shipping, the canal was completely closed for only a week and was restored to full service after a month. At 5.9 m., immediately after crossing the bridge, is the junction with the road into Chesapeake City South and with old Md. 213.

● Go right 0.2 m. at the intersection, then left into **Chesapeake City South;** at 0.7 m. turn right, then left (just after crossing a small bridge) at 1.1 m. At 1.3 m. is the U.S. Army Corps of Engineers Station. Here in the stone **Pumphouse** (1837) is a wooden waterwheel (1851), thirty-eight feet in diameter, that formerly ran day and night lifting water into the canal to replace the water lost every time a vessel passed through the lock. It is undoubtedly one of the largest waterwheels ever constructed. A plaque on the Pumphouse commemorates the opening of the canal, describing some of the difficulties overcome in its construction. One room is occupied by a museum. Tours are available to the public.

● Go left on what was once Md. 213 to **St. Basil's Catholic Church** (R), 0.4 m., which has an onion-shaped dome that can be seen above the treetops from the main highway a few hundred feet to the east. It served a small colony of Ukrainians who settled here about 1900 and who converted a wilderness of marsh and scrub into farmland.

At 7.5 m. is the junction with Court House Point Road.

● Go right on this road to **Courthouse Point,** 2.8 m., site of the second courthouse of Cecil County. As a matter of convenience to the county's residents, the first courthouse at Oldtown on the Sassafras River was superseded in 1719 by a building here in which court was held until 1781. Ephraim Augustine Herman, the builder, received more than 60,000 pounds of tobacco for his work. According to local tradition, bricks from this structure were used in building its successor in Elkton. During the eighteenth century, the ferry running from Elk Ferry on Oldfield Point across the Elk River to Courthouse Point was one of the most important in the county. Gen. William Howe's invading army landed at Elk Ferry on August 25, 1777, and on August 28, Howe marched with part of his army to Head of Elk, now Elkton (*see* Tour 2a). Gen. Wilhelm Knyphausen and Gen. James Agnew crossed to Courthouse Point on August 20. Their men removed some court records but left the building intact. There is a local story that nineteen deserting Hessians were captured and shot (presumably by the British) at Welsh Point, across the mouth of Back Creek from Courthouse Point, and buried in a common grave. A depression at the spot, said to be the grave, is called "The Hessians' Hole."

The hamlet of **CAYOTS,** 8.9 m., marks the northern edge of the Labadie Tract. This fertile farmland formerly belonged to a colony founded by the followers of Jean de Labadie, a seventeenth-century religious mystic who advocated community ownership of property. In 1679, after several forced migrations in Europe, the Labadists sent Jaspar Dankers and Peter Sluyter, two of their leaders, to New Netherlands in search of land. They met and converted Ephraim Herman, son of Augustine Herman, who was at that point planning to establish a town at Bohemia Manor. Herman, who was interested in attracting as many settlers as possible, agreed to grant a tract of some 3,700 acres to the Labadists. Dankers and Sluyter returned to Holland and came back in 1683 with a group of colonists to take up the land.

Herman refused to honor his promise, however, and the Labadists were forced to take the case to court before a deed was finally executed on August 11, 1684.

Most Labadists came from Holland, a few came from New Amsterdam (New York City), and some were recruited from the surrounding countryside, but the group never exceeded one hundred. Life in the Labadist colony was austere. Hardworking members followed a rule of silence at meals, and men and women ate at separate tables. Each gave all his belongings to the community and in return was issued only bare necessities. All shared equally in the work without regard to their former station in life. They raised corn, hemp, flax, and cattle, and despite their strong religious convictions, they used slaves to cultivate tobacco. Largely because of poor leadership, the community disintegrated before the end of the seventeenth century. In violation of the rules of the mother church in Holland, Sluyter made himself a dictator. In addition, as one colonist complained, "Sluyter would not allow them to have any fire in order to harden them and mortify and subdue the sins of the body . . . but . . . had his own hearth well provided night and day." Even though Sluyter was a man of some genuine religious enthusiasm, he succumbed to mercenary desires. In 1698, he divided the property among the more prominent members of the community, keeping for himself a portion upon which he grew wealthy. Five years after his death in 1722, the colony had completely disappeared.

At Cayots is the junction with Md. 310.

● Go left on this 2.2 m. to St. Augustine, and the small frame **St. Augustine Protestant Episcopal Church** (church office open Tues., Wed., and Thurs. mornings; call otherwise) of Bohemia Manor. A "Mannour Chapel" was authorized and built here as a chapel of ease for North Sassafras Parish in 1695, and the brick chapel that replaced this early structure about 1735 became the church of St. Augustine's Parish when it was formed out of the North Sassafras Parish in 1744. This church fell into decay in the early nineteenth century when Methodism began to attract large numbers in this part of Maryland. In 1816, only the arch of the chancel stood. The present simple frame church was built in 1838 and consecrated by Bishop Whittingham in 1841. From 1893 to 1924 and from 1930 to 1962 the church was in disuse, but in 1963 it was restored, and regular services have resumed. According to local tradition, a walled grave in the cemetery contains the remains of a dissolute young man, who, when dying in 1861, requested that his coffin lid be left unscrewed, that no dirt be thrown over the coffin, and that a brick wall be set up about the grave with one brick left out in order that he might escape if the devil came after him. Bricks mortared into the space from time to time by sextons of the church supposedly always disappeared.

Along Bohemia River is part of the land patented by Augustine Herman (1621–86). The manor and the river are named for the kingdom of Bohemia, Herman's birthplace. In the area is the site of the house Herman built in 1684, which burned in 1816. His broken grave stone, reset in marble, is also here, but the exact site of his grave is not certain.

Augustine Herman was born in Prague about 1621. In 1643 he moved to New Netherlands, first visiting Maryland in 1659 as an envoy from the Dutch at New Netherlands to Lord Baltimore at

Chesapeake & Delaware Canal

St. Mary's. Herman was so charmed by the region that he applied to the Calverts for a large tract, offering in return an "exact mapp" of the entire province. The Calverts accepted, and Herman spent ten years surveying the shore lines and other boundaries for his excellent map of Maryland and Virginia. Many place names he noted have survived to this day.

On June 19, 1662, Herman was granted the 4,000-acre tract of Bohemia Manor, which was regranted in 1676 in the amount of 6,000 acres. In order to make the grant, Lord Baltimore decreed Herman a resident of Maryland in 1660. In 1666, Herman and his family were listed in the first Act of Naturalization passed by the Maryland Assembly, which expressed concern that the lack of legal rights for aliens was "Foreslowing the peopleing of the Province with useful Artificers & handicrafts men." By the time of his death about 1686, Herman had acquired over 25,000 acres in Maryland. In the 1670s and 1680s, Herman took part in peace negotiations with the Indians and boundary disputes with the Penns, and legends of his personal exploits as hunter and horseman survive to this day. His map of the province was of utmost importance to the Calverts in maintaining the boundaries of their grant, and it was referred to as late as 1873 in Maryland's border controversies with Virginia.

At 14.1 m. on the right is **The Anchorage** (private, but visible from the road), home of the Lusbys in the early 1700s. Com. Jacob Jones, commander of the sloop *Wasp* during the War of 1812, married Ruth Lusby in 1821. The couple resided at The Anchorage and enlarged the house in 1835.

CECILTON, 15.0 m., the third and only successful town to be named for the second Lord Baltimore, Cecilius, is a crossroad village with several houses that appear to date from the late eighteenth century.

Here is the junction with Md. 282 at 15.5 m.

● Go left on Md. 282 to a road (historical marker), 2.3 m., leading to **Worsell Manor;** to **WARWICK,** 5.1 m., and **Quinn House;** and **St. Francis Xavier** (Old Bohemia Church), 7.3 m. (*see* Tour 24).

● Go right on Md. 282 to a fork at 2.4 m.

Go left (straight ahead) at the fork to **Rose Hill,** 2.7 m., one of eight Maryland houses to bear this name. The small frame, gambrel-roofed section was built by Thomas Marsh about 1683. In 1830, Gen. Thomas Marsh Forman (1758–1845) added the 2½-story brick town house, with its molded plaster ceilings and marble fireplaces. General Forman, who joined Washington's army at the age of eighteen and served in the War of 1812, is buried in the family graveyard. House and graveyard, shaded by great trees, look out across wide fields to the Sassafras River.

● Continue on Md. 282; at 3.3 m. turn right to **St. Stephen's Protestant Episcopal Church,** 3.6 m., which serves what was once North Sassafras Parish, one of the original parishes of Maryland. The present church was built in 1873. In 1724, a commission of neighboring clergymen tried to oust the rector, John Urmston, for habitual drunkenness. Urmston brought suit to regain his living, but before his case could be heard in court he fell into the fire when drunk and burned to death.

At 16.6 m. on Md. 213, **Greenfields,** or **Greenfield Castle** (private), can be seen from the road. This large hip-roofed brick mansion may have been built in the 1740s, and it is located on a tract of land patented to John Ward about 1674. A narrow pedimented pavilion gives emphasis to the entrance on the approach front and the underside of the cornice is decorated with "nails of the Parthenon." The one-story brick wings, each with a wide doorway topped by a long elliptical fanlight, were post-Revolutionary additions. The unusually handsome and complete Georgian interior is well preserved.

FREDERICKTOWN, 18.2 m. on the north bank of the Sassafras River, was laid out in 1736 and served travelers on the post route from Annapolis to Philadelphia via Rock Hall (*see* Tour 13). For some years this area was the home of thirty or more Acadian families, people of French descent who came as refugees from Nova Scotia in 1755 during the French and Indian War. The town is now a center for boat-building and repairing, and the river is lined with boathouses and docks. Dozens of small boats of all kinds lie at anchor on the quiet water. On a pier at the right is an old granary that now houses a restaurant. At the northern end of the bridge over the river is a stone monument commemorating the explorations (1607–9) of Capt. John Smith up the Sassafras River.

GEORGETOWN, 18.7 m., located on the opposite side of the Sassafras from Fredericktown and laid out at the same time, was an active port during the eighteenth century. On May 6, 1813, both Georgetown and Fredericktown were almost totally destroyed by a British landing party from Adm. George Cockburn's fleet. Only two houses were left standing in Georgetown, the **Kitty Knight House** and its neighbor (now a part of the Kitty Knight House). Kitty Knight is supposed to have extinguished the fires with a broom as fast as the soldiers lit them, until a sympathetic officer ordered the house spared. The house still stands overlooking the Sassafras at the end of the bridge, a rambling brick building with a gambrel roof now used as an inn (open Mon.–Thurs., 5–9; Fri., 5–10:30; Sat.–Sun., 2–9).

In **GALENA** (formerly Georgetown Crossroads), 20.5 m. (at the junction with Md. 290 and Md. 313), is the **Site of Down's Cross Roads Tavern,** built by 1763 on the water and stage route from Annapolis to Philadelphia. In 1774, George Washington stopped here on his way both to and from the first Continental Congress. The tavern burned in 1893.

At the crossroads, Md. 213 turns sharp right. Md. 313 (temporarily combined with Md. 290, which is a side tour of Tour 24, *see* Shorewood Gardens), continues straight ahead to a junction with U.S. 301 and Tour 24 at 2.5 m. This is the fastest route to the Chesapeake Bay Bridge.

At 25.4 m. on Md. 213 is the junction with a paved road (R) that leads to **Shrewsbury Church** (sign).

● Go right to Shrewsbury Church (L) (open), 0.4 m., which serves one of the original parishes of Maryland laid out in 1692 when the General Assembly passed the first act for establishing the Anglican Church. According to tradition, a pre-establishment church was located on the Sassafras River a few miles away. The present plain brick church was built in 1832 on the site of the one erected in 1692–93, and it is surrounded by the graves of parishioners buried over a period of two centuries. Among them is the **Grave of Gen. John Cadwalader** (1742–86), a revolutionary soldier and close friend of George Washington. Cadwalader challenged the leader of the "Conway Cabal," Gen. Thomas Conway, to a duel and wounded him in the mouth. When Cadwalader saw Conway lying on the ground with blood gushing from his mouth, he is supposed to have said, "I have stopped the damned rascal's lying tongue, at any rate." The eulogy on Cadwalader's tombstone was written by Thomas Paine, his bitter political opponent.

At 25.5 m. on Md. 213, **Blay's Range** (L) (private, but visible from the road) is a 2½-story brick house with the date 1727 in glazed headers on the south gable.

From the Sassafras River to this point, Md. 213 has passed through a large vegetable-producing area. South of here for the next thirty miles or more, fields are usually sown in feed or cash grain crops, especially corn, or they are used as pasture for milk cows. During winter the cornfields are feeding grounds for countless thousands of migratory birds. Acreage in wheat, once the largest cash grain crop, has decreased by one-half since 1950, but dairy farming has become a big business. Bulk milk tanks and trucks have hastened the trend away from small producers. The milk is pumped from holding tanks into trucks, which then rush the product to processing plants in Wilmington, Philadelphia, and southern New Jersey as well as Washington and Baltimore. From the highway, one can see the high-quality Holstein herds in adjoining pastures. About the time of World War I, Kent County was famous for its orchards, but these have almost entirely disappeared.

In the neighborhood of **KENNEDYVILLE**, 27.7 m., a community of Amish settled in 1954. A sweet corn cannery is the economic mainstay of the village.

In Kennedyville is the junction with Md. 448.

● To the right on Md. 448 are several old houses, all visible from the road during most seasons. **Suffolk** (L) (private), 2.0 m., is a narrow 2½-story brick house built sometime after the Revolution. It stands in the middle of cornfields that conceal it from the road at harvest time. **Janvier House** (L) (office of **Turner Creek Park**), 3.8 m., stands at the top of a high bluff above Turner Creek. The 1½-story section built of logs in the late seventeenth century was enlarged with a brick addition about 1800. Turner Creek was purchased in 1972 by the Kent County commissioners. The county now owns 163 acres and offers recreational opportunities (swimming, crabbing, fishing, and boating).

At 29.2 m. is the junction with Md. 292 (*see* Tour 13).

At 30.3 m. is the **Thomas Perkins House** (R). Part of this long, narrow, whitewashed brick dwelling with a steep gabled roof was built in 1720 by Thomas Perkins, whose son Col. Isaac Perkins was known as the Flaming Patriot during the Revolution. Colonel Perkins was one of the commissioners appointed by the Maryland Council of Safety to raise supplies for Washington's army, and much of the flour supplied from the Eastern Shore was ground in the mills on his property. On June 29, 1780, Perkins wrote the council that "the precarious supply that our Army has had for some time past and the Considerable Consequence my Mills has been in the Manufacturing such large Quantitys of grain for the Army and french fleet . . . has caused those Villains [the Tories] to hire some Abandoned Wretch to set those Mills on fire." In the burial ground is the grave of Thomas Perkins's daughter Mary, whose ghost is said to walk on the anniversary of her death, January 8. Many local residents believe that wishes made in good faith at her grave will come true. Open by appointment: Mr. and Mrs. Arthur F. Pinder, Chestertown.

Locust Grove Farm (R) (private), 30.9 m., is two old 1½-story frame houses joined together. The larger of the two wings retains some original early woodwork, and the owners have also used floors and paneling from an old Chestertown house in restoring the dwelling.

CHESTERTOWN (22' alt., 3,476 pop.), 36.0 m. at the junction with Md. 20, is a gracious town that faces the broad and tranquil Chester River. Chestertown has been the county seat of Kent County since 1706. The town represents the very essence of the Eastern Shore, with mellow combinations of sights, feelings, tastes, and smells that recall centuries of pleasant living. Along the waterfront, eighteenth-century brick houses overlook the river. On Courthouse Square is a row of one-story law offices whose occupants are the descendants of lawyers who practiced the profession here for generations. Social life and sports are important to the area's residents. In the fall, lawyers, doctors, and merchants leave their work for days at a time to shoot doves and quail, ducks and geese. Nearly everyone has some kind of boat, ranging from the smallest sloop to a cabin cruiser. Late in July, the Chester River Yacht and Country Club hosts scores of sailboats and powerboats that arrive here for the Chester River Regatta, one of a series of regattas held on the Bay.

When the first lots in Chestertown were laid out in 1707, the courthouse had already been standing for nine years. Apparently

Palmer House

the site originally selected for the town was several miles down the river, but it was soon abandoned in favor of this spot by the courthouse. In 1708, Newtown, as it was then called, was made a port of entry for Cecil, Kent, and Queen Anne's counties. In 1730 the assembly ordered the town resurveyed, and by mid-century it had become a center for horse racing and for performances by traveling theatrical groups. In 1766, Selim, owned by Samuel Galloway of Tulip Hill (*see* Tour 25b) and up to that time undefeated, beat Yorick, a famous horse owned by John Tayloe of Mount Airy, Virginia, for a purse of 100 pistoles. In his journal for the year 1786, Rev. Francis Asbury noted: "Sunday 9. I preached at Kent Old Chapel . . . in the afternoon and at night in Chestertown. I always have an enlargement in preaching in this very wicked place."

A Chestertown tea party was staged here on May 13, 1774, when tea brought into port by the brigantine *Geddes* was thrown overboard after an indignant meeting of citizens. A short while later, Chestertown sent vessels loaded with provisions to the people of Boston, who were suffering from the effects of the Boston Port Act.

After the Revolution, Chestertown, like other Bay ports, lost its foreign trade to Baltimore, and there are only the Georgian mansions along the water to remind us of its cosmopolitan past. During the nineteenth century, sailing packets and then steamboats carried grain and passengers to Baltimore. When the railroad finally arrived after the Civil War, Chestertown became linked to Wilmington and Philadelphia, a pattern that still remains. Many residents commute to jobs in northern Delaware. The town itself has a large pickle plant, a chemical plant, and feed and fertilizer factories.

On an eminence overlooking the town as one approaches on Md. 213 is the fifty-acre campus of **Washington College** (open), a coeducational nonsectarian institution. It confers A.B. and B.S. degrees.

The Reverend William Smith founded Washington College in 1782. He had come to Chestertown in 1780 as rector of Chester Parish and was made director of the Kent County Free School, first established in 1723, when the Maryland Assembly offered an endowment of 100 acres of land for a free school in each county. (There is some evidence that the Kent school had already been established in 1707.) By 1782, the school had 140 pupils, and the assembly agreed to charter it as a college if a £10,000 endowment could be raised within five years. The Reverend Smith collected the money within five months, and the charter was granted. The first commencement was held in May, 1783, when six graduates delivered their orations in both Latin and French. The college was named in honor of George Washington with his express permission, and in 1784 he visited it as a member of the Board of Governors. In 1789, the college gave Washington the honorary degree of Doctor of Laws, *in absentia.* Presidents Franklin D. Roosevelt and Harry S. Truman received honorary doctorates of law in 1933 and 1946 respectively.

Washington College and St. John's College, the latter founded in Annapolis in 1784, were apparently intended as part of a state-supported system of public education. But in 1805 Maryland ceased the annual subsidy guaranteed to the two schools, which proved a serious blow to both institutions. Both have had state financial aid from time to time, however, and since 1839 the state has provided Washington College with scholarships.

In 1827, Washington College burned, but classes continued in other quarters until the construction of Middle Hall in 1844. East and West halls were erected in 1854.

Md. 213 runs through the college campus as it enters Chestertown from the north. On the left are the women's dormitories. To the right on Washington Avenue are East, Middle, and West halls, now used as fraternity houses and men's dormitories. On College Avenue, which runs parallel to Md. 213, is the William Smith building, containing classrooms and administrative offices. In the president's office hangs a portrait of George Washington by Rembrandt Peale (1778–1860) (*see* Downtown Baltimore, Municipal Museum), which was painted in 1803 while Peale was studying in the London studio of the American painter Benjamin West. Peale devoted much of his life to painting portraits of Washington. His father, Charles Willson Peale (1741–1826), was a good friend of Washington and painted several portraits of Washington from life. Rembrandt Peale's grandfather, Charles Peale, taught in the Kent County Free School in Chestertown from 1742 until his death in 1749. Next to the William Smith building is the library, which houses over 100,000 volumes.

Md. 213 makes a junction with Md. 20 three blocks from the bridge across the Chester River; turn right on Md. 20 to reach the town square. A courthouse and Episcopal church have stood on the square since 1698 and 1768 respectively. The present courthouse was built in 1860, and although numerous additions and changes have been made since then, its facade has remained unchanged. In front of the courthouse is the **Civil War Monument,** erected in 1917 by Judge James Alfred Pearce to honor the soldiers of Kent County who fought on both sides.

The inscription for the Federals faces north; for the Confederates, south.

Also on the green, at the junction of High and Cross streets, is **Emmanuel Episcopal Church** (open), which has stood here since its erection as a chapel of ease for Chester Parish in 1768 (it became the parish church in 1809). Several additions, new windows, and a completely altered interior largely conceal the church's eighteenth-century identity, but the original walls, two of them laid in all-header bond, can still be seen.

In 1780 Rev. William Smith (*see above*) became rector of Chester Parish. He had come from Scotland to the colonies in 1751 and was the first provost of the College of Philadelphia (now the University of Pennsylvania) until its charter was revoked. In November, 1780, Smith called the preliminary convention of the Maryland Episcopal Church, which met at Chestertown in an effort to reorganize a church that could no longer be headed by the king of England. Of the fifty-four Anglican clergymen active in Maryland in 1775, only sixteen had taken the Oath of Allegiance and only fifteen were still active by 1780. One of these men, in addition to a new incumbent and twenty-four laymen, joined Smith at this meeting at which a new title for the Anglican church in the former colonies was adopted. The name chosen was the Protestant Episcopal Church of America.

In 1783 the General Assembly authorized the clergy to make changes in the church's liturgy and to provide for the continuation of the ministry. Until he left Maryland in 1789, Smith was president of the convention that undertook this work. In 1783, Smith was nominated bishop of Maryland. Smith had made enemies, however, and his participation in the 1785 revision of the Book of Common Prayer, which had a deistical cast and was rejected by the American clergy, increased his unpopularity. Finally, Smith was forced to withdraw his name from nomination as bishop. In 1789 he returned to the University of Pennsylvania, where he was provost until his death in 1803.

The oldest part of Chestertown, where town lots were first sold, is the hill to the west of the town square. Local residents suspect that many of the small frame houses along High Street as it descends this hill are among the oldest surviving buildings in the town, although they have been much changed over time and many have lost their chimneys. Only one, the stone **Ship Ballast House,** or **Palmer House** (L) (private), 532 W. High Street, has the appearance today of an early-eighteenth-century house. The stone used in its construction is believed to have been brought into the country as ship ballast, since nothing like it is to be found in the vicinity. A representation of the house is embossed on the silver service presented to the battleship *Maryland*. **411 W. High Street** (R) (private) is a house with Flemish bond brickwork and large chimneys that may have been built soon after the Revolution. **414 W. High Street** (L) (private) resembles the others but has many Victorian details.

Partway down the hill, Mill Street turns off High Street to the right. **101** and **103 Mill Street** (private) are frame houses with large chimneys and old window sashes containing some old panes of glass. Mill Street runs into Cannon Street, and one block east on Cannon Street is a large brick house (private) of considerable interest. The common bond of its brickwork suggests an early-nineteenth-century construction date, but its very steep roof and heavy chimneys with elaborate multiple hips are characteristic of much earlier styles.

Back on High Street, **320 W. High Street** (L), on the northwest side of the town square, is a plain brick building raised in 1803 as a Methodist meeting house and now used as a clothes shop and hearing aid center. The **Eliason Building** (R), 231–35 E. High Street, a white brick building across from the courthouse, was once the White Swan Tavern and appears to have been built before the Revolution. It has two stories in front, where shops have long supplanted the public rooms of the tavern, but the roof slopes to one story in the rear. The occupants of the building have refrained from sacrificing the old window sashes with their antique glass, in spite of the fact that they are less than ideal for modern usage.

The **Masonic Building** has stood on the southeast corner of the courthouse green since 1827; it now houses real estate and insurance offices. On the third floor front and sides are symbols of the Freemasons. One block east of the green, Queen Street crosses High Street, and in the Queen Street block between High and Maple streets are several old houses. Among the most interesting are **109 Queen Street** and the **Nicholson House,** 111 Queen Street (private), both brick town houses with brick cornices, which were probably built soon after the Revolution. Number 109 was the Episcopal rectory from 1850 to 1910. On Church Street, a very short alley leading from Queen Street to the courthouse green, stands the **Geddes-Piper House,** a handsome three-story brick house built between 1730 and 1754. The house was restored and is occupied by the **Kent County Historical Society** (open May–Aug., Sun., 2–5). **135** and **137 Queen Street** (private) are frame houses, now shingled, built about the time of the Revolution.

On the block of E. High Street between Queen Street and the waterfront and along Water Street, which borders the Chester River, are the mid- and late-eighteenth-century mansions for which Chestertown is famous. The first floor of the **William Barroll House** (private), 108–10 E. High Street, is believed to have been built about 1735; the line of the old catslide roof can still be seen in the brickwork. The first floor of the **Wickes House,** or **Burrell House** (private), 102 E. High Street on the corner of Water Street, is believed to be a pre-Revolutionary tavern operated by Samuel Beck. The **Burrell Garden,** 102 E. High Street, is an unusually beautiful formal garden laid out by the present owners.

High Street ends at the river just beyond Water Street. A block to the right on the corner of Front and Cannon streets stands the **Abbey,** or the **Hynson-Ringgold House** (open for periodic tours), now the official home of the president of Washington College. The rear portion of the house on Cannon Street was probably built about 1735 by Nathaniel Palmer, and the section on Water Street was erected at a later date by Nathaniel

Hynson. In 1767 Thomas Ringgold bought both these brick houses and connected them. He made the Palmer house into a kitchen, installing a beautiful divided staircase in the connecting section, which was probably designed by William Buckland, whose woodwork decorates many famous Annapolis houses (*see* Annapolis Tour). Buckland certainly designed one of the two front rooms in the Hynson wing, for his initials, with the date 1771, were found on the back of the paneling when the woodwork was loaned to the Baltimore Museum of Art in 1932. The room is noted for its chimney piece—duplicated in the house—with its eared and pedimented overmantel flanked by delicate floral plaster designs. The original woodwork of the other main room is done in a less elaborate earlier style.

Thomas Ringgold was a prominent Chestertown merchant and a member of the Stamp Act Congress of 1765. In 1854, U.S. senator James Alfred Pearce (1805–67) bought the house, and his descendants lived here until the twentieth century; the house is still sometimes called the Pearce House.

At 103 High Street is the **Chestertown Customhouse,** a long, three-story brick building, once a warehouse owned by the Ringgolds and now used as an apartment house. The earliest section was built sometime after 1719 and the remainder was completed before the Revolution. The Ringgolds are supposed to have rented a room here to the port authorities, hence accounting for the building's name.

Widehall (private), 101 Water Street, is an imposing brick mansion with a double hipped roof and a facade laid in all-header bond, probably built sometime in the 1760s. The Georgian doorway, with its fluted engaged columns and carved pediment, is a beautiful example of eighteenth-century craftsmanship. The present owners removed Victorian modifications that had been made to the house and added the Ionic portico on the river front. The interior is remarkable for the beauty of its Georgian woodwork. The entrance hall, which takes up nearly one quarter of the house, is set off from the transverse hall by two arches, a plan similar to that of the Pratt Mansion (*see* Tour 24) a few miles away. A former owner, Col. Thomas Smythe, was a merchant of importance in Chestertown and a member of the Council of Safety during the Revolution.

103 Water Street (private) is a late-eighteenth-century house once occupied by Charles Hackett, watchmaker and silversmith. Part of **River House,** 107 Water Street, is believed to have been standing in the 1740s. The building was a combination home and warehouse, perhaps built for the merchant William Trimbrill, who purchased the land it stands on in 1737. The present three-story house is believed to have been finished by 1753. The first floor was commercial; the upper floors were living quarters. The woodwork from one of the rooms is now in the Winterthur Museum. The house is owned by the Maryland Historical Trust (public access is limited).

Several other houses in this block of Water Street are of interest. The **Meteer House** (private), 110 Water Street, is believed to have been built about 1780, and the **Perkins House** (private), 115 Water Street, may date back to 1736; the fronts of both houses are laid in all-header bond. **201 Water Street,** built about 1785 but much altered thereafter, houses a collection of ship models.

● Md. 289 leaves Chestertown on Queen Street and travels through Quaker Neck, a peninsula formed by the Chester River and Langford Bay, where a number of old houses still stand. On the outskirts of Chestertown **Stephney Manor** (R) (private), 0.2 m., was once the dwelling plantation of the Wilmers, who owned the tract on which Chestertown was built. Incorporated into the rear wing of this great brick structure is the small gambrel-roofed house that Charles Willson Peale (*see above*) depicted in his painting of the Reverend Simon Wilmer and his wife. The oval track by the gate is believed to be on the site of the colonial Chestertown race track (*see above*), which was located many years ago by aerial photography.

Radcliffe Cross (R) (private, but visible from the road), 0.8 m., is a large white brick house of uncertain date, built on a tract granted to Mark Pensax, "Marriner," in 1659.

Wilkens Lane branches left at 2.1 m. and crosses **Godlington Manor** (private, but visible from the road), granted to Thomas Godlington in 1659. Two old houses still stand on the property, one a frame brick-nogged gambrel-roofed building believed to have been built in the middle or late eighteenth century.

● At 4.7 m. on Md. 289 is the junction with Md. 661, which travels through pleasant countryside to **QUAKER NECK LANDING,** 2.2 m., a tranquil haven on the Chester River. At the old steamboat landing there are fishing boats for hire, and there is a striking view of the Hollyday mansion *Readbourne* (1730s) across the broad Chester.

● The road to **Reward** (R) (private) branches off Md. 289 on Walnut Point Road at 6.9 m. This brick house, 1.6 m., was built in the 1740s on the east branch of Langford Creek by the Charles Tilden family and is now restored. The front is laid in Flemish bond with glazed headers, with English bond on the sides. Mullioned chimneys rise from the peak of a steep catslide roof. The interior, which is divided into four rooms with no hall or passage, retains its excellent paneling and chimney pieces.

● At 7.6 m. Johnsontown Road branches off Md. 289 on the left. The second left leads to the **Comegys Bight House** (private), 1.3 m., a well-known Kent County house with a dated gable reading 1768.

● **Clark's Conveniency** (R) (private, but visible from the road), 7.9 m. on Md. 289, may have been standing as early as 1704 and is a beautiful example of the many two-wing, 1½-story brick houses built in this area during the colonial period. The mullioned chimneys and dormers that slope from the ridgepole on the lower wing are characteristic of these houses. Near here is the **Site of the Quaker Neck Meeting House,** erected by Friends living in the area between the Cecil Meeting at Lynch and the Third Haven Meeting at Easton.

12b. CHESTERTOWN–WYE MILLS; 22.6 m.
Md. 213

Md. 213 leaves Chestertown at 0.0 m. by crossing the bridge over the river. From the Queen Anne's County shore, 0.5 m., the quiet waters reflect the old houses and gardens of the town river front.

Like Kent County, Queen Anne's County is mostly dairy country, with fields sown in feed crops, especially corn and hay. The acreage devoted to cash grain crops, especially wheat, is declining but is still next in importance. Small amounts of barley, essential for dairy feed, are also grown.

In winter the pale rose-colored bricks of **Chester Hall** (L) (private), 1.5 m., are a striking contrast to the dark green of the cedars that line its entrance lane. The hip-roofed brick house was built about 1790, with a wide roof-pediment on the facade set off by two-story brick pilasters that are repeated at the corners. The trim is otherwise quite simple. Although the house is not large, the overall effect is one of great dignity.

Ripley (private, but close to the road), 5.9 m., at the end of a long lane of cedars, is a 2½-story brick house built in 1806 by Col. James Brown.

CHURCH HILL, a center for rural trade, is named for the venerable **St. Luke's Protestant Episcopal Church** (open on request), 0.8 m., around which it grew. St. Luke's Parish was created in 1728, and the present brick church was finished in 1732 at a cost of 140,000 pounds of tobacco. A heavy gambrel roof covers walls laid in Flemish bond. In the apse and in the south wall, which once contained the entrance, glazed headers create a checkerboard pattern. The long round-arch windows are set off by narrow buttresses. Inside the church, the chancel is recessed in the apse and is framed by a great arch. On either side of the arch hang two wooden tablets. On two are written the Creed and the Lord's Prayer; on the other two, the Ten Commandments. During the early nineteenth century, St. Luke's fell into disrepair, but it was restored in 1842. Union cavalry wrecked the interior during the Civil War, but the church was restored again in 1881, at which time the entrance was moved from the south to the west end, where the present bell tower was erected. In 1957, the stained-glass windows were replaced by beautiful panes of hand-blown clear glass, which flood the church with light.

Behind the church is a small brick parish house built in 1817 and used as the first public school in the county.

At 8.4 m. Island Creek Road branches right off Md. 213.

● Follow this road to its end at the junction with Land's End Road, 3.2 m. Turn left on Land's End Road to the drive (marked by a sign) into **Readbourne** (R) (private), 4.5 m. This massive T-shaped house, with hip roof and modillioned cornice, was built about 1734 on a knoll overlooking the Chester River. The smaller hyphen and wing were added in 1791, with the larger one being constructed in 1948 to house a collection of Vernet murals. The high-ceilinged central hall ends in two archways that open into the T-wing. Beyond one arch rises a beautiful staircase, a copy of the original, which is now at the Winterthur Museum; the other arch leads to a small reception room called the stone-step room. Most of Readbourne's exceptionally handsome paneling is also at Winterthur. Duplication of the paneling proved impractical, but the interior has been restored in the mid-eighteenth-century style. The furnishings are unusually beautiful. Readbourne was built by Col. James Hollyday and his wife, Sarah Covington Lloyd, widow of Edward Lloyd of Wye House (*see* Tour 15). Their son, Henry Hollyday, built Ratcliffe Manor, another famous Eastern Shore house (*see* Tour 16).

A left turn from Land's End Road on to Spaniards Neck Road leads to Md. 213, 3.5 m.

On Md. 213 stands an unrestored stuccoed brick farmhouse known as **Bloomfield** (L) (private, but visible from the road).

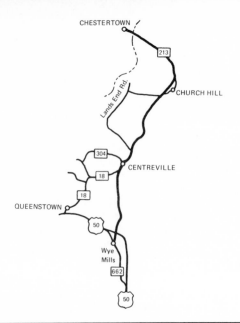

The southern end of the house is believed to have been built before 1760 by William Bourke Young.

CENTREVILLE (1,853 pop.), 14.8 m., county seat of Queen Anne's County, is a well-kept, quiet town typical of the Eastern Shore. Business consists chiefly of supplying the needs of public officials and farmers; besides the stores typical of any small market town, there are flour mills and a small fertilizer factory.

The original county seat was Queenstown (*see* Tour 24), but in 1782 the legislature authorized the sale of the courthouse and jail at Queenstown and the construction of new buildings more centrally located at the head of the Corsica River. The **Courthouse** (open Mon.–Fri.), 120 N. Commerce Street, was completed in 1792 after many delays, and in 1794 the town of Centreville was laid out. Fire has destroyed most of the older houses, but the courthouse itself remains. One of only two eighteenth-century courthouses left standing in Maryland, the building sits on a tree-shaded square, its white-painted bricks contrasting with the green lawn and boxwood hedge. A modillioned cornice runs under the hip roof of the central section, and a handsome iron balcony, added in the nineteenth century, ornaments the second story. The wings, also hip-roofed, are somewhat lower, with smaller windows. The brick is laid in Flemish bond along the whole facade. The interior of the building has been completely remodeled.

Md. 213 divides in Centreville: southbound traffic flows down Liberty Street, northbound up Commerce Street. These streets, plus Water Street (Md. 304), which crosses them one block below the courthouse, are the original streets of Centreville. A few houses built not long after the town was established still stand along these traffic arteries. The **Yellow Brick House** (private), northeast corner of Water Street and Banjo Lane (one block east of Commerce Street), is a 2½-story brick house

with double chimneys, which is believed to have been
built in the late eighteenth century. Judge Richard Bennett
Carmichael (1807–84), a well-known Queen Anne's County jurist
who, even though he supported the right of secession, believed
that Maryland should stay in the Union during the Civil War,
lived in the house. His courageous action as judge of the Circuit
Court in instructing grand juries to indict officers of the law
guilty of illegal search and seizure led to his arrest for treason
while actually sitting on the bench during a session of court
at Easton on May 27, 1862. According to Carmichael's obituary
published in the *Baltimore Sun* in 1884, "Marshal McPhail gave
the order to seize the judge and drag him from the bench.
Deputy Marshal Bishop at once seized the judge by the throat,
but was repulsed. The other deputies then closed in upon the
judge and beat him over the head with the butts of their re-
volvers. Deputy Marshal Cassell interfered for his protection,
but not until five wounds had been inflicted, and the judge,
stunned and bleeding, had been dragged from the recess behind
the desk at which he was sitting." No warrant was ever served
on the judge and no specific charge ever made against him.
Finally, on December 2, he was released from prison and at
once resumed his judicial duties.

The **Palmer House** (private), on the west side of Commerce
Street (Md. 213 N) south of Water Street, is another old house.

Across the street is **Wright's Chance,** 119 S. Commerce Street,
a frame, gambrel-roofed house probably built in the 1740s,
which has been given to the **Queen Anne's County Historical
Society** for its headquarters. The original site of the house is
some miles away. The society has restored the building, which
retains some good paneling, and has furnished it with period
pieces (open summer, Fri., 11–4 and on request). **202 Liberty
Street** (private), a gable-roofed brick house with huge double
chimneys, was built about 1800. The recessed doorway contains
a lovely half-moon fanlight. **208 Liberty Street** (private), similar
to the house at 202 but somewhat smaller, was built in 1792
and retains all its original woodwork. Across the street from 208
is the stuccoed brick **St. Paul's Church,** built in 1834–35. The
transept and chancel were added in 1862 and enlarged in 1892,
when the interior was remodeled. St. Paul's serves one of the
original parishes of Maryland, St. Paul's Parish, erected in 1692.
Before 1834, the church stood near the intersection of Md. 213
and Md. 18 (*see below*), the road from Queenstown to Corsica
Neck. Another church, known as Old Chester Church, is believed
to have occupied that site before 1692.

Before the courthouse, Md. 213 S (Liberty Street) intersects
Broadway Street. Turn right. Broadway becomes Md. 304.

● Go right on Md. 304 to **Thompson House** (R) (private, but near the
road), 0.7 m., a brick house built about the time of the Revolution,
probably by Elizabeth Nicholson. The house, two and one-half stories of
brick laid in Flemish bond, is one room deep with a central hall containing a handsome stairway.

At Thompson House a side road branches right, and at 0.5 m. on the
left is **Paschall's Chance** (private), a handsome yellow brick house, the
central part of which is believed to be eighteenth century.

● At 2.5 m. on Md. 304, turn right on N. Hibernia Road. At 0.2 m. is a fork.

Go right to **Gunston School,** 0.8 m., a school for girls from fourteen to eighteen years of age.

● Go left (straight ahead) at the fork to **Corsica** (R) (private), 1.2 m. This simple brick house, one room deep, stands on a high bluff overlooking the Corsica River. The first section was built about 1780, but the two wings are modern.

● At 3.0 m. on Md. 304 **Melfield** (R) (private) can be seen from the road during the fall, winter, and spring. It is a two-story brick house, painted white; according to tradition it was intended to be the library of a much larger house that was never completed because of the outbreak of the American Revolution. The Doric portico was added about the time of the Civil War.

Just beyond Melfield, at 3.2 m., state maintenance ends. The road turns sharply to the right, and Spider Web Road (paved) and the tour branch left. To the right the road leads to **Pioneer Point,** once a great estate belonging to the late Jacob Raskob, financier and Du Pont associate, and now the location of research facilities for United Nuclear, Inc.—a change symptomatic of times to come on the Eastern Shore, where an increasing number of firms are opening offices.

The tour continues left on Spider Web Road to its end at Wright's Neck Road (graveled), 4.5 m. To the right on Wright's Neck Road is **Walnut Grove** (L), 4.8 m., a historic dwelling believed by many to be the oldest in Queen Anne's County. It is a small frame structure with brick gables and steep catslide roof, near Reed Creek, perhaps built by a member of the Wright family. Nearby is a handsome brick house of the Revolutionary period also built by the Wright family, known as the **Reed's Creek House.** The house has been restored and is now open to the public by appointment. From the junction with Spider Web Road, Wright's Neck Road is 1.5 m. from Md. 18 (*see below*).

At 16.6 m. on Md. 213, Md. 18 branches right.

● At 2.7 m. on Md. 18 two roads branch right. The second of these, Wright's Neck Road, leads to *Walnut Grove* and *Reed's Creek House.*

At 3.1 m. Tilghman's Neck Road (paved) turns right. At 1.1 m. the paving ends and the road forks.

Go right from the fork to the lane (L) of **The Hermitage** (private, but often open on the House and Garden Pilgrimage), granted in 1659 to Dr. Richard Tilghman. Matthew Tilghman (*see* Tour 16, Rich Neck), Lt. Col. Tench Tilghman, and Tench Francis Tilghman (*see* Tour 17, Plinhimmon) were all descended from him. His gravestone, dated 1675, is in the family burying ground.

● Go left at the fork on De Coursey Tom Road to the **Site of Blakeford.** When Lord Baltimore granted Henry DeCourcey (Coursey) as much land as his thumb would cover on a map (*see* Tour 24, My Lord's Gift), the extreme tip of his thumb extended across Queenstown Creek and included this tract. In 1696 it was sold to Charles Blake, whose family gave the property its present name.

● Md. 18 continues to Queenstown, 5.9 m. (*see* Tour 24).

Md. 213 crosses U.S. 301 and Tour 24 at 18.1 m., and passes by **Peace and Plenty** (L) (private, but visible from the road) (*see* Tour 24), 18.4 m. It intersects U.S. 50 at 22.6 m., just outside of Wye Mills. The tour continues south (L) on U.S. 50.

● Go north (R) on U.S. 50. At 2.4 m. is the junction with Carmichael Road, which junctions with Wye Neck Road and Cheston Lane. Bear right on Cheston Lane to the **Wye Institute,** an agricultural experiment station of the University of Maryland. Research is conducted on vegetables, corn, soybeans, and other field crops.

Old Wye Grist Mill

● At 4.0 m. on Wye Neck Road are the gates (L) to **Wye Planta-tion,** a large estate on the Wye River where purebred Angus cattle are raised. The original house, a portion of which was built in the seven-teenth century, was owned by the Tilghman family. In 1811 the prop-erty came into the possession of Julianna Tilghman Paca, wife of John Philemon Paca. His father, William Paca, was a signer of the Declara-tion of Independence and a three-term governor of Maryland. In 1911 the Maryland Society, Sons of the American Revolution, erected a monument to Paca in the graveyard in front of the house where many of his descendants were buried.

Among the famous visitors to Wye Plantation when owned by the Tilghmans and Pacas were Col. Tench Tilghman (*see* Tour 17), General Lafayette, and the two Carrolls. William Paca's own Eastern Shore man-sion, Wye Hall, was located nearby on Wye Island. The dwelling was probably the most magnificent in the United States when completed in the early 1790s. The house was destroyed in 1879 when workmen repair-ing the roof accidentally started a fire.

Though united solidly during the War of Independence, the Paca family was split by the War between the States. At the close of the war the Unionist William B. Paca of nearby Wye Hall attempted to take over the lands of Edward Paca of Wye Plantation. In the resulting feud two members of the Edward Paca family were killed, and William Paca, though acquitted after a trial for murder, soon died. Shortly afterward two of his sons committed suicide, and a daughter died of accidental poisoning.

A visitor's center explains the story of Wye Plantation as an exten-

sive Angus beef cattle operation. The new house is privately owned
and is closed to the public.

● At approximately 2.5 m., continuing north on U.S. 50, is **Bloomingdale** (R) (private, but visible from the road), called Mount Mill when it
was built by the Seth family in 1792. This large, hip-roofed brick house
has an unusual two-story octagonal portico. A one-story hyphen leads
to a wing believed to be older than the main house. From Bloomingdale
Road, which turns right here, there is a closer view of the house.

● Go straight ahead on Md. 213 to **Old Wye Grist Mill** (open during summer; during school sessions on Wed., 10–5, and Sat.), 0.9 m.
A mill is known to have stood on this site since early colonial days,
but the date of erection of the existing building is uncertain. Old
records reveal that the mill ground grain for General Washington's
troops during the Revolution. It remained in private ownership and
continuous operation for an estimated 250 years, finally closing down
in 1953. The state then acquired the mill, and a local organization, the
Old Wye Mills Society, Inc., restored it. It has been reopened due to
the efforts of two students of Chesapeake College. Flour is still ground
here as it was during the Revolutionary period.

At 0.9 m. is **WYE MILLS,** which grew up around the mill and now
contains a cannery that employs about 400 people in season. Here is
a junction with Md. 404.

To the right on Md. 404 is Foremans Landing Road, which leads to
Clover Fields (L) (private), a well-known old house famous for its
woodwork, which belonged to William Hemsley, sheriff of Queen Anne's
County.

● Almost opposite the junction of Md. 404 and Md. 662 in Wye Mills
is **Wye Oak House,** believed to have been built about 1720 as a schoolhouse. The building has been restored by the garden clubs of Talbot
and Queen Anne's counties.

At 1.2 m. on Md. 662 is the **Wye Oak,** the largest white oak in
Maryland and one of the largest in the United States. Believed to be
nearly 400 years old, the tree is 104 feet high with a horizontal spread
of 160 feet and a trunk 32 feet in circumference. The tree and a 1½-
acre area surrounding it were acquired by the state in 1939 and now
constitute **Wye Oak State Park.** In 1941 the Maryland legislature
honored the Wye Oak by formally designating the white oak as the
official state tree. In August, 1959, a massive limb crashed to the
ground, but the ancient tree's vitality appears to be unimpaired.

Old Wye Church (also known as **Wye Chapel**), 7.3 m., was consecrated as a chapel of ease for St. Paul's Parish (*see above,* St. Paul's
Church, Centreville) on October 18, 1721. A letter, copied into the
vestry minutes of Shrewsbury Parish from Rev. Christopher Wilkinson
to Rev. James Williamson of Shrewsbury, invited Williamson to assist
at the ceremony and to lodge with the writer "ye night before." The
small red brick structure was restored in 1949 through the generosity
of Arthur Amory Houghton, Jr., of nearby *Wye Plantation.* The Boston
firm of Perry, Shaw, and Hepburn undertook the work. This church,
with its brick floors, unusual box pews, magnificent hanging pulpit and
pulpit canopy, and slave gallery, is now regarded as a near-perfect
example of rural colonial church architecture. The chancel contains two
chairs dating from the time of James II. The Baskerville Bible at the
reading desk is contemporary with the church. Nearby are a reconstructed vestry house, erected on the original 1763 foundations and
furnished with eighteenth-century antiques, and the parish house, built
in 1957 in an eighteenth-century style. The church is open in the summer, Thurs.–Fri., 3–5; Sat., 11–5; Sun., 2–5. Services are held every
Sunday at 11, and Holy Communion is given the first Sunday of each
month.

At 2.5 m. on Md. 662 is the junction with the graveled Wye Landing Lane.

Wye Oak

Right on this road to **Wye Landing Farm,** also called **King Hays Farm** (L) (private, but near the road), 2.3 m. This old brick telescope house stands under great trees just above the Wye River. The largest section, two and one-half stories with a hall on one side, appears to have been built about the end of the eighteenth century. The wing retains its original woodwork including two handsome mantels, and the ten windows in the gable permit a view of the river from each room. The lower wings are doubtless older, but their original interiors are gone. Behind the house is an old brick dairy with a roof that overhangs its walls by almost five feet.

An old dock and warehouse mark **WYE LANDING,** 2.5 m., once a busy shipping point for this farming section.

At 3.8 m. Md. 662 rejoins U.S. 50.

12c. WYE MILLS–EASTON–CAMBRIDGE–SALISBURY; 58.6 m. U.S. 50

This tour begins at the junction of U.S. 50 and Maryland Route 213, 0.0 m.

East of Wye Mills U.S. 50 intersects Md. 404 (*see* Tour 14) at 1.5 m. As U.S. 50 continues southward it passes through the gently rolling land of a prosperous farming area. Southeast of the Choptank River, the route travels by low-lying truck farms.

At 4.7 m. another section of Md. 662 branches right.

● Go right to **LONGWOODS** (45 pop.), 1.3 m. A little red schoolhouse is to the right at 1.4 m. In the village is a junction with two roads.

Make a sharp right at the junction to **Wye Heights,** or **Cleghorne-on-Wye** (private), 2.1 m., a three-story structure built by the Lloyds of Wye House in 1823 and enlarged in the 1930s. The gardens along the Wye River are bordered by boxwood and are among the most beautiful in Maryland. A magnificent view of the water can be seen through the 300-foot-long rose arbor.

● At 3.5 m. on Md. 662 is the junction with Hailem School Road. Turn right and continue to the intersection with Goldsborough Neck Road, 0.9 m. Turn right again to **Myrtle Grove** (private), 1.9 m., the ancestral home of the Goldsboroughs. The small house was built in 1734; the 2½-story addition was built in 1790. The earlier house, built

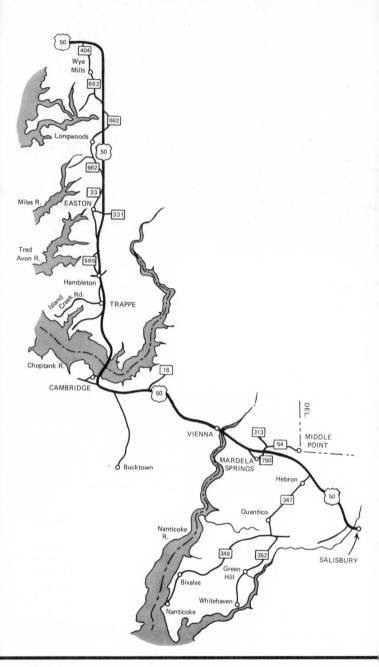

TOUR 12c

of logs covered with wide clapboards, still retains part of its original paneling. The addition is a handsome brick building with a modillioned cornice that extends completely around the house, thus enabling the gables to be treated as pediments with oval windows in the center. Inside, the hall is distinguished by a beautiful hanging staircase, and both the hall and the parlors have Adam-style plaster cornices and molded ceilings. From the house the gardens slope to the waters of the Miles River. At the end of the greensward is one of the largest swamp chestnut oaks in the United States and a state champion loblolly pine.

At 4.6 m. Md. 662 merges with U.S. 50.

At 8.8 m. on U.S. 50 is the entrance (R) to the **Easton Municipal Airport.**

At 8.9 m. is the junction with Md. 309 (L) to Cordova and Queen Anne.

On the right is a housing development, the beginning of the Easton metropolitan area.

At 9.6 m. is Md. 33, the principal north entrance to Easton. In Easton, Md. 33 branches at Bay Street toward St. Michaels and Claiborne (*see* Tour 16).

At 11.1 m. is Md. 328, which runs into Easton via Goldsborough Street (R) and to Chapel and Denton via Easton-Denton Road (L).

At the traffic light, 11.4 m., is Md. 331 which leads into the center of Easton via Dover Road (R) and to Dover Bridge, Bethlehem and Preston (*see* Tour 18) via Easton-Preston Road (L).

EASTON (35′ alt., 8,000 pop.), the county seat of Talbot, was once the capital of the Eastern Shore. It now serves the surrounding area as a commercial center. Although it is not an industrial town, the variety of small enterprises that have located here, combined with the extension of the town boundaries, has increased the town's population in recent years. In addition to its growing industrial capacity, the town is a banking and medical center, but most of all, Easton is the trading and distribution point for a four-county area. The importance of its many service establishments are enhanced by the trade of numerous wealthy people from New York, Pittsburgh, Cleveland, and other cities who have bought waterfront plantations in the county over the past half-century. Many of these people actively support local cultural and philanthropic affairs, and they and their guests help support Easton's restaurants and antique shops. During the duck-hunting season, Easton's hotels and guest houses are filled with sportsmen from throughout the East.

Most of the larger Eastern Shore towns are located on rivers, but Easton is situated inland, with the nearest waterfront, Easton Point on the Tred Avon River, a mile away. The old docks and warehouses at the point have largely been supplanted by modern oil company installations.

Easton arose around the Talbot County Courthouse, which was erected in 1710–12 near what was then known as Pitt's Bridge. The bridge spanned a small arm of the Tred Avon on the main road north from Oxford, and its location is now marked by a plaque on the wall of a shopping center on N. Washington Street. At the time the original courthouse was built the only structure of importance in the neighborhood was the *Third Haven Quaker Meeting House*, erected in 1682–84. Establishment of the courthouse provided an impetus for growth, and by 1723 the court justices were forced to forbid "the Publick Houses at the Court House" from "keeping their nine pins in the streets during the sitting of this Court" and likewise to forbid the playing of ninepins during court sessions. During the intense American resistance to the British-imposed stamp tax in 1765, the freemen of Talbot County met in the courthouse and adopted a resolution declaring that they would "detest, abhor, and hold in the utmost contempt" anyone having anything to do with enforcement of the obnoxious Stamp Act. And, the resolution continued, "in testimony of their fixed and unalterable resolution, they have this day erected a gibbet, twenty feet high, before the Court House door, and hung in chains thereon the effigy of a stamp informer, there to remain *in terrorem,* till the Stamp Act shall be repealed." When the Revolution came ten years later, the Declaration of Independence was read from the courthouse steps, and Talbot County troops drilled on the dusty road in front of the courthouse before marching off to join Washington's army.

Early in its history, the village was known as Talbot Court House. For convenience, the name was later shortened to Talbot Town or Talbottown, and still later to Talbotton or just plain Talbot. The village grew slowly in colonial times, and not a single pre-Revolutionary building survives except the old Quaker meeting house.

After the Revolution, the village entered a period of rapid development, largely because its central location led the state to establish the administrative offices for the Eastern Shore counties here. Thus, the town became in effect the "capital" of the Eastern Shore. In 1788, the legislature renamed the town Easton, probably a contraction of East-town. The old courthouse of 1710–12 was too small for the Court of Appeals, the federal courts, and the state offices centered here, so in 1794 a new courthouse was finished at a cost of £3,000, the state providing five-sixths of that sum. Some Eastern Shore residents thought that the legislature intended to hold alternate sessions here and in Annapolis, but this never materialized.

For a century Easton was the largest and most important and progressive town on the Eastern Shore. The first newspaper on the Eastern Shore was established here (1790), the first bank (1805), and the first steamboat line to Baltimore (1817). Most of the buildings facing the courthouse, in the heart of the business section, were built between 1790 and 1820, although their fronts have been remodeled. The checkerboard street plan of the central section of Easton dates back to 1785. Col. Jeremiah Banning, a wealthy landowner of Talbot County, "had the honour" of naming the streets, giving the name of Washington to the principal business thoroughfare.

The Protestant Episcopal Diocese of Easton, covering the nine counties of the Eastern Shore, takes its name from the town and has its cathedral here. The headquarters of the Easton District of the Peninsula Conference of the Methodist Church is also located in town. In addition to the cathedral, Easton has about fifteen other churches and a synagogue, modern schools (five public, one parochial, one private), an orphans' home operated by the Diocese of Easton, an aged women's home, two motion picture theaters, a state armory, a "Little Theater" group known as the Easton Players, a yacht club, a country club, a women's club, veterans' clubs, fraternal organizations, civic and service organizations, a public park and several playgrounds, a fully organized city police department, and an active fire department with nine pieces of equipment. The city runs its own waterworks, electric plant, and gas plant.

On Md. 50, as one approaches Easton, is the **Talbot County Chamber of Commerce and Information Center.** The building that houses the chamber of commerce originally stood on the tract Tilghman's Fortune. When it was restored, the structure was made to resemble a nineteenth-century farmhouse.

Talbot County Courthouse (open Mon.–Fri., 8:30–4:00), located on a square—or "courthouse green"—in the center of town, is the "capital" building of 1794 enlarged in 1958 by the addition of wings to the north and south. During the Civil War, Federal troops shocked Marylanders by mounting an assault on the second-floor courtroom, where they dragged Judge Richard B. Carmichael, who was believed to have Southern sympathies, from the bench (*see above*, Centreville).

The **Talbot County Free Library** (open weekdays) is considered the best nonmetropolitan library in Maryland. Its Maryland collection and children's library are especially good.

In 1954, citizens and businessmen, supported by the county historical society, the garden club, and other agencies, began a project to restore the buildings on the central courthouse square to their approximate appearance during the Federal period. The restoration project aroused such interest that many new buildings beyond the courthouse square have been built in the Federal style, including a shopping center, a hotel, various office buildings and stores, and even service stations.

As one approaches the courthouse, chimneys of a series of Federal period houses on the right make a striking pattern against the sky. Of these, the **Thomas Perrin Smith House** (private), 119 N. Washington Street, built in 1803 by the founder of the newspaper from which the present *Easton Star–Democrat* grew, has been the home of the **Chesapeake Bay Yacht Club** since 1912. Beyond it, on the corner of Washington and Federal streets, is the **Brick Hotel,** completed in 1812 and used as a hotel until the late nineteenth or early twentieth century, when it was converted into an office building. In this same block on the corner of Goldsborough and Washington streets is the **Old Frame Hotel** (now Nevius Hardware), believed to be more than 150 years old.

South of the courthouse one block, at 29 S. Washington Street, is **Stevens House,** home of the **Historical Society of Talbot County,** which restored the building (originally built around 1800) during the late 1950s. On display are pieces of furniture and artifacts that illustrate Talbot County history. Just off S. Washington Street, at 26 South Street, is the **Hughlett-Henry House,** another building dating from the 1790s. **105, 107,** and **109 S. Washington Street** (private) are well-proportioned brick buildings that retain some attractive original external woodwork.

Third Haven Quaker Meeting House (open by request to caretaker), entrance on S. Washington Street immediately beyond the railway overpass, is a clapboard structure erected between 1682 and 1684 and enlarged in 1792. It is one of the oldest frame houses of worship in the United States. William Penn once held meetings here under one of the massive oaks on the parklike grounds. Preserved in the old house are the original broad-plank floors and straightbacked benches. The stove was a source of contention in 1781 when some members thought that religious zeal should give sufficient warmth without artificial heating. The Third Haven Meeting no longer uses the old house, meeting instead in the brick house adjacent. The meeting's records, which date from the mid-seventeenth century, are now at the Hall of Records in Annapolis.

Washington Street continues to a traffic light and a junction with Md. 333 and Tour 17.

The **Old Market House,** Harrison Street and Magazine Alley, is a small 1½-story stuccoed brick building erected in 1791. The Grand Lodge of Maryland of the Masonic Order, organized in Easton in 1783 (formally organized in 1787), held its first meetings in the old courthouse but moved to the Market House while the courthouse of 1794 was being constructed. Dr. John Coats, the first Grand Master of the Grand Lodge, is commemorated here with a monument. The building also contains a museum.

The old **Cannon** in front of the American Legion home on Dover Street east of the Tidewater Inn is believed to have been part of the armament of Fort Stokes which was built in 1813 on the Tred Avon River opposite Easton Point to protect the town from the British fleet.

Easton Utilities, 11 S. Harrison Street near Dover Street, was formerly an old firehouse; the cupola of the building still contains the old fire bell that summoned the town's volunteer firemen.

The 2½-story brick **Bullitt** or **Chamberlain House,** Dover and Harrison streets, was erected about 1790 by Thomas James Bullitt, progenitor of the famous Bullitt family of Philadelphia. One of his descendants was William C. Bullitt, American ambassador to the U.S.S.R. (1933–36) and to France (1936–41).

Foxley Hall (private), N. Aurora and Goldsborough streets, is a distinguished brick dwelling built about 1794 by Mrs. Henry Dickinson, whose husband was uncle to the Charles Dickinson killed by Andrew Jackson in a duel (*see* Tour 14).

Trinity Cathedral, Goldsborough Street east of Aurora Street, primary church of the Protestant Episcopal Diocese of Easton, was consecrated in 1894. An unpretentious stone building of Romanesque design, the church has notable stained-glass windows. The small one-story frame building behind it, now used as a parish house, was the original cathedral, built in 1876.

Leaving Easton, at the intersection with Md. 331, U.S. 50 runs southward through land sown mostly in field crops. The region abounds in legends, folklore, and well-preserved eighteenth-century buildings.

At 13.5 m. on U.S. 50 (L) the brick buildings constitute the substation of Troop I, Maryland State Police (information and first aid). Troop I is responsible for the northern portion of the Eastern Shore.

The small hexagonal frame structure, 14.2 m., is **Peachblossom Church** (L), built in 1881 and formerly used alternately every fourth Sunday by Methodist, Reformed Lutheran, Swedenborgian, and Church of the Brethren congregations. According to tradi-

Third Haven Quaker Meeting House, Easton

tion, the devil can make himself invisible by hiding in a right-angled corner; therefore the six-sided, wide-angled edifice was built "so that the devil would have no corner to sit in and hatch evil."

At 14.9 m., Md. 565 (R) (formerly Md. 213) branches to parallel U.S. 50 to *Trappe.*

At 14.9 m. is the junction with Landing Neck Road.

● Left on this road, through the crossroads of Ivytown to the junction with Lloyds Landing Road opposite a cannery at 2.3 m. Go left to **Lloyds Landing** (private), 4.6 m., built about 1720 by a member of the Lloyd family when the landing was a shipping point on the Choptank. The steep pitch of the roof of this hall-and-parlor brick cottage makes evident its medieval character even at a distance. The living room has interesting wainscoting and overmantel paneling, projecting window seats, and twenty-four-pane windows. Capt. James Lloyd sailed his own ships from the wharf nearby in the mid-eighteenth century.

At 18.4 m. is a crossroads. Under the shade trees on the left, the ruins of **White Marsh Church** (open to public) stand among well-tended graves. The original church may have been built as early as 1685, and parish records show that White Marsh had an Anglican rector at least by 1690. The church was abandoned during the Civil War, and partly burned in 1896. Annual services are now held here. In the churchyard is the **Grave of Robert Morris, Sr.** (d. July 12, 1750), father of Robert Morris, the Revolutionary War financier (*see* Tour 17).

Among provincial rectors of White Marsh was Rev. Thomas Bacon (1746–68), compiler of *Bacon's Laws,* a compendium of Maryland's colonial statutes that was for many decades an authoritative guide for the state courts. The first rector (1716–45) after establishment was Rev. Daniel Maynadier, believed to have been a Huguenot. It is said that the night after Maynadier's wife was buried in the churchyard here, two strangers opened her grave to steal a valuable old ring from her hand. Unable to slip it off, they severed her finger. Suddenly revived by the shock, the woman arose, gathered up her shroud, and made her way to the rectory, where she survived for several years after the ordeal.

To the right is **HAMBLETON** (52' alt., 20 pop.), locally known for more than two centuries as Hole-in-the-Wall. According to one tradition, the town got its name because sailors formerly sold smuggled goods through a hole in a wall here, by which precaution the buyer and seller were concealed from each other. Another more likely explanation is that the town was named after an inn that operated here about 1750, which had appropriated the name of a well-known English tavern. On the corner, visible from U.S. 50, is a shingled telescope house, the two lower wings of which are believed to be nearly 200 years old.

TRAPPE (56' alt., 426 pop.), 19.3 m. at the junction with Maple Street (unmarked), an inland farming community, is known to baseball fans as the home of J. Franklin "Home Run" Baker. Baker was born here on March 13, 1886, and won fame as third baseman with the "$100,000 infield" of the then Philadelphia Athletics. During the World Series of 1911 against the New York Giants, Baker won two games with timely home runs. Baker's name and achievements are now enshrined in the Baseball Hall of Fame at Cooperstown, New York.

U.S. 50 by-passes Trappe on the east. Maple Street serves as the town's northernmost street, extending (right) to Md. 565.

● At 0.2 m. on Maple Street is **Dickinson House** (private, but visible from the road), a quaint gambrel-roofed frame house with picturesque chimneys that once belonged to the family of John Dickinson (*see below*, Site of Crosiadore).

Maple Street continues through Trappe into Island Creek Neck, where a number of old houses remain. Continue straight ahead at the intersection of Main and Maple streets in Trappe at 1.0 m. At 1.1 m. is a fork; bear left. At 1.7 m. is another fork; bear left on Island Creek Road. At 2.6 m. is the lane to **Hampden** (private), a 1½-story brick house believed to be the oldest house in Talbot County. Part of the building dates from the very early eighteenth century. The woodwork in the interior of the dwelling is noteworthy. The **Wilderness** (private), 4.1 m., a handsome 2½-story brick house with a lower two-story wing, is beautifully situated on a bluff above the Choptank. The main house was built in 1810 by Daniel Martin (1780–1831), twice governor of Maryland (1829–31). The wing dates from about 1700, but it has been widened and much altered.

● The main side route turns left at the intersection of Maple and Main streets. At 1.6 m. just beyond Trappe a road bears right into Grubin Neck. At 1.9 m. is the **Site of Crosiadore,** once a Dickinson homestead and the birthplace of John Dickinson (1732–1808). Dickinson's *Letters from a Pennsylvania Farmer* (1767), written after he had moved to Delaware, was an attack on British taxes that fomented much anti-British feeling in the colonies. Dickinson resisted declaring the colonies independent, however, although once the break had been made he espoused the American cause and became a signer of the Constitution of Delaware. In 1781 Dickinson served as president of the State of Delaware and from 1782 to 1786, he was president of the State of Pennsylvania. The tract on which Crosiadore was built remained in the Dickinson family for nearly 300 years, finally passing to a new owner in 1959. The dwelling was destroyed in April, 1976.

Compton (open by appointment: Conrad W., James M., and Charles C. Arensberg), 2.5 m., belonged to the Stevens family from 1679 to

1860. William Stevens (d. 1701) was a prominent Quaker, but his great-grandson, John, was expelled from the meeting in 1759 for having "a dark and Libertine spirit" that allowed "fiddling and dancing . . . and also the poppets to be shown in his house." John inherited Compton in 1782 and may have built the present brick house in which he is said to have held lavish parties. His son, Samuel, Jr. (1778–1860), served three one-year terms as governor of Maryland (1822–25). While governor, Samuel Stevens invited Lafayette to Maryland during his farewell visit to America in 1824.

The **Gov. Emerson C. Harrington Bridge,** 26.1 m., across the Choptank, was completed in 1935 at a cost of $1,500,000, one-third defrayed by the state and the remainder by the Public Works Administration. President Franklin D. Roosevelt attended the dedication.

Below the Choptank, U.S. 50 crosses the flat vegetable-growing farms of Dorchester, Wicomico, and Worcester counties. Most of the truck crops—especially tomatoes, snap beans, sweet potatoes, and sweet corn—are grown for freezing and canning, with the processors usually contracting for the crops in advance. Because competition from the irrigated, year-round-producing valleys of California has made quality control crucial, the packer may supply the grower with seed and fertilizer, supervise their use, and harvest the crop. Until recently, harvesting had been done almost entirely by hand by migrant pickers, who came by the thousands each summer and fall from the South (*see* Tours 20 and 22). Pea and snap-bean harvesters and sweet-corn pickers have now been perfected, but such machinery is often too expensive for a single grower, so much of it is owned by the processors. The long-run effect of mechanized harvesting cannot be predicted, but it may ultimately result in greater acreage being planted in truck crops and a decrease in the number of jobs for migrant pickers. Mechanization will certainly increase the industrial character of truck farming in the area, enhancing the processors' influence on the agricultural economy. Because of the cost of mechanized harvesting and the need for precise quality control, processors must now invest large sums of capital in the operations, and as a result the small crossroads cannery, once important on the Eastern Shore, has nearly disappeared.

At the present time, vegetable acreage is declining on the Lower Shore, in part because the packers tend to make contracts with the more efficient growers, leaving the others without a market for their produce. Soybeans have proved to be an excellent crop for farmers who have been forced to abandon truck gardening, because the crop can be harvested with relatively inexpensive machinery that the small producer can either purchase himself or rent from a neighbor. Another advantage of soybeans is that, unlike truck gardening, the farmer does not have to depend on migrant laborers to harvest his crops.

From the **Harrington Bridge** on the Choptank, U.S. 50 skirts **CAMBRIDGE.** At 28.4 m. is the junction with Md. 16 (*see* Tour 19). Here the long low buildings and high chimneys of several food-processing companies (*see* Cambridge) line the road.

The steep roof line of the three-story **Shoal Creek House** can be seen across the fields on the left at 28.8 m. In the early nineteenth century this was the home of Charles Goldsborough, governor of Maryland in 1818.

The **Eastern Shore Hospital Center** (L), 29.1 m., a hospital for the mentally ill, admitted its first patient in 1915.

At 29.8 m. is the junction (R) with paved Bucktown Road.

● This route takes the traveler into the flat marshes of central Dorchester County, where several eighteenth-century brick houses can be seen. Not far off this road is a small log house, now covered with shingles, which local tradition claims was the home of Henry Airey, an early convert to Methodism. In 1781, Airey offered this house to the Methodist evangelist Freeborn Garrettson for services. During one of the services, Garrettson was arrested as a Tory and imprisoned in Cambridge.

At 7.4 m. is **BUCKTOWN,** birthplace of Harriet Tubman, a black woman famous for her role in the Underground Railroad and as a coconspirator with John Brown. After her escape to the North in 1849, Harriet made nearly twenty trips back to Maryland to help other slaves escape, especially from this area of Dorchester County. Although she was illiterate and suffered from blackouts resulting from a severe head injury inflicted upon her by a slave overseer, Harriet was considered highly dangerous by Maryland planters, who offered large rewards for her capture. John Brown counted upon her to lead an army of escaped slaves down from Canada to join him in his raid upon Harpers Ferry. When the time came, Harriet was sick and could not carry out her part of the mission. During the Civil War, she nursed the wounded and acted as a spy for the Southern Department of the Union Army near Charleston, South Carolina, but because she was not officially a soldier, Congress refused to recognize or compensate her for her services. She lived until 1913, most of the time in Auburn, New York. At her death, the people of Auburn erected a bronze tablet in her honor, inscribing it with her own statement that in her work for the Underground Railroad, she "never ran her train off the track and never lost a passenger."

At 32.0 m., Md. 16 branches off U.S. 50.

● Turn left, and return on U.S. 50 toward Cambridge 0.3 m. Here Whitehall Road branches off to the right. At 0.8 m. is **Whitehall** (private), a long, narrow whitewashed brick three-story house on the banks of a creek. The central portion, gable to front, has an unusually large lunette window in the triangle. Bricked-up windows in the inside partitions indicate that the wings at each side of the main block are later additions. The frame wing in the back contains the old kitchen. According to local legend, one of Patty Cannon's henchmen (see Tour 18) owned this house and hid some of her kidnapped Negroes in a barred room in the basement. There was supposed to have been a tunnel from the basement to the creek.

At 43.3 m. on U.S. 50 **VIENNA** (358 pop.) is at the junction with Md. 331 and Tour 18. Although some believe there was a settlement here before the end of the seventeenth century, the proceedings of the General Assembly make no mention of the town until the law of 1706, which ordered the area to be laid out as one of the sites established "for the advancement of Trade." The land, which was duly "apportioned into One hundred Equal lotts, Streets, Lanes with a Reserve of fifteen Acres for publick uses," bordered the reservation laid off for the Nanticoke Indians in 1698. The site had formerly been called Emperors Landing, and the name of Vienna is believed to have been derived from the name of the Nanticoke Emperor, Vinnacokasimmon. By 1709 some houses and a chapel of ease had been

built in the town, and Vienna's location on the navigable Nanticoke River kept it from dying out like so many of the other
towns that the General Assembly tried to legislate into existence. About 1768, Vienna became a port of entry with its own
customs official, and by 1781 its shipyards were considered
worthy of attack by the British. The English troops burned a
brig in the shipyard and in the ensuing skirmish killed Levin
Dorsey, the only man to die in battle on Dorchester soil during
the Revolution.

Vienna was a stopping point on the inland route from the
northern to the southern Eastern Shore, with a ferry operating
across the Nanticoke River until 1828, when a wooden bridge was
built. The introduction of steamboats made the bridge such a
menace to navigation that it was eventually destroyed, and ferry
service was resumed in 1860. The present span was not constructed until 1931 and only then because of persistent pressure
from residents of the area. The flood of telegrams supporting
the project is supposed to have driven Gov. Albert C. Ritchie to
wire in return, "For God's sake stop the telegrams, we'll give
you the damned bridge."

From the bridge one has a view of Vienna, both old and new.
The new is represented on the north by the giant plant of the
Eastern Shore Public Service Company, built in 1927–28. Its great
smokestacks, which seem to scrape the sky above the low-
lying marshes, dwarf the old Vienna, represented by a row of
houses to the south along Water Street fronting on the Nanticoke. These frame buildings, with their heavy outside brick
chimneys, appear to antedate the Civil War, and several must
be much older. At the end of Water Street is the small frame
customshouse built in 1791 and used until 1866. Across the
way is perhaps the most handsome of the early buildings, a
weatherboarded frame house, two stories under a steep roof,
with a delicately carved cornice. Concealed under the wide
screened porch is a beautifully carved doorway done in the light
Federal style.

From the bridge at Vienna U.S. 50 travels a long causeway
through the marshes into Wicomico County.

At 46.5 m. is the junction with Md. 750 (unmarked).

● Go right (straight ahead) 1.0 m. to **MARDELA SPRINGS,** formerly
the village of Barren Creek. At 1.5 m. is the octagonal **Spring House**
(R) which covers a natural spring that made this a stopping place for
Indians traveling on the Eastern Shore long before white settlers
arrived. During the nineteenth century, the supposedly beneficial effects
of the water made the village into a small health resort. In 1906, the
General Assembly incorporated the town as Mardela Springs, the name
being a combination of Maryland and Delaware. Although road maintenance was rapidly becoming a specialized task, the town's charter
still followed the ancient form in specifying that every able-bodied
male between the ages of twenty-one and sixty should contribute two
days of work on the town roads, either in person or by substitute, or
pay the bailiff a dollar for each day missed.

At 1.6 m. Md. 750 rejoins U.S. 50.

At 48.1 m. is the junction of U.S. 50 and Md. 313.

● Go left on Md. 313, 0.1 m., then right on Md. 54 to the **Mason-
Dixon Middlestone** (L), 3.4 m., protected from the weather by a brick

shelter. The two stones here mark the mid-point of a line surveyed in 1750–51 from Fenwick Island on the Delaware Bay due west to the Chesapeake (*see* Tour 12d, Delaware Line). From this mid-point, the east-west boundary of Delaware and Maryland was to run north to a point where it would be tangent to a circle of twelve miles radius centered in New Castle. The mid-point stone could not be placed, however, until the dispute as to where the line should terminate was settled. The Maryland commissioners claimed that Slaughter Creek, which divides Taylor's Island from the mainland of Dorchester County, should be the terminus. The Pennsylvania surveyors, however, argued that since water in the creek at low tide was less than two feet deep, the Bay shore of Taylor's Island should be the end point. The question was settled in favor of the Penns in 1760, and the smaller of the two stones was then placed here. When Charles Mason and Jeremiah Dixon resumed the survey in 1763 (delayed by the death of the fifth Lord Baltimore and by the minority of the sixth), they accepted this transpeninsular line as the mid-point, placing the second stone, marked with a double crown, here in 1768. Both stones have the Calvert arms on the south side and those of the Penns on the north.

Spring Hill Church (L), 53.0 m., built in 1771–72 as a chapel of ease of Stepney Parish, is a white frame rectangular structure with little visible on the exterior to distinguish it from more recent buildings except its elliptical-headed windows full of old glass. The unpainted pine interior, however, retains some of the woodwork that was here in 1772 when the vestry paid the builder John Hobbs £506, deducting £3 "for Bad work." At one time the interior of the church was stripped bare, but later, when church services were resumed in the building, the old hand-pegged box pews were found and restored to their proper places. The railing around the chancel is held together with pegs. The wall behind is paneled—partly with old pew doors— and a narrow band of the paneling rises twelve or more feet to a small canopy over the altar. Canopies are found over the pulpits of many pre-Revolutionary churches, and this one may once have served that purpose here. The original center section of box pews has been converted into row pews by taking off the pew doors and placing the benches directly on the floor, but the change is hardly noticeable. Luckily, the congregation never had enough money for serious remodeling or even a coat of paint in the days when colonial interiors were considered old-fashioned. Vesting rooms added recently on either side of the church under the balcony are unpainted pine in keeping with the rest of the interior.

At Spring Hill Church is the junction with Quantico Road (Md. 347). Turn right.

● This road leads into a low pine-wooded neck of land between the Wicomico River on the south and Nanticoke River and its creeks on the north and northwest. Along the upper reaches of the Wicomico, the land has been tilled for more than two hundred years, and a few old houses still dot the landscape. On lower ground, alternating with marshes, are the watermen's villages, situated close to the water's edge. Inland along the highway, old-fashioned farmhouses alternate with newer houses and barns of truck, dairy, and poultry farmers.

HEBRON (705 pop.), 0.8 m., is a railroad village dating from the 1890s. Several of the houses in **QUANTICO** (300 pop.), 5.2 m., indicate that this town may be nearly a century older than Hebron. Two attractive boxwood gardens can be seen from the road.

Tonging for oysters

At 6.9 m., Md. 347 comes to an end at the junction with Md. 349.
Go left 0.6 m. to the junction with Md. 352. Go right on Md. 352
to a crossroads at 4.6 m. A left turn here on to Green Hill Church
Road leads to **Green Hill Episcopal Church** (called St. Bartholomew's
in 1887), 1.0 m., built on the banks of the Wicomico River in 1733 and
virtually unchanged since then. The walls are laid in Flemish bond with
glazed headers on the entrance gable. The brick-floored, unpainted pine
interior, with its high box pews, high pulpit, and clerk's desk on the
south wall and hand-pegged rail around the altar, are all original. The
first church, built about 1698, stood nearby. In 1706, the assembly
ordered a town named Green Hill to be laid out here, but no trace of
it can be found today.

● Md. 352 bears right outside **WHITEHAVEN.** Continue straight ahead,
bearing left on Whitehaven Road to the ferry. Whitehaven was once an
active fishing and fishpacking center. A three-car ferry now provides
transportation across the Wicomico River.

● Go right on Md. 349 to **BIVALVE,** 10.2 m., and **NANTICOKE** (450
pop.), 11.9 m., typical of the oystering, fishing, and muskrat-trapping
villages that occupy the narrow strip of fastland along the southeast
shore of the mouth of the Nanticoke River where it flows into Tangier
Sound. Small boat marinas and other facilities for water sports also
provide an income for some of the area's residents.

SALISBURY is 58.6 m. at the junction with Md. 349.

● Go right on Md. 349. At 0.1 m. is the junction with Pemberton Drive. Go left on Pemberton Drive. At 1.9 m. a farm lane (L) leads past a frame house to **Pemberton** (open by request), a small gambrel-roofed brick house built in 1741 (date on gable) by the Handy family, founders of Handy's Landing, the forerunner of Salisbury (*see* Salisbury). Under a cove cornice—one of the few original cove cornices remaining on a Maryland building—the brick is laid in Flemish bond with glazed headers. Originally, the living room took up more than one-half the house, but a later partition now makes a central hall out of one end. The living room chimney wall and the wall opposite (now in the hall) are paneled, but the cupboard that once stood next to the fireplace has been removed. Paneled chimney pieces remain in the two rooms that occupy the other side of the house.

According to local tradition, a Civil War occupant of Pemberton, Capt. Allison Parsons, used the house as a rendezvous point for Confederate sympathizers, even though Union troops were stationed nearby in Salisbury. Parsons's practice of firing a cannon at the news of each Confederate victory brought him repeated warnings from Union commanders, who finally raided the house. The defiant captain, his brother Milton, and a loyal slave claimed that they had buried an arsenal of small arms on the property, although the cache was never found.

Another mile or so down the Wicomico River is **New Nithsdale** (private), an old brick house that has been extensively altered by later additions. In 1730, Capt. Levin Gale, the owner of the farm, was homeward bound in his vessel from Glasgow, Scotland. When he stopped in Bermuda for water and supplies, he found that the island was embroiled in a slave revolt. Several white residents prevailed upon Captain Gale to take them to Baltimore, and that night, a four-year-old boy and a six-year-old girl arrived with some baggage. After waiting as long as he dared for the children's parents, the captain finally hoisted sail and departed without them. The children knew their names only as John and Frances, but the name North appeared on a trunk and in some of their books, and other articles bore a family crest. Gale brought the children to this farm, returning to Bermuda the next year to find their parents, but without success. John was lost at sea when a young man. Frances married Capt. William Murray, a Scottish sea captain, who is believed to have named this place New Nithsdale after his native Nithsdale in Scotland.

12d. SALISBURY–OCEAN CITY; 29.6 m.
U.S. 50

From Salisbury to the Pocomoke River one passes through a vegetable-growing area; east of the river and its swamp, grain farming and lumbering and some fruit growing predominate. Along the whole route, broiler raising is also still important.

U.S. 50 continues east from Division Street, 0.0 m., in **SALISBURY** (*see* Salisbury Tour).

At 0.1 m. is the junction with U.S. 13 and Tour 20.

Near **PARSONSBURG**, 8.0 m., farmers who have dug wells over the last fifty years have occasionally tapped reservoirs of natural marsh gas, but hopes of finding gas and oil resources of any importance have been disappointed.

PITTSVILLE, 9.5 m. at the Main Street exit, is a center for gathering large quantities of holly and other Christmas evergreens brought in by farmers during November and December.

U.S. 50 crosses the narrow Pocomoke River at 15.2 m. From

its source in the **Great Pocomoke Swamp** of Delaware and Maryland, this deep and treacherous stream twists and turns for thirty-three miles through the pine, gum, white cedar, bald cypress, and holly of the ever-broadening Pocomoke River to its mouth in Pocomoke Sound. From early colonial days, the chief activity of those living near the swamp was making cypress shingles riven out by hand with heavy iron blades called frows and then drawknifed to the required thinness. Most old-time Pocomoke shingles were thirty inches or longer (modern shingles are eighteen inches in length) and were used throughout the region not only for roofs but also for siding. Many houses on the Lower Eastern Shore still have shingled walls that are more than a century old; the handshaved cypress shingle wears out in time—it becomes paper thin—but it never decays.

By 1860 most of the old-growth standing timber suitable for shingles was gone, but layers of windfalls of bald cypress and white cedar were found in the deep peat of the Great Pocomoke Swamp, which covers about fifty square miles chiefly north of the Delaware line. Rotting vegetation and sphagnum moss had perfectly preserved the trunks for hundreds of years. When winter rains flooded the swamp, men working with oxen scooped the muck off the logs, which then floated to the surface. Later the logs were dragged to the crosscut saws of nearby mills. The logs were cut into large cylinders that were then split into bolts and finally into shingle blocks from which an expert with a drawknife could rip out 500 long shingles a day. When he had 1,000, the workman could trade them at the store in Whaleysville for $2.50 worth of calico, sugar, tobacco, whiskey, or other commodities.

In 1930, after drainage and drought had lowered the water level of the swamp, a great fire—allegedly started by an exploding moonshine still—burned for several months through from five to ten feet of tinder-dry peat, destroying most of the remaining buried cypress and cedar. Foresters say it will take several thousand years for the swamp to regenerate itself. The fire of 1930 destroyed the Eastern Shore cypress shingle industry; redwood shingles from the West Coast now supply most of the nation's demand.

Bear, deer, and wildcats survived in the depths of the Great Pocomoke Swamp until the mid-nineteenth century, long after they were virtually extinct elsewhere on the peninsula. Locally forged bear traps are still kept by the sons and grandsons of men who in earlier days trekked perilous miles in the swamp in search of the prized fur-bearing animals.

At 16.1 m. is the junction with Md. 610.

● Turn left to Sheppards Crossing Road, 1.2 m. Turn left on Sheppards Crossing Road. At 1.3 m. bear left to a Methodist church for which P. Dale Wimbrow, a young black man from Whaleysville and an entertainer well known for his phonograph records and radio performances in the 1930s, once put on a benefit that by his own account outdid any of the performances that later brought him fame:

Those colored people plastered posters from Curtis's Chapel to Sugar Hill. Every telephone pole shouted in red letters that *"The Real Honorable Peter Dale Wimbrow Esquire"* would entertain at Whaleys-

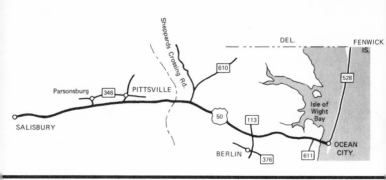

TOUR 12d

ville Schoolhouse—looked as if I was running for sheriff in a Democratic primary. On the night appointed they came from Parsonsburg in busses, from Jenkins Neck in carryalls, from the swamp in oxcarts and one-lung jalopies. They were jammed in the schoolhouse and standing about fifty deep outside. . . . So I uked—and New York never heard that much uking from me. I sang, danced, whistled, told stories, and did impersonations for a solid hour. When I had to sign off, limp and wet with sweat . . . up came the master of ceremonies, all worried, and whispered: "What we gonna do about all de folks dat couldn't git in?" So I told him to clear the hall and let in another helping. There was a second show from start to finish, and a third. The money they raised not only put the new wing on the church—it painted the whole works.

The 2½-story stuccoed brick wing of **Caleb's Discovery** (L) (private, but visible from the road), 20.1 m., has the handsome proportions of a house raised sometime between 1800 and 1825, the year its builder died; the small hall-and-parlor brick cottage adjacent may well be a hundred years older. The larger wing contains stairhall and living room and a handsome Federal mantel that is said to be a duplicate, made by the same joiner, of one made for Almodington in Somerset County (*see* Tour 21) and now in the Metropolitan Museum of Art in New York. To the right at the same point the former U.S. 213 leads into Berlin (*see* Tour 23).

At 21.4 m. is the junction with a paved road, formerly U.S. 113, which leads into the center of Berlin.

At 21.7 m. is the junction with new, dualized U.S. 113 and Tour 23.

At 27.6 m. is the junction with Md. 611, called the Stephen Decatur Highway, which was named for the naval hero of the Tripolitan War and the War of 1812. Decatur was born on a nearby farm on January 5, 1779. His father, a Revolutionary naval officer, had sent his wife there for safety during her confinement, and she returned to Philadelphia with young Stephen when he was four months old. In the war against the Tripolitan pirates of the Mediterranean in 1804, Decatur won fame for his dashing leadership in hand-to-hand combat with pirate crews, and during the War of 1812 his duels with the British fleet added to his luster, although he was ultimately defeated when greatly outnumbered. At a dinner in Norfolk in 1815, Decatur offered the toast that every school child knows: "Our country! In her intercourse with foreign nations may she always be in the right; but our country, right or wrong!" That same year he commanded the fleet sent to Algiers, where he was successful in bringing the Bey of Algiers to terms that ended the tribute being paid to the Tripolitans by American ships in the Mediterranean. In 1820, Decatur lost his life in a dual with Com. James Barron (*see* Tour 27). His body lies in St. Peter's churchyard, Philadelphia.

OCEAN CITY (5′ alt., 1,493 pop.), 29.6 m., Maryland's large seashore resort, has a population of over 150,000 on summer weekends. It is primarily a hotel, motel, apartment-house, and condominium resort built on a three-mile section of the coastal barrier reef, at this point hardly a quarter-mile wide, that protects Worcester County from the ocean. Beginning in the late nineteenth century, the U.S. Coast and Geodetic Survey experimented here with jetties, building up a sand bar at the surfline that has made this beach one of the finest and safest on the Atlantic seaboard. A boardwalk stretches two miles along the beach; its southern end is lined with amusement places and refreshment stands. Sunning, swimming, and fishing are the chief attractions at Ocean City, but there is also a semipublic golf course nearby on the mainland, and small sailboats can be rented.

Before the 1870s, Ocean City was nothing but a tract of sand originally patented under the name "The Ladies Resort to the Ocean." A group of promoters laid out a ten-acre development on the site in 1872, but few people visited the area until another group built the Atlantic Hotel, which had over 400 rooms, in 1875. By 1878 the railroad had reached the shores of Sinepuxent Bay, and the completion of a railroad bridge in 1881 enabled summer visitors to travel directly into the town. Every hotel had its hacks, whose drivers corralled as many guests as possible at the railroad depot. By the 1930s, however, the highways had so undermined the business of the railroad that the destruction of the bridge in the great hurricane of 1933 caused no great hardship. U.S. 50 from Washington, D.C., to Ocean City, now dual highway, today enables residents of the Baltimore-Washington metropolitan area to reach the ocean in less than three hours.

Storm tides from the Atlantic have always posed a threat to Maryland's coastal beaches. The *Maryland Gazette* of October 18, 1749, tells of tides that reached two miles inland in Worcester County. The great tides of March 6, 7, and 8, 1962, which devastated the whole East Coast, did their greatest damage on the section of shore line from Rehoboth Beach, Delaware, to Chincoteague, Virginia. Much of the sand from Ocean City's beach was washed into the town, the boardwalk was destroyed, and many of the ocean front buildings were ruined. Yet the resort was ready for visitors by May 30, the traditional opening day, with rebuilt waterfront motels and apartments and a new boardwalk. The surf line now reaches almost to the boardwalk at high tide, but the jetties built at the turn of the century have enabled ocean currents to replace the long gentle sandy slope for which Ocean City is famous.

The great storm of 1933 was a blessing for Ocean City, despite the enormous damage it caused, because it opened up the inlet which had been silted up since 1819. Since then, boats have protected anchorages on the Sinepuxent Bay side of the town yet enjoy immediate access to the ocean through the inlet. Improvements financed with state and federal funds have made the opening in the inlet permanent, so Ocean City has become a major center for deep-sea fishing. Channel bass (drum) and large tuna are frequently taken, with white marlin being a prime attraction from June through September. A famous fighting fish, the marlin is sought for the sport of landing it rather than for eating, and most of those caught are tagged and returned to the water to fight another day. For marlin fishing, cruisers are equipped with tall, flexible outrigger poles fastened upright amidship; from the fisherman's rod the heavy line goes to the top of an outrigger for trolling outside the boat's wake. When a marlin strikes the bait—usually squid—with its long, sharp bill, the line is knocked from the outrigger. For an instant, the fish leaps into the air, then dives deep under the water running with the line. The angler uses both arms and nearly every muscle in his body to play the fish, which must be allowed to wear itself out before it is brought close enough to the boat to be hoisted aboard by its bill. Such battles last from twenty minutes to two hours or more. Any craft on which a fisherman has caught and landed a marlin flies a blue flag coming home, even though the fish itself may have been released. A white marlin tournament is sponsored by Ocean City early each September.

Less expensive, yet still exciting, fishing can be had from "head boats." These leave the docks each day during the summer months for the "wrecks," where porgy and sea bass are to be found. In addition surf fishermen catch flounder and rock, and the quiet Sinepuxent Bay provides excellent angling for whitefish for those who enjoy the relaxation of a rowboat or beach chair.

The U.S. Coast Guard Station here, established on August 4, 1790, is one of the oldest in the United States.

● At Ocean City, go left on Md. 528, the Ocean Highway, which leads up the coastal barrier reef into Delaware. At the **Delaware Line,** approximately 10.0 m., is the **Fenwick Island Lighthouse**—no longer in use—and at its foot is the **First Maryland-Delaware Boundary Marker,** erected in 1751 to mark the survey made by John Watson and William Parsons for Pennsylvania (which claimed the territory that is now Delaware) and by John Emory and Thomas Jones for Maryland. The placing of this stone and the running of the line due west from it across the peninsula ended the first stage in the settlement of the conflict between the Calverts and the Penns over the boundaries of their respective colonies. The conflict began in 1682 when William Penn bought the lands on the western shore of the Delaware River from the Duke of York. In 1685, the Privy Council established Cape Henlopen as the southern boundary of Pennsylvania, but the map used by the council, published by Nicholas Visscher in 1651, showed the cape as being located on what is now known as Fenwick Island. As early as 1670, Augustine Herman, in a map drawn on commission for Lord Baltimore, placed Cape Henlopen at its present location fifteen miles north of Fenwick Island. But as late as 1732, when both parties signed a preliminary agreement for surveying the boundary between the two colonies, the reference map used still placed Cape Henlopen on Fenwick Island. In 1750, the English Court of Chancery settled the dispute in favor of the Penns; the fifth Lord Baltimore died, however, before any but the southernmost boundary had been surveyed. Com-

Surf fishing in the Atlantic

pletion of the survey was delayed until Frederick, sixth Lord Baltimore, came of age, finally ending with the famous survey by Jeremiah Dixon and Charles Mason (1763–68) (*see* Tour 12c, Mason-Dixon Middlestone).

The boundary stone at Fenwick Island is not a Mason-Dixon marker; it records the work of Watson and his colleagues, who, in December of 1750, began the survey that Mason and Dixon finished. Watson's diary tells of December storm tides that nearly drowned the first surveyors and of a fire from which they barely escaped with their lives and in which one of them lost his shoes—a catastrophe in that time and weather. After spending twenty-two midwinter days surveying about six miles, the surveyors found the icy swamps impassable, which forced them to postpone the rest of the work until late April, 1751. Commissioners appointed by the two proprietors then met with the surveyors and accepted the line they had run. This stone is the first boundary marker on the line. On the north side are carved the arms of the Penns; on the south, the arms of the Calverts. In 1952, the State of Delaware had the badly weathered stone recut.

JUNCTION OF MD. 292 AND U.S. 213–FAIRLEE–EASTERN NECK ISLAND; 28.9 m.
Md. 292, 298, 20, 21, and 445

This route, never far from the broad Chesapeake, which can be glimpsed now and then, passes through fertile land devoted to general farming and dairying. Some large estates maintain prize-winning herds of Aberdeen Angus beef cattle. In the summer, people from Baltimore make regular excursions to Betterton for swimming and to Rock Hall for sport fishing, and in winter sportsmen from all over the East come to shoot ducks and geese that arrive by the hundreds of thousands to feed and rest in the fields and creeks. An avid hunter will shiver in a duck blind located in a cornfield or in a cove off the shores in an effort to capture his prize. Oyster dredging and tonging, com-

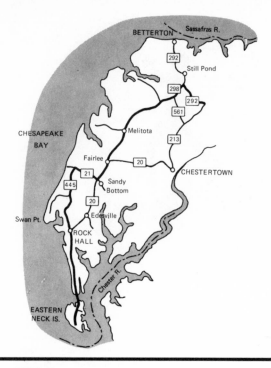

TOUR 13

mercial fishing, and fishpacking are the main commercial activities in the area.

Md. 292 branches west from a junction with Md. 213 (*see* Tour 12a), 0.0 m., at a point 1.5 m. south of Kennedyville. Turn left to **Friendship Manor Farms,** formerly Runnymede (R) (private, but visible from the road), 0.6 m. This 2½-story brick house with a frame wing is believed to have been built shortly after 1700. At 1.2 m. **Hedgewood Farm,** or **Valentine Farm** (L) (private), is visible across the fields. This 2½-story brick house, which stands on land patented to James Hebourne in 1683, is believed to have been built sometime after 1713 by James Corse, Quaker son of Col. Henry de Courcy (*see* Tour 24, My Lord's Gift, and 12b, Blakeford) and a founder in 1696 of the Cecil Friends Meeting.

One of the well-known houses of the area is **Shepherd's Delight** (L) (private, but visible from the road), 1.7 m., a narrow 1½-story frame brick-nogged house with a steep roof that sweeps down over porches on each side. The living room features a mantel carved by hand with nineteen different-sized auger bits and a chair rail with 5,000 handmade holes. Handsome boxwood behind the house once enclosed a garden. This was the home of Rev. Sewell S. Hepburn, one-time pastor of *I. U. Church* and grandfather of the actress, Katharine Hepburn.

At 2.9 m. is the junction with Md. 298, which to the left becomes the main route.

● Go right on Md. 298 to **Lamb's Meadows** (R) (private, but visible from the road), 0.9 m., a simple brick farmhouse built in 1733 by a

Quaker, Pearce Lamb, on land patented to him in 1694. The main house, which is covered by a steep gambrel roof, has beautiful paneling on the fireplace walls of both the living and dining rooms. The date 1733 is written in glazed headers in the gable of the lower kitchen wing.

● Go straight ahead on Md. 292 to **STILL POND,** 0.9 m. For generations, the inhabitants of this crossroads town have believed it was named for a neighboring pond, now mostly a marsh, that was supposed to be bottomless and haunted by the ghost of an Indian chief. However, a more likely derivation for the town's name is the nearby Still Pond Creek, which was labeled Steel Pone Creek on Augustine Herman's map of 1673 and mentioned as such in many seventeenth-century records.

Md. 292 ends at **BETTERTON,** 3.1 m., at one time a small Edwardian summer resort. The road descends a steep hill, past mansard-roofed houses and sprawling white-painted residences, to the beach and pier.

The main route, Md. 298, turns left. Just beyond the junction with Md. 561 (Hassengers Corner Road), 4.7 m., is the **Site of the Cecil Meeting House,** built by Friends in 1696, and the location of a weekly and monthly meeting until 1900.

At 5.8 m. is the junction with an improved road.

● Go right to **Drayton Manor** (open by appointment: Rev. Walter H. Stone), 3.5 m., an original manor of 1,200 acres granted to Charles James in 1677. The handsome brick house was built from an eighteenth-century plan and contains beautiful paneling from an old Rhode Island house. Aberdeen Angus cattle were once raised here, and orchards such as those that made Kent County famous were maintained. An anonymous buyer gave the house to the United Methodist Church for use as a Retreat Center.

From the gardens, one can look down the bluff to **Rocky Point,** which is located at the mouth of Still Pond Creek. In 1849, Rocky Point was the site of a prize fight in which Tom Hyer defeated Yankee Sullivan for a purse of $10,000. The fight was originally scheduled to be held on Poole's Island off Harford County, but the State of Maryland dispatched militia via steamboat to disperse principals and spectators. The steamboat went aground, however, and Sullivan, Hyer, and their most avid fans went by boat to Rocky Point, where Hyer thrashed his opponent so severely that he had to be sent to the hospital.

Old **I. U. Church** (R), 6.1 m., may have received the name because of initials found on a large boundary stone nearby. The first church was built about 1768 to serve Chester Parish, which was erected in 1765. In 1809, the chapel of ease at Chestertown (*see* Tour 12a, Emmanuel Church) replaced I. U. Church as the parish church, and soon thereafter the building decayed. The present structure was consecrated in 1860, being designated the parish church for the newly established I. U. Parish in 1863.

At 6.5 m. is the junction with Md. 297, and at 10.2 m., in **MELITOTA,** is the junction with the paved Handy Point Road.

● Go right on this 1.9 m. to the entrance (L) of **Great Oak** (members and guests only), a large estate that has been converted into a marina and country club with a beautiful Bay waterfront. The original Great Oak Manor was granted to John Van Heck in 1673. The British burned the building and crops of Richard Frisby's farm on this property in August, 1814, shortly before the Battle of Caulk's Field (*see below*).

Carvill Hall, once called Little Fairlee, which stands on Fairlee Creek on the property, was built in the late seventeenth or early eighteenth century.

Manor Shore (private), 3.1 m., formerly Handy Point, is a well-known Kent County house.

In **FAIRLEE**, 13.9 m., is the junction with Md. 20, which becomes the main route.

To the left, Md. 20 is a fast route to Chestertown. At 6.0 m. in Chestertown there is a junction with Md. 213 and Tour 12a.

At 15.2 m. is the junction with Md. 21 (R), which now becomes the main route.

● Go left on Sandy Bottom Road to **St. Paul's Protestant Episcopal Church** (L), 0.9 m. This beautiful little brick church sits among great oaks and sycamores that were standing when the building opened in 1713. The building is believed to be the oldest Episcopal church in Maryland that has been used continuously as a place of worship. Under a steep gable roof, with kicked eaves, the brick walls are laid in Flemish bond and pierced by great roundheaded windows, and at the rear of the church is an apse. Thirty-four pews were constructed in 1714 and rented for a stipulated number of pounds of tobacco; an entire pew could be bought for 1,000 pounds of tobacco. A few yards away stands the vestry house, a small 1½-story brick building with the date 1766 in one gable. In the graveyard is the tomb of Tallulah Bankhead, a famous actress.

Just beyond the church the road forks, and a right turn leads to the **Remington Farms** (L) (open Oct.–Mar. during daylight hours), 1.1 m. In 1957, the Remington Arms Corporation took possession of the game sanctuary established here by Glenn L. Martin. Remington established a demonstration program for raising and harvesting field crops in such a way as to provide food and cover for game, especially quail, doves, geese, and ducks. On the property is **Broadnox** (private), a two-wing, 1½-story brick house, now restored, believed to have been built between 1704 and 1708 by Robert Dunn on land surveyed in 1659 for Thomas Broadnox. Broadnox, a notoriously cruel master, died while being tried for beating one of his servants to death. He was one of only three people in all of Maryland's history known to have been subjected to the so-called blood test, the ancient English procedure whereby the suspect was forced to put his hand upon the slain person, who was supposed to bleed if touched by the real murderer. Broadnox thrust his thumb into the corpse to show "how the flesh did dent," but no blood appeared.

At 1.7 m. is the junction with Md. 20, which again becomes the main side route (L). The road passes the **Rees Corner House** (private), 2.2 m., a handsome brick house built about 1800, and then makes a junction at the crossroads of **EDESVILLE**, 3.6 m., with the Edesville-Piney Neck Road (L). At 1.0 m. on this road is the entrance (L) to **Bungay** (private, but visible from the road), a 2½-story brick house that may have been built by Charles and Phoebe Hynson. On a brick in the gable appears "HCP 1757." Md. 20 continues to *Rock Hall*, 6.9 m., and a junction with Md. 445.

The main route continues on Md. 21. On Md. 21, beyond the junction with Md. 20, is the junction with the graveled Caulk's Field Road (R).

● To the right, a granite monument marks **Caulk's Battlefield**, scene of a skirmish between English and American forces on August 31, 1814. Sir Peter Parker, commander of the ship *Menelaus*, landed with a force of 260 men to engage in what he termed a "frolic with the Yankees." The landing was an attempt to prevent Eastern Shore militia from aiding the beseiged troops at Baltimore. Twice the British attacked the American force. After Parker died from a thigh wound his troops retired, not knowing that the Americans were out of ammunition. British losses were fourteen killed and twenty-eight wounded; Ameri-

Decoys resting beside the Bay

can casualties totaled only three wounded. For many decades the battle was referred to as "Marse Peter Parker's War."

From the marker there is a view of **Caulk's Field House.** Like many other old houses of Kent County, Caulk's Field House is two stories high under a steep gable roof, with a 1½-story wing with dormers that slope from the ridge pole. On the gable of the house in glazed headers is written the date 1743.

The tour turns left on Md. 445 at 17.0 m. and at 18.9 m. is the entrance to **Hinchingham** (open by appointment: Mr. Elwood McCann), a handsome brick house of two and one-half stories and a well-preserved interior with the date 1774 written in glazed headers on the gable. The lower 1½-story wing with dormers may have been built before 1700. The house stands on a grant of 2,000 acres made to Thomas Hynson in 1659.

The junction with Swan Creek Road and Reeses Corner Road is at 19.6 m.

● Go right on Swan Creek Road to **Hinchingham Farmhouse** (L) (private), 0.3 m., a three-part frame telescope dwelling. The earliest part of the structure, a 1½-story wing made of squared logs covered with weatherboarding, may have been standing when Michael Miller bought the farm in 1675, but recent study indicates that this is unlikely. Miller was at various times a county justice, the high sheriff, a delegate to the Maryland General Assembly, and one of the original vestrymen of St. Paul's Parish, to which he donated the land for the church (*see below*). The largest and most recent wing, two and one-half stories high, is believed to date from about 1725.

Rosedale (R) (private), 20.9 m., is another 2½-story structure of handsome proportions with a 1½-story wing. The house is

believed to have been built about 1730 by Ralph and Elizabeth
Miller Page.

At 21.3 m. is a junction with Humphreys Point Road.

● Go right on this to **William's Venture,** 0.5 m., originally a 1½-story
brick house that was raised to two stories before the close of the
eighteenth century; the lower frame wing is modern. In the old house,
the paneled fireplace wall, recessed paneled windows, and mahogany
staircase are of interest. Open by appointment: Ms. Sylvia Bothe, Rock
Hall.

ROCK HALL, 22.1 m., on the shore of Chesapeake Bay, offers
excellent facilities for fishing and is a leading center for processing fish, crabs, and oysters. Some say the name was originally
Rock Haul because of the large hauls of rockfish taken here.
The historic marker on the site, however, states that the town
was named for Rock Hall Mansion, which stood at the landing
a mile west of the town. Used as a landing as early as 1707,
Rock Hall was the Eastern Shore terminus of a post road from
the North for many years, and thus the point of departure for
passengers for Annapolis and the South. George Washington
crossed here many times, and Lt. Col. Tench Tilghman crossed
on the Rock Hall Ferry in October, 1781, as he was taking the
news of Cornwallis's surrender at Yorktown to the Continental
Congress sitting at Philadelphia. In 1790 Thomas Shippen of
Virginia wrote about eating "delicious crabs" here in the company of Jefferson and Madison while awaiting the ferryboat.

At Rock Hall is the junction with Md. 20.

By Gray's Inn Creek along Md. 445 is the **Site of New Yarmouth** (L), a seventeenth-century settlement. In 1674, Charles
Calvert ordered the removal of court sessions from *Eastern
Neck Island* to the mainland, and by 1679 the first Kent County
courthouse had been built at New Yarmouth. Until 1696, when
the court moved to New Town (now Chestertown), New Yarmouth was a town of some importance, but once the county
seat was moved the town rapidly declined.

Md. 445 continues down the peninsula created by Gray's Inn
Creek, the Chester River, and the Bay. The peninsula is one of
the earliest areas of settlement on the Eastern Shore.

Trumpington (R) (private), 28.0 m., is a 2½-story brick house
built on the shores of the Bay in 1723 by Thomas Smythe, a
member of the council and one of the important figures of early-
eighteenth-century Maryland. The interior of the house retains its
beautiful old woodwork.

A bridge, 28.9 m., crosses to **Eastern Neck Island,** which now
serves as a National Wildlife Refuge.

Continue down the road, through the game refuge, to the
road's end at the **Site of Wickliffe.** Built on a large grant made
jointly to Joseph Wickes and Thomas Hynson in 1659, Wickliffe
was the home of the Wickes family for many generations. In
the Wickes house that once stood here the Kent County Court
met sometime before 1674. Lambert Wickes, commander of the
American vessel *Reprisal,* which carried Benjamin Franklin to
France, was born here. After capturing several British merchant
ships, Wickes went down with his vessel in a storm off Newfoundland in 1777. In the summer of 1975, the site was commemorated as the birthplace of Lambert Wickes.

14

JUNCTION OF MD. 404 AND U.S. 50–DENTON–DELAWARE LINE; 22.6 m.
Md. 404

Maryland Route 404 is a link in the most direct route between the metropolitan areas of the Western Shore and the Delaware ocean beaches. Now that the Chesapeake Bay bridges have replaced the Bay ferries, thousands of city dwellers make the round trip to the Delaware and Maryland ocean beaches each weekend. The county is tabletop flat, and the road runs straight for seemingly endless miles through farmlands planted in wheat, corn, soybeans, and hay. Dairying and the production of meat animals, broilers, and vegetables are important major industries in this area.

After the Bay Bridge, Md. 404 leaves U.S. 50 (L), 0.0 m. At 6.2 m. the road crosses Tuckahoe Creek, a branch of the Choptank River, and at 7.0 m. is the junction with Md. 480 (L) and Ridgely Road (R).

● Turn right on Ridgely Road. At 0.3 m. on Ridgely Road is a junction with Alternate 404. Turn right to **HILLSBORO,** 0.5 m., an old settlement on the banks of navigable Tuckahoe Creek. A chapel of ease stood across the creek as early as 1694 and there was a bridge across the creek in the mid-eighteenth century. The sand-colored brick house near the present bridge is believed to have been built just after the Revolution by a Scottish merchant, Francis Sellers, and at that time there was also a tobacco warehouse and a tavern. During steamboat days, steamers unloaded four miles south of Hillsboro, but smaller vessels carried freight to the town wharf. In 1797 local citizens founded Hillsboro Academy, which offered a classical education for over thirty years; with the advent of public schools it lost pupils and was absorbed into the county school system in 1878.

From Hillsboro, Tuckahoe Road runs left (south) into Tuckahoe Neck, an area of good farmland between Tuckahoe Creek and the Choptank River. **Daffin House** (private, but visible from the road), 3.0 m., is a handsome brick house, long and narrow, and decorated with Victorian-Gothic icing trim that was retained in the restoration. Charles Daffin is believed to have begun the house in 1774 and to have finished it just after the Revolution. Andrew Jackson, while visiting here, first met Charles Dickinson, Rebecca Daffin's brother. In 1806 Jackson and Dickinson quarreled over payment of a racing bet and met in a duel on the banks of the Red River in Kentucky. Jackson allowed Dickinson, known as an excellent shot, to fire first; then, ignoring his own wound, he took deliberate aim and killed Dickinson. Even in the rough society of the frontier Jackson's act seemed brutal, and it clouded his reputation for some years.

At 9.3 m. along Md. 404 is the junction with Md. 312.

● Go left to **RIDGELY** (822 pop.), 2.0 m. Md. 312 becomes the main street. Ridgely is a forwarding point for farm produce and a center for processing canned and frozen vegetables. Ridgely was laid out in 1867 in what was then an isolated section of Caroline County as a land speculation of the Maryland Baltimore Land Association and Rev. Greenbury W. Ridgely, who owned several thousand acres of land in the area. The promoters persuaded the Maryland and Delaware Railway to extend its line from *Greensboro,* about five miles away, to Ridgely,

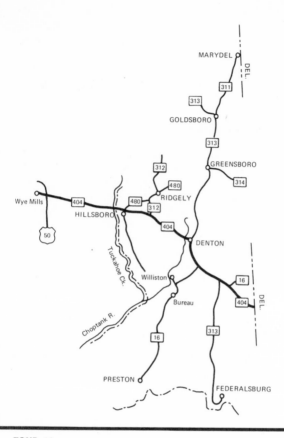

TOUR 14

agreeing to supply the ties for the road; but by the time the track was finished in 1868, the land company had gone bankrupt. Eventually, as the surrounding farmland became more heavily populated, the town developed along the lines of the original plan—hence the broad Main Street. After 1890 the railroad brought industries. Today, a vegetable-processing plant, a feed company, a shirt factory, a beverage company, and a fishery employ a large number of people.

At 5.1 m. on Md. 312, the private road to **Cedarhurst** (private) turns off to the right. Just beyond, there is a good view of this late-eighteenth-century house.

● At 5.5 m. on Md. 312 are the gates to **Oak Lawn** (L) (private), a brick house built in 1783 (date on brick) by Benjamin Sylvester and attractive in neglect. The 2½-story main house is connected to a smaller two-story kitchen wing at the back by a brick hyphen, one side of which is a fine arcade of four arches. Oak Lawn was the home of Rev. Greenbury W. Ridgely, who, before he became a clergyman, was for a short while a law partner of Henry Clay in Lexington, Kentucky.

DENTON (1,561 pop.), 13.2 m. at the **Caroline County Courthouse,** was known as Pig Point in 1773, when the General Assembly named it the seat of the newly established county and renamed it Edentown after Gov. Robert Eden. The Revolution postponed construction of a courthouse, and afterwards there was considerable pressure to put the county seat at what is now

Greensboro, farther up the Choptank River. The issue was finally settled in favor of Pig Point by local referendum in 1790. Denton was adopted as the official name of the town at that time. The courthouse that was finished in 1797, a handsome Georgian structure possibly built from plans made by William Buckland (see Annapolis Tour), was replaced in 1895 by the present late-Victorian building (extensively enlarged in the past few years). Surrounded by trees, this stands, like its predecessor, on the public square shown in a map of 1807. The map pictures a community of forty-nine buildings including "storehouses," a smithy, a cartwright shop, a linenwheel shop, a currying shop, "a tanners house and seler," and a saddler's shop. There was a schoolhouse lot on the public square, but no schoolhouse. Little remains of this early Denton, partly because of a fire in 1863 that was started when Union soldiers celebrated the fourth of July with skyrockets. The two-masted schooner drawn on the map was probably typical of the craft that traded on the upper Choptank at that time, bringing this inland county into contact with ports on the Bay. After 1850 steamboats came as far as Denton, but today railroads and trucks have supplanted ships. However, tankers still come up the river to Denton.

Although the railroads brought small industries to many communities in Caroline County after the Civil War, the county seat has always retained the flavor of a rural trading center. However, companies that manufacture electric heating elements, sheet metal, signs, and plastic products employ about 215 people here today.

At 13.6 m. is the junction with Md. 313.

● Go left on Md. 313 to a junction with Md. 314 at 6.8 m. in **GREENS-BORO** (1,173 pop.), first laid out in 1732. It was known as Bridgetown in Revolutionary times when it was competing against Pig Point for the county courthouse, but a legislative act changed the name in 1791. In the days of the sailing packet, Greensboro was a port, and even today oil and fertilizer barges occasionally make their way here. Greensboro is typical of the inland towns on the Shore that owe their chief development to the railroads of the post–Civil War era and are the centers for small industries. A sausage and scrapple plant, a garment factory, and a sporting goods factory employ about 100 people.

GOLDSBORO (231 pop.), 11.2 m. at the junction with Md. 311, once a crossroads called Oldtown, became a canning center when the railroad arrived in 1867. In 1870 it was renamed for Dr. G. W. Goldsborough, a large landowner in the community. Tomatoes, once a huge crop in this section of Maryland, are disappearing and with them the crossroads canneries, but a sizable plant founded in the 1870s still flourishes here.

The route turns right on Md. 311. **Castle Hall** (L) (private, but visible from the road), 12.3 m., is a four-wing brick telescope house, painted white, that was finished in 1781 by Thomas Hardcastle, a county justice. On the approach front of the main wing, the brick is laid in all-header bond under a handsome modillioned cornice decorated with wall-of-Troy trim; the effect is somewhat marred by large dormer windows of a later period.

Md. 311 continues to **MARYDEL**, 17.3 m., named for its geographical position on the Maryland-Delaware line. This village, established in the 1850s, was the scene on January 3, 1877, of a duel—by then illegal —between James Gordon Bennett, owner of the *New York Herald,* and Frederick May, a well-known explorer. The two men had quarreled in New York City over May's broken engagement to Bennett's sister. Both men fired wildly, and neither was hit. Afterwards Bennett exiled himself to Paris.

Back on Md. 404, **Plaindealing** (R) (private), 14.2 m., is a brick house, now an antique shop, that was built as a "pore, or alms House" for the county in 1790. In 1823, it was purchased by James Dukes, who converted it into a private dwelling.

At 16.3 m. is the junction with Md. 16.

● Go right on Md. 16 to a junction with Williston Road (R) at 2.3 m. Go right on this to **Williston,** 0.8 m., formerly known as Potter's Landing after the first settler here, a Rhode Island sea captain named Zabdiel Potter. In the mid-eighteenth century, Captain Potter built the small log wing of the **Potter Mansion** (private), which stands by the Choptank River, and he made his landing a place of commercial importance. At the end of the road, by the water, there is an excellent view of the handsome brick house the captain's grandson Gen. William Potter built about 1808. The village is now named for Col. Arthur John Willis, who bought the mansion in 1849 and maintained a line of sailing packets that traded to Baltimore. As late as 1900 two steamboats a day stopped here, but the railroads put the steamers out of business, and the fortunes of Williston declined.

● At 2.4 m. on Md. 16 is **Williston Mill Lake**—a lake created in part by a mill dam that Gen. William Potter enlarged. A mill was in operation here by 1778, and General Potter attempted to make a ship channel to the mill race, but due to the cost the project was left unfinished and its sponsor in financial difficulty.

At 3.4 m. on Md. 16 is the crossroads still marked on the maps as **Bureau,** though no building stands here now. In the field on the southwest corner are the foundations of a school built by the Freedmen's Bureau before 1870 as part of a federal government program for the care and education of emancipated slaves. It is said that the school was erected here because a Choptank River boat captain unloaded the lumber at a nearby wharf instead of at Denton, as intended. The reason may also have been proximity to Potter's Landing, where Col. A. J. Willis (*see above*) had raised four Union companies in an area where Confederate sympathies were dominant.

The road to the right at Bureau leads to **Two Johns** (private), a landing on the Choptank where once stood a large Victorian mansion owned in the 1880s by John Stewart Crossey and John Hart, noted comedians of the period. The two Johns each weighed over 300 pounds, and one of their later shows was called *The Fat Men's Club.* This landing became a regular stop for the Baltimore-Denton steamers, and stage folk came for gay holidays. Neighboring farm families were fascinated but reserved.

Md. 16 continues through farmlands to Preston and a junction with Md. 331 and Tour 18, 11.8 m.

At 18.5 m. Md. 313 branches right of Md. 404—Md. 16.

Md. 313 travels the flatlands off Caroline County to Federalsburg (*see* Tour 18), 10.5 m. at the junction with Md. 307. This is a vegetable-growing area. Acreage in tomatoes has been greatly reduced since World War II, but other vegetables are still important. Some farmers manage two crops a season, starting with early tomatoes or peas and finishing with beans.

Md. 16 branches left off Md. 404 at 19.4 m.

At 22.6 m. Md. 404 crosses the **Delaware Line.**

Harvesting corn

15

JUNCTION OF MD. 662 AND U.S. 50–TUNIS MILLS–JUNCTION OF MD. 370 AND 33; 11.8 m.
Md. 662 and 370 and unmarked roads

This route follows country roads that twist among the flat fields and woodlands of Miles River Neck, never more than a mile from tidewater. The motorist catches frequent glimpses of the inlets that cut back into the level country, forming an intricate pattern of rivers and coves. At times a mast or a sail can be seen, apparently gliding across fields as a boat travels a hidden creek. As elsewhere in Talbot County, the most notable houses in the area are more easily approached by water than by land. Few of them are visible from the county roads, which pass by scrub forest and fields and tumbledown shacks that give little indication of the elegant old houses that sit by the water not far away. This is the land of the Lloyds and the Tilghmans, whose families provided many of Maryland's colonial and Revolutionary statesmen.

Sharp Road branches west from Md. 662 at 0.5 m. south of **LONGWOODS** and 1.8 m. south of the junction with U.S. 50. Follow the macadam road; at 2.1 m. is a junction. Bear left, continuing on Sharp Road.

At 3.4 m. the road forks.

Turn left at the fork on Little Park Road. At about 3.9 m. is the junction with Todds Corner Road. Turn right. At the next junction bear left on Gross Coate Road.

TOUR 15

● **Gross' Coate** (private) stands on a tract granted to Roger Gross in 1658. The land was acquired by the Tilghmans in the eighteenth century, and the family has owned it ever since. The large brick house, its main section a full three stories high under a low hip roof, stands among towering old trees. The oldest section of the house was built in the mid-eighteenth century, and each succeeding generation has made additions to it. In 1790, Charles Willson Peale visited here and painted three portraits, which hung in the house until the twentieth century. The portrait of Mary Tilghman he painted at that time is considered one of his finest. Peale was then a forty-nine-year-old widower in search of a new mother for his six young children. He fell in love with Mary, but her family expected her to marry a member of her own class, and she finally refused him.

The main route, which is Todds Corner Road, bears left at 3.9 m. and right at 4.2 m. and right again at 5.3 m.

At 6.4 m. is the junction with Bruffs Island Road, an improved road.

● Go right (straight ahead) to the iron gates of **Wye House** (R) (private), 1.5 m., which has belonged to the Lloyd family since the first Col. Edward Lloyd received a grant of thousands of acres in the area in 1658. Beyond the entrance gates, a formal avenue lined with oaks and beeches leads to the Palladian portico of the mansion three-quarters of a mile away. The two balanced lower wings of the five-part frame house form an imposing facade rising from the smooth turf. The pedimented gable of the main building is repeated on the wings, which were originally separate structures that were later connected to the main block by hyphens. Paneled overmantels extend to the high ceilings in all the first floor rooms, and the woodwork throughout is beautifully executed. The great windows of the drawing room and dining room create an effect of spaciousness and dignity ordinarily found only in rooms of much larger size.

The fourth Edward Lloyd built Wye House sometime between 1770, when he inherited the plantation, and 1792, when two of his children scratched their initials and the date on a window pane. The house was probably finished about 1784, when some of the present furnishings were ordered from England. Many of the other furnishings came from an earlier Wye House, including the grandfather clock in the hall, which was made by a clockmaker who died in 1725.

The porch across the back of Wye House faces a bowling green, beyond which is the **Orangery.** This stucco-covered brick building, decidedly French Renaissance in style, was probably erected by Edward Lloyd IV. The two-story, hip-roofed central portion of the Orangery features piers of rusticated stonework dividing the floor-length windows at the first story, and the stone quoins running up to the cornice at the corners give the structure a monumental effect. The one-story flanking hip-roofed wings, raised just one step above grade, have large arched windows that give the appearance of glass-enclosed arcades. A central heating system once augmented the sun's heat, and the orange and lemon trees that were grown here were planted in square tubs identical in design to those at Versailles.

Extensive boxwood gardens flank both sides of the Orangery. The boxwood is laid out on the axis of the first Wye House mansion, which stood just to the east of the Orangery. The small 1½-story brick structure, probably built before 1700, is believed to be the north dependency of the earlier house.

Through an arched gate in a high brick wall behind the Orangery is the family graveyard, one of the oldest in America. Ten generations of Lloyds are buried here, including the first American-born Edward Lloyd, who died in 1696. From 1664 to 1907, seven successive Edward Lloyds owned Wye House; all seven served in the provincial or state legislature and all seven are buried here. Edward II (1670–1718) served as acting governor of Maryland from 1709 to 1714. Edward IV (1744–96) was a member of the first Council of Safety, a delegate to the Continental Congress, and from 1781 until his death, a member of the Maryland Senate. In 1790, Edward IV owned 305 slaves, 225 more than the second-largest slaveholder in Talbot County. Frederick Douglass (1817–95), who was owned by an employee of the Lloyds, spent his childhood at Wye House. In his book *My Bondage and My Freedom* (New York, 1855), Douglass provides a graphic picture of slave life on Edward Lloyd V's (1779–1834) plantation. Edward V was governor of Maryland in 1809 and a U.S. senator from 1819 to 1826. The Confederate admiral Franklin Buchanan (*see below,* The Rest), son-in-law of Edward V, is buried at the left of the entrance gate to the cemetery. Nearby is the grave of Edward V's grandson, Confederate general Charles S. Winder. The earliest stone in the cemetery marks the grave of Capt. James Strong (1684), the most recent having been placed here in the 1960s.

At 2.3 m. on Bruffs Island Road is the entrance to **Bruffs Island** (private). Inside the gate, where the road reaches the shore, is the **Site of Doncaster,** a town laid out in 1684, again in 1707, and finally abandoned. A plat of 1695 shows several houses in Doncaster, as well as a Roman Catholic "chapple" built by Henrietta Maria Lloyd (1647–97), daughter-in-law of the first Lloyd and perhaps the best known of all the Lloyds today. Henrietta Maria was supposedly a namesake and godchild of Queen Henrietta Maria, wife of Charles I. Because of her exceptional character and charm, she shares the honor, along with Margaret Brent (*see* Tour 29), of being among the best-known women of early Maryland.

The main route turns left from the junction at 6.4 m. to the tiny settlement of **COPPERVILLE,** 7.2 m.

At 7.6 m. is the junction with two graveled roads and a macadam road (L) that becomes the main route.

● Go straight on the graveled road, which ends at the entrance to **Fairview** (private), 1.5 m. The large brick house is said to have been built in 1729; in the early nineteenth century, the two-story portico and Federal-style doorway with fanlight and sidelights were added and much of the delicate interior woodwork was installed. The grounds are planted with a great variety of beautiful trees, including a thirty-eight-year-old Chinaberry, an Irish yew, and a Nordman fir. The garden is famous for the great variety of shrubs it contains as well as for its large collection of camellias.

● Returning to the junction, go right to another road, 0.5 m.; to the right on this is **Hope House** (private), said to have been built about 1748. The dwelling is one of the most unusual five-part brick houses in Maryland. The hyphens connecting the main house with the wings have serpentine rooflines that sweep down in a wavelike curve, a design unique in Maryland. Only the 2½-story gable-roofed central portion of the house is original, because the wings and hyphens were rebuilt between 1906 and 1910. The line of the cornice was carefully restored, however, although the roofs themselves were slightly raised. The property belonged to the Lloyd and Tilghman families for more than 200 years.

The narrow head of **Leeds Creek,** 7.9 m., is crossed on a wooden bridge, from which can be seen the remnants of the wharf from which steamers once set out for Baltimore.

TUNIS MILLS, 8.1 m., was once a shipping center and post office for farmers.

At 8.3 m. is the junction with Marengo-Gregory Road.

● Turn right. Along this road is the **Site of Marengo,** for generations the home of the Gibson family (*see* Tour 17). Fayette Gibson, the last of his name to live here, was, according to local historians, the inventor of the first reaper. His machine was exhibited at the Easton Fairgrounds in 1833, where it was examined by Obed Hussey, whose own reaper, patented in December of that year, is generally considered the earlier. Gibson's machine and his models were destroyed when the Marengo house burned in 1847.

The main route continues straight to an intersection at 9.5 m. in Unionville. Turn right. Continue straight to Md. 370. On Md. 370, before the bridge which crosses the Miles River, is **The Anchorage** (R) (private), 10.7 m., a five-part frame house that incorporates in its central section a house built in the mid-eighteenth century, probably by Richard Bruff. In the 1830s, Edward Lloyd V gave the property to his daughter Sarah and her husband, Lt. Charles Lowndes (d. 1885). The Lowndeses added the two-story portico and the hyphens and wings, converting the house into the present-day antebellum mansion. Lowndes retired from the navy just after the Civil War began, but because of his Union sympathies he was awarded the rank of commodore on the retired list in 1862.

From The Anchorage, Sarah Lloyd Lowndes, wife of the Union commodore, could look across the Miles River to **The Rest** (private), home of her sister Ann Catherine, wife of the Confederate admiral Franklin Buchanan (1800–1874). Buchanan entered the U.S. Navy at the age of fourteen, and when he died, it was said that he had seen more varied sea service than any other naval officer. Buchanan was the first superintendent of the U.S. Naval Academy at Annapolis (1845), but he offered his services to the Confederate side during the Civil War. In the Battle of Hampton Roads, he commanded the ironclad *Virginia* (*Merrimac*). Seriously wounded, Buchanan was incapacitated the day before his ship's encounter with the *Monitor*. Buchanan was later named admiral and ranking officer of the Confederate navy, and he was in command when Admiral Farragut defeated the Confederates at the Battle of Mobile Bay, August 5, 1864. After the war, Buchanan returned to The Rest, rebuilt after a fire in 1863, and he died there in 1874. Buchanan is buried in the graveyard at *Wye House.*

Directly across the road from The Anchorage are the ruins of **St. John's Protestant Episcopal Church,** so close to the shore that on still days its low crenelated tower and crumbling walls are reflected in the river's waters.

In 1839, the wealthy planters of Miles River Neck donated the money to build this chapel on land given by Commodore Lowndes (*see above*) in order to save themselves the long trip to their parish church in St. Michaels. By the late nineteenth century, however, the dwindling congregation, unable to afford repairs to an unsafe roof, had abandoned the church. The present frame church at *Tunis Mills* eventually replaced the chapel.

A concrete bridge spans the **Miles River,** originally called St. Michaels in honor of the saint upon whose feast day the semi-annual rents for lands granted the colonists were paid to the lord proprietor. Perhaps due to the influence of Quaker settlers, the word *Saint* was dropped and the name corrupted to Miles. As early as 1677, a ferry operated at this crossing. At first it was "a canowe," later a flat scow pulled by a rope. In 1858, the General Assembly authorized some of the Miles River planters to issue stock in a company to build a toll bridge, which was finished in 1859. The toll was as high as forty cents for a vehicle; a pedestrian with a cow, mule, or horse had to pay six cents, and a sheep or a pig could be driven across for three cents.

From the bridge the tract once called **Ending of the Controversie** can be seen up the Miles River where Glebe Creek branches off to the right. The land was given to the famous Quaker Wenlocke Christison in 1670, and until recently the ruins of Christison's house stood nearby. In 1660 and again in 1661 and 1665 Christison was one of the Quakers whipped through the streets of Boston and then banished for "Rebellion, which is as the Sin of Witchcraft." By 1670 he was in Talbot County, where he acquired land and servants, and was active in the Third Haven Meeting. At his death, about 1679, he was a delegate to the General Assembly.

Further up Glebe Creek a pile of bricks on the shore is all that remains of **Fausley,** birthplace of Col. Tench Tilghman (*see* Tour 17).

At 11.8 m. Md. 370 joins Md. 33 (*see* Tour 16), 2.5 m. west of Easton.

EASTON–ST. MICHAELS–TILGHMAN ISLAND; 28.7 m.
Md. 33

Most of Md. 33 was at one time part of a main route between Ocean City and the Annapolis ferry terminal at Claiborne. Now that the ferry has been discontinued, this route is the principal entrance into an area famous among sportsmen: the St. Michaels and Bay Hundred districts of Talbot County. The road passes through the flat fields and pine woods of a region that is more picturesque along its waterfront than along its highways.

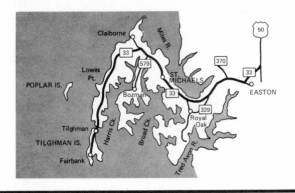

The road skirts the headwaters of creeks that are frequented by yachtsmen, hunters, and fishermen.

Branching from U.S. 50 at 0.0 m., Md. 33 enters a new section of Easton, which has grown up along what used to be U.S. 213. At 1.5 m. is Easton's municipally owned electric plant and water pumping station.

In Easton at 2.2 m., Md. 33 branches west (R) at Bay Street. Beyond the small bridge over the headwaters of the Tred Avon River are several small industrial plants.

At 2.6 m. is the junction with a gravel road.

● Go left on this to the catalpa-bordered lane (straight ahead) of **Ratcliffe Manor** (private), 0.7 m., a handsome brick house with distinctive clipped gables built in 1755–56 by Henry Hollyday, son of James Hollyday of Readbourne (*see* Tour 12b). The house may be the work of John Ariss, who is believed to have designed a number of famous Virginia houses, including Kenmore in Fredericksburg and possibly Mount Vernon. Ratcliffe Manor retains nearly all of its beautiful interior woodwork. All four walls of the living room are paneled; on the chimney wall, pilasters mark off the fireplace, with its eared frame and paneled overmantel, from the flanking corner cupboard and closet. The adjoining "plantation room" has a corner fireplace, again flanked by pilasters, and projecting paneled window seats.

At 3.8 m. is the junction with Md. 370 and Tour 15.

At 4.0 m. is the junction with North Bend Road, which leads to the North Bend Estates and the **Site of the Betty Cove Meeting House.** This meeting was perhaps the first in Talbot County, the meeting house having been built sometime between 1653, when the first Quakers settled in Talbot, and 1676, when, according to still extant records, it was expanded. In 1684, this meeting house was superseded by the one near Easton (*see* Tour 12c). Nearby was the first free school in Talbot County. Both the meeting house and the school have long since disappeared.

At 4.8 m. is the junction with Bloomfield Road.

● Go left on this to **Old Bloomfield** (L) (private), 1.1 m., a white-plastered, one-room-and-loft brick house with an unusual steeply pitched roof that projects nearly four feet beyond the northwest wall. The lower frame wing appears to have been built about a hundred years after the main portion of the house, the two-story wing having been added more recently.

At 6.2 m. on Md. 33 is the junction with Md. 329.

● Turn left (right at fork) to **ROYAL OAK** (6′ alt., 600 pop.), 2.4 m., a town named for a giant tree that supposedly stopped two British cannonballs during the bombardment of nearby *St. Michaels.*

At Royal Oak is the junction with Bellevue Road.

Go left (at fork, 1.9 m., keep left). At 2.9 m. at another fork bear left to **Clay's Hope** (L) (private, but near the road), 3.1 m., a plain but handsome 2½-story brick house laid in Flemish bond. The house, believed to have been built about 1726, is painted white, and it has an old, but much altered, frame wing. At **BELLEVUE** (5′ alt., 300 pop.), 3.5 m., a fishing and farming community, is the terminus of the small Bellevue-Oxford Ferry, which is hailed by a signal raised from the dock. A ferry has been in operation here since 1760. In the coves and up the creeks of this neck of land are sites of many seventeenth- and eighteenth-century shipyards.

At 7.3 m. on Md. 329 is the junction with Md. 33 again.

At 9.6 m. on Md. 33 is the junction with the lower end of Md. 329.

ST. MICHAELS (8′ alt., 1,456 pop.), 12.4 m. at Cherry Street and Railroad Avenue, on a neck of land between Miles River and Broad Creek, is one of the best-known yachting centers on the East Coast. Thousands visit here annually in early August for a regatta held on the broad Miles River west of the town. In addition to the boatyards and other services that meet the needs of these visitors, the town has three seafood packing plants and a small grain mill.

The St. Michaels area, accessible by water on both sides and once heavily timbered, has been a shipbuilding center since the last half of the seventeenth century, although the town itself did not develop until the time of the American Revolution. One of the first buildings on the site of the town was an Episcopal church, which, according to depositions taken in 1736, was built in the late 1680s by Edward Elliott. It was not until 1778, however, that the English merchant, James Braddock, bought land by the church and had it surveyed into lots. In 1805, the town was sufficiently populous to secure a charter of incorporation, with the town lands being resurveyed two years later. About 1810, when ship construction was at its height in St. Michaels, craft of all kinds came down the waterways, including schooners of the type later known as Baltimore clippers, the fastest ships afloat for their time. By 1820, however, diminishing supplies of local timber and the rise of Baltimore as a major shipbuilding center signaled the decline of St. Michaels, and shipyard activity had almost ceased by 1830. When the Chesapeake & Delaware Canal opened northern markets to the Bay area in 1829, oystering became a new source of income for the town, and after 1840 the building of small water craft revived. But ocean-going vessels no longer anchored in the harbor, and St. Michaels never grew to be more than a small village.

The pungies, sloops, and two-masted schooners built at St. Michaels and in other Bay villages were of first importance to the Bay economy in the nineteenth century. They provided fast, low-cost transportation for shipping Eastern Shore grain, farm produce, and seafood to the markets in Baltimore. After the Civil War, when oyster dredging from sail craft was made legal in Maryland waters, St. Michaels shipyards began producing "buckeyes," or "bugeyes." These long, low vessels with two raked masts developed from the log canoes that had been used for more than a century in oyster tonging. The bugeye was heavy enough to haul a dredge, and its thick log hull could withstand the sharp edges of the oyster shell cargo, which quickly tore the hulls of framed vessels. During the off-season, the shallow bottom of the bugeye enabled it to be used for transporting crops from the farms along the small tributaries of the Bay. A few bugeyes and some other locally built sailing vessels are still used for oyster dredging, although gasoline-powered craft have superseded them for most other purposes. Sailing is now a pastime in St. Michaels rather than an occupation. Nevertheless, each year in August a regatta is held commemorating earlier days in which appear nearly all of the old craft that remain afloat.

St. Michaels was the scene of a major British attack during the War of 1812. On the night of August 9, 1813, British troops landed in an attempt to assault the town, but they sustained heavy losses when the local militia fired a cannon into their ranks at point-blank range. British barges on the Miles River bombarded the town during the night. According to tradition, residents extinguished all lights near the ground and hung lanterns in upper story windows and treetops, causing the British to overshoot the town. Contemporary accounts make no mention of the ruse, but in any case the town escaped serious damage from the attack.

Md. 33 is known as Talbot Street inside the town of St. Michaels. On the corner of Chestnut and Talbot streets is the **Newman Funeral Home** (private), a white brick house built about 1803. Across the street is another white brick house built in 1842. A block further up the street, on the corner of Grace and Talbot streets, is the **Harrington Funeral Home** (private), a frame telescope house, the two lower sections of which date from the eighteenth century. The red brick house across the street on the corner of Talbot and Mulberry streets is called **The Inn** (private). Built in 1817 by Wrightson Jones, the house is distinguished by an inset two-story gallery. On the opposite corner of Talbot and Mulberry streets is a white brick house built in 1806, which was considerably altered in the late nineteenth century.

Down Mulberry Street four houses on the right is the **Cannon Ball House** (ca. 1800–1810, private), an elegant 2½-story brick house laid in Flemish bond. The house got its name as a result of the 1813 bombardment of the town, during which a cannon-ball dropped through the roof and bounced down the stairs past the owner's wife. The **Amelia Welby House** (private), a 1½-story frame house at the foot of Mulberry Street on the left, was the birthplace in 1819 of Amelia Ball Coppuck, a poet praised by Poe. The street ends at the harbor, where fishing and pleasure boats lie at anchor.

The Cannon Ball House stands at the corner of a lane leading into **St. Mary's Square,** the original public square of St. Michaels. In the middle of the green is a rectangular brick structure built in 1832 for the Methodist Episcopal Church, a denomination that has flourished in St. Michaels since the late eighteenth century.

Log canoe racing

The building later served as the public school, then as the Masonic Temple, and it is now used by Grand Lodge #177 A.F. and A.M. In front of the temple, under the trees, is a small cannon mounted on a concrete base. This cannon is said to be one of two given to St. Michaels by Jacob Gibson in compensation for a prank he had perpetrated on the town (*see* Tour 17), and it is thought to have been one of the artillery pieces used in the defense against the British attack of 1813.

The **St. Mary's Square Museum** (open Fri., Sat., Sun., and holidays; other days by appointment) on St. Mary's Square includes the **St. Michael's Bell,** cast in 1842 and once used in the local shipyards to signal the beginning of the workday, lunch break, and quitting time for the workers. It is still rung three times each day.

On Talbot Street, between Mulberry and Willow streets, is the **Protestant Episcopal Church** (1878), which is situated on the site of a church built by Edward Elliott in the seventeenth century. From 1749 until his death in 1790, Rev. John Gordon served the Anglicans of St. Michaels Parish. Since he was a patriot, he was one of the few Church of England rectors who kept his parish throughout the Revolution. It is said that Gordon was also a racing enthusiast, maintaining a track near the church where he and members of his congregation bet on each other's horses after services.

At one time, the harbor came up to the back of the Episcopal church, but during the nineteenth century the townspeople dumped their refuse here and the area was finally filled. The town office and fire department stand on the land thus reclaimed from the river.

At Willow Street, just beyond the church, the pre-Revolutionary part of the town begins. On the corner of Willow and Locust streets is a small 1½-story brick house, which is said to be the dwelling built by Edward Elliott about 1680. Across the street is a log house now covered with shingles. At the corner of Locust and Cherry streets is the **Smither House,** a 2½-story brick dwelling, part of which was built before 1810. Two of the houses across Cherry Street from the Smither House are constructed of hewn logs covered by shingles.

On Navy Point at the end of Mill Street, which turns (R) off Talbot Street (Md. 33) beyond Cherry Street, is the **Chesapeake Bay Maritime Museum** (open daily, except Mon., 10–4; 10–5 in summer), which exhibits drawings, models, and examples of Bay craft of all kinds. There are twenty-eight principal types of Bay craft, all of which are represented.

Opposite the intersection of Talbot Street (Md. 33) and Cherry Street, Railroad Avenue branches east.

● Follow Railroad Avenue 0.4 m. to the gates of **Crooked Intention,** which stands on the banks of Broad Creek. The original house, probably built soon after 1717 by Robert Harrison, was a simple hall-and-parlor dwelling with a kitchen wing, but after the middle of the eighteenth century, additions at the rear of the house created the present quaint roof line. Paneling and a built-in cupboard were installed in the main room of the house at this time. After the Revolution, the box stair behind the fireplace in the dining room was removed and a china cupboard and a new mantel and overmantel were built. Later, a wing was added on the right of the house to balance the kitchen wing on the left.

The Harrisons, who acquired Crooked Intention in 1696, were merchants, and their extensive business transactions contributed substantially to the development of St. Michaels. In 1802, Thomas Harrison left his son Samuel a large fortune, which he employed not only in trade but in buying up mortgages and lending capital to shipbuilders. In 1819, Samuel built the first steam-powered mill in Talbot County, producing flour for export to the West Indies.

At 13.0 m. on Md. 33 is **Perry Cabin** (R), a dwelling that incorporates a pre-Revolutionary structure, although the house was greatly expanded in 1860 and 1870. The building was given its name by Samuel Hambleton, who was paymaster on Com. O. H. Perry's flagship in the Battle of Lake Erie. The place is now used by a riding school.

At 13.5 m. is the junction with Yacht Club Road.

● Go right to the **Miles River Yacht Club,** site of the Miles River Regatta (sail and motor) which is held each August.

Martingham (R) (private), 14.5 m., appears to have been built in the seventeenth century, perhaps by Samuel Hambleton, who patented the land in 1659. The 1½-story weatherboarded house has a narrow box stair that rises from the small central hall. In both living room and dining room the corner posts of the house frame are exposed.

At 15.2 m., turn left at the junction with Md. 579.

● **BOZMAN,** at 2.7 m., is a small summer resort.

At 3.7 m., **Lostock** (private), at the end of a long wooded lane, can

Chesapeake Bay Maritime Museum

be seen standing in the middle of a field. The roof of this narrow 2½-story brick house runs across its two rooms, creating the effect of a much larger dwelling as one approaches the gable end with its seven windows. Maj. William Caulk, an officer in the War of 1812, may have built Lostock. His son, John Caulk, a sea captain, is credited with the introduction of Muscovy ducks into this country.

At 15.9 m. is a junction with Md. 451, which leads to Claiborne.

● **CLAIBORNE** (5′ alt.), 1.3 m., was named for William Claiborne, the English merchant who, in 1631, established a trading post on Kent Island, which is visible across Eastern Bay. The village was established in 1886 by the Baltimore & Eastern Shore Railroad as a ferry point on its boat-and-rail line between Baltimore and Ocean City. Later, Claiborne became the terminus of a state-operated ferry line to Annapolis. Still later, when the ferry's Eastern Shore terminus was moved to Matapeake on Kent Island, an auxiliary ferry ran from Romancoke on Lower Kent Island to Claiborne. When this ferry ceased operations several years ago, Claiborne became a quiet residential village.

Outside Claiborne is **Rich Neck Manor** (open by appointment: Mrs. E. P. Burling), home of the Tilghmans in the eighteenth and nineteenth centuries. The tiny gambrel-roofed wing may have been built prior to the main section, but the large white brick house was erected by Matthew Tilghman (1718–90) in the late eighteenth century. Tilghman was a delegate to the Continental Congress, president of the Maryland Constitutional Convention, and one of the most influential men on the Eastern Shore during the Revolutionary period.

Along Md. 33 stands **Webley** (private), an old house that has had modern wings added to it. The house was purchased by Dr. Absalom Thompson in 1826, and four years later he converted the dwelling into the first hospital on the Eastern Shore. Although Thompson was a famous surgeon, contemporaries described him riding bareback and barefoot on a mule on his way to visit patients, carrying a jar of calomel, a lancet, and a syringe with a nozzle as large as a gun barrel.

At 21.9 m. is the junction with Lowes Wharf Road.

● Go right 0.4 m. to **Lowe's Point.** Two miles offshore is **POPLAR ISLAND,** patented in 1640 by Richard Thompson, kinsman and follower of William Claiborne. A few years later, Thompson lost his family in an Indian massacre here. In 1669, Alexander D'Hinoyossa, the Dutch director of Delaware who came to Maryland when the English captured New Amstel (New Castle) in 1664, purchased Poplar Island and lived here for several years. Tidal erosion has reduced the 1,000-acre tract of Thompson's time to three small islets.

At 22.7 m. is the entrance (L) to **Langdon** (private), famous for its gardens laid out near the shores of Harris Creek. The large Georgian-style mansion was built around a much smaller eighteenth-century house.

The bridge at 25.9 m. on Md. 33 crosses Knapps Narrows to **TILGHMAN ISLAND,** a 3½-mile expanse of low sandy ground favored by hunters and fishermen. The only villages on the island are **TILGHMAN** (4′ alt., 1,200 pop.), 26.3 m., **AVALON** (4′ alt.), 26.8 m., and **FAIRBANK** (4′ alt.), 28.7 m. The island's residents engage in fishing, crabbing, and oystering. Boats and guides can be hired here throughout the fishing season in summer and the hunting season in autumn.

17

EASTON–OXFORD; 8.8 m.
Md. 333

This route crosses three small peninsulas cut by the Tred Avon River and its branches. The low flatland, thickly wooded along the stream banks, is well adapted to farming, which, along with fishing, furnishes a livelihood for many of the area's residents. Sport fishing and yachting attract numerous summer visitors.

Md. 333 branches right at 0.0 m. from the junction with S. Washington Street, Harrison Street, and Idlewild Avenue in Easton. Locally, Md. 333 is known as Oxford or Peachblossom Road. On the right, just before reaching the Easton city limits, is the Easton Junior-Senior High School. Across the road is **St. Mark's Methodist Church.**

At 0.5 m. there is a branch of the Tred Avon River known as Paper Mill Pond, so-called because a paper mill once stood on its banks.

At 2.3 m. is the concrete bridge over Peachblossom Creek. Along this tidal tributary of the Tred Avon River are many country houses amid dense woods.

At 3.1 m. is the junction with Country Club Road (R) that leads to the **Talbot Country Club** (L). The club is on land formerly called Llandaff, once owned by Richard Tilghman Goldsborough.

At 3.8 m. the road crosses Trippe Creek, which runs into the Tred Avon River at Turner's Point, granted in 1659 to the Quaker, William Turner. Between 1663, the year of Turner's death, and 1697, Thomas Skillington established a shipyard here that is believed to have built and supplied ships for buccaneers.

At the junction with Otwell Road is **Trappe Station,** 5.6 m., once a railroad shipping point.

● Go right on Otwell Road to **Otwell** (private), a Goldsborough estate for more than two centuries. The gambrel-roofed wing predates the main section of the house.

At 6.1 m. **Anderton** (R) (private) can be seen from the road. The old part of this frame house was built in two sections of one and one-half stories each, one weatherboarded, the other covered with wide fitted boards. The weatherboarded section, which may have been built sometime in the early eighteenth century, has an outside door only four feet high and an interior "cell" nineteen feet long but only five feet wide.

Jena (R) (private), 7.3 m., presents a dramatic appearance from the road because of the high peak of its roof from which the dormers near the bottom seem to peer like eyes nearly lost under a huge forehead. It is a small 1½-story yellow brick house built after 1700, with a catslide roof and windows of all different sizes but each with the same number of panes. The property was christened Jena by Jacob Gibson, a well-known Talbot County eccentric, who named his various estates in the county after victories won by Bonaparte; others were Marengo (see Tour 15), Austerlitz, and Friedland.

During the War of 1812, Gibson owned Sharp's Island near the mouth of the Choptank River. When British cruisers under Adm. John Borlase Warren raided the island and carried off some of the cattle, Gibson persuaded the admiral to reimburse him. Gossips claimed that Gibson had sold out to the enemy. With animosity against him at its height and at a time when the people of the town (see Tour 16) were fearing an attack any minute, Gibson sailed up Broad Creek to St. Michaels with a red bandanna at the masthead of his boat and an empty rum barrel for a drum on its deck. The town thought the attack had come; women and children were sent to the country and the militia had assembled before Gibson's prank was discovered. Angry soldiers nearly shot Gibson, but after a public apology and explanation he was allowed to depart. Immediately afterwards he presented the town of St. Michaels with two cannon for its defense.

Gibson is also remembered for his proposal to open a bank, with part of the profits to be used for a fund to manumit slaves. He offered to supply the capital for the bank and to put the direction of it into the hands of four men of the county, who would themselves have no financial interest in the institution. The citizens of Easton were to fill vacancies on the board of directors by election. Once all the slaves in the area had been freed, the fund was to be used to support clergymen.

At 8.4 m. is the gate to **Plinhimmon** (private); the name on the gatepost is concealed by a boxwood bush. The lane crosses fields to the house, which sits in a grove of enormous old trees. The frame wings, built about seventy-five years ago, replaced a much older frame house. The 2½-story main block, laid in Flemish bond and painted yellow, appears to have been built after the Revolution.

Plinhimmon was purchased in 1719 by John Coward, whose

EASTON

333

Tred Avon R.

Trappe Station

OXFORD

Choptank R.

son John was captain of the *Integrity,* a ship that carried cargo between Oxford and London. According to local lore, a young girl, disguised as a man but of genteel rearing, stowed away on the *Integrity* in 1763 in pursuit of a sailor. When her disguise was discovered, Captain Coward protected her and took her home to Plinhimmon, where she was consigned by his less compassionate wife to duties in the kitchen. Later, with the help of another sailor, the girl stowed away on the *Hazard* and returned to London. After hearing the tale from Gen. Tench Tilghman when visiting at Plinhimmon about 1825, Theodore Sedgewick repeated it to his sister Catherine, who embroidered the tale into her famous story, "Perdita."

Capt. John Coward's son, Thomas, was captain of the *Choptank,* one of the last ships to trade out of Oxford before the Revolution. In 1786, Thomas sold Plinhimmon to Matthew Tilghman, who gave it to his daughter Anna Maria, widow of Washington's aide-de-camp, Col. Tench Tilghman (*see below*); she may have built the remaining brick wing of the house. Upon her death in 1843, Anna Maria willed the estate to her grandson, Gen. Tench Tilghman (1810–74), who was the first Talbot County farmer to fertilize with Peruvian guano, as well as the first Marylander (1836) to use the newly invented Hussey reaper. In the 1850s, he also built on Tilghman Island (*see* Tour 16) the first steam-powered sawmills on the Eastern Shore. His son Tench was an aide to Jefferson Davis during the Civil War. The younger Tench Tilghman left a diary describing the flight of Davis and the Confederate cabinet in the last days of the war, his own capture by Negro troops, and his determination to leave the scene of past humiliations to seek his fortune in South America.

At 8.5 m. is the junction with a paved road.

● Go right to **Oxford Cemetery,** 0.3 m., a green refuge by the waters of the Tred Avon, once part of Plinhimmon and a Tilghman family burying ground. Here is the monument erected to the memory of Col. Tench Tilghman (1744–86) and his wife, Anna Maria, by their descendants. Tilghman was born at Fausley near the Miles River in Talbot County (*see* Tour 15) but went with his father, James Tilghman, to Philadelphia in 1762. There he became a merchant, acquiring a great fortune before the outbreak of the Revolution, when he liquidated his business. Though his father was a firm Loyalist, Tench Tilghman warmly supported independence and from 1776 until the end of the war served first as Washington's secretary, then as his aide-de-camp. After the victory at Yorktown it was he who carried the news to Congress, going by boat from Yorktown, via Annapolis, to Rock Hall, and thence overland to Philadelphia. Legend has it that he rode without a break, stopping every three or four hours at the nearest farmhouse with the cry "Cornwallis is taken; a fresh horse for the Congress!" After the Revolution, Tilghman went into business in Baltimore with Robert Morris (*see below*), a partnership that terminated with Tilghman's death in 1786. Washington said of him, "He had as fair a reputation as ever belonged to a human character."

Just inside the town limits of *Oxford* a left turn leads to the **U.S. Bureau of Commercial Fisheries Biological Laboratory,** established in 1960 on Boone Creek to study oyster culture and diseases. The drastic decline of the oyster catch in Chesapeake waters threatens the whole industry, and research here may determine how Bay fishermen can create oyster "farms" similar to those successfully operated in Japan. Shells with spat (baby oysters) are strung on ropes, which are lowered into the water to a point a few inches above the creek floor. So suspended, the shellfish grow much faster than those on natural oyster beds.

OXFORD, 8.8 m., located on the southern tip of a peninsula between the Choptank and Tred Avon rivers, has a landlocked harbor that protects a fishing and oyster fleet. In appearance, Oxford reflects the nineteenth, rather than the eighteenth, century. The town's great charm derives from the trees and lawns that line its main street, from the shipyards and harbor, and from the minimum number of twentieth-century plate glass windows, neon signs, and chromium decoration.

In spite of the peaceful aspect of present-day Oxford, the town was rivaled only by Annapolis among pre-Revolutionary Maryland ports. The site of the town was probably occupied as early as 1668; at least there was land for a town at that date somewhere on the Tred Avon (then called Thread Haven, or Third Haven). In 1683, this town was made an official port of entry into the colony, with the site being officially laid out in 1684 and again in 1694, when its name was changed briefly to Williamstadt, in honor of King William. Large London and Liverpool commercial houses established branch stores here, exchanging articles of necessity for cargoes of tobacco. Two record books kept by the port collectors between 1747 and 1775 show almost 200 vessels registering at the customs house. By the time of the Revolution, however, Oxford, which had no extensive back country depending upon it, had begun to decline. The outbreak of war and subsequent rise of Baltimore, which had access to the rapidly developing West, accelerated the decline. Before his death in 1798, Jeremiah Banning, a sea captain who had long sailed out of Oxford, wrote in his diary: "Oxford's streets and strands were once covered by busy crowds ushering in commerce from almost every quarter of the globe. The once well-worn streets are now grown in grass, save a few narrow tracks made by sheep and swine; and the strands have more the appearance of an uninhabited island than where human feet have ever trod."

By 1825, Oxford had declined to such a state that municipal government had ceased to function. In order to revive local government, the town was incorporated in that year and the streets were resurveyed. After the Civil War, Oxford began to grow again. Shipbuilding revived, oystering and fishpacking became important occupations, and summer visitors came to enjoy "the salubrity of the air."

Boatbuilding and fishing are still primary occupations of Oxford residents today, and an inn and tourist homes cater to sport fishermen. Every August, the **Tred Avon Yacht Club** holds a three-day regatta, which includes races for log canoes (*see* Tour 16, St. Michaels).

At the foot of Morris Street at The Strand is the Tred Avon Ferry. This ferry is believed to be the oldest ferry in the United States that runs "free"—not attached to a cable. The line, which connects Oxford and Bellevue, was started in 1760 by Elizabeth Skinner.

The main street of Oxford is named for Robert Morris (1711–50) and his son and namesake (1734–1806), who became the so-called financier of the American Revolution. The senior Morris, who came to Oxford in 1738 as a factor for the Liverpool house of Foster Cunliffe, Esq., and Sons, became a successful merchant in his own right. His death resulted from an accidental wound he received from a cannon, which had been shot in salute upon his departure from a ship in the service of his own company. At least one contemporary attributed Oxford's decline to Morris's death. Robert Morris, the younger, is believed to have come to Oxford at about thirteen years of age and to have attended school here briefly before entering the Greenway countinghouse in Philadelphia. He became one of the wealthiest merchants in the colonies and was a signer of the Declaration of Independence and finance minister for the Confederation. In spite of his fortune, Morris lost everything in land speculation and was finally sentenced to debtor's prison.

The remains of the **Morris House** (1774) at Morris Street and The Strand are embodied in a three-story frame hotel with a mansard roof, restored and refurnished in 1952 and now known as the **Robert Morris Inn.** Ancient wooden beams of great size, evidently part of the original house, are visible in the basement beneath the old portion of the building. During the building's restoration, many hand-wrought iron nails and a few English copper coins were found.

On the south side of Morris Street, three doors from The Strand, is the **Grapevine House,** where there is an ancient but still productive grapevine believed to have been planted about 1808 by John Willis, who introduced many new and improved varieties of fruit into Talbot County.

Four doors further up Morris Street from The Strand, the gray clapboard **Academy (Bratt) House** (private), with its pilastered facade and cupola atop a low hipped roof, is a distinctive landmark. The academy was built about 1848 as part of the Maryland Military School established under the sponsorship of Gen. Tench Tilghman of *Plinhimmon*. The main house, which stood in what is now the box garden, burned down in 1855, and shortly thereafter the school closed. The box hedge leading up to the wrought-iron front porch has completely overgrown the walk.

Almost opposite the Bratt House on the north side of Morris Street is **Barnaby House,** supposed to have been built by a Captain Barnaby, who is noted as owner of the lot in a plat of

Oxford made in 1707. It is a small 1½-story house covered with weatherboarding and shingles. Although the exterior of the building does not distinguish it from more recently constructed houses nearby, its interior retains the old floors and staircase, paneled chimney pieces, and a hand-carved corner cupboard.

At the end of Tilghman Street, tall trees and shrubs enclose **Wiley's Shipyard.** Perched at the water's edge is **Byberry,** a shingled 1½-story house that is said to have been standing in 1695.

The **Oxford Town Museum** is open without charge on Fri., Sat., and Sun., 2–5 and by appointment for groups.

EASTON–HURLOCK–VIENNA; 29.2 m.
Md. 331

This tour follows part of what was once the main route from Easton and points north to Ocean City. The route crosses the southern part of Caroline County and the northern tip of Dorchester County, traveling through flat country from the Choptank to the Nanticoke and always near water. In the fields, rye and wheat in spring give way to corn and soybeans in summer and fall. Chicken raising and vegetable canning and freezing are important sources of income in the area, although the acreage devoted to vegetable crops has diminished in recent years (*see* Tour 12c, Harrington Bridge). From time to time, the road passes by steep-roofed cottages with large chimneys, indicating considerable age despite the disguise of modern shingles.

Md. 331 branches left from U.S. 301 in Easton at 0.0 m. Md. 331 crosses the Choptank River, 3.8 m., on the **Dover Bridge,** which was built in 1860. Until 1865, when Talbot and Caroline counties bought the company stock and made the bridge free, foot passengers, horses, and cows were charged a five-cent toll for crossing the bridge, while a sheep or a pig could cross for three cents. The gradual adoption of heavy farm machinery, as well as the use of trucks and cars, caused the maintenance of the bridge to become increasingly expensive, and supervision of repairs began to require technical knowledge beyond that of the ordinary citizen. In 1898, the two counties paid nearly $9,000 to put iron spans in part of Dover Bridge. One of the Talbot commissioners was appointed to check on the progress of the repairs, and the two counties tested the finished bridge by sending two "traction engines" across it side by side. Even though the bridge was judged sound, a year and a half later a traction engine with a threshing rig fell through.

Two miles below on the west bank of the Choptank is the **Site of Dover.** Local historians believe that Dover was a port of considerable foreign trade during the eighteenth century. Seagoing vessels supposedly tied up at its wharves so that the fresh river water would kill the barnacles on their bottoms. During the Revolution, when the Eastern Shore began its long agitation for autonomy from the rest of the state, Dover was

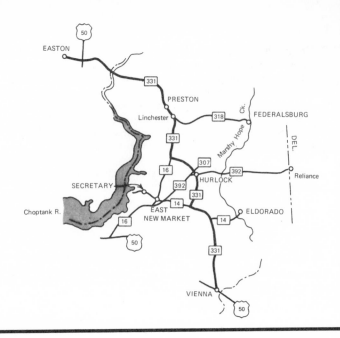

TOUR 18

proposed as the capital for the Shore. In 1778, the General Assembly authorized construction of a courthouse and prison at Dover for use by the General Court, which was scheduled to meet on the Eastern Shore in alternate years. The law was not heeded, however, and the General Court continued to use the county courthouse at Talbottown, later renamed Easton (*see* Tour 12c). As new shipping routes developed and the harbor shoaled, Dover's role as a Chesapeake Bay port ended.

Beyond Dover, William Frazier (1756–1807), who was a captain in the Revolution and prominent in Caroline County Methodism, built a home. Bishop Francis Asbury records in his diary numerous visits to Frazier's house between 1801 and 1813. Religious meetings were often held in the second-story front room of the house, often called the Church Room.

Before 1856, **PRESTON** (509 pop.), 9.7 m., had been a tiny settlement known as Snow Hill. With the advent of the railroad, which opened the interior of the Delmarva Peninsula after the Civil War, Preston started to grow. Now the town is a marketing center for a broiler-raising and truck-gardening district with canning factories, canned goods brokerage houses, and a trucking firm that transports local produce to markets on the Eastern seaboard.

The **Bethesda Methodist Church** (L), at the junction of Md. 16 and Main Street, is a large brick building with a square belfry. It stands on the site of one of the first Methodist churches in America, the Bethesda Chapel.

LINCHESTER, 11.4 m., one of the oldest settlements in Caroline County, was formerly called Murray's Mill because of the grist mill (R) (open Mon., Tues., Wed., Fri., 8–5) established here in 1681. By legislative act the town was renamed Linchester, a combination of the names of Caroline and Dorchester counties (CaroLINe, DorCHESTER). The present mill building (on the old road to the right) was probably constructed in the early nineteenth century, although according to oral tradition it is the original mill, which formerly stood farther upstream until it was swept from its foundations to its present site during a flood. The date 1847 is carved on one of the wooden hoppers. The present water wheel is made of steel rather than wood, but the mill still grinds wheat and corn in the traditional manner. Water from the millpond on the other side of the road flows through a pipe into the mill race, and then through another pipe to the wheel.

At 11.6 m. is the junction with Md. 318.

● Go left (straight ahead) on Md. 318 to **FEDERALSBURG**, 6.3 m., situated on Marshy Hope Creek. Federalsburg now lies in Caroline County, but until 1891 the Caroline-Dorchester county line followed the creek, which ran through the middle of the town. In the late eighteenth century, a bridge crossed the Northwest Fork (Marshy Hope Creek), and a settlement developed around a general store opened in 1789 by Cloudsberry Jones. In the records of both counties, ordinaries, or taverns, were authorized at Northwest Fork Bridge; but in 1793, the name of the settlement appears as Federalsburgh, probably named after the Federalist Party. Although the water at Federalsburgh was too shallow for launching boats, a shipbuilding business using top grade white oak flourished here before the Civil War. Hulls were conveyed on lighters and scows to a point about four miles down river for launching. Tanbark, cordwood, and mill products were other sources of income, and there was a large slave-trading station at the east bridgehead. Today, more than half of the town's residents are employed in various small industries, especially at the canneries and a poultry-dressing plant.

At 15.0 m. Md. 331 turns off Md. 16.

● Go straight on Md. 16, a country road that passes a number of frame houses with outside pyramidic chimneys, suggestive of ante-bellum origin. **EAST NEW MARKET**, 3.8 m., a small market town, was in existence by 1800, since there are several buildings that predate this time. The old houses, set back from the road, are almost concealed by great trees, and the motorist can easily drive by the town without realizing that he has passed a late-eighteenth-century settlement.

At the junction with Md. 14, in the center of town, go left about 0.1 m. to **Friendship Hall** (R) (private, but visible from the road), the best-known and most elaborate of the houses in this area. This 2½-story brick mansion, with a 1½-story brick curtain and kitchen wing, was built about 1790 by James Sulivane, quartermaster general of Dorchester County during the Revolution. From the end of the lane, the ivy-covered facade, a half mile away, looks black and forbidding, but a closer view reveals a pink brick building of excellent proportions. Brick pilasters near each end run up to the stringcourse on the otherwise plain entrance front. The cornice goes around the gables and in the triangle of the end gable are two oval windows. The elaborate interior features a paneled staircase rising from a wide central hall. The two drawing rooms have paneled wainscoting, projecting window seats, and ornate mantels and overmantels on the corner fireplaces.

Across the road from Friendship Hall, **Maurice Manor** (private, but visible from the road), with its A-window and transomed door with sidelights, appears from the road to be a Victorian structure. From the garden, however, the house shows its true eighteenth-century style. The dwelling is a solid frame house, two stories in front and one story behind, with chimneys at the lower corners of the catslide roof as well as at the ridge pole. Inside, a tiny, incredibly steep paneled staircase runs up one side of a central hall. The usual curtain and kitchen wing run off one side.

● Continuing west, at 1.2 m. on Md. 14 is the fishing village of **SECRETARY,** supposedly named for Henry Sewall, secretary of Maryland under Gov. Charles Calvert. At the end of Willow Street sits a small 1½-story brick house. This is **My Lady Sewall's Manor House** (private, but visible from the road), so called because it was long believed to have been built by Sewall in 1661. Its fine paneling, installed about 1720 or 1730, is in the Brooklyn Museum of Art. "My Lady Sewall" married Charles Calvert, later the third Lord Baltimore, shortly after her first husband's death in 1664.

Md. 14 crosses Secretary Creek by the local crab house. At 2.2 m. turn right on Greens Point Road. At 0.4 m. is a fork; bear left. At 0.7 m. is the lane (R) to **Indian Purchase** (private), formerly known as Goose Creek Farm. This handsome brick house built in the 1790s is typical of many houses built on the Lower Eastern Shore at the end of the eighteenth century. The entrance on the gable end, with its transom and sidelights, leads to a hall running across the whole front of the house. Attractive mantels distinguish the two parlors beyond. The 1½-story kitchen wing runs off one side, and a modern two-story frame wing provides additional living space on the opposite side. Goose Creek Farm was originally part of a tract reserved by treaty for the Choptank Indians, with Chief Hatchwop and his queen signing the deed transferring the land to Francis Taylor in 1693.

● Just beyond the blinker light on Md. 16 in East New Market is the **Old House of the Hinges** (private), locally known as the Brick Hotel. This white-painted brick structure sits back from the road almost concealed under the trees. Under the steep roof and over a carved frieze is a cornice of tapering modillions, accentuated with guttae. The effect of the elaborate carving is light and delicate. Behind the 1½-story kitchen wing is an old meat house, which has the enormous old hinges for which the house is named. The Old House of the Hinges is said to have been built in the late eighteenth century by one of the Ennalls; later, it came into the possession of Anthony L. Manning, an officer in the War of 1812. During the 1920s the building served as the East New Market Hotel.

Farther along on Md. 16 on the left is another brick house, called **Edmondson House,** or **Jacob's House** (private). Like many houses built near the turn of the eighteenth century on the Lower Eastern Shore, the gable faces the road and contains the entrance. Off one side runs the curtain and kitchen wing, which contains a huge fireplace.

Across the street is the **Smith House** (private), built before 1797. A small frame 1½-story house with a very steep roof, it has outside end chimneys with elaborate pyramidic hips. Curtain and kitchen wings extend from the back. According to local legend, a nineteenth-century owner swapped this house plus his nagging wife for a new wife and a feather bed.

Just beyond East New Market, Md. 16 passes by several old cottages somewhat disguised by modern shingles. Bear right at the fork in East New Market. At the junction of Md. 16 and Md. 392, turn right.

At 5.5 m. on Md. 16, the white frame house with low-pitched hip roof and balustraded roof deck is **Sherman Institute** (private, but visible from the road), built in 1825 by Capt. Thomas Sherman as part of a private school for the education of his two sons. The children of other prominent families were also educated here, and the school flourished for some years.

Md. 16 continues to a junction with U.S. 50 and Tour 12b on the east side of Cambridge.

Linchester Mill

HURLOCK (45′ alt., 1,056 pop.), 17.4 m. at the junction of Md. 331 and Md. 307, is a busy, modern town in the midst of prosperous farming country. Developed around a railroad station built here in 1867, the town was named for John M. Hurlock, who erected the town's first store in 1869 and its first dwelling in 1872, twenty years before the town was incorporated.

Hurlock is primarily a vegetable-processing center but a tin-can factory and shirt factory are also located here. The **Hurlock Free Library,** established in 1900 and now a branch of the Dorchester County Library, is the oldest public library on the Eastern Shore.

At 17.9 m. in Hurlock is the junction with Md. 392.

● Go left on Md. 392 to **RELIANCE,** 8.5 m., a hamlet on the Maryland-Delaware line. The old plain frame building here is supposed to be the tavern that served as headquarters for the gang led by the notorious Lucretia ("Patty") Cannon and her son-in-law and partner, Joe Johnson. An Eastern Shore legend, Patty Cannon was a handsome woman of extraordinary charm, physical strength, and power. She masterminded the gang's operations, which included smuggling and kidnapping slaves and free Negroes for resale. According to local tradition, a combined raid by Delaware and Maryland police was necessary to bring about Patty's arrest, because the state line ran through the tavern, enabling members of the gang to elude Maryland police by moving into the Delaware half of the tavern, and vice versa. Joe Johnson escaped arrest, but Patty and the other gang members were tried at Georgetown, Delaware, and sentenced to be hanged, a fate that Patty avoided by committing suicide.

At 20.8 m. is the junction with Md. 14.

Md. 331 and Md. 14 turn left. At 22.8 m. Md. 14 continues straight ahead and Md. 331, the main route, turns right.

● At 2.5 m. Md. 14 crosses Marshy Hope Creek and at 3.1 m. makes a junction with Md. 313 (straight ahead and right) and a narrow paved road (L) in **ELDORADO.** On the narrow road at 3.5 m. just beyond the farmhouse, a lane crosses a field and passes through a wooded area to **Rehoboth** (private), a handsome brick house that once may have been one and one-half stories with a catslide roof. The earlier structure was the home of the Lee family, who patented the land in 1673, built the house about 1725, and lived here until 1787. A fire in 1917 destroyed the old interior. On the lawn by Marshy Hope Creek stand several old cannons.

At 29.1 m. on Md. 331 is **VIENNA** and the junction with U.S. 50 (*see* Tour 12c).

CAMBRIDGE–CHURCH CREEK–HOOPERSVILLE; 31.1 m.
Md. 16 and 335

Md. 16 and Md. 335 pass through tidewater country popular with hunters and fishermen. Much of the land is fresh- or salt-water marsh, where muskrats and other game of all kinds flourish. The farmland in the area, which was never exceptionally fertile, suffered severely from salt water during recent hurricanes. Many farmers eke out a living by trapping muskrats and tonging for oysters in the winter. Waterfront communities on the Little Choptank and Honga rivers, once centers of shipbuilding before local forests were depleted, depend on crabs and oysters and the packing, canning, and freezing of seafood. In fall and winter, the marshes below Church Creek have an austere beauty, but the mosquitoes and humidity often make them uncomfortable for tourists during the summer.

● In **CAMBRIDGE** (*see* Cambridge Tour), from its junction with Md. 341, Md. 343 (Washington Street) runs through the level peninsula formed by the Choptank and the Little Choptank rivers, which are lined with numerous beautiful private estates. **Horn Point,** about two miles below Cambridge on the Choptank, was developed by Coleman Du Pont (1863–1930), U.S. senator, industrialist, and pioneer in modern roadbuilding. The late Francis P. Du Pont gave this 720-acre site to the city of Cambridge, and in 1971, Cambridge conveyed the property to the State of Maryland for use by the University of Maryland. The Center for Environmental and Estuarine Studies located here conducts studies of environmental problems pertinent to the state.

● Three miles farther along Md. 343, on the Little Choptank, is **Spocot**, patented to Stephen Gary in 1662. Part of the house, which can be seen in the distance from Md. 343 during the winter, is believed to have been built in the seventeenth century. There was once a self-contained community here with shipyard, sawmill, blacksmith shop, and large slave quarters, but all of the buildings have disappeared except for two of the slave houses, now combined to form a tenant house.

On Castle Haven Road is **Castle Haven** (private), one of the famous pre-Revolutionary houses of the county. The land is part of a grant made in 1659 to Anthony LeCompte, a French Huguenot who came to Maryland from England in 1655 and eventually settled in Dorchester.

Most year-round residents of this area divide their time between working on the estates of summer residents and farming and fishing during the remainder of the year. Many live in frame houses built around much older structures.

In Cambridge, turn left at the junction of Md. 343 and 341. Md. 341 (Race Street) joins Md. 16, 0.0 m., which is the main route of the tour.

At 3.0 m. on Md. 16 is the junction with a narrow, asphalt-paved road.

● Off this road stands **Woolford House,** or **Hull Farm** (private). This small brick house, with its steep roof and small, twenty-four-pane windows, was built in the late eighteenth century on the banks of Fishing Creek. Architecturally, the dwelling is reminiscent of an earlier style.

The houses of **CHURCH CREEK** (est. 130 pop.), 5.1 m. (at the junction with Md. 335), stand along either side of Md. 16 and Md. 335. Church Creek is an old settlement, perhaps having developed around *Trinity Protestant Church* before 1692. Town lots in Church Creek are mentioned in the land records by 1700. A shipyard in the town is mentioned in a deed of 1766, and the yards remained in operation until the supply of lumber began to decline in the first half of the nineteenth century. Today a tomato cannery and crabbing and oystering provide the chief sources of income for the town's residents. At the crossroads stands **Sam Jones's Store,** made famous by Arthur Godfrey when he presented Mr. Jones on his television program in the 1950s. In addition to general merchandise, Mr. Jones sold the inspirational sayings that had resulted in his conversion from a wayward life.

A number of old houses can be seen in Church Creek, and portions of old houses have been incorporated in many newer buildings. The heavy end chimneys of the two-story frame **Gibson House** (private, but visible from the road), opposite the Methodist Episcopal Church at the east end of town, are nearly 100 years old. Daniel T. Owen, an ardent abolitionist and Republican who was delegate to the convention that nominated Lincoln, built the main part of the house just after the Civil War, supposedly modeling it after Lincoln's house in Springfield, Illinois. The back wing, which once occupied the site of the present main house, was built much earlier. Surviving documents show that local residents believed Owen was building his house for use as a Negro college, and he did in fact furnish the land and a teacher for a school in Church Creek.

At the junction with Md. 335, Orion Road runs off to the right. Two houses down is the **Richardson House** (private, but visible from the road), a small 1½-story frame structure that sits back from the road behind a green lawn, boxwood, and a profusion of flowering shrubs, including a green rose. Two Richardson brothers, ship carpenters from New England, bought the property in 1812 and may have built the house that now stands here. All four walls of one room in the house are paneled ship-style with random-width boards. Next to the Richardson House is a two-story shingled frame house that may be as old. Around the corner is another 1½-story frame house. In both buildings the chimney on the free gable is exposed below the second floor, a feature common to many old houses in this area. At 0.7 m. the road ends at the shores of Church Creek by the **Richardson Graveyard,** a well-tended green full of beautiful

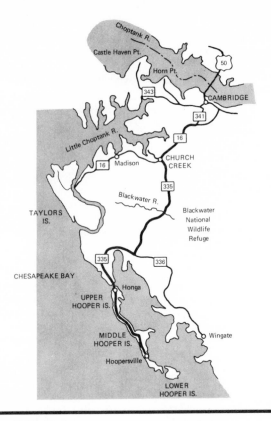

TOUR 19

boxwood. Behind the fenced area surrounded by thick honey-suckle is the grave of the Nathan Richardson who, according to his stone, was "one who followed the Apostolic injunction, Bretheren [*sic*] mind your own business & in connexion with it he took care to let other people's business alone."

Steamboats once docked at this point on the creek, and prior to that shipyards were located here. Now, a pile of lumber and two ship railways indicate the location of a boat repair yard. Across the creek is the **Dorsey House,** a 1½-story frame house built around the end of the eighteenth century.

In Church Creek, Md. 335 becomes the main route.

● Go right (straight ahead) on Md. 16. At 0.4 m. the frame tele-scope **Wyvill House** (R) (private, but visible from the road) stands behind large trees that shade the farmyard. Dr. Dorsey Wyvill, one of the founders in 1799 of the Medical and Chirurgical Faculty of Maryland, lived in this house and may have installed some of its exceptional woodwork and plaster moldings.

On the shore of Church Creek at 1.0 m. on Md. 16 is **Trinity Protestant Church** (R) (open daily except Tues.; service, Sun. 9:00, except third Sun. in month), the oldest Episcopal church still standing in Maryland. Built before 1692 (1675 is the tentative date of construction), it was long believed that the church had originally been cross-shaped. In 1956, however, Col. Edgar Garbish undertook the restoration of the then T-shaped church as a memorial to his father-in-law, Walter P. Chrysler, and excavations made at that time failed to show any sign of the missing wing. The existing T-wing was removed as part of the restoration, and in so doing the foundations of the original entrance to the church were uncovered as well as evidence indicating that the T-wing had been added about 100 years after the main section of the church had been built. As a result, the church has been restored without the T-wing.

The north wall of the church had to be rebuilt during the restoration because it had begun to bulge dangerously. Before it was taken down, however, the wall was measured and photographed so that it could be rebuilt precisely like the original.

All the church's walls are laid in Flemish bond. The south wall features a glazed-header checkerboard; the other walls have random glazed bricks. The west gable is decorated with nested triangles made with glazed headers. The medieval-style lancet windows that had been added in the nineteenth century were replaced by more appropriate casement windows during the restoration. The altar table in the church is believed to be original, although the top was apparently replaced at some point in its history.

Trinity Church still has a communion chalice presented by Queen Anne. A cushion, supposedly used by Queen Anne at her coronation and so highly valued that it once was kept on the altar, was destroyed when the Thomas King Carroll house burned in 1939.

Thomas King Carroll (1793–1873) lies in the tree-shaded graveyard at Trinity Church. Carroll was governor of Maryland in 1830, moving to Church Creek from Kingston Hall in Somerset County (see Tour 22) in the last years of his life. Nearby is the grave of his daughter, Anna Ella Carroll. One other point of interest in the cemetery is the millstones marking the grave of an early miller.

The brick section of the **Busick House,** 1.4 m., just across the cove from Trinity Church, is said to have been standing since 1700, but the brickwork appears to postdate the Revolution. The frame extension with its central chimney was added later. Old mantels, vertical paneling, and old floors grace rooms that members of Trinity Church now use for parish activities.

MADISON, 4.6 m., once a shipping and boat-building community, now depends entirely on crabbing, oystering, and tomato and oyster canning. In existence before 1760, Madison was originally called Tobacco Stick after the creek that flows into the Little Choptank River here. According to local tradition, the creek was named after the feat of an Indian who escaped pursuers by vaulting across the channel at the mouth of the cove on a tobacco stick. Emerson C. Harrington (1864–1945), governor of Maryland (1916–20), was born here.

A farm near Madison was the home of the legendary stubborn white mule that successfully resisted every attempt to harness him. According to the story, a Negro who once tried to harness the mule fell to the ground in a coma, proving that the mule was an incarnation of Satan. The mule is said to have galloped about the neighborhood at night, until he was finally driven into the marshes by a posse. Here he sank from view, but his ghost later appeared before the town drunkard, who was so overcome by the experience that he stopped drinking and became a parson.

At 5.5 m. on the right is the **Site of the Hodson House,** which is believed to have been built in 1673 by John Hodson, an early justice, as the first Dorchester County Courthouse; before that time the court had met in private homes. As late as 1814 the building was used as a jail. In 1814, men from Madison and Taylor's Island captured the eighteen-man crew of a British tender from the ship *Dauntless* that had gone aground near James Point, detaining them in this jail until they could be marched to Easton the next day.

From Madison to **Slaughter Creek,** 10.0 m., the road passes through flat marshes full of the shrub baccharis. On a misty fall day, the layers of grey baccharis, water, and sky create a dreamlike landscape where grasses sometime seem to float on air while their tips drown in water. A small oyster fleet rides at anchor on the island side of the bridge across the creek. By the shore stands the **Becky-Phipps Cannon,** captured with the British tender from the *Dauntless* in 1814 and named for Lieutenant Phipps, who commanded the crew, and for a Negro slave, Becky, whom they had taken prisoner.

Pioneers from the Western Shore were cultivating crops on **TAYLOR'S ISLAND,** 10.2 m., as early as 1659, and one or two early-eighteenth-century houses are still standing. From 1700 to about 1850, timber for shipyards was a major source of income for the island's residents, but since then fishing and farming have provided most people's livelihood. In summer and fall the island is renowned for sport fishing and duck hunting. The Page Communications Laboratory has an experiment station on the northern tip of the island.

At 10.8 m. is the second of two crossroads. Turn right on Hooper Neck Road to the **Chapel of Ease, Grace Protestant Episcopal Church** (R), 11.2 m. This simple one-room frame structure with a freestanding chimney is believed to be the chapel of ease erected soon after 1709 for Dorchester Parish. In 1959, the chapel was moved from its original site about one quarter mile away to this location by Grace Church. The chapel was then restored by the Grace Church Foundation, which had been established for that purpose. The chapel is one of the earliest buildings for worship still standing in Maryland, the Third Haven Meeting House in Easton (*see* Tour 12c) being the only frame church that is older.

Md. 335, now the main route, branches south from Md. 16 at Church Creek at 7.3 m. Just past the junction is another old Richardson house (private, but visible from the road), similar in style to *Richardson House.*

Along the Big Blackwater River, 9.0 m., the **Blackwater Migratory Bird Refuge** (refuge open, 8–8; visitor center, 8–4:30) stretches over more than 10,000 acres of marsh filled with wild fowl and muskrats. The refuge, established by the federal government in 1933, raises Canadian geese, mallards, blue-winged teal, and black ducks and is a migratory place for other varieties of wild fowl. Hundreds of thousands of muskrats populate the marshes, and a research station here is studying how best to manage and harvest this valuable animal, which has been steadily decreasing in numbers in recent years. Marshland in this area is considered to be as valuable for its game as adjoining farmland is for its crops.

At 16.0 m., Md. 335 turns sharp right at the junction with Md. 336.

● To the left Md. 336 travels the Lakes and Straits Neck districts, a peninsula full of quaint place names, such as Crapo, World's End Creek, Tedious Creek, Honga (Hunger) River, and Bishops Head. The name *Lakes* itself derives from a well-known family rather than from the watery character of the landscape. Capt. Henry Lake fought in the Revolution, and his daughter Lavinia, or Lovey, became a local Revolutionary heroine. According to tradition, although she was only in her early teens, Lovey fought off British soldiers who were trying to steal the silver buckles on her shoes. When the soldiers set fire to her house, she supposedly extinguished the fire by herself. Later, to prevent her father's capture, Lavinia brought members of his militia company to the rescue. Twenty-one of Captain Lake's descendants are said to have fought on the Confederate side during the Civil War.

WINGATE (est. 450 pop.), 10.0 m., is a center for oyster shucking

Blackwater National Wildlife Refuge

and seafood packing. From here county roads continue into the marshes. Inhabitants of this area are mostly descended from early British settlers. Although good roads keep them in touch with the rest of the world, their speech retains the back-of-the-throat quality often found in isolated areas (*see* Tour 22).

At 17.8 m. on Md. 335 the sprawling frame **Applegarth House** (private) stands near the road. Richard Tubman, an early Catholic settler from St. Mary's County, received a patent for the land here in 1670 as payment for his services as an Indian fighter. Tubman is believed to have built part of the present house, although it was much expanded during the nineteenth century. Even though the house is built on a high basement because of the marshy land, tides from the hurricane of October, 1954, reached the first floor. Most of the farmland in this area was flooded during this storm.

Just beyond the Applegarth House the road crosses Great Marsh Creek to **Meekins Neck,** 19.3 m., an area first settled in the last quarter of the seventeenth century by a group of Catholics from St. Mary's County including the Tubmans (*see above*), the Meekins, the Hoopers, and others. **St. Mary's Star of the Sea Church,** 19.4 m., serves a community of their descendants. The church is a white frame building (1872) with a rose window over the entrance and a tower on the corner, and it stands near the site of the first Catholic church in the county, which is said to have been built by Richard Tubman II in 1769.

At 22.4 m., where a wooden drawbridge crosses Fishing Creek to Upper Hooper Island, is the **Site of Plymouth,** laid out in 1707 on "Philips his pointe." In 1683 and again in 1706, the General Assembly passed acts "for the advancement of trade"— later disallowed by the Crown as likely to encourage local manufactures injurious to British commerce—ordering the erection of towns throughout the province. Temporary tax exemptions were allowed to "Tradesmen and Artificers" who would "live and inhabit in" the new towns, and all local business transactions were to take place at these spots and no others. Like most of these towns, however, Plymouth could not be legislated into existence. According to the records that remain, during the first three years local planters took up only eight of the one hundred lots ordered to be laid out. Nevertheless, the location was still referred to as Plymouth Town in 1748 when the assembly ordered a public tobacco warehouse built there; but later it became known simply as Plymouth Warehouse. The tobacco inspector was obliged to be on duty only three days a week, and in 1773 the assembly ordered the sale of the warehouse. The town's name was kept alive a while longer, however, because the militia company formed in 1776 called itself the Plymouth Greens.

Upper Hooper Island is part of a chain of three islands that are parallel to the mainland and separated from it by an estuary of the Bay called the Honga (formerly Hunger) River. These islands lie in an area that has one of the largest concentrations of wild ducks and geese in the United States. Most of the present residents, like those near *Wingate* across the Honga River, are descended from early settlers of pure British stock, and their speech has a soft, back-of-the-throat tone. Originally the islanders were farmers, but now almost all of them make their living from the water as crabbers, oyster tongers, and seafood packers. The villages on Upper and Middle Hooper islands came into existence after the Civil War, when improved transportation connected the islands with seafood markets. Good roads, radio and television, and mail-order houses have brought twentieth-century comforts to this corner of Dorchester. However, it still remains a special world in its orientation to the water rather than the land.

On the island side of the bridge the village of **HONGA** consists of a gasoline station, a general store, and fishermen's cottages and gardens. Next to the bridge, a retaining wall enables trucks to back up to the water's edge. Toward the end of the day during the oyster season, tongers dock their boats at the wall, using hand pulleys to unload directly into the trucks. The trucks then transport the catch to oyster shucking houses at Wingate or Cambridge.

Turn right at **FISHING CREEK** (est. 750 pop.), 24.2 m., the main settlement on the islands. Here the land is so narrow that the backyards of houses merge with the Bay while front yards border the Honga River. Along the road that skirts the river are retaining walls that enable trucks to park next to the boats for loading. Five crab houses operate here. Crabs are steamed and the meat picked out by hand. Then the crabmeat is packed in cans that are refrigerated for shipment to the supermarkets of Eastern cities. Beyond Fishing Creek, the road winds through marsh onto the narrow causeway leading to **Middle Hooper Island.** In misty weather only the tonging boats and duck blinds in Tar Bay and Honga River separate the water from the sky. The long, narrow one-way plank bridge, 26.0 m., that connects the causeway to Middle Hooper Island, does not look as if it could support the great trucks that cross it daily.

HOOPERSVILLE (est. 250 pop.), 31.1 m., on Middle Hooper Island, is a watermen's town. In addition to tonging craft, oyster dredge boats—sailing craft that dredge for oysters in waters too deep for tonging (*see* Tour 21, Deal Island)—are used by residents of Hoopersville. Two crab houses here employ people during the season.

Lower Hooper Island, isolated since the connecting bridge washed out more than thirty years ago, is frequented only by hunters, who reach it in private boats. Applegarth, once a small village of watermen here, was abandoned during World War I.

DELAWARE LINE–PRINCESS ANNE–POCOMOKE CITY–VIRGINIA LINE; 38.9 m.
U.S. 13

U.S. 13 crosses the southernmost part of Maryland's Eastern Shore, connecting towns on the navigable or once-navigable reaches of Chesapeake Bay rivers that flow into broad estuaries and sounds a few miles to the west. On the necks of land between these rivers, seventeenth-century settlers cleared small patches of pine land for pasture and crops. This part of Maryland, less well suited than the rest to produce high-quality tobacco, developed a trade in grain and livestock with Barbados and New England and was an early center of shipbuilding. Most of the earliest settlers in the area were Englishmen who had initially settled in Virginia, and among them were a considerable number of Quakers. Outlawed in Virginia during the 1600s, Quakers were welcomed by Lord Baltimore, who was anxious to strengthen his claim to territory on the Virginia border by attracting settlers. Settlement in the region was slower than farther north on the Shore, however, where the higher bluffs offered more tempting homesites and the land was generally richer and better drained. Rivers in this southern section of the Eastern Shore are often separated from the upland by broad expanses of marsh. After the Civil War, fishing villages grew up along the rivers and the Bay, but many of these have been affected by the declining yield of oysters and the centralization of seafood processing in a few towns such as Crisfield (*see* Tour 22).

East of U.S. 13 to the Pocomoke was nearly all wilderness until the railroad came through after the Civil War making possible the marketing of forest and farm products. There are still large areas of second-growth or cutover woodlands (mostly loblolly pines), but this central section, as well as the necks of land that were settled first, contain numerous truck farms that produce beans, tomatoes, melons, peppers, and sweet and white potatoes. At harvest time, migrant pickers are hired to supplement the regular farm workers. The migrants come from the South by the truckload, following the ripening crops from Florida through the Carolinas and Virginia to Maryland and New Jersey. Pressure from the federal government has forced

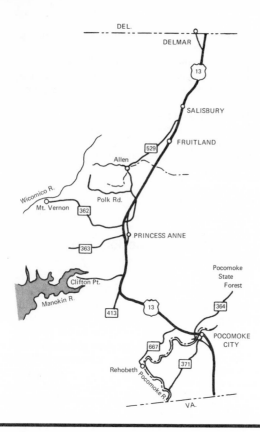

residents of the area to provide decent housing and community services for migrants. As elsewhere on the Lower Shore, some farmers faced with the cost of building acceptable housing for their workers have turned to field crops such as corn and soybeans and to livestock raising (*see* Tour 12c, Harrington Bridge), which do not depend on migrant labor.

Somerset County is trying to attract light industry that will provide employment and widen the tax base. Indicative of the region's poverty, several of the old houses that still stand along the rivers have been purchased and restored by affluent outsiders.

U.S. 13 crosses the **Delaware Line** in **DELMAR** (57' alt., 2,134 pop.), 0.0 m., a town with two mayors, two town councils, and two school systems, although the post office address for both sections is Delmar, Delaware. State Street, the main thoroughfare, is the state boundary. The site was a pine forest in 1858, when the Delaware Railroad reached the state line and opened repair shops here; it has been a railroad center ever since. After 1884, when the New York, Philadelphia, and Norfolk Railroad was extended to Cape Charles and a ferry line established from there to Norfolk, Delmar enjoyed a period of fast growth. Not long after the Pennsylvania Railroad acquired the whole line in 1918, the town's business began to feel the competition from trucks on the new paved highways, resulting in an increased economic dependence on the surrounding farmlands.

The combination bridge and tunnel across the mouth of the Chesapeake Bay that opened in 1964 has altered the economy of the Lower Eastern Shore because U.S. 13 is now a through north-south highway.

At 6.6 m. in **SALISBURY** (23′ alt., 15,252 pop.) (*see* Salisbury Tour) is the junction with U.S. 50 and Tour 12d.

At 8.0 m. College Avenue turns right at Salisbury State College.

● Go right to Md. 529 (Camden Avenue), 0.5 m., an alternate to U.S. 13. Go left on Md. 529. In **ALLEN** (10′ alt.), 6.6 m., turn right on the paved Cooper Road to the entrance lane (L), 3.3 m., of **Bennett's Adventure,** formerly known as the Paul Jones House (open by appointment: Thomas Horner). This gambrel-roofed brick house, now restored, has stood here since 1733. The house is well known for the excellence of its interior paneling and for the diamond patterns formed by the glazed headers in the brick of its front wall.

Cooper Road becomes Riverside Road and at about 4.3 m. makes a very sharp left turn. Just beyond is the private road (L) into **Bounds Chance** (private), believed to have been the rectory of Somerset Parish during the incumbency (1739–45) of Rev. Thomas Chase. It thus may have been the early childhood home of his son Samuel (1741–1811), signer of the Declaration of Independence and associate justice of the Supreme Court of the United States (1796–1811).

● From Allen, Md. 529 continues to Passerdyke Creek, 7.1 m. Near the bridge, a grassy bank (R) is all that remains of a bridge abutment constructed in 1835 for what was to have been the Eastern Shore Railroad. In 1833, the state legislature agreed to underwrite an $8,000,000 bond issue for the railroad as part of a successful effort to induce the Eastern Shore counties into abandoning the idea of uniting with Delaware. The Panic of 1837 brought the railroad project to an end.

Brentwood Farm (R) (private), 8.1 m., is visible from the road. Rev. Alexander Adams of Stepney Parish supposedly built the brick part of the house in 1738 (date on board in attic stair, now removed). Although the dwelling is two and one-half stories high, it is dwarfed by the early-twentieth-century shingled additions. From the lawn, **Anderson House** on the Tull Farm can be seen. A large brick dwelling of distinguished appearance, Anderson House is said to have been built about 1730. The gable ends, once stuccoed, extend to form the walls of a great built-in porch.

Md. 529 continues to a junction with Polks Road, 9.0 m. Go right to **White Hall** (private), 3.0 m. a 2½-story frame house with one brick gable built sometime in the eighteenth century by a member of the Polk family. It stands on the banks of Wicomico Creek. James Knox Polk (1795–1849), eleventh president of the United States, was a member of this family.

At 3.9 m. on Polks Road is the junction with Redden Ferry Road (unmarked). Turn right on Redden Ferry Road; along the road is the probable **Site of the Birthplace of Samuel Chase** (L) (*see above*), 4.5 m. (not marked). The house, now destroyed, belonged to Chase's maternal grandfather.

At 9.8 m. on Md. 529 is the southern junction with U.S. 13.

The first few miles of U.S. 13 south of Salisbury are a dense commercial area. **FRUITLAND** (42′ alt., 2,315 pop.), 9.5 m., is a busy canning and freezing center. In December, holly and Christmas greens from all the Lower Shore counties are sold here at two great auctions. Open country prevails from Fruitland to *Pocomoke City*, for the main highway now by-passes *Princess Anne.*

At 17.6 m. Md. 529 turns left into the center of *Princess Anne.*

At 18.8 m. is the junction with Md. 362.

● Go right on Md. 362 to **Waterloo,** formerly called Moni or Carey's Purchase (private, but visible from the road), 3.3 m., and probably built by Henry Waggaman shortly after 1741. The house, nearly square in shape with a hip roof and modillioned cornice, stands by a mill pond, and the glazed headers of its facade and the plastered quoins on the corners are resplendent in the afternoon sunlight. A curtain and kitchen wing on one side have been matched by corresponding modern structures on the other side, making the house a five-part mansion. The building served as the Somerset County Almshouse for many years, during which time the county commissioners sold the paneling from the interior of the house; some original woodwork and a very interesting stairway still remain.

Just beyond Waterloo is the **Site of Hackland** (L), 3.5 m., home of Levin Denwood, a Quaker leader whose house was designated a Friends meeting house by the Somerset County Court in 1704.

The road continues a meandering course through the marshes, passing through the settlement of **MT. VERNON,** 6.1 m., and ending in a cluster of houses near the water.

At 19.4 m. is the junction with Md. 363 and Tour 21 in **PRINCESS ANNE** (18′ alt., 975 pop.). To reach the center of town, turn left on Md. 363, following Mansion and Prince William streets to Somerset Avenue. Princess Anne is the county seat of Somerset County and, except for the two-block "downtown" along Somerset Avenue, is predominantly nineteenth century in appearance. Federal and Victorian houses are shaded by magnificent sycamores that line Somerset Avenue and Prince William Street, and both the trees and houses symbolize a town of venerable age and dignity. The future of Princess Anne seems to depend on attracting light industries that will provide jobs and widen the tax base. The new bridge and tunnel across the mouth of the Chesapeake Bay has increased the area's potential for economic development.

Aside from one garment factory, present industries in Princess Anne center around agriculture, fishing, and lumber resources. Three vegetable canneries, a pickle factory, a seafood processing plant, five lumber yards, and three poultry feed plants employ many of the town's residents. As late as 1900, three-masted schooners could sail up the Manokin River almost to the main street to unload fertilizer and manufactured goods and to load lumber and agricultural products. Now a rowboat can scarcely navigate at low tide, and weeds almost conceal the river from view. A truck body shop reflects the town's dependence upon trucking for transportation, although railroad freight service is still available. Tourism is a new resource for the area. Each October, a weekend is devoted to "Princess Anne Days," with many homes in the town and surrounding countryside being opened to visitors.

The General Assembly ordered the town to be laid out in 1733, but the site did not become the county seat until 1742. In that year, Worcester County was created from part of Somerset County, causing the courthouse at Dividing Creek to be no longer centrally located in the county. Since travel was slow and often hazardous in eighteenth-century Maryland, geographically central county seats were considered highly desirable. As a result, when Worcester County was erected, Princess Anne was named the new county seat of Somerset.

The town was named in honor of George II's daughter Anne (1709–59). Few colonial buildings still stand, but the town may never have contained very many. Perhaps the earliest is the **Tunstall Cottage** (private), on the corner of Church and Broad streets, one block west of Somerset Avenue, a picturesque 1½-story frame house with curiously pyramidic outside chimneys that are freestanding above the first floor. The house was built in 1705 and is the oldest inhabited dwelling in Princess Anne. The rear wing is a later, but still very old, addition. The hall and parlor of the original house retain their old chimney pieces, box stair, and some paneling.

Around the corner from Tunstall Cottage on N. Somerset Avenue is the **Washington Hotel** (open daily), a 2½-story frame structure with heavy outside brick chimneys that was built in 1744. The hotel has been used as an inn since the late eighteenth century and served as a rendezvous for several prominent men. A ledger dated 1780 is preserved by the owners.

The most handsome pre-Revolutionary building in this area and one of the best-known houses south of the Nanticoke is **Beckford** (private), most easily seen from U.S. 13, which passes a few feet from its entrance. Henry Jackson, a merchant, is supposed to have built Beckford about 1776. The Doric frieze under the cornice of this large, hip-roofed brick house and the wooden keystone lintels over the windows contribute to its sumptuous and imposing character. White panels between the first and second floor windows replace a stringcourse, a variation found on many late-eighteenth- and early-nineteenth-century houses of this area but rarely seen elsewhere in Maryland.

The most famous house in Princess Anne is the **Teackle Mansion** (foot of Prince William Street, along Mansion Street and adjoining Beckford), a magnificent five-part brick house built in 1801 by Littleton Dennis Teackle. The main block and the wings all have gables to the front, and the cornice crosses the center gable to create a pediment pierced by a bull's-eye window. The hyphens are two stories high on the Mansion Street front but drop to one story on the garden front. The reeded cornice, keystone lintels over the windows, and the white panels that replace the stringcourse in the center block add to the elegant appearance of the house. The Teackle Mansion is featured in George Alfred ("Gath") Townsend's *The Entailed Hat,* a locally famous novel of the antebellum lower peninsula based on the kidnappings and other criminal exploits of Patty Cannon (*see* Tour 18, Reliance). The living room of the house illustrates the obsession with symmetry characteristic of late Georgian architecture, the garden windows being balanced by false window openings in the opposite partition. Old Princess Anne Days, Inc., has purchased the central block of the mansion (open Sun., 2–4, and by request) for a museum.

Contemporary with the Teackle Mansion is the **Johnston House,** 205 S. Somerset Avenue, corner of Antioch Street, a

2½-story frame house with a pedimented gable and a handsome fanlight over the entrance. The builder, William Johnston, is believed to have copied the interior stairway from one on exhibit in the Peale Museum in Baltimore.

One block north from the Johnston House on Somerset Avenue is the **Handy Garden,** a formal box garden planted in 1842 by Gen. George Handy. Across the street is a handsome frame house, with a pedimented front gable and two brick chimneys in the rear, which appears to be at least as old as the garden. On the corner of Somerset Avenue and Prince William Street is the **Somerset County Courthouse** (open Mon.–Fri.), built in 1905 in a simplified Renaissance-Revival style. A portrait of Queen Anne attributed to Sir Geoffrey Kneller hangs in the courtroom.

At the eastern end of Prince William Street, one block to the right off Somerset Avenue, **East Glen** (private) faces the Teackle Mansion. The well-kept white frame house with its pedimented front gable and double chimneys in the rear is said to have been built about 1795 by Col. Mathias Jones.

On the left off Somerset Avenue just beyond the bridge over the Manokin (here scarcely a brook) is **Nutter's Purchase,** a small eighteenth-century house recently restored. Beyond is one of the two eighteenth-century churches in Princess Anne, the **Manokin Presbyterian Church** (open), which serves a congregation founded by Rev. Thomas Wilson in 1683. The first church on this site is believed to have been built in 1690; in 1697 it was described to Gov. Francis Nicholson as a "plain country building" belonging to the "dissenters." Only the walls of the present structure date as early as 1765. The tower was added in 1888, and there have been many other alterations to both the interior and exterior.

The second colonial church is **St. Andrew's Protestant Episcopal Church** (open by request) on Church Street (parallel to Somerset Avenue), one block south of Prince William Street. In 1767, the Somerset Parish vestry contracted for a chapel of ease on this site, to be sixty by forty feet with a "Simey Circle" for the communion table. The brick walls, laid in Flemish bond, still stand, but the "Simey Circle," or apse, has been enlarged and the interior remodeled in the Victorian style. While rector here, Rev. Clayton Torrence wrote *Old Somerset* (1935), a standard book on the early history of the Lower Eastern Shore.

● Turn west off Somerset Avenue on Broad Street to the **University of Maryland, Eastern Shore (UMES),** a coeducational state college. The school was founded by Methodists in 1886 as the Delaware Conference Academy, a preparatory branch for the Methodist-sponsored Centenary Bible Institute, which in 1890 was renamed Morgan College (*see* East Baltimore and Northeast Baltimore). Under provisions of the Morrill Act, the academy became a land grant college in 1890, taking the name Princess Anne Academy. In 1919, the University of Maryland assumed control of the college, and in 1935 the state acquired full title to the school from Morgan College. Courses offered lead to bachelor's degrees in agriculture, home economics, industrial and mechanic arts, and the liberal arts and sciences.

At 19.5 m., U.S. 13 passes *Beckford* (L) and at 21.3 m. joins Alt. U.S. 13 as it emerges from Princess Anne. At 22.0 m. the

Beverly of Somerset

road crosses Jones Creek. To the left a short distance up the creek is the second **Site of Washington Academy.** A brick house was built here in 1803 to replace the group of buildings, erected sometime before 1779 on Back Creek a few miles away, that had burned—along with a newly acquired "Philosophical Apparatus"—in 1797. For a while at least, the school (chartered in 1779) appears to have served the whole Lower Shore. Funds for the school were collected from the two adjoining Virginia counties and Sussex County in Delaware as well as from Somerset, Worcester, and Dorchester counties in Maryland. Representatives from each of these areas were appointed to the governing board of the school in 1785. In 1819, forty-five students, twenty-five of them boarders, took courses in mathematics, Latin grammar, and rhetoric, studying Homer, Horace, Cicero, Virgil, and the Greek Testament. The school rules of 1823 were in some ways similar to those of a modern boys' boarding school. Most rules governed "hallowing" in the dormitory and destruction of school property, but visits to billiard or gaming rooms in Princess Anne were listed as major offenses; surprisingly, there was no mention of alcoholic beverages! In 1843 the academy discontinued boarding the students and moved to Princess Anne. In 1872 the school was closed, but by agreement with the school commissioners of Somerset County, it was reopened a few months later as a public high school. In 1891, bricks and timbers from both the "Old Academy" and the buildings in Princess Anne were used in the construction of a new public school building, which was torn down in 1939. The bricks were then used once again as backing for the wall of the present Washington High School.

KING'S CREEK, 22.1 m., is a hamlet at the junction of the Crisfield branch of the Pennsylvania Railroad. Just beyond is the entrance lane (R), 22.5 m., of **Beverly of Somerset** (private), so called to distinguish it from *Beverly* in Worcester. When completed in 1796, this mansion was a great house by any American standard, reflecting the wealth of its builder, Nehemiah King II (1755–1802), who at his death was one of the largest slave-holders in Maryland. The house, hip-roofed with modillioned and dentiled cornice, is distinguished by a two-story octagonal entrance bay. The semicircular fanlight of the doorway, which breaks into the delicately carved pediment, is repeated in the round head of the second-story window above. The narrow windows in each side of the bay create a Palladian effect. The entrance hall is magnificent. No stairway is visible to obstruct the sumptuous effect of space and airiness created by the four-teen-foot ceilings, the wide elliptical central arch, and the elaborate but delicate carving on cornice, chair rail, and door and window frames. The woodwork of the living room is equally well done, and the stair in a transverse hall (off the main hall, behind the arch) has a simple elegance. In 1938, just after the building had been thoroughly renovated and restored, a dis-gruntled former employee of the owner flooded the house with coal oil and set it afire. The present interior is an exact restora-tion based on drawings and descriptions made before the fire.

The house is alleged to have figured in one of the many schemes to rescue Napoleon from St. Helena Island. In 1803, while awaiting an opportunity to return to the scene of his brother's triumphs, Jerome Bonaparte married Betsy Patterson of Baltimore (*see* Downtown Baltimore). When he was finally able to return to Europe two years later, Jerome had the marriage annulled even though Betsy had already borne him a son. In spite of his abandonment of Betsy, Jerome retained the friend-ship of many Americans, including the Kings of Beverly. When Napoleon was finally confined to St. Helena, some of his ad-mirers plotted to rescue him. According to tradition, the friends raised funds to build a fast sloop, studied plans of the island and its fortifications, and carefully rehearsed details of the escape. Once Napoleon was rescued, he was to be brought across the Atlantic to Beverly, where he would hide in a secret room until he could be safely taken to New Orleans. Before the sloop sailed in 1821, however, word of Napoleon's death was received.

At 23.0 m. is the junction (R) with Revell's Neck Road.

● This road leads into Revells Neck, where Randall Revell, one of the earliest Somerset County settlers, patented a large tract of land, naming it Double Purchase. One of the seventeenth-century court-houses and the first town of Somerset County, called Somerset Town (established 1668), were built on Double Purchase. The exact location of Deep Point, the site of the town, is not known. It probably stood on Clifton Point, where an old brick house, **Clifton** (private, but visible from the road), 4.2 m., still stands. Although some say this large 2½-story dwelling has been here since 1700, when the town was still in existence, the details of its construction resemble those of houses built in this area about 1800. Just across the Manokin River from here stand Elmwood and Almodington (*see* Tour 21), homes built by descendants of John Elzey who, with Randall Revell, was a leading figure in the first settlement of the Maryland Lower Shore by Englishmen moving up from Virginia. Elzey and Revell were named in the first commissions for granting land and keeping the peace in this region (1661–62), which were issued prior to the establishment of county government. Revell later lost his position and influence because he was suspected of supporting Edmund Scarborough, the surveyor general and treasurer of Virginia who in 1663 invaded Maryland in the name of the Virginia government (*see* Tour 21, Almodington). Revell continued to reside on Double Purchase, however, holding the office of sheriff of Somerset County in 1670.

At 24.2 m. is the junction with Md. 413 and Tour 22.

At 30.5 m. on U.S. 13 is the junction with Md. 667.

● Turn right. At 4.9 m. bear left (there is a sign for Rehoboth Church). At 5.4 m. bear left again to the **Ruins of Coventry Church**, brick walls of a church built between 1784 and 1792 on the banks of the Pocomoke for Coventry Parish. The building continued in use until about 1900. In 1928 the ragged walls were capped with cement and a brick altar was built within the roofless rectangle. The double tier of windows that once lighted this fine church can still be seen on one wall. About four feet to the south is the site of the first church, which was probably standing by 1696. In 1933, the foundations of the old church were excavated and marked with four cement posts. Farther up the river, but within sight of these ruins, is **Rehoboth Presbyterian Church** (open), notable as the oldest house of worship (1705–6) in the United States that has remained exclusively Presbyterian and as one of the meeting houses built by the Presbyterian zealot, Francis Makemie (ca. 1658–1708). This small church, with random glazed headers in the Flemish bond brickwork, was partially restored in 1954–55. The stained-glass windows were added during a Victorian remodeling, but the plain walls, white paneled pews, and plain paneled reading desk have the simple character of an early-eighteenth-century dissenters' house of prayer. Makemie owned the land on which the church was built, which proved important when the Anglican ministry protested to the governor and the council that a dissenting church should not be allowed within half a mile of an established church (Coventry Church is less than 200 yards away). Pending action by the bishop of London, temporary permission was finally granted to Makemie "to preach in his house according to the Tolleration," and in 1708 the county court certified the meeting house without waiting for the bishop's decision.

Francis Makemie (pronounced M'Kemmy), born of Scottish parents in Ireland, immigrated to the Eastern Shore in 1683. He came in response to a plea sent to the presbytery at Laggan by Col. William Stevens—himself Anglican—asking that someone be sent to minister to the spiritual needs of the Presbyterians who were fast settling in the area. Makemie traveled to the South shortly after he arrived, while Samuel Davis (*see* Tour 23, Snow Hill), William Traile, and Thomas Wilson (*see above*, Princess Anne), all of whom had arrived by 1686, carried on his work in Somerset County. By 1687 or 1688, however, Makemie had settled in nearby Accomac County, Virginia, ministering to the Presbyterians there as well as to a congregation here at Rehobeth. During the 1690s, Makemie continued his missionary endeavors in the colonies, including Barbados. In 1706, after returning from Europe, Makemie helped found the presbytery of Philadelphia, from which organized Presbyterianism in America grew.

The name *Rehoboth*, meaning "there is room," was given by Col. William Stevens (1630–87) to the Pocomoke River plantation he patented in 1665. Stevens was appointed a county justice the year he arrived in Maryland and from 1679 until his death he served as a member of the council. Stevens utilized the political influence he derived from these important county and provincial offices to amass a large fortune from real estate and merchandising.

At 32.3 m. is the junction with Md. 364 and old U.S. 13.

● Go left on this road. At 5.5 m. state maintenance ends and the county road continues into Pocomoke State Forest. Just before this point, a narrow private dirt road turns right to **Cellar House** (private), a late-seventeenth- or early-eighteenth-century frame house with brick ends, distinguished by its excellent early interior woodwork. The house stands on a high bank above the Pocomoke at one of the few places along the river not bordered by marsh.

The county road forks at 6.1 m.; bear right and then right again at 6.5 m. (follow signs) to **Milburn Landing Recreation Area** (camping, picnicking, fishing; no swimming) on the Pocomoke River within the **Pocomoke State Forest.** The forest, over 12,000 acres, was cutover and unimproved woodland when it was acquired by the state in the 1930s. Forest management is directed at creating a self-sustaining yield of loblolly pine. Trails into the forest from Milburn Landing lead to swamp and woodland areas that are rewarding for nature study, especially birdwatching, with the close proximity of swamp and upland bringing together a great variety of plants, animals, and birds.

● Go right on old U.S. 13 and cross the Pocomoke River into the downtown area of **POCOMOKE CITY** (8′ alt., 3,573 pop.), 0.5 m., the largest town in Worcester County. A landing has been located here since the seventeenth century, because the deep Pocomoke River was a center of shipping and shipbuilding from the earliest days of settlement in the region. Even with the competition from railroads and trucks, small oil tankers still bring petroleum to the port. The town was called Newtown when it was first laid out about 1780. Finally incorporated in 1865, the town changed its name to Pocomoke City in 1878. A poultry freezing plant here employs about 700 people, with a shirt factory and four vegetable canneries accounting for another 600 workers. Aspiring to further economic development, the active Pocomoke City Chamber of Commerce is aggressively seeking new industry.

Fires in 1888, 1892, and 1922 destroyed most of the old structures in Pocomoke City. Citizens are proud of the **City Hall,** on the east side of Clarke Avenue near Market Street, a Georgian-Colonial-style building erected in 1936.

At 0.7 m. Fourth Street turns right off Market Street. After one-half mile, Fourth Street becomes Md. 371 (Cedarhall Wharf Road). Follow this to a junction with Colona Road and Cedarhall Wharf Road, 4.9 m. Continue straight ahead on Cedarhall Wharf Road to the entrance lane (L) to **Beverly** in Worcester (private, but visible from the road), 5.2 m., standing on the banks of the Pocomoke River. Both inside and out, this two-story brick mansion reflects the date of its construction (ca. 1774), with its good proportions, modillioned cornice, and paneled walls and chimney pieces executed in balanced designs. The two-story Greek-Revival portico on the land approach is a later addition. The Beverly tract, which once extended across the line into Virginia, belonged to the Dennis family until the twentieth century. Donnoch Dennis moved to Somerset from Accomac, Virginia, taking out his first land patent in 1669. Donnoch's great-grandson, Littleton Dennis, merchant and planter, started construction on the present house before his death. Later descendants served on the Maryland Court of Appeals (Littleton Dennis served 1801–6), in other judgeships, and in Congress. John Dennis, elected to Congress at the age of twenty-five (1797–1805), was one of the five Federalists who switched his vote in the presidential election of 1800 to Jefferson, thus breaking the deadlock with Aaron Burr. John Upshur Dennis (1797–1851), an exporter of cypress and molasses, sired twenty-one children and is said to have won his third wife in competition with his oldest son. According to family tradition, a tombstone for John Upshur's second wife and a carriage for his

third arrived on the same ship. The brick-walled Dennis family graveyard is near the house.

U.S. 13 crosses the Pocomoke at 32.6 m., traversing the outskirts of Pocomoke City. At 34.3 m. the road makes a junction
with the southern terminal of U.S. 113 (Tour 23), and at 38.9 m.
it crosses the **Virginia Line.**

PRINCESS ANNE–DEAL ISLAND; 16.2 m.
Md. 363

From U.S. 13 in Princess Anne, 0.0 m., Md. 363 crosses farmlands and forested lowlands that recede into marshes. At 5.1
m. is the junction with Md. 627.

● Go left 1.2 m. to a graveled road to **Almodington** (open by appointment: Mrs. Wayne L. Benedict), one of the well-known houses of
Somerset County. This long, narrow, 2½-story brick house is believed
to have been built by Arnold Elzey, who died in 1733. The magnificent
woodwork of the dining room, executed in the eighteenth century, and
a mantel of the early Federal period are in the American wing of the
Metropolitan Museum of Art in New York City. Arnold Elzey's father,
John Elzey, who patented the tract in 1661, was one of the commissioners appointed by the Maryland governor and council in 1661 to
govern the Manokin and nearby Quaker Annemessex settlements,
newly established by Englishmen from Virginia. These first Lower Eastern Shore Maryland settlements had to contend not only with the
rigors of a frontier existence and the fear of Indians but also with
Virginia imperialism. Col. Edmund Scarborough, surveyor general and
treasurer of Virginia, demanded that Elzey acknowledge the Virginia
government and pay fees for his land grant. Elzey barely escaped
arrest with a vaguely worded submission (that Scarborough compared to the "Oracle at Delphos") and begged Lord Baltimore's government "to consider our condition, how we lie between Scylla and
Charibdis, not knowing how to get out of this labarynth." The Maryland
Council protested to Virginia's Governor Berkeley but sent no one to
protect the Eastern Shore residents. In 1663, Scarborough invaded
Manokin and Annemessex with forty horsemen and placed "the broad
arrow of confiscation" on the door of all who would not submit to
Virginia authority. The Annemessex Quakers resisted; most of the
Manokin settlers submitted, but John Elzey asked for time to turn in
his Maryland commission first. The Virginia government refused to
support Scarborough's invasion, and shortly thereafter the Virginia-
Maryland boundary was set well to the south, near its present location.
Elzey retained his influence and his place on the Maryland commission
until his death in 1664.

South of Almodington on the Manokin River is **Elmwood** (private),
1.3 m., an exceptionally handsome brick house built about 1800 by another Elzey. Offshore, and now covered by water, lies the site of the
first church of Somerset Parish. Across the river can be seen Clifton
(*see* Tour 20).

At 8.3 m. on Md. 363, the great marshes almost reach the
road; flat miles of grass and water reach to the horizon. On
the left, at times adjoining the road, is the **Deal Island Wildlife**

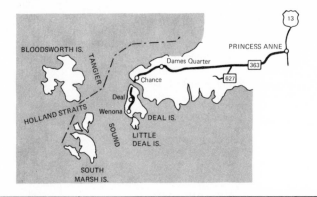

Management Area (entrance at 10.3 m.), over 10,200 acres of marsh abounding in wildlife. Belonging to the state, it is the responsibility of the Department of Natural Resources and is administered by the Wildlife Management Administration. Part of this marsh is a game refuge, with the remainder open to hunters in season. The Deal area is one of thirty-five wildlife management areas the state has purchased.

DAMES QUARTER (2′ alt.), 9.9 m., a fishing and farming village, was formerly known as Damned Quarter—perhaps because of its proximity to Devil Island, later known as Deal Island.

CHANCE (2′ alt.), 12.6 m., at the tip of the neck, may be named for an early land patent.

A wooden bridge crosses a narrows called Upper Thorofare to Deal Island. Most of the year, a dozen or so skipjacks are moored in the Upper Thorofare, a portion of the five dozen or so commercial sail craft left in Somerset County waters. Skipjacks are sloop-rigged vessels that vary in length from thirty to sixty feet. With their raked masts, white hulls, and "trail boards"—that is, name boards on the bows painted with gold leaf and brilliant colors—skipjacks are an arresting sight. The boats are equipped with iron-pronged dredges that are lowered overside to scrape oysters from the deepwater bottom. Maryland conservation laws require that deepwater oyster dredging be carried on by sail craft only. In 1940 there were about 150 skipjacks at Deal Island; today hardly a third of these are left. Few new boats are being built, partly because the oysters are disappearing, but also in the expectation that the Maryland restrictions against power-driven dredges will eventually be lifted. About 1960, the Deal Island skippers, mourning a dying skill, established a skipjack race on Labor Day that has since become an annual event.

On the left of the bridge over Upper Thorofare are moored tonging boats—low, power-driven craft from which watermen use giant hand tongs to harvest oysters in shallow waters. The tongs lift as much as fifty pounds of shellfish at a time. Since oystering is a winter activity, few occupations require more physical endurance. Still in use at Deal Island for tonging are some sailing canoes (called cunners) made long ago out of hewed-out logs of cypress or heart-pine and now unmasted.

Dredging for oysters from a skipjack

Tonging in the Wicomico River was outlawed as of September 14, 1975, because of the Wicomico-Somerset boundary dispute.

Crabbing is nearly as important as oystering to watermen here and elsewhere. The soft-crab season runs from May to October. Crabbers set out latticed shedder-floats, which are stacked in piles on land during the winter, in which crabs are kept until they shed their old shells; then while soft they are packed in seaweed and crushed ice and shipped live to market.

DEAL ISLAND (2' alt., 957 pop.), 13.8 m. in Tangier Sound, is approximately one-half marshland. Most of the people live on a "high" strip a mile wide and three miles long on the western side of the island. The main population clusters are Deal on the north and Wenona on the south. Most houses on the island are white-painted frame structures that appear to have been built no earlier than the late nineteenth or early twentieth century, though there were settlers here in the eighteenth century. Nearly everyone makes his living by catching, packing, or shipping oysters and crabs, by trapping muskrats on the great marshes, or by taking out parties of salt-water anglers in summer and hunters in winter. Some pleasure craft anchor in the harbors, but for the most part, Deal Island is still an out-of-the-way place for city people.

Two crab and oyster packing houses on Deal Island employed about 100 people in 1974, nearly one-fifth of the people employed in these industries in the county. Thousands of barrels of hard-shelled crabs are annually brought to the packing houses by water and truck. They are steamed in huge vats, and the meat is picked out by hand. Skilled workers can earn over $100 a week shucking oysters and picking crabs, but the work is only seasonal (*see* Tour 22, Crisfield). Incomes of those who harvest shellfish are impossible to determine accurately. A few watermen—probably very few—do very well, but fluctuations in the size of the catch and in the price it will command are extreme.

From the shore of Deal Island one can look out to South Marsh Island and Bloodsworth Island. Between these are the **Holland Straits,** the primary location of a major experiment undertaken by the Maryland Department of Tidewater Fisheries (now the Maryland Fisheries Administration) to revive the oyster beds. Since 1954, oyster packers have by law turned over half their shells for replanting in areas where oyster larvae are likely to "set" and grow. This program proved insufficient, so the department started dredging unproductive reefs of old oyster shells in the Bay in 1960. In 1961 over 5,000,000 bushels of shells were dredged and planted, and more than 3,500,000 of these went into Holland Straits. When the seed oysters had grown for a year or so on these shells, they were moved to natural oyster bars where growing conditions were favorable. This program was so successful that the state established the Shellfish Propagation Program.

At 14.6 m. Md. 363 passes in front of one of the three Methodist churches and graveyards on the island. Here, and in the two other island cemeteries, the dead are buried in sarcophagi that rise above the surface of the marshy ground. Behind the church that is used today is a frame chapel built in 1850, and beside it is the **Grave of Joshua Thomas** (1776–1853), called the Parson of the Islands. Thomas was largely responsible for establishing Methodism as the deep-rooted faith of lower Chesapeake Bay islanders. A fisherman like his neighbors and, like most of them, almost illiterate, Thomas converted to evangelical Methodism in 1807, soon after the Great Revival reached this part of America. He "managed" yearly camp meetings on Tangier Island, his home until 1825, and carried preachers in his log canoe, *The Methodist,* from island to island and to the mainland. Thomas is famous for his sermon to the British expeditionary force encamped on Tangier Island during the War of 1812, in which he boldly predicted (divine guidance, say the islanders) that they would fail to capture Baltimore.

An elder of this church, it is said, was responsible for changing the name of the island from Devil to Deal to avoid the implication that Satan had any right or property on the island.

In **WENONA,** 16.2 m., there is an anchorage for skipjacks and other craft on Lower Thorofare, which divides Deal Island from Little Deal Island. Besides fishpacking houses, there is a sail loft in town where sails for pleasure boats as well as for oyster craft are made. Joshua Thomas lived on Little Deal Island from 1825 until his death and was presiding elder of the congregation of the area.

JUNCTION OF U.S. 13 AND MD. 413–WESTOVER–CRISFIELD–SMITH ISLAND; 24.6 m.
Md. 413 and boat

This route travels the neck of land between the Annemessex and Pocomoke rivers, which empty into Tangier Sound on the Chesapeake Bay. The north side of the peninsula was the first area of the Maryland Lower Shore to be settled. Harsh laws against Quakers passed by the Virginia Assembly in 1661 drove these pioneers to petition Lord Baltimore's government for permission to take up lands in Maryland, and the Annemessex colony was founded by January of 1661/62, a few weeks before the Manokin settlers appeared a few miles north on Revell Neck (*see* Tour 20, Clifton, and Tour 21, Almodington). The land today produces truck crops, corn, and soybeans, while the marshes harbor muskrats and are feeding grounds for countless thousands of ducks and geese during the winter. From the surrounding waters, fishermen harvest hundreds of thousands of dollars worth of crabs and oysters each year. *Crisfield,* at the tip of the peninsula, is a busy headquarters for the Maryland and Virginia seafood industry.

Md. 413 branches south from U.S. 13 (*see* Tour 20), 0.0 m., at a point about five miles south of Princess Anne.

WESTOVER, 0.4 m., is a rail and highway shipping point for farm and forest products in the heart of this agricultural area. In 1959, in accordance with federal guidelines, the State of Maryland finally took steps to improve the living quarters and community services offered to migrant laborers, many of whom work in this area. The Governor's Committee for the Regulation and Study of Migratory Labor in Maryland was created. This committee develops and recommends standards for housing, sanitation, health, and welfare for farm laborers.

Maryland is in the middle of the East Coast migrant labor stream. Pickers travel as families either in their own cars or in crews traveling by truck. Crew leaders usually carry on the negotiations with the growers, often through the mediation of the U.S. Employment Service. The pickers work the winter crops in Florida and move north through the Carolinas, Virginia, and Maryland to New Jersey during the summer and fall (*see* Tour 12c, Harrington Bridge). They are paid either by the hour or by the quantity harvested, depending upon the crop. Employers need not pay a minimum wage because the federal law applies only to plants and factories where workers are employed more than eight weeks each year. One worker cannot earn enough to support a family by sharecropping at home in Florida or Georgia, but when the whole family takes to the road as pickers they can earn enough to get by, although they rarely are able to save much of their income.

Sometime after the mid-eighteenth century, Thomas King built a brick house named **Kingston Hall** in the vicinity of Westover. Thomas King Carroll (1793–1873), governor of Maryland (1830–

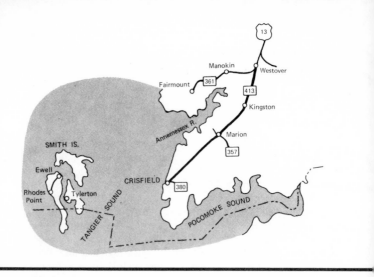

31), lived here until 1837, and here he raised his famous daughter, Anna Ella Carroll (1815–94).

Anna Ella Carroll, oldest child and favorite daughter of Thomas King Carroll, was educated from the books in her father's library, including his law books. When financial difficulties, partly the result of Carroll's unwillingness to sell slaves or free them without adequate provision, forced the sale of Kingston Hall after the Panic of 1837, his daughter embarked on a career that today would be described as that of a public relations expert. Her eminent social connections gave her an unquestioned entrée into Baltimore and Washington society; her pen was skilled, and she was knowledgeable in law. These assets made her especially useful to various railroad interests, for which she wrote and lobbied. In addition, after 1850 she became an active force in Whig and American (Know-Nothing) party politics.

When the Civil War broke out, Anna Carroll turned her talents to helping the Union cause. Her pamphlet, *Reply to Breckinridge* (1861), which accused Southern leaders of preparing for secession as early as 1850, was considered so effective in persuading Marylanders to stay in the Union that the federal government bought ten thousand copies for distribution throughout the North. Some claim that Anna Ella Carroll became one of Lincoln's secret advisors at this time. She was commissioned as a writer for the War Department, although she was never able to collect more than token payment for her work. Her *War Powers of the General Government* (1862) contained the first published justification for the extraordinary executive powers Lincoln was forced to exercise. Carroll also traveled to St. Louis in the summer of 1861 to assist in devising a plan for invading the South through Tennessee rather than by the heavily fortified Mississippi, the plan that was actually used during the winter of 1862. When the capture of Vicksburg seemed impossible, she drew plans for attacking it from the land, and in 1863, Vicksburg fell to a land attack. It is claimed that these and Anna Carroll's other contributions to the war strategy were a well-kept secret that Lincoln would have revealed had he lived. Congress never officially recognized her role in the war, and much of the correspondence with Lincoln that would have proved her case has disappeared if it ever existed. In 1876, Anna Carroll was finally granted a small pension, and she lived her last years paralyzed, supported by her sister who worked as a government clerk.

At 1.3 m. is the junction with Md. 361, the Fairmount Road.

● Go right on Md. 361 into Fairmount Neck, where a number of old brick and frame houses remain along the shores of the Annemessex. At 1.4 m. turn left onto a dirt road; then left again to the gates of **Liberty Hall,** a small frame house, originally one and one-half stories but raised to two and one-half stories in a remodeling about 1795. The mantel and other handsome woodwork in the living room must have been installed in 1795, although the pre-Revolutionary mantel in the dining room may have been in the living room at an earlier date. The first house on the tract was built in the seventeenth century, and the owners believe the living room of the present house incorporates the earlier dwelling, which was expanded in the mid-eighteenth century to include a dining room and stair hall. Open by appointment: Mr. and Mrs. Theodore Dorman, Manokin.

● **MANOKIN,** at 2.3 m., is a crossroads hamlet.

At 5.6 m. Md. 361 becomes a county road that continues to **FAIR-MOUNT,** a small village of farmers and watermen bordering the edge of a great marsh on Tangier Sound and the Annemessex River. Part of this marsh is now the **Fairmount Wildlife Management Area** (*see* Tour 21, Deal Wildlife Management Area).

KINGSTON (est. 140 pop.), 4.7 m., is a railroad stop with a lumberyard and two canneries. In May, **MARION,** 7.9 m., is the auction center for strawberries, one of the major crops grown in this area. Here is the junction with Md. 357.

● The right branch of Md. 357, which is Cannon Road, joins Coulbourn Creek Road, 1.0 m. (L). This route leads to the mouth of Colbourn Creek, along which Stephen Horsey, the first known settler in Maryland below the Choptank River, patented the tract Coulbourne in 1663. Horsey (ca. 1620–71), a vigorous and independent cooper, arrived in Northampton County, Virginia, about 1643. In 1652, he was one of the Committee of Six that drafted the celebrated Northampton Protest, opposing the taxation of Eastern Shore settlers when they were unrepresented in the Virginia Assembly. In 1653, he was one of those "elected a Burgess by ye Common Crowd," but he was "thrown out by ye Assembly for a factious and tumultuous person; a man repugnant to all Govm^t." After several arrests for refusing to pay Church of England levies, Horsey moved to the shores of the Annemessex about 1661. He became a defiant leader of this Maryland settlement by resisting Col. Edmund Scarborough's attempts to make the residents swear allegiance to Virginia (*see* Tour 20, Clifton, and Tour 21, Almodington).

CRISFIELD (5′ alt., 3,540 pop.), 13.6 m. at the pier at the end of Main Street, is a distinctive town that derives its livelihood from oysters, crabs, and fish. All the waters of the lower Chesapeake Bay are its salty domain, and in recent years seafood processing has become concentrated here to the detriment of the small plants that used to operate in marsh and island villages. Vessels of many sizes and riggings bring thousands of tons of marine edibles each year to this self-styled Seafood Capital of the Country. They come from the Bay islands and sounds, the rivers and coves of the Eastern Shore of Maryland

and Virginia, the waters of the Western Shore in Southern Maryland, and the great rivers below—the Potomac and the Rappahannock of the Virginia mainland.

The upper part of the town resembles other Eastern Shore settlements, with its narrow tree-lined streets, modest business section, and small frame houses. There is a well-equipped hospital, a public library, a municipal building, and a post office and customhouse. Eighteen churches serve five different denominations; the Baptist Temple, built in 1920, is sometimes mistaken for City Hall. Upper Crisfield is built on tracts surveyed in 1663 for John Roach and Benjamin Summer (Somers), and Somers Cove was the name of the wharf-hamlet that was here in 1868 when the railroad arrived. The town, renamed for John W. Crisfield, a promoter of the railroad, began to grow steadily after it was incorporated in 1872. Seven disastrous fires swept through the frame buildings and sheds of Crisfield between 1883 and 1928, and many of the structures built in their place are constructed of less flammable brick or cinder-block.

It is the lower section at the waterfront that gives Crisfield its character. Here the town is more water than land. Even the site is made of oyster shells, the residue of years of oyster shucking along the marshy shores. Somers Cove Marina, a $750,000 project completed jointly by local citizens and the Maryland Port Authority, provides complete facilities for pleasure craft. Along the Annemessex River, work boats of many sizes lie at anchor from sunset to sunrise, hours when the harvesting of shellfish is illegal. Some of the "gas boats" are dismasted skipjacks (called sailing bateaux here). Few sailing craft now work out of Crisfield, although in 1910 it had one of the largest registries of sailing vessels in the United States.

The railroad track, which runs down the middle of Main Street to the railroad pier, provides transportation for fresh and processed seafood. Trucks arrive with fresh seafood for processing, which is then shipped to market. From the pier, a passenger and freight vessel leaves daily for *Smith Island* and *Tangier Island*, returning the next morning.

Near the waterfront along the Little Annemessex and the passage into Somers Cove are the wooden or concrete block buildings where oysters and crabs are prepared for shipment up the peninsula. Over a quarter of the people employed in processing Maryland seafood—a thousand or more—work in Crisfield. Some plants here and elsewhere are heavily mechanized, sometimes with equipment of ingenious local design. But no machines have been devised to shuck oysters, and no mechanical device has proved practical for picking the meat out of hard crabs. These operations are done by the knives and deft fingers of hundreds of workers. The extremely perishable nature of crabs and oysters requires the most rigid sanitary regulations. Speed and cleanliness are the inflexible goals of every seafood packer.

Crab meat, graded from back fin to claw, is picked from steamed hard crabs by people who work at long stainless-steel tables in the large sheds. Fertilizer makers collect the shells and other residue daily. Although the wages for crab picking and

Hauling oyster shells

oyster shucking are the same, oyster shucking apparently carries more prestige, because men as well as women will work at that job. The shuckers rapidly stab open the oysters at the risk of gashing their fingers with the sharp oyster knives (*see* Tour 21, Deal Island).

The crab catch and the oyster population fluctuate from year to year. Small catches bring higher prices for the watermen, but seafood-processing workers lose their jobs when yields are low. The fin-fish catch is also important to Crisfield, although its value is but a fraction of that of the shellfish. In spring and summer hundreds of barrels and boxes of shad, herring, croakers (hardhead), and other fish are sent to market both fresh and frozen, and sportsmen board charter boats that run to the fishing grounds of Tangier Sound.

Crisfield also manufactures oyster tongs, oyster dredges, oyster knives, muskrat traps, and other equipment for local industries. The firm that produces most of these products started as a blacksmith shop in the 1890s and during World War II produced rockets for bazookas. Three clothing factories are the other chief employers of Crisfield residents. The state is cooperating with the Crisfield citizens in an attempt to induce more industries to locate in or near Crisfield in an effort to bolster the economy, which has suffered from the decline of the oyster supply.

Native marine arts, such as the carving and painting of amazingly lifelike decoy geese and ducks, flourish in Crisfield. Now almost lost is the art of carving, painting, and gilding the fancy name boards under the bowsprits of sailing vessels.

Each year on the Saturday before Labor Day, Crisfield publicizes its industries with hard crab races. The crabs are set on a wet inclined platform that encourages them to scuttle towards the finish line at the bottom, although stubborn entries occasionally attempt an offside foul. The Hard Crab Derby takes all entries; in the Governor's Cup, there is one entry from each crab-producing state. In 1964, the last race was run between LBJ (Lyndon B. Johnson) and Barry (Barry Goldwater). The governor of Maryland accepted the prize for the president. Speeches by political figures, parades, and fireworks round out the occasion, which attracts many spectators.

● From the intersection of Main Street and Somerset Avenue, go east on Main Street 1.1 m. to the junction with Md. 380. Take Md. 380 to the junction with Johnson Creek Road. Go left on this to **Makepeace** (private), overlooking the green marshes of Johnson Creek, which empties into Pocomoke Sound. Built in the late seventeenth or early eighteenth century, this 1½-story house with walls laid in Flemish bond stands on the 150-acre tract that John Roach called Makepeace in his patent of 1663. According to tradition, Roach chose the name to commemorate the peace the white men negotiated with the Indians of the region at the time of the Annemessex settlement.

Makepeace is one of the finest and best-preserved of the modest, early Virginia-type houses on the peninsula. Two adjoining front doors lead into the two large rooms of the first floor. The gable ends are notable for their glazed-header bricks in a diamond grid pattern at one end and an inverted V-pattern on the other. Inside the house are two enormous fireplaces. The fine interior paneling is similar to the paneling of Eastern Shore houses built in the Revolutionary period and may have replaced earlier woodwork.

At the railroad pier at the foot of Main Street is the berth for the boat that carries passengers, mail, and freight, but no vehicles, to Smith Island (the boat to the island leaves at 12:30 and 3. Call [301] 968–1636 for reservations and tour information). Charter boats are available for a one-day trip. The boats travel west from Crisfield across Tangier Sound eleven miles to **SMITH ISLAND** (2′ alt., 688 pop.), 24.6 m., the most remote and distinctive of all Maryland islands in the Chesapeake. Named for Capt. John Smith (1580–1631), who explored the Bay in 1608, Smith Island is actually a compact group of islands extending about eight miles north and south and four miles east and west. Nearly all of the land is salt marsh or meadow, cut and indented by dozens of thoroughfares, guts, ditches, and coves. The southern fringe of the island stretches across the border into Virginia. On several occasions, great storm tides have flooded the entire island, damaging truck gardens, oyster boats, and crab houses, even drowning unsuspecting islanders working on the Bay or the sound. After the waters recede, however, these hardy, strongly religious people go on living in the same manner as their ancestors before them.

As a boat approaches Smith Island there appear beyond the marshes the villages of **EWELL, TYLERTON,** and **RHODES POINT,** each separated from the others by a mile or more of marsh and water. A few sparse pine groves are seen, but the most prominent objects are the three Methodist churches, each rising high above the small frame dwellings of its village. Offshore along the front of each village is a row of small buildings on pilings; these are crab houses where soft crabs are packed in ice for shipment to Crisfield. Between and behind the crab houses are fenced crab pounds in which scores of latticework shedding-floats contain thousands of crabs that are carefully separated daily according to their stage in shedding their hard shells. At Tylerton the effect is that of a main street of water, one side with crab houses and pounds, the other side with the houses and stores on shore, each with its little pier. The busy

Smith Island oysterman

traffic of small boats moves up, down, and across this "street." At Ewell, the largest of the settlements, white picket fences mark off small yards and vegetable patches from the two or three narrow roads. The white frame houses resemble those in Crisfield, Deal Island, and other fishing settlements. Although settlers have lived here since the seventeenth century, fires, storms, and floods have destroyed most, if not all, of the old structures. Motor vehicles can use the two miles of road to Rhodes (originally Rogue's) Point, but Tylerton must be reached by water. Because the islanders maintain their own roads the state does not enforce the law requiring license plates. Most of the firewood and much of the food must be brought by boat from the mainland. Radios and television have brought welcome entertainment, especially when the island is made inaccessible by occasional freezes lasting several weeks. However, this is one of the intrusions by the outside world that threatens a way of life which, in some ways, has remained unchanged for two centuries.

The islanders are almost entirely of British ancestry. Their speech, like that in fishing settlements on Hooper Island and in the Lakes District, is spoken from the back of the throat and is punctuated with unusual, often archaic, words and grammatical constructions. *Either* and *neither* are used in perplexing constructions of double and triple negatives. "I didn't ketch neither fish," a comparatively simple form, means the speaker had no luck at all.

The whole population of the island has always derived its livelihood from the water. Before the Civil War, the islanders lived off their small gardens and the fish they caught, trading fish and produce for their other needs in a local market. As the nineteenth century progressed, however, residents began taking boatloads of oysters to Baltimore, which had fifty-eight raw-oyster packing houses and several steamed oyster canneries in the 1860s. The quantities of shellfish being harvested led to fears that the supply of oysters might be in danger; but in 1860, most people agreed with a Somerset County Methodist preacher who believed that "there seems very little probability that this providential product . . . will be cut off for many generations, if ever."

By the 1890s, however, providence had begun to fail the watermen. In 1865, the assembly had authorized dredging in state waters, a practice that had been banned in 1820 because New England dredge boats were exploiting Maryland oyster beds. The oyster yields increased tenfold by 1884, when 15,-000,000 bushels were harvested, but thereafter the decline in supply was rapid. By 1904, the oyster catch amounted to only 4,500,000 bushels. In 1906, the Haman Act provided for a state survey of oyster beds and for a program whereby persons willing to seed them could lease unproductive oyster beds for a dollar per acre. The survey, which took six years, has been described as one of the most thorough studies ever made of any natural resource, but the leasing program was a failure. Although experts believed that the submerged lands could produce 40,000,000 bushels of oysters a year through private management, the oystermen feared—and with reason—that large corporations would take over, reducing the watermen to little better than hired help. Since 1912, the state itself has undertaken a small amount of oyster farming financed by a tax on yields taken from the planted areas. The program has never really paid for itself, however; nor has the acreage planted ever been large enough to increase the oyster yield.

From 1915 to 1950, the annual oyster harvest averaged something under 3,000,000 bushels, but from 1950 to 1961 the quantity dropped to less than half this amount. In order to save the oyster industry, the state was faced with two alternatives: stop oyster farming and all attempts to maintain a public oyster fishery, thereby compelling watermen to adopt private oyster farming; or vastly increase state oyster farming to revive the public fishery. In 1960, the state chose the second plan and began a large-scale program of shell planting to create new oyster beds (see Tour 21, Deal Island). The program has proved successful and Maryland now has a major shellfish propagation effort underway.

Crabbing for market did not begin until after the Civil War, and as late as the 1890s crabs were considered more of a nuisance than an asset because they clogged fish nets. Marked variations in the annual crab catch, which ranged from 5,000,000 to 30,000,000 pounds between 1915 and 1950, reflect fluctuations of unknown causes in the crab population. Nevertheless, Maryland's crab catch is second in value to the annual oyster catch, and on average the supply is not declining. Should the oyster industry die, some residents of the seafood areas would have to find new jobs or move to new localities. To what degree the fishing communities on the Eastern Shore and its islands can maintain their traditional reliance on harvesting the bounties of the Bay remains to be seen.

Until about 1800, the people of Smith Island were largely neglected by government and church alike. Lawlessness, violence, and drunkenness typified the fiercely independent men who struggled to make a living from the surrounding waters. Then the Great Revival reached the islands about 1807, and revival meetings and hymn singing replaced drinking and dancing as forms of community activities. Methodism is the island religion to this day, partially as a result of a nearly illiterate fisherman, Joshua Thomas (1776–1853), who was converted in 1807 and spent the rest of his life spreading the Methodist word by example and exhortation (see Tour 21, Deal Island). Religious faith is still powerful on the island. When the church in Ewell burned in 1938 and the wind changed in time to save the rest of the village, the entire population, which had been kneeling in the road for hours, gave thanks that their prayers had been answered. All three congregations on the island are served by one preacher, whose salary is raised by a head tax. The minister is the most respected man on the island, an arbiter and counselor as well as a man of God. There is no mayor, no city council, no jail. Children attend public school on the mainland, with a boat providing transportation from the island to the mainland and back.

The spirit of independence characteristic of early Smith Island residents did not disappear with the rise of religion. The Black and Jenkins Award of 1877 forced Maryland to cede Virginia 23,000 acres of fine oyster bottoms, chiefly at the behest of Tangier Island, but the Smith Island men kept on dredging there for more than thirty years despite repeated attacks by Virginia patrol boats and interisland battles in which oystermen on both sides were killed. The warfare ended about 1910 when the oysters in the area died, a calamity that the islanders interpreted as the hand of God protesting strife. Although the killing of wild ducks for market was outlawed in 1918, the slaughter continued for twenty years or more on Smith Island. Game wardens enforcing the ban risked their lives when they entered the lonely island marshes in an attempt to silence the powerful swivel guns that islanders used to kill ducks by the hundreds.

The independence of the Chesapeake Bay watermen is illustrated by their refusal to accept any other type of job, even though they would often be better paid, and by their resistance to any law or regulation that threatens their traditional way of life.

DELAWARE LINE–BERLIN–SNOW HILL–JUNCTION OF U.S. 113 AND 13; 39.8 m.

U.S. 113

This route along the seaside of Maryland's Eastern Shore runs through Worcester County between the coast and the Pocomoke River, which approaches within a few miles of the ocean yet empties into the Chesapeake Bay. The area was set-

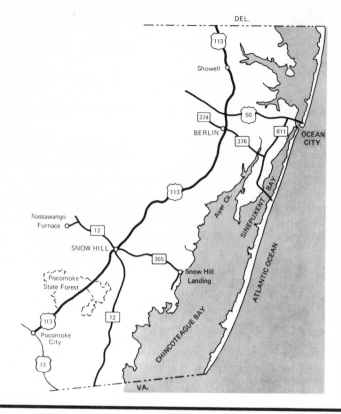

TOUR 23

tled—mostly by Eastern Shore Virginians—in the latter part of the seventeenth century as part of Somerset County; Worcester County was erected from Somerset in 1742.

Between the eastern chain of small, salty bays—noted for fish, oysters, and waterfowl—and the Pocomoke's cypress swamps, the country is low, flat, and considerably wooded. The old-growth loblolly pine was used for the paneling and wide flooring of the old houses. New growth keeps sawmills running. Holly abounds and is a source of pre-Christmas revenue. Most of the hard-shell clams harvested in Maryland come from Worcester County, but the oysters for which it has long been famous were recently infected with the MSX disease; consequently, the oyster population of Delaware Bay has been decimated.

Unlike the Southern Maryland counties (*see* Tour 26a), this was never tobacco country; the earliest settlers raised grain and livestock. Since 1900, with the introduction of the refrigerated railroad car, this has been a vegetable- and fruit-growing area. The tempering effect of the ocean and the Chesapeake allows a growing season (210 days or so) as long as that of inland regions much farther south. When the sandy soil is heavily fertilized, it can produce two crops of vegetables in a season—two crops of potatoes, for instance, or a crop of early tomatoes followed by beans. Acreage in vegetables has been halved, however, in the last thirty-five years, and the potato crop has diminished by 90 percent. Apple and peach orchards have dwindled since World War II. Field crops, on the other hand, especially corn and soybeans, have greatly increased. Labor difficulties accounted in part for the change. Vegetable growers were necessarily dependent at harvest time upon migrant pickers, who in the past were brought from the South by the truckload at low rates of pay and provided with primitive accommodations. Attempts by the federal government to require better living arrangements threatened to make labor more costly and aroused great antagonism on the Lower Shore.

Raising and marketing broilers is big business in Worcester County, which ranks second in the state in the number sold per year. Summer visitors to the ocean are even bigger business, especially at Ocean City (*see* Tour 12d), which has a population of 150,000 or more on summer weekends.

Isolated by geography and until the 1930s by poor roads, the people are friendly and hospitable. The speech of educated as well as uneducated persons is spiced with archaic words and phrases, and the peculiar rhythm and slurring of common speech can be difficult for a Baltimorean to follow. People call each other "honey" on first acquaintance as casually as a New York policeman calls a stranger "buddy."

U.S. 113 crosses the **Maryland-Delaware Line,** 0.0 m., at a point twenty-two miles south of Georgetown, Delaware.

Just south of **SHOWELL,** 4.5 m., **St. Martin's Episcopal Church** (annual services held in June; otherwise not open) stands solitarily on the edge of a pine woods by the side of the road. It is forty-four by fifty-four feet—the first specifications called for a forty-four foot square—unusual dimensions for an Anglican church but customary in seventeenth-century New England meeting houses. A high gable roof with kicked eaves and cove cornice covers brick walls laid in Flemish bond with glazed headers. The six great forty-eight-pane windows are usually covered by their huge shutters, for the church is rarely used for services. The interior is austere, almost barnlike. The specifications signed in 1756 by the vestry and the builder, James Johnson, mention no paneling or decoration of any kind, and there is no sign that any such frills were ever added. The appearance of the church is closer to that of the Puritans of seventeenth-century New England than most other eighteenth-century Anglican churches in Maryland, perhaps reflecting the influence of the many Presbyterians who were among the early settlers of the Lower Shore.

At 8.4 m. U.S. 113 makes a junction with U.S. 50 and Tour 12c. At 9.8 m. is the junction with Md. 376.

● Go right on Md. 376 to the center of **BERLIN** (pronounced Bér/lin) (45′ alt., 1,942 pop.), a pleasant town of shady, winding streets that radiate from a compact little business section. The town grew up during the early nineteenth century around a public stable, blacksmith shop, and tavern and acquired its name from Burleigh, the tract on which the town stands. A number of houses, mostly frame, remain from antebellum times. Poultry-processing plants, a slacks factory, and millwork and building materials are main sources of income. **Buckingham Presbyterian Church,** on the west side of Main Street, is the fourth church to serve a congregation organized by Francis Makemie soon after 1683. The first church, in use by 1696, stood in the cemetery at the southern end of town (*see below*) on land that was then part of the tract called Buckingham. A later church was literally blown down in 1857 by the high winds and heavy snow of a blizzard. The present structure was built in 1906.

On Main Street north of Burley Street, **Burley Cottage** (L) (private, but visible from the street) is a 1½-story brick house, two rooms deep, built in 1834. Protecting the front door is a delightful porch decorated with dogteeth and sunbursts.

Just south of Burley Street on Main Street is **Burley Manor** (private, but visible from the street), or **Hammond House,** a dignified house of stucco-covered brick with a quaint arrangement of wings. The kitchen may have been built about 1814, but the house as it stands was not finished until shortly before it was sold to the Hammonds in 1833. Like Burley Cottage, it has an entrance porch trimmed with dogteeth and sunbursts. Still standing at the back are the shingled barn, built in 1835, the carriage house, the summer kitchen, the brick ash house, the smokehouse, and the "necessary."

Where Main Street joins U.S. 113 is **Buckingham Cemetery,** the earlier location of *Buckingham Presbyterian Church.*

● Go left on Md. 376 into Sinepuxent Neck, a very low, wooded, marsh-fringed peninsula protected from the Atlantic Ocean by the great sandbar called *Assateague Island.* The colonial and postcolonial plantation houses built here were once the most important group on the Maryland seaside, but long years of tenancy and neglect have destroyed many of them and reduced others to hay barns. Before World War II the neck was devoted to moonshining, coon hunting, and duck hunting as well as farming; today it is beginning to exploit the summer tourist trade.

Just before the bridge across Ayer Creek at 3.3 m., **Golden Quarter** (R) (private), shaded by the great Ayers Elm, is almost concealed from the road by a bamboo hedge. The 1½-story pre-Revolutionary brick wing, now stuccoed and painted white, retains four corner fireplaces with paneled chimney pieces and, in one room, a handsome paneled wall and medieval-style box stair. Delicately carved trim on the cornice and on a frieze between the second-story windows adds elegance to the good lines of the nineteenth-century frame wing. Near the creek a small gravestone mourns the death in 1770 of the infant son of Ebenezer and Naomi Campbell: "Youth thou forward flipt, But Death soon thee nipt."

At 4.1 m. is a T-junction with Md. 611 (the Stephen Decatur Highway) (*see* Tour 12d).

● Bear right at the T-junction to a private road immediately on the left. **Fassit House** (R) (private), 0.4 m., is an early seventeenth-century, 1½-story house well known for elaborate patterns of glazed headers in its brickwork; such brickwork is to be found in many English houses of the early sixteenth century. The present owners, descendants of the Fassits who built the house, have constructed a marina on the site. One of their ancestors is believed to be the Fassit who shot Gen. Edward Braddock in the back during the western campaign of 1755; he was avenging the death of his brother, cut down by Braddock for advancing, Indian style, behind trees.

● Go right on Md. 611 at the T-junction. At 1.3 m. is the road (L) into **Bayside Farm** (private), where purebred Welsh ponies are raised. At the end of the entrance lane, a distance of over half a mile, is **Henry's Grove** (private). A plaque on the south wall tells that it was built in 1792.

At 2.2 m. on Md. 611, **Genesar** (R), built, according to tradition, in 1732, stands lonely in a cornfield, hay protruding from its windows. From the front this two-story brick house is early Georgian, though the modillions and dentils of its cornice are now tattered, and what was once a balanced arrangement of windows and doors has been altered; the high narrow profile, however, with its brick patterns of

Wild ponies on Assateague Island

nested triangles in the gable, creates a Tudor—even Gothic—rather than a Georgian effect. Before a nineteenth-century coating of stucco eroded the surface of the bricks, an elaborate lozenge pattern in the brickwork of the front must have accentuated the Tudor character. The kitchen wing (nineteenth century) has crumbled, and the interior was long ago robbed of its fine woodwork.

At 3.0 m., the road turns left on to the bridge that crosses Sinepuxent Bay to **ASSATEAGUE ISLAND,** a great sand bar in most places less than a mile wide, which stretches thirty-five miles from Ocean City on the north to Chincoteague on the south. The southern twelve miles are in Virginia. This primitive wilderness of beach, sand dunes, and marshes is frequented mostly by fishermen and campers. Its only permanent residents are the Chincoteague ponies, wild descendants of horses brought to Maryland by seventeenth-century settlers. Uncontrolled breeding among these wild herds has reduced the size of the ponies, a result foreseen by the colonists as early as 1699, when they first attempted to legislate the erection of fences. The ponies belong to the Chincoteague National Wildlife Refuge on Chincoteague Island, which is located between the southern end of Assateague and the mainland of Virginia. During the late 1940s an enterprising real estate speculator bought up property on Assateague and sold hundreds of lots in a proposed resort development. Business and political leaders of Worcester County with state aid have built a bridge that makes access to the island feasible. The great storm tides of March 6, 7, and 8, 1962, however, shifted tons of sand from the ocean to the bay side of the island, in places moving the shore line more than four hundred feet. Any resort would have been washed away, and since then, the U.S. Army Corps of Engineers have declared Assateague unsuited for commercial development. About 700 acres of the island is now a state park. Conservation groups hope the federal and state governments will supply funds to make more of the island parkland.

SNOW HILL (2,201 pop.), 27.2 m. at the courthouse, first laid out in 1686, was a commercial center for the Lower Shore before Worcester County was created in 1742 and has been the county seat ever since. The site is on a tract called Snow Hill by Col.

William Stevens (*see* Tour 20), who patented it in 1676 and may have named it for the Snow Hill section of London. Scottish Presbyterians from Northern Ireland were early settlers in Somerset and undoubtedly helped develop the town. We know, at least, that by 1687 the Presbyterian minister Samuel Davis was preaching at a church in Snow Hill (*see below*) that has remained in existence ever since.

Early wills and inventories show that merchants in or near the town carried on an active trade with England and with Barbados. In 1700, for example, James Round, brother of a London iron-monger and a parishioner of Samuel Davis, left an estate of more than £1,700, much of which was tied up in his store. A list of its contents suggests how much the colonists depended on imports for all kinds of supplies, despite English fears that Scotch-Irish weavers in Somerset were establishing home indus-tries that might diminish English markets. Mr. Rounds imported great quantities of cloth, from "Irish Linnens" at 17 pence a yard to "Course Ozenbriggs" at 9 pence per yard. Thirty-seven quires of "whyte paper," 5 dozen "Ivory Combs of sorts," 10 gross of "Coal Gimp buttons," 8 "Irons of Casem^t," 11 primers and 5 hornbooks, I dozen "lock & ketches," I dozen saddles and bridles, 22 "sheephead hooks," 9 saws and thousands of nails are among the great variety of goods listed in his inventory. Besides such commercial ventures, we know of grist mills and a public tobacco warehouse and inspection station (established in 1753) located at Snow Hill in the colonial period.

During the Revolution this part of the Eastern Shore produced many Tory sympathizers, and Loyalists who could not afford the trip to England came here to hide in the swamps. Nevertheless, on July 26, 1775, about sixty leading men of the county met at Snow Hill and signed the Association of Freemen, and several battalions were recruited in Worcester during the course of the war. During the Civil War, Snow Hill was a center of Confederate sympathy.

Destructive fires in 1834 and 1893 burned most of the old Snow Hill, but the numerous large houses in more outlying areas testify to the wealth in the town at the time they were built, some in the late eighteenth and early nineteenth cen-turies, others in Victorian times. Nevertheless, the rise of Baltimore as the chief port in Maryland after the Revolution must have brought a decline in shipping here as it did at other colonial ports. Whereas eighteenth-century residents of Snow Hill had regular contact with London, nineteenth-century resi-dents lived in a remote outpost. However, some coastwise shipping evidently survived. A wagon route from Snow Hill on the Pocomoke River, a Chesapeake tributary, to Chincoteague Bay on the Atlantic only seven miles away, offered a portage that greatly shortened the water route north for goods that could travel on sailing vessels small enough to negotiate the exit from the Bay at Chincoteague. After the Civil War, steam-ship service from Snow Hill to Baltimore was established. Good roads and fast motor vehicles have since supplanted water transportation. These days the drawbridge across the Pocomoke rises only for barges carrying oil.

Contemporary Snow Hill is a quiet town in which life for

several generations has reflected the rural activities of the county free from any urban aspirations. Most industries are allied to local farm products. One chicken hatchery supplies broiler farms. There is also a fertilizer plant and feed mill and a sizable lumber yard. Recently the town has tried to attract light industry; a manufacturer of business forms has established a branch, and one small clothing factory has joined an older one. Local businessmen are urging the county to sponsor a canal along the old wagon road from Snow Hill to Chincoteague Bay to revive this route for coastwise shipping. Nevertheless, Snow Hill shows little desire to emulate Salisbury in industrial and commercial expansion, and many people who value the quiet come here to retire. The town commissioners pride themselves on the town's small debt and its excellent services, including a municipally owned waterworks.

Except for the brick business section squeezed between the courthouse and the river, Snow Hill is a town of shingled frame houses, many built in the Victorian era and quaintly decorated with elaborate icing. Houses that remain from still earlier days can be identified by large outside chimneys and separate kitchen buildings connected to the main house by curtains, all characteristics of early-nineteenth-century houses of the lower peninsula. Several houses have two-story galleries across the front.

At the junction of Market Street (U.S. 113) and Washington Street (Md. 12 W) is the brick **Makemie Memorial Presbyterian Church,** built in 1890 as one of the successors to a "plain country building" erected some time between 1686 and 1697. A church has stood on the present site since 1742. The screened porch on the white frame house at **116 Market Street** (private) conceals a handsomely carved Federal doorway.

On Market Street at the corner of Church Street (Md. 12 E) is the **All Hallows Protestant Episcopal Church** (open), a building that blends Georgian and Victorian features. The walls, laid in Flemish bond with glazed headers on the long sides, stand as they did when the building was completed in 1755 after seven years of work. In the 1870s a remodeling added the chancel and the slate roof and took away the belfry. The bell now hangs in the churchyard. At the same time the parishioners "modernized" the interior, but they kept it simple. In 1899 they installed amber and purple panes in the great roundheaded windows.

On either side of the paneled door hangs an old tablet, one commemorating the death of Margaret Rosse (1762–69), the other the death of her mother, Elizabeth (1747–71), respectively the daughter and wife of John Rosse, minister of All Hallows from 1755 to 1775. The Rosses mourned their small daughter with a quotation: "Death, that does sin and sorrow thus prevent, Is the next blessing to a life well spent." In a glass case on one wall is a Bible, printed in London in 1701, given to the church by Queen Anne.

Beyond the church at 208 Market Street, the **Julia Purnell Museum** (open daily in summer, 1–5; in winter, Sun., 1–5) occupies the old election house. When Mrs. Purnell died in 1943 at the age of 100, she had embroidered more than 3,000 pieces of work, some of which are on display. In addition the museum houses artifacts and memorabilia of all kinds from eighteenth- and nineteenth-century Snow Hill.

Parallel to Market Street, one block east, runs Federal Street, heavily shaded by old trees and lined with roomy nineteenth-century houses set back on large green lawns. South of Church Street, **Widehaul** (private), on the corner of Federal and Gunby streets, is a handsome house built about 1814. Under the high gable roof of the main house runs a modillioned cornice above a frieze of garlands made with tiny holes—a motif found in several houses in Snow Hill built about this time. The cornice runs across the gable, which contains the main entrance, its fanlight and sidelights under a square portico. A curtain runs off the back of the main house to a small kitchen with a huge outside chimney.

A few doors further south, **Chanceford** (L) (private) is a majestic stuccoed Greek-Revival brick house built sometime in the latter half of the eighteenth century and known for its exceptional woodwork. The house is composed of three sections: the first is three and one-half stories, the second is two stories, and the third is two and one-half stories. Its modillioned and dentiled cornice runs across the gable, which faces the street and contains the main entrance. The paneled double door of the entrance opens into a hall that runs across the whole front of the house with an additional entrance at each end. This plan is frequently found in Eastern Shore houses of this period. The two living rooms behind have handsomely carved chair rails, mantels, and cornices. The crown molding and mantels are identical. In the room on the right, the windows, frames and all, were replaced some years ago; the original windows were doubtless like those in the other room, with ridged, eared frames that rest on pilasters with recessed panels. Beyond the drawing rooms, the large, high-ceilinged dining room takes up the whole middle section of the house. Here the carving on chair rail, cornice, and mantel is much lighter than that in the parlors. The richness of the detail in so spacious and well-proportioned a setting creates an effect of light, restrained elegance. The last section of the house contains another hallway. Here the delicately carved stair with reeded balusters is considerably more elaborate than the main case in the entrance hall. Beyond the hall is the ballroom, now used as the kitchen. Cornice and chair rail in this room are like those in the dining room, but the mantel is a later addition with heavy free-standing pillars. The original kitchen, now destroyed, was in a separate building off to the right.

Slightly further south on the southwest corner of Federal and Morris streets stands the white frame **Whaley House** (private), with a two-story gallery on the main wing. The lower wing, off of which runs the standard curtain and kitchen, has heavy outside chimneys.

On Church Street, two blocks east of Federal Street, Ironshire Street branches right. At **207 Ironshire Street** (private) is an eighteenth-century frame dwelling that stands incognito in a row of twentieth-century houses. Originally it was gambrel-roofed with a curtain and kitchen wing at the rear. About 1840 the

Nassawango Furnace

two-story gallery was added and the entrance was put in the gable end.

North of Church Street on Federal Street are several houses that predate the Civil War. The right hand part of **109 Federal Street** (private) is decorated with a dentil cornice over delicate garlands made with tiny holes. Wings of the houses on the southeast and northwest corners of Federal and Washington streets have old lines and heavy outside chimneys. One block west on Washington Street is the courthouse.

From Market Street north of the courthouse one can see the **Seltzer Cottage** (private), a short distance down Green Street. This small 1½-story house, with its blue shutters, quaintly paneled front door, and great outside brick chimney looks older than most other houses in town, but little is known of its history. On the northern edge of town, Park Row turns off Market Street (U.S. 113) on the right. This was once the drive leading to the **Timmons House** (private), a shingled frame building with a two-story gallery across the front. As one enters town from the north on U.S. 113, its three chimneys are a landmark.

● At the northern end of U.S. 113, Md. 365 branches left to **SNOW HILL LANDING**, 6.4 m., formerly called Public Landing, on the shore of Chincoteague Bay, here five miles wide. This was the terminus of the nineteenth-century portage from Snow Hill. On the water, concealed behind green shrubbery, is the **Mansion House** (R) (private), built in stages during the eighteenth and nineteenth centuries by the Spence family, long prominent in Maryland affairs. For many years it was a hotel, and Public Landing was a small summer resort.

Turn right on Bayside Road, which skirts the water, to **Mount Ephraim** (L) (private, but visible from the road), 7.5 m., an old 1½-story brick house located at the water's edge. It is one of several houses on the Worcester County seaside associated with a legendary rescue from the British—or from pirates—through a ruse: all the occupants paraded the shore with cornstalks and guns to simulate a large force of soldiers.

Historians believe that the shore of Chincoteague Bay may be the "Arcadia" described by Giovanni da Verrazano, who explored eight miles inland when he landed in 1524 while in the service of the king of France. Assateague Island may have been pierced by many inlets at the time.

● Back at the courthouse, go west from Snow Hill on Md. 12, the "airline" to Salisbury. At 4.1 m. Old Furnace Road turns left (a historical marker gives a short history of the Nassawango Furnace); follow this across Nassawango Creek to a dirt road, 5.2 m.; go left to a clearing (L). A few feet down a path out of the clearing is the crumbling brick chimney of the **Nassawango Furnace,** established in 1832 to process bog ore from Nassawango Creek. Only high prices for iron could make processing of such low quality ore profitable, however, and by 1847 the furnace had to be abandoned. The hotel and houses that once graced the town here have disappeared entirely. There are plans to make a small park here. The local historical society is restoring the furnace.

● Md. 12 going southeast (from the courthouse it goes south one block on Market Street, then east on Church Street) travels through field-crop country; side roads lead to the shores of Chincoteague Bay, here marshy, where crabbing, oystering, and clamming are important. From time to time the highway passes by old houses. It crosses the Virginia line.

U.S. 113 continues south through generally wooded country and makes a junction with U.S. 13 at 39.8 m. outside of Pocomoke City (*see* Tour 20).

DELAWARE LINE–KENT NARROWS–CHESAPEAKE BAY BRIDGE–DISTRICT OF COLUMBIA LINE; 86.7 m.
U.S. 301 and 50

This tour follows one of the main routes from New York to Washington. The dual highway, which by-passes all towns, has been built in Maryland since World War II. From the Maryland-Delaware line to the Bay Bridge, the route crosses flat country, most of which is planted with feed crops (*see* Tour 12a).

U.S. 301 crosses the **Maryland-Delaware Line** at 0.0 m. In Delaware, 1.1 m. from the state line, is the junction of U.S. 301 with Delaware Route 299.

● Go right on Del. 299 (which becomes Md. 282) to the junction with Bohemia Church Road in **WARWICK,** 1.2 m. on the Maryland side of the state line.

Near Warwick is the birthplace of James Rumsey (1743–92), inventor of an early marine steam engine. On two occasions in December, 1787, twenty years before Robert Fulton operated his *Clermont* on the Hudson, Rumsey demonstrated on the Potomac River a boat propelled by a stream of water forced out through the stern by a steam pump. As far as is known, Rumsey's experiment was the first application of the principle of jet propulsion.

Go right from Warwick on Bohemia Church Road to **St. Francis Xavier (Old Bohemia) Church** (open third Sun. during June, July, Aug., Sept., 11–6; also on request), 2.0 m., a beautiful brick church with a bell tower on the gable end, built about 1790 on a hill above the Little Bohemia River. A fire in 1912 gutted the interior, but the church was rebuilt within the old walls. It originally served a Roman Catholic mission established here in 1704 by the Jesuit Thomas Mansell. In 1745—secretly, since Catholic schools were illegal—the mission opened Bohemia Academy, whose students included John Carroll, first American Catholic archbishop (see Downtown Baltimore), and perhaps Charles Carroll of Carrollton (see Tour 2b), signer of the Declaration of Independence. The brick rectory to one side was erected in 1825 from the bricks of the old schoolhouse. At the back of the church under a great clump of boxwood are the graves of eight of the early Jesuit priests. Nearby is the tomb of Kitty Knight (see Tour 12a). The Jesuits turned the church and buildings over to the Wilmington Diocese in 1898 but regular services were discontinued during the 1920s. The Old Bohemia Historical Society now maintains the church and has made excavations to discover the sites of the other mission buildings. A small museum in the rectory is open on the same days as the church.

● Back in Warwick, past the intersection with Bohemia Church Road, is a brick house on the right (private, but visible from the road), built about 1750 by Daniel Charles Heath (see below) for his son. The original house consisted of a passageway along one gable that opened into one large room downstairs and two small rooms above. About 1800, the house was extended to make the long narrow 2½-story building that now stands.

Go straight ahead on Md. 282 to the junction with Worsell Manor Road, 4.2 m. To the right on this is **Worsell Manor** (L) (private, but visible from the road), 1.3 m., a simple 2½-story brick house surrounded by beautiful trees. Daniel Charles Heath entertained George Washington here on May 14, 1773, when Washington was traveling to New York to enter his stepson, John Parke Custis, at Kings College.

Md. 282 continues to a junction with U.S. 213 and Tour 12a in Cecilton, 6.4 m.

At 4.8 m. from the Delaware line, Md. 290 turns off U.S. 301.

● Go right on Md. 290. At the stop sign, go right to the junction with Wilson Point Road, 1.5 m. Go right on this to the end of the macadam road at 0.7 m. Go straight to **Shorewood**, 1.1 m., an estate laid out amid beautiful gardens on the steep banks of the Sassafras River. Paths along the river lead westward through carefully pruned and watered woodlands planted with azaleas and other flowering shrubs and many varieties of flowers. Eastward from the house, which dates from the Civil War period, are Italian walled gardens with fountains and statuary of Roman and Renaissance styles, some of which are antique pieces. Gardens open to the public.

Md. 290 meets U.S. 213 and Tour 12a at Galena, 4.1 m., and continues through *Chesterville* and *Crumpton* to a reunion with U.S. 301 at 15.8 m.

At 8.3 m. on U.S. 301 is the junction with Md. 313.

Go right to the junction with U.S. 213 and Tour 12a in Galena, 2.5 m.

At 11.4 m. on U.S. 301 is the junction with Md. 291.

● Go left on Md. 291 to **MILLINGTON** (474 pop.), 1.5 m., on the headwaters of the Chester River and once called Head of Chester. A

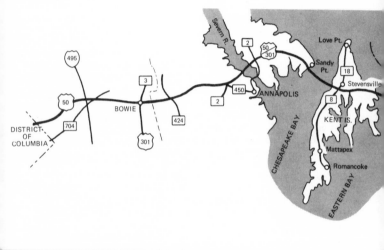

fire in 1904 destroyed all save the westernmost portion of the town, but several houses here attest to the existence of Head of Chester in the late eighteenth and early nineteenth centuries. On the outskirts of Millington on Md. 291 is **Sunset Hall** (L) (private, but visible from the road), a brick 2½-story town house with the street front laid in Flemish bond. The house is known to have been standing in 1797, and it may be somewhat older. Just before the junction with Md. 313 in the center of town, a two-wing brick house of excellent proportions stands across the street from an old frame house with a gambrel roof. To the right on Md. 313 a few hundred feet, the **Higman Mill** (L), with foundations believed to date from the 1760s, stands on the river bank. Until the early 1950s, the mill ground corn with water wheel and grindstone. Millington is a shopping and service center for surrounding farms, with two lumber companies, a wood products company, a hardware and farm implement store, and a steel company.

The route turns left on Md. 313 to **London Bridge** (R) (private, but

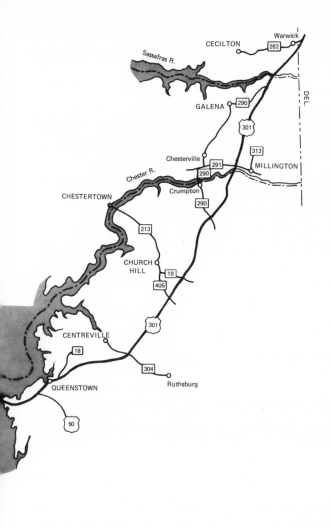

visible from the road), 2.2 m., a 2½-story brick house laid in Flemish bond and said to have been built not long after the London Bridge tract was patented to Daniel Massey in 1754.

● Go right on Md. 291 to a junction with Md. 290 at 2.7 m.

Go right on Md. 290 to **CHESTERVILLE**, 1.3 m., a country crossroads containing some old houses. Maps indicate that in 1860 the town contained a hotel, stores, and a blacksmith's shop. Straight ahead on Md. 290 is a house on the left with glazed-header brickwork on the gable, which appears to date from the mid-eighteenth century. Go left at Chesterville on Morgnec Road to **Mount Hermon** (R) (private), 2.2 m., a well-proportioned brick farmhouse containing some good handcarved cornices and mantels, which is believed to have been built in the 1700s.

● At 4.0 m. on Md. 291, go left on Md. 290 S to the **Comegys House** (private, but visible from the road), 1.0 m., an ancient brick cottage on the banks of the Chester River. Its aura of antiquity refuses to depart despite a remodeling that destroyed its old interior and added a huge dormer window to the long slope of the catslide roof. This was probably the house on the dwelling plantation of William Comegys, Jr., who acquired the land from his father in 1728. A much smaller gambrel-roofed house, the lines of which can still be seen in the brick, may antedate this period.

Directly across the bridge from the Comegys House is **CRUMPTON,** 1.3 m., a nineteenth-century town of white frame houses clustered on one or two tree-lined streets. The village grew up around McAllister's Ferry, which preceded the bridge built in 1856, and evidently was once the focus of elaborate plans for expansion. A map of 1877 shows about 600 lots in the town, most of them unoccupied. At 4.8 m. Md. 290 S makes a junction with U.S. 301.

At 22.6 m. U.S. 301 makes a junction with Md. 19.

● Go right on Md. 19 to a junction with U.S. 213 and Tour 12a in Church Hill, 2.9 m. At this intersection is **St. Luke's Protestant Church** (1732). To the right on U.S. 213 at 7.1 m. is the eighteenth-century port of Chestertown (*see* Tour 12a).

At 24.6 m. is the junction with Md. 405.

To the right on Md. 405 two eighteenth-century brick houses (L) (private) can be seen from the road. Md. 405 joins Md. 19 at 2.5 m.

At 30.8 m. is the junction with Md. 304.

To the right on Md. 304 is the junction with U.S. 213 and Tour 12a in Centreville, at 2.5 m.
● Go left to **RUTHSBURG,** 4.3 m., named for the Routh, or Ruth, family, who built the oldest section of the **Pratt Mansion** (private). A merchant, Christopher Cross Routh, may have begun the large hip-roofed main house before his death in 1777, but it was probably finished after the Revolution by his stepson, Henry Pratt. The house is approached through an aisle of great linden and maple trees. The narrow pedimented front door on the facade is framed by a pilastered doorway above which a frieze of thirteen stars is carved in stone. This design is supposed to represent the original thirteen colonies. The interior woodwork is unusually handsome. The entrance hall, like that at Widehall in Chestertown (*see* Tour 12a), occupies a quarter of the house and is marked off from the transverse hall by two great arches, giving the effect of great space and airiness. The wing at the back, with its huge fireplaces and box stair, probably dates from about 1730. From 1832 until the 1950s, this house served as the county almshouse.

At 33.8 m. U.S. 301 makes a junction with U.S. 213 and Tour 12b. On the left, **Peace and Plenty** (private) can be seen in a grove of large trees. This handsome two-story brick house was built shortly before the Revolution by Christopher Cox, whose daughter married a Wright, and it greatly resembles the nearby Reed's Creek House built at the same time by the same family (*see* Tour 12b).

At 38.5 m. is the junction with Md. 456.

● Go right to **QUEENSTOWN** (387 pop.), 0.4 m., first county seat of Queen Anne's County (*see* Tour 12b, Centreville). During the eighteenth century, although never more than a village, Queenstown's shipping facilities on the then-navigable Queenstown Creek made it an outlet for cargoes of grain, hemp, and tobacco as well as a receiving point for manufactured goods from Europe. For these reasons, Queenstown was considered so important by the British in the War of 1812 that they launched a land and sea attack on the town. Two miles south of the village the British encountered a band of pickets, who were able to check the British advance at Slippery Hill, even though they were greatly outnumbered. The British finally captured the town, but in contrast to their policy at Havre de Grace (*see* Tour 2a), they did little damage. At the crossroads, adjoining a ramshackle frame store, is a 1½-story brick and frame house, part of which may have been the Queen Anne's County jail built about 1709. Gallows Field, on the outskirts of Queenstown, survives in name as a memento of the days when the gallows, stocks, and pillory were in regular operation in this former court town.

At Queenstown, Md. 456 ends at a junction with Md. 18. Turn right at the intersection to **Bowlingly** (L), 0.1 m., a long, narrow, 2½-story brick house one room deep that was built in 1733 (written in glazed headers on the gable). The British burned the house when they attacked Queenstown in 1813, destroying the interior and the roof, and when the house was restored in 1820 its plan was somewhat altered. More changes were made later, especially when the house was used as a hotel during the 1890s and early 1900s. Most of the later additions were removed in a careful restoration of the house undertaken in 1954. The brick is laid in Flemish bond with glazed headers on the water side and in English bond on the land side. Originally a separate structure, the kitchen was connected to the main house in the 1820s and a second story was later added. The wing that forms the L was probably built soon after 1820. From the doorway (restored) of the main house, on the river front, the green lawns shaded by great trees stretch to the banks of the Chester River. A willow oak and an American linden, said to be the largest in the United States, grow here.

The central hall of Bowlingly contains a double staircase, which replaced the original single stairway in the 1820 remodeling. The original kitchen, now used as a living room, contains two eighteenth-century mantels from a Rhode Island house. The house is furnished with eighteenth-century pieces, mostly English, French, and Chinese. Open by written or telephoned appointment: Mrs. W. Randolph Burgess, Queenstown.

At the stop sign, turn right. At the junction with Md. 18, turn left, 0.3 m. Md. 18 continues to a junction with Wright's Neck Road, which leads to Walnut Grove and Reed's Creek House (*see* Tour 12b).

● Go left on Md. 18 to the gates of **My Lord's Gift** (private), 0.4 m. just before Md. 18 crosses U.S. 301. This is the principal estate in the "thumb" grant made in 1658 by the third Lord Baltimore to Henry DeCoursey. DeCoursey received as much land as his thumb covered on a map of the province (*see* Tour 12b, Blakeford). The delapidated old house still stands on the property, but its interior woodwork and staircase have been removed.

At 39.9 m. U.S. 301 joins U.S. 50. At 44.2 m. U.S. 301–U.S. 50 crosses the **Kent Narrows.** Here several packing plants process the catch from a large oyster, crab, and clam fleet. Soft-shell clamming in the Bay was made possible by the development of a hydraulic dredge that sucks the clams out of the mud. A fisherman in the Eastern Bay–Miles River area between Kent Island and the mainland perfected the dredge in 1951. The dredge was first used commercially the following year, and by 1956 there were ninety-three dredges operating out of the narrows. Since clam dredging kills oysters within twenty-five feet of the site, the General Assembly passed legislation in 1955 strictly regulating the new industry. Clam beds can be self-sustaining, especially since soft clams grow three times as fast in the Chesapeake Bay as in New England waters. Dredging equipment is expensive, however, and the yield must be large for a profitable operation. In 1968, Queen Anne's County watermen operated almost half of the dredges in the state's waters.

In 1631, William Claiborne established a trading post on Kent Island, three years before Lord Baltimore's settlers landed at St. Mary's. Thus, Kent Island is the site of the first permanent European settlement within the present boundaries of Maryland. Claiborne traded here by permission of the Crown, and as an influential member of the Virginia Company he preferred to recognize its claim to the Chesapeake Bay area rather than that of the Calverts. Claiborne became Lord Baltimore's most troublesome rival, and in 1635 two of his ships and two Calvert ships fought a miniature sea battle off Kent Island. The following year, however, Claiborne's partners in the Kent Island venture replaced him with George Evelyn, who invited Leonard Calvert to take control of the island. Claiborne regained the island for Virginia during Ingle's Rebellion in 1644 but lost it again when Ingle returned to England. No trace remains of Claiborne's settlement, nor has it been precisely located, but it is known that several mills and a fort were built on the site.

Today farming and fishing are the chief sources of income for the island's residents. Fishing and sailing attract visitors and even some commuters, who can now reach Baltimore or Washington in little more than an hour. In the future, commuters will doubtless swell the population, thereby changing the character of the island.

At 48.2 m. is the junction with Md. 18 and Md. 8.

● Go right on Md. 18 to **STEVENSVILLE** (est. 500 pop.), 0.3 m., the chief town on Kent Island, which was named for Stevens Adventure, the tract on which it was built. Stevensville may originally have been the town of *Broad Creek,* but the present village contains no old buildings. At 1.7 m. an imposing 2½-story brick house with a 1½-story wing is silhouetted against the sky (L) (private, but visible from the road). **Scillin** (L) (private, but visible from the road), 3.7 m., was built in three stages. The earliest section, a seventeenth-century cottage of one and one-half stories, may have been built by Thomas Broadnox (*see* Tour 13, Broadnox) soon after he patented the land in 1650, but if so, it was later moved from a site on the shore that has now eroded away. The second section was built in the eighteenth century, and the last section in 1820. **LOVE POINT,** on the tip of the island, lost the reason for its name when the ferry from Baltimore ceased to run after World War II. It is now a small village.

● Go left on Md. 8. At 0.7 m. the road passes part of **Broad Creek.** By 1686, there was a settlement in this area that became a stop on the postal route established by the Maryland Assembly in 1695. By the mid-eighteenth century, Broad Creek was the terminus for two ferries from Annapolis. An inn here served travelers, many of whom were traversing the main route to and from the northern colonies. By the time of the Revolution, however, the main route had shifted, and Kent Island became a backwater settlement. Ferry service continued until 1858 and was resumed in the twentieth century.

An Anglican church was standing at Broad Creek by 1651, and a later building was still in use in 1880 when the present church in *Stevensville* was built.

At 1.9 m. on Md. 8 is the junction with a graveled road. To the left is **Great Neck Farm** (R) (private), a handsome brick telescope house on a point of land completely surrounded by Warehouse Creek. The main wing was probably built in the early eighteenth century, but the

Chesapeake Bay Bridge

first floor of the middle wing is much earlier. The lowest wing replaces a log structure believed to have dated from the seventeenth century. The present owner believes he has found the foundations of the early warehouse from which the creek derived its name. The brick pilings form a foundation that measures thirty-two by sixty-four feet. Some of the bricks have seventeenth-century dates on them.

At 2.5 m. is the junction with a paved road that goes 0.3 m. to the slips for the ferries that crossed the Bay to Annapolis before the Bay Bridge was finished (picnic site). At 5.6 m. turn left on Shipping Creek Road. **Mattapex** (R) (private, but visible from the road) is a small brick house that may have been built in the seventeenth century. The house retains some good paneling.

● Md. 8 continues to **ROMANCOKE,** 8.2 m., once the terminus for a ferry from Claiborne in Talbot County to the mainland (*see* Tour 16). There is a small park here where one can fish off the pier.

At 49.2 m., U.S. 301–U.S. 50 moves on to the **Chesapeake Bay Bridge** (William Preston Lane, Jr., Memorial Bridge). In the shallow waters just off Kent Island, flocks of swan, geese, and ducks often rest and feed during the winter. At this point the Chesapeake Bay is four miles wide, and on clear days the view is spectacular. Freighters move along the channel to and from Baltimore, passing under the bridge, held 198.5 feet above the water by suspension towers. In winter, the grey sails of skipjacks dredging for oysters near the island blend with the waves, and on summer weekends white sails of pleasure boats make gay patterns on the blue water. When the haze is thick, the freighters sometimes seem to float on clouds, and the bridge recedes into the gloom. Completed in 1952 at a cost of $45,-000,000, the bridge is one of the largest continuous overwater steel structures in the world. The long curve at its Western Shore end was made necessary by the Enabling Act, which required that the bridge cross at right angles to the shipping channel and at the same time have its present terminal points. On June 28, 1973, the parallel Bay Bridge was opened to traffic. As one descends towards the Western Shore, the sky ahead is dominated by the radio towers of the Naval Experiment Station on Greenbury Point (*see* Tour 25a). To the right, *Sandy Point* beach stretches north for nearly two miles. Sandy Point is part of a grant patented in 1667 as Rattle Snake Point. Baptist Mesick of Baltimore bought the property in 1833 and opened Mesick's Wharf; the pond just north of the bridge bears his name. In 1858, Mesick sold two acres to the United States for the Sandy Point Lighthouse. The mainland lighthouse was replaced in 1883 by the present lighthouse, which still warns boats off the great sand bar that reaches far out into the Bay.

At 53.9 m. is the tollgate (toll for passenger cars and all other vehicles).

At 54.3 m. is the exit (R) to **Sandy Point State Park.** Turn left at the stop sign, then right into the park (nominal admission charged; summer hours, 5–9; fishing season, 6–8:30; Dec.–Mar., 8–5; bath houses open; sandwich and soft drink concession; lifeguards on duty). State operated, the beach is man-made. When the state acquired the land in 1949 the shore was marsh, and most of the sand has been brought in by truck, not washed in by the waves. Stone jetties protect the shore from erosion and provide perches for fishermen. Those parts of the marsh that have been preserved for nature study contain many varieties of aquatic plants and are stopping points for migratory birds. The great expanse of sand stretches around the point for nearly two miles, providing a striking vantage point of the Bay Bridge and the freighters that travel to and from Baltimore.

Near the beach is **Sandy Point Farm,** a lovely late-eighteenth-century brick house. The house is being considered for restoration.

At 55.2 m. on U.S. 301–U.S. 50, narrow Whitehall Road turns off to the left.

● Go left to **Whitehall** (private), 1.1 m., one of the famous mansions of America, designated by the secretary of the interior in 1960 as a National Historic Landmark. The five-part brick house is nearly 200 feet long, built on rising ground that looks out across green lawns to the Chesapeake Bay. Horatio Sharpe (1718–90), governor of Maryland from 1753 to 1769, built the central block of Whitehall in 1764–65 as a summer pleasure retreat. A garden pavilion in Roman temple form, the house resembles the structures Colon Campbell designed for the estates of eighteenth-century English noblemen. A central salon, entered through a great portico covered with a pedimented gable roof, is flanked on each side by a smaller withdrawing room with a lower hipped roof concealed behind a roof balustrade. The Corinthian columns of the portico support a superb entablature. Under the portico, the outside wall projects slightly with white-painted wooden quoins decorating the angles. The bricks around the window frames and at the corners of the building are also painted white. Viewed closely, the house seems overdecorated with trim to the twentieth-century **eye,**

Skipjacks

but at a distance and from the water the result is impressive, even princely. The interior of the house is equally splendid. The coved ceiling of the central salon reaches into the roof space, and in its center is a gilded plaster phoenix representing the Egyptian sun god. In the four corners of the ceiling are carved masks representing the four winds. Under an elaborate plaster cornice, the walls, painted red in an effort to reproduce what are believed to have been the original colors, are decorated with white festoons of flowers and fruit carved in wood. Chair rails, baseboards, window frames, and door frames are delicately carved, both in the salon and in the two withdrawing rooms.

Although there was a small dining room, a kitchen, and an office or bedroom in the basement, Whitehall was not a house for daily living. It was a garden temple, an eighteenth-century gentleman's tribute to nature that a more bourgeois era might find extravagant. Soon after the building had been completed, the governor decided to expand it into a mansion, adding the hyphens and wings that provided the necessary rooms for daily living. The result was a seven-part house, with the "temple" as a central block from which hyphens on each side led to square, hip-roofed wings. Additional hyphens led from each wing to a springhouse on the east and a water closet—unusual in the colonies —on the west.

The facade of the temple is magnificent when approached from the water. The land side of the house is more severe but equally impressive. The ground falls away from the land side of the house, and the basement, which is nearly one-story high, creates the appearance of a two-story structure. The white-painted bricks around the windows and on the corners of the central block give the house a monumental character, with less gingerbread effect than this trim creates on the garden front. Transforming the whole into a baronial fantasy are the fortifications that have been excavated and partly restored. Enclosing a courtyard that runs the whole length of the present house is a semi-octagonal bank of earth with a bastion for a small cannon at each of four corners. A ditch originally followed the outside perimeter, and according to surviving plans other components included ha-has, chevaux-de-frise fences, and petard gates.

Whitehall is thus a fortified castle on one side and a pastoral temple on the other. Within and without it expresses the position and character of its builder—his status as a ruler, his military prowess, his love of gardens, his flair for elegance and luxury, and his taste for the whimsical and fantastic.

To create what he called his "elegant lodge," Governor Sharpe obtained the services of the two most talented professionals available. The present owner possesses unsigned plans and specifications for Whitehall that experts believe are the work of Joseph Horatio Anderson, who may have been the first architect for the present Maryland State House. Drawings for the decorations in the salon are attributed to William Buckland (see Annapolis Tour), and he was doubtless responsible for all the woodwork and plasterwork. Sharpe retired to Whitehall in 1769, intending to live out his days here. But in 1773 he visited England and was detained there because of the Revolution. Upon his death in 1790, Sharpe willed the estate to John Ridout, his former secretary and close friend, who had come from England with him in 1759 and had cared for Whitehall in his absence. The Ridouts took down the springhouse and water closet and used the bricks to raise the withdrawing rooms to two stories. This alteration reduced the seven-part house to five parts, but it created more living space than the bachelor governor had required. The present owner has returned the central block to its temple form but has not rebuilt the extensions.

The temple form and the giant portico establish Whitehall as a landmark in American architecture. The only other pre-Revolutionary portico known to have graced a private American dwelling was that on the Roger Morris house in New York City, but that house was not in temple form. Contemporaneous temple-form houses in Virginia did not have porticoes. Thus, Whitehall stands as the first true Classic-Revival dwelling in America.

At 56.6 m. is the junction with Md. 179.

● Go left to **St. Margaret's Church** (L), 1.1 m., a white frame building with a shingled tower, built in 1895. This is the fourth building to house the congregation of Westminster Parish (formerly Broad Neck) since 1696. Each fall a tilting tournament is held in a nearby field for the benefit of the church. Like the late-medieval jousters, riders on horseback aim lances at rings suspended in the air, a sport probably introduced into Maryland in the 1840s. Jousting is now Maryland's official sport.

Below the chancel of the second Westminster Parish church, which stood near the banks of the Severn River several miles away, was buried Sir Robert Eden, last governor of the Province of Maryland. Eden, accompanied by his brother-in-law Henry Harford, proprietary heir-at-law, returned to Maryland after the Revolution to press their claim to their estates, which had been confiscated by the State of Maryland. Eden died at the home of Dr. Upton Scott in Annapolis on September 2, 1784. Since the vestry of St. Anne's had just closed the churchyard to further burials and refused to make an exception for Eden, he was interred in this country parish church. The building burned in 1803, and when Eden's relatives came to Annapolis some years later to seek his grave, it could not be found. In 1923, Mr. Daniel Randall excavated the site of the church, and in 1925, with the aid of the Society of Colonial Wars, he uncovered a skeleton under

Jousting

the site of the pulpit that has been tentatively identified as Eden's. In 1926, the remains were moved to the churchyard at St. Anne's, where Eden on his deathbed had asked to be buried.

At the present church is a crossroads. Pleasant Plains Road, to the left, penetrates a neck of farmland, much of it owned by people who live in large houses along the water. At 1.8 m. are the gates of **Pleasant Plains** (L), a brick house of excellent proportions built in the early nineteenth century. The wing, with its great fireplace and box stair, probably dates from much earlier. Open by appointment: Mrs. Charles Dodds, St. Margarets, Annapolis.

To the right at the crossroads on Md. 179 the road turns to U.S. 301–U.S. 50.

At 59.2 m. is the interchange with Md. 2 and at 59.4 m. is the interchange with Md. 450 and a junction with Tour 25a.

Go right on Md. 2 (Ritchie Highway) to Baltimore, 17.6 m. at the city line; Md. 2 enters downtown Baltimore on Hanover Street.

Go right on Md. 450 (Ritchie Highway) to Annapolis, 3.3 m. at Church Circle.

At 60.0 m., U.S. 301–U.S. 50 (now called the John Hanson Highway) crosses the Severn River. From the bridge one can look down the river to Annapolis and the Bay and on clear days across to the Eastern Shore. In summer the brilliant blue of the river is dotted with white sails.

At 61.3 m. is the interchange with divided-access highway Md. 70 (Rowe Boulevard) into Annapolis (*see* Annapolis Tour), 1.7 m. at Church Circle.

At 62.2 m., Md. 2 and Tour 25 turn south off U.S. 301–U.S. 50. From the Bay Bridge to this point the route is commercial, but from here to Washington, D.C., access to the Hanson Highway is limited. Since state law forbids billboards close to federally subsidized highways, crops and woodlands still dominate the scenery.

At 63.1 m. is the interchange with Md. 450 (Defense Highway) and Tour 27.

At 69.3 m. is the interchange with Md. 424, a side route of Tour 27.

At 72.9 m. is the interchange with Md. 3 N and Tour 26a. At 73.1 m. U.S. 301 turns south and becomes part of Tour 26a.

U.S. 50 and the tour continue straight ahead through open countryside, some of it still in cropland. At 74.1 m., **Belair,** a Levitt subdivision, suddenly appears in the fields of what was once a great estate and racing stable (*see* Tour 27). By 1980, the Baltimore-Annapolis-Washington triangle will probably be heavily developed, but if regional planners have their way, the built-up areas will be confined to the main highway corridors, with "green space," either farmland or parks, being preserved in between.

At 79.9 m. is the junction with Md. 704 N and at 80.2 m. is the interchange with Md. 704 S, and the sprawl of the Washington metropolitan area begins. There is a junction with the Capital Beltway at 80.7 m. (to Baltimore) and at 81.0 m. (to Richmond); with Md. 202, the route to Bladensburg (*see* Tour 27), at 83.3 m.; and with Kenilworth Avenue N (Md. 201) at 85.6 m. Kenilworth Avenue S, 85.8 m., leads to E. Capitol Street, which is the fastest route to the Capitol, the areas near Constitution Avenue, the Virginia bridges, and Georgetown. At 86.2 m., U.S. 50 joins the Baltimore-Washington Parkway and Tour S 1. The traveler enters Washington via New York Avenue, the fastest route to the center of the city, at 86.7 m.

BALTIMORE CITY LINE–ANNAPOLIS–PRINCE FREDERICK–SOLOMONS ISLAND; 78.1 m.
Md. 2

Md. 2, the main route between Baltimore and Annapolis, is paralleled for most of the distance by narrow, winding old Md. 2, now known as Md. 648. The dual highway, without a curve for three-quarters of its length, rises and dips across low, rolling Anne Arundel County. Side roads lead to the Magothy River on the east and the Severn River on the west and to waterfront resorts ranging from fashionable Gibson Island houses to clusters of weekend cabins. The highway itself is heavily commercial as far south as Glen Burnie, and the rest of the distance is rapidly developing.

From Annapolis to Solomons Island, Md. 2 winds through tobacco country. In this part of agricultural Maryland there are no towns of importance; farmers ride to the crossroads to church or the post office. In the villages along the creeks and the Bay, fishing, boat building, and the summer vacation trade are sources of income.

Since World War II, the isolated character of Calvert County, the southern part of this tour, has begun to change. With the establishment of the Navy Mine Test Center and the Amphibious Training Base (now disbanded) at the mouth of the Patuxent River, Solomons, once a remote fishing village, has been connected to Washington by a highspeed highway. Some of the oldest houses in Maryland stand in Calvert County, which was one of the earliest areas of the province to be settled.

25a. BALTIMORE–ANNAPOLIS; 21.3 m.
Md. 2

Between Baltimore and Annapolis, Md. 2 is named for Albert Cabell Ritchie (1876–1936), four-time governor of Maryland (1920–35). The route crosses the **Baltimore City Line** at 0.0 m. and traverses the suburb of Brooklyn Park. At 2.4 m. is the junction with I-695, the Baltimore Beltway, and at 2.8 m. is a junction with Md. 710. This leads into the heavily industrialized Curtis Bay area of Baltimore City on the lower harbor, and from there via Md. 172 and Md. 173 into the Marley Neck section of Anne Arundel County. The copper refinery of the Kennecott Copper Corporation, built in 1961 on the shores of the Bay just below Hawkins Point, is only one of several large industrial complexes recently constructed in the area.

At 3.1 m. traffic coming from the south can enter the Harbor Tunnel Thruway, from which there is no exit before passing under the Patapsco River, which enables traffic to by-pass downtown Baltimore (see S 2, Harbor Tunnel Thruway). Just beyond this point are a series of shopping centers with large discount department stores.

FURNACE BRANCH, 4.3 m. at the junction with Md. 270, is at the head of the Furnace Creek, which flows into Curtis Creek. Town and creek are named for the iron furnace founded in 1759 by Caleb and Edward Dorsey, which operated until 1851.

GLEN BURNIE (38,608 pop.), 5.7 m. at the junction with Md. 648, was named for John Glenn, who acquired an estate here in the 1880s, and is the center of an area that was rapidly subdivided and developed into small residential lots. Just outside the town is the **Harundale Mall,** 6.5 m., a shopping center opened in 1958 which features an indoor landscaped mall. The mall was the first of its kind in the area, and it still attracts business as far away as Annapolis.

At 8.0 m. is the junction with Md. 177 (Mountain Road) and with an entrance to Md. 100, a limited-access highway that connects Md. 2 and Md. 3 (see Tour 26a).

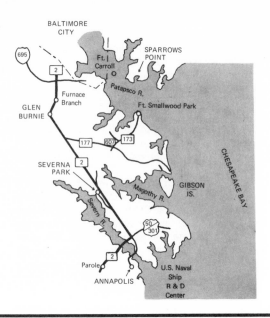

TOUR 25a

● Turn left on Md. 177. At 4.3 m. is a junction with Md. 607. Turn left on Md. 607 to a junction at 0.7 m. with Md. 173; go right on Md. 173 to the junction with Bayside Beach Road, 2.4 m. Turn right again to **Hancock's Resolution** (R) (private), 2.3 m., a rugged seventeenth- or early-eighteenth-century house built of local fieldstone with a gambrel roof. A frame wing was added between 1830 and 1850. Hancock family tradition tells that the stone wing may have been a fort built in the 1670s for protection against the Susquehannocks, but the interior woodwork appears to date from about 1720, when Anne Arundel County was no longer an exposed frontier. The Hancock family has given the house to Historic Annapolis, Inc.

● Md. 173 continues to **Fort Smallwood Park,** 3.8 m., named in honor of Gen. William Smallwood (*see* Tour 31, Smallwood's Retreat State Park). In 1896, the U.S. government acquired one hundred acres here on Rock Point, erecting fortifications at the mouth of Rock Creek. In 1926 the government sold the property to Baltimore City for use as a public park. The fortifications still stand. Scattered under the trees of this charming, rather European-looking park, are white frame picnic huts, each equipped with a table and benches. The view of the Patapsco River at its confluence with the Bay is striking, and the procession of freighters leaving the river on an ebb tide presents an impressive sight. Directly across are the smokestacks of industrial Sparrows Point (*see* Tour 2a), and to the left of the point is **Fort Carroll,** a man-made island begun in 1847 on a shoal, called Sollers Flats, in the middle of the Patapsco River. From 1849 to 1852 Robert E. Lee, then a brevet colonel of engineers in the U.S. Army, supervised construction of this fort, which was intended as a full military post but was never completed. Two batteries of soldiers from Fort McHenry manned the island in 1898, but subsequently it was used solely as a lighthouse and fog-bell station. In 1920 the lighthouse service took it over and installed an automatic light.

● Md. 177 continues to the gate, 11.1 m. at the end of a causeway, to **GIBSON ISLAND** (private), a quiet, fashionable resort open to members and their guests. Much futile digging has been done on this island in search of Captain Kidd's treasure.

At 12.3 m. is a junction with Md. 648 in **SEVERNA PARK** (16,358 pop.), a suburb of Annapolis.

At 17.6 m., Md. 2 branches right to join U.S. 50–U.S. 301 and Tour 24.

● To by-pass Annapolis, follow Md. 2 on to U.S. 50–U.S. 301, which is at this point a limited-access dual highway. From the high bridge across the Severn River there is a magnificent view of the broad river, which is almost always a brilliant blue. At 1.9 m. is the exit into Annapolis. Here the by-pass rejoins the tour as it emerges from the city.

The Ritchie Highway now becomes Md. 450 and passes over U.S. 50–U.S. 301, turning right off the overpass at 17.9 m. (follow signs to U.S. Naval Academy). At 19.2 m., where the road descends steeply to the Severn River, is the **Ritchie Memorial,** a small park in the dividing strip established in memory of Governor Ritchie. From here there is a spectacular view of Annapolis across the Severn. The massive gray buildings of the Naval Academy seem to rise from the water. Behind them are the red brick chimneys of a colonial town and the white dome of the State House, which, when illuminated at night, can be seen for miles. In summer the water is filled with the white sails of navy yawls and knockabouts and private sailboats.

At the bottom of the hill, 19.4 m., is another junction with Md. 648.

● Turn left for 0.5 m., then right on Md. 672 to the **Naval Ship Research and Development Center** (pass must be applied for at main gate). The nine towers of the radio station, one of the most powerful on the East Coast, are visible from the Bay and from points on the low-lying Eastern Shore nearly thirty miles away. The radio station can reach any naval vessel in the world. Extensive research in marine engineering problems is carried on here.

The Experiment Station—as it is called locally—is on **Greenbury Point,** a site settled by Puritans from Virginia in 1649.

At 19.5 m. Md. 450 crosses the Severn River. It then winds round the Naval Academy grounds and St. John's College (R) to Church Circle, and the center of **ANNAPOLIS,** 21.3 m. (*see* Annapolis Tour).

25b. ANNAPOLIS–PRINCE FREDERICK–SOLOMONS ISLAND; 56.8 m.
Md. 2

Leave Annapolis on Bladen Street where it crosses Md. 450 near the State House, 0.0 m. At 1.9 m. the road joins U.S. 50–U.S. 301–Md. 2 and Tour 24. Follow Md. 2 off U.S. 50–U.S. 301 at 2.6 m. Md. 2 turns south and is the main route for the whole tour.

At 3.5 m. is **PAROLE,** the **Site of Camp Parole,** where, from 1862 until the end of the Civil War, Union prisoners paroled by the Confederate government were confined until they were exchanged and returned to duty (*see* Tour 27).

At 5.4 m. the highway crosses the South River (beach concession, boats for hire), here a half mile wide.

At 6.5 m. is the junction with Md. 253 (Mayo Road).

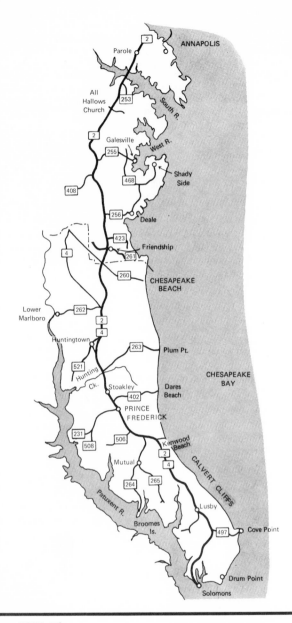

TOUR 25b

● Turn left to Popham's Store (unmarked), 0.9 m., then left at Londontowne Road, 2.1 m., to the **London Towne Publick House** (open daily, 10–4; nominal fee) on the banks of the South River. Supposedly built about 1747, this severe but handsome Georgian building is built of brick laid in all-header bond, two stories high with double-hipped roof and a pavilion with pediment on the facade. The cornice with its carved frieze adds elegance to the otherwise plain exterior. The Town Hall, if such it ever was, is the last building that remains of Londontown, one of the towns established by the Maryland Assembly in 1683. For years the building served as the Anne Arundel County Almshouse.

From 1689 to about 1695, the Anne Arundel County Court met at Londontown, and local residents may have hoped that the government of Maryland would locate here rather than at Annapolis. During the first half of the eighteenth century, Londontown rivaled Annapolis in importance, but as ships grew in tonnage and the river silted up, the town began to decline and today even its ruins are hard to find.

At 7.5 m. Md. 2 crosses Md. 214 and Tour 28.

At 8.9 m. **All Hallows Church** (R) (open by request), in a grove of oaks beside the road, is a small brick church (ca. 1729) of beautiful proportions. A low hip roof covers walls laid in Flemish bond and decorated at the corners with brick quoins, an unusually elegant feature in a country church. A square brick porch protects the entrance on one of the sides. Such porches, common in England, are found on several churches built between 1730 and 1760 near the Patuxent River. The Victorian interior was destroyed by fire in 1940, and the present colonial interior was modeled after other surviving eighteenth-century churches.

Rev. Joseph Colebatch, rector of All Hallows from 1698 to 1734, was designated first bishop of Maryland in 1724 by the bishop of London, but the Maryland courts are believed to have issued a writ of *ne exeat* that prevented his going to England for consecration. This action terminated a series of efforts to provide the Anglican Church in Maryland with a diocesan government. The Charter of Maryland gave the lord proprietor such power over the clergy that he successfully prevented any ecclesiastical interference with an institution he considered a legitimate part of his patronage. Under Anglican canon law, however, only a diocesan court could hear charges against a rector and dismiss him. Thus, during the whole period of colonial establishment (1702–76), Lord Baltimore appointed the rectors, but neither he nor any other authority in Maryland could remove a minister who was unsuitable. From 1784 to 1792, the rector of All Hallows was Mason Locke Weems (1759–1825), an itinerant preacher, tract writer, and book peddler. Weems's biography of George Washington, which contains the famous bit of fiction about the cherry tree, has gone through more than seventy editions, perpetuating for over 150 years the stereotype of Washington as an individual who was austere and truthful above all else.

● At All Hallows turn left onto S. River Club Road, 0.2 m. to a fork, then left to the **South River Club** (not open, but visible from the road), 1.4 m., a one-room frame building raised in 1742 to house what is probably the oldest club still active in America. The club, founded early in the eighteenth century, met for dinner every two weeks until 1760, and then once every four weeks except when membership fell very low. From 1875 to 1895 no meetings were held, but since 1895, twenty-five members, most of them descendants of former clubmen, have held four dinner meetings annually. Since 1801, one of the dinners has always been held on July 4. Club rules have always forbidden the discussion of religion or politics, but in the eighteenth century meetings were enlivened by debates. Mason Locke Weems introduced the question for July 6, 1786: "Is not the use of Spiritus Liquor, except in cases of ill health, an Idle and Unnecessary practice?" For the following meeting the question was "Whether ought the Ladies to court the Gentlemen, or the Gentlemen the Ladies?" The rules of the club, which have hung on the walls at least since 1793, require that members provide the dinner in rotation. The athletically inclined still play quoits with bronze rings given to the club over a hundred years ago. Inside, the fireplace has the original cranes and other equipment of the colonial kitchen. Other furnishings include old chairs and china and a great silver punchbowl that has been used since 1776.

At 10.7 m. is the junction with Mill Swamp Road.

● Turn left to **Larkins Hundred** (L) (private), 1.0 m., believed to have been built by 1704. This two-story brick house with massive chimneys at the gable ends was occupied by Rev. Joseph Colebatch while he was rector of All Hallows. The interior of the dwelling is notable for its excellent paneling and walnut staircase.

At 10.9 m. on Md. 2 is **Obligation Farm** (R) (private), a two-story brick house possibly of late-seventeenth-century origin but enlarged in the 1730s and again in the early nineteenth century. Originally only one and one-half stories high, the old roof lines of the house can be seen in the brick.

Opposite Obligation is **Larkins Hill** (L) (private), believed to have been built in the late seventeenth century. The brick house is laid in all-header and English bond, with tall chimneys and a gambrel roof. In 1683, Charles, Lord Baltimore, and his council met the assembly "at Larkin's place on the Ridge"—if not this house, doubtless one near it.

Just beyond Obligation, **Etowah Farm** (R) (private), 11.1 m., was built about 1824 following a plan characteristic of English town houses: square, gable-roofed, two rooms deep with the hall on one side. This house once belonged to Anna Lee Marshall, sister of Robert E. Lee. In 1682, William Penn and Charles Calvert, Lord Baltimore, met nearby to discuss the boundaries between Pennsylvania and Maryland.

At 14.5 m. is the junction with Md. 255.

● Turn left on Md. 255. At 3.2 m. is the **West River Quaker Burial Ground** (L) and the junction with Md. 468. The earliest graves in the cemetery are unmarked. The meeting house that once stood here burned during the Civil War, but the West River Meeting that it served was founded at least by 1671. In 1672, the first general meeting of Friends in Maryland was held here, nine years before the first general meeting was organized in Pennsylvania. George Fox himself addressed the meeting and helped establish procedures and discipline for Maryland Quakers. Quakers were predominant in the West River area during the seventeenth and early eighteenth centuries, but many had become members of the Protestant Episcopal Church by the time of the Revolution. In 1785, the meeting merged with the Baltimore Yearly Meeting of Friends.

● Turn right on Md. 468. At 3.4 m. Md. 468 intersects Md. 256, which passes through **DEALE**, 2.6 m., a picturesque fishing and boat-building community, and continues to a junction with Md. 2 at 5.4 m.

● Md. 468 continues to **SHADY SIDE** (1,562 pop.), 6.4 m., a waterfront community and resort on West River. Anne Arundel County ranks fifth in Maryland in the number of watermen, with many of them living in the West River area and near *Deale*. The water cannot supply a single activity that will provide a year-round living for these families. Many tong for oysters in the winter and then turn to crabbing in the spring and summer. Some dredge for soft clams, but equipment for this is expensive (*see* Tour 24, Kent Narrows), and others do some net fishing or take out fishing parties.

● At the Quaker Burial Ground, turn left on Md. 468 0.4 m. to

Tulip Hill (R) (private), one of the famous five-part Georgian mansions of Maryland. Samuel Galloway, a wealthy merchant and member of a Quaker family, began the central section of the house about 1756. Samuel's son John built the wings with connecting passageways after the Revolution. The central section, two and one-half stories of brick laid in Flemish bond, has a double-hipped roof and chimneys pierced by arches, a feature found on few colonial houses. A bull's-eye window in the eave pediment of the facade is balanced by carved white panels set into the brick. The one-story entrance portico with a carved white cupid in its pediment was added later. On each side of the main block, curtains, or covered passageways, with inset brick arches, lead to a low two-story gabled wing. Over the door on the garden front is an arched canopy with cresting and a carved tulip on the finial, a unique decoration in colonial Maryland houses. From the house, the gardens sweep down to the West River in a series of terraces.

The house is named for the giant tulip poplars that surround it, and the tulip motif appears everywhere in the carvings that ornament the house; tulip poplar wood is used in the framing. The central hall is famous for the great shell cupboard and the double arch leading to a fine stairway with tulips carved on the balusters. The similarity of this hall to that in George Mason's Gunston Hall in Virginia suggests that the woodwork at Tulip Hill may have been carved by William Buckland, who did the famous woodwork in Mason's house while serving as an indentured servant.

George Washington often stopped here to dine with Samuel Galloway, who owned Selim, one of the finest horses of his day.

At 0.6 m. on Md. 468, turn right on Cumberstone Road to a fork, 0.4 m. Go left (straight ahead) and then sharp left for a view of **Cedar Park** (R) (private, but visible from the road). From the road one looks down the fields to this ancient dwelling, which seems never to have heard a twentieth-century voice. When the Quaker Richard Galloway bought the tract in 1697, the house was probably a 1½-story T-shaped structure with a fishscale-shingled roof, most of which is still enclosed within the present brick walls. Galloway probably added the two back rooms immediately, at the same time bricking over the original house in all-header and English bond and decorating each corner of the front wall with a Jacobean pilaster—a detail that suggests the early date for these changes. John Francis Mercer, governor of Maryland (1801–3), later lived in the house and made several additions and changes, although most are not visible from the road. From the road, Cedar Park, with its roof pitched at sixty degrees and its towering end chimneys, still resembles an English Tudor country house.

A short distance further along the road is the "park" (R) from which Cedar Park took its name—a stand of virgin timber supposedly once part of an English-style deer park. At 1.2 m. is **Parkhurst** (R) (private, but visible from the road), built by Richard Mercer in 1848 on a hill overlooking the West River. This white frame house, shaded by great trees, has a two-story entrance portico supported by four Ionic columns.

● Md. 255 continues to **GALESVILLE** (10′ alt., est. 670 pop.), 4.2 m., originally called West River Landing. The assembly designated the site a town in 1684, but as with other legislated towns, growth was slow. The site was a shipping center for the area through the steamboat era, and is now devoted to fishing and boatbuilding.

At 15.8 m. on Md. 2 is the junction with Md. 408 and Md. 422.

● Go straight ahead on Md. 408 to **Lothian** (R) (private, but visible from the road), 0.3 m., built by the Quaker Philip Thomas in 1804. Like *Etowah Farm,* the original house follows the traditional English town house plan, with the hallway to one side. The rooms on the opposite side of the hall were added about 1840. The house has an early central-heating system. A furnace in the cellar, no longer in use, sent hot air through brick ducts in the walls and out registers in the floors, some of which still remain.

Along Md. 408 is located part of **Portland Manor,** 1,000 acres of which was granted in 1697 by Lord Baltimore to his "Receiving General, Chief Agent and Keeper of our great seal at Arms in our Province," Col. Henry Darnall. At 5.5 m. Md. 408 joins Md. 4. Continue on Md. 4 to the exit for Upper Marlboro, 8.0 m., and a junction with Tour 26a.

At the junction with Md. 408, Md. 2 turns sharp left. South of this point, almost any side road leads past tobacco fields, where, after rain in late May or early June, farmers can be seen driving tractors that pull tobacco-transplanting machines. The young plants, started in special plots early in spring, must be transplanted while the ground is moist. Until the end of World War II, transplanting was a hand operation. Now, two people sitting on a carriage pulled by a tractor drop plants into holes dug by the machine, which then automatically waters each plant. Many of the tobacco barns that can be seen in fields along the roads were built in the nineteenth century, and the fundamental design of the buildings has changed little since then. Maryland tobacco is air dried, so air circulation is crucial. The sides of the barns have slats that may be open or closed, depending upon the humidity, and the best constructed barns also have roof ventilators. Air drying, a curing method unique to Maryland, gives tobacco the capacity to stay lit, and as a result, some Maryland leaf is used in most cigarette mixtures (*see* Upper Marlboro, Tour 26a).

The smaller structure near many tobacco barns is called the stripping shed, where cured tobacco is stripped from the stalks and graded according to quality. Stripping and grading are hand operations requiring great care. The amount of hand labor required to produce cured leaf is the most important factor limiting the size of the crop a farmer can plant. A farmer can use his tractor to plow and fertilize the land and to transplant his seedlings, but other steps in the production of tobacco differ little from those followed by his seventeenth-century predecessors.

At 16.7 m., **Tudor Hall** (L) (private) can be glimpsed on a hill. Edward Hall is supposed to have built the smallest wing of this frame telescope house in 1722.

The road passes little **St. James Church** (L) (open by request), 18.8 m., which was finished in 1765 and has now been restored. In the vestry minutes, the church contract of 1762 reads as follows: "Mr. John Weems has undertak[en] the Building of the Breek Church in the sd Parrish according to the Draft of the Plan that was this Day layd Before the Vestry, and is to Build the sd Church att fourteen hundred pounds Cur[rent money], Without any further Charges to the said parrish In any Shape Whatever In Case that the sd Vestry git ann Acte of Assembly, for What Tob. Will be wanting of the Sum that is to Build the sd Church for as they hant Tob. Enufe in hand for the finniching of the sd Church."

Two walls of this simple rectangular building are laid in all-header bond. The hip roof ends in graceful swallowtail eaves,

and as at *All Hallows Church,* a brick porch protects the entrance on one of the long sides. Nearby among the trees is a
freestanding belfry, the third built for this church.

At 19.6 m. is the junction with Md. 256 (*see above*).

At 21.6 m. is the junction with Md. 423.

● Left on this at 0.3 m., an old house (R) (private), with great double
chimneys and a steep roof that sweeps down over porches, is framed
by a double row of old trees. Md. 423 continues to **FAIRHAVEN,** a
small cluster of houses on Herring Bay.

At **FRIENDSHIP** (150' alt.), 23.0 m., is the junction with Md.
261 and Sansbury Road.

● Turn left on Md. 261 (Friendship Road) to **Holly Hill** (R) (private),
1.7 m., one of the most interesting seventeenth-century houses in
Maryland. The original clapboard frame house, probably built by the
Quaker Richard Harrison about 1667, was one room with a loft that
was covered by a very steep roof. A few years later Harrison added another room and loft, and in the early 1700s the front wall and one
end wall were covered with brick over the original clapboards. In
1733, the wing that forms the L was constructed. Inside the house is
excellent paneling and other woodwork, as well as several early wall
paintings. Especially interesting is the end wall of one of the second
floor bedrooms, which is covered with paneling painted to look like
marble, set around a huge fireplace. The panel above the fireplace is
a mural depicting an English country scene. Above the fireplace in
the library on the first floor is another old painting on canvas which
shows the Holly Hill property and an inset of the house.

● Turn right from Md. 2 onto Sansbury Road. At the fork bear left
to Md. 260, 1.5 m. Turn right onto Md. 260 to **Maidstone** (private),
2.0 m. The house was built soon after the Quaker Benjamin Chew
willed the farm to his wife in 1699. The dramatic appearance of the
house is derived from its great roof, which rises at a pitch at 56°️ and
covers both a second story and a twelve-foot attic. The porches were
added about one hundred years ago, and the house was extended and
renovated so drastically at that time that little remains of the early
woodwork except the chimney piece in the dining room. Dr. Samuel
Chew (1693–1744), only son of Benjamin, lived here until 1735, when
he moved to Dover. In 1741, Samuel was appointed chief justice for
the Pennsylvania counties that now compose the State of Delaware. He
advocated self-defense during King George's War (1740–48) and as
a result was read out of the Friends Meeting. His son Benjamin (1722–
1810), brought up at Maidstone, became chief justice (1774) and president of the High Court of Errors and Appeals (1791–1808) of Pennsylvania. Benjamin's sister Anne married Samuel Galloway of *Tulip
Hill.*

From Maidstone, turn left, continuing on Md. 260. At 3.1 m. turn left
onto Brickhouse Road. At 1.4 m. is the entrance to **Highlands** (R)
(private), a great brick house with double chimneys on each gable
probably built by Fielder Bowie Smith about 1800.

At 1.5 m. on Brickhouse Road is the junction with Md. 4. Turn left
on Md. 4. At 1.1 m. is Ferry Landing Road. Turn right to **Smithville
Methodist Church** (R), a plain brick church of good proportions built
in 1835.

● At 1.3 m. on Md. 4 is the junction with Ward Road (L). Turn left
onto Ward Road to **Red Hall** (L) (private), 0.7 m., a frame, gambrel-
roofed house not far from Maidstone and probably built in the same
period by William Lyles. Originally, the house was only one room and
a loft with a single chimney. Later, each floor was partitioned into
three rooms, the single chimney was taken down, and double chimneys
with pent were put in its place. Coins and artifacts found in the ground

beneath the double chimneys appear to have been buried there since 1720 or earlier, and the wainscoting and other woodwork in the "greate" room are of the same period. The curtain and kitchen wing were probably added at the same time. The stone basement, originally divided into four stone cells, had no exit except through a trapdoor to the first floor of the house. Small wood carvings of a pig and a horse were found in the dirt when the present cement floor was laid.

Go right from Maidstone on Md. 260 to the junction with Md. 2 at Owings.

On Md. 2, at 24.3 m., turn left to **OWINGS.** Here is the junction with Md. 260.

Straight ahead on Md. 260 is **CHESAPEAKE BEACH** (15' alt., 934 pop.) (beach concession, amusements, boats for hire).

At 28.5 m. is the junction with Md. 262.

● Turn right on Md. 262 to **LOWER MARLBORO,** 4.4 m., on the Patuxent. This was a port before the river silted up with top soil, and it was the location of Lower Marlboro Academy (ca. 1775–1860), one of the few schools in eighteenth-century Maryland. In a field **Graham House** (R) (private), on the outskirts of the village, is a striking 1½-story brick house with catslide roof, built about 1744 by Malcolm Graham on Patuxent Manor. The river side of the house, with its glazed headers and well-proportioned doors and windows, can be seen in the fall, winter, and spring months from the road by turning right at the intersection. The original paneling is at the Winterthur Museum in Wilmington, Delaware.

In the triangle where Md. 2, Md. 262, and Md. 4 meet is **All Saints Protestant Episcopal Church** (open by request), shaded by impressive Canadian hemlocks. The original church, erected on a different site, was built before 1695. The present church was built between 1774 and 1777. The rectangular brick building achieves the graceful effect of height and airiness from two-story surface arches, which on the side walls enclose two tiers of windows. The interior, remodeled in 1857 and restored in 1950, has a gallery running along each side. By the side of the road is a sundial presented by Thomas John Claggett, rector of the church from 1767 to 1776 and 1788 to 1792, upon his consecration as first bishop of Maryland (*see* Tour 26a, Upper Marlboro).

At 28.6 m. Md. 2 joins Md. 4.

In **HUNTINGTOWN,** 31.5 m., is the junction with Md. 524 that leads to Md. 521.

● Take Md. 524 to Md. 521. Turn right on Md. 521 to the junction with Lowery Road at 2.2 m. Turn left, then right at 2.4 m. at the fork. At 3.0 m. is **Huntingfields** (L) (private), a frame house with a puzzling architectural history. The two-story wing was built about 1820, but the two smaller wings are perhaps a century or more older.

Islington (L) (private, but beside the road), 33.2 m., is a small, 1½-story frame house with a steep gable roof believed to date from the late seventeenth century.

At 34.4 m. is a junction with Md. 263 (L), which leads to **Plum Point** at the beginning of the *Calvert Cliffs.*

At **STOAKLEY** on Md. 2, 36.3 m., is the junction with Stoakley Road.

To the left is the **Calvert County Hospital.**

● Go right 2.2 m. to a fork; bear left on Barstow Road; then left at the next fork, 3.7 m. Turn left again to **Cedar Hill** (L) (private), or

Gantt House, 3.9 m., built about 1730 in a seventeenth-century style with steep pitched roof and very tall outside chimneys. The house is cross-shaped, a familiar plan in Tudor and Stuart England. The cross is formed by a 2-story enclosed porch and an upstairs porch chamber in front and a 1½-story wing behind. Some good woodwork remains in the interior, including benches with Jacobean-style supports built into the porch.

Md. 402 branches left at 37.2 m.

● This travels 4.2 m. to **DARES BEACH,** a resort on the Bay where a hollow in the cliffs makes the narrow beach accessible and allows a view of Calvert Cliffs as they curve to the south. The earliest land patents in this area were issued to Puritans in the mid-seventeenth century, but by the 1670s the neighborhood was a center of early Quakerism. What was probably the earliest Friends Meeting in Maryland had been established in the vicinity by 1672.

On Md. 2 at 37.3 m. is the junction with Md. 765.

● Go left 0.2 m. to **PRINCE FREDERICK** (150′ alt., 600 pop.), county seat of Calvert County since 1725. The town was named in honor of a son of King George II. Prince Frederick was burnt by British raiders in 1814, and another fire in 1882 so destroyed the town that no old buildings remain. The handsome white portico of the present brick courthouse, built in 1915 and remodeled in 1948, shows through the trees planted on the site of the prior courthouses.

Md. 765 rejoins Md. 2 at 2.2 m.

At 37.9 m. on Md. 2 is the junction with Md. 231.

● Turn right on Md. 231 to the junction with Md. 508. Turn left on this road to the **Taney Place** (private), 0.7 m., birthplace in 1777 of Roger Brooke Taney, who served as chief justice of the U.S. Supreme Court from 1836 to 1864. The house, which overlooks the Patuxent on the west side of Battle Creek, has brick end walls two feet thick and frame sides filled with brick nogging covered by clapboard.

Near here on Battle Creek was the first Calvert County seat, Battle Town, or Calvert Town, established in 1652 by Robert Brooke. Brooke came to Maryland at Lord Baltimore's invitation in 1650, bringing with him his wife, ten children, and twenty-eight servants (and, legend has it, a pack of foxhounds). He was made "commander" of a new county, called Charles County, which occupied what is now Calvert County. When the Parliamentary commission took over the Maryland government in 1652 (*see below,* Preston-on-Patuxent), Brooke was named to the new council. After Gov. Thomas Stone had been reinstated, he dismissed Brooke and declared that Charles County no longer existed, erecting Calvert County in its place. Battle Town remained the county seat until 1725, but all traces of it have disappeared.

Brooke lived at **Brooke Place Manor** just across Battle Creek. His son Roger and his descendants continued to live here until recent times. Roger Brooke Taney was a descendant.

Md. 231 crosses the Patuxent River to Benedict (*see* Tour 29) at 5.6 m.

At 40.1 m. on Md. 2 is the junction with Md. 506.

● Go right to a bridge over the **Battle Creek Cypress Swamp,** 2.1 m. Paths from the bridge penetrate some distance into the swamp, where a stand of cypress trees, rare at this latitude, has maintained itself since the Pleistocene epoch. This being the most northerly habitat of such trees, the swamp has been designated a registered National Natural Landmark.

At 41.5 m. on Md. 2 is **PORT REPUBLIC** and the junction with Md. 264.

● Turn right on Md. 264 to **Christ Protestant Episcopal Church** (L),
0.5 m., which serves one of the original parishes of Maryland. The
first church on this site was built before 1692. A second, built in
1735, fell into disrepair, and the present church was started in 1769
using bricks from the old structure. The Victorian surfacing of stucco
and the brown-painted bracketed cornices obscure the lines of the old
buttressed walls. On the front of the church are the dates 1772, 1881,
and 1906.

Continue on Md. 264 to **MUTUAL**, 2.4 m. Once a year, usually in
August, a tilting tournament (*see* Tour 24, St. Margaret's Church) is
held here for the benefit of one of the local churches.

At Mutual, continue on Md. 264 to **BROOMES ISLAND** (20' alt., est.
250 pop.), 4.8 m., a waterfront community of oystermen and fishermen, some of whom act as guides for sportsmen. From the "island"—
a narrow point that juts into the Patuxent—the view extends for miles
up and down the river.

● At Mutual turn left on Md. 265. At 4.2 m. is the gate (R) to **The
Cage** (private), a brick house on the shores of the Patuxent long believed to date from 1652, but probably built some fifty years later.
One part of the house is typical of others built about the same time,
being one-room deep and one and one-half stories high with a steep
gable roof. The brick walls are laid in Flemish bond with glazed
headers. Inside, the original exposed and beaded rafters remain in all
but one room. The horizontal-board wainscoting and the paneled fireplace wall in the "greate" room were destroyed years ago, but the
room has been reconstructed with the help of those who remembered
how it looked. Modern wings on each side blend well with the old
section of the house.

At 42.6 m. on Md. 2 is the junction with Md. 509.

● Turn left to **KENWOOD BEACH**, where there is access to **Calvert
Cliffs** (not open to the public), first described by Capt. John Smith
following his exploration of the Chesapeake in 1608. From here the
bluffs, varying in height up to 150 feet, stretch out in a great thirty-
mile arc from Chesapeake Beach to Cove Point. The cliffs are famous
among paleontologists for their exposure of Miocene fossils, including
whale bones, crocodile plates, shark teeth, and other remains of life
15 to 20 million years old.

In 1967, the Baltimore Gas and Electric Company announced its
intention of building a nuclear power plant at Calvert Cliffs. Before
construction started, environmental studies were conducted so that the
plant could be designed, built, and operated without harm to the Bay.
In 1968, construction was started, and in 1975 the first unit was placed
in operation. The second unit is scheduled for completion in 1977.
Environmental studies are still being conducted to insure that the Bay
does not suffer any harmful effects.

Outside the main gates the Baltimore Gas and Electric Company has
a visitors center. An old tobacco barn is now used as a museum in
which are housed displays of fossils found in the cliffs. Tours of the
plant are available.

At **LUSBY** (100' alt.), 50.0 m. on Md. 2, is the junction with
Sollers Road.

● Go right on this 0.3 m., then right on a dirt road to **Morgan Hill
Farm** (private), a frame house built about 1670 on a bluff above St.
Leonard Creek which has now been restored. The foundation is dark
red native "Iron Rock," the walls are of random-width siding, and a
steep-pitched roof with dormers sweeps down over a one-story front
porch. Posts and rafters in the interior are exposed and beaded. The
owners have added twentieth-century conveniences without destroying

Battle Creek Cypress Swamp

the simplicity that befits a colonial farmhouse. Not long ago a telegraph instrument was found on the property, suggesting that during the Civil War the farm, with its splendid view of St. Leonard Creek, was used as a lookout.

● Continue on Sollers Road about 2.0 m. to a fork.

Go straight ahead on Sollers Road to **Spout Farm** (private), 3.3 m., situated on a cliff above St. Leonard Creek. The old section of the house, said to have been built in 1700, is well known for the giant chimneys on the east end of the building. The chimneys narrow at the third-floor line and are connected at that point by a two-story windowless pent. Lovely boxwood gardens adorn the ground, from which may be had a spectacular view of St. Leonard Creek as it joins the Patuxent.

On the river below here, British warships in 1814 blockaded part of the flotilla of Com. Joshua Barney, which was anchored up the creek. The flotilla, consisting of about twenty-seven gunboats and barges, was all the U.S. Navy had available to cope with the British squadron that was blockading the Chesapeake Bay. Aided by a battery of guns on the bluff across the creek, Barney forced the British to retire long enough to enable his fleet to escape up the Patuxent River. A few days later, however, he was forced to burn a cutter, a gunboat, and thirteen barges to prevent capture by the British, who had gathered in strength at Benedict (see Tour 29) before their attack on Washington, D.C. Barney's men joined Gen. William H. Winder's command and fought at the Battle of Bladensburg (see Tour 27). According to British accounts, Winder's men provided the only significant resistance they faced.

At the foot of the bluff at **Sollers Wharf** is a "spout," or spring that has been in use for almost 300 years.

● Turn left at the fork onto Mill Bridge Road. About 1652, Richard

Preston built a house near here. From 1654 to 1657, Preston's house was the provincial seat of government. During this period, Lord Baltimore lost control of his province to a group of Puritans who, at the invitation of Governor Stone, left Virginia in 1649 to settle in Maryland. Although Cecilius Calvert had been prompt to express allegiance to the Commonwealth after the execution of Charles I, his deputy governor in Maryland followed Virginia's example by proclaiming Charles II king. Governor Stone attempted to undo the mistake by proclaiming Maryland's loyalty to the Commonwealth, and Lord Baltimore succeeded in having the province omitted from the commission Parliament authorized in 1650 to establish loyal government in Virginia and the Chesapeake Bay area.

Nevertheless, in 1652, the Parliamentary commissioners, among them Lord Baltimore's old enemy William Claiborne and the Puritan leader Richard Bennett, used their influence to overthrow the "Papist" proprietary government and reopen Virginia's old claim to the Maryland patent (see Tour 24, Kent Island). At first, the commissioners reappointed Governor Stone, who was himself a Puritan. Stone attempted to reassert the charter rights of the lord proprietor, however, because his patent, contrary to the commissioner's expectations, was not voided. As a result, Bennett and Claiborne deposed Stone and his councillors in 1654, appointing ten Puritan commissioners to replace them. Richard Preston was named one of the ten, and the colony's records were soon moved from St. Mary's City to his house, where the assembly and the Provincial Court met until 1657. In 1655, Governor Stone unsuccessfully took up arms against the Puritans. His men temporarily retrieved the records from Preston's house, however, and on another occasion raided it for arms. During these attacks some of the colony's records and the Great Seal of the Province were lost.

In 1656, Lord Baltimore appointed Josias Fendall governor of Maryland, but Fendall was powerless to act until the spring of 1658. By then it was clear that the English government intended to support Lord Baltimore's claim to the province, so the Puritans in Maryland peacefully relinquished their claims in return for amnesty and confirmation of lands granted, taxes levied, and other actions taken by the courts and the assembly under their rule.

In 1656, one of America's first juries of women was impaneled at this house for the trial of Judith Catchpole on the charge of infanticide. Their report stated: "[We] have according to our charge searched the body of Judith Catchpole, doe give in our verdict that according to our best judgement [she] hath not had any child within the time charged."

At 51.4 m. on Md. 2, **Middleham Chapel** (L) (open on request) stands in a grove of shellbark hickory trees. In 1746, the vestry of Christ Church (see above) petitioned the assembly to levy the sum of 80,000 pounds of tobacco to build a new chapel of ease here because the old one had "by length of Time become ruinous and by increase of Inhabitants, too small for the congregation." The present chapel was built in 1748, with the date inscribed in the brick of the gable above the entrance. The church bell bears the inscription, "The gift of John Holdsworth of Middleham [England] to Middleham Chapel, Anno Do 1699." The communion service was a gift from Queen Anne's Bounty in 1714.

At **BERTHA,** 52.3 m., is the junction with Md. 497.

● Go left on Md. 497 to **Cove Point** at the end of *Calvert Cliffs,* where the U.S. Coast Guard maintains a lighthouse. A large beach runs along both sides of the point, and there is a small community of summer cottages here.

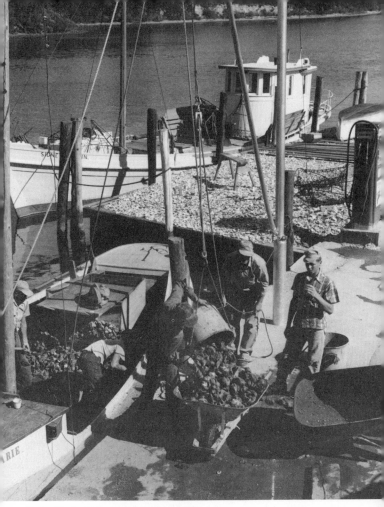

Unloading oysters on Solomons Island

Md. 2 continues to **SOLOMONS ISLAND** (10′ alt., 183 pop.), 56.8 m., a small island named for Isaac Solomon, who established an oyster cannery here after the Civil War. Solomon settled the island with people from the Eastern Shore who fished and canned for him. Solomons is reached from the mainland by a causeway lined with a single row of houses. On the mainland side of the island is a landlocked harbor, which serves as an anchorage for a fishing fleet and the many small boats that make Solomons a stop on the Inland Waterway. The new Reginald V. Truitt Environmental Laboratory has been established here to conduct estuarine studies.

On the Patuxent side of the island is one of the great natural harbors of the East Coast, too far from railroads and cities and yet too near to Baltimore and Norfolk to make its development profitable. The harbor is two miles wide and in places over one hundred feet deep. The drydock *Dewey* was tested here in 1905, and in 1942 the deep waters were used for mine testing. The Navy Mine Test Station at Point Patience is just up the river. During 1942–45, the Navy Amphibious Training Base operated nearby, and thousands of sailors and marines who practiced landings on the beaches of Drum and Cove points went from Solomons in the Patuxent to the Solomons in the South Pacific. Across the river is the Patuxent Naval Air Test Station (*see* Tour 30), which formerly was connected to Solomons by ferry. During World War II, navy dependents increased the population of Solomons tenfold, but now the island has once again become a quiet fishing village.

The **Chesapeake Biological Laboratory** (open all year; Mon.–Fri., 9–5; closed 12:30–1:30; open Sat., June–Aug.), conducted by the Natural Resources Institute of the University of Maryland, is housed on Solomons in a large brick building with a 750-foot pier on the Patuxent waterfront. Here experts study the marine life of the Bay area and its problems, such as water pollution.

From the tip of the island, **Rousby Hall** can be seen on the mainland. A large brick house with outbuildings and gardens, the whole surrounded by a brick wall for defense, was once located here. The British burned Rousby Hall in 1780, and it was replaced by the present whitewashed, weatherboard farmhouse with a steep roof that sweeps down over porches on each side. In the garden is the grave of John Rousby, "who departed this Life the 28th day of January Anno Domini 1750 Aged 23 years and 10 months." His widow married Col. William Fitzhugh after a stormy courtship, during which he is said to have seized her baby, rowed with it out into the river, and threatened to throw it overboard unless she promised to marry him. Colonel Fitzhugh was a close friend of Gov. Robert Eden, who was a frequent visitor at Rousby Hall. In 1776, Fitzhugh was a member of the convention that framed the first Maryland State Constitution, and in 1778 he was Speaker of the House of Delegates. In 1890 the property was laid out in lots for a proposed city that was to be called "Rousby on Patuxent." The town was to be served by the Baltimore-Drum Point Railroad, but the railroad was never completed and the city never materialized.

BALTIMORE CITY LINE–UPPER MARLBORO–LA PLATA–POTOMAC RIVER; 74.6 m.
Md. 3 and U.S. 301

Md. 3 is part of a north-south artery from Baltimore to Florida that crosses **Harry W. Nice Memorial Bridge,** formerly known as the Potomac River Bridge. After the highway leaves the suburbs of Baltimore below Glen Burnie, it travels twenty miles or so through the open rolling countryside. Some of the surrounding land is still being farmed, but all of it may soon be developed into suburban housing. Regional and local planners, however, hope to preserve fingers of open space for farm or park land. South of the interchange with U.S. 50, the route becomes U.S. 301.

26a. BALTIMORE CITY LINE–UPPER MARLBORO; 33.0 m.
Md. 3 and U.S. 301

In Baltimore, Md. 3 (Greene Street) branches off U.S. 40 (Franklin Street or Mulberry Street); Greene Street joins Russell Street. At the intersection of Russell and Bush streets can be seen the orange and yellow **Baltimore City Solid-Waste Disposal Plant** (L). Built by the Monsanto Company at the cost of 16 million dollars, the plant can process 1,000 tons of refuse daily. After the refuse has been shredded, it undergoes pyrolysis (the term is emblazoned in huge letters on the side of the building), during which it is baked at 1,800° F. The resulting gases are mixed with air, then burned to produce steam. The steam will eventually provide heat and air conditioning for about half of the buildings in downtown Baltimore. The solid wastes, including iron, steel, and glass, are sold for recycling, while the small quantity of carbon char residue, now buried in a landfill, may prove valuable for reconditioning soil.

As part of the Baltimore-Washington Parkway, Md. 3 crosses the **Baltimore City Line** at 0.0 m., but at 2.3 m. it moves on to the Baltimore Beltway (I-695), which it leaves at 4.3 m. At 6.1 m. is an exit onto Md. 648 in Glen Burnie (*see* Tour 25a).

At 13.9 m. is the junction with Md. 178, a side route of Tour 27, at Dorr's Corner.

At 15.7 m. is the junction with Md. 175, which leads past Fort George G. Meade to a junction with the Baltimore-Washington Parkway and Tour S 1.

Johns Hopkins Road turns left off a Md. 3 crossover at 18.1 m.

● Take this road to **Whites Hall** (R) (private), 0.9 m., formerly known as Whitehall. Here Johns Hopkins, founder of The Johns Hopkins University, was born in 1795. The white-painted brick central portion is the old house, probably built by his grandfather in the 1760s and certainly standing in 1784 when it was inherited by his father. The Hopkinses were Quakers, and in 1778, after the Baltimore Yearly Meeting had condemned slavery (1777), Hopkins's grandfather freed his forty-two slaves, thus depriving the family of a considerable portion of its capital wealth. Johns, one of eleven children, left the farm in 1812 to work in the wholesale grocery business of his uncle Gerard in Baltimore. In 1819, he started his own wholesale grocery business, amassing through trade with the West the fortune that enabled him to found the university that bears his name. Continuing on Johns Hopkins Road, bear left at the junction with Underwood Road. At 1.5 m. bear left again onto St. Stephen's Church Road. At 1.6 m. is **St. Stephen's Church** (L), built in 1845 when St. Anne's Parish was divided.

At 18.9 m. is the junction with Md. 424, a side route of Tour 27.

At 20.9 m. Md. 450 (Tour 27) joins Md. 3; it departs at 21.4 m.

At 23.6 m. and 23.8 m. are the junctions with U.S. 50–U.S. 301 and Tour 24. Here the route becomes U.S. 301, passing through tobacco-growing country.

Nearly all Maryland tobacco is grown in the five southern Maryland counties, where it has been the chief money crop from the first days of settlement. Soil exhaustion has been an ever-present problem because tobacco rapidly depletes the land, and by the nineteenth century much of the Southern Maryland soil was worn out. Proper care and heavy fertilizing can solve

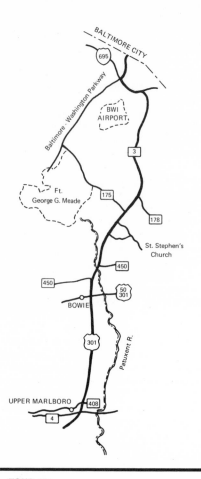

TOUR 26a

the problem, but vestiges of past abuses can be seen everywhere.

The future of Maryland tobacco is uncertain despite its superior ability to hold fire, which keeps it in steady if limited demand. Given government price supports, tobacco is still the best-paying field crop. But from thirteen to fifteen months are required from the time tobacco is sown until it reaches the market place, and the crop requires as much as 270 man-hours of labor per acre (*see* Tour 25, before Tudor Hall), far more than any other crop. The amount of his land a farmer plants in tobacco is directly related to the amount of labor he can command. Good roads have brought much of Southern Maryland sufficiently near to better paying jobs in Baltimore and Washington, so many tobacco planters are finding it increasingly difficult to hire reliable farmhands. Although the average Southern Maryland farm encompasses from 85 to 130 acres, the great majority of farmers plant fewer than 12 acres in tobacco. When a farmer stops planting tobacco the reason most often given is that he could not find suitable labor to help tend the crop.

Price fluctuations are another problem faced by tobacco growers. Attempts to establish acreage and quality controls in an effort to stabilize tobacco prices date back to the 1660s in Maryland. Little was accomplished until the Tobacco Inspection Act of 1747 provided for public warehouses at which public inspectors examined and graded all tobacco before shipment to market. The effectiveness of the inspection system is debatable, but nothing better was devised until the Federal Agricultural Adjustment Act of 1938 was passed. This act and later amendments to it established a voluntary program combining quality controls, acreage controls, and price supports. In the years that Maryland tobacco growers have voted to abide by the provisions of this program, each farmer has been limited in the number of acres he could plant in tobacco based on the quantity of land he had devoted to the crop in previous years. In the long run, however, a shortage of labor and the rising value of land due to suburban residential expansion are liable to have more effect than any government regulations on reducing the amount of tobacco grown in the area.

At 27.5 m. and 27.7 m. are the junctions with Md. 214 and Tour 28 and at 33.0 m. is the junction with Md. 408 at Upper Marlboro.

UPPER MARLBORO (39' alt., 646 pop.), first laid out in 1706 and named for the Duke of Marlborough, has been the county seat of Prince George's County since 1721. The town has always been a tobacco marketing center. During the eighteenth century, shallow draft boats carried hogsheads of tobacco from the town down Western Branch to the Patuxent River, where ocean-going vessels anchored. From 1748 until about 1818, all locally grown tobacco was inspected here at a public warehouse before shipment overseas, and today two leaf-tobacco auction houses are located at the intersection of U.S. 301 and Md. 408.

The tobacco auctions, held from late April until mid-July, are of prime economic importance to the farmers in the area. In low warehouses with flat roofs full of skylights that enable buyers to examine the leaf in full daylight, shallow slat baskets holding about 140 pounds of tobacco lie in long lines. Each basket is marked with the weight and grade of the tobacco it contains. The starter, who calls out the starting price, and the auctioneer, who chants the bidding, move rapidly down the rows selling as many as 400 baskets an hour. A planter's whole income from a crop sown at least 12 months before is thus determined in a matter of minutes. If he feels that the price offered is too low, he has thirty minutes in which to void the sale by tearing the bid price off the identifying ticket on the basket. He can then put the tobacco up for sale again.

The auction method of marketing tobacco first appeared in Maryland in 1939 and immediately became predominant because it brought a quick income. Formerly, all tobacco had been shipped in hogsheads to Baltimore warehouses where it sometimes sat for months before being sold. Now, 90 percent of tobacco grown in Southern Maryland is sold at leaf auctions. In years when price supports are not in effect, planters who can afford to wait find that the older marketing system has some advantages. A state subsidy reduces marketing costs, and if prices are low the tobacco can be held until they rise. Under the present price support program, the Maryland Tobacco Co-operative, using funds lent at interest by the Commodity Credit Corporation, purchases at auction any leaf that will not sell above support prices.

In the mid-eighteenth century, Upper Marlboro was a busy, almost cosmopolitan, urban center. Theatrical companies gave occasional performances here, and every spring and fall the races attracted some of the outstanding horses of the time. In 1768, Samuel Galloway's Selim (*see* Tour 25b), a grandson of the great Godolphin Arabian and until then undefeated, lost to Figure, who had an unbeaten record in England. A number of stores in the town offered "European and West Indian" goods for sale, occasionally advertising "silks of the newest Patterns." In 1771, Mahon and Connor, Staymakers, promised to make house calls to any lady who lived within a ten-mile radius of the town. On the other hand, there was neither church nor chapel of ease in Upper Marlboro until 1810, which suggests that the number of permanent residents in the town must have been small.

During the nineteenth century, stagecoaches and then rail-roads brought Upper Marlboro closer to Washington and Balti-more, making the town less isolated, but at the same time more provincial. "Silks of the newest Patterns" no longer came direct from London, and people traveled to the city to attend the theater. Today, even though it is the administrative center of a large and rapidly expanding metropolitan area with easy access to Washington, D.C., Upper Marlboro is still a country town in the middle of rolling farmlands.

● Go right on Md. 408 into the center of Upper Marlboro. Hidden under trees behind commercial buildings and the new County Office Building is the **Harry Buck House** (R), one of the showplaces of the town in the 1850s and still a handsome building with a Greek-Revival porch and doorway. It is now owned by Maryland-National Capital Park and Planning Commission.

In the center of town, still on Md. 408 (Main Street), is the **Court-house.** The present building incorporates the courthouse of 1881, but it was completely enlarged and remodeled in 1940. Additions in the rear were completed in 1949, 1958, and 1973. On the courthouse lawn a marker commemorates John and Daniel Carroll, who were born in a house that once stood on this site. John Carroll (1735–1815) became the first bishop and then archbishop of the Roman Catholic Church in the United States (*see* Downtown Baltimore); Daniel (1730–96) was a signer of the U.S. Constitution. The father deeded the courthouse lot to the county in 1730. The brick part of the building to the right of the courthouse was built for the Register of Wills in the 1830s. In the Post Office across the street is a mural, painted as a WPA project, depicting workers loading tobacco leaves on wagons in the field. Since tobacco is harvested by the stalk, not the leaf, the picture is a subject of much local derision.

Beyond the courthouse on Md. 408 is the intersection with Elm Street. Turning to the right, Elm Street ends at Academy Hill, where the **Grave of Dr. William Beanes** and his wife is now surrounded by an iron railing. In 1814, Dr. Beanes was the leading physician in Upper Marlboro, and when the British occupied the town before the attack on Bladensburg, his house was used as the headquarters for Gen. Robert Ross and his staff. After the British had continued to

Tobacco auction

Nottingham to camp for the night, some stragglers attempted to steal refreshments from a party being given at Dr. Beanes's house. Dr. Beanes headed a posse to capture the British stragglers. The British, interpreting this act as a breach of faith, imprisoned Beanes on board ship. Beanes's old friend, Francis Scott Key, visited Adm. Sir Alexander Cochrane in an effort to procure his release. At this point, the ships set sail for the attack on Baltimore. The British admiral agreed to let Dr. Beanes go, but stipulated that none of the Americans could leave the fleet until the battle was over. It was while he and Beanes watched the bombardment of Fort McHenry that Key conceived "The Star-Spangled Banner."

To the right a few hundred feet on Church Street is **Trinity Protestant Episcopal Church** (L), built about 1846. The bell tower was added in 1898 to commemorate Rev. Thomas John Claggett (1743–1814), who founded the church as a separate congregation (not part of any parish) in 1810. Claggett, although enough of a Tory to retire from preaching for a while during the Revolution, was consecrated the first bishop of Maryland in 1792. Claggett founded Trinity after age had forced him to retire from the larger parish of St. Paul's at Baden (*see below*). At his death he was buried on his estate, Croome, but in 1919 his remains were removed to the National Cathedral in Washington.

Across the street from Trinity Church is the frame house **Content** (private, but visible from the road), with a pair of great outside brick chimneys connected by a one-story pent with window. The house is believed to have been built about 1787.

Church Street ends at the junction of Md. 408 with Old Crain Highway, and in the Y formed in the intersection is the **Claggett House** (private), a 1½-story frame building with double chimneys on each gable, which is believed to have been built before the Revolution by one of the founding fathers of Upper Marlboro, David Craufurd. The quaint gingerbread trim on the house's porches and dormers is clearly a Victorian alteration.

● On Md. 408 (Marlboro Pike) is the **Mount Carmel Cemetery** (R). Gov. Thomas Sim Lee (1745–1819), the second governor of Maryland (1779–83 and 1792–94), is buried here. The Prince George's County Chapter of the Daughters of the American Revolution recently unveiled a bronze marker at the site.

Go right on Md. 408 to **Melwood Park** (R) (private), 4.0 m., visible through the great trees that surround it. The long narrow stuccoed brick house is two stories in front, one and one-half behind. Now deteriorating (for many years it was used for grain storage), the house was once owned by Ignatius Digges, who entertained George Washington here several times during the early 1770s.

At 5.9 m. on Md. 408 is a junction with Md. 223. Turn left on Md. 223–Md. 408. Then turn right on Md. 408 (Md. 223 continues straight). At the stoplight, turn right to Md. 4. Turn left on Md. 4 to the junction with Md. 337, 6.7 m. Turn left on Md. 337 (Suitland Parkway) to Andrews Airforce Base (*see* Tour 29). Md. 4 continues to the **District of Columbia Line,** 12.6 m.

● Go left on Old Crain Highway, now unmarked. At 0.4 m., the **Overseer's House** (private), a frame house with heavy brick chimneys, sits on a ridge above the road. Coming downhill towards Upper Marlboro it can be seen from some distance. At 1.6 m. **The Claggett Family Burying Ground** (R) is silhouetted against the sky, and just beyond is **Weston** (private), situated on a tract owned almost continuously by the Claggetts since the seventeenth century. At 1.9 m., just past the tree-lined driveway, a better view of this handsome brick dwelling can be had in the winter. The house was built between 1805 and 1810 incorporating the foundations of a dwelling built about 1702.

Old Md. 3 rejoins U.S. 301 at 2.4 m.

● Go left on Md. 408. At 1.1 m. is a fork; bear left. In winter, the eighteenth-century brick chapel at **Compton Bassett** (L) (private), 0.1 m., can be seen through the trees. Before the Revolution, when by an act of 1704 Catholic services were not permitted except in private homes, this was a chapel for the descendants of Clement Hill, surveyor general of Maryland. Concealed by the woods is a handsome house built by the Hills in 1789.

● Continue on Md. 408. At 1.3 m. turn left to Md. 4. At 2.0 m. is a fork; bear left to **WAYSON'S CORNER,** 2.4 m., a tobacco auction center. Here is the junction with Md. 4, which becomes the main route of the side tour and leads to summer resorts along the Chesapeake Bay and the Patuxent River.

At 13.0 m. Md. 4 ends at a junction with Md. 2 and Tour 25.

26b. UPPER MARLBORO–LA PLATA–POTOMAC RIVER; 41.6 m.
U.S. 301

At 3.8 m. from the junction of U.S. 301 and Md. 408, just beyond the junction with Old Crain Highway, is the lane leading to **Sasscers Green** (L) (private), a small frame house with interesting hipped chimneys built about 1820.

At 4.5 m. is the junction with Md. 382 (L).

● This road travels through rich farmland along the Patuxent River. At 2.5 m. is a junction with Mt. Calvert Road Spur. Go left 0.2 m. to the **Croom Vocational School,** 1.0 m. This was formerly Croom Nike Site, one of the many missile installations that protected the Washington-Baltimore area.

At 1.4 m. on Mt. Calvert Road, go left at a fork. At the next fork, 2.5 m., bear left and continue to **Mount Calvert** (private), a brick house of uncertain date which can be seen in a field at the confluence of Western Branch with the Patuxent River. The great end chimneys are connected by a one-story windowless pent. Staircase, chair rails, cornices, and mantels in the hall and living room were evidently hand-carved in the late eighteenth century. The house, on land surveyed for Philip Calvert in 1652 and designated a manor in 1657, is on the site of Charlestown, the county seat of Prince George's County from 1695 to 1721.

Elizabeth Fowler, the only person ever executed for witchcraft in Maryland, lived in Mount Calvert Hundred on this manor. At a meeting of the Provincial Court in 1685, a grand jury agreed that she, "having not the feare of God before her eyes but being led by the instigation of the Divell certaine evil & dyabolicall artes called witchcrafts . . . did use and practice & exercise in upon & against one Francis Sandsbury . . . & several others . . . [so that] his & their bodyes were very much the worse, consumed, pined & lamed against the peace." She was convicted and hanged. Only four other men and women were tried for witchcraft in Maryland, all before 1713. One of the four was reprieved and the other three were acquitted, a good record for an age that genuinely believed in witchcraft.

This site on the Patuxent is slated to be one of the developed areas in the projected Patuxent River Park, which planners hope will keep the stream valley of the Patuxent a nature preserve and recreation area in the rapidly developing Baltimore and Washington suburbs.

● At 3.9 m. on Md. 382 in the village of **CROOM** is the junction with Duley Station Road. Go right 0.9 m. for an excellent view of **Bellefields** (R) (private), built on a tract formerly known as Sim's Delight. This is a handsome house of brick laid in Flemish bond throughout, with double end chimneys. The wings are later additions. Dr. Patrick Sim, believed to have been a refugee from the Scottish rebellion of 1715, is supposed to have built at least part of the house before his death. Then as now, medical care was costly, and patients often delayed paying their doctor's bills. In 1740, Dr. Sim sued Richard Marsham Waring for £97, the unpaid portion of a £192 bill run up by Waring's father for "journeys," "potio purges," "Mixt.^{r} Nervos," "Mixt.^{r} paragoric," "mixtor Castor," and other remedies for his family and slaves over a twelve-year period. Dr. Sim's great-grandson sold this part of the property to Benjamin Bowie Oden in 1799, and either Oden or his Bowie in-laws who lived here after him were responsible for the present interior of the house. The present owners breed race horses.

At 4.2 m. on Md. 382 is the junction with St. Thomas Church Road. Go left 0.1 m. to **St. Thomas Church** (L), finished in 1745 as a chapel of ease for St. Paul's Parish. Except for bell tower and chancel, the basic structure of this little brick church remains as described in the specifications recorded in the vestry minutes for 1742. Several years ago the parish restored the building, replacing the barrel ceiling, box pews and brick-paved "alleys." Good stained glass creates a pleasing effect in the white interior of the church. The exterior cornice was always plain, although perhaps not as heavy as now. In 1744, the vestry agreed to forgo modillions or other trim if the contractor, Daniel Page, would clear the churchyard. The bell tower, added in 1888, is a memorial to Bishop Thomas John Claggett (*see* Tour 26a). In the churchyard, shaded by great trees, are the graves of many of Maryland's outstanding families—Odens, Bowies, Sims; members of the Calvert family are buried under the church floor.

St. Thomas Church Road continues through well-tended rolling farmland. At about 0.9 m. the Bowie mansion **Mattaponi** (private, but visible from the road) comes into view. At 1.0 m. is the junction with Matapони Road. Go right to the lane to the house, a 2½-story building with hipped roof, believed to have been constructed by William Bowie about 1745 but greatly altered in 1820 when the one-story wings were added. The front door, with its handsome elliptical fanlight, leads into

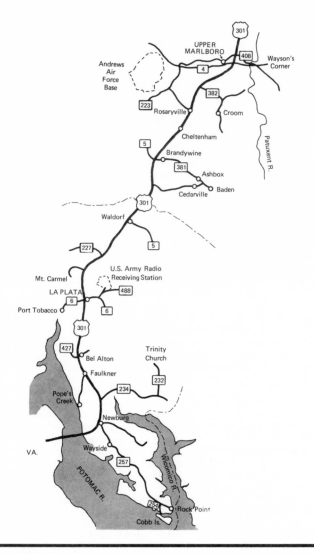

TOUR 26b

a hall that runs across the whole front of the house and contains a finely proportioned stairway.

On U.S. 301 at **ROSARYVILLE** (200' alt.), 6.8 m., is the junction with Rosaryville Road.

● At 2.8 m. on Rosaryville Road, turn left on Md. 223. At 3.1 m. a graveled road on the left leads to **His Lordship's Kindness** (also known as **Poplar Hill**) (private), 3.4 m., believed to have been built before 1735 by George, fourteenth Earl of Shrewsbury, for his niece Anne Talbot on her marriage to Henry Darnall. The house is a handsome five-part brick mansion notable for its beautiful proportions. The right wing was once a Roman Catholic chapel; the left is still used as a kitchen. On the approach front, the main house has a central projecting bay with a half-moon window in the pediment. Both the approach and the garden fronts have Palladian windows on the second floor and white doorways, each with a fanlight, reached by low flights of stone steps. The entrance portal, however, with its fluted pilasters and pediment, is more elaborate. The central hall is so well proportioned that its great size is not overwhelming. The wide staircase with carved balusters leads to unusually large second-story rooms with ceilings and windows as high as those on the first floor. Nearly all of the richly carved woodwork is original.

At 8.5 m. is **CHELTENHAM** (237' alt.).

● Turn right to **Boys' Village of Maryland** (formerly Cheltenham School for Boys), established in 1870 as a private institution for delinquent boys and taken over by the state in 1937.

At **T.B.** (225' alt.), 11.9 m., apparently named for an old boundary stone on the property of Thomas Brooke, an eighteenth-century landowner with extensive holdings, is the junction with Md. 381.

● Go left on Md. 381 to **BRANDYWINE,** 1.0 m.

At 4.8 m. is the junction with Ash Box Road. Go right 0.7 m. to **CEDARVILLE** (240' alt.), then right on Cedarville Road to a gravel road, 1.2 m., which leads into **Cedarville Natural Resources Management Area** (camping grounds, picnic areas, and hiking trails), a 3,000-acre tract of woodland and swamp.

● Md. 381 continues to **BADEN** (220' alt.) and the Baden-Westwood Road, 6.1 m. Turn left here to **St. Paul's Protestant Episcopal Church** (L) (open) (1733–35), 0.4 m. According to the specifications outlined in the vestry minutes of 1733, the church was originally like its chapel of ease, *St. Thomas Church* at Croom, a rectangle made cruciform by a square porch on each side. Between 1793 and 1795 the vestry took down the south porch, replacing it with a thirty-foot addition. About 1852, the north porch was replaced by the present chancel, and pews were placed in both ends of the original nave, converting it into a transept. The marks of the original door, of the windows in the west end, and of the first triple window in the east end can still be seen. The present east window is a memorial to Bishop Claggett (*see above*), rector of St. Paul's Parish from 1780 to 1786 and from 1793 to 1806. The sun dial, or "changing Dial," above the present entrance, was part of the church "furniture" ordered from London in 1753. The vestry requested "the following Motto to be on ye Dial Vist Sic Transit Gloria Mundi."

Md. 381 continues to a junction with Md. 231, 16.0 m., and Tour 29.

On U.S. 301 just beyond the junction with Md. 381 is the junction with Md. 5 and Tour 29, which unites with U.S. 301 southward to Waldorf.

At 14.6 m. on U.S. 301 is an entrance (L) to *Cedarville Natural Wildlife Management Area.*

WALDORF (200' alt., 7,368 pop.), 18.0 m., developed after 1870 as a trading and shipping center for tobacco growers, is one of the four tobacco auction centers in Maryland. Today the area is surrounded by restaurants and motels, part of "Million Dollar Motel Row" that stretches along U.S. 301 from Waldorf to the Potomac River Bridge twenty miles to the south. Prior to 1968, in any place of business on the "row," day or night, the clank of slot machines could be heard. Charles County legalized gambling in this form in 1949, and in 1960 more than 20 percent of the county budget was based upon the revenues from slot machine licenses. Some casinos contained as many as 250 machines. Now that gambling is no longer legal in the area, many of the motels and casinos have gone out of business or have been converted to other uses.

Md. 5 and Tour 29 turn left at Waldorf.

At 21.8 m. is the junction with Md. 227.

● Turn right. At 2.2 m. **Linden** (R) (private, but visible from the road) can be seen from the road amid a housing development. This 2½-story frame house, with a pair of huge outside chimneys, is believed to have been built by John Mitchell late in the eighteenth century. The oldest wing is of logs, now covered with clapboard.

On U.S. 301 turn right on Mitchell Road.

● Go left 1.8 m. to the gravel lane leading uphill to **Mount Carmel** (tours available by appointment), founded in 1790 by four Carmelite nuns, Anne Matthews, her two nieces, and an English associate. The first three women were born in Charles County and, like many Southern Maryland Roman Catholics, went to Belgium for a Catholic education. There they joined the Carmelite order, and in 1790 they obtained permission to establish a nunnery in Maryland. Fr. Charles Neale brought the four nuns to his family home at Chandler's Hope (*see* Tour 31) until a proper residence could be found for them. By October, 1790, the nuns were able to move to unfinished buildings on this site. For a generation, the farm was worked by slaves belonging to supporters, with Father Neale providing spiritual guidance. By the 1820s, however, some of the leaders had died and the farm had ceased to provide for the community's needs. In 1831 the convent moved to Baltimore, and the buildings here lay abandoned for a hundred years.

In 1931, two of the seven original buildings still remained, and they have since been joined together and restored to make the present brick-nogged frame house. The larger section was the dormitory with nuns' rooms on the second floor; the smaller was the infirmary. The floor and fireplaces are original. In 1954 the Restorers of Mount Carmel built the rose brick Pilgrim's Chapel, which is maintained as a shrine.

LA PLATA (pronounced La Playta) (192' alt., 1,561 pop.), 26.6 m. at the junction with Md. 6, came into existence in 1873, and shortly thereafter the Pope's Creek Railroad connected it with Baltimore. In 1895, La Plata replaced Port Tobacco (*see* Tour 31) as the county seat of Charles County.

To the right is Port Tobacco (*see* Tour 31), 2.6 m.
● Go left 1.4 m. on Md. 6 and then left again on Md. 488 to the **U.S. Army Radio Receiving Station** (not open to the public), which receives messages for the Washington area from all parts of the world. The most conspicuous antenna is the tapered Aperture Horn Antenna, a horn-shaped grid of intermeshing wires that covers twenty-seven acres. The antenna is supported by several towers, some as high as 350 feet.

At 31.6 m. in **BEL ALTON** is the junction with Md. 427.

● Go right to **St. Ignatius Roman Catholic Church** (L) (open) and **St. Thomas Manor House** (L) (not open), 2.1 m., buildings of a Jesuit mission established on the Port Tobacco River in 1662. Like other large landholders, the Jesuits acquired their land from the proprietors in exchange for transporting settlers. At first the Jesuits had attempted to buy land directly from the Indians, but Lord Baltimore, who was anxious to avoid the appearance of establishing a Roman Catholic state, not only stood firm on his right to grant all lands on his own terms but also insisted on applying the English statute of mortmain to his property. This statute, first passed in 1279 to limit the power of the papacy in England, forbade corporate bodies from acquiring land.

Rigid application of the statute in Maryland would have prevented the Society of Jesus from holding any lands at all, since Jesuits as individuals were not allowed to own property. The Society circumvented this problem by registering their land in the names of individual priests or members of their households. In 1649, Fr. Thomas Copley established his right to 8,500 acres, 4,000 of which he then assigned to Thomas Matthews, for whom this plantation was surveyed. Matthews held the land in trusteeship until 1662, when Fr. Henry Warren took possession and built the first chapel.

The manor house has been enlarged several times. The marks of the original roof line on the gable of the lower wing and the glaze of the headers on its lower front wall show that this was once a 1½-story house, perhaps the earliest building erected here. The larger wing may be the "palace" begun in 1741, which became a source of complaint by other Jesuit priests. A statement by Gov. Thomas Sim Lee in April, 1781, that the British "have burnt Priest Hunter's house at the mouth of Port Tobacco Creek," however, suggests that the dwelling must have been rebuilt after the Revolution. The projecting bay on the facade and the stone quoins at the corners give the house an imposing aspect. A fire in 1866 destroyed the original hipped roof. The church was built in 1790, but at a later date its roof was evidently raised, perhaps to make room for the pointed-arch windows. The hyphen connecting the church and the house was once a chapel, believed built before 1692 but considerably altered after the fire. The view here of the Port Tobacco and Potomac rivers was enthusiastically described in 1784 as "the most majestic, grand and elegant in the whole world."

In 1773 the Catholic Church suppressed the Jesuit order except in the White Russian provinces, so a "Corporation of Roman Catholic Clergymen" was formed to hold this property. In 1805, the few surviving Jesuit priests succeeded in reestablishing the Jesuit order in America by joining the Russian Province. The first three of the Jesuits, one of whom was Fr. Charles Neale, took their oaths here on August 18, 1805.

At 32.5 m. on U.S. 301 is the junction with Mt. Air Road.

● To the right on this road is **Mount Air** (private), a large brick-nogged, frame house with a pent between two outside chimneys. The house was built early in the nineteenth century by Luke Francis Matthews on a precipitous bluff overlooking the Potomac River. Much of its original, exquisitely carved woodwork remains in the house.

Between Bel Alton and Faulkner, along Pope's Creek Road, John Wilkes Booth and his accomplice, David Herold, hid in the woods for over a week after Lincoln's assassination until Thomas Jones of Pope's Creek could provide them with a boat to enable them to escape across the Potomac River to Virginia.

At **FAULKNER,** 33.1 m., is the junction with Md. 429 (Pope's Creek Road).

● Go right on this to **POPE'S CREEK** (10′ alt.), 3.0 m., terminus of the Pope's Creek Branch of the Pennsylvania Railroad, which ran from Bowie to the confluence of Pope's Creek and the Potomac River. When the Pennsylvania Railroad bought the line from the Baltimore and Potomac, it did so because of a clause in the franchise that allowed construction of branch lines no longer than twenty miles in length. The Pennsylvania wanted a "branch" from Bowie to Washington because its own charter did not permit a terminus in the District, but to keep this "branch" open it had to continue service on its "main line" to Pope's Creek.

Long before Europeans came to Maryland, Indian tribes gathered at Pope's Creek to eat oysters. The shell heap that accumulated for centuries once covered thirty acres and at places was fifteen feet high. In recent years, most of the shell has been trucked away for use in road building and fertilizer, or for *cultch,* that is, material to which oyster larvae will attach. Archeological excavations have uncovered artifacts of people who lived here long before the arrival of Europeans.

At 35.8 m. is the junction with Md. 234.

● Turn left on this winding road, which passes through well-tended farmlands. At 4.2 m. is the gate to **Sarum** (R) (private). A plaque recounts that Sarum, encompassing 1,150 acres, was granted to Joseph Pile, Esq., on November 2, 1680, with power "to hold Court Leet and Court Baron with all liberties privileges and Immunities whatsoever by the laws and customs of the Kingdom of England to a Manor belonging."

At 5.7 m. go left on Md. 232 to **Trinity Protestant Episcopal Church** (R) (open for services only), 2.8 m., which sits in a tree-shaded churchyard at a crossroads in the middle of green fields. All that remains of the original church, built in 1793, are the brick walls laid in Flemish bond. At some later period, the walls were raised to permit installation of pointed-arch windows, and the eighteenth-century interior was remodeled.

At 37.8 m. Md. 257 branches left off U.S. 301 and becomes the main route of a side tour.

● At 0.2 m. on Md. 257 at **NEWBURG** (120' alt.) is the junction with Mt. Victoria Road.

Go left on Mt. Victoria Road, 3.6 m., to the lane (L) leading to **Society Hill** (private) and its splendid view of the Wicomico River valley. This frame house is believed to have been built early in the eighteenth century, although it was later raised to two stories. Two doorways have been cut through its great chimney.

At 3.1 m. on Mt. Victoria Road turn left on W. Hatton Road. **West Hatton** (private), 5.0 m., is a well-known brick house built on the banks of the Wicomico River about 1790 by Maj. William Truman Stoddert. The wings are later additions. The 2½-story central section, gable-roofed with brick roof curtains between the chimneys, is two rooms deep with the entrance hall at one side. The river facade has a two-story gallery with tapering brick columns; the approach front has a square porch before an inset doorway with fanlight and sidelights. In the hall, a fragile-looking mahogany stairway rises to the third floor. Between the drawing room and dining room is a double door with an elaborate fanlight.

● On Md. 257, **Mount Republican** (R) (private), 1.2 m., is a large 2½-story house with a two-story wing. The house has stood here since 1792, overlooking the Potomac at the end of an avenue of great elms. In plan the house resembles its neighbor *West Hatton,* but the roof curtains extend on each side to the cornice to form parapets on each gable. The doorways on both fronts are set into wide paneled archways and have large fanlights and sidelights, and together with the elaborately carved cornice they give elegance to the two facades. The house was built by Theophilus Yates and was once the home of Franklin Weems, one of the great *bons vivants* of nineteenth-century Southern Maryland. According to local tradition, Weems kept a poker game going continuously for forty years.

In **WAYSIDE** (10' alt.), 2.0 m., behind a low brick wall in a church-yard planted with cedars, is **Christ Protestant Episcopal Church** (L), a plain little brick rectangle with steep gable roof, built before 1750 and remodeled in 1871. It is the second church to stand on this site since 1691. The communion service was imported from England in 1740.

Mount Republican

At 9.6 m. on Md. 257 is the junction with Md. 254 (Cobb Island Road).

Go right to **COBB ISLAND,** 1.2 m., a summer resort on an island at the confluence of the Wicomico and Potomac rivers.

ROCK POINT (10′ alt.), 11.0 m., is a small resort well-known to fishermen on the Wicomico River just above Cobb Island.

U.S. 301 continues to Virginia across the **Potomac River** at 41.6 m.

ANNAPOLIS–BLADENSBURG–DISTRICT OF COLUMBIA LINE; 28.0 m.
Md. 450

This route, known as Defense Highway, follows what used to be a main thoroughfare from Annapolis to the District of Columbia, although it has now been supplanted by the limited-access dual highway (U.S. 301–U.S. 50) that is part of Tour 24. Few of the houses along the highway are of interest, but side roads pass by eighteenth-century dwellings built when the soil yielded bountiful crops of tobacco and maize.

Leave Annapolis on Md. 450 at Church Circle, 0.0 m. In the **National Cemetery,** 0.7 m., established in 1862, are buried veterans from the Civil War through the Korean War. This green, tree-shaded spot contains about 2,800 graves, including the graves of 24 Confederate and 206 unknown soldiers.

In **PAROLE,** 2.4 m., is the junction with Md. 2 and Tour 25b. In 1861, D'Epeneuil's Zouaves encamped and trained on a farm located here. The Zouaves were a special unit of the Union army, recruited in New York City from nationals of nearly every

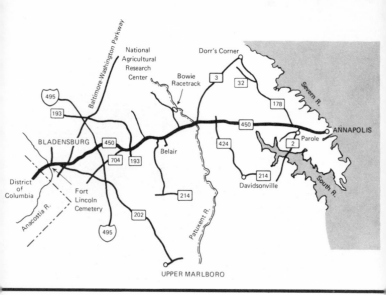

European country. Their uniforms consisted of baggy blue trousers, yellow leggings, bright blue blouses, and a little red cap with a long yellow tassel. The Zouaves never had a chance to fight as a regiment, because the unit was disbanded and its men distributed among other commands.

About 700 feet from the intersection is the **Site of Camp Parole,** which was moved here in 1863 from South River. Until the end of the Civil War, Union prisoners paroled by the Confederate government were kept in this camp until they could be returned to duty. The U.S. government established the camp because it suspected that soldiers were purposely allowing themselves to be captured so that they could return to their homes on parole. Once home, many of the soldiers were able to avoid returning to their units. About 70,000 soldiers passed through Camp Parole, although there were never more than about 8,000 at any one time.

At 2.7 m. is the junction with Riva Road.

● Go left on Riva Road to **Old Bloomfield** (L) (private, but visible from the road), 2.4 m., a striking two-story brick Georgian house that is only one room deep. From the hilltop the house looks down on South River and the Riva Bridge. Across the bridge the road leads into farmland between the Patuxent and South rivers.

At 3.1 m. is the junction with Md. 178. **Three-Mile Oak** (L) is the blackened stump, set in concrete, of the tree under which George Washington met Generals Horatio Gates and William Smallwood and a welcoming committee of Annapolitans on September 19, 1783. Washington was on his way to resign his commission before the Continental Congress, which was meeting in Annapolis.

● Go right on Md. 178, known locally as the Generals' Highway because both Rochambeau and Washington traveled it to Annapolis—Rochambeau in 1781 on his way with his troops to embark for Yorktown and Washington in 1783.

Iglehart (L), 2.1 m., is a two-story gable-roofed frame house built before 1809. The two-story recessed porch is part of the original house, as is the projecting brick pent that adjoins the single chimney. These architectural features are distinctive elements of design in old Southern Maryland houses.

At 3.2 m. the narrow dirt road to **Belvoir** (private) turns off on the right. The house was built on the ridge overlooking Little Round Bay about 1730 by John Ross, great-grandfather of Francis Scott Key (1779–1843). The oldest section of the house is the gambrel-roofed brick wing at the back, which may date back to the seventeenth century. The main house, a six-bay building with unusually thick brick walls laid in English bond, also once had a gambrel roof. When the gambrel was removed to make a full two stories, the house was extended to the left. The frame wing on the right is modern. Fine mantels and a canti-levered staircase distinguish the interior. The fenced-in **Grave of Ann Arnold Key,** Francis Scott Key's grandmother, is on the property.

At 5.2 m. is the junction with Herald Harbor Road, which leads to waterfront communities on Little Round Bay.

At 5.5 m. is the junction of Md. 178 and Md. 32. Make a right, continuing on Md. 178. The middle section of **Part of Providence** (R) (private), at 5.9 m., a small, 1½-story gable-roofed house of board and batten construction, was built about 1800. The wings on each side are modern.

The **Rising Sun Inn** (L) (private, but visible from the road), 6.1 m., is a 1½-story frame building, one-half with a steep gable roof, the other half with a gambrel. The gable-roofed end wall is brick laid in all-header bond. The Peggy Stewart Tea Party Chapter of the D.A.R. has restored the building.

At **SEVERN CROSS ROADS,** 7.1 m., is the stone **Baldwin Memorial Methodist Episcopal Church** (1861).

Md. 178 joins Md. 3 and Tour 26a.

At 10.5 m. is the junction with Md. 424.

● Go right on Md. 424 to **Bright Seat** (R), 0.3 m., which can be seen from the road. The 1½-story wing of this frame house may date from 1690 and is believed to have once been a tavern. The 2½-story main house with its great double chimneys was built one hundred years later. Open by appointment: Mrs. Benjamin King, Conaways.

● Go left on Md. 424 through well-tended farm country. At 2.0 m. a brick house (ca. 1812) with a great double chimney stands impos-ingly on a hilltop (L) (private). At 6.0 m. Md. 424 ends at a junction with Md. 214 at Davidsonville (*see* Tour 28).

At 12.3 m., Md. 450 turns left on Md. 3, and at 12.7 m. turns right.

At 13.4 m. a paved road turns left.

● Follow this road up a steep hill to **Whitemarsh Church,** a rectangu-lar brick and stone building erected in 1856 on the foundations of a church that had been built about 1742 and destroyed by fire in 1853. In 1728, James Carroll bequeathed the 2,000 acres that the church stood on, along with 100 slaves, to the Jesuits at St. Thomas Manor House, Port Tobacco (*see* Tour 26b). In 1783, a delegation of the Roman Catholic clergy met at Whitemarsh to draw up a plan for the govern-ment of the church in the newly created United States. Here on May 18, 1789, Fr. John Carroll was nominated first bishop of the Roman Catholic Church in North America.

At 13.9 m. Race Track Road turns right.

● Take this to **Bowie Race Track,** 1.7 m., one of Maryland's three one-mile tracks. The Southern Maryland Agricultural Association estab-lished the track in 1914, remodeling and expanding it in 1956. The road passes between barns and the track itself, which is flanked on the homestretch side by the grandstand.

At 2.7 m. on Race Track Road is the junction with Jericho Park Road. Go right to **Bowie State College,** 3.0 m., first established in Baltimore in 1867 as the Baltimore Normal School. Founded with a $2,500 bequest from the estate of Nelson Wells, a black, the institution began as a training school for Negro teachers. Privately supported until 1908, the school was then purchased by the State of Maryland and moved to Bowie. Until 1925 it was largely an industrial school, but since then it has become an accredited four-year college specializing in teacher education.

At 14.7 m. on Md. 450, make a left onto Belair Road.

● At 0.8 m. on Belair Road turn right onto Tulip Drive. To the left on Tulip Drive at 1.0 m. is **Belair,** famous for its race horses since the eighteenth century. Benjamin Tasker built the house for his son-in-law, Gov. Samuel Ogle (1694–1752). A long double avenue of venerable tulip poplars leads to the house, which is a handsome example of mid-eighteenth-century Georgian architecture. The central section, with its double-hipped roof, modillioned cornice, and central pediments that break the roof on each facade, was built in 1746. The hyphens and two-story wings were added after 1900.

Samuel Ogle was governor of Maryland from 1731 to 1732, 1733 to 1742, and 1747 to 1752. An enthusiastic horseman, Ogle imported two famous thoroughbreds, Spark and Queen Mab, from England in 1747. Much of the horseflesh that has made Maryland famous on American tracks is descended from these two horses. Benjamin Tasker, Jr., Ogle's brother-in-law and the next occupant of Belair, owned the notable mare Selima. The Belair stables were maintained until the untimely death in 1955 of William Woodward, Jr.

At 0.9 m. on Belair Road is the **Belair Stables Museum** (L). The museum houses a collection of horse-raising memorabilia from the Belair stables. It is open during May, June, Sept., and Oct. on Sun., 2–4, and by appointment.

At 16.1 m. is the narrow paved Church Road on the left.

● Church Road leads through another belt of farmland, which is rapidly being developed into suburban housing. At about 1.0 m. a narrow lane leads to **Fairview** (L) (private), built about 1790 by Baruch Duckett. Duckett left the house to his son-in-law, William Bowie, with the unusual restriction that he not "suffer to be cut down the enclosed woods below my dwelling house for cultivation." Oden Bowie (1826–94), governor of Maryland from 1868 to 1872, maintained a famous stable here that bred such horses as Compensation, Belle D'Or, Oriole, and Crickmore.

Church Road continues to a junction with Md. 214 and Tour 28.

At 16.8 m. is a junction with a road on the right.

● Turn right to **Holy Trinity Church,** an ivy-covered brick building erected in 1836. The first church on this site was a small family chapel built by Mareen Duvall, a Huguenot. In 1737, the land was deeded by Rev. Jacob Henderson for the use of Queen Anne's Parish. Nearby is the rectory, a brick house built in the 1820s. Both buildings are visible from the highway.

At 17.3 m. turn right onto Hillmeade Road.

● Go 1.7 m. to Prospect Hill Road. Make a left and, at 2.4 m., make another left onto Old Prospect Hill Road. This takes one to **Prospect Hill** (R), a handsome eighteenth-century brick house with a Palladian window and a gambrel-roofed frame wing. The house, with its slave quarters and other old farm buildings, stands on the highest hill between Washington, D.C., and New York City. The building is the clubhouse for the Glenn Dale Golf and Country Club (members only).

At 17.9 m. is the junction with Bell Station Road on the right.

● Turn right to **Marietta,** 0.4 m., a handsome 2½-story gable-roofed house with walls laid in Flemish bond and handsome interior woodwork. Gabriel Duvall (1752–1844), who served on the U.S. Supreme Court from 1811 to 1835, lived in the house for a number of years, dying here in 1844. The house is owned by the Maryland–National Capital Park and Planning Commission. Open by appointment.

At 19.2 m. is the junction with the Glenn Dale Road.

● Glenn Dale Road travels through rural areas, passing through part of the National Agricultural Research Center to a junction with Greenbelt Road in Greenbelt (*see* Tour S 1).

At 19.6 m. on Md. 450 is the junction with Md. 704 (L), and at 22.3 m. the junction with the Capital Beltway and Tour S 3.

At 25.5 m. is the junction with the Baltimore-Washington Parkway and Tour S 1.

At 25.9 m. is the junction with Md. 202, Landover Road.

● Make a sharp left on Landover Road to a junction (the second) with Old Landover Road, 2.1 m. Off Old Landover Road stands **Beall's Pleasure** (private). The handsome brick house with double chimneys was built about 1795 by Benjamin Stoddert (1751–1813), first secretary of the navy. The handsome doorway with elliptical fanlight and sidelights is noteworthy.

Landover Road continues to Upper Marlboro (*see* Tour 26a), crossing Md. 214 and Tour 28. The road follows the route which the British took in 1814 on their march to *Bladensburg.*

BLADENSBURG (7,488 pop.), 27.0 m. at the junction of Md. 450 and Alt. U.S. 1, was a prosperous port in the eighteenth century. Called Garrison's Landing on the Anacostia River when it was founded in 1742, the town was renamed in honor of Thomas Bladen, governor of Maryland from 1742 to 1747. By the end of the eighteenth century, silt from surrounding tobacco land had made the river at Bladensburg impassable, and flooding was a recurring problem for the town until 1959. For a time, the town continued to prosper because it was located on the main north-south coach road, but with the coming of railroads the importance of the turnpike declined. Bladensburg served as a terminus of the Baltimore & Ohio Railroad for a few years, with freight and passengers for Washington being discharged here. After 1835, however, with the completion of a terminus within the District, local business declined. Partly because of the floods, the town grew little before 1920. Bladensburg is now a suburb of Washington, D.C., and flood control measures completed in 1959 included the construction of a handsome small-boat marina. Highway improvements made at the same time make the center of town hard to recognize, and quick food services, gas stations, and industrial enterprises have largely destroyed what eighteenth-century character the old houses that remain might provide.

On August 24, 1814, one of the famous engagements of the War of 1812 took place at Bladensburg. The American forces, more than twice as numerous as the British, were well entrenched on the heights outside the town; however, except for the troops led by Com. Joshua Barney (see Tour 25b, Spout Farm), who made a good account of themselves, they were poorly trained and organized. The Americans suffered a disastrous defeat, enabling the British to march directly on Washington, D.C., where they burned the Capitol, the White House, and other public buildings.

Turn left off Md. 450 on 48th Street (formerly River Road), just before the overpass.

● The **Market Master's House** (R) (private) at 4006 Forty-Eighth Street (near the corner of 48th Street and Md. 450), a small stone cottage set back from the road, is believed to have been built by the merchant Christopher Lowndes. It was known as the market master's office before the Revolution. Further along on 48th Street, on a terraced hill, is **Bostwick House** (L) (private). This great yellow-painted brick house with single end chimneys was also built by Lowndes. Erected in 1746, the house retains some excellent walnut paneling in the drawing room.

On Md. 450, just beyond the overpass, is the **Old Stone House** (L), a 1½-story, gambrel-roofed dwelling covered with stucco, which is believed to have been built in the 1740s. The house is now an antique shop.

In the interchange of Md. 450 and Alt. U.S. 1 at 27.0 m. is the **Peace Cross,** erected in 1925 to commemorate the Prince George's County men who died in World War I.

● To the right on Alt. U.S. 1 is the **Indian Queen Tavern,** also known as the **George Washington House,** 0.1 m. This narrow, two-story brick house was built between 1755 and 1765 and was used as a store and a tavern when Bladensburg was a port and railroad depot. It is at present a hotel and is undergoing restoration. The tavern was probably built by Jacob Wirt, father of William Wirt (1772–1834), lawyer, attorney general of the United States, and anti-Masonic candidate for president of the United States in 1832. The younger Wirt, who lived in the tavern during his boyhood, served as counsel in such famous cases as *McCulloh* v. *Maryland*, *Gibbons* v. *Ogden*, and the Dartmouth College case.

To the left at the Peace Cross is the entrance to the boat marina.

The tour turns left on to Alt. U.S. 1 at the Peace Cross. Near **Fort Lincoln Cemetery** is the site of many famous duels, some fought after Maryland had outlawed dueling in 1816. It was here on March 22, 1820, that Com. James Barron shot and killed the naval hero Stephen Decatur. The preceding year, Gen. Armistead T. Mason, a senator from Virginia, had challenged and was killed by Col. John M. McCarty. McCarty had tried to laugh Mason out of the duel, first by suggesting that they leap from the dome of the Capitol, then by proposing that they fight with lighted matches on a barrel of gunpowder. The weapons finally chosen were muskets at twelve paces.

At 27.8 is the entrance to Fort Lincoln Cemetery. Of interest are the floral clock, the old spring house (ca. 1683), the Civil War fortifications, and the bronze statue of Abraham Lincoln.

Alt. U.S. 1 crosses the **District of Columbia Line** at approximately 28.0 m. and enters downtown Washington via New York Avenue.

JUNCTION OF MD. 2 AND 214–PAROLE–DISTRICT OF COLUMBIA LINE; 19.9 m.
Md. 214

Md. 214, an east-west highway crossing Anne Arundel and Prince George's counties, is one of the direct routes between Washington, D.C., and the Annapolis area. The road passes through farmland and residential areas, but the high banks of the dual highway and honeysuckle hedges bordering the old road conceal the surrounding landscape from the occupants of passenger cars.

Md. 214 branches west from Md. 2 (*see* Tour 25b), 0.0 m., at a point about 7.0 m. southwest of Annapolis. Here the road is a general access dual highway.

DAVIDSONVILLE (185′ alt., est. 350 pop.), 3.4 m., is a scattered farming community located in excellent dove-shooting country. On the right at the junction with Md. 424 is an interesting nineteenth-century house, a frame structure one room deep, with a great two-story built-in portico on each side and a 1½-story wing with a heavy chimney (private, but visible from the road).

At 4.1 m. is the junction (L) with the paved but narrow Queen Anne Bridge Road.

● Go left to **Friends Choice** (R) (private), 0.6 m., a small, 1½-story frame house on a brick foundation with brick ends, a gambrel roof, and a pair of massive outside end chimneys connected by a projecting brick pent. These chimneys, which dominate the house, taper to a point beyond the roof line, rising to a great height. Two lower wings slope off to the right, one gabled, one with a gambrel roof.

At 1.1 m. Queen Anne Bridge Road forks.

Go left on Wayson Road to another fork, 2.3 m., then right on Harwood Road to **Roedown** (private), 2.5 m., a 2½-story beautifully proportioned brick house, with a gable roof and entrance and hall on one side. Built about 1780, the house is now restored and furnished with Dutch antiques from the owner's ancestral home in Holland. Jerome Bonaparte and his wife, the former Betsy Patterson (*see* Downtown Baltimore), honeymooned here. It is the homeplace for an extensive beef cattle and race horse operation. The Marlboro Hunt Club Point-to-Point Races were held here in March, 1975.

● A left on Harwood Road continues through farmland and some exceptionally beautiful woods to a junction with Md. 2 and Tour 25b.

At 4.3 m. on Md. 214 the **Duckett House** (Tilden Farm) (R) (private) can be seen among the trees. More than a century old, the white frame house has tall brick chimneys on each gable end of the main house.

Md. 214 crosses the Patuxent River at 6.2 m. and U.S. 301 and Tour 24 at 8.9 m. and 9.2 m. Here the dual highway ends. At 11.3 m. is the junction with Church Road.

● Go left on Church Road 1.0 m. to **Bowieville** (L) (private), a stuccoed brick mansion, now almost neglected, that commands the rolling countryside from a rise shaded by great oaks. The hip roof is topped by a roof deck with a wooden balustrade. A pavilion with

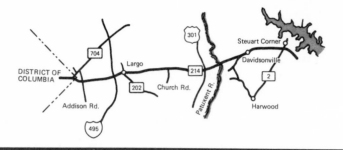

broken pediment on the facade emphasizes the pleasing arrangement of doorway and windows. From the road on a sunny day the white woodwork gleams magnificently.

Continuing on Church Road, at 1.9 m. is **St. Barnabas Church** (open every day), which serves a parish (Queen Anne's) formed from St. Paul's Parish, Prince George's County, by an Act of Assembly in 1704. Construction of the first brick church, which replaced a wooden chapel, was begun in 1708. Gustavus Hesselius (1682–1755), the Swedish artist who came to America in 1711, painted an altarpiece of the *Last Supper* between 1721 and 1722 on commission from the vestry. However, when the present church was built in 1773, during the incumbency of Rev. Jonathan Boucher (*see below*), the picture disappeared, and it was not rediscovered until 1848. The church is built of brick laid in Flemish bond and is a full two stories high with a steep double-hipped roof that flares at the eaves. The belfry, a small separate structure of brick, was erected in 1930 in honor of Dr. John Contee Fairfax, eleventh Baron of Cameron. The parish has a communion service dated 1718.

LARGO, 15.4 m., is at the junction with Md. 202.

● Go left on Md. 202 to **Mount Lubentia** (R) (private), 1.5 m., a large hip-roofed brick house with a balustraded roof deck. The pilastered and pedimented doorway is now partly concealed by a one-story porch.

Ninian Beall patented Mount Lubentia in 1696, naming it for his birthplace in Fifeshire, Scotland. Beall had been captured at the Battle of Dunbar in 1650 and transported to America, but as soon as his years of servitude were over, he began to patent land and take part in civil and military affairs. Eventually he became commander in chief of the rangers, who protected the northern and western frontier. The estate was purchased by the Magruders, one of whom built the present house sometime before 1770. It is now owned by the Bowie family.

From 1770 to 1774, Mount Lubentia was rented to Jonathan Boucher (1737–1804), rector of *St. Barnabas Church* and noted tutor, whose three pupils—Washington's stepson John Custis; Charles, eldest son of Benedict Calvert; and Overton Carr of Virginia—named the house Castle Magruder. In 1772, Boucher married Nelly Addison, niece of Henry Addison, a prominent planter. Boucher, a man of violent temper and strong prejudices and an ardent Tory sympathizer, had made himself very unpopular while rector at St. Anne's in Annapolis, and his reputation had preceded him to St. Barnabas. As he recorded in the reminiscences he wrote after his return to England: "The very first Sunday I found the church doors shut against me; and not many Sundays thereafter a turbulent fellow had paid eight dollars for as many loads of stones to drive me and my friends from the church by force." Feeling grew so strong that in 1774 Boucher moved his family, and a year later he hired a curate for his own parish, becoming curate to his brother-in-law, Rev. Henry Addison, at St. John's Church, Piscataway. There, Boucher recorded, "for more than six months I preached, when I did preach, with a pair of loaded pistols lying on the cushion."

At the particular request of Governor Eden, however, Boucher returned to his own pulpit at St. Barnabas to preach a sermon on the day of a public fast, but he found that Osborn Sprigg, former sheriff of the county, and two hundred armed men had filled the church determined to prevent him from preaching. As he climbed to his pulpit, a friend, David Crauford, restrained him. As Boucher stepped down, he was surrounded by a violent and hostile crowd. "There was but one way to save my life," Boucher later wrote, and this was "by seizing Sprigg . . . by the collar, and with my cocked pistol in the other hand, assuring him that if any violence was offered to me I would instantly blow his brains out, as I most certainly would have done. I then told him that if he pleased he might conduct me to my horse, and I would leave them. This he did, and we marched together upwards of a hundred yards, I with one hand fastened in his collar and a pistol in the other, guarded by his whole company, whom he had the meanness to order to play on their drums the Rogues' March all the way we went, which they did."

When Revolution finally broke out, Boucher decided to return to England, sailing with his wife on September 10, 1775. Boucher considered George Washington a friend but characterized him as a man who always acquitted himself "decently, but never greatly." As a result, Boucher viewed Washington's military and political achievements with astonishment.

At 19.0 m. is the junction with Md. 389 (Addison Road).

● Go right on Addison Road, 0.8 m., make a left onto Md. 704; at 0.9 m. turn right onto Addison Road to **St. Matthew's Protestant Episcopal Church,** 1.1 m., often called **Addison's Chapel,** which stands on a hill overlooking a residential area. William Scott donated the land to King George's Parish in 1731. The parish received its name from the Addison family, at whose home the organizational meeting of the parish was held. Local tradition dates the simple brick church, third on this site, about 1801, but it was not consecrated until 1833. The brick walls, weathered to a beautiful shade of rose, are laid in Flemish bond under a steep gable roof. In the cemetery are the graves of Christopher Lowndes (see Tour 27, Bladensburg), Benjamin Stoddert (see Tour 27, Beall's Pleasure), who was first secretary of the navy, as well as numerous Lowndes and Stoddert descendants.

CAPITOL HEIGHTS (125' alt., 2,852 pop.), 19.5 m., is a suburban section of Washington, D.C.

Md. 214 crosses the **District of Columbia Line,** 19.9 m., and joins E. Capitol Street, entering downtown Washington via E. Capitol Street.

DISTRICT OF COLUMBIA LINE–WALDORF–LEONARDTOWN–ST. MARY'S CITY–POINT LOOKOUT; 78.4 m.
Md. 5

For the first part of this tour the traveler crosses the Washington suburbs in Prince George's County, which are built on land that only a generation ago was sown to tobacco. Md. 5

crosses the **District of Columbia Line** as Branch Avenue at 0.0 m. and crosses the Suitland Parkway at 0.2 m.

● Take the second exit on the beautifully landscaped parkway to the main gate of **Andrews Air Force Base,** 5.9 m., built in the winter of 1942–43 to protect Washington. The base was first named for Camp Springs, a nearby village so named because it was the site of a Methodist camp meeting. Union soldiers during the Civil War were billeted in the church that now serves the base as Chapel No. 2. In February, 1945, the installation was renamed for Lt. Gen. Frank Maxwell Andrews, who at his death in May, 1943, was commanding general of the U.S. forces in the European theater of operations. Foreign dignitaries who visit the capital often arrive at and depart from Andrews Field. Here, too, is the home base of Air Force One, the president's plane.

At 1.3 m. on Md. 5, Md. 458 branches left.

● At 1.2 m. on Md. 458 begins a complex of federal buildings (L) that houses, among other agencies, the research facilities of the Bureau of the Census, including its computers, and the U.S. Weather Bureau and its National Weather Satellite Center.

At 7.5 m. on Md. 5 is the junction with Md. 223.

● Go right to **CLINTON** (240′ alt., est. 4,670 pop.), 0.8 m., and the junction with Md. 381. Go left on Md. 381 to **The Surratt House** (L) (under restoration). This red frame house was once a tavern, store, and post office owned by Mrs. Mary Surratt, who was hanged for alleged complicity in Lincoln's assassination. In 1864 she and her son John rented the property to John Lloyd and moved to Washington, D.C. In March of 1865, John Surratt and fellow conspirators hid two guns and some ammunition at the tavern as part of a plot to kidnap Lincoln. Lee's surrender at Appomattox on April 9 ended all hope for the South, and John Wilkes Booth murdered Lincoln two days later, apparently as an act of revenge. It is now generally believed that Mrs. Surratt was innocent and that although her son John was party to the plans for the kidnapping, he had no hand in the assassination. He escaped to Europe and was not caught and returned for trial until 1867, after the Supreme Court's *Ex Parte Milligan* decision assured him a civilian trial. The jury could not agree on a verdict, and Surratt went free. He lived in Maryland until his death in 1916.

At 13.1 m. Md. 5 joins U.S. 301 and Tour 26, from which it branches left at **WALDORF,** 18.4 m.

At **BEANTOWN,** 20.2 m., is the junction with Md. 382.

● Go left on Md. 382 to the junction with Md. 232 at 3.3 m. Go right on Md. 232. In the frame house **Rock Hill** (R) (private), 3.8 m., built about 1857, Dr. Samuel Mudd set John Wilkes Booth's leg on the morning of April 15, 1865. Mudd was found guilty as an accessory to Lincoln's assassination and sentenced to life imprisonment at Fort Jefferson in the Dry Tortugas, a sentence that many now believe to have been a miscarriage of justice. President Andrew Johnson pardoned Mudd in 1869 after he had rendered great services during a yellow fever epidemic at the fort.

Md. 232 continues to the lane leading to *Mount Eagle* (L) at 6.5 m. and to a junction with Md. 5 at *Bryantown,* 8.3 m.

At 24.4 m. Md. 5 follows a route across the Zekiah Swamp that has been in use since the seventeenth century.

On the right at the crossroads in **BRYANTOWN** (est. 150 pop.), 25.2 m., are two brick houses built at the beginning of the nineteenth century. Here is the junction with Md. 232.

● Go left on Md. 232 to the lane (R) to **Mount Eagle** (private), 1.8 m., a restored brick farmhouse. Although built in 1796, it resembles houses built nearly a century earlier, with its steep gable roof and cells, or narrow chambers, behind the two main rooms. The house still has its original floors, mantels, corner cupboards, and other woodwork. The wings were added in 1940.

At 27.8 m. Gallant Green Road, or Chapelear Road, joins Md. 5 at an acute angle at the left.

● Go left to a fork, 0.6 m., then left (straight ahead) to the lane (R), 1.3 m., to the **Manour of Truman's Place** (private). In 1832 the owner of this brick house transformed a 1½-story brick cottage into a handsome 2½-story residence with a lower wing that included what was once the outside kitchen. Most of the interior woodwork dates from the period of the remodeling, but the stairway appears to have been retained from the earlier house.

At **HUGHESVILLE** (193′ alt., est. 350 pop.), 29.0 m., a tobacco auction center, is the junction with Md. 231.

● Go left on Md. 231 to **BENEDICT** (5′ alt.), 6.5 m., a Patuxent River shipping center during the eighteenth century. This is the birthplace of Gen. James Wilkinson (1757–1825), who at nineteen joined the Revolutionary army and was a general by the age of twenty. After the Revolution he settled in Kentucky and procured the right, where Congress had failed, for Kentucky settlers to trade with Spanish New Orleans. In return he promised to persuade Kentucky to secede from the Union and join the Spanish colony. Despite his conspiracy with the Spanish, which was suspected by his contemporaries, Wilkinson became an officer in the American army in 1792 under Gen. Anthony Wayne. In 1797, after Wayne's death, Wilkinson was named commanding officer, although he was still receiving payment from the Spanish. Wilkinson is best known for his part in the Burr conspiracy (1806), which he probably planned while he was governor of northern Louisiana and later betrayed. Wilkinson ended his military career under a cloud of suspicion after displaying incompetence during the War of 1812, living out his last years in Mexico.

The British anchored at Benedict on December 26, 1812, while blockading the Potomac River and Chesapeake Bay. On August 19, 1814, British troops under Gen. Robert Ross landed here for the march to Bladensburg and Washington, D.C. (*see* Tour 27).

Md. 231 crosses the Patuxent River and joins Md. 2 and Tour 25b near Prince Frederick.

The tour now traverses the oldest section of Maryland, St. Mary's County. A large proportion of its population is Roman Catholic, descended from Roman Catholic families of the colonial period. Tobacco is still the chief source of income, and lumbering, fishing, and oystering are also important. In 1969, St. Mary's county ranked first in the state in the number of licensed oystermen. Summer visitors are also a growing business in the county. In addition, the Patuxent Naval Air Test Center, established in 1942 at the mouth of the Patuxent, has brought many new residents, and high-speed roads now connect St. Mary's, once a backwater county, to metropolitan Washington and Baltimore. In 1940 there were fewer people in the county than in 1790, but since then the population has more than doubled.

At 32.9 m. is the junction with a paved side road.

● Go right to **Charlotte Hall**, 0.2 m. The "Coole Springs of St. Maries," which still flow here, became a health resort for a few years after the pestilence of 1697–98, when many recoveries were attributed to the exceptionally pure water. In October, 1698, the assembly appropriated money to buy the springs and build cottages to hospitalize indigent citizens who became ill. There is no proof that the cottages were ever built, but old court records show that several other counties appropriated public funds to board the indigent sick.

The springs now supply water to the **Charlotte Hall School,** named for Queen Charlotte of England and chartered in 1774 as a "free" school for Charles, St. Mary's, and Prince George's counties. As early as 1723 the assembly had passed legislation ordering the establishment of a free school in each county, but few had actually been built. In 1772, the inhabitants of the southern counties agreed to sell the lands set aside for the support of the individual county free schools and to use the proceeds to establish a consolidated school. There is some doubt about the meaning of the word *free,* but it does not seem to have meant free tuition for every student. Perhaps the word referred to the curriculum, which in such schools was based on the classical and modern languages and mathematics. Under the charter of 1774, the trustees of Charlotte Hall met, but the Revolution postponed the project. The school finally opened in 1797, and in 1798, with some help from the state, it was expanded. By 1802 there were ninety-four students, but the enrollment dropped to less than fifty later in the century. About 1850, Charlotte Hall became a military school. In 1975, it became a coeducational, college preparatory school. It still offers military training as an elective.

On the grounds is the **Old White House,** erected in 1803 as a classroom building and residence for the headmaster. Restored in 1938, the gambrel-roofed brick house, painted white, has been the continuous meeting place of one of the oldest literary societies in the country, the Washington Stonewall Society, founded before 1800.

In 1939–40 a group of Amish moved from Pennsylvania, where land had become too expensive, into the neighborhood of Charlotte Hall. By 1952, about fifty Amish families were settled near here. The beliefs of the Amish restrict their use of modern farm equipment, and the older generation, at least, uses animals rather than tractors to pull the plows, and windmills rather than electric motors to pump the water. Through resourcefulness and hard work, the Amish have had considerable success reclaiming the worn-out tobacco lands of Southern Maryland. Their horse-drawn buggies, lit at night by lamps, can occasionally be seen on the highway.

At 33.3 m. is the junction with Md. 6.

● Go left on Md. 6 to **All Faith Church** (R), 2.6 m., built in 1766–68 by Samuel Abell, Jr., according to a plan made by Richard Boulton, to serve one of the original parishes of Maryland. It is a rectangular building of brick laid in Flemish bond with a steep gable roof and a "venetien" window (somewhat changed from the original) over the front door. Between 1881 and 1900 stained glass replaced the crown glass originally installed in the roundheaded windows, but clear glass has recently been reinstalled. The hurricane of 1954 blew out the chancel window, which has been replaced by a five-part rose window that depicts the various crops grown in the neighborhood. The interior of the church was renovated in 1881, at which time the box pews were removed—if they were still in place—and the chancel remodeled. Nevertheless, much of the original interior described in the specifications of 1766 remains. Eight fluted square pillars with capitals "wrought in the Ionick order" still hold up the barrel ceiling of the nave, and the "flatt" ceilings of the side aisles are still decorated with a "dental cornish." In many ways the interior resembles that of St. Andrew's Church (*see* Tour 30) twenty miles away, which was built at the same time by the same builder and architect.

At 37.8 m. is the junction with Three Notch Road (Md. 235 and Tour 30). Proceeding south on Md. 5 one comes to **HELEN**, 40.8 m., and the junction with Md. 238.

● Go right on Md. 238 to **CHAPTICO**, 8.8 m., an attractive country village named for the friendly Chaptico Indians, who apparently had a town here that was visited by Gov. Charles Calvert in 1663. John Coode made the Chaptico area a muster spot for his soldiers before the coup of 1689 (*see below*, Reconstructed State House), and during the eighteenth century it was a shipping point.

At Chaptico, cross Md. 234, continuing on Md. 238. Take the first left at 3.9 m. on Md. 238 to **Christ Church** (R), built in 1737 of brick laid in Flemish bond. The church is unusual for its apse at the rear and for the great wooden columns, topped by elaborately carved caps of mixed Corinthian and Ionic design, which hold up the arched ceiling of the nave. In 1813, British soldiers used the building as a stable, causing extensive damage that aroused newspaper comment as far away as Boston. The present pews and woodwork in the chancel date from 1839, the bell tower from 1913. The cemetery contains the **Grave of Gilbert Ireland,** high sheriff of St. Mary's County, who requested in his will probated in 1755 "That a Cheap black Marble Stone may be Sent for to Philadelphia." According to tradition, the stone, now gone, recorded that he was buried upright at his own wish.

● Continue on Md. 238 to Manor Road, 6.3 m. Go left on this 1.4 m. to **Bachelor's Hope** (L) (private), which can be seen from the road. Historians of architecture find this house exceptionally interesting. It was probably built as a hunting lodge early in the eighteenth century, although local tradition sets a much earlier date. The two-story central section has a steep roof with clipped gables, while the one-story wings are hipped. Set into the front of the main house is a one-story portico with four brick pillars topped by a narrow classic entablature with a carved frieze. The stairway within the portico provides the only access to the second floor.

● At 11.1 m. is the junction with Md. 242. Go right to the junction with Md. 239 at 0.9 m.

Go right on Md. 239 to **Ocean Hall** (L), 1.5 m., an ancient brick house, one and one-half stories with a steep gable roof, located on the shore of the Wicomico River at Bushwood Wharf. The house stands on the plantation owned by the merchant Robert Slye at the time of his death in 1671 and may be the "new house" mentioned in his inventory. If so, he used it as a store, with sleeping quarters for servants in the loft. Slye was the first husband of Susannah Gerard, whose father, Thomas Gerard, was owner of St. Clement's Manor and one of the wealthiest and most important early colonists. Susannah's second husband was John Coode, leader of the Revolution of 1689 in Maryland. The house is extraordinary for its upper-cruck roof construction. The living room paneling was installed early in the eighteenth century and is the first covering ever put on the walls. Evidently the ceiling was always plastered. These two facts would suggest that the house was new when the paneling was installed except that the window openings were moved to their present locations at that time. Over the delicately carved mantel (ca. 1830) a mural painted at that time supposedly represents the view of the river as seen from the house. The house is privately owned.

● Md. 242 continues to **COLTON POINT** (20' alt., est. 118 pop.), 5.4 m. at a T-intersection, a small summer resort and fish-packing center. Turn left at the intersection. To the right is **St. Clement's Island** (no ferry) in the Potomac River, a short distance from Colton Point. Here the *Ark* and the *Dove*, carrying the first Maryland settlers, dropped anchor on March 25, 1634, after a stormy passage across the Atlantic. "This we called St. Clement," wrote Fr. Andrew White, one

Ocean Hall

of the Jesuit priests who accompanied the expedition, "here we first came ashoare; here by the overturning of a shallop we had allmost lost our mades which we brought along. The linnen they went to wash was much of it lost, which is noe small matter in these parts. . . . In this place we first offered [the sacrifice of the mass], erected a crosse, and with devotion took solemn possession of the Country." A large cross erected on the island in the Tercentenary year 1934 commemorates these events.

Across the road is the **St. Clement's and Potomac River Museum** (L).

● From the junction of Md. 238 and Md. 234, turn right on Md. 234 1.5 m. to **Deep Falls** (L) (private), a house with giant outside end chimneys and triple one-story pents with windows. The chimneys completely cover the gable ends up to the second floor. Maj. William Thomas is believed to have built the house about 1745. Md. 234 joins Md. 5 and the main tour.

At 48.1 m. on Md. 5 is the junction with Md. 243.

● Go right on this 4.7 m. to **St. Francis Xavier Church** (still in use and open to the public), the oldest Roman Catholic church in Maryland, and **Newtown Manor** (closed), dating from the mid-eighteenth century. They stand at the end of the state highway in the midst of the green farmlands and blue water vistas of Newtown Neck. The neck was granted to William Bretton in 1640, and some believe that he built the old building, whose lines can still be seen in the gables of the present building. However, the gambrel shape of the roof, the eleven-foot ceilings of the first floor rooms, and the considerable size of the cells suggest mid-eighteenth century. The second story was added in 1816, and the stair and cornice in the wide central hall, as well as the mantel in the parlor, may have been installed then.

William Bretton (d. 1672), "gentleman," was clerk of the Lower House Assembly (1637–66), clerk of the Council of Maryland (1637–49), and clerk of the Provincial Court (1649–63). In 1662 he gave one and one-half acres for a Catholic church, and in 1668 he granted his whole tract "with edifices and buildings" to the Jesuits. The neck was an area of early population in Maryland, and in 1657 Ralph Crouch established here what may have been the first school of humanities in the colony. How long the school lasted is unknown, but in 1677 the Jesuits had either taken it over or started another, which was probably held in this house or an earlier structure on the site. The

Act to Prevent the Growth of Popery, passed in 1704, forced the school to close, and thereafter the neck declined in importance, but the Jesuit priests remained. Since modification of the act passed soon afterwards permitted mass to be celebrated in a private home, they doubtless then built a chapel attached to the house, the foundations of which may still be seen.

It is believed that Fr. James Ashby built the present shingled frame church just before his death in 1767. The brick half hexagons at each end were added in 1767 and 1816, one for a choir loft, the other for a confessional. In the steeple hangs a bell, inscribed "1791, S. T. Joannes Arden," which once belonged to the first church. The foundations of this first structure were discovered some years ago in the old cemetery a half mile back on the state highway. Priests of the mission were buried in the graveyard here from 1685 to 1862. In 1868, a decline in the congregation, most of whom came by water from other areas, induced the priest to move his residence to Leonardtown, but services are still held in the church of 1767. Near the entrance is a stone monument to the early "soldiers of Ignatius" who labored to bring religion and learning to a wilderness. Tenants rent the house and farm the land for the benefit of the parish.

In 1708 the assembly ordered **LEONARDTOWN** (50' alt., 1,406 pop.), 49.5 m., then a site called Shepherd's Old Fields, to be laid out as the new St. Mary's County seat. By 1710, when the new courthouse was finished, the town was called Seymour Town after Col. John Seymour, governor of the province. In 1728 the name was changed to Leonardtown in honor of Benedict Leonard Calvert, fourth Lord Baltimore. The British raided Leonardtown during the War of 1812. Today its business centers around tobacco, seafood, and summer visitors. From the present courthouse, built between 1899 and 1901 and rebuilt in 1957, is a splendid view of Breton Bay and the waterfront, where until World War II tobacco hauled by oxen from neighboring farms was shipped to Baltimore.

The original house at **Tudor Hall** (open Mon.–Thurs., 10–9; Fri.–Sat., 10–5), corner of Library Place and E. Key Way, a 1½-story frame structure overlooking Breton Bay, may have been built early in the eighteenth century. In 1744, the property was acquired by Abraham Barnes (ca. 1715–78), long a delegate to the Provincial Assembly and in 1774, chairman of the Committee of Observation for St. Mary's County. Either Barnes or his son may have added the one-story brick wings described in a tax list of 1798. Soon after 1815, Philip Key (d. 1820) bought Tudor Hall, and either he or his son Henry Greenfield Sotheron Key replaced the central frame section of the house and raised the whole structure to two stories of brick. In 1950, through the generosity of Mrs. Howard C. Davidson, Tudor Hall was restored and remodeled and given to the county for a library in memory of men from St. Mary's County killed during the two world wars. The waterfront facade is interesting for its central recessed portico with four columns, reminiscent of *Bachelor's Hope* and St. Andrew's Church (*see* Tour 30). In the central hall is a graceful hanging staircase with shallow risers. The eighteenth-century kitchen with its huge fireplace and Dutch oven also remains.

The part of the house occupied by the *St. Mary's Beacon*, a newspaper begun in 1839, is believed to have been built in 1704, the other part having been added later in the eighteenth century. The county court is supposed to have sat here in 1709–10 while the courthouse was being built.

At 57.4 m. is the junction with Md. 249 in **CALLAWAY.**

● Turn right on Md. 249 to a junction with Md. 244, at 3.2 m. Continuing on Md. 249 just beyond the junction, Md. 244 also turns left.

Go right (west) on Md. 244 to **St. George's Protestant Episcopal Church** (L) (1799) (open by request at rectory; otherwise closed except for services), 0.3 m., which serves one of the oldest Anglican congregations in Maryland. There is record of a church standing here or nearby before the mid-seventeenth century. At that time there were only two other Anglican congregations, one on St. Clement's Manor, where the Catholic leader Thomas Gerard had built a chapel for his Protestant wife and daughters, the other south of St. Mary's City. In 1650, William Wilkinson became the first Anglican rector to make a permanent home in Maryland, serving the congregations here and near St. Mary's City. The tombstone of his successor, Francis Sourton (rector 1663–79), was discovered in the ground twenty-five feet or so from the present building and now rests in one of its aisles. In the chancel is the tombstone, moved from a spot close to that where Sourton's was found, of Leigh Massey (d. 1732–33), who "was Educated at Oxford, Rector of this Parish the darling of his Flock and Beloved by all that knew him." It is believed that the three previous churches built by this parish stood where these stones were found and that the Reverend Mr. Sourton had been buried in the aisle of the first church, the Reverend Mr. Massey in the chancel of the second. The third church, built of brick about 1760, probably burned about 1799, when the present structure was built.

This beautiful little brick church, with walls laid in Flemish bond and a handsome, if modern, modillioned and dentiled cornice, has a lovely setting in the woods under great oak trees. The church was extensively repaired in 1884, when the pillars that divide the side aisles from the arched nave were replaced, the gallery taken down, and the walls strengthened with iron supports. By then windows had replaced the doors that had originally stood in the center of each side. In 1958, the interior was replastered and repainted, the pulpit was restored, and the "alleys" were laid with brick, as was customary when the church was first built.

At 4.1 m. on Md. 244 is the lane (L) into **Mulberry Fields** (private), 4.0 m., a well-known 2½-story, hip-roofed house with handsome interior paneling. John Anthony Clarke is believed to have built the house between 1760 and 1770. Under the modillioned cornice the walls are laid in all-header bond. The little brick cottages on each side of the main house were designated as a kitchen and workhouse on a tax list of 1798. A portico added on the river front about 1830 looks down a steep bluff landscaped into terraces, or "falles," which descend to fields divided by two rows of giant mulberry trees that once supported a small silk industry. These rows of trees appear parallel but are actually four times as far apart at the river as at the house.

● Returning to the junction of Md. 244 and Md. 249, turn right. Bear left on Md. 244 to a fork. Bear right. At 2.9 m. there is a sharp curve to the left. Go right to **Porto Bello** (private), built after 1740 by William Hebb, who may have fought under Adm. Edward Vernon in the War of Austrian Succession and who named his home after the town in the West Indies captured by Admiral Vernon in 1740.

● Further down the St. Mary's River from Porto Bello is West St. Mary's Manor Road, 3.1 m. Turn right to **West St. Mary's Manor,** a 1½-story frame house with brick ends from which rise beautifully proportioned double chimneys with one-story pents. The 2,000-acre manor was granted to Capt. Henry Fleet in 1634. The house itself must have been built sometime in the eighteenth century. The arrangement of hall and stair and the design of the newel and stair rail greatly resemble counterparts at *Mulberry Fields*. The wallpaper in one room is a Williamsburg reproduction of paper found on the walls and dated 1765. Open by appointment: Col. and Mrs. Miodrag Blagojevich, Drayden.

● Continuing straight ahead on Md. 249 one comes to **PINEY POINT,** 7.4 m.; turn right on Md. 498 to the resort that served as a summer social center for Washington dignitaries between 1820 and 1853. President James Monroe stayed here, first in the hotel and later in a cottage that became in effect the summer White House. The cottage was destroyed by a hurricane in 1933. John C. Calhoun, Henry Clay, Daniel Webster, President Franklin Pierce, and President Theodore Roosevelt also visited here.

In the waters off the point oil tankers regularly anchor and pipe oil to the tanks of the **Steuart Petroleum Company** on Piney Point Creek.

● At 7.6 m. on Md. 249 is the **Harry Lundeberg School of Seamanship** (L) for training merchant seamen.

Md. 249 continues 7.7 m. to **ST. GEORGE ISLAND,** which is reached by a steel and concrete bridge. Until 1862 this island at the confluence of the St. Mary's and Potomac rivers belonged to the Jesuits as part of *St. Inigoes Manor*. The British raided the island several times during the Revolutionary War and the War of 1812.

The waters of this area, rich with oysters, have been a source of conflict between Maryland and Virginia since the eighteenth century. In 1785 the two states signed a compact allowing watermen from both states to fish in the Potomac, even though Maryland claimed Potomac waters to the low-tide watermark on the Virginia shore. Fishery regulations were to be agreed upon by the legislatures of both states, but as the oyster supply diminished and conservation measures became critical, Maryland passed laws that Virginia refused to honor. In 1957, the Maryland legislature finally abrogated the Compact of 1785, and in 1958 the two states drew up a new compact, ratified by the two legislatures in 1959 and accepted in Maryland after a statewide referendum in 1960. A joint commission now regulates the Potomac fisheries, and patrol boats from both states enforce the laws. Related to the negotiations over the fisheries was the act passed by Maryland in 1958 outlawing the slot-machine casinos that had been operating at the ends of piers extending from the Virginia mainland to points just beyond the low-tide watermarks. Slot machines were illegal in Virginia, but technically these casinos were located in Maryland.

At 64.3 m. on Md. 5 beside the junction with Fr. Andrew White Memorial Road the **Father Andrew White Memorial,** erected to honor one of the Jesuit priests who came with the *Ark* and the *Dove* in 1634, stands on the left overlooking the river. Father White (1579–1653) worked among the Indians, first at Piscataway, then at Port Tobacco (*see* Tour 31), before Richard Ingle returned him to England in chains (*see below,* St. Inigoes Manor). At Port Tobacco in 1642, White converted the "Queen" and nearly the whole Indian village, later writing an Indian catechism and a grammar of the Indian language.

● Go right on Fr. Andrew White Memorial Road to the **Jesuit Memorial Altar** (L), 0.2 m., a concave brick wall topped by a white stone slab. Dedicated in 1933 by the Pilgrims of Maryland Society, the memorial commemorates Fathers Andrew White and John Altham and Brother Thomas Gervase. Father Altham (1589–1640) came with Father White on the *Ark* and worked on Kent Island before his death. Brother Gervase, also one of the original immigrants, died in 1637.

On the left at 64.7 m. is **Pope's Freehold** (stabilized archaeological site, open), a 100-acre tract patented in 1641 by Nathaniel Pope, a maternal ancestor of George Washington. From 1649 this was the home of two of the most powerful men in the province: Thomas Hatton, secretary of Maryland, who was killed at the Battle of the Severn in 1654, and the chancellor, Philip Calvert, youngest son of the first proprietor. Calvert lived at Pope's Freehold from his arrival in 1658 until 1679, when he finished the "Great House at St. Peter's" (*see below*, St. Peter's) a half mile away.

After Calvert's death (1682) without heirs, Pope's Freehold reverted to the proprietor, who retained it as part of his personal holdings, leasing the tract to tenants. In 1763, Moses Tabbs (d. 1779), rector of William and Mary Parish, purchased the tract with its house and orchard. Archaeological excavations undertaken in 1972–73 uncovered the house and the additions Tabbs made to it. The earliest portion—built sometime in the eighteenth century—was frame, twenty-eight by sixteen feet, with brick chimneys. Tabbs enlarged the structure into a house that was twenty-eight by thirty-two feet with four rooms on each floor. Since Tabbs had ten children, even the enlargement must have provided cramped quarters by modern standards. Yet Tabbs's income from parish taxes made him one of the wealthiest men in the area. Late in the eighteenth century, the house was once again used as a tenement until it was abandoned sometime after the middle of the nineteenth century. The artifacts found during excavations, mostly ceramic shards, all date from the nineteenth century.

Pope's Freehold borders on Fisherman Creek, a boundary of the seventeenth-century **St. Mary's Town Lands.** The Town Lands comprised about 1,200 acres which in 1636 Lord Baltimore ordered granted on special terms to early settlers. By 1640, at least ten dwellings, a forge, a mill, and a Catholic chapel were scattered over thirteen separate tracts. The seventeenth-century Maryland capital was located here, although no clustered development began before the 1660s. A village, called St. Mary's City (*see below*, Reconstructed State House), then slowly came into being, but it disappeared soon after the capital had been moved to Annapolis in 1695. In 1966, the Maryland legislature established the St. Mary's City Commission to preserve the Town Lands and to develop them into an outdoor history museum.

The St. Mary's Town Lands offered a major opportunity to excavate a seventeenth-century area because no urban development had destroyed the sites. The commission is undertaking archaeological excavations, and the artifacts recovered will be displayed in a museum where they will be used to interpret local history. Questions being explored by the commission include: How and why did settlers come? How did planters sell their tobacco in a market that lay across 3,000 miles of ocean? What role did St. Mary's, Maryland, and the Chesapeake in general play in developing the British imperial system and then in aiding the growth of a new nation? What were the consequences for the inhabitants here? What changes occurred here from generation to generation as people multiplied and resources accumulated or were wasted? The plans include a visitors' center, seventeenth-, eighteenth-, and nineteenth-century working farms, waterfront exhibits that will focus on commerce and shipping, and stabilized archaeological excavations of buildings that once actually stood on the Town Lands.

At 64.9 m. is the junction with Fisher Road.

● Go left 0.1 m. to the **Site of St. John's** (stabilized archaeological site, open). John Lewgar, an ex-Anglican minister turned Catholic, whom Lord Baltimore had made provincial secretary, had built St. John's by 1638. Archaeological excavations made by Dr. Henry Chandlee Forman in the early 1960s and by the commission in 1972–74 have found vestiges of a hall-and-parlor frame house, 52 by 20.6 feet and one and one-half stories high. A central brick chimney served both rooms, a plan common in contemporary farmhouses of southern England. (The end chimneys found in later Maryland houses were an adaptation of west-country English houses, more suited to the heat and humidity of Chesapeake summers.) A remarkable feature for such an early period in Maryland settlement is a cellar under the east end built with dressed stone walls. In the main room—or hall—of this house the freemen of the colony met to elect an assembly in February, 1639. Through the 1640s Lewgar's house was often used as a meeting place for the assembly, council, and Provincial Court—that is, for the handful of men who ran the affairs of a colony inhabited by little more than 400 to 600 souls. Lewgar left Maryland about 1649. By 1653 or 1654 the house belonged to a Dutch merchant, Simon Overzee, who died early in 1660. In 1661 Charles Calvert, the new young governor of Maryland, who became the third Lord Baltimore in 1676, acquired and lived in the house. An imaginative geographer of the period who had never visited St. Mary's called it the "Palace of St. John's." But by 1667, Calvert had moved to a new house he had built at Mattapany on the Patuxent (*see* Tour 30). Thereafter, St. John's was usually used for public offices or was leased to men who kept an inn here to accommodate visitors in assembly and court time.

The archaeological record shows extensive changes at St. John's after Lewgar's time, but who made them is unknown. The central chimney was moved, a new stairway built, and the house raised to two full stories. A separate kitchen, a nursery, and a quartering house are alluded to in an innkeeper's lease of 1678. By that time, an orchard and a kitchen garden were in need of new palings to enclose them against foraging animals and the house was in need of a new roof, specified to be of tiles. After the capital had been moved to Annapolis in 1695, occupation of some kind continued at St. John's through part of the first decade of the eighteenth century. The house then collapsed or was torn down.

At 0.3 m. on Fisher Road, between two dormitories of *St. Mary's College of Maryland* (R), is the stabilized **Site of John Hicks House** (open), excavated in 1969–70. This frame house, sixteen by forty feet with brick end chimneys, was probably built about 1723 by Capt. John Hicks, a sea captain from Whitehaven in northern England. By that time St. Mary's City had disappeared and Hicks was settling in a rural neighborhood. He served a term in the lucrative post of sheriff and sat briefly on the Provincial Court. At his death in 1753, a personal estate of about £400 made him one of the wealthiest men in the area. About 1746 Hicks built a new house nearby, and his old dwelling was then dismantled. Hicks had a brother in the tobacco trade in Whitehaven and may have been a merchant-planter. Surviving accounts prove that Hicks's son, William, functioned in such a capacity during the 1750s in some kind of partnership with his uncle. There was excellent harborage here and several ships a year came from London and

Freedom of Conscience Monument

Whitehaven to bring in goods and carry away tobacco. William Hicks purchased the crops of his neighbors and sold them goods in return, thus providing the necessary link between planters and distant markets.

Md. 5 passes Mill Creek at 65.0 m. On the borders of the pond at its mouth are a dormitory, library, and student union of *St. Mary's College of Maryland.* Near this creek the *Ark* and *Dove* anchored late in March of 1634, and Gov. Leonard Calvert and about 140 settlers set foot on ground they had just purchased from a local Indian village. The early narratives describe the harbor and their walk "in land" half a mile south to the *Site of St. Mary's Fort,* which they built for immediate protection.

In the Y of the junction between Md. 5 and Md. 584, 65.1 m., is the **Freedom of Conscience Monument,** a massive limestone figure of a youth with face uplifted designed by the Baltimore sculptor Hans Schuler. Erected in 1934 by the counties of Maryland in celebration of the Tercentenary, the statue commemorates the passage on April 21, 1649, of the Act Concerning Religion. In an age of religious intolerance, when in England itself Puritans were at war with Catholics, this act provided that "noe person or p[er]sons whatsoever within this Province . . . professing to believe in Jesus Christ, shall from hence forth be any waies troubled Molested or discountenanced for or in respect of his or her religion nor in the free exercise thereof." Lord Baltimore gained much by this pioneering move: he demonstrated to a Protestant regime in England that he was not establishing a Roman Catholic state, and he attracted much-needed colonists. Quakers and Catholics, unwelcome elsewhere, settled by the side of Anglicans and Presbyterians and shared in public responsibilities. Until 1689, when Protestant rebels overthrew the proprietary government and enforced English laws restricting the political liberty of Catholics, Maryland demonstrated to the Christian world that a state could practice religious toleration and survive.

● Go right on Md. 584 to **St. Mary's College of Maryland,** established in 1840 as St. Mary's Female Seminary to commemorate the founding of Maryland and the religious toleration practiced throughout most of the seventeenth century. The seminary, begun as an academy for young ladies, is now a four-year coeducational state college. **Calvert Hall** (R), 0.2 m., where the road angles left, is a partial reconstruction of the first school building erected in 1844 and destroyed by fire in 1924.

Trinity Protestant Episcopal Church, on Church Point beyond Calvert Hall, was built shortly after 1829 with brick salvaged from its predecessor, the State House of 1676, which the assembly had turned over to the parish in 1720. In the churchyard, the **Leonard Calvert Monument** marks the site of a mulberry tree near which the settlers from the *Ark* and the *Dove* are supposed to have assembled to hear the Royal Charter read soon after their arrival.

The **Copley Vault** at the rear of the church is believed to hold the remains of Sir Lionel Copley and his wife. Copley (d. 1693) was the first royal governor of Maryland during the twenty-five years of crown government that followed the Revolution of 1689.

Between the church and the monument, mixed in with the gravestones, are granite markers that show the outlines of the **Site of the State House of 1676.** Capt. John Quigly built it for 300,000 pounds of tobacco, then worth about £1,250. This was a huge public expenditure for the time. Excavations made in 1933 revealed walls laid out much as required by the contract recorded in the assembly journal of 1674. The cross-shaped brick building had two full stories and an attic. The main section was forty-five feet by thirty feet; the stair tower and porch tower that made the cross extended the width to more than sixty-one feet. The location on Church Point must have made the State House a landmark from the water, a fitting sign that a traveler was approaching Lord Baltimore's seat of government. Unfortunately, the masons available had insufficient skill for so grand a structure, and it was constantly in need of repairs. Its condition in 1693—the walls were reported to "leane out on each side the Staire Case"—partly contributed to the decision to construct a new capital in a more central location. Nevertheless, the building stood for another 135 years, serving for most of that time as a chapel of ease for William and Mary Parish.

Adjacent to the churchyard is the **Reconstructed State House** of 1676 (open daily, May–Oct., 10–5; Nov.–Apr., 10–4; rest rooms), built in 1934 to celebrate the Maryland Tercentenary. The reconstruction, the work of Herbert Crist, James Edmunds, Jr., and Horace Peaslee, is based on the recorded construction contract and on archaeological studies of the original building. Exhibits illustrating seventeenth-century Maryland history are presently housed on the second floor. The late-sixteenth-century cannon on the bluff in front of the building is one of several salvaged from the river in 1824. The cannon quite possibly is one of those known to have been shipped on the *Ark* with the first settlers in 1633–34.

By the time the State House of 1676 was built, St. Mary's City had come into being. During the 1660s, the rapidly growing population of the colony required and could support the construction of public buildings, and accommodations for visitors were also necessary. In 1662 the

St. Mary's State House

province purchased a building for use both as the First State House and as an inn. This house, called from that time the Country's House, may have been the dwelling Leonard Calvert had built by the time of his death in 1647. Around it a cluster of new buildings had appeared by 1668: the secretary's office and the Council Chamber—which for a while served as a Second State House—another inn, lawyers' offices, and a lawyer's house. To encourage the town's development, Gov. Charles Calvert chartered St. Mary's City in 1669, rechartering it in 1671 and giving it the right to send two representatives to the assembly, although the city was still little more than a village. Lots were laid out and taken up along two streets. Aldermanbury Street, which started near where Trinity Church now stands on Church Point, ran south near the river, passing the river entrance of the Reconstructed State House. Middle Street ran from the landing near the mouth of Mill Creek inland to the Country's House, near the *Site of St. Mary's Fort.* Nevertheless, in 1678 there were at most eighteen structures in St. Mary's City and perhaps not more than eleven. Three of these— the State House, the secretary's office, and a prison—were devoted to public uses. Most of the others were inns, offices, or lodgings for clerks and lawyers, all essential to a seat of government.

In 1683 and 1684, acts of assembly to encourage the development of towns had little effect, but they may have encouraged some growth at St. Mary's City. One hundred lots were laid out, in addition to those already taken up, and some are known to have been put to use. William Nuthead, prohibited by royal order from printing in Virginia, set up his press in St. Mary's City in 1685, thus becoming the colony's first printer. Construction also began on a water mill on Mill Creek.

City bylaws passed in 1685 provide some picture of the village. They required all housekeepers to "provide to their Chimneys two ladders, one twenty four foote, and the other twelve foote in length" and to see that "all Chimneys . . . be lathed, filled, dawb'd and plaistered." Most chimneys evidently were not of brick, which must have presented a major fire hazard. The bylaws also complained that hogs roamed freely, "killing the Poultrey, rooteing up the Gardens and fields." Hogpens were required, and the constable was to impound any hogs found wandering. There were provisions for maintaining the "highwaies" and the landing, but no market regulations, although a space was set aside for markets and fairs and the charter permitted the use of a *court of pie powder*, a judicial procedure whereby persons apprehended for criminal activities during market or fair days could be tried expeditiously. Evidently St. Mary's City did not encourage the sale of local produce, and a market did not come into being. Such commerce as was carried on did not center on the sale of local goods but on the exportation of tobacco and the importation of foreign products.

St. Mary's City was one of several official ports of entry. Nevertheless, it did not offer centralized economic services. The landing here was only one of dozens scattered over the province, and ship captains came by small boat or on horseback from anchorages elsewhere to enter and clear their vessels here.

In July of 1689, St. Mary's City was the scene of a revolution. News of the Glorious Revolution in England and the flight of James II to France aroused anti-Catholic fears in the predominantly Protestant population of Maryland. In 1689, the council was dominated by Catholics, and it lacked strong leadership. These circumstances provided a small group of agitators and ambitious men with the opportunity to overturn the government. In mid-July, Capt. John Coode began raising troops. Col. William Digges, a member of the council, led about eighty militiamen to St. Mary's City to protect the State House, but attempts to mobilize other troops to march against Coode failed. The rebels accused Lord Baltimore's council of plotting to deliver Maryland to the French and the northern Indians, and for a time these fears prevailed. On July 27, Coode and several hundred men reached St. Mary's City and demanded that Digges surrender. Digges's men refused to fight, and he was obliged to turn over the State House and the colony's records without firing a shot. Four days later the rest of the council surrendered at Mattapany (*see* Tour 30). As a result of the coup, Catholic-Protestant cooperation was ended, and Catholics lost their political rights until the American Revolution restored them. The Crown ruled Maryland until 1715, when the third Lord Baltimore died and his Protestant heir was allowed to reassume control of the province.

Among the second-floor exhibits in the Reconstructed State House is a late-seventeenth-century saker that has been purposely disabled. It is one of the cannon found in the river in 1824 and may well have been part of the State House defenses when Digges surrendered to Coode.

In 1695 the second royal governor, Francis Nicholson, moved the capital to Annapolis, a site more centrally located for the colony's expanded population. Once the capital was gone, so was the economic base of St. Mary's City. By 1708 there were no voters to hold an election, and the city lost its representation in the assembly. By 1720, the town had disappeared completely.

Between the Reconstructed State House and the churchyard, a road leads to **Broome's Wharf.** From the late nineteenth century until 1935, steamboats brought passengers and freight to the landing. This will be the site of the St. Mary's City Commission's waterfront exhibits.

● At 0.6 m. on Md. 584, by a private driveway (R), is a view of the probable **Site of St. Mary's Fort** (private), as yet identified only from aerial photographs. The traces found in the photographs fit Leonard Calvert's description of a "pallizado of one hundred and twentie yards square, with fower flankes." Here the first settlers lived temporarily, but by early 1638, when the assembly journal begins, they had scattered over several miles of the surrounding countryside. When Richard Ingle plundered the St. Mary's settlement in 1645 (*see below,* Sister's Freehold), the fort had disappeared. By the river bank, beyond the site of the fort, is the **Broome House** (private), built in the 1840s by

Dr. John MacKall Broome, a large landowner. South of the house is a frame slave quarter of the same date. The central chimney served two families, one on each side.

At 65.8 m., Mattapany Street branches left. In the field on the right once stood the Roman Catholic Chapel built in the 1660s to replace the first chapel, which burned in Ingle's Rebellion (*see below,* Sister's Freehold). Excavations by Dr. Henry Chandlee Forman in the 1930s revealed that the church was built of brick in the form of a great Latin cross, fifty-five feet long and fifty-seven feet wide. The chapel was torn down after 1705, when the Maryland Assembly passed a law prohibiting Catholic services except in private houses.

Just beyond Mattapany Street at 65.9 m. is the junction with Rosecroft Road. In a field opposite this junction are the buried foundations of St. Peter's, excavated by Dr. Forman in 1940. Chancellor Philip Calvert finished this imposing brick house in 1679. It was fifty-four feet square with interior chimneys and was equal in size to the governor's palace built at Williamsburg twenty-five years later. The chancellor's "Great House" was the finest building in Maryland and probably one of the best in any colony at the time. The first royal governors, Lionel Copley and Francis Nicholson, lived in St. Peter's. A few months after the capital was moved to Annapolis, St. Peter's was destroyed when gunpowder stored here exploded. No effort was ever made to rebuild the house.

● Go right on Rosecroft Road, which travels by several of the Town Land tracts occupied by 1740. Among them is **Sister's Freehold,** granted in 1639 to Margaret and Mary Brent, upon which they had already built their house. Margaret Brent (ca. 1600–1670/1), an exceptionally able woman, had arrived in 1638 with her sister Mary and her brothers Giles and Fulke. She acquired a great deal of land, and her energy and ability won her the confidence of the governor. When Leonard Calvert died suddenly early in 1647, he named her his sole executor, with responsibility for paying the soldiers he had imported from Virginia to reestablish his authority after the so-called Ingle's Rebellion. In 1645, the adventurer Richard Ingle had plundered the colony in the name of Parliament, forcing most of the settlers to flee into Virginia. It was more than a year before Calvert was able to return, and later depositions referred to the intervening period as "the time of plunder." After Calvert's death, the restored government was weak and unable to cope with a severe corn shortage. Furthermore, the governor's estate fund was found to be insufficient to pay the soldiers he had imported. Unfed and unpaid men posed the threat of mutiny. Margaret Brent imported corn for the soldiers from Virginia and had herself declared attorney for Lord Baltimore in place of the former governor. She was then able to use the proprietor's cattle to help pay the men, because Leonard Calvert had pledged his brother's estate as well as his own for the purpose. The assembly later gave her sole credit for having kept the soldiers in line until the government became securely established. If she had failed, it might have been the end of the Calvert regime, for by 1647 there were fewer settlers in Maryland than had arrived on the *Ark* and the *Dove* thirteen years before.

Mistress Brent's reward for undertaking these responsibilities was angry complaint from Lord Baltimore at her "meddling" in his affairs, although the assembly vigorously defended her. Giles Brent, who was at odds with the proprietor over various matters, including the rights of the Jesuits (*see below,* St. Inigoes Manor), moved to Virginia in 1650, and his sisters followed him there in 1651. Margaret Brent never married, an astonishing feat in a society where men outnumbered women about six to one. Her will, dated December, 1663, was probated in Virginia on May 19, 1671. Margaret Brent is most famous today for her unsuccessful effort on January 21, 1648, to claim two votes in the Maryland Assembly, one as a landowner in her own right, the other as the attorney for Lord Baltimore. This is the first recorded case in America of a woman seeking the legal prerogatives of a man. When the story first became widely known in the 1880s, supporters of the movement for women's rights claimed Margaret as the first American feminist.

About 150 acres in this area were owned by Daniel Clocker, a carpenter whose successful career in Maryland resembled those of many early immigrants. At his arrival in 1636, Clocker was a servant indentured to Thomas Cornwallis. By 1660, he owned 200 acres of land, and at his death in 1675 he was a member of the Common Council of St. Mary's City, even though he was illiterate. Mortality was shockingly high in seventeenth-century Maryland, but for those who survived, opportunity was great in the expanding tobacco economy, even for those starting at the bottom. After the mid-1660s, opportunity for poor men first declined and then virtually disappeared as the early period of expansion ended. Thereafter, most men found it increasingly difficult to climb the social and economic ladder. None of Clocker's descendants were able to surpass Daniel's achievements, even though he had started with nothing except physical stamina and the skills of a carpenter. A house (private) built before 1766 by his grandson or great-grandson, both also named Daniel Clocker, is still standing.

At 1.6 m. Rosecroft Road makes an abrupt left. Bear right on a dirt road to **Chancellor Point,** 0.5 m. (walking trail, public beach, rest rooms). A walk along the beach to the point allows a view of the whole sweep of the St. Mary's River. In the 1640s, a plantation house stood on the bluff above, and ceramic fragments found in the plow zone indicate that an eighteenth-century planter also lived here. The present house (not open to the public) was built in the 1940s.

At 67.0 m. Bauer Road branches right.

● Turn right and go 0.5 m. to **Fenwick Farm** (L) (private). The first structure here may have been a tenant farmer's house built late in the seventeenth century. Later it was a "quarter" for servants and slaves of the wealthy planter and royal collector of customs William Deacon, who lived on the town lands from 1722 until his death in 1759. Deacon's executor, Ignatius Fenwick, bought the property and gave it to his son Edward, who built the present structure, probably shortly after 1772. Two great brick chimneys, shown in an old photograph, have been removed.

At 68.1 m. on Md. 5 is the junction with Villa Road.

● Turn right to an intersection with Grayson's Road, 1.5 m. Turn right to **Cross Manor** (private), 0.7 m. (left at the bend where Grayson's Road becomes Cross Manor Road), long believed to be the oldest brick house in Maryland, but it is now considered to be of late-eighteenth-century construction. The 2½-story house has a gable roof and outside chimneys connected by a windowless pent. Some good paneling is still preserved in the interior. The structure stands on a grant made in 1638 to Thomas Cornwaleys, one of the leaders who came with the *Ark* and *Dove* and one of the early colony's largest landholders. In 1638, Cornwaleys wrote Lord Baltimore that having "hithertoe imployde myself and Servants in Publick works" including the construction of a grist mill, "I am building of A house toe put my head in, of sawn timber framed A story and half hygh, with A seller and chimnies of brick toe Encourage others toe follow my Example, for hithertoe wee liue in cottages." The house may have stood nearby but cannot have been the present brick structure.

● Returning to the intersection of Grayson's and Villa roads, go straight ahead on Villa Road to **St. Ignatius Church** (R), 1.9 m., built in 1788 on St. Inigoes Manor and restored in 1953 by volunteers from *Webster Field.*

Webster Field (no admittance), a naval airfield established during World War II as part of the Patuxent Naval Air Test Center (*see* Tour 30), is on the **Site of St. Inigoes Manor,** a large tract of land patented in 1641 and 1651 to Cuthbert Fenwick and Ralph Crouch, who held it in trust for the Jesuits (*see* St. Thomas Manor House, Tour 26b). Fr. Thomas Copley (1594–1653), who came to Maryland in 1636 and served as superior of the mission, moved his headquarters to St. Inigoes from St. Mary's City in 1644, just before Ingle's Rebellion. The mission remained active into the nineteenth century, although the Jesuit order itself was suppressed from 1772 to 1805.

Thomas Copley was an aggressive leader who antagonized both Protestants and Catholics. He and his colleagues attempted to acquire large tracts of land directly from the Indians and to establish for themselves the freedom from secular law that was enjoyed by the church in Catholic parts of Europe. These efforts brought the Jesuits into conflict with the lord proprietor and contributed to Protestant fears engendered by living under a Catholic proprietor during the English Civil War. When Richard Ingle drove Gov. Leonard Calvert and other Catholic leaders to Virginia in 1645 (*see above*), he sent Father Copley and Father White to England in chains. Calvert reasserted proprietary power in 1646 and the priests were released upon their arrival in England. But the proprietor was determined that Jesuit activity should not continue to endanger his position, and by 1648, when Copley returned to Maryland, Lord Baltimore had won this battle. With the approval of the authorities in Rome, the Jesuits formally renounced their claims to any right to hold land except by grant from the proprietor, and the theoretical power of ecclesiastical courts—courts that never were established in Maryland—did not again become an issue. Father Copley seems to have spent his remaining years trying to recover Jesuit property, valued at over £2,000, that had been stolen or destroyed during Ingle's Rebellion.

In **RIDGE,** 71.5 m., is the southern junction with Three Notch Road (*see* Tour 30).

At about 75.4 m. is **Point Lookout Confederate Cemetery,** where the bodies of the Confederate prisoners who died at *Point Lookout* are interred. Two monuments, one erected by the federal government, the other by the State of Maryland, commemorate their suffering. At 76.1 m. is **Point Lookout State Park.**

Point Lookout, 78.4 m., in the 1850s was the site of a flourishing summer resort, which enjoyed the magnificent view of the Potomac as it empties into the Chesapeake Bay. During the Civil War, the Union government maintained a hospital and a prisoner of war camp here, in which the poet Sidney Lanier was held prisoner. More than 3,000 Confederate soldiers died at the camp. Conditions at the camp were insanitary, the water was polluted, and due to poor administration there was insufficient food, clothing, and shelter. In 1867, the dead were moved to the national cemetery three miles away.

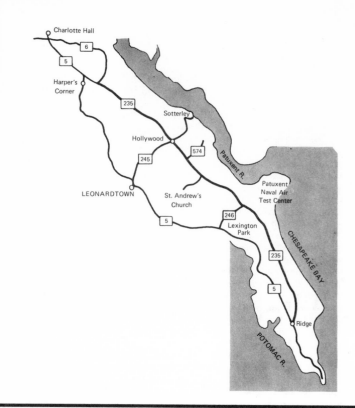

HARPER'S CORNER–LEXINGTON PARK–RIDGE; 30.7 m.
Md. 235

Md. 235, the alternate to Md. 5 between Harper's Corner and Ridge, follows a trail laid out in 1672 from Mattapany Landing near the mouth of the Patuxent to the more northern settlements. In 1702, a road-marking law prescribed three equidistant notches on the face of a tree to indicate a road to a ferry, two notches with a third high above for a road to a courthouse, and two notches near the ground with a slit down the face for a road to a church. To this day, this route is known as Three Notch Road.

Md. 235, which is 4.9 m. below Charlotte Hall, branches off Md. 5 at 0.0 m. At 1.3 m. on Md. 235 is the junction with Md. 6.

● Go left on Md. 6 to Delabrooke Road, 1.3 m.

Turn right onto Delabrooke Road. At 2.1 m. on the left is **De Le Brooke Manor,** surveyed in 1650 for Robert Brooke, commander of old Charles County (1650–54) and a member of the Provincial Council under the Puritans (*see* Tour 25b, Site of Battletown). When Gov. Thomas Stone reasserted Lord Baltimore's authority in 1654, Brooke lost his position, but his son, Baker Brooke, who settled at De Le Brooke, married Ann Calvert, daughter of Leonard (*see* Tour 29, St. Mary's City). In 1657, Baker Brooke was appointed to the Provincial Council, the beginning of a long and powerful career in Maryland politics. The council met in Brooke's house with Gov. Charles Calvert on March 19, 1662.

In **HOLLYWOOD**, 9.8 m., is a junction with Md. 245.

● Go left 2.5 m. to **Sotterley** (open daily, June–Sept., 11–5, and by appointment, Apr., May, Oct., and Nov.). The merchant James Bowles built the oldest section of the house between 1710, when he acquired the land, and 1727, when he died. His widow married George Plater II (d. 1755), who with his son George Plater III (1735–92), governor of Maryland (1791), enlarged the house. Bowles's dwelling was framed, one and one-half stories, with two rooms on a floor. A wing that gives the house a T-shape was added before Bowles's death and retains paneling he installed. George Plater II probably added the dining room at the south end of the house. About 1760 his son remodeled the original main room of the house, adding fourteen feet to create a central stair hall with a drawing room on the north. In the drawing room is some of the finest woodwork in Maryland. The fireplace, with bracketed mantel and a large carved overmantel panel, is flanked by deep shell-topped alcoves. Local lore has it that the Chippendale stairway in the hall was the work of Richard Boulton, designer of All Faith and St. Andrew's churches in the 1760s (*see below*, St. Andrew's Church and Tour 29). George Plater III named Sotterley for the Plater family home in England. His profligate grandson lost the property in 1820. The present owner, a member of the fourth family to own Sotterley, has created the Sotterley Foundation to maintain the house as a museum.

At 11.9 m. on Md. 235 is the junction with Md. 574.

● Go left on Md. 574 1.5 m. to an unmarked paved road, then right to **Resurrection Manor** (L), 2.4 m., 4,000 acres granted to Thomas Cornwaleys in 1651. It has been long believed that part of the house was built in 1651, and if correct, it is probably the oldest existing structure in Maryland. Originally, the house contained only one room and a loft and was built of brick with a steep gable roof. Later, another room was added to make the hall-and-parlor dwelling that now stands.

At 14.0 m. on Md. 235 is the junction with St. Andrew's Church Road.

● Turn right on this to **St. Andrew's Church** (R), 2.3 m., built by Samuel Abell, Jr., between 1766 and 1768 and standing today almost exactly as it was described in "Richard Boulton's Plann" accepted by the vestry in 1766. The brick, gable-roofed building has an unusual facade, with two towers (the stubby steeples are probably modern) flanking an inset portico. The wall above the portico conceals the roof of the church and has a Palladian window that projects up into a pediment. A third tower was planned, perhaps at the end of the nave looking down on the chancel roof. The third tower would have completed the resemblance of the plan to that of a medieval church. In the interior, a gallery fits into the space above the portico and is lit by the Palladian window. Two rows of square fluted pillars with Ionic capitals mark off the barrel-ceilinged nave from the side aisles and lead to the chancel, which is set off from the nave by an arch. The altarpiece, an elaborate pilastered and pedimented tablet containing the Lord's Prayer, the Ten Commandments, the Apostles' Creed, and selections from Exodus, was painted by John Friech, "Limner." Friech agreed with the vestry on July 29, 1771, to finish the work for his board and £16 10s. currency, the vestry supplying him with "Lamp Black white Vitriol and a Book of Gold leaf." Boulton and Abell also constructed All Faith Church, which was built at the same time twenty miles away (*see* Tour 29), and except for the facade, the two churches resemble each other. St. Andrew's Parish, erected from All Faith and William and Mary parishes in 1744, included Leonardtown, the county seat. However, this little church in the woods continued to be the parish church until World War II, when the chapel of ease in Leonardtown, which was not built until about 1870, became the main church.

At 18.7 m. is the junction with Md. 246 in **LEXINGTON PARK** (110′ alt., 9,136 pop.), formerly a tiny crossroads village named Jarboesville and now the home of many workers at the **Patuxent Naval Air Test Center** (no admittance). This installation was begun in 1941 as part of the Potomac River Naval Command.

Within the grounds of the Naval Air Center is **Mattapany,** built early in the nineteenth century. A handsome stuccoed brick 2½-story house with roof curtains between flush chimneys on the gables, it now serves as the official residence of the commandant of the Naval Air Test Center.

The land on which the house stands was the site of a Mattapany Indian village acquired from the Indians by Fr. Andrew White (*see* Tours 29 and 31, Father Andrew White) and his associates, who established a storehouse and mission here. Lord Baltimore reclaimed the land in 1641 in a move designed to prevent the Jesuits from establishing independent communities on lands they had obtained from the Indians (*see* Tour 29, St. Inigoes Manor). In 1663, the proprietor granted Mattapany to Henry Sewall, secretary of the province, whose widow married Gov. Charles Calvert three years later. Calvert then built the "fair House of Brick and Timber" to which he had moved from St. John's in St. Mary's City (*see* Tour 29) by 1668. He also erected a fort and a magazine. When the Maryland councillors were driven from St. Mary's during the Revolution of 1689, they took refuge here, and here the proprietary government surrendered to the Protestant rebels. About 250 yards south of the present dwelling are the foundations and cellar of an old building, probably Calvert's house, which was described as dilapidated in 1773. The site of the garrison building can be seen about 100 yards nearer the river, as well as the remains of old earthworks on the river bank itself.

RIDGE, 30.7 m., is at the southern junction with Md. 5 (*see* Tour 29).

DISTRICT OF COLUMBIA LINE–PORT TOBACCO–LA PLATA; 46.3 m.
Md. 210, 225, 224, 334, and 6

Until the mid-1930s, the area crossed by this tour, which includes southwestern Prince George's County and Charles County, was an isolated and unprosperous tobacco and woodlot country. The establishment of the Southern Electric Cooperative in 1938 brought cheap electricity to the region, and although tobacco and lumber are still the chief products, both counties are making vigorous efforts to attract more industrial develop-

Sotterley

ment. The extension of water and sewer lines several miles south along the river after World War II has brought over 50,000 people to the areas near the city, and more intensive development is coming. The suburbs of Washington are reaching down into Charles County, where the expanded production of the U.S. Naval Propellant Plant at the Indian Head Naval Reservation has also attracted many new residents. South and east of Indian Head, Charles County remains mostly forest and farmland.

Leave Washington, D.C., on Md. 210, which is an extension of S. Capitol Street. Its route crosses the **District of Columbia Line,** 0.0 m., at a point 7.7 m. south of the White House. At 1.0 m. is the junction with the Capital Beltway, Tour S 3.

● Go right to the **Woodrow Wilson Bridge,** 1.4 m., a Potomac River crossing to Alexandria, Virginia, completed in 1962 as part of the beltway around the nation's capital. The area on the right of the beltway between the river and Md. 210 has been purchased by the Department of the Interior for parkland. **Mount Welby** (1805), an old brick house, is on the grounds of the proposed park.

At 1.4 m. is the junction with Oxon Hill Road.

Near the intersection of the Capital Beltway and Md. 210 is the **Oxon Hill Children's Farm** (open daily all year). This is a working farm typical of those in this area around the turn of the century. Examples of every kind of farm animal may be seen.

● Turn right on Oxon Hill Road into an area that until the 1950s was dominated by estates. In the eighteenth century it was part of **Oxon Hill,** originally known as St. Elizabeth's, which was purchased by Col. John Addison, the first settler of a family long prominent in Southern Maryland life. His great-grandson had the Addison lands resurveyed and incorporated in 1767 into the estate known as Oxon Hill Manor. The old Oxon Hill house built by his son, Thomas Addison, stood about half a mile away in the direction of the Potomac until it burned in 1895. John Hanson (*see below,* Mulberry Grove), president of the Congress of the Confederation of the United States (1781–82), died at Oxon Hill on November 15, 1783, and is buried here. In recent

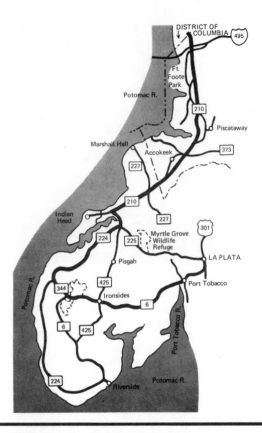

TOUR 31

years, Oxon Hill Manor was owned by Sumner Welles (1892–1960), President Franklin Roosevelt's undersecretary of state from 1937 to 1943.

At 1.8 m. is the junction with Fort Foote Road. Go right to **Fort Foote Park,** 1.5 m. (picnic tables and fireplaces). To the left of the parking area in the woods that now crowd the steep bluff along the river are the crude concrete and stone gun emplacements and remains of reinforced earthworks at Fort Foote, which was built during the Civil War as one of the defenses of the capital. William H. Seward, Jr., son of Lincoln's secretary of state, a young man of twenty-four, supervised its construction. Two twenty-five-ton Rodman guns, never used, lie on the ground at the back of the fort.

At 4.0 m. on Md. 210 is a junction with Livingston Road, once the main road (Md. 224) before Md. 210 was built.

● Turn right on Livingston Road. At 0.8 m. turn right on Old St. John's Way to **St. John's Protestant Episcopal Church** (open), which stands on the side of the road at the edge of the woods. This rectangular brick building with a steep hip roof and kicked eaves was built in 1723 and rebuilt and enlarged between 1765 and 1768. The interior was remodeled in 1820, and later, colored glass replaced the earlier clear panes. The church serves one of the original parishes of Maryland, first called Piscataway, then St. John's, and finally King George's Parish. In the churchyard is the faded stone of Enoch M.

Lyles, who was killed by John Frazer Bowie on August 7, 1805, in a duel Lyles is said to have precipitated at the insistence of his father, who expected the excellent marksmanship of his son to make him the survivor. The stone reads in part:

> Yet oh, what hand can paint thy parents' woe,
> God only can punish the hand that gave the blow.

● **Harmony Hall** (R) (private), 1.5 m., formerly known as Battersea, is visible from Livingston Road. This 2½-story brick house is believed to have been built by Enoch Magruder about 1750. It is an early Georgian house with narrow gable ends, but it has a symmetrical floor plan, and the sash windows are carefully balanced on either side of the front door. Walter Dulany Addison and his brother John, grandsons of John Addison of *Oxon Hill,* are said to have brought their brides here in 1792. The two couples are supposed to have lived in harmony in the house for a year, giving the place its present name.

At 1.7 m. is the junction with Fort Washington Road. Go right to **Fort Washington** (open; museum, picnic grounds), 3.5 m., first called Fort Warburton after the estate on which it was built. Warburton Manor, patented in 1661, was the home of the Digges family, who were descended from Edward Digges, governor of Virginia from 1652 to 1689. The site of the fort, a high promontory on a bend in the Potomac that commands a view up and down the river for many miles, was selected by George Washington in 1795. The land was not purchased until 1808, however, and the fortifications were old-fashioned and inadequate. In August, 1814, the British advanced up the Potomac and landed a reconnaissance party near here. The commander of the fort spiked his guns, blew up his ammunition, and withdrew to Washington without firing a shot. Immediately after this fiasco, Maj. Charles L'Enfant, who laid out the city of Washington, began constructing the present fort, but in 1815 he quarreled with the War Department, and Lt. Col. Walker K. Armistead replaced him. The fort was completed in 1824, and it is one of the most interesting old military structures in the country. A deep dry moat, which encircles the whole fort, is crossed by a drawbridge leading to a massive Roman arch trimmed with rusticated stone quoins and key block. The entrance is guarded by a medievallike portcullis, flanked by high brick guardhouses built into the thick walls. At intervals the walls with their gun emplacements jut starlike over the wooded river bank. Within the fort are a parade ground, storehouses, and old barracks.

In 1939, the Department of the Interior took over the fort as a park, but from 1943 to 1944 the army located the Adjutant General's School here, and later in the war the fort was used as a prisoner of war camp. It is now part of the National Capital Park System.

Md. 210 makes a second junction with Livingston Road at 6.8 m.

● Go left on Livingston Road to a junction with Md. 223, 2.4 m.; turn left again (an acute angle) to the town of **PISCATAWAY,** 0.7 m., which in the eighteenth century was a shipping center, until *Piscataway Creek* became filled with silt. Philip Fithian, the New Jersey tutor hired by Robert Carter of Virginia, noted in 1774 that the tavern here was kept by a woman with two bouncing daughters eagerly angling for husbands among the Scottish merchants. Today the town is little more than a crossroads. About seven old houses remain, but they have been much altered since they were constructed.

● Livingston Road passes **St. James Hill** (L) (private, but visible from the road), 2.6 m., a brick house with great chimneys built about 1740. The road continues to a junction with Md. 210.

Md. 210 crosses **Piscataway Creek,** 8.7 m., now merely a trickle but deep enough in colonial days to float vessels of considerable size to the town of *Piscataway*. Somewhere nearby on this creek is the site of the Piscataway village visited by Gov. Leonard Calvert when he negotiated the agreement with the "Emperor" of the Piscataways, which spared Maryland from much of the Indian terror that menaced other colonies. Excavations along the creek have uncovered hundreds of Indian skeletons and artifacts as well as evidence of early trade with Europeans. Thousands of tiny blue trade beads with brilliant glaze, possibly Venetian in origin, have been found. The oddest relics are a few small thin disks stamped with the rose and thistle—tokens used for admission to the ceremony of the "King's touch" for the cure of scrofula during the reign of Charles I. After the king lost his throne, some canny trader may have offered them as money to the American Indians.

Somewhere in the neighborhood of the creek, possibly as far north as the Fort Washington reservation, the Susquehannock Indians built a fort of a primitive European type after their defeat by the Iroquois in 1673. Raids in the area on both sides of the Potomac, possibly by the Seneca, were blamed on the Susquehannock. A joint force of Virginia militia under Col. John Washington and Maryland militia under Thomas Truman sought to drive the Susquehannock away. They beseiged the fort for seven weeks before five Susquehannock leaders came out to negotiate under a flag of truce. What followed is not certainly known, but for some reason the Indian leaders were murdered, and their followers fled to Virginia. Seeking revenge, the Susquehannock carried out the raids that touched off Bacon's Rebellion.

At 11.1 m. on Md. 210 is the junction with Bryan Point Road.

● Go right 0.7 m., then right again to **Christ Church** (R) at the junction of Bryan Point Road and Farmington Road. The brick walls are all that remain of the original church built in 1745, but the woodwork in the ceiling of the nave, installed after a fire in 1857, is especially noteworthy. The first church here was a private chapel built in 1698, which was officially named a chapel of ease for Piscataway Parish (*see above*) in 1729.

Continue on Bryan Point Road. Along the route, close to the river, is the **Site of Moyaone,** an Indian village marked on Capt. John Smith's map with a "king's house." The village was burned during the reprisals following the 1622 Indian uprising in Virginia, and those Piscataways who survived established their next home along Piscataway Creek, where they were still living when Calvert arrived. Extensive archaeological and anthropological study has been done here with the cooperation of the Smithsonian Institution. More than a thousand skeletons and many artifacts have been recovered. Studies indicate that the site was occupied for hundreds of years by people of varying cultural levels, some of them possibly dating back to the early Christian era. A portion of the artifacts are on display in the museum at *Accokeek.*

Near the end of the road is the **Colonial National Farm Museum,** operated by the Accokeek Foundation, an example of a mid-eighteenth-century farm (open Sat. and Sun., 1–5).

The road continues a short distance to **Bryan Point,** which affords a view of Mount Vernon, slightly to the south on the opposite shore.

Also at 11.1 m. is another junction with Livingston Road (formerly Md. 224).

● Go right to **ACCOKEEK** (19′ alt., est. 400 pop.) and the **Public Library** (open) housed in the Accokeek Elementary School (L), where artifacts from Moyaone (*see above*) are on display.

Rose Hill

At 15.6 m. is the junction with Md. 227.

● Go right on Md. 227 to **Marshall Hall** (open Fri., Sat., and Sun.), 4.2 m., an amusement park located on what is believed to be the estate granted to William Marshall in 1690. The Marshall family occupied the property until the 1860s, and the old brick house and its outbuildings appear to date from the colonial period. The Pot of Gold Casino here once housed hundreds of slot machines, attracting customers from a wide area, for between 1949 and 1968 Southern Maryland was the only place in the United States outside of Nevada where gambling in this form was legal. Charles County laws were considerably more liberal than those of any other Maryland county that had attempted to raise revenue in this way, and more than 20 percent of the county's revenue was derived from fees obtained from slot machine owners. In 1963, however, the Maryland legislature passed a law that outlawed slot machines by 1968.

At 19.4 m. is the junction with Md. 225. The main route turns left here.

● Md. 210 goes straight ahead to **INDIAN HEAD** (780 pop.), 0.8 m., and the **U.S. Naval Ordnance Station** established in 1890 as a proving ground for naval ordnance. In 1921, the proving ground was moved to Dahlgren, Virginia, where a larger range is available. The powder manufacturing plant established in 1898 and now used to produce rocket fuel is still operated here and is of great importance to the economic life of Charles County.

At 21.1 m. on Md. 225 is the junction with Md. 224, which now becomes the main route.

● Continue on Md. 225 to the **Myrtle Grove Wildlife Refuge** (L), 3.3 m., 800 acres of game preserve owned by the state. Md. 225 continues to a junction with U.S. 301 in La Plata, 9.0 m. (*see* Tour 26b).

At 21.2 m., just beyond the intersection of Md. 225 and Md. 224, is the junction with Md. 425.

● Go left on Md. 425 to the driveway (L) of **Araby,** 0.3 m., built before 1720 and now handsomely restored. The main house was originally only one and one-half stories, but sometime later in the eighteenth century it was raised to two stories. A lower brick wing has a long recessed porch, from which steps rise to the main entrance of the house. The woodwork is notable, particularly in the study. Washington's diary refers to Araby as the home of the Widow Eilbeck, whose daughter became the wife of George Mason, the master of Gunston Hall across the Potomac and the author of the Virginia Bill of Rights.

Md. 425 continues through **PISGAH**, 3.1 m., to a junction with Md. 6 at *Ironsides*.

Md. 224 continues through country covered by scrub and pine. At 25.0 m. is the junction with a paved road and a sign marking the way to Smallwood State Park.

● Go right on this to **Smallwood State Park** (open daily, June–Sept., 10–6; Mar.–May and Sept.–Dec., Sat.–Sun., 10–5; closed Dec.–Mar.), 0.9 m., established in 1957 on part of the tract owned by Gen. William Smallwood (1732–92). At the Battle of Long Island (August 27, 1776), Smallwood's battalion lost 256 of its 684 men in covering the American army's retreat to Brooklyn. The courageous actions of Smallwood's inexperienced troops earned Maryland the title "Old Line State," in honor of the Maryalnd Line of the Continental Army. Thereafter Smallwood and his men were often chosen for the most dangerous assignments, with Smallwood becoming a brigadier general in 1776 and a major general in 1780. The legislature elected Smallwood governor of Maryland from 1785 to 1788, and thereafter he retired to the little house that stands here. In 1898, the Sons of the American Revolution erected a five-foot granite monument at his grave, until then unmarked.

The Smallwood Foundation and the State of Maryland have restored the 1½-story **House** (open daily, 10–6), which was little more than a pile of bricks in 1956. The steep roof, dark glazed headers, and tiny rooms supplementing its two main chambers resemble those of very early structures. The first floor is furnished with pieces dating from the Revolutionary period, some of which came from the Smallwood family.

The state hopes to double the size of the park, now 316 acres, and to provide facilities for boating, picnicking, and camping.

At 29.7 m. is the junction with Md. 344 (L), which now becomes the main route.

Md. 224 follows the shore of the Potomac River to a junction with Md. 6, 19.7 m., near *Riverside*.

At 31.9 m. Md. 344 joins Md. 6. The main route turns left on Md. 6.

Md. 6 passes through **Doncaster State Forest**, over 1,500 acres of woodland, much of it pine, which offers limited picnic and camping facilities.

At **IRONSIDES**, 34.9 m., is a junction with Md. 425.

● Go right on Md. 425. At 1.3 m., **Old Durham Church** (open) comes into view through the woods. This plain two-story brick building was erected about 1732, although the walls were raised four feet in 1791 to accommodate a second tier of windows. In 1932, the church was restored as a memorial to Gen. William Smallwood (*see above*), one of its vestrymen. The well-tended churchyard served an even earlier church; tombstones for two sons of William and Elizabeth Dent are dated 1690 and 1695. The latest addition to the present church is the Smallwood Memorial Bell Tower, constructed of bricks salvaged from the ruined house that belonged to General Smallwood's sister.

The minutes of the Old Durham vestry reveal that the time for beginning Sunday church services was established by a sundial in the churchyard, although other measures had to be taken on overcast days. According to the vestry book for 1779, the vestrymen had resolved "that 12 oClock be the Houre of Meeting until the snd Monday in March next, and that the Dial in the Church Yard to determine the Time of Day—and in Case it is cloudy, the majority of Watches which the Owners, on their Honor, think right."

Md. 425 continues to another junction with Md. 6, 4.8 m. Go left on Md. 6 to **RIVERSIDE** (10' alt.), 10.5 m., one of several small river resorts on the peninsula.

Md. 6 descends through wooded country to a junction with Poor House Road, 42.4 m.

● Go left on this to **Retreat,** 0.2 m., the home of Daniel of St. Thomas Jenifer (1723–90), member of the Continental Congress and signer of the U.S. Constitution. He is the only signer whose place of burial is unknown. The origin of his name is uncertain but it is believed that the first Maryland settler of this branch of the Jenifers came from St. Thomas in the Virgin Islands. When the colonists' dispute with England grew bitter, Jenifer was at first inclined toward reconciliation, but when the breach came, he espoused the Revolutionary cause. He was president of the Maryland Council of Safety (1775–76), and first president of the state senate (1777–81). According to tradition, Jenifer built this frame house, and the land was certainly owned by the Jenifer family in 1750. Tall chimneys, connected by a pent with a window, tower over a great roof punctured by tiny dormers. The curtain and wing off the back cannot be seen from the road. The house has been repaired and retains some attractive mantels and other old woodwork. Open by appointment: Mrs. William G. Moore, Port Tobacco.

At 43.7 m. is the junction with Rose Hill Road.

● Go left on this route up a hill. At 0.7 m., go left on a gravel road to **Betty's Delight** and **Rose Hill.** Betty's Delight (private) is an early frame house, possibly dating from the seventeenth century, with an interesting battened front door. Rose Hill (private), on land originally part of Betty's Delight, is one of the best five-part mansions in Maryland. Dr. Gustavus Richard Brown, George Washington's friend and physician, bought the property in 1773, constructing the frame brick-nogged house with brick gables, hyphens, and wings soon thereafter. On the garden facade, a projecting bay with pediment adds prominence to the handsome doorway with fanlight framed by pilasters and pediment and to the Palladian window above it. Narrow windows on either side of the doorway light the spacious first floor hall. Rather than being located in the hall, staircases to the upper floor are set into small passageways on either side of the door on the driveway side. The hall and sitting room retain handsome cornices, window and door trim, and mantels. Dr. Brown and his wife are buried in a corner of the great boxwood garden that overlooks the Port Tobacco valley.

At 1.6 m. on the paved road is the gate to **Habre de Venture** (L) (private), built by Thomas Stone (1743–87) in the early 1770s. The five-part house is laid out along a curve. The main section is a brick 1½-story house one room deep with a gambrel roof. A one-story curtain leads to a frame wing with gambrel roof that once served as Thomas Stone's office. The balancing wing on the other side was replaced by the present two-story brick and frame structure. In the curtain leading to this wing is a huge chimney with a retreating breast. From the columned porch on the garden front one can look out over meadows where race horses graze.

Thomas Stone, who bought Habre de Venture in 1770, was a signer of the Declaration of Independence. He and his wife are buried on the property.

At 44.0 m. is the junction with a paved road.

● Turn right on this, then right again onto Chapel Point Road to **PORT TOBACCO**, a town built on one of the oldest sites of settlement in Maryland. The Potopaco Indians had a village here when the first Europeans arrived, and Fr. Andrew White (*see* Tour 29, Father Andrew White Memorial) made it the headquarters for some of his early missionary work. In 1727, the county seat, previously located according to the Maryland Assembly in a spot "remote from any landing," was laid out here. Originally called Charlestown, the present name of Port Tobacco was not officially adopted until 1820. The marsh that is now the head of the Port Tobacco River was an active port during the eighteenth century, and the town also served as a station on the water and coach route between Philadelphia and the South. Late in the eighteenth century, the town contained fifty or so houses and several hotels. The future of the town was foreshadowed in 1775, however, when a traveler observed that the creek "only carried small craft now."

An active Confederate underground operated out of Port Tobacco during the Civil War, and the conspirators who planned to kidnap Lincoln counted on using boats owned by Port Tobacco residents to ferry the president across the Potomac. By 1868, silting of the creek had caused a serious decline in the town's population and after the courthouse burned in 1892, the county seat was moved (1895) to nearby La Plata (*see* Tour 26b). When the Society for the Restoration of Port Tobacco was formed in 1949, only a handful of houses remained, mostly near the site of the old courthouse. Tobacco grew on the spot where once had stood the St. Charles Hotel, with its twenty-five guest rooms and a dining room that seated two hundred people.

Today, two eighteenth-century houses and a reconstruction of a third stand on the borders of the pleasant green that was once the public square. **Chimney House** (private) is a 2½-story frame dwelling believed to predate the Revolution. The house is conventional in appearance except for the enormous double chimney with a two-story brick pent that almost covers one gable. Cut into the pent are two tiny windows on each story and a great door into the basement. **Stagg Hall** (private) next door may be slightly later in date, although its steep gambrel roof and heavy hipped chimney freestanding above the second floor make it appear older. The smaller gabled wing was once a separate building, and it has now been almost completely rebuilt. The living room paneling has been acquired by the Chicago Art Institute. The present mantelpiece is said to have come from the courthouse.

Quinsell House (private) across the green is a reconstruction of the "salt box" frame house that once stood on the same foundations. On the third side, a small brick well house stands on the site of the hydrant that once supplied the village with fresh water piped from springs in the nearby hills. The structure was built in 1958 to celebrate the Charles County Tercentenary.

Destroyed by fire in 1892, the courthouse of 1820 has been rebuilt by the Society for the Restoration of Port Tobacco, Inc. The society purchased the courthouse land and reconstructed the present structure on the old foundations.

In Port Tobacco continue to a dirt road, 0.7 m. This road leads to **Chandler's Hope,** commanding a glorious view of the Port Tobacco valley below. The smallest section of the house, now carefully restored, may have been built in 1639 by Job Chandler, who patented 6,000 acres on both sides of the river. It is a little brick-nogged frame house with a six-foot fireplace, exposed rafters, and batten doors. The rest of the building, probably built before 1790, has been considerably

Port Tobacco

altered. During the eighteenth century, this house was the home of the Neales, a Catholic family that produced a generation of famous sons, all of whom devoted themselves to the religious life. In 1815, Fr. Leonard Neale (1745–1817) succeeded Fr. John Carroll (*see* Baltimore) as archbishop of Baltimore. His brother, Francis Neale, became vice-president (1799) and then president (1809) of Georgetown College. Fr. Charles Neale, who at the time of his death in 1823 was superior of the Jesuit Mission in America, helped found the Mount Carmel nunnery (*see* Tour 26b). Before the Revolution, candles in the windows that could be seen for miles down the river are supposed to have indicated when masses were being held.

At 2.0 m. on Chapel Point Road is the precipitous graveled entrance road to **Mulberry Grove** (L) (private, but visible from the road), birthplace of John Hanson (1721–83). The old house burned in 1934, but a similar building was erected on the same foundation with a chimney made from bricks of the first house. At the edge of the steep bluff, overlooking the Port Tobacco and Potomac rivers, is a monument to John Hanson. Erected in 1959 by the Swedish order Sons of Vasa, the monument commemorates Hanson's contributions to the Revolutionary cause and his years (1781–82) as president of the United States under the Articles of Confederation.

Chapel Point Road continues down the Port Tobacco valley; it turns abruptly left and becomes Md. 427, joining a side route of Tour 27.

At 44.3 m. on Md. 6, **Plenty** (private), an early-nineteenth-century frame house, can be seen atop a great hill.

La Grange (R) (private), 45.8 m., is visible from the road. Dr. James Craik (1730–1814), a close friend of George Washington, who served with him in the French and Indian War and later in the Continental Army, bought the property in 1763 and probably built the house soon afterwards. The main house resembles *Rose Hill*, with its brick-nogged, clapboard-covered frame with brick ends, gable roof, and pavilion (projecting bay) with pediment on the facade. The arrangement of windows, pilasters, and doorway on the pavilion adds a touch of elegance to the structure. A five-part plan may have been intended, but if so it was never carried out. The main house is flanked by a two-story brick-gabled building, but the curtain, which runs from a brick pent between the end chimneys, is a modern addition. A stable on the other side of the main house once provided symmetry to the plan. All brickwork is common bond.

The **Site of the McDonough Institute** (L), 46.1 m., is occupied by the Roman Catholic **Archbishop Neale School.** Maurice James McDonough, a peddler who lived at Pomfret near *Indian Head*, walked the western part of the county selling small goods. His will, probated in 1804, ordered that after the death of his wife his estate was to be sold, the proceeds invested, and the income used to educate as many poor children of the "McDonough District" as possible. One hundred years later, the $2,000 or so he left had grown to $50,000. In 1903, with the aid of an annual appropriation from the state, the trustees opened ·the McDonough Institute, which taught children from kindergarten through tenth grade. Until 1924, the Institute provided the only high school education in the county. Since the establishment of public high schools, the trustees have used the income to grant scholarships to children of the district for college or business education.

At 46.3 m. is the junction with U.S. 301 in **LA PLATA** (*see* Tour 26b).

BALTIMORE CITY LINE–TOWSON–COCKEYSVILLE–PENNSYLVANIA LINE–(York); 26.2 m.
Md. 45

Md. 45, the York Road, runs through the Piedmont, a country of green hillsides in the northern part of the state but a gently rolling terrain in the vicinity of Baltimore. Opened in 1743 as the Susquehanna Road and converted to a turnpike about 1807, this road became an outlet to the Chesapeake for fertile Pennsylvania and Maryland farmlands and thus contributed considerably to the growth of Baltimore. Trucks now travel the parallel I-83 with vegetables, poultry, and milk as well as factory products from the industrial centers. In recent years there has been considerable suburban and exurban development of Baltimore County, but beyond the commercial strips and clustered housing developments, the land retains its beauty. The valleys and vistas accessible from side roads resemble typical English countryside and the sound of the hunting horn and the baying of hounds enhances this illusion.

Hunts are still popular, and cross-country races held here attract thousands of sportsmen from all sections of the East. The races draw the best of the country's steeplechasers. Billy Barton, a starter some years ago in the famous Grand National at Aintree in England, was trained in the valley. Although old "Baltimore Countians" disdained flat racing, there are now several estates that breed and train thoroughbreds and race on the country's major tracks.

Maryland's state sport, jousting, is practiced here. Tournaments are modeled after the jousting contests of knights. The rider, armed with a lance and with his mount at a run, must spear rings that are hung from overarms. The most skillful rider is permitted to designate the Queen of Love and Beauty of the carnival. Riders spend much time practicing for the contests and they will pay a handsome price for the type of horse most likely to carry them to victory. A thick-set, short-coupled horse with a "lot of nerve" is the choice of most riders.

Cockfighting was formerly a popular, though illegal, pastime, carried on in a more or less clandestine manner, although most bird owners made little secret of the fact that they had a pen of "breeding birds." In several pits in the county, Baltimore County cock owners competed with Pennsylvanians.

Horse and pony shows are held at a dozen places in the valley and children are taught to ride at an early age. Many of the "squires" of the neighborhood have taken up cattle breeding as a hobby and some of the finest herds in the East are to be found on nearby farms.

The tour begins at the **Baltimore City Line,** 0.0 m.

● Just before Towson State College, make a left on St. Joseph Hospital Road. This road leads to the **Sheppard and Enoch Pratt Hospital,** which is situated on a beautifully landscaped tract. This institution for the treatment of mental and nervous disorders was opened in 1891 and named the Sheppard Asylum for its founder, Moses Sheppard. In 1898 the institution received the residuary estate of Enoch Pratt.

At 1.5 m. on Md. 45 (York Road) is **Towson State College.** Begun as a state teacher's college in 1866, it now offers a full liberal arts program. The college moved from Baltimore to its present site in 1915. The older buildings, made of red brick, are designed in the Tudor-Gothic style.

TOWSON (465′ alt., 77,809 pop.), 2.2 m. at the junction of Md. 45, 146, and Joppa Road, seat of Baltimore County since 1854, was founded by Ezekiel Towson. Manufacturers of building materials have grown with the county, and modern industrial plants have taken advantage of Towson's location. One of the principal manufacturers makes ticket-issuing and automatic odds-calculating machines for race tracks. Many people are employed by government offices. The green spaces provided by school campuses and Towson's noted hospitals vary the scenery.

● The **Blue Cross–Blue Shield Building** (Medical Insurance) on Joppa Road, east of the main intersection in Towson, is a striking modern office block. Its massive squared shape is covered in blue-tinted reflecting glass, merging the ultrastark contours with reflections of its surroundings. As an accent, the architects placed a small red-glazed block beside it, in which some service facilities are housed.

● Along Md. 146 to the northeast, **Goucher College** is on a tract of more than 300 acres purchased in 1935. Beginning in the early 1940s, the college gradually moved its facilities to this lovely campus. A women's school, Goucher offers some courses in conjunction with The Johns Hopkins University. Goucher has earned a national reputation for quality education. It opened in 1888 as the Woman's College of Baltimore, a Methodist institution, at St. Paul and 23rd streets in the city. In 1914 the school became nonsectarian and the name was changed to Goucher College after its president from 1890 to 1907, John F. Goucher.

Md. 146 north from Towson crosses the Baltimore Beltway (I-695) at 0.8 m. just north of the Goucher College campus. Immediately

TOUR 32

beyond the cloverleaf, turn right on Hampton Estate Lane to the **Hampton National Historic Site** (R).

Hampton (open Tues.–Sat., 11–5; Sun., 1–5; closed Mon.) was for more than 150 years the home of the Ridgeley family. One of the largest colonial mansions of Maryland, Hampton was completed in 1790 by Charles Ridgeley (the builder) whose forebears were early settlers who had made large fortunes in iron and land. Charles, the builder, was assisted by Mr. John Howell, a master builder and amateur architect. The plan is simple: a huge central hall with four square rooms on either side. The service quarters are housed in two wings flanking the central building. The proportions of the mansion have been unfavorably criticized, but the magnificence of the central portion and the nobility of the interior are universally admired. The house is made of stone that has been stuccoed, an unusual feature in early Maryland houses. The furnishings are remarkable, many of the pieces having belonged to the Ridgeley family. There are interesting displays of china and *objets d'art,* some gifts and some on loan. Hampton, with its grounds and gardens, was purchased in 1948 by Mrs. Ailsa Mellon Bruce and presented to the nation. It is under the direction of the National Parks Service, which has turned over the administration to the Society for the Preservation of Maryland Antiquities. In one of the wings is a tearoom (luncheon); in the other an antique shop.

● North of the beltway, Md. 146 continues through the beautiful Dulaney Valley and crosses the **Loch Raven Reservoir** at 4.8 m. In **HESS**, at 11.7 m., just over the Harford County line, turn left on Hess Road to **Breezewood** (R), 1.3 m. Here the splendid Breezewood Collection of Oriental Art is open to the public on the first Sunday of each month in the summer season.

● On Md. 146, at 13.6 m., are the **Ladew Topiary Gardens** (R) (open May–Oct., Sat. and Sun., 11–4:30; weekdays by appointment). Here, spread over fourteen acres, are elaborate horticultural displays, featur-

Hampton

ing the intricately shaped shrubbery known as topiary. Among the living sculptures are a full-sized fox hunt and formal geometric designs.

At 3.6 m. on Md. 45, the main route (York Road) in **LUTHER-VILLE**, a well-to-do suburb, is the **Fire Museum of Maryland** (open weekends Apr. 1–Nov. 1; also by appointment), 1301 York Road (R). The museum, with its displays of antique fire-fighting apparatus and alarm equipment, is one of the finest collections of its type in the area.

The **Timonium Fairgrounds** (L), 5.5 m., is the site of the ten-day annual state fair held by the Maryland State Fair and Agricultural Society of Baltimore County. The focus of the grounds is on the Timonium Race Track, run by the nonprofit society. It is an odd and endearing little track, with no pretentions whatsoever. The track is one of three half-mile tracks in Maryland.

COCKEYSVILLE (264′ alt., 3,623 pop.), 8.2 m., is a developing industrial center that originally grew up around the Beaver Dam quarries. High-grade marble from Cockeysville was used in the construction of the Washington Monument in the District of Columbia, and St. Patrick's Cathedral in New York City.

● Turn left on Ivy Hill Road in Cockeysville to **Ivy Hill Forest,** which was founded in 1944. One hundred acres of woodland have been set aside as a demonstration area for sound conservation practices developed by the Maryland Conservation Federation.

The stone **Sherwood Episcopal Church,** at the corner of York and Sherwood roads, was erected in 1830. The church was named for the English home of the Cockey family, one of whose members donated the land and money for it. In 1876 the building was enlarged and the belfry added. A museum is open every weekend.

Shawan Road, 9.4 m. on the left, runs under I-83 through a valley famed for fox hunting in the nineteenth century.

The Elkridge Hounds was formed in 1878 as the Elkridge Kennels with headquarters at Elkridge Landing. In the early days the huntsmen-members in their red coats, white breeches, and black boots, and the ladies riding sidesaddle were a familiar Sunday morning sight as they rode from the Washington Monument in Baltimore toward the open country.

● **Oregon Ridge Park,** about 2.0 m. on Shawan Road, is on the ridge overlooking the valley. Merryman's Lane to the south from Shawan Road between I-83 and Oregon Ridge Park was named for the family of Lt. John Merryman. Merryman, who lived here, was the central figure in a celebrated Civil War legal struggle. Arrested and detained without formal charges, he obtained a writ of habeas corpus from Chief Justice Roger B. Taney to force his release. The military authorities controlling the government ignored the court order and successfully maintained that the ancient writ, guarantor of the liberties of Englishmen and Americans for centuries, was suspended during times of national emergency.

Continuing northward on Md. 45, an entrance lane (R), bordered by tall Norway spruce, leads to the gray stone **Jessop Church** on a high hill. The main part of this Methodist church was erected in 1811, although the present Gothic-type vestibule, the steeply pitched dormered roof, and the belfry were added in 1887.

The **Milton Inn** (R), 12.2 m., a large 2½-story stone building with dormers, was once the Milton Academy, where John Wilkes Booth and his brother Edwin received their early education. The institution, usually called Lamb's School, was founded in 1847 by John E. and Eli M. Lamb and was conducted by them until 1877. In 1885 the academy was moved to Baltimore and continued there until 1899.

Old Gorsuch Tavern (R) (private, but visible from the road), 14.3 m., is a 2½-story T-shaped brick house whose north wing was built about 1810 by Capt. Joshua Gorsuch. Beneath the tavern are brick-arched chambers where, it is said, Captain Gorsuch stored the silks, spices, and other goods he brought from his voyages to the East. Across the road from the tavern is the 3½-story **Gorsuch Stone Barn,** where Edward Gorsuch, slave-trader and son of Joshua, kept his "merchandise." In September, 1851, two Negroes escaped and with the aid of the Underground Railroad made their way to Lancaster County, Pennsylvania. In the attempt to retake them from their protectors, Edward Gorsuch was killed and his son Dickerson and several members of their party were wounded. The incident is known as the Christiana Massacre.

On the **Hereford Farm** (L) is the **Grand National Steeplechase Course.** Eighteen fences and two water jumps make the three-mile course one of the most hazardous in the United States.

HEREFORD is at the junction with concrete-paved Monkton Road.

● Right on this road to **MONKTON,** 3.0 m. Between Monkton and **SHEPPERD,** 6.2 m., is the northern boundary of My Lady's Manor, a tract the third Lord Baltimore bestowed in 1713 upon his fourth wife, Margaret. The 10,000 acres are now subdivided into farms and estates.

On **My Lady's Manor Course** the most important race is the My Lady's Manor Point-to-Point, a four-mile test for hunters. Other important races on the annual card are the Right Royal Cup, three miles over timber, and the John Rush Street Memorial, a two-mile steeple-chase over brush jumps.

At 3.3 m. on Monkton Road is the junction of Monkton Road and Shepperd Road; right 4.3 m. on Monkton Road to **St. James Church** (L), a T-shaped brick structure erected about 1750. The belfry is of much later construction. This was once within St. John's Parish, the mother church of which was at Joppa Town (*see* Tour 2a).

Areas of the **Gunpowder State Park** are on both sides of Md. 45 north of Hereford. The **Prettyboy Reservoir,** within the park, can be reached by turning left at 16.4 m. on Mt. Carmel Road (Md. 137) to **MOUNT CARMEL,** 4.5 m.

● At the intersection turn right (north) on Mt. Carmel Road; at 5.5 m. is a junction with Parkton Road. Go straight to a fork with Backbone Road and Prettyboy Dam Road at 6.0 m. Go right (straight) on Prettyboy Dam Road to the reservoir, 7.1 m.

Md. 45 continues north, crossing the **Pennsylvania Line** at 26.2 m. about eighteen miles south of York, Pennsylvania.

I-695 (Exit 20)–REISTERSTOWN–WESTMINSTER–PENNSYLVANIA LINE–(Gettysburg); 33.0 m.
U.S. 140

U.S. 140, the most direct route between Baltimore and Gettysburg, has four lanes from the beltway to Reisterstown and from Finksburg to Westminster; elsewhere there are two lanes. There is a by-pass around Westminster. A frontier trail in use by 1741, the route was first improved for year-round wagon travel in 1802 by a private toll road company, the state legislature having refused to vote public funds. Before the construction of rail-roads and the development of new farming country beyond the Appalachians, this was an important trade route linking the productive farms of central Maryland and Pennsylvania with the market and port of Baltimore.

Lining the highway between Baltimore and Reisterstown are housing developments, shopping centers, and the grounds of institutions and country estates. The only significant industrial concentration is in Owings Mills. Beyond Reisterstown most of the land is still being farmed, although with the extension of the metropolitan area the farms are gradually being broken up into commuters' residences. Agricultural activity is primarily dairy, poultry, and livestock husbandry; many thoroughbred horses are raised in the area. The rolling countryside along the highway affords pleasant vistas of wooded hills, cultivated fields, grassy pastures, ponds, and neat farm buildings.

To the right on U.S. 140 at Exit 20 of the Baltimore Beltway (I-695) is **PIKESVILLE** (516′ alt., 18,737 pop.), 0.0 m., settled before the Revolution but not named until after the War of 1812. Dr. James Smith, who owned much land in this vicinity, named

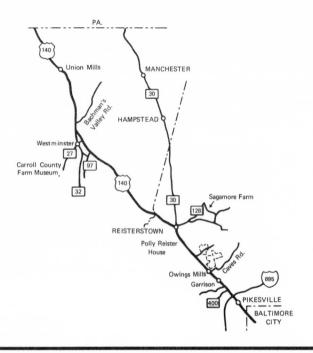

the village for his friend Gen. Zebulon Pike, who had been killed during the burning and seige of York (now Toronto), Canada. Before the war, Pike had led several expeditions into territory west of the Mississippi newly acquired by the United States. One of his discoveries was Pike's Peak in Colorado, which also is named for him.

Near the southern end of town is the **Pikesville Armory** (L), 0.6 m., a training center for military reserve units. The group of gray stone structures, erected in 1903, is dominated by the massive central building, where indoor polo was played for many years. During World War II prisoners of war were housed here.

Near the center of town is the old **U.S. Arsenal** (R), 1.0 m., erected by the federal government in 1816. The complex of red brick buildings served as a military post until 1879, when it was conveyed to the State of Maryland. In 1888 the General Assembly turned the property over to the Association of the Maryland Line, which operated it as a home for Confederate veterans. The old soldiers were moved to private nursing homes in 1932, and the usable buildings were subsequently occupied by several government and civic agencies. After World War II the Maryland State Police selected this historic site as its new headquarters, establishing themselves here in 1950, when considerable renovation and new construction were completed. In addition to administrative offices, the old arsenal now houses a training school for recruits to the State Police, other police departments, and certain state agencies.

In **Druid Ridge Cemetery** (L), 1.4 m., is the **Grave of Mary**

Barroll Washington, wife of Lewis Washington (1825–71), a great-grandnephew of George Washington. Lewis Washington was held hostage by John Brown at Harpers Ferry in 1859. Nearby is the **Queen Victoria Monument,** erected in 1903 by the St. George's Society of Baltimore and said to be the only monument to that venerable monarch in the United States.

At 2.5 m. is the junction with Md. 400.

● Turn left on this road to **Mount Wilson State Hospital,** 1.5 m. Mount Wilson was opened in 1884 as a summer resort for poor children of Baltimore with a bequest from a wealthy Quaker merchant, Thomas Wilson. In 1925 the state established a tuberculosis hospital here. Parts of the hospital are now used for geriatric and mentally retarded patients.

At 2.7 m. is the junction with Stone Chapel Road.

● Turn right on this road to **Old Stone Chapel** (L), a well-proportioned Classic-Revival structure with a Doric portico. This stuccoed church, white with gray trim, was built in 1862 with stones from an earlier chapel (1785). Robert Strawbridge, one of the founders of Methodism in America, preached in the first church on this site.

At 3.0 m. is the junction with McDonogh Road and Cradocks Lane.

● On McDonogh Road (L) at 1.5 m. is the **McDonogh School,** endowed in 1850 by John McDonogh, a wealthy New Orleans merchant who was born in Baltimore. After litigation over McDonogh's will, the school was established in 1873 to give a free education to "poor boys, of good character," who also were required to work on the extensive farmlands of the school. Now McDonogh is a preparatory school, open to those who can pay, and is styled a "Boarding and Country Day School."

● Turn right on Cradocks Lane to **Trentham** (L) (private, but visible from the road), 0.4 m., a square 2½-story stuccoed house with a hip roof, erected in 1860. Trentham stands on the site of a house built in 1746 by Rev. Thomas Cradock (1718–70), who named his home for the Free School of Trentham in Staffordshire, England, where he had taught before coming to America. In 1747 he opened a school here that was attended by boys of prominent Maryland families, including the Dulanys of Annapolis and the Cresaps of the frontier. Between the house and the road is an octagonal bathhouse, built about 1750 and equipped with two mahogany bathtubs.

The old **Ten-Mile House** (L), 3.3 m., a 2½-story stone tavern with a low gable roof and wide windows, was built about 1810. The foundations are thick, and the original staircases, fireplaces, and mantels are still in place. When the Reisterstown Pike was a main artery of trade, the tavern catered to wagon drivers and poorer travelers. This was the first home of the Green Spring Valley Hunt Club, and here Jake Kilrain had several workouts while training for his fight with John L. Sullivan in 1889.

The **Garrison Forest School** (R), 4.0 m., is a private day and boarding school for girls, founded in 1910.

At 4.5 m. is the junction with St. Thomas Lane.

● Turn right on this road to the **Garrison Forest Protestant Episcopal Church** (L), 0.8 m., a red brick cruciform building with a steeply pitched roof and a cupola belfry. The church, built in 1743, forms the present nave, but many changes and additions have been made. Established as a frontier "chapel of ease for the forest inhabitants" of St. Paul's

Parish, Baltimore, the church became a separate parish in 1745, taking the name of St. Thomas.

The Reverend Thomas Cradock (*see above*) was appointed first rector. Cradock (1718–70) was born in England on an estate of the Duke of Bedford and was sponsored by the duke for a career in the Anglican Church. His powerful patron sent him to Oxford and secured him a promising position after his ordination. Cradock was almost certain to become a bishop; however, upon the development of an attachment between himself and a sister of the Duchess of Bedford, he was induced to emigrate to Maryland.

To the right from the church on Garrison Forest Road is the junction with Caves Road, 0.4 m.

Along Caves Road, **The Caves** (L) (private) was the home of Charles Carroll, Barrister (1723–83), framer of Maryland's Declaration of Rights, and outstanding citizen during the Revolutionary period. Carroll lived here until 1754, when Mount Clare in Baltimore was completed. This tract, Bear Run, was patented in 1710. Part of the manor house built in 1730 has been incorporated into the present main structure. Banks of iron ore on the property were mined in the nineteenth century.

OWINGS MILLS, 4.6 m., an unincorporated center of light industry, now has manufacturers producing paper cups, soda straws, book matches, ice cream cones, and embroidered insignia. An industrial park site has been established, and new plants are being sought by local developers. In Owings Mills is the junction with Painters Mill Road, 4.7 m.

● To the left on this road is **Ulm House** (R), 0.3 m., a two-story brick home with a gable roof and awning, built in 1765 by Samuel Owings. The name *Ulm* is derived from the Upper, Lower, and Middle Mills owned by Owings and was long the trade name of the flour he milled. The building now houses a restaurant.

At 4.8 m. is the junction with the road (R) leading to the entrance of the **Rosewood State Hospital.** Established in 1888 as the Asylum and Training School for the Feeble-minded of the State of Maryland, the hospital now is devoted to the care, education, and training of mentally retarded children. Also on the grounds are centers providing intensive in-patient psychiatric treatment for children of normal mentality with serious emotional illnesses.

At 6.5 m. is the junction with Gwynnbrook Avenue (R) leading to the **Gwynnbrook State Game Farm**, where regional administrative offices of the Maryland Department of Game and Inland Fish are located. On exhibit here are various animals native to Maryland.

The **Hannah More Academy** (R), 8.2 m., until its closing in 1974, was the oldest existing Protestant Episcopal school for girls in the United States. It was founded in 1832 as a school for the poor by a Baltimorean, Ann Van Bibber Neilson. She named the school for an English bluestocking, Hannah More (1745–1833), who wrote plays and a novel before turning to philanthropy and writing religious tracts. The oldest structure on the campus, St. Michael's Chapel, was built in 1854.

The two parts of the unincorporated area of **REISTERSTOWN-GLYNDON** (735' alt., 4,216 pop.), 8.3 m., though both are primarily residential, differ considerably in character. Glyndon's peaceful, shady streets have changed little in appearance over the years. In Reisterstown, which lies on both sides of U.S. 140,

Ulm House

new houses, gas stations, and other buildings are constantly being constructed, while many of the older buildings have been demolished.

Reisterstown is named for the family of John Reister, a German immigrant who settled just north of Cockey's Mill Road in 1758. With the completion of the road through Reisterstown connecting Baltimore with Gettysburg and Hanover, the settlement became a regular stopping point for travelers. Among the inns established here was Forney Tavern, noted for the excellence of its food and liquors and patronized by "persons of wealth and fashion."

At the intersection of U.S. 140 and Cockey's Mill Road in Reisterstown, 9.4 m., the highway bends sharply. Jacob Medairy, who sought to prevent the road from coming through the town, built a house here in its path about 1804. The roadbuilders simply went around the house, and the deflection has been preserved through the many alterations of the road. At the bend is **Beckley's Blacksmith Shop** and the **Polly Reister House** (L), a 2½-story brick building with a one-story wing, erected in 1779. Originally the house and blacksmith shop were separated by a lane. The land on which the house was built was given by John Reister to his son-in-law, John Beckley, the village blacksmith.

On Cockey's Mill Road (L), which follows the old Indian trail from Patapsco Falls, is the old **Lutheran Cemetery** (L), surrounded by a low brick wall. It developed around a log cabin used for Lutheran services as early as 1765. By the cemetery is the former **Franklin Academy,** founded in 1820. It is said that Edgar Allan Poe (1809–49), while eking out a livelihood in Baltimore, applied for the advertised position of principal of the academy but was rejected. The academy became a public school in 1849 and now houses a branch of the Baltimore County Public Library.

In Reisterstown is the junction with Md. 30 at 9.7 m.

● In the northern part of Reisterstown is the junction of Md. 30 with Md. 128 (Butler Avenue), 0.5 m.

Turn right on this into Glyndon. To the left on Waugh Avenue, 0.9 m., is **Emory Grove,** a Methodist camp meeting ground since the end of the eighteenth century. The large frame Victorian hotel and cottages replaced tents that from 1870 annually accommodated thousands on two-week pilgrimages. Emory Grove is named for Bishop John Emory, who died in 1835 of a fractured skull, probably received from a horse's kick, while traveling from Reisterstown to Baltimore on the Reisterstown Pike.

At 1.3 m., Worthington Avenue junctions with Md. 128 (Butler Road). Go straight ahead on Worthington Avenue through the Worthington Valley. **Montmorenci** (L) (private), 2.4 m., a 2½-story fieldstone house covered with painted stucco, was one of the original estates of the Worthington family. The earliest part of the house, incorporated into the present structure, was possibly built in 1742.

At the junction with Tufton Avenue, 3.6 m., turn left to Belmont Road, 4.4 m. To the left on this is **Sagamore Farm** (closed to public as of June 1, 1976), a horse-breeding and training stables belonging to the Alfred G. Vanderbilt family. These are the home stables of several noted race horses, including Discovery and Native Dancer. The main building of the extensive physical plant contains a quarter-mile track and ninety box stalls.

● At 1.0 m. on Tufton Avenue is the western boundary of the **Maryland Hunt Cup Course.** Preparing the four-mile course for the race, which is over in less than ten minutes, takes two months. There is no pari-mutuel betting.

● On Md. 30, continuing northward from Reisterstown, is the junction with Montrose Road, a private road (no trespassing), 2.4 m. Along this road is **Anderson Chapel** (R), a small, plain, rectangular structure of stone with a square tower and a tin roof, surrounded by a wall. It was erected in 1854 for Col. Franklin Anderson, one of the owners of *Montrose.* Also on Montrose Road is the **Montrose School** (no trespassing), a state training school for delinquent girls and children. The gray stone buildings form a quadrangle around attractive lawns and gardens. The institution, established in 1886 as the Female House of Refuge, was purchased in 1918 by the state. The school received its present name when it was moved to this estate from Baltimore in 1922.

On the eastern end of the grounds is **Montrose,** a 2½-story stone mansion with a French roof and dormers. It is named for the Marquis of Montrose, a Scottish nobleman and Royalist military leader who was hanged by order of Parliament under Cromwell's Protectorate. The property was part of the extensive real estate held by William Patterson, a Baltimore shipping magnate and father of Elizabeth (Betsy) Patterson Bonaparte (*see* Downtown Baltimore). Betsy's son Jerome inherited the estate and lived on it several years, setting himself up in the manner of an English country gentleman. In 1840 he sold Montrose to Col. Richard Anderson; it subsequently was owned by Jerome's son, Charles Joseph Bonaparte (1851–1921), who served as secretary of the navy and attorney general in Theodore Roosevelt's cabinet.

● Md. 30 continues through farming country and small towns into Carroll County at 7.6 m. The only indication of industrialization visible from the road is the manufacturing plant of the Black and Decker Company (L), one of the largest producers of portable electric tools in the country.

HAMPSTEAD (913′ alt., 961 pop.), 9.1 m., one of the larger villages in the area, adjoins the Western Maryland Railroad. The town site was part of the tract Spring Garden patented to Dutton Lane in 1748. The first settlers were predominantly of English background, but they were joined before the end of the eighteenth century by Germans from Pennsylvania.

MANCHESTER (975′ alt., 1,466 pop.), 13.4 m., is near the site of one of the Susquehannock tribe's towns, Cepowig, at the headwaters of the Gunpowder River. Despite the aid of the Maryland authorities with whom the Susquehannock were on friendly terms, the tribe lost in a long and bitter war with the Iroquois and in 1675 was forced to seek refuge in the South. Settlers there, invaded by the homeless Indians and frequently victimized by their foraging, attempted to drive them elsewhere. During the hostilities the chiefs of the tribe, under a flag of truce seeking negotiations, were massacred by a company led by Col. John Washington and Maj. Thomas Truman. (The latter was impeached for his participation in this crime, but his punishment was very light.) The Indians then crossed into Virginia, where the settlers' discontent with insufficient protection given by the government against the tribe's depredations was a principal cause of Bacon's Rebellion. Surviving Susquehannock later returned to the north; one band settled within a mile of Manchester, near their old town, but moved on about 1750.

The first colonists in the area of Manchester were English; many Germans came here in the mid-eighteenth century. In 1758 a tract of land, now a part of the town, was patented to the "German churche," a combined Lutheran and Evangelical Reformed body that had built a church on the site by 1760, thus making this one of the oldest religious centers in Carroll County. In 1765 Capt. Richard Richards laid out a town on land patented to him, naming it after the English city of Manchester, where his family had lived. Though the town was a stopping point on the wagon road between Baltimore and Hanover for a while, it has primarily grown through the trade of local farmers. The railroad did not come through Manchester, thereby impeding the development of industry. The only significant manufacturers in the town are two clothing plants.

The buildings of the farms along the roadside become increasingly Pennsylvania Dutch in character as Md. 30 approaches the Pennsylvania line; the highway crosses the state line at 18.1 m. at a point about six miles south of Hanover.

On U.S. 140 is the **Children's Rehabilitation Institute, Inc.** (a development of the John F. Kennedy Institute), a specialized hospital for children with cerebral palsy. It is affiliated with The Johns Hopkins School of Medicine and Hospital. Established in 1937, the hospital treats children from all over the world.

The exit from U.S. 140 for Westminster is at 20.3 m. **WESTMINSTER** (744' alt., 7,207 pop.), the seat of Carroll County, was founded in 1764 by William Winchester, who on the original plat named it Westminster. However, it seems to have been known as Winchester during its early years. It became the county seat when Carroll County was erected from parts of Frederick and Baltimore counties in 1837. When the railroad came through in 1861, Westminster had 2,500 inhabitants, 40 stores, 3 banks, and several factories. Other factories, including a cannery first established at *Union Mills*, soon moved to Westminster to take advantage of the rail transportation available. Wheat was the principal crop of the county in the mid-nineteenth century; its production was sufficient to support five cooper shops in Westminster, making barrels to hold grain for shipping and storage.

During the Civil War Westminster was occupied three times in three successive years (1862–64) by soldiers of both armies. In 1863 a battle was expected in the Pipe Creek valley (by chance, it was fought at Gettysburg); the town was also an important Union supply depot. Quartered in and about Westminster at this time was a supply group of an estimated 5,000 wagons, 30,000 mules, and 10,000 men. The only significant action in the immediate vicinity during the war occurred when Confederate Gen. J. E. B. Stuart, on his way to join Lee in 1863, encountered the First Delaware Cavalry. Though Stuart's seasoned cavalry easily defeated the Union force, the engagement delayed his meeting with Lee, who had crucial information on the movements of the Union troops to give him, and thus was probably a contributory factor in the Confederate defeat at Gettysburg.

Westminster suffered little during the war and quickly returned to peacetime conditions afterwards. Changes occasioned by the extension of agriculture into the middle western wheat belt and the urbanization of the Baltimore area gradually transformed the county's farms from wheat producers to dairy and poultry establishments. This is still primarily an agricultural area, but a few manufacturers, producing clothing, electric controls, floor covering, shoes, and advertising material employ a number of county residents. Others commute to jobs in and around Baltimore.

Church Street (L) intersects Main Street in the southern part of town. At its end is the **Westminster Cemetery.** On a knoll at the entrance is an urn marking the **Site of the Union Church,** erected in 1755 to replace a log church, and for many years used by several congregations. Here Lorenzo Dow (1777–1834), the eccentric Methodist evangelist, held a number of revivals where many conversions were recorded. It is said that his success was due not only to the strength of his exhortations but also to a certain skill in dramatics. While preaching of the Day of Judgment, when the trumpet of Gabriel would blow and the regenerate separate forever from the unrepentant, he would have his assistants, hidden in leafy treetops on the grounds, blow louder and louder trumpet blasts. Near the urn is the grave of the town's founder, William Winchester.

At 206 E. Main Street is the **Shellman House** (L) (open Tues.–Sun., 1–4), headquarters of the **Carroll County Historical Society.** A 2½-story brick town house built in 1807, it is furnished as a residence with authentic period pieces. It was the home of a noted local character, Miss Mary Shellman, who reportedly gave Gen. J. E. B. Stuart a "piece of her mind" when his troops occupied the town in 1863. As the operator of the town's first telephone service, she entertained Alexander Graham Bell here when he visited Westminster. On display at the house are collections of nineteenth-century dolls, early household implements and farm tools, hobnail glass, and a few rare flags.

Behind the Shellman House is a replica of **God's Well,** which received its name during a protracted drought in 1806. The few fortunate owners of wells that had not gone dry locked their pumps and refused water to travelers and neighbors. Only the aged daughters of the town's founder, Lydia and Betsy Winchester, opened their gates. They placed a sign on their well, "Free Admittance to All. Water belongs to God." Eventually, the story goes, all other wells in town went dry, but "God's Well" furnished enough pure, cool water for all.

The pump of this well was originally installed at the Pipe Creek Church of the Brethren and is of a type once common in

Shriver Homestead

the area. The shafts of these pumps, which have been sunk up to ninety feet into the ground, are constructed of sections of logs, each about twenty feet long and one foot in diameter. The bore, augered out by hand, increases from about two and one-half inches at the bottom to four and one-half inches at the top, where the drawing apparatus is attached.

On N. Court Street one block (R) from Main Street is the **Carroll County Courthouse,** a handsome Classic-Revival structure built in 1838. The columned portico, the steps, the cupola, and the wings have been added to the original building. Diagonally across from the courthouse is the **Church of the Ascension,** a rectangular stone building with large arched windows that was erected in 1844.

On the lawn of the **Westminster Post Office** (R), at Main Street and Longwell Avenue, is a marker noting that Carroll County was the first county in the country to have complete rural free delivery service. Inaugurated in 1899, it operated with four two-horse wagons, each carrying a driver and a mail clerk. Extensive material on the early mail service is in the custody of the County Commissioners at the courthouse annex.

Continuing along Main Street is **Western Maryland College** (R), a private liberal arts school. It has been coeducational since it was founded in 1867 as a successor to a small academy organized in 1860. Not until well into the twentieth century, however, did students of both sexes actually attend the same classes together. The college was the first school in Maryland to employ trained athletic instructors and to build a gymnasium. The grounds of the college were once the "Commons," the site of the local race track and a favorite political meeting ground in the early 1800s.

From U.S. 140 take the exit for Md. 97 (south).

● At 0.4 m. turn right onto Main Street. At 0.8 m. turn left onto Washington Avenue (Md. 32) to Gist Road (R), 1.5 m.; turn right on this to **Friendship Valley Farm** (private, but visible from the road). This two-story brick house was built in 1795 by Col. Joshua Gist on the part of the Gist family land bequeathed to him. The log house originally on the site is believed to have been destroyed in a fire set by a kitchen servant who was homesick for Baltimore and hoped the family would move to the city rather than rebuild.

Colonel Gist, in the last years of his life, frequently had his man-servant lay him out in his coffin, which, according to general custom, had been built in advance in order to be ready for its inevitable, but unpredictably timed, function. When properly attired and arranged, he would summon his family to comment upon the effect. On these occasions he would solemnly enjoin them not to bury him until the third day after his death. It seems that when his brother, Gen. Mordecai Gist, died, his burial was delayed until his closest friend, Gen. Nathaniel Greene, could come to pay his final respects. General Greene, arriving the third day after his friend's death, asked to view the body. He noted an eyelid twitching. General Gist was revived and lived to marry a third time and have another child.

On U.S. 140 take the Center Street exit. Just out of West-minster to the southwest, at 500 S. Center Street, between Md. 32 and 27, is the delightful **Carroll County Farm Museum** (open May–Oct., weekdays and holidays, 12–5; July–Aug., 10–4, except Mon.). Antique equipment and a marvelous barn are on display. A community pond is also on the property.

At 25.0 m. on U.S. 140 north of Westminster is the junction with Bachman's Valley Road.

● To the right on this road is the farm that belonged to Whittaker Chambers (L). On the farm was the pumpkin patch where, in 1948, Chambers, in the presence of a House investigating committee, opened a hollowed-out pumpkin and produced several spools of microfilm. These, along with similar documents, came to be known as the "Pumpkin Papers" and were important evidence in the widely pub-licized case of Alger Hiss. Hiss, a former State Department official, was convicted of perjury charges after denying that he had passed information to Chambers, a former magazine editor, for transmission to a communist spy ring.

At 28.3 m. on U.S. 140 is the **Shriver Homestead** (R) (open May–Nov., Mon.–Sat., 10–5; Sun., 12–5) in the village of Union Mills on Big Pipe Creek. The rambling, clapboard-sheathed structure has been the Shriver family home since the first part of it was built in 1797 by the first Shrivers to settle in the area. As the family increased, additions were made to the house with little regard for the overall form. It now has twenty-three rooms, which are interestingly furnished with pieces of the various fashions of the nineteenth and early twentieth centuries. All the furnishings are from the storerooms of the house itself. In continuous use as a residence, the house has also served as inn, store, post office, magistrate's office, and school. The old mill was built in 1797 with bricks made on the property. Other mills and houses were constructed along the creek, and a Shriver descendant established a cannery here that was later moved to Westminster. Both Union and Confederate troops camped here on the way to Gettysburg.

U.S. 140 crosses the **Pennsylvania Line** at 33.0 m., beside a Mason-Dixon line marker at a point about twelve miles south-east of Gettysburg.

⑤CHEMATIC TOURS

The three schematic tours, which take the driver along I-95, the Harbor Tunnel Thruway, and the Baltimore-Washington Parkway (S 1); I-695, the Baltimore Beltway (S 2); and I-495, the Washington Beltway (S 3), are intended mainly to indicate access routes to tours that can be joined from these express-ways.

S 1. (Wilmington)–DELAWARE LINE–BALTIMORE–DISTRICT OF COLUMBIA LINE; 85.9 m.

I-95 (through toll from Delaware Memorial Bridge), Harbor Tun-nel Thruway (toll), and Baltimore-Washington Parkway) limited access)

Restaurant-service area south of Aberdeen; new restaurant-service area now under construction near Perryville

This route across Maryland is the one a traveler passing through is most likely to take and the one from which he is least likely to see anything of interest, with the notable excep-tion of the Baltimore outer harbor. The first part of the route, the Kennedy Expressway (Interstate 95), was opened Novem-ber 14, 1963, by President John F. Kennedy a week before his assassination. Aside from a short commercial stretch near Hartford, Connecticut, it is the last link in a system of limited-access and toll roads that runs from Washington, D.C., to Augusta, Maine.

For travelers who are sightseeing the expressway is not con-venient, especially beyond the Susquehanna River, where a toll must be paid regardless of where one intends to exit. Once off the highway, another toll must be paid to reenter.

I-95 crosses the **Maryland-Delaware Line,** 0.0 m., at a point about fifteen miles from the Delaware Bridge. At 0.8 m. is the interchange with Md. 279.

North on Md. 279 is the **Delaware Line,** 1.2 m., and **NEWARK, DELA-WARE,** 3.8 m.
To the south is **ELKTON** and a junction with Tour 2a, 3.3 m.

At 9.5 m. is the interchange with Md. 272.

To the north is **CALVERT,** 5.3 m., and the junction with a side tour of Tour 1a.
To the south is a junction with U.S. 40, 1.7 m., and Tour 2a.

The interchange with U.S. 222 is at 16.1 m.

To the north is **PORT DEPOSIT,** 3.7 m., and **CONOWINGO,** 9.2 m., and a junction with Tour 1a.
To the south is the junction with U.S. 40, 1.9 m., and Tour 2a.

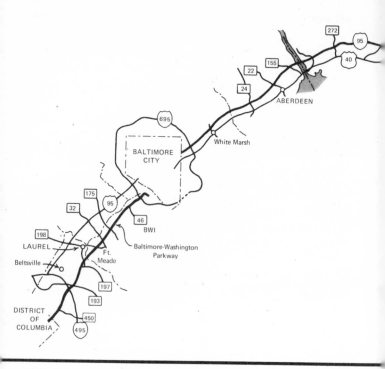

TOUR S 1

Just beyond the interchange is the tollgate.

The Kennedy Expressway crosses the **Susquehanna River** at 17.3 m. on a great bridge that spans the high bluffs and offers a magnificent view and reaches the interchange with Md. 155 at 19.3 m.

North on Md. 155 is **CHURCHVILLE**, 6.6 m., and the junction with a side tour of Tour 1a.

To the south is **HAVRE DE GRACE**, 2.5 m., and the junction with U.S. 40 and Tour 2a.

At 23.6 m. is the interchange with Md. 22.

To the north is **CHURCHVILLE**, 4.3 m., and the junction with a side tour of Tour 1a.

To the south is the junction with U.S. 40 and Tour 2a in **ABERDEEN**, 2.0 m.

The **Restaurant and Service Area** provides food, rest rooms, gasoline, and other services to motorists traveling along this route.

The interchange with Md. 24 is at 31.7 m.

To the north is **BEL AIR**, 6.0 m., and the junction with U.S. 1 and Tour 1a.

To the south is the junction with U.S. 40 and Tour 2a at 1.7 m.

At 41.3 m. is the White Marsh interchange. This is the first toll paying entrance.

Go north 2.5 m. to the junction with U.S. 1 and Tour 1a.
Go south 1.0 m. to the junction with U.S. 40 and Tour 2a.

At 44.5 m. is the junction with the Baltimore Beltway (I-695) and Tour S 2 (no toll). The last exit off the Kennedy Expressway (no toll) is at 48.3 m., a little more than a mile within the limits of Baltimore City; it connects the traveler with U.S. 40 and Tour 2a. This interchange is the beginning of the Harbor Tunnel Thruway (still I-95), seventeen miles of limited-access highway and tunnel, opened November 29, 1957, which provides a fast route through Baltimore.

Going south on the thruway, entrance but no exit is possible until after the tunnel, which crosses the Patapsco River.

Going north, however, there are five exits from the tunnel mouth to this point.

Exit 1 leads to Holabird Avenue and **Fort Holabird** (no admittance), established during World War I and named for Brig. Gen. Samuel Beckley Holabird of the Quartermaster Department during the Civil War. During World War II this was the largest U.S. Army Signal Corps Depot in the world; it was the home of the Army Intelligence Corps, including the Intelligence School, facilities for research in intelligence equipment, and storage for records of some 7.5 million people who had received clearance from the army since the start of World War II. Fort Holabird was also the induction center for the Baltimore-Washington area. Exits 2 and 3 lead to O'Donnell Street. To the east O'Donnell Street is a route into the Dundalk section of Baltimore County just beyond the city limits. To the west the street leads into the harbor area along the Northwest Branch of the Patapsco. Exit 4, at Lombard and Ponca streets, is the route to the Baltimore City Hospitals, established by the city as the Bay View Asylum in 1867; several of the recent additions can be seen from the highway on the right. Via Exit 5 the traveler can turn onto U.S. 40 and join Tour 2a going east or he can turn onto Md. 151. Going north, Md. 151 is Erdman Avenue, which leads to Northwest Baltimore. Going south Md. 151 becomes North Point Boulevard and a side route of Tour 2a, which leads to **SPARROWS POINT** and **Fort Howard.**

From the end of the Kennedy Expressway (at the connection with U.S. 40) to the mouth of the **Baltimore Harbor Tunnel,** the Thruway passes through an area of heavy industry. The tunnel itself, 6,300 feet long, is the longest open-trench tunnel ever built. Its twin steel tubes, each with two lanes, were constructed in shipyards in 300-foot sections, each launched into the water like a ship. The sections were then towed to a basin near the tunnel site, where they were covered with concrete inside and out, and the foundations were laid for the roadbeds. When heavy enough, the sections were sunk into the prepared and precisely graded trench, and divers joined the pieces together with steel pins.

Beyond the southern mouth of the tunnel, at 54.1 m., is the tollgate and a series of exits from the Thruway for travelers going south; going north, motorists may enter the Thruway but may not leave before passing through the tunnel.

From this section of the highway the Baltimore skyline (R) and the harbor present a dramatic view.

Exits 1 and 2 are interchanges with Frankfurst Avenue, which lead west towards Brooklyn Park and east into the Fairfield area of the harbor. Exit 3, 55.1 m., is an interchange with Md. 2 and Tour 25 at **BROOKLYN PARK,** and Exit 4, 56.3 m., is (A) another exit to Md. 2 and Tour 25, just above **GLEN BURNIE** and

(B) an exit to Md. 3 and Tour 26. At Exit 5, 57.8 m., the tour turns off the Harbor Tunnel Thruway and I-95 on to the Baltimore-Washington Parkway.

I-95, the Harbor Tunnel Thruway, continues to Exit 6, 1.0 m., an interchange with I-695 (the Baltimore Beltway) and Tour S 2, and to Exit 7 at U.S. 1 and Tour 1b, 3.4 m. in Elkridge.

The Baltimore-Washington Parkway goes north into **BALTIMORE** via Russell Street, and makes a junction with U.S. 40 and Tour 2a (Franklin Street going west and Mulberry Street going east) in the center of the city.

The Baltimore-Washington Parkway south is a beautifully engineered and landscaped limited-access highway that in 1954 replaced U.S. 1—one of the ugliest and most dangerous highways in the United States—as the through route to Washington, D.C.

At 58.9 m. is the interchange with I-695 and Tour S 2, and at 61.1 m. is the interchange with Md. 46.

Md. 46 leads to **Baltimore-Washington International Airport** (BWI), 2.0 m., a 3,200-acre field opened on June 24, 1950. It is one of the largest airfields in the United States and one of the few in the area capable of accommodating large jet airliners. Turn right on Md. 170 to reach the facilities of the Electronics Division of Westinghouse Electric Company, where more than 8,100 people work in the development of military electronic systems of all kinds. Westinghouse employs nearly ten times more people than any other firm in Anne Arundel County, and its economic impact on the area has been large.

At 66.7 m. is the junction with Md. 175.

To the east is **Fort George G. Meade,** 1.2 m., a 13,000-acre installation named after the major general who commanded the Army of the Potomac during the Civil War battle of Gettysburg. Established in 1917 to train troops for World War I, Fort Meade was enormously expanded during World War II. By 1945 almost 70,000 soldiers were on its rosters. During World War II it was primarily a reception center, replacement depot, special training center, and finally a separation center. It is now headquarters for First Army Command and the location of the National Security Agency.

To the west on Md. 175 is a junction with U.S. 1 and Tour 1a at **JESSUP,** 3.0 m. To the left of this short stretch of road lies the **Maryland Institution for Women,** established in 1941 as the Women's Prison of the State of Maryland; the **House of Correction,** a medium-security prison created in 1874; and the **Clifton T. Perkins State Hospital,** which opened in 1960 as a maximum-security mental hospital for those found not guilty of crimes by reason of insanity and for inmates of prisons who have become mentally ill.

On the right, just before U.S. 1, is the **Patuxent Institution,** an experimental detention center in Maryland begun in 1959 providing for psychiatric treatment of offenders under indeterminate sentence judged to be "defective delinquents"—that is, people whose unstable personalities have led them to persist in crime.

At 68.9 m. is the interchange with Md. 32.

To the east is **Fort George G. Meade,** 1.6 m.
To the west is the junction with U.S. 1 and Tour 1b at 2.8 m.

At 70.7 m. is the interchange with Md. 198.

To the east, Md. 198 is another entrance to **Fort Meade,** 2.0 m.
To the west, Md. 198 joins U.S. 1 and Tour 1b at **LAUREL,** 2.7 m.

At 74.0 m. is the interchange with Md. 197.

Going east on Md. 197, on the left for two miles is the **Patuxent Wildlife Research Center,** a marshy area along the Patuxent River used by the U.S. Fish and Wildlife Service to study wildlife problems related to agriculture.

Md. 197 makes a junction with Jericho Park Road, 3.8 m. To the left on Jericho Park Road is a junction with Bowie Race Track Road, 5.4 m.; a left turn (straight ahead) here leads to **Bowie Race Track,** 6.9 m. (*see* Tour 27).

To the west, Md. 197 backtracks to **LAUREL** and a junction with U.S. 1 and Tour 1b, 3.2 m.

At 76.4 m. is the interchange with Powder Mill Road, which crosses the National Agricultural Research Center of the U.S. Department of Agriculture—more than 10,000 acres of experimental pastures, ranges, orchards, gardens, field crops, forest, and soil treatment plots (*see* Tour 1b).

At 79.1 m. is the interchange with Md. 193.

To the east on Md. 193 is the **Goddard Space Flight Center** of the National Aeronautics and Space Administration. This opened in 1960 on 550 acres adjoining the Agricultural Research Center. Work is done on the design and development of satellite and rocket systems, which included the U.S. program for sending a rocket to the moon. Next to the flight center is the **Bureau of Standards Radio Station, WWV.**

Going west on Md. 193, to the right of the interchange is **GREEN-BELT,** one of the three experiments in building a planned community undertaken by the Resettlement Administration of the New Deal. On about 3,300 acres in what was then a nearly rural section, about 885 houses and apartments housing some 3,000 people were built from 1935 to 1938. The design of the project was greatly influenced by that of Radburn, New Jersey, a planning experiment of the late twenties undone by the depression. The houses were grouped around open space into which no vehicles could enter, and pedestrian walks crossed over the roads between these "super blocks." The landscaping utilized the small stream that winds through the town. Schools, a community center, and a shopping center—one of the first of its kind—were built as a part of the project, and the whole development was incorporated as the self-governing town of Greenbelt in 1937.

Originally Greenbelt was built for families who earned not more than $1,250 a year, but in 1941, to relieve the housing shortage created by defense operations near Washington, the Public Works Administration added 1,000 more units (and about 4,000 more people) for which there were no income restrictions; priorities were set according to the essential nature of the defense work done by the head of the family. This new area of Greenbelt did not receive the care in planning that had been given the original section. In 1953 the U.S. government sold all the land and improvements to the residents of the town, and the houses are now individually owned. Various nonprofit groups purchased the open space that had originally served the whole community and have developed much of it in apartments and houses.

At 1.0 m. is the junction with Md. 201 (Kenilworth Avenue); a left turn here to Good Luck Road, 1.8 m., then another left brings the traveler to the entrance to **Greenbelt Regional Park,** 2.6 m., 6501 Greenbelt Road, an 1,100-acre wildlife sanctuary that opened in 1964.

Md. 193 continues to a junction with U.S. 1 and Tour 1b in **COLLEGE PARK,** 2.9 m. From here it is a dualized route through the outer northern suburbs of Washington; eventually it enters the District of Columbia via Connecticut Avenue.

At 79.5 m. is the interchange with the Washington Beltway (I-495) and Tour S 3.

The interchange with Riverdale Road is at 81.9 m. and with

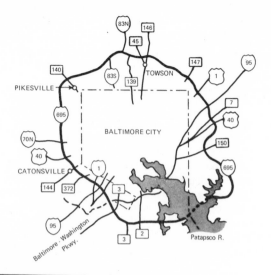

Md. 450 (Defense Highway) and Tour 27 at 83.6 m. At 83.9 m. is the interchange with Md. 202.

To the east on Md. 202 (R) is the **Prince George's County Hospital** (follow signs), which lies next to the highway at the southeastern edge of the interchange. Further east, Md. 202 intersects U.S. 50 and Tour 24, 1.2 m., and Md. 214 and Tour 28, 5.9 m., and traverses tobacco country to **UPPER MARLBORO** and a junction with Tour 26, 13.5 m.

To the west, Md. 202 intersects Md. 450 and Tour 29 just outside of **BLADENSBURG,** 0.5 m.

The Baltimore-Washington Parkway makes a junction with Kenilworth Avenue at 85.4 m.

Kenilworth Avenue intersects U.S. 50 and Tour 24 and crosses the **District of Columbia Line** at 0.5 m. It is the fastest route, via E. Capitol Street (which turns off at 2.6 m.) to the Capitol Hill section of Washington. Beyond E. Capitol Street it continues as the Anacostia Freeway, which joins the Capital Beltway at the Woodrow Wilson Bridge to Alexandria, Virginia.

The Baltimore-Washington Parkway crosses the **District of Columbia Line** at 85.9 m. and enters downtown Washington via New York Avenue.

S 2. I-695, THE BALTIMORE BELTWAY; 37.2 m.

The Baltimore Beltway (Interstate 695) is a quick route around Baltimore City. It allows easy access into the city at various points. This schematic tour plots the access routes to tours that can be approached by the beltway.

I-695 intersects Md. 2 and Tour 25a at 0.0 m.

Baltimore City (*see various Baltimore tours*) is north on Md. 2.
Md. 2 enters the city via Hanover Street.
Tour 25a turns south on Md. 2.

At 1.1 m. the Baltimore Beltway intersects Md. 3 and Tour 26a. Md. 3 joins the beltway at this point.

At 3.0 m. is the intersection of the beltway with Md. 3 N (Tour 26a) which becomes part of the Baltimore-Washington Parkway.

Turn north on the Baltimore-Washington Parkway (Tour S 1) and Md. 3 (Tour 26a) to enter Baltimore City via Russell Street.

Turn south on the Baltimore-Washington Parkway (Tour S 1) to reach the District of Columbia, 27.0 m.

At 4.2 m. is the junction with the **Harbor Tunnel Thruway.** The Thruway was opened to traffic on November 30, 1957, providing a by-pass around Baltimore. Each of the two tunnels that runs under the Patapsco River is 1.7 miles long. Access roads are available only to tunnel patrons. The Tunnel Thruway becomes I-95 (Tour S 1), the John F. Kennedy Expressway.

At 5.1 m. is the intersection of the beltway and Alt. U.S. 1, which joins U.S. 1 and Tour 1b at 1.5 m.

At 5.7 m. the beltway intersects I-95, a fast, limited-access route to the Washington Beltway, 22.5 m.

At 6.3 m. is the junction with U.S. 1 and Tour 1a.

To the right U.S. 1 enters Baltimore and crosses town on Wilkens Avenue, Fulton Avenue, North Avenue, and leaves via Belair Road. Tour 1a continues northeast of the city.

Tour 1b turns left off the beltway.

At 7.3 m. is the intersection with Md. 372, which crosses the city line on Wilkens Avenue and joins U.S. 1 at 1.5 m.

At 8.5 m. is the intersection with Md. 144 and Tour 2b.

To the right Md. 144 enters the city at 0.8 m. as Frederick Avenue. Tour 2b continues to the left in **CATONSVILLE.**

At 9.8 m. is the intersection with U.S. 40.

US. 40 enters Baltimore at 1.5 m. via Edmondson Avenue and crosses the city on Mulberry and Orleans streets.

At 8.9 m. U.S. 40 joins Tour 2a.

At 11.2 m. is the intersection with I-70 N, a fast, limited-access route to points west.

At 16.9 m. is the intersection with U.S. 140 and Tour 33.

To the right U.S. 140 enters the city as Reisterstown Road, 1.9 m. Tour 33 continues to the left.

At 20.9 m. is the intersection with I-83 S, which enters Baltimore via the Jones Falls Expressway, 3.1 m.

At 22.3 m. is the intersection with I-83 N, the Baltimore-Harrisburg Expressway, which leads to points north.

At 22.9 m. is the intersection with Md. 139 (Charles Street), a fast route into Baltimore City. Charles Street crosses the city line at 3.5 m. and junctions with U.S. 1 and Tour 1a at 8.0 m.

At 23.9 m. is the intersection with Md. 45 and Tour 32.

To the right Md. 45 enters Baltimore at 3.2 m. via York Road. Tour 32 continues to the left.

At 24.5 m. is the intersection with Dulaney Valley Road, a side route of Tour 32.

At 28.9 m. is the intersection with Md. 147 (Harford Road), a side route of Tour 1a.

Turn right to Baltimore, 1.4 m.

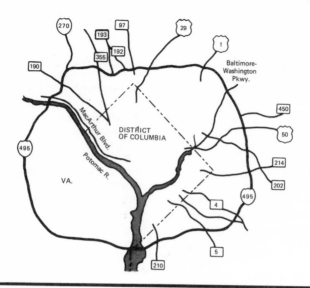

TOUR S 3

To the left Md. 147 is a side route of Tour 1a.

At 30.5 m. is the intersection with U.S. 1 and Tour 1a.

To the right U.S. 1 enters Baltimore as Belair Road, 1.4 m.
To the left U.S. 1 is the main route of Tour 1a.

At 32.1 m. is the intersection with I-95 and Tour S 1.

To the right is the Harbor Tunnel Thruway, which crosses the city line at 2.8 m.
To the left I-95 is the main route of Tour S 1.

At 33.5 m. is the intersection with Md. 7, a side route of Tour 2a.

To the right Md. 7 joins U.S. 40 at the city line, 3.4 m.
To the left Md. 7 is a side route of Tour 2a.

At 33.8 m. is the intersection with U.S. 40 and Tour 2a.

To the right U.S. 40 enters the city at 2.8 m.
To the left U.S. 40 is the main route of Tour 2a.

At 34.5 m. bear right, continuing on the Baltimore Beltway (Windlass Freeway).

At 37.2 m. is the intersection with Md. 150, Eastern Boulevard, a side route of Tour 2a.

Bear right on Md. 150 to the interchange with the Harbor Tunnel Thruway, which rejoins the Baltimore Beltway after passing through the tunnel.

S 3. I-495, THE WASHINGTON BELTWAY; 40.6 m.

Interstate 495, the Washington, or Capital, Beltway, provides a quick route around the city of Washington, D.C., as well as access to routes extending across Maryland and Virginia. This schematic tour lists access routes to tours in Maryland.

I-495 crosses the Potomac River from Virginia, 0.0 m., and enters Montgomery County, Maryland. Immediately after entering Montgomery County is the junction with MacArthur Boulevard.

To the left on MacArthur Boulevard past the **Naval Ship Research and Development Center** (*see* Tour 4) is the junction with Md. 189, a side route of Tour 4, 4.3 m.

At 5.5 m. is **Great Falls** (*see* Tour 4).

To the right MacArthur Boulevard leads to **Cabin John Bridge,** 1.2 m., and **GLEN ECHO** and the **Clara Barton House,** 1.7 m.

At 2.3 m. I-495 intersects Md. 190.

To the right, at 6.2 m., Md. 190 enters the District of Columbia and joins Wisconsin Avenue.

At 3.9 m. there is an interchange with I-270.

To the north I-270 parallels Md. 355 and Tour 4. I-270 also connects with routes north and west of **FREDERICK** (*see* Frederick Tour and Tours 2b, 2c, 3, 4, and 5).

At 5.6 m. the beltway intersects Old Georgetown Road (Md. 187), a side route of Tour 4 (*see* Josiah Henson).

At 6.5 m. the beltway intersects I-270 and Md. 355.

To the left Md. 355 is the main route of Tour 4.

To the right Md. 355 (Tour 4) passes the **National Institutes of Health** and the **Naval Medical Center** and enters **BETHESDA,** a Washington suburb. At 4.2 m. Md. 355 enters Washington, D.C., via Wisconsin Avenue.

Between Md. 193 and Md. 192 stands the **Washington Temple of the Latter Day Saints** (*see* Tour 4), on the north side of the beltway.

At 10.3 m. is the intersection with Md. 192, a side route of Tour 4.

To the left on Md. 192 is **FOREST GLEN.** A right turn on Forest Glen Road leads to **St. John's Cemetery** (*see* Tour 4).

At the intersection with Md. 97 (Georgia Avenue), turn north to the intersection with Md. 144 and Tour 2b in **COOKSVILLE,** 23.4 m.

U.S. 29 and the beltway intersect at 11.7 m.

North on U.S. 29 is **COLUMBIA,** and a connection can be made with Old Columbia Pike, a side route of Tour 2b, at 19.2 m.

At 14.3 m. is the Montgomery–Prince George's County Line.

At 16.8 m. is the intersection with U.S. 1 and Tour 1b.

To the north is a junction with Md. 212 in **BELTSVILLE** and the **National Agricultural Research Center,** 1.6 m. (*see* Tour 1b).

To the south is the interchange with Md. 193 in **COLLEGE PARK.**

At 19.9 m. is the intersection with Md. 295, the Baltimore-Washington Parkway, and Tour S 1.

To the north, 5.5 m., is the intersection with Md. 198, a side route of Tour 1b.

To the south, 4.1 m., is the interchange with Md. 450 and Tour 27; at 4.4 m. is the interchange with Md. 202, a side route of Tour 27 (Landover Road). Continue south to Washington via Kenilworth Avenue, 6.4 m.

At 22.4 m. is the intersection with Md. 450 and Tour 27.

To the left Md. 450 crosses Prince George's County and Anne Arundel County to **ANNAPOLIS** (*see* Annapolis Tour), 22.3 m. at Church Circle.

To the right is the junction with the Baltimore-Washington Parkway and Tour S 1, 3.2 m. At 3.8 m. is the junction with Md. 202 and Tour 27 in **BLADENSBURG.**

At 23.5 m. I-495 intersects U.S. 50 and Tour 24.

To the left are **BOWIE** and Tour 27, 6.5 m.; Md. 3 and Tour 26b, 7.8 m.; Md. 424, a side route of Tour 27; Md. 2, 18.3 m.; and **ANNAPOLIS,** 19.4 m.

To the right is Md. 202 (*see* Tour 27, Bladensburg), 2.5 m. U.S. 50 intersects the Baltimore-Washington Parkway and Tour S 1 just before entering Washington. U.S. 50 enters Washington via New York Avenue.

At 25.5 m. the beltway intersects Md. 202 and Tour 27.

Go left to a junction with Md. 408, a side route of Tour 26a in **UPPER MARLBORO,** 9.6 m., to reach Md. 214 and Tour 28 in **LARGO.**

At 27.3 m. is the intersection with Md. 214 and Tour 28.

Turn left to cross Md. 202 and Tour 27 in **LARGO,** 0.9 m.

Turn right to Capitol Heights, a suburb of Washington, and enter the District of Columbia via E. Capitol Street, 3.7 m.

At 31.3 m. is the intersection with Md. 4 and Tour 26a.

To the left Md. 4 intersects Md. 223, a side route of Tour 29, 2.3 m. Turn left, then right on Md. 408 to reach **UPPER MARLBORO,** 4.3 m.

To the right, Pennsylvania Avenue leads to the **District of Columbia Line,** 5.0 m.

The Washington Beltway crosses Suitland Parkway, a side route of Tour 29 (*see* Andrews Air Force Base).

At 33.8 m. is the intersection with Md. 5 and Tour 29.

Left on Md. 5 to Md. 223, a side route of Tour 29, which leads to **CLINTON,** 4.1 m.

To the right is the Suitland Parkway and **Andrews Air Force Base,** a side route of Tour 29, 2.7 m.

At 38.3 m. is the intersection with Md. 210 and Tour 31.

To the left is Washington, D.C., 1.3 m.

Tour 31 continues to the right.

At 40.6 m. is the **Maryland-Virginia Line.**

ANNAPOLIS

ANNAPOLIS (20′ alt., 29,592 pop.), capital of the State of Maryland and site of the U.S. Naval Academy, is a small city of dignified, gracious, and attractive character, greatly influenced by its distinguished history. Unlike the neighboring cities of Washington (described by President John F. Kennedy as a city of Northern charm and Southern efficiency) and of Baltimore, which was cut off from its Southern commercial connections during the Civil War and became an eastern extension of the Midwest, Annapolis has remained essentially Southern in character. The past is evident in the present appearance of the city. When it was designated a National Historic Landmark in 1965 by the Department of the Interior, Secretary Stewart Udall noted: "Annapolis has the greatest concentration of eighteenth-century buildings anywhere in the United States." These buildings remain because Annapolis has maintained a sufficient degree of affluence and importance as the center of state government and, in later years, through the substantial presence of the Naval Academy. Annapolis has become a pleasure-boating center, attracting yachtsmen from nearby metropolitan areas and developing into a major stopping point on the Inland Waterway. Thus the maritime orientation of the city, vital for trade in its early years and important until recently for the seafood industry, has been renewed and gives Annapolis yet another attraction and source of income.

During the winter months political maneuvering is the primary activity and major topic of conversation. The legislature meets then, and debate rages between representatives from the rural and urban sectors of the state. Politics, with compromises, deals, lobbying, and a hectic social schedule, though commonly found wherever politicians gather in the world, is a traditional pastime of the South, where it is considered natural and respectable and where the participants go about their activities with relish. In contrast, after the legislature adjourns, especially during the long, balmy days of summer, the pace of life changes dramatically. Inhabitants and visitors sit or sail, converse and drink, in unhurried, peaceful enjoyment of life.

Puritans fleeing from intolerance and persecution in Virginia were the first white settlers in the Annapolis area. They came in 1649, welcomed by Lord Baltimore, who collected a tax (quit rent) on their land, and by the Provincial Assembly, which, on April 21, 1649, passed the Toleration Act, which allowed the free exercise of religion by all who believed Jesus Christ divine. They chose a site (now covered by water) on the north bank of the Severn River, calling it Providence. Within a year, population throughout the region had grown so rapidly that a new county was created, named "Annarundell" after the wife of Cecilius, second Lord Baltimore.

Across the Atlantic, Puritans were staging a successful rebellion that kept the affairs of Maryland in a constant state of turmoil and confusion. Its leader, Oliver Cromwell, perhaps influenced by Lord Baltimore's practice of toleration (beneficial to both his fellow Catholics and to Puritans), did not annul the proprietary charter, although in 1654 his government did send commissioners to take over the administration of the colony. The ousted governor, William Stone, led a military force against the Puritan stronghold at Providence. During the ensuing Battle of the Severn, which took place on March 25, 1655, the Puritans seized two ships that had been anchored in the river, an armed merchant ship, the *Golden Lion,* and a small New England vessel with two guns. The greater firepower this gave them proved decisive, and the proprietary force was routed, probably off Horn Point. Stone and nearly all his men were captured. The encounter was perhaps the first pitched battle fought between white men in North America and the last ever fought near Annapolis. The issue of who should govern the colony was not resolved, however, and Puritan authority continued to be disputed until a formal agreement in favor of the proprietor was signed in 1658.

By 1670, a map of the colony revealed a new settlement called Arundelton, across the Severn from Providence, which was soon to overshadow and ultimately replace its predecessor. In 1684 this point of land between Acton's (now Spa) Creek and Deep (now College) Creek was laid out by surveyor Richard Beard as Anne Arundel Town from 100 acres donated by Robert Proctor, an innkeeper, Richard Hill, a merchant, and the lord proprietor. In 1694 it became the capital of the province.

Attempts were made as early as 1662 to move the seat of provincial government to Anne Arundel County. In 1683 one session of the assembly actually met at a house on the ridge near West River; but not until another decade passed was the capital moved permanently from Catholic St. Mary's City to Protestant Anne Arundel Town. By then the majority of the colony's population was non-Catholic. Anne Arundel Town was centrally located and close to the narrowest part of the Bay, making it more convenient for people residing on the Eastern Shore. Most important, there was a new royal governor, Sir Francis Nicholson, an experienced and skillful administrator, who convinced the assembly that the move was necessary. A year later, in 1695, he was probably instrumental in changing the name of the new capital to Annapolis, in honor of the future queen of England, Princess Anne.

Nicholson had a profound influence on the development of the town. He took Beard's uninspired survey and added several distinctive features that have endured to the present, including two circles on the high knoll where the church and State House were to be built and the streets radiating from each that followed the main points of the compass. It was an aesthetically pleasing and functional design, even if it did create some rather odd-shaped lots and now contributes to the traffic congestion of the automobile age. Imposing vistas of the State House and St. Anne's Church, both made of brick burned from local clay, resulted along East, West, Main, and Francis streets. Sections of the town were designated for different purposes in Nicholson's plan. To the north, away from the harbor, were small lots for tradesmen, collectively called Bloomsbury Square. Today this area is filled with government structures, including the imposing new House of Delegates building.

Potentially obnoxious neighbors such as tanners and brewers were relegated to the perimeter of town. Along the basin that was to become the harbor was a "shipcarpenter's lot." Tobacco warehouses and customs offices were planned for the waterfront. Two regular market days were set aside each week. In 1696, Nicholson persuaded the assembly to charter a school, which they named after King William. About the same time Dinah Nuthead moved her late husband's printing press from St. Mary's City in order to supply all the forms that government needed, even then, in order to function.

From the beginning there was a lively male social life in the capital, especially during meetings of the assembly and on occasions when the planters and their families came to town to inspect the latest imports or to transact business. As the wealth of the colony and the amenities of its capital increased during the eighteenth century, planters' wives came to town to enjoy the social events while the assembly was in session. By the 1740s the gayest and most socially conscious people from all over Maryland converged on Annapolis to attend the theater, dance at balls, and wager on the races. The breeding of fast horses was a primary concern to the gentlemen of the colony, and government officials from the governor down enthusiastically joined the planters in the competition to import fine thoroughbreds in order to improve the local stock. By 1744, visitors were commenting on the elegance of the clothing worn by the young ladies at assembly balls, which were held in a house with "a back room for wines, punch and sweetmeats, and the playing of cards, dice and backgammon." Balls lasted well past midnight, and it was the custom for the gentlemen to escort their partners home. Indeed, for all its celebrated urbanity and its brilliant legal minds, Annapolis in its eighteenth-century Golden Age was no solemn center of intellectual activity. The most eminent and able men of the province did not debate philosophical questions in their club meetings but exerted themselves to produce sallies of satirical wit and light and sophisticated conversation to accompany the superb meals liberally accented with liquor. In the decades before the Revolution well-connected lawyers and opulent tobacco planters built elegant town houses, many of which still stand, in which the gay, frivolous life of London society was cultivated with all the exaggerated enthusiasm of a provincial capital. These beautifully proportioned buildings reflect the great wealth, education, and taste of the men of the period, who produced little else in the way of the arts or literature but who thoroughly enjoyed and appreciated all the cultural achievements of European society.

The French and Indian War did not greatly disturb the lives of most Annapolitans, although Gov. Horatio Sharpe, preoccupied with the safety of the western borders of the colony, had little opportunity to give the grand parties that were his delight. Even the weighty events leading up to the Revolution did not disrupt the social life of the city. Although there was high feeling and much debate on the issues, men who were soon to become radicals or firm Tories remained close friends in nonpolitical pursuits. Racing, dancing, and gaming went on more briskly than ever. When George Washington arrived for the September races in 1771, he lost money (eight pounds) but consoled himself by going to the theater four times and attending three balls. A year later he returned with somewhat better luck, winning thirteen pounds on the horses but losing five pounds at cards, as well as attending the theater four times and appearing at one ball.

Underlying issues and conflicting interests between the colonists and the British king and Parliament occasioned increasingly violent debates and demonstrations as Marylanders were inexorably propelled toward revolution. When the Stamp Act was passed in 1765, Zachariah Hood, a former Annapolis merchant, was sent from England as stamp agent. A crowd of Annapolitans led by Samuel Chase, then an aspiring young attorney, paraded an effigy of the agent to the shipping post, pillory, and gibbet, finally burning the hanging figure over a flaming tar barrel. Several days later a more violent mob ransacked the stamp agent's new office. This convinced Hood, who had landed secretly, that he could not safely remain in Annapolis, much less execute his duties, and he fled to Long Island. A majority of Marylanders favored the nonimportation agreements with other colonies, which in 1765 and 1774 demonstrated opposition to Parliament's restraints on colonial trade. In these agreements the colonists agreed to boycott all taxed articles, including tea. On October 14, 1774, the brig *Peggy Stewart* reached Annapolis. Anthony Stewart, part owner of the brig named for his daughter, defied public sentiment and paid the despised duty on its cargo of tea. Radical patriots gathered in a threatening mob, demanding that the tea be destroyed. Stewart, in an effort to save his family and home from harm, allowed his ship to run aground on the far side of Spa Creek and set fire to it. The ensuing conflagration destroyed ship and cargo and provided a more dramatic spectacle than the Boston Tea Party.

The tide of resistance soon mounted to the point of open rebellion. A revolutionary government was set up in Maryland in which William Paca, Samuel Chase, and Charles Carroll of Carrollton, all trained as lawyers, took leading roles. These men, whose houses still may be seen, were all signers of the Declaration of Independence. Thomas Stone, the fourth Maryland signer, also had Annapolis connections, having studied law here as a young man and having lived here again later in his career.

No battles of the Revolutionary War were fought in Maryland, but many Marylanders served gallantly in the Continental Army. During the War, Annapolis, in addition to being the headquarters of the Maryland government and military organization, was an assembly point for soldiers of the state before they marched to the front. In 1781, French and American troops of the main allied army passed through the city. The French officers were charmed by the elegance and appearance of the capital and its young ladies, who were in turn quite taken with the polite manners and dashing uniforms of the Frenchmen.

Peace and acknowledged independence came to the United States in 1783. In November the Continental Congress, as yet lacking a permanent meeting place of its own, convened in the

Maryland State House. On December 23, 1783, George Washington came before them in a formal ceremony in the Senate Chambers to resign his commission as commander in chief of the Continental Army. Although Congress departed in June, 1784, Annapolis, because of its central location in the new country, for a time remained a contender for the site of the nation's capital. But political considerations eventually resulted in the creation of a new city on the banks of the Potomac. In 1786, delegates of five states met in Annapolis to discuss the need for stronger federal government. They planned the convention that met in Philadelphia in 1787 that drew up the Constitution of the United States, ratified by Maryland in April, 1788.

Soon after the Revolution, first commerce, then wealth and social influence, deserted Annapolis for Baltimore, the state's rapidly growing center of trade. The Annapolis institution perhaps most seriously affected by this change was St. John's College, which was grandly planned to be the center of higher learning for the Western Shore of Maryland when it was chartered in 1784. The state granted the school a generous yearly allowance from public funds, but an economy-minded legislature withdrew it in 1806. The school then went through more than a century of financial difficulties, occasionally so intense as to cause a temporary closing. With surprising tenacity it always managed to reopen and has educated many of Maryland's most eminent citizens. Similar spirit rallied the citizens and supporters of Annapolis to stave off attempts to move the seat of the state government to Baltimore.

In 1808, after the H.M.S. *Leopard* had attacked the U.S.S. *Chesapeake* and when war with Great Britain seemed imminent, the federal government built Fort Severn on Windmill Point, on the site of rudimentary fortifications that had been erected for the defense of the harbor during the Revolution. This stronghold possibly prevented the British from attacking the city during the War of 1812. More than once British squadrons anchored near the mouth of the river, but none made any attempt to take the capital.

Fort Severn was garrisoned by the army until 1845, when the historian and secretary of the navy, George Bancroft, selected it as the site for the new naval school he was planning. There was much opposition in Congress to his plan, so he accomplished the transfer of Fort Severn to the navy quietly within the War Department. Adroitly he secured funds, instructors, and facilities in ways that would not require the school to be brought up for debate before Congress. It soon became well-established as the U.S. Naval Academy, with such a reputation as an efficient and patriotic institution that few politicians who wished to be reelected dared oppose its appropriation requests.

During the Civil War, the Naval Academy was moved to Newport, Rhode Island, in order to protect the young men from the hostile atmosphere, for Annapolis was thoroughly in sympathy with the South. In 1861, Annapolis was occupied by Massachusetts troops under Gen. Benjamin F. Butler, who arrived by the Perryville–Havre de Grace ferryboat that he had commandeered in order to avoid rioting Southern sympathizers in Baltimore. No acts of violence met him in Annapolis, although support for the

Confederacy remained strong. It is said that one old gentleman, refusing to take the oath of allegiance to the Union required of all passengers on the local railroad, walked the thirty miles between Annapolis and Baltimore twice each week to and from his job. Though Annapolis saw no military action, it shared in the efforts and privations of the war. A large military hospital and camp were set up on the grounds and in the buildings of the Naval Academy and St. John's College. After 1862, thousands of paroled prisoners awaited formal exchange while confined to the area around the Annapolis suburb now called Parole. Early in the war, the Fifty-third New York Infantry, known as D'Epeneuil's Zouaves, was stationed at Annapolis. Their colorful uniforms— baggy blue pants, blue coats with yellow lapels, yellow leggings and red kepis with yellow tassels—matched their colorful be- havior. Nearly all the Zouaves were of European origin, and many were professional adventurers and soldiers of fortune. Their drinking and gambling parties and fiscal irresponsibility were long remembered by the city. Perhaps the most enduring tale of the Zouaves' stay concerned the time the officers of the regiment became suspicious of the number of beardless, slender young soldiers swathed in the unit's baggy uniform and, upon questioning them, found that they were young women.

When the war ended Annapolis returned to its earlier pattern of life, centered on the state government and the Naval Acad- emy. Although the fortunes of the old families and the impor- tance of the seafood industry steadily declined, the growth of the government and the academy compensated sufficiently for the losses to the economy. The quick and popular victory in the one-sided Spanish-American War in 1898 gave the navy new prestige. Shortly thereafter when Theodore Roosevelt, who had long advocated a more powerful navy, became president of the United States, the Naval Academy was greatly enlarged and completely rebuilt. Several square blocks of the city were en- closed within the new walls. The displaced residents and new academy personnel occasioned a minor real estate boom as new houses were constructed on small lots carved out of the large old lots between the State House and the Academy. Construc- tion to the west and in other outward directions continued, and much of the surrounding area soon became heavily built up, though it was not incorporated into the city proper until the 1950s.

In the course of the twentieth century, Annapolis has gradually become a modern city. Old roads leading to Washington and Baltimore were improved, then high-speed, four-lane highways were built, thus more efficiently connecting Annapolis to those cities and to points beyond. The completion of the Chesapeake Bay Bridge in 1952 followed by a second span in 1973 caused Annapolis and the Eastern Shore to be linked far more effec- tively than they had been by the old ferry. New apartment com- plexes on and near the city's waterways attract commuters from the nearby large cities. Many navy personnel retire here, and in general real estate in the town has a good, possibly an inflated, value.

Among the factors making Annapolis an enjoyable place to live is the lack of air pollution; very little manufacturing is done here. The principal industries are the tourist trade, government, and the building, outfitting, and refitting of boats. Some of the finest yachts in the country are built in Annapolis.

Many changes in Annapolis over the years are visible to the discerning eye: the old brick patterns showing where walls have been extended in both large and small buildings; the widened but still narrow streets; the broad chimneys rising above houses which are covered with modern asbestos siding and which almost surely no longer depend upon fireplaces for heat and cooking. The presence of numerous small details such as these give an even greater authenticity to the atmosphere of continuity with the past. They complement the many striking large houses that have been preserved, and in some cases, restored. The age of the city is apparent in the earlier forms, and the vitality of the city is shown by the alterations that have been made to accommodate the changing needs of its residents through the years. And so Annapolis, protected from decay by its institutions and at least partially insulated from the radical changes of rapid commercial development, remains to please its residents and its visitors.

ANNAPOLIS TOUR

The tour of Annapolis is divided into four sections. The first section covers the area between Main and Hanover streets and between St. John's campus and Market Space. The second section covers the area bounded by Compromise, Main, and South streets. The Naval Academy is discussed in the third section, and other points of interest are listed in the final section.

The **Harbor** of Annapolis, the scene of the earliest activities and first buildings of the city, is still an important center of economic and social life. Although ocean-going freighters and trading vessels have long since grown too large for its shallow waters, many oystering and fishing boats tie up year-round at the city dock. In the summer hundreds of pleasure craft move in and out of the harbor and hold space at public and private facilities. The warehouses, where tobacco was stored before shipment to Europe and imported goods kept until sold to the colonists, have disappeared. At the head of the city dock is the **Market Space.** The first market house here was built in 1728. The present **Market House** (1), restored in 1970, is a long, one-story structure completed in 1858 on a site next to that of the market of 1728.

Across the Market Space, at the corner of Green Street, stands the **Frederick Grammar House** (2). The three-story structure, of brick laid in Flemish bond, was built in the 1790s by Frederick Grammar, a German immigrant who came to Annapolis during the Revolution and made his living as a baker. Typically Georgian in style, the house has a rectangular floor plan and chimneys placed symmetrically at each end.

On the opposite side of the Market Space on the corner of Randall Street is the **Middleton-Randall Building** (3), begun by Samuel Horatio Middleton early in the eighteenth century as a tavern and remodeled in the 1790s as a store and Federal Customs House. The building, now a restaurant, has survived a fire and undergone many alterations since its earliest portion was constructed. The all-header bond in which the bricks in the facade are laid gives evidence of the first period of construction.

Leading off from Market Space at the corner just above the Middleton-Randall Building is a narrow twisted street that has borne several names over the centuries but which today is called Pinkney Street.

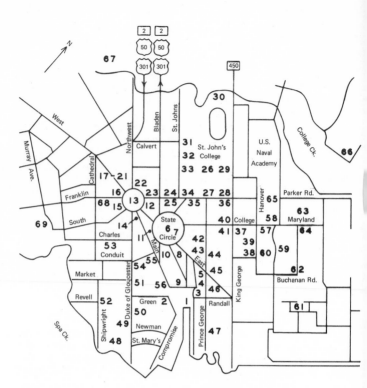

KEY

1. Market House
2. Frederick Grammar House
3. Middleton-Randall Building
4. Barber Store
5. Slicer-Shiplap House
6. State House
7. Old Treasury Building
8. Monroe and Callahan Houses
9. Wallace, Davidson, and Johnson Building
10. Donaldson-Steuart House
11. Brooksby-Shaw House
12. Governor's Mansion
13. St. Anne's Church
14. Maryland Inn
15. Anne Arundel County Courthouse
16. Reynolds Tavern
17. Claude House
18. Frances Bryce Boarding House
19. Ghiselin Boarding House
20. Golder House
21. Quynn House
22. Post Office
23. William S. James Senate Office Building
24. House of Delegates Building
25. Legislative services building
26. McDowell Hall
27. Liberty Tree
28. Library (Woodward Hall)
29. Charles Carroll the Barrister House
30. French Soldiers Memorial
31. Mellon Hall
32. Francis Scott Key Memorial Hall
33. Johnson House
34. Maryland Hall of Records
35. Bordley-Randall House
36. Ogle House
37. Lockerman-Tilton House
38. Peggy Stewart House
39. Rectory of St. Anne's Parish
40. Chase-Lloyd House
41. Hammond-Harwood House
42. John Brice III House
43. John Brice II House
44. Paca House
45. James Brice House
46. Patrick Creagh House
47. Sands House
48. Carroll Mansion
49. St. Mary's Church
50. Ridout House
51. City Hall, or Ballroom
52. Upton Scott House
53. Jonas Green House
54. Lloyd Dulany House
55. Callahan House
56. Price House
57. United States Naval Academy
58. Naval Academy Museum
59. Herndon Monument
60. Naval Academy Chapel
61. Bancroft Hall
62. Tecumseh
63. Mahan Hall
64. Macedonian Monument
65. Tripoli Monument
66. Jeannette Monument
67. Navy–Marine Corps Memorial Stadium
68. Mount Moriah A.M.E. Church
69. Acton

ANNAPOLIS TOUR

At the intersection of Pinkney Street and Market Space is the **Barber Store,** or **Tobacco Prize House** (4), which dates from the 1830s. The **Slicer-Shiplap House** (5) (R), 18 Pinkney Street, one of the few surviving large houses of its period, has been restored. Probably built in 1723, the 2½-story house has several notable features: the unusual shiplap siding, the steeply pitched roof, the gable end, and the alternating rows of headers and stretchers (English bond) that are characteristic of English construction in the seventeenth century. The house, erected on land belonging to colonial Gov. Sir Thomas Bladen, was first occupied by Edward Smith, who kept a tavern here. Its present name derives from a Golden Age occupant, William Slicer, a Scottish cabinetmaker whose work was advertised in the *Maryland Gazette* in 1769. Late in the nineteenth century, Frank B. Mayer, a locally well-known painter whose *Burning of the Peggy Stewart* hangs in the State House, lived here. Historic Annapolis, Inc., now uses the house as an office.

Continue up Pinkney Street to the corner and look up East Street to the left for one of the vistas intentionally created by Governor Nicholson's seventeenth-century plan. At the end of the street on top of the hill is the imposing brick **State House** (6) (open daily except Christmas Day, 9–5), surmounted by a tall, white-painted octagonal dome and cupola. The first State House on the site, called the Stadt House in deference to King William's Dutch origin, was completed in 1698. In 1699 lightning struck it, killing a member of the House of Delegates and injuring several others. Damages from the lightning and the fire that resulted were repaired, and the building continued in use until 1704, when it was completely gutted by fire. The second State House was completed in 1707, but the construction was evidently not of the best quality, for only fifty-nine years later Thomas Jefferson wrote that the State House, "judging from its form and appearance, was built in the year one. . . ." Described in 1769 as "an emblem of public poverty," the dilapidated structure was slated for demolition later that year and a new State House planned by the legislature. The cornerstone for the present State House was laid in 1772, but construction was delayed by the Revolution and the building probably was not occupied by the legislature until 1780. The intricate wooden dome designed by Joseph Clark was not completed until 1793.

The main entrance to the State House, facing Francis Street, is protected by a one-story pedimented Corinthian portico with marble floor, wooden columns, iron capitals, and cast-iron railing, all of which were later additions. The portal opens into a wide arcaded hall of similar classic order under the central dome, which has arched and oval windows. The delicate plaster ornament in the Adam style is primarily the work of the artisan Thomas Dance, who was killed in a fall from the scaffold as he was finishing the job.

From the hall, one enters the beautiful **Old Senate Chamber,** which has been painstakingly restored to its original appearance. Over the entrance is a curved balustraded visitors' gallery supported by fluted Ionic columns. Opposite the entrance is a circular, stepped speaker's platform with its chair in a pedimented niche. The walls of the chamber are painted plaster. Typical of late-Georgian design are the twenty-four-pane sashed windows with deep paneled window seats, shutters, and elaborately ornamented cornices. Two of the desks and one of the chairs are all that remain of the original furnishings made by the noted Annapolis cabinetmaker John Shaw. The others are reproductions. The Congress of the United States met here from November 16, 1783, to June 3, 1784.

George Washington resigned his commission as commander in chief of the Continental Army on December 23, 1783, in this room, and on January 14, 1784, the Congress ratified the Treaty of Paris here, formally ending the Revolutionary War. Over the fireplace hangs a portrait by Charles Willson Peale of Washington, Lafayette, and Col. Tench Tilghman, a Marylander who served as one of Washington's aides. Peale began his career as a saddler in Annapolis. His talents as a painter soon became known, and several prominent Annapolitans provided the money that made it possible for him to study art in London at the school of Benjamin West. On his return, Peale painted many of the leading figures of the Revolutionary War era.

The present Senate Chamber and Chamber of the House of Delegates are in the large, west extension of the capitol, completed in 1905. The two square chambers are decorated in a modified Italian-Renaissance style with marble columns and vaulted arcades. Both have sky-lighted ceilings of stained glass.

Standing before the main entrance is a bronze statue of Roger Brooke Taney (1777–1864), one of the finest legal minds Maryland has produced. The statue is the work of William H. Rinehart, "Father of Maryland Sculpture." A duplicate of the statue stands in Mount Vernon Place, Baltimore. To the left is a statue by Baltimore's Ephraim Keyser of Baron de Kalb, who was killed while leading Maryland and Delaware troops at the Battle of Camden, South Carolina, on August 16, 1780. To the right is a cannon taken from St. Mary's River and identified as one of the field pieces possibly brought over on the *Ark* in 1634 to defend the first settlers of Maryland.

The only other structure on State House hill is the **Old Treasury Building** (7), completed in 1737 as the Office of the Commissioners for Emitting Bills of Credit. As its present name indicates, it later became the Office of the Treasurer. It is a small cruciform building of brick laid in Flemish bond with a barrel-arched ceiling. The weight of the ceiling repeatedly caused damage to the walls. In 1949 a complete rehabilitation and restoration of the Old Treasury was authorized, and the building is now both structurally sound and beautiful. It is used as the Tour Office of Historic Annapolis, Inc.

Leading off from State Circle to the east-southeast, toward the waterfront, is Cornhill, a charming street of eighteenth- and early-nineteenth-century houses, many of which have been restored in recent years to their original appearance. The adjacent **Monroe and Callahan Houses** (8) at 49 and 53 Cornhill Street are good examples of dwellings built by craftsmen living in late-eighteenth-century Annapolis. Thomas Callahan was a prosperous tailor and William Monroe was a moderately successful carpenter. Both leased the lots on which they built their homes from the merchant Charles Wallace. In 1769, Wallace purchased a tract of largely undeveloped land that ran from the marshy basin at the foot of Main Street up the hill to State House Circle. Almost immediately, he laid out the property into lots along two new streets, Cornhill and Fleet, which ran from the circle to the water. Undoubtedly he chose the names carefully, hoping that the area would soon resemble (in miniature at least) its London counterpart. At the foot of Cornhill and Fleet streets, Wallace envisioned an impressive row of four stores situated on the new wharf, housing goods transferred by open shallow-draft boats from ships anchored out in the Severn. All that remains of the four houses known collectively as the **Wallace, Davidson, and Johnson Building** (9) is approximately two-thirds of the brick shell of 26–28 Market Space, which today is a restaurant.

Walk to Main Street, turn right and continue to Francis Street (R). The **Donaldson-Steuart House** (10) (R), 10 Francis Street, is probably one of the three or four oldest brick buildings in Annapolis. It was completed before 1738 on land that Governor Nicholson had given for a free school. The builder was probably Henry Donaldson, who, with his brother James, was a prominent Annapolis merchant. In 1738, Dr. George Steuart took over Donaldson's lease to the property and in turn sublet to a number of innkeepers including Isaac McHard, who kept his "Sign of the Indian King" here in 1773.

Maryland State House

Continue on Main Street to **Chancery Lane** (R), the best known of the alleys that connect the streets of Annapolis at convenient points. Walk up Chancery Lane to State Circle. On the left is the **Brooksby-Shaw House** (11) (L), a two-story frame building with a captain's walk on the crest of the gambrel roof. It is named for its first owner, Cornelius Brooksby, and the well-known Annapolis cabinetmaker John Shaw, who occupied the house at the time of his death in 1829. The house, which was probably constructed in the 1720s, is owned and used by the Maryland Historical Trust.

Walk around State Circle to the **Governor's Mansion** (12), which was completed by 1870 and extensively remodeled in 1936, when the mansard roof and other mid-Victorian features were replaced by broad gables, chimneys, Palladian windows, and other features of the Georgian five-part house. The five-part form was the most popular design in Maryland for large residences of the eighteenth century. Essentially a plan for country houses, it was successfully brought into the city and can be seen in the Hammond-Harwood, Brice, and Paca houses in Annapolis. It consists of a large central block with symmetrically designed outbuildings on each side connected to the central section by the fourth and fifth parts—one-story passage halls called hyphens, or curtains. This carefully balanced design satisfied the classically attuned eye of the eighteenth-century man of culture. Its length provided for a sufficient number of rooms to accommodate the household without making any part more than two rooms deep, thus allowing cross ventilation in the hot summers of the Tidewater country.

Turn left on School Street and proceed to **St. Anne's Church** (13) (open to the public). It has a square clock tower, octagonal steeple, and circular apse. This is the third church built here for St. Anne's, or Middle Neck, Parish since the parish was established in 1692. The first appropriations for the original church were made in 1695, but construction proceeded erratically. In 1699 the situation had reached such scandalous proportions that the assembly assessed a substantial fine on the contractor, Edward Dorsey, for "negligence and omission" and

"Disengaged" him from building the church. Under new supervision the church was probably ready for use in 1704 and was definitely completed by 1706. By the 1770s the building had deteriorated seriously. Its condition was especially apparent in contrast to the fine new houses and the nearby theater built during this opulent Golden Age of Annapolis. A poet complained in the pages of the *Maryland Gazette:* "Here, in Annapolis alone, God has the meanest house in town." Plans for a new church were made and in 1775 the old structure was razed. Many materials collected for the new church were taken for private use during the Revolutionary War, and the building was not completed until 1792. In the interim, the Annapolis theater was used for worship. The second church burned in 1858. Construction of the present church, incorporating the walls and tower of the older building, was completed in 1859. The steeple was added in 1865–66. The silver communion service, given to the parish by King William III, escaped the fire, because it was stored in a bank vault. The service, now used every Sunday, was made in 1695/6 by George and Francis Garthorne, prominent London makers of royal plate, and bears the royal arms and cipher.

St. Anne's Parish was relatively small compared to other Maryland parishes in the colonial period. The population of a parish, assessed at a flat rate per taxable head to support the established church, determined the income of the rector. An unusually large number of men held the rectorship of St. Anne's, generally staying here only until a richer parish was open. The notorious Bennett Allen, inducted in 1767, left a year later for All Saints' Parish in Frederick County. While in Annapolis Allen began his feud with the Dulany family that culminated in London during the American Revolution when he killed Lloyd Dulany (*see below* [54]) in a duel. Another well-known rector of St. Anne's Parish was Jonathan Boucher (*see Tour 28*), inducted in 1770, who supplemented the meager income of his rectorship by keeping a boarding school for the sons of the gentry. The most notable of his pupils was John Custis, George Washington's stepson. Washington himself frequently stayed with Boucher in the rectory on his visits to Annapolis before the Revolution (*see below* [39]).

Gravestones in the small churchyard mark the final resting place of several seventeenth-century residents of Annapolis and also some members of prominent eighteenth-century families. The remains of Robert Eden, the last colonial governor of Maryland, were reinterred here in 1926.

The **Maryland Inn** (14), Church Circle and Main Street, was built in the 1770s as an inn by Thomas Hyde, who advertised it in the *Maryland Gazette* as an "elegant brick house" that was "100 feet front, 3 story high, has 20 fire places, the rooms mostly large and well finished, and is one of the first houses in the state for a house of entertainment." This "flatiron" type building has been one of the leading hotels in Annapolis ever since, with modifications being made as necessary. It was restored in 1953.

The **Anne Arundel County Courthouse** (15), Church Circle and Franklin Street, is a large brick block with a domed cupola and a two-story arcaded entrance porch. The original part of the building was completed in 1824. It was remodeled in 1892, and some parts of it were made fire-resistant in 1925. A large annex that looms behind the older structure was completed in 1952.

Reynolds Tavern (16), Church Circle and Franklin Street, was standing in 1747. Its first owner, William Reynolds, was a "hatter" as well as an innkeeper. The two-story building has a dormered gambrel roof and broad end chimneys. The facade, laid in all-header bond, is marked between the first and second stories by the unusual stringcourse that arches over the windows. Well preserved in the basement is the original kitchen, with two huge fireplaces, a brick "stove," and a patterned brick floor. The building is owned by the National Trust for Historic Preservation.

For almost 200 years, the only road to Annapolis was **West Street,** which intersects Church Circle to the north of Reynolds Tavern. Once called Cowpens Lane, in the eighteenth century West Street was lined with boardinghouses, taverns, and homes of storekeepers and craftsmen.

Philip Syng, noted Maryland silversmith, lived on West Street in the early eighteenth century, as did William Faris and Abraham Claude, rival watchmakers. The **Claude House** (17) still stands at 26 West Street. Above it at number 18 is the **Frances Bryce Boarding House** (18), built soon after the Revolution, and just below it, at numbers 28–30, is **Ghiselin Boarding House** (19). The most notable of widow Ghiselin's boarders was Thomas Jefferson, who lodged with her during January and February of 1784 while he was attending the Continental Congress, then meeting in Annapolis. Jefferson's diary notes that he paid five shillings per day for a room plus an additional two shillings and sixpence for firewood, and that he often dined with Mrs. Ghiselin during these months (even though she had earlier been accused by a local resident of serving oyster shells in her stew).

At 42–50 West Street is the **Golder House** (20). Golder lived and kept a store here at the "Sign of the Waggon and Horse" until 1765, when he died an untimely and ghastly death from eating poisonous mushrooms. His son ran the store after the Revolution, and then for many years the house was used as a tavern, first known as the Sign of the Pennsylvania Farmer and later as Hunter's Tavern.

On the opposite (north) side of West Street are the sites of Annapolis's second colonial theater, the home of Samuel Chase in the 1770s, and William Faris's shop. The lower end of the triangle formed by Cathedral and West streets was developed by Allen Quynn, a prosperous cordwainer (shoemaker) who served as a vestryman of St. Anne's Parish, mayor, and long-time delegate to the General Assembly. By the late 1700s, Quynn owned property on both sides of West Street and lived in the imposing brick house (21) on the north side. It was this building that housed William Rind's library in the 1760s and that was later owned and enlarged by John Johnson, Jr., chancellor of Maryland in the mid-1800s.

At the end of the first block on the south side of West Street stood the original town gates, which were closed each night to discourage marauders and strays, and just beyond the gates was the old racecourse where the finest American horses vied for the Jockey Club Purse each fall.

Around Church Circle from West Street, just beyond the intersection with Northwest Street, is the **Post Office** (22), a dignified two-story brick building with wood and sandstone trim designed in the late-Georgian style. The rectangular structure, completed in 1910, is crowned with a dormered hip roof surrounded by a balustrade. On the roof is an octagonal cupola with gilded dome and weather vane. Beyond the post office is the **William S. James Senate Office Building** (23), dedicated in 1974. One block further on College Avenue is the **House of Delegates Office Building** (24) (L), completed in 1975, and across the street is the new legislative services building (25) (R), completed in 1976.

Continuing east on College Avenue, one block beyond the new House of Delegates building, is **St. John's College,** between St. John's and King George streets. St. John's is a nonsectarian, coeducational school with an unusual curriculum based on the classical idea of liberal education. Graduates of the college complete a four-year study of philosophy and mathematics, science, music, language, and literature taught by tutors. The "textbooks" are the works of the most eminent Western thinkers, from Plato and Aristotle to Einstein and

Freud. Classes are small and the size of the college is restricted to 400 students in order to preserve the atmosphere of an intimate, intellectual community. Rather than expand on its present site, in 1964 the school established a new campus in Santa Fe, New Mexico, with the same curriculum as the Annapolis campus and, through a faculty exchange program, with some of the same tutors.

St. John's has had a long and eventful history. It is usually regarded as a successor to King William's School, a grammar school established in 1696. There are few records available for King William's School in the eighteenth century. Although it may not have operated continuously, it survived in some form until 1786 when some of its funds and books were transferred to St. John's College, chartered in 1784. Many colleges were established in the United States immediately after the Revolution to educate the youth of the new nation, and St. John's was one of these. The act chartering St. John's gave the college a building —the old shell of "Bladens Folly" (*see below* [26])—state funds, and permission to raise the balance of its expenses through private subscriptions.

Like King William's School, established under the guidance of Governor Nicholson and other prominent members of the colonial government, St. John's enjoyed eminent patronage, numbering all the Maryland signers of the Declaration of Independence among the petitioners for its establishment. George Washington sent his nephews, Fairfax and Lawrence Washington, to St. John's in 1794, and his wife's grandson, George Washington Parke Custis, in 1798. Other early alumni were Francis Scott Key and Reverdy Johnson.

Difficulties beset the college almost from the beginning. The private subscriptions so generously made were not easily collected; the board of the College finally hired a collector, and the sheriffs of the counties dragged a number of backsliders into court. The legislature revoked its annual subsidy, and only occasionally provided modest sums for the college's support. Although it closed briefly in 1818, St. John's managed to keep going until the Civil War, when its physical plant was taken over by the military authorities for camp and hospital purposes. During the war, the college continued to operate on an irregular basis, with one master and a few students for a time meeting in a private house in Annapolis.

Regular classes were resumed after the war, although only after the Naval Academy's effort to take over the college's property had been partially defeated. The academy did manage to obtain a portion of the campus lying east of present-day King George Street, which up to that time had been a cow pasture and from which the college had derived a small income by renting it to townspeople who grazed stock there.

From 1886 to 1923 the school was a military academy. In 1923, it adopted a system of open electives, specializing in preprofessional education. During these years St. John's emphasized its athletic program and fielded successful football and lacrosse teams. The 1930s was a time of financial crisis for the college. Hard hit by the depression, its enrollment dropped and it lost accreditation. Stringfellow Barr and Scott Buchanan, educational innovators from the University of Chicago, were made president and dean. They dropped intercollegiate athletics and initiated the Great Books Program, which is the basis of the present curriculum. In 1951 the school became coeducational.

McDowell Hall (26), the administration building, was named for the first president of the college. The large square brick building, with its broad hip roof and octagonal cupola, has an air of complacent dignity. Its history goes back to 1742 when the assembly authorized Gov. Thomas Bladen to buy four acres of land and build "a Dwelling House and other Conveniences for the Residence of the Governor of Maryland for the Time being," the cost not to exceed £4,000. Bladen employed Simon Duff, a Scot, to build the house. Two years later a request for

£2,000 more to complete the mansion turned the assembly against the project, and the building was left unroofed. Benjamin Mifflin, a Philadelphian visiting Annapolis in 1762, "Viewd Bladens Folly as the Inhabitants Call it, the ruins of a Spacious Building began by Govr Bladen but carried no further than the Brick Work & Joists 2 Stories High but if Finished would have been a Beautiful Edifice." After forty years of neglect the building was turned over to the college and completed. When Lafayette visited Annapolis in 1824, the hall was the scene of two banquets and a ball in his honor. During the Civil War, it was used as a clearing station for exchanged Union prisoners. It was gutted by fire in 1909 and subsequently reconstructed on the undamaged foundation, incorporating remains of the original walls.

The **Liberty Tree** (27), in front of the library, Woodward Hall, is a tulip poplar roughly thirty feet in circumference that is believed to be nearly 400 years old. Revolutionary meetings held in its shade earned it its present name. In 1840 boys ignited gunpowder in its hollow trunk, setting it afire; citizens rushed out with as much zeal as if a public building were threatened and succeeded in saving the tree. The next spring, having been freed of parasites by the heat, it burst into leaf with exceptional vigor.

At the eastern end of the campus, **Woodward Hall,** which houses the **Library** (28), contains 70,000 volumes. The facade is embellished by a two-story Corinthian colonade and makes a handsome balance to the Hall of Records at the west end of the campus.

The **Charles Carroll the Barrister House** (29), on the King George Street side of the campus, is a 2½-story, T-shaped yellow frame building with two of its brick ends and chimneys in English bond and the third in all-header bond. It was built for Dr. Charles Carroll in 1722/3 on the corner of Main and Conduit streets. In 1724, Dr. Carroll's son Charles was born in the house. This Charles Carroll, known as the Barrister to distinguish him from his distant cousin Charles Carroll of Carrollton, became a noted lawyer and patriot. He may have written the Maryland Declaration of Rights, adopted on November 3, 1776, which later that month was incorporated into Maryland's first constitution. The building was moved to its present site in 1955 to preserve it from demolition, and it now houses administrative offices of the college.

The **French Soldiers Memorial** (30), at the rear of the campus on a knoll overlooking College Creek and King George Street, was erected in 1911 by the Sons of the American Revolution. This memorial honors the Frenchmen who were buried in Annapolis after having aided the Americans in their fight for independence from Britain.

Mellon Hall (31), on the St. John's Street side of the campus, houses classrooms and laboratories. In the center of the stairwell at the northwest corner of the building hangs a replica of the pendulum devised in 1851 by the French physicist Jean Foucault in the first non-astronomical demonstration of the rotation of the earth. At the latitude of Annapolis the pendulum performs a complete rotation of 360° in thirty-eight hours. The **McKeldin Planetarium** adjoins Mellon Hall, and the **Francis Scott Key Memorial Hall** (32) is also part of the same complex of buildings.

The **Johnson House** (33), on St. John's Street next to the Key Auditorium, once stood on property owned by John Johnson, a chancellor of Maryland, and brother of the prominent lawyer, Reverdy Johnson, but neither ever lived in the house. The charming 1½-story white frame structure with a gambrel roof is typical of early-eighteenth-century domestic architecture. It was moved here from Northwest Street in 1937 and is now a student residence.

The **Maryland Hall of Records** (34), on St. John's College campus, has in its custody a large collection of public and private records including the surviving books from the collection bought by Thomas

Bray in 1696 to found the first public library in Maryland. The Public Search Room of the Hall of Records is open Mon.—Sat., 8:30—4:30, except on specified holidays.

From the very beginning of Maryland government, a great concern was shown by the General Assembly and the chief executive for the safety of its records, but their concern was often negated by carelessness on the part of record custodians. Although the transfer of the records from St. Mary's City to Annapolis in 1695—96 was very carefully planned, on the journey some items fell into the Patuxent.

The disastrous fire that destroyed the State House in 1704, consuming along with it a great quantity of records, stimulated plans for a detached, "fire-proof" records' depository. In those days legislative wheels ground slowly when appropriations for a new building were involved, and the "repository" for old records was not finally authorized until 1729.

The first central depository seems to have been in use until after the Revolution, when the state's records were lodged in the new State House. By 1854, these rooms were filled to capacity, and a legislative committee urged the construction of a fireproof building to house these records, which had by that time deteriorated badly. Several years later this building was erected on State Circle and served at least in part as a records depository until it was razed in the first years of this century.

The idea of a centralized archival agency remained very much alive in the minds of many Maryland citizens, but no opportunity presented itself for carrying out such an extensive project until the 300th anniversary of the founding of the province. Preparations were begun in 1928, for celebrations to be held in 1934, with the appointment of a Tercentenary Commission by Gov. Albert C. Ritchie. On February 21, 1934, the visitors and governors of St. John's College deeded land to the State of Maryland, and on October 1, 1935, the present building was occupied by the Hall of Records Commission.

When Governor Ritchie's Tercentenary Commission estimated the size of the proposed building it did so by measuring the accumulation of historical records then known to be in existence and allowing for a twenty-five-years' subsequent accumulation. The Hall of Records is now filled to capacity and plans are underway for a new building to house at least another twenty-five-years' collection of historical records.

The rambling **Bordley-Randall House** (35) (not open), on Randall Place between College Avenue and State Circle, is a 2½-story five-part brick town house standing amid magnolias and evergreens. The oldest wing (R) may have been completed by 1717 and is known to have been standing in 1726. A two-story columned porch on the main unit was replaced in 1860 by a smaller enclosed porch floored with marble from the State House, which was undergoing repairs at the time. On the left, connected by a low passage, is an L-shaped gambrel-roofed wing. The original part of the house was built by Thomas Bordley, one of the petitioners for the incorporation of Annapolis. His son Stephen (1709—64) inherited the house and developed it to suit his elegant tastes. Stephen Bordley was one of the foremost lawyers in colonial Maryland. Thomas Johnson and William Paca, who both became governors of Maryland after the Revolution, received their legal training in his office. The house was bought in 1804 by John Randall, whose descendants owned it for about 125 years. Randall's son Alexander (1803—81) was a representative in the Twenty-seventh Congress. Another son, Richard (1796—1829), was appointed governor of Liberia, where he died of malignant fever. Reverdy Johnson (1796—1876), born here and a playmate of the young Randalls, was one of the defense lawyers in the Dred Scott case. Maryland sent Johnson to the U.S. Senate in 1845, where he served until he was named U.S. attorney general in

Annapolis Harbor

1849. He again served in the Senate from 1863 to 1868, when he became the U.S. minister to Great Britain. More recently the house became the home of Capt. P. V. H. Weems, a specialist in navigation methods and inventor of widely used navigation instruments.

The **Ogle House** (36), 247 King George Street, is a 2½-story house of brick laid in Flemish bond with a steep gable roof and wide built-in end chimneys. The main entrance on King George Street is flanked by engaged Doric columns and topped with a triglyphed entablature. A later addition is set back from the original five-bay facade. An entrance on the College Avenue side is protected by a hooded and pedimented portico with two slender columns, similar to the entrance of the Reynolds Tavern. The narrow doorway opening from a corner bedroom onto a small wooden balcony is probably of later construction. The rooms in the original part of the building are relatively austere, but the ballroom, added on the rear in the late eighteenth century, is richly ornamented in the fashion of that period. Lafayette is supposed to have found it to be the most beautiful ballroom in America. It was traditionally said that the house was built in 1742 for Samuel Ogle, three-time colonial governor of Maryland. Ogle did occupy it for several years until his death in 1752, but further research revealed that it was built in 1739 for a Dr. William Stephenson. The house is now the headquarters of the U.S. Naval Academy Alumni Association.

Walk down King George Street to Maryland Avenue. Turn left.

The **Lockerman-Tilton House** (37), 9–11 Maryland Avenue, is an un-dated brick home built on six levels with a hyphen having three levels and a kitchen wing. It resembles buildings of the mid-eighteenth century, and the little information available indicates that it was built before 1770. It was owned for a time by John Rogers, first chancellor of the State of Maryland. A later owner was Josephine Tilton. Her husband, Edward McLane Tilton, accompanied Admiral Perry on his historic trip to Japan. The kitchen wing, converted into a separate house, was the home of Comm. Gordon Ellyson, the navy's first aviator.

Continue along Maryland Avenue to Hanover Street and turn right.

The **Peggy Stewart House** (38), 207 Hanover Street, is a 2½-story brick structure built between 1761 and 1764 by an Anne Arundel County planter, Thomas Rutland. Its facade, laid in all-header bond, is accented by a projecting stringcourse. The house was extensively altered in 1894, when the roof was changed from gable to hip form. In 1774 the house was purchased by Anthony Stewart, the merchant whose importation of tea that same year created such a public uproar that he was compelled to set fire to both the tea and the ship that carried it (see Annapolis). Stewart fled to England at the beginning of the Revolution and the house became the property of Thomas Stone, one of Maryland's signers of the Declaration of Independence.

The old **Rectory of St. Anne's Parish** (39), 215–17 Hanover Street, is a handsome brick residence, its facade laid in all-header bond, built about 1760. Originally the house had a gable roof with end chimneys, which was later altered to the present mansard roof line. Philip Key, great-grandfather of Francis Scott Key, sold the land to the Episcopal Church in 1759. The house built soon thereafter was the rectory until 1885. Perhaps the most notable of the resident rectors was Rev. Jonathan Boucher, clergyman, teacher, active social figure, and Loyalist. Before the Revolution, when Boucher held the incumbency of St. Anne's, he kept a school here at his home for the sons of the gentry.

Return to Maryland Avenue and proceed toward the State House.

The **Chase-Lloyd House** (40) (not open), King George Street and Maryland Avenue, is one of the few three-story Georgian-Colonial town houses south of New England. It is said that the third story was added to the original plan by Edward Lloyd IV so that his view of the harbor would not be obstructed. Samuel Chase began the house in 1769 but sold it unfinished in 1771 to Lloyd. Charles Carroll of Carrollton wrote to Charles Carroll the Barrister that the house was likely to cost Lloyd £6,000 to complete and commented that Chase had rid himself of a ruinous encumbrance. Lloyd hired the noted architect, William Buckland, to work on the house, and Buckland's masterly hand is evident in the rich interior ornamentation.

The massive facade rises behind a white picket fence to a dentiled and modillioned cornice, topped by a hip-on-hip roof. A pedimented central pavilion shows the width of the central hall. The brick walls, laid in Flemish bond, are accented by window headings and projecting stringcourses of hand-rubbed brick. At the left side is a three-story, white-columned portico, the upper stories of which are a much later addition, as are the modern screening and iron fire escape. The kitchen wing to the rear on the right is also obviously of later construction. Just behind the kitchen structure is the "party wall," which was built at the same time as the house to separate its grounds from those of the Ogle House. The garden facade is organized around a large, graceful Palladian window, which forms an impressive background to the interior central hall. The fanlighted and sidelighted street entrance is framed with Ionic columns and pilasters, cornice and pediment. It opens onto a wide hall with an Ionic colonnaded screen opposite and a staircase beyond leading up to the Palladian window on a landing above. Notable interior features include a fine Adam-style coffered ceiling in the parlor (L) and the magnificent trim of the dining room

(R). The paneled doors in this room, of dark mahogany, have handles of silver and are crowned with broken pediments. The frames are trimmed with rope twists, ears, and heavy molded architraves. The paneled window shutters, with octagonal medallions and rosettes, are of similar pattern to those in the Hammond-Harwood House and are from the workshop of William Buckland.

The massive simplicity of the facade and floor plan possibly reflects the taste of Chase, the son of a poor Anglican clergyman, while the rich, elegant detail of the interior trim and perfectly positioned Palladian window-stair-screen ensemble more closely resemble Lloyd's aristocratic background. Chase made his fortune as a first-generation lawyer and rose to become associate justice of the U.S. Supreme Court. Lloyd, the sophisticated product of a long line of wealthy planters, lived his life at a much more leisurely and refined pace than Chase, serving in a number of public offices and managing his large Eastern Shore estate. In 1802, Lloyd's youngest daughter, Mary Tayloe, married Francis Scott Key, who later wrote "The Star-Spangled Banner." Today the house is an Episcopal Church home for elderly ladies.

The **Hammond-Harwood House** (41) (open to the public; entrance fee), across Maryland Avenue from the Chase-Lloyd House at the corner of King George Street, has been described as one of the finest medium-sized houses in the world. Its perfect Georgian proportions, designed by William Buckland, have been preserved from later additions and "improvements." The symmetrical building consists of a five-bay central section with two-story flankers connected by enclosed passages. The street ends of the flankers are octagonal bays. Like the central unit, the facade is accented by rubbed brick stringcourses and window headings. The brick of the house, laid in Flemish bond, is of the distinctive salmon color indicating a base of local Maryland clay. The main entrance is framed by slender engaged Ionic columns and a pediment. Beautifully carved egg-and-dart molding surrounds the door and fanlight; falls of roses ornament the spandrels. The second-story window above the door is trimmed with sill brackets, a wide architrave, and a cornice. A bull's-eye window in the central eave pediment is framed with a trim almost rococo in style.

The floor plan of the main block is unusually asymmetrical. A short central hall, with front sitting rooms and an enclosed stairway (R) opening off it, leads back to a large room overlooking the garden. This room was used as the dining room when large dinners were given; a smaller dining room is to the right. The kitchen, in the right flanker, has a brick paved floor and a huge fireplace.

The interior woodwork is more delicately and intricately carved than that of the Chase-Lloyd House. The windows are set with quite high sills, permitting a wide wainscot of matched boarding with a heavy chair rail and base mold. The most elaborate rooms are the large dining room and the ballroom directly above it. Their trim is richly carved with beads, acanthus leaves, scrolls, interlaces, and gauge work, showing Buckland's mastery of Georgian patterns as well as his ability to execute them fully while avoiding excessive ornamentation. Especially notable are the headings of the dining room doors and the overmantel panel in that room. The frieze of the ballroom is embellished with Adam-style urns and festoons.

The house is one of the few of the period that can be directly attributed to an architect. A portrait of Buckland by Charles Willson Peale, now at Yale University, shows the architect working on clearly identifiable plans of this house, his masterpiece. Buckland completed the Hammond-Harwood House in 1774 for a young lawyer, Matthias Hammond. Although the Hammonds were a wealthy colonial family that had been closely associated with the proprietary interests, Matthias was already actively allied with the proprietary opposition. In 1773 he was elected to the assembly and played an active part in events leading up to the Revolution. Hammond apparently undertook to build the house when he was planning to marry a Miss Chase. Tradition says that he became so engrossed in the house plans that he neglected the young lady and she jilted him. A journal of James Nourse, who subsequently rented the house from Hammond, notes that while Hammond was in Philadelphia buying furniture for the house, Miss Chase eloped with another man. Hammond remained a bachelor. In 1776 he suddenly retired from political and military affairs, remaining in quiet obscurity at the family plantation in Anne Arundel County until his death ten years later at the age of thirty-eight. Subsequent owners of the house were Ninian Pinkney, brother of the noted lawyer and diplomat William Pinkney, and Jeremiah Townley Chase, cousin of Samuel Chase and chief judge of the Court of Appeals for twenty-five years. The house passed to J. T. Chase's granddaughter, who married William Harwood, a grandson of William Buckland. Their daughter Hester Ann inherited the house and lived in it till her death in 1924. Since then it has been kept as a historical landmark, first by St. John's College and most recently by a nonprofit organization called the Hammond-Harwood House Association, Inc.

Continue on Maryland Avenue to Prince George Street and turn left.

The **John Brice III House** (42) (formerly known as the Dorsey House), 211 Prince George Street, is a three-story structure of brick, painted grey, with a double-curved flight of iron steps to the entrance. It was long believed that the house was built before 1700 by Col. Edward Dorsey, but careful research indicated that it was constructed after 1766 by John Brice III and remodeled extensively after the Civil War.

The **John Brice II House** (43) (formerly known as the Jenings House), 195 Prince George Street, is a small 1½-story house of typical early-eighteenth-century design, with a gambrel roof and four tall chimneys. It is set back from the street, an unusual feature for a small house in Annapolis. Houses on smaller lots were generally set close to the street in order to provide as much space as possible for a garden in the rear. The house may have been built as early as 1728 by Amos Garrett, first mayor of Annapolis and a prominent merchant. His heirs sold this lot, which included a house, to John Brice II in 1737, and it is with the Brice family that it is most closely associated. John Brice II maintained a store next door and lived in this house until his death in 1766. His descendants owned the house until 1841.

The **Paca House** (44) (open to the public; admission fee), 192 Prince George Street, across the street from the John Brice II House, is one of Maryland's chief historic and architectural landmarks. Begun in 1763, the house was the home of William Paca from the time it was completed in 1765 until he sold it in 1780. Paca was born near Abingdon, Harford County, in 1740. He served as a member of the Maryland Provincial Assembly from 1767 to 1774. In 1774 he became a member of the Committee of Correspondence and a year later served on the Council of Safety. He represented Maryland in the Continental Congress from 1774 to 1779 and signed the Declaration of Independence. In August, 1776, Paca was appointed to a committee "to prepare a declaration and charter of rights and form a government for Maryland," and he served as a state senator under the Constitution of 1776. He assisted in planning naval armaments in the Revolution and in 1778 was appointed chief justice of the General Court of Maryland. Paca also served three times as governor of Maryland and was chosen a member of the Maryland Convention that ratified the Constitution of the United States.

Paca sold his house in 1780 to Thomas Jenings, a fellow attorney. In the year following his death in 1796, Jening's heirs rented the house to Baron Henri de Stier. Throughout most of the nineteenth century the house was rental property, serving during the last quarter as a boardinghouse. In 1907 a long hotel building was attached to the garden front of the house, and the whole complex became known as Carvel Hall. It was given this name because it was said that the house was used as background in the American Winston Churchill's novel *Richard Carvel*. In 1965 the house and its hotel wing were slated for demolition. Through the efforts of Historic Annapolis, Inc., sufficient funds were secured for the purchase and preservation of the house. Since then the house and its grounds have been the focus of one of the most thorough research and restoration projects ever undertaken in Maryland. At present, restoration of the spectacular garden behind the house, the house's exterior, and the interior of the main block has been completed. The hyphens and wings are currently being restored.

The **James Brice House** (45) (private), Prince George and East streets, is the largest of the Georgian-Colonial town houses of Annapolis. Unusually broad end chimneys tower ninety feet above the ground, flanking a steep gable roof. The facade, in all-header bond, is ornamented by an intricate eared cornice and a small, elaborate, pedimented window. The five-part house extends over 180 feet along East Street.

By 1766, when John Brice II died, various building materials had been assembled on the site. Actual construction, detailed in a full account book now among the collections of the Maryland Hall of Records, was started in 1767 by his son James. The house was virtually complete by 1775.

The parlor has a heavy and unusually elaborate cornice. The carved ornament of the fireplaces is varied, delicate, and graceful. Plaster wall panels, with edges beveled to simulate wood, have been restored to their original paint shade, one of the many details in the careful and extensive restoration done by the present owners of the house.

The **Patrick Creagh House** (46) (not open to the public), 160 Prince George Street, was built between 1735 and 1747 and affords an interesting, even dramatic, contrast to the James Brice House built two decades later at a much more affluent time. Patrick Creagh began his career in Annapolis as a painter and in time expanded his business to include the slave trade, shipbuilding, and house construction. By the time he built this comparatively modest "dwelling house," he was probably at the height of his career and perhaps as wealthy as any man in town. Creagh died in 1760, deeply in debt, and in 1788 the house was sold by the sheriff to Absalom Ridgely. In 1798 Ridgely's tenant was John Smith, a free Negro, whose wife (or close relative), known locally as Aunt Lucy, kept a bakeshop here for a number of years.

The **Sands House** (47), 130 Prince George Street, is a small, yellow-painted clapboard frame structure with a gambrel roof. The original part of the house is thought to have been built in the 1680s by Richard Hill, whose land, together with that of Robert Proctor and the proprietor, comprised the original town of Annapolis when it was laid out in 1685. It is possible that Col. Edward Dorsey rented this house and that the first meeting of the General Assembly in Annapolis was held here in 1695. The unusual and charming roof line is a result of some of the many additions and changes made over the years. The Sands family has owned the house since the Revolution.

From Market Space, cross to the corner of Main and Green streets. Turn left on Main Street to Compromise Street. Walk along Compromise Street to St. Mary's Street and turn right. Standing on a rise, which was Robert Proctor's contribution to the town lands in 1685, is the **Carroll Mansion** (48). The house, on the grounds of St. Mary's Church between Duke of Gloucester and Shipwright streets, is the probable birthplace and home, until 1820, of Charles Carroll of Carrollton, Catholic signer of the Declaration of Independence and one of the richest men of his day.

The oldest section of the Carroll Mansion may have been built in the late 1720s, but the house was extensively remodeled and expanded in the late 1760s. Today it is a massive brick structure of three and one-half stories, with a dormered gable roof. A chapel on the upper floor, forty feet long, was the first Roman Catholic place of worship in Annapolis. The Carrolls were closely allied with the Catholic Lords Baltimore, and much of the early family wealth was amassed because of proprietary favors. In 1852, Carroll's grandchildren devised the property to the Congregation of the Most Holy Redeemer (Redemptorists), and the mansion is now the House of the Second Novitiate.

St. Mary's Church (49), Duke of Gloucester and Chestnut streets, possibly built on or near the site of Robert Proctor's seventeenth-century tavern, is on the property acquired by the Redemptorists from the Carroll family. A small church was built here in 1825 where the parish school is today. The present church, dedicated in 1860, is a charming Victorian-Gothic building with pleasing proportions. The design of the interior evokes an appropriate atmosphere of solemn reverence.

The **Ridout House** (50), 120 Duke of Gloucester Street, was built around 1765 by John Ridout, secretary and lifelong friend of Gov. Horatio Sharpe. The 2½-story mansion has a gable roof and two massive end chimneys. The brickwork on the street facade is laid in all-header bond and is accented by a projecting stringcourse, rubbed brick arches over the regularly spaced windows, and a wide overhanging cornice. A flight of stone steps with wrought-iron handrails ascends to the Doric entrance under a beautifully simple pediment with dentils and modillions. The garden facade is more elaborate than the front. A Doric portico ornamented with triglyphs protects the entrance to the main floor above a long flight of steps going down to the garden level. Above it is a Palladian window that breaks through the cornice line. The flankers (buildings at each end) are completely separate from the main house and may be of a later date.

To the right of the Ridout House, **110-14 Duke of Gloucester Street**, are three town houses in a row constructed by 1786 as rental property by John Ridout. In that year a serious attempt was made to move the capital to Baltimore, an effort that caused Ridout "uneasiness on account of my houses in this place and makes me regret I ever built them." The houses, of brick laid in Flemish bond, have long since passed into separate ownership. Still the basic unity of design predominates over the individualizing touches of later additions. Each of the houses has a similar floor plan with a large, well-proportioned drawing room to the rear overlooking what was once the extensive formal garden shared by all the Ridout houses.

The **City Hall** (51), or **Ballroom,** Duke of Gloucester and Market streets, is a two-story brick building with a cupola on the site of the old "Assembly Rooms." This center for social gatherings is said to have been built in 1764 as a ballroom. Many gala functions were held here during the Revolutionary War era, attended by such notables as George Washington. The building burned during the Civil War while it was being used as the provost marshal's headquarters. Three original walls left standing after the fire were incorporated into the present structure.

Turn left on Market Street and continue to Shipwright Street. Turn left.

The **Upton Scott House** (52), 4 Shipwright Street, is a square hip-roofed building with two tall chimneys and a pedimented doorway. The facade, in all-header bond, is accented by a slightly projecting central pavilion and an unusual bracketed cornice, which may be of later date. The house was built about 1765 for Dr. Upton Scott, who came to

Maryland in the retinue of Gov. Horatio Sharpe. Scott had been a poor Belfast physician, but with Governor Sharpe's patronage he developed an extensive medical practice and obtained various fee-collecting offices in the proprietary government that, together, made him a wealthy man. Scott was a Loyalist during the Revolution, but through the influence of his many Patriot friends and by not being conspicuously vocal in his Tory views, he was for the most part left in peace by the new state government. In 1784 Robert Eden, the last provincial governor, who had returned to Maryland to reclaim his property, which had been confiscated by the state during the war, died suddenly in this house. Francis Scott Key lived here while a student at St. John's College. More recently the building was occupied by the Sisters of Notre Dame and today it is privately owned.

Return to Market Street. Turn right, then left on Union Street. Turn left on Conduit Street, then right on Cathedral Street. Proceed to Charles Street and turn right.

The **Jonas Green House** (53), 124 Charles Street, is a gambrel-roofed building in the Dutch-Colonial style, believed to have been built around 1700. It is one story high to the eaves, with another full story above. Twin end chimneys rise above the brick ends. The rear of the house is also of brick, with additions. The street side originally was clapboard. It was the home of Jonas Green, who came to Annapolis in 1738 and in 1745 began publishing the long-lived *Maryland Gazette.* Benjamin Mifflin, while visiting from Philadelphia in 1762, "Went with Jonas Green to View his p[r]inting office which is all below Capacious Airy & Convenient took a Walk in his garden. . . ." Green was the official "Poet, Printer, Punster, Purveyor and Punchmaker" of the Tuesday Club, and contributed to the hilarity of its uproarious proceedings.

Continue on Charles Street to Duke of Gloucester Street. Turn right and proceed to Conduit Street. Turn left.

The **Lloyd Dulany House** (54), 162 Conduit Street, was built around 1771 on land which Lloyd Dulany had inherited from his mother in 1766. Dulany was much criticized for the ostentatious display of his newly acquired wealth. Even a fellow Annapolitan, Charles Carroll of Annapolis, who was said to be the wealthiest man in the colonies, was shocked at the construction costs. In a 1771 letter to his son, Carroll wrote: "Were Lloyd my son, I should not like his sinking £10,000 in a house." Not only the house but its costly furnishings and Dulany's gay social life confirmed the opinions of more prudent Annapolitans that Dulany was spending his money recklessly. Unfortunately for Dulany, an avowed Tory, he was not to enjoy his fine home for long. His property was confiscated during the Revolution, and he was killed in a duel in London in 1782 by the former rector of St. Anne's, Bennett Allen.

In 1783 Dulany's house with outbuildings and adjoining lot was sold by the Commissioners of Confiscated Property to George Mann, an innkeeper. Soon afterwards, the house was incorporated as a wing into the extensive Mann's Tavern, later to become the City Hotel. George Washington stayed at Mann's when he came to Annapolis in 1783 to resign his commission, as well as on several other occasions.

The house remained part of the City Hotel complex until the main part was destroyed by fire in 1902. The Dulany House escaped the fire without damage. Following demolition of the remainder of the hotel in 1918, the Freemasons converted the Dulany House into a temple, and it is still used as such today.

The Lloyd Dulany House is a massive, three-story, five-bay rectangular structure covered by a gable roof. A proper town house, the building has no front yard but was built directly on Conduit Street. The exterior walls contain especially fine brickwork. The main portions are laid in Flemish bond without glazed headers, and the floor levels are indicated with belt courses of header bond. Below the molded water table the brick is laid in English bond. All the windows are topped with brick arches. The only wooden ornament on the exterior is the dentil cornice and the handsome Georgian doorway in the west facade.

Despite alterations to the interior, the Lloyd Dulany House remains an impressive example of Annapolis town house architecture. Its refined sophistication and lack of extensive exterior ornament recall the town houses of Georgian London. The building's great size stands as evidence of the prosperity and the grand scale of living achieved in Annapolis during the decade preceding the Revolution.

The **Callahan House** (55), Conduit Street, a 2½-story brick structure with a pedimented doorway, is said to have been built according to the design of John Callahan. William Pinkney (1764–1822) was born here. After rising to eminence in the Maryland bar, Pinkney served his country as U.S. attorney general, representative and senator from Maryland, and minister to Great Britain, Naples, and Russia. The house was moved twice: first from its original site across from the new legislative services building on College Avenue to St. John's Street, where the new House of Delegates building now stands; then in 1972 to its present location on Conduit Street.

Proceed to Main Street and turn right.

The brick half of the **Price House** (56), 230–36 Main Street, was constructed between 1821 and 1832 by Henry Price, a third generation Annapolitan and "a free man of color." It is possible that the frame part of the structure may have been erected before 1780 by Archibald Chisholm, once partner of the noted cabinetmaker John Shaw. Henry Price, a lay minister in the Annapolis Station Methodist Episcopal Church, subsequently was one of the founders of the present Asbury United Methodist Church. The property was owned by Price from 1819 until his death in 1863.

The third section of the tour covers the **United States Naval Academy** (57), whose main entrance is at Maryland Avenue and Hanover Street. The academy occupies a tract of approximately 300 acres along the Severn River. The buildings, forming an imposing group, were designed in the late-French-Renaissance style by Ernest Flagg of New York City. The decorations throughout are symbolic of the sea and of naval warfare.

Largely through the influence of Secretary of the Navy George Bancroft, the Naval School, as it was called until 1850, was opened here at Fort Severn on October 10, 1845. Franklin Buchanan, who was later to become the ranking admiral of the Confederate navy, was superintendent.

The Civil War disrupted the school, with midshipmen from the seceding states resigning. As preparations were being made to transfer the remaining students to Newport, Rhode Island, in the old frigate *Constitution,* Union Gen. Ben Butler appeared on the ferryboat he had commandeered at Perryville, and Com. G. S. Blake, the superintendent, at first mistook him for a Confederate raider. During the war, the academy buildings and grounds were used as a military hospital and camp.

When the school was brought back to Annapolis in September of 1865 with Rear Adm. David Dixon Porter as superintendent, the curriculum was revised to permit athletics and more recreation. A department of steam engineering was begun, indicative of the navy's transition from sail to steam. The Spanish-American War, the first foreign war fought by the United States since the conflict with Mexico, demonstrated the importance of the navy and caused a considerable expansion of facilities. An entire new layout of buildings was planned and construction of the first new unit was begun in 1899. Fort Severn, the old chapel, the former governor's mansion, and other mellow red

United States Naval Academy

brick landmarks were swept away. Meanwhile the student body increased from a few dozen to hundreds.

Admission to the academy as a midshipman may be gained in various ways. All candidates must be high school graduates or the equivalent, citizens of the United States, unmarried, between seventeen and twenty-one years old and of good moral character. Nominations to the academy are made by the president, vice-president and congressman of the United States. Appointments are also made by governors of the Commonwealth of Puerto Rico and the territories of the Canal Zone and the Virgin Islands. In addition, there are appointments available to men in the navy and the Marine Corps and in reserve units. Special regulations provide for the appointment of sons of Medal of Honor winners and for sons of armed forces members killed or totally disabled in the service. After the appointments are made, usually on a principal / alternate basis, the academic and physical qualifications of the candidate are examined. The academic standard requires a college preparatory course and college work (if applicable) as well as college entrance exam boards. The physical standard is strict. Twenty-twenty vision is generally required.

The academy is primarily a professional school for the preparation of naval officers. Mounting pressures in recent years have brought about a liberalization in the curriculum, which now offers a number of academic courses and electives and allows greater flexibility to exceptional upper classmen. As a result of a law signed by President Ford in October, 1975, women were admitted to the academy for the first time in 1976.

The great event of the academy year is June Week, when the fourth-year men receive their commissions, an event commemorated by the tossing of midshipmen's caps high into the air. Relatives and visitors crowd the academy grounds, snapping pictures of midshipmen in immaculate white uniforms. Parades, dances and other traditional activities entertain not only the "middies" and their dates, but also parents, alumni, and other onlookers. One of the features of June Week is the performance of the graduation march and Navy Anthem "Anchors Aweigh," composed in 1907 by the bandmaster, Lt. Charles A. Zimmerman, in collaboration with Midshipman Alfred H. Miles.

The **Naval Academy Museum** (58), just inside the Maryland Avenue entrance, contains more than 50,000 items, including a large collection of some of the finest ship models in the world.

To the right along Lovers' Lane, the traditional promenade for middies and their guests, is the **Herndon Monument** (59), a granite obelisk commemorating Comm. W. L. Herndon, who, in 1857, helped save the passengers of his ship the *Central America* before he went down with it. Also to the right from the Maryland Avenue entrance is the huge **Naval Academy Chapel** (60), where Protestant and Catholic services are held for the midshipmen. The dome rises more than 200 feet above the chapel floor. Stained-glass windows in the apse and transepts commemorate naval heroes—Sampson, Mason, Porter, Farragut—and other academy men who have served in the wars. Under the chapel is the crypt, a round colonnaded chamber containing the bronze and marble sarcophagus of John Paul Jones, who was originally interred in Paris in 1792. In 1905 the coffin was ceremoniously transferred to America.

Beyond the chapel one sees the tremendous mass of **Bancroft Hall** (61), the home of all midshipmen. It was named for George Bancroft, noted historian and secretary of the navy, who promoted the establishment of the academy. **Tecumseh** (62), facing the entrance, is a bronze copy (1930) of the U.S.S. *Delaware*'s figurehead.

The immense dormitory, with miles of corridors, is approached by a broad flight of steps and has a large forecourt before its three arched doorways flanked by gray granite columns. Under the mansard roof broken by many dormers is an elaborate cornice and frieze. From a lofty colonnaded hall with domed and vaulted ceiling and an inlaid polished marble floor rises a grand staircase turned at a central landing. A monumental doorway on the landing leads into the spacious Memorial Hall, where relics and memorials of naval heroes are displayed. Notable is Perry's battle flag with its rather crudely lettered motto Don't Give Up the Ship. In the lunettes at the ends of the hall are paintings of the battles between the frigate *Constitution* and H.M.S. *Java* on December 29, 1812, and between the frigate *Constellation* and the French frigate *L'Insurgente* on February 9, 1799.

Mahan Hall (63), across The Yard from Bancroft Hall, was named for Alfred T. Mahan, naval historian and president of the Naval War College in 1886–89 and 1892–93. This building houses an extensive collection of books supporting the midshipmen's curriculum in both its technical and academic aspects. In the Annex, government documents, back files, and related data are stored. On display are ship models and numerous historic flags, including the only known captured British Royal Standard. Opposite the entrance is the **Macedonian Monument** (64), a marble copy of the figurehead of the British frigate *Macedonian,* captured by Decatur near Madeira on October 12, 1812. Adjacent to Bancroft Hall is the **Brigade Library,** which has additional library facilities.

Near the museum is the **Tripoli Monument** (65), an eagle-surmounted marble shaft surrounded by symbolic figures and standing on a high broad base. It commemorates five young American officers killed in the war with Tripoli. Made in Italy, the shaft was brought to America on the *Constitution* and erected in the Washington Navy Yard in 1808; it stood on the Capitol grounds after the War of 1812 and was brought here in 1860.

Across College Creek is the Naval Cemetery. The **Jeannette Monument** (66) in the cemetery is a cairn similar to that raised in Siberia over the bodies of Lt. George W. DeLong and part of the *Jeannette* crew, who died with him. In 1879, DeLong set out for the North Pole by way of the Bering Strait, but his ship was icebound for twenty-one months and finally crushed. A lifeboat under Chief Engineer Melville and another under DeLong reached land at different points. When Melville found DeLong's party, they were dead, and all that survived to tell the story were the notes DeLong had written as he froze to death.

Other points of interest include the **Navy–Marine Corps Memorial Stadium** (67), in West Annapolis on Rowe Boulevard, where Navy plays its home football and lacrosse games. The stadium, constructed with privately donated funds, seats approximately 30,000 people.

Mount Moriah A.M.E. Church (68) backs the courthouse on the first block of Franklin Street. Completed in 1876, it is typical of a small-scale Victorian-Gothic church of the period. The Mount Moriah congregation was formed by 1804 when the free blacks of Annapolis were already worshiping in their own meeting house located in the Franklin–West Street area. Since 1970, when a new church was erected for the Mount Moriah congregation on Forest Drive, concerted efforts have been made by Historic Annapolis, Inc., and the Maryland Commission on Afro-Indian History and Culture, to preserve the building for use as a museum and as a center for black culture in Annapolis.

Acton (69), on Acton Place off Franklin Street, is a large two-story brick mansion showing yet another variation of the highly flexible Georgian-Colonial style. Its broad chimneys rise above the hip roof parallel to the facade. The five-bay facade, in Flemish bond, is of tripartite design. The central entrance is protected by a simple pedimented portico supported by four slender columns. On either side are projecting two-bay pavilions surmounted by twin pediments. A hyphen and wing of later date extend from the right of the house. Acton was built around 1770 for Philip Hammond, a relative of Matthias Hammond, the builder of the Hammond-Harwood House. At that time it was a country house, being situated well beyond the town limits of Annapolis.

BALTIMORE (20′ alt., 905,759 pop.), the seventh-largest city in the United States, has been termed Charm City because of its residents' long-established concern for good food, beautiful city parks and buildings, and other elements enhancing the quality of life. Another side of Baltimore is shown in the nickname Mobtown, descriptive of bloody nineteenth-century rioting arising from narrow-minded political dissension. One slogan is relatively accurate in its comprehensive description: "Baltimore is the northernmost southern city, the southernmost northern city, the westernmost eastern city and the easternmost western city." Its border location on the north-south axis is relatively clear, both geographically and historically. However, a look at a map may be required to confirm that it is nearer to the Middle West than any other major Atlantic port. Transportation, commerce, and industry have exploited the economics of distance; the link thus forged, together with the period of expansion that Baltimore shared with the Midwest (somewhat later than the other major Eastern ports and earlier than the beginnings of development in the Far West and Southwest), gives Baltimore a degree of midwestern flavor in its physical structures and demography.

Its border position, combined with its size and history, gives diversity to Baltimore life. Some of that diversity is shown by its famous native and adoptive citizens: Babe Ruth, Emily Post, Edgar Allan Poe, Billie "Lady Day" Holiday, the Duchess of Windsor, "Mama" Cass Elliot, Francis Scott Key and his twentieth-century relative F. Scott Fitzgerald, Cab Calloway, H. L. Mencken, Jacob Epstein, Ogden Nash, Dashiell Hammett, Gertrude Stein, Francis X. Bushman, John Wilkes Booth as well as public servants Alger Hiss and Spiro T. Agnew, stripper Blaze Starr, and Frank Zappa, a Mother of Invention.

The working heart of the city employs thousands of unpublicized Baltimoreans in the transportation services that constitute the lifeline of the city and in the commercial and industrial development stimulated by access to full-range transportation. The port of Baltimore handles thousands of ships annually, ranking fourth among U.S. ports in total tonnage. Major railroads and trucking lines supply and distribute metals, chemicals, heavy equipment and electrical machinery, stone, glass, rubber, textiles and apparel, paper products and foods—all processed by Baltimore manufacturers. Baltimore's trade and factories have enriched its banks, insurance companies, and other service-sector enterprises. The Johns Hopkins University and the University of Maryland professional schools, together with more than thirty other institutions of higher learning in the area, draw students from the entire country. Still, the cosmopolitan influences of its geography, economy, and cultural life are conditioned in the Baltimore setting to a markedly local orientation. Baltimoreans tend to have roots and a sense of local identification that counter the alienation associated with modern city life. Clearly defined neighborhoods exist and frequently organize for political and social action. Geographic mobility is less common than in most American cities. In all economic and ethnic groups, most Baltimoreans were born in the city.

Group structure is one of the significant elements of a city's personality, creating a characteristic mosaic of political interests, housing patterns, life-styles, community organizations, religious and intellectual institutions. Baltimore's black, British, European, Catholic, Protestant, Jewish, labor, management, and self-employed groups are accustomed to dealing with one another. The pattern of Baltimore's mosaic can perhaps be described as more diverse than that of inland or smaller cities yet better-fitted than that of other large port cities because groups in Baltimore have lessened some of the points of conflict by long contact.

The neighborhoods of Baltimore vary in appearance from the maritime potpourri of Fells Point to the towers of Charles Center, from the rolling garden development of Roland Park to the monotonous and frequently substandard row housing of many sections of the city. The geographically and chronologically piecemeal development of the physical structure of the city has contributed to its consciousness of neighborhood. While the essential shape of Baltimore's street plan is elusive at street level (to the frustration of visitors), a city map shows it to be defined around the harbor and the downtown core, from which expressways and the older commercial arteries radiate. The radial pattern was imposed by growth along the main routes stimulated by the extension of public transportation during the era of streetcar lines. It effectively forestalled the orderly development of a continuous grid network of streets crossing regularly at right angles. The radiating streets are, ultimately, named for their destination. Thus, clockwise from the harbor in the southeast corner of the city, there is the Old Annapolis Road, Washington Boulevard, Frederick Avenue, Liberty Road, Reisterstown Road, York Road, Harford Road, Belair Road, Philadelphia Road, North Point Boulevard, and Dundalk Avenue. Disorientation arising from the radial pattern is compounded because those roads do not extend into the downtown area under the same names, or they may originate as branches off downtown streets. Gay Street becomes Belair Road, and Greenmount Avenue turns into York Road. Privately owned cars permitted residential development between the rays of the principal streets as they diverged. Interstitial housing developments, each with its own street pattern, were built decades after housing and commerce had stretched out along the streetcar lines. Loch Raven Boulevard, Cold Spring Lane, Belvedere Avenue, and Hilton Parkway were among the streets constructed or upgraded during the 1920s to serve the automobile age.

Some of today's neighborhoods began as independent settlements that were enveloped as the city grew. In the eighteenth century, "Old Town" east of Jones Falls and Fells Point were united with Baltimore's original area west of the falls. More recently, the charming eighteenth-century mill town of Dickeyville and the early twentieth-century community of Roland Park were among the neighborhoods annexed in the last expansion of the city in 1918.

Many of Baltimore's neighborhoods have an ethnic focus. Perhaps the earliest of these was French Town, along S. Charles Street, where a boatload of Acadians, exiled from Nova Scotia by the English, settled in 1755. Succeeding waves of immigrants, dominated by the Irish after 1820, by Germans after 1848, by Central Europeans around the turn of the century, and by Italians early in the twentieth century, also tended to establish communities. Black settlement was concentrated first around Gay and High streets, then on lower Pennsylvania Avenue. All groups in the city have dispersed outward from the core as their economic status has improved. Among those cores that can still be discerned are Little Italy, around the intersection of High and Baltimore streets, and Little Lithuania, around Pratt Street and Fremont Avenue. A significant reason for continued residential grouping by race and religion in the past has been conscious discrimination, with ugly episodes of blockbusting exploitation. These irrationalities have been muted to a degree by modern laws and the realities of power, causing the city to exert effective pressure on financial institutions. Internal factors, including economic status and affiliation with a community religious institution, still combine with discrimination to produce distinct neighborhoods. Some areas have a predominantly middle-class white population, while others are mostly middle-class black. There are also working-class neighborhoods, dominated by one race or the other, together with a few integrated communities. Perhaps the best known, and certainly one of the most influential, of the existing group neighborhoods is the "Gilded Ghetto."

Some neighborhoods have historical unity; they include Federal Hill and the elegant town houses of the mid-nineteenth-century elite on Mount Vernon Place. Others have grown up around city improvements, the landscaped boulevards of Eutaw Place, or the green spaces of Union and Lafayette squares. Among twentieth-century realtor developments are Guilford, Homeland, and Cross Keys, and redevelopments such as Charles Village and Harlem Park. Individual private renovation is going on in many picturesque older areas; Bolton Hill is an attractive example.

The history of the growth of Baltimore is exciting, involving wars, sleek ships, canny traders, sturdy millers, aggressive railroad men, and a constant ferment of human activity and antagonism. Baltimore's growing pains required creative social solutions among its people. That it happened as it did was determined by the particular conjunction of place, time, and people. The town is on the fall line, the point where the harder rocks of the Piedmont plateau drop off to the softer terrain of the coastal plain. The wide estuary of the Patapsco River cuts in from the Chesapeake Bay to the fall line, affording a large, sheltered harbor. Streams descending the fall line had the velocity to provide power for early mills; the harbor, connected to the Chesapeake, the C & O Canal, the Susquehanna River system, and ultimately the open sea toward Europe, the West Indies, and South America, supplied the mills and distributed their flour and other products. Baltimore was also a depot for the transfer of cargo from Bay and river boats and the inland roads to and from the ocean-going ships that could anchor in the deep harbor and, at the same time, rid themselves of the boring shipworm that threatened wooden hulls (the constant flow of fresh water lessened the salinity of the water in Baltimore Harbor, killing the shipworms). North and south of Baltimore most centers of population established in the early industrial days of the first part of the nineteenth century developed along the fall line; roads and railroads connecting those centers were bound to pass through Baltimore.

When Baltimore County was laid out in 1659—to embrace a much larger area than the present county—the uninhabited land here was partly meadow and partly marsh at the foot of irregular wooded bluffs divided by the brawling creek later called Jones Falls. Below the bluff the falls meandered sharply westward then eastward before turning south to the broad cove later named the Northwest Branch of the Patapsco River. Patapsco Falls flowed from the west, emptying into the cove later named the Middle Branch. Between the two bodies of water lay a low peninsula called Whetstone Neck.

Many of the early characteristics of the terrain have now disappeared; creeks have been diverted, marshes filled in, bluffs graded. Even the ravine of Jones Falls is hardly noticeable.

In June, 1661, land on the west side of Jones Falls near the water was surveyed for David Jones, who soon went there to live. Shortly before this Charles Gorsuch, a Quaker, had patented a tract out on the toe of the little peninsula. During the next sixty years numerous tracts were patented in what is now the City of Baltimore; these were exchanged, broken up, and re-patented without, however, producing much settlement. Among the names denominating the holdings were Haphazard, Hale's Folly, Luns Lot, Ridgeley's Delight, Fell's Prospect, Gallow Bar, David's Fancy, and The Choice.

Settlement progressed in the region but the possibilities of this site for a town were ignored; the county seat was not even in the present-day Baltimore County. In 1696 Charles and Daniel Carroll resurveyed and patented 1,000 acres on the west side of Jones Falls, including part of an earlier patent called Cole's Harbor. By 1726 there was a grist mill on the east bank of the Falls and near it were three dwellings, a store, and some tobacco "houses"—whether barns or storehouses for shippers is not clear. Tobacco growers to the north were anxious to have a cus-toms house established here to enable them to shop without hav-ing to roll their tobacco needless miles to some duly constituted port. Local landholders therefore united, with Daniel and Charles Carroll as leaders, to petition the assembly for establishment of a town on the north side of the Patapsco. They had first chosen a site on the Middle Branch, but the owner, an English merchant named John Moale, was one of many who had specu-lated in warrants along the Patapsco in the hope of uncovering rich deposits of iron ore, and he refused to sell. The site se-lected for the new town was land held by the Carrolls. The bill was passed and was signed by Gov. Benedict Leonard Calvert on August 8, 1729.

It was largely an accident that the future metropolis of the state was given the name of Lord Baltimore's titular seat in Ireland. Most early Maryland county names honored the Cal-verts, and *Charles, Calvert,* and *Anne Arundel* had already been assigned when the county at the head of the Chesapeake was erected. It was natural for the town founders to attempt to establish their real estate development as the town of Baltimore County, though little Joppa to the north seemed to have had a head start in the race for prominence.

By 1730 the town established a year before had been laid out roughly in the shape of an arrowhead, with the tip near the intersection of Hopkins Place and Redwood Street, which is now Charles Center. This original town site of sixty acres, for which the Carrolls were paid the equivalent of about £600, is now bounded by Gay Street on the east, Saratoga Street on the north, Liberty Street and Hopkins Place on the west, and Pratt Street on the south. At that time the town grew so slowly that some of the lots were not taken up for years. The Basin then curved up to what is now Water Street. Harrison's Marsh was a good place for snipe and woodcock and not a business street. John Flemming, a tenant of the Carrolls, was probably the only man then living in the vicinity. Soon after the first lots were taken up a causeway across Harrison's Marsh and a bridge across Jones Falls, where Gay Street now crosses the Fallsway, were constructed to link the new town with Jones Town, the older settlement east of the falls.

In 1732 the residents of Jones Town, watching what was happening on the other side of the stream, persuaded the assembly to pass a bill erecting their settlement into "a town on a Creek Divided on the East from the Town lately laid out in Baltimore County called Baltimore Town on the Land whereon Edward Fell keeps Store." The town on the creek was to occupy twenty acres, the area now roughly bounded by the Fallsway on the west, Hillen Street on the north, Exeter Street on the east, and Lexington Street on the south. This section, an older place of settlement than Baltimore Town, is still called Old Town.

Perhaps there was some rivalry for a time but in 1745 the assembly, on a joint petition of the citizens of both towns, united the two, making them "one entire Town, and for the future called and known by the Name of Baltimore-Town, and by no other Name. . . ."

A tobacco-based trade proved inadequate to support a town of any size. English mercantile policies forbade the development of manufactures competitive with the mother country. Planters lived most of the year on their lands, the ordinary ones being almost self-sufficient and the powerful ones importing their goods directly from England. When the planters did congregate, it was either for social purposes at each other's homes or for mixed social and governmental duties in the provincial capital of Annapolis. The clearing and farming of land above the harbor led to a constant silting problem, threatening the most important feature of the new town in an era of poor roads and dependence upon water transport.

In 1750 John Stevenson, an Irish immigrant, sent a consignment of flour back to Ireland. This was the turning point in the town's fortunes. Stevenson, encouraged by the commercial success of his venture, backed the construction of a public wharf that would extend over the marshes to deep water, and a retaining wall was built to prevent further silting. In 1752, a picture attributed to John Moale, son of the man who did not want the town on his land, showed Baltimore Town to have twenty-five houses, one church, and two taverns. Four of the buildings were made of brick, the rest of wood. Rudimentary heating and cooking arrangements in the flammable buildings, together with the crooked, irregular streets, posed a constant danger of fire. The Provincial Assembly required that each citizen keep a ladder tall enough to reach the top of his chimney. About 200 persons lived here at the time. The French-speaking Acadians arrived in 1755 and added their numbers to the Englishmen, Scots, and Germans living in the colony where the Roman Catholic religion had long been tolerated. The Anglican religion had been officially established, however, at royal insistence, and the parish church of St. Paul's looked over the town and harbor from up the hill.

The town grew steadily. In 1756, a Baltimore ship sailed for the British West Indies with a mixed cargo consisting of flour from the mills along the Patapsco and Jones Falls, corn, beans, hams, bread, iron, barrel staves, peas, and, of course, tobacco; it returned with sugar, rum, and slaves. Thus began one of the mainstays of Baltimore commerce for a century, supplying the foodstuffs and goods for the Caribbean Islands. Baltimore traders traveled through the high, well-watered valleys of the Piedmont, in Maryland and southern Pennsylvania, dealing for the wheat crops that flourished in the region. Not only was wheat a suitable crop for the land but it was also a far more stable commodity in the markets of the day than tobacco. The backlands filled with settlers from the coastal region and Europe. Much of their grain was shipped through Baltimore, and the trade stimulated the growth of flour mills and other related light industry. The land also provided sound wood for barrels, and the iron to bind them.

In a few years Baltimore had a pottery and a distillery. An educator from London was teaching young men "writing, arithmetic (both vulgar and decimal), merchants' accounts, geometry, etc.," and young ladies the "Italian hand," while selling "choice West India rum by the hogshead, loaf-sugar, coffee, chocolate, Madeira wine, and cedar desks" on the side.

In July, 1762, a visitor, Benjamin Mifflin, noted in his diary that the town had about 150 houses, mostly of brick, and 30 or 40 under construction:

> . . . it seems to Encrease very Fast. there are 2 Bridges over the creek which Joyns the 2 Parts of the Town together the Creek so shoal that only Boats or Flats can go up, & runs such a short distance in the Country that there is but very Little Currant to keep it clear so that its my Oppinion both that & the Bason to the S. of the Town must in a Few Years be Choak'd up Except a small Stream that the Creek which they call the Falls will keep open sufficient perhaps for Flat Bottom Craft & in that case the Sea Trade will draw down to a point Call'd Fells Point where the Shipping now Lye there being at this time 3 Ships & a Snow from London Loading with Tobacco. for other Sea Trade there is very Little now the bent of the Inhabitants not being as yet that way but I think a very considerable one might be carried on here there being Two Merch^t Mills now Building on the above Creek contiguous to the Town and another ab^t 2 Mile off the First by Willm Moore the second by John Burgess & co & the Third by —— the Back Country will amply supply them with wheat & Indian Corn in very Plenty. as to Lumber altho there seem to be very good Timber about the Country the people has not fell Into making Staves, & as to Fells Point about a Mile below the Town the Owner has such a High notion of it, has Laid it out into such small Lotts proposing a perpetual Ground rent of £3 Ster^g for the water & 30/ Ster^g for the Inner Lotts that he has Let but 2 or 3 & I believe in his time will not Let many, without he Lowers his Terms or Inlarges his Lotts. . . .

William Fell, nephew of the storekeeper, had laid out these lots on Fells Point, and in spite of Mifflin's prophecy a wharf, warehouse, and shipyard had been established within a few years. For a time there was intense rivalry between the point and Baltimore Town, but in 1773 the assembly added eighty acres, including Fells Point, to the town.

Baltimore had been made the county seat in 1768, and a courthouse was built near the site of the Battle Monument, on a bluff that was then some thirty or forty feet above the present street level. By this time the town had 3,000–4,000 inhabitants, but it was still possible to catch crabs with a stick at what is now the intersection of Charles and Lombard streets, or to drown, as one citizen did, at the place where Calvert now crosses Lexington Street.

It was natural that Mifflin, a Philadelphian, should have surveyed Baltimore's business possibilities with a sharp eye, for the little city was beginning to divert some trade from his own home, which with its suburbs had about 30,000 people at the time. Baltimore's importance by 1769 is attested by the fact that the Merchants' Committee of Philadelphia believed it necessary to get the cooperation of Baltimore merchants to strengthen their own nonimportation agreement made to force repeal of the Townshend Acts. The temper of Baltimoreans was vigorous; they not only responded promptly to the appeal but took the lead in obtaining agreement throughout Maryland.

In 1765 citizens hanged in effigy the man appointed stamp distributor for Maryland. When two sloops with contraband arrived in 1770 they were forced to leave the port, and Baltimoreans passed a resolution not to trade with Rhode Island when the New England colony violated the intercolonial nonimportation agreement. In 1774 a Committee of Correspondence was appointed and resolutions were passed recommending that all trade with Great Britain and the West Indies cease, even though the trade with the West Indies was then the most profitable carried on by Baltimore citizens. Only four days after the Virginia House of Burgesses had made a similar recommendation and before the news had been brought up the Bay, Baltimore citizens in a general meeting went on record as favoring a convention of representatives from all the colonies.

In December, 1774, a company of militia was formed and Mordecai Gist was elected captain. These "Baltimore Independent Cadets" were "impress'd with a sense of the unhappy [state] of our Suffering Bretheren in Boston" and they firmly resolved "to Procure at our own Expense a Uniform Suit of Cloths, (vizt) [a coat] turned up with Buff, and trim'd with Yellow Metal, or Gold Buttons, White Stockings and black Cloth half Boots; likewise a good Gun with Cartouch Pouch, a pair of Pistolls Belt and Cutlass, with 4 pounds of powder and 16 pounds of lead." Six months later, after the news of Lexington and Concord had reached the town, there were seven companies drilling in Baltimore.

Many of these boys, and others later recruited by Lafayette and Pulaski, became dependable soldiers in the Revolutionary army, distinguishing themselves in many battles. In July, 1783, the veterans returned from the war "penniless and in rags," under the command of Mordecai Gist, then a brigadier general.

Meanwhile the folks at home had had their adventures. Several times the town had with good reason been thrown into a state of excitement by the approach of British men-of-war. General Greene, passing through the town in 1780, reported that Baltimore was in "so defenseless a state" that "a twenty-gun ship might lay the town under contribution." But perhaps the most gloomy period of the war had been December, 1776, when Baltimore was host to Congress, which had fled southward before the British advance, and there seemed little hope for the cause of independence. The representatives of the new states had met in a three-story building at Sharp (then correctly spelled Sharpe) and Baltimore streets. And to add to Baltimore's problems, not all of the distinguished guests had been polite. A Virginia delegate had written, "If you desire to keep out of the damnedest hole on earth come not here!" But the Congress had accomplished much during its brief stay. A New Hampshire delegate wrote, "Congress is now doing business with more spirit than they have for some time past. I hope the air of this place, which is much finer than Philadelphia, will brace up the weak nerves."

Baltimore, however, had made her greatest contribution on the sea. In October, 1775, the Continental Congress had passed an act for the formation of a navy, and in the same month the Continental Marine Committee at Baltimore had fitted out two of the first cruisers of the American navy. A new flag had been sent down from Philadelphia to be used on one of these vessels, the *Hornet,* and Joshua Barney, the recruiting officer of the ship, had unfurled this flag to the music of fifes and drums. "The heart-stirring sounds of the Martial instruments, there a novel incident in Baltimore," wrote Barney's wife "and the still more novel sight of the REBEL COLORS gracefully waving in the breeze, attracted crowds of all ranks and eyes to the gay scene of the rendezvous, and before the setting of the same day's sun, the young recruiting-officer had enlisted a full crew of jolly 'rebels' for the HORNET."

There was also a Maryland navy that did good service in keeping down plunderers in the Bay and at times in suppressing Tory uprisings. Many of these vessels were built and equipped at Baltimore. They ranged in size from tiny barges carrying six to a dozen crewmen with perhaps as many muskets, to cruisers of twenty-two guns. The larger vessels often had such mild names as *Defence, Friendship,* or *Amelia,* but the barges bore mighty names like *Revenge, Terrible, Intrepid, Fearnaught.*

In March, 1776, Congress had authorized the fitting out of "private armed vessels," and this act, in the words of a nineteenth-century historian, "offered to the enterprise and patriotism of the citizens of Baltimore an opportunity of acquiring wealth, while defending their commerce and protecting the people from the depredations of the common enemy. Under this act *privateering* became a business as well of fortune as of patriotism." Here indeed was a business exactly to the taste of Revolutionary Baltimore.

Between April 1, 1777, and March 14, 1783, a total of 248 vessels, most of them owned by Baltimoreans, sailed from the Patapsco to capture what they could from the British, and they succeeded so well that British merchants for more than thirty years referred to Baltimore as a "nest of pirates." When a prize was captured it might be manned by a skeleton crew and sent to the nearest American port, or if this was impossible, it was burned or sunk. The damage done to English shipping during this period has been estimated at a million pounds.

Baltimore Town had contributed perhaps more than its share of the money needed to carry on the war and, like all other American towns of the period, had suffered from the disruption of business. But Baltimoreans had learned to build fast ships and were to profit much by this knowledge during the succeeding period of privateering and slave running.

In 1776 the town had some 6,700 inhabitants. By 1790, the population had more than doubled, and the census of 1800 showed it to have doubled again, to 31,514. The federal census of 1810 showed a population of 45,000. From the outbreak of the French Revolution to the close of the Napoleonic Wars there was a good European and West Indian market for foodstuffs. Land to the south and west of Baltimore supplied grain and other necessities. The citizens of Baltimore loaded this merchandise on their fast ships and profited when the ships returned with manufactured goods to be auctioned on the wharves.

There was, of course, great building activity within the town. In 1784 Baltimore underpinned the courthouse, leaving it standing upon stone stilts, and carted away the hill to open up Calvert Street beneath it. "At that time," says a historian, "the arch under the court house was supplied with stocks, pillory, and whipping post, and Justice straddled over the city's center like Gulliver in Lilliput."

A writer described the Baltimore of the 1780s as "so conceited so bustling and *debonnaire,* growing up like a saucy, chubby boy, with his dumpling cheeks and short, grinning face, fat and mischievous, and bursting incontinently out of his clothes."

For a decade there was a spirited battle between the conservative and well-to-do citizens on the one hand and the "mechanical, Republican, and carpenters' societies" on the other over the problem of incorporation, the latter groups objecting strenuously to provisions in the proposed act of incorporation "contrary to reason and good policy, to the spirit of equal liberty and our free constitution." Finally, in 1796, the assembly passed the act "to erect Baltimore Town . . . into a city, and to incorporate the inhabitants thereof." The new act had many, though not all, of the provisions to which the mechanics and carpenters had objected.

The following year the newly elected mayor approved an ordinance to prepare "a scheme of lottery, to raise a sum of money for the use of the city of Baltimore." For a long time Baltimore enjoyed lotteries. They were held to raise money for churches, schools, colleges, and all manner of civic improvements, including the Washington Monument. One winter a lottery was held for its own sake, the money to be used for any suitable enterprise in the spring.

Baltimoreans continued to hate the British. In 1808, after passage of the Embargo Act, in a huge ceremony attended by virtually all citizens—1,200 of them on horseback—the city burned 720 gallons of gin because the master of a vessel had paid duty on it in an English port. After the declaration of the War of 1812 patriotism ran so high that the office of a Federalist newspaper that was opposed to the war was raided. During the ensuing riot there was loss of life on both sides. The editor and his friends were tortured. One of the latter, Gen. James M. Lingan, died. Another, Gen. "Light-Horse Harry" Lee, father of Robert E. Lee, remained a cripple for life.

Besides contributing to the federal navy, Baltimore enthusiastically resumed its old business of privateering. Four months after the declaration of war 42 privateers, carrying 330 guns and about 3,000 men, had put out from Baltimore, and some of them preyed on English shipping within a few miles of the British coast.

A British statesman called Baltimore "the great depository of the hostile spirit of the United States against England." A British admiral said, "Baltimore is a doomed town," and a London paper declared that "the truculent inhabitants of Baltimore must be tamed."

The "truculent inhabitants" were worried. Fort McHenry had been neglected. Big guns were scarce. The federal government had sent many of Baltimore's fighting men on the disastrous Canadian expedition and was in no condition to aid the city; Baltimore would have to fight its own battle. Fort McHenry was repaired as soon as possible, and the guns of an abandoned French frigate were borrowed from the consul. Furnaces were built to make the forty-two-pound balls. Forty pieces of artillery were stationed on elevated ground east of the city (now Patterson Park), and every man and boy was assigned to military duty. A Baltimore seamstress made a big flag for Fort McHenry.

Then the news came that Washington had been captured and partly burned. The British army landed on North Point under the command of General Ross, and the British fleet came up the Patapsco. "The citizen-soldiery of Baltimore on that gloomy Sunday bade a tearful adieu to their wives and children, put on the harness of battle, and went forth to meet the insolent invader." But General Ross, who was going to eat dinner "in Baltimore or in hell," was knocked off his horse by Baltimore marksmen and died a few hours later. The British, who had just defeated Napoleon's army, found to their dismay not only that the citizen-soldiers were good shots but that they loaded their cannon with "grape and canister, shot, old locks, pieces of broken muskets, and everything which they could cram into their guns."

After a preliminary skirmish the British spent a miserable twenty-four hours in a cold rain without even blankets to protect them and contemplated the earthworks behind which Baltimoreans and soldiers from Pennsylvania and Western Maryland waited to shoot their metallic scrap. Meanwhile, the British fleet fired more than 1,500 bombs at Fort McHenry, and the garrison could not reply because the fleet was out of range of the borrowed French guns.

But by dawn's early light it appeared that the flag made by the seamstress was still there, and the British army had sneaked off in the middle of the night. The "truculent" citizens were greatly relieved and within a few days were attempting to learn the difficult tune to which Francis Scott Key had written some new words.

The Peace of Ghent ended the War of 1812, and once more vessels leaving the port of Baltimore carried on a vigorous foreign trade. The principal export was flour. With abundant water power and easy access to large wheat-growing areas, Baltimore became one of the largest milling centers in the country. By 1825, when the population had grown to about 72,000, making Baltimore the second-largest city in the country, there were some sixty mills within a few miles of the city. The soft flour produced was especially well suited to tropical conditions;

this characteristic, combined with Baltimore's advantageous position, made Baltimore the largest exporter of flour to Antillean and South American ports. Returning vessels brought coffee from Brazil and guano from Peru. The latter commodity, bird dung deposited through thousands of years and preserved in the dry altitudes of Peru, made a superior concentrated fertilizer. It was first introduced to the country through Baltimore in 1824. The demand for guano was greatest in the Southern states, and until the Civil War Baltimore enjoyed a monopoly in its importation and distribution.

Baltimoreans had played a vigorous part in obtaining federal funds to build the Cumberland Road (the first across the mountains to the west) and had also improved the road between Baltimore and Cumberland to draw the trade to and from the new settlements beyond the mountains. Conestoga wagons were bringing wheat, corn, and pork and leaving with manufactured wares for the Ohio Valley. Then the Erie Canal, completed in 1825, cut deeply into this western trade, and local merchants were much concerned to find a means of recovering their advantage. At a meeting in February, 1827, at the home of the banker George Brown, a committee was appointed to determine whether a railroad would be practicable. The committee reported favorably, and a charter incorporating the Baltimore & Ohio Railroad Company was obtained from the assembly on February 28. This was probably the most decisive event in the city's history. The railroad, completed to Ellicotts' Mills in 1830, to Cumberland in 1842, and to Chicago in 1874, enabled the city to retain its hold on the western market.

During the nineteenth century Baltimore acquired several nicknames, each based on some aspect of the city's life. The Washington Monument, begun in 1815, and the Battle Monument, among others, gave it the name Monumental City. Baltimore also became known as the Convention City. Because of its central position on the Atlantic seaboard and its accessibility by train from the West, and also because it was in a border state with mixed agricultural enterprises and with a business center, reflecting all the opposed interests of the country, political parties frequently chose it for their national conventions. Presidents Jackson, Van Buren, Tyler, Polk, Pierce, Lincoln (for his second term), and Wilson were nominated in Baltimore, as were several unsuccessful candidates.

A less enviable title was Mobtown. Vitality and violence were inextricably associated with each other amid the tensions of a rapidly growing, changing city. Rioting in the streets of Baltimore had occurred, at various intervals, since Revolutionary days. Around the middle of the century, violence and fraud became a regularly exercised technique in the political action of several groups and, in response, elicited violence from the opposition. Edgar Allan Poe was accidentally and tragically involved in one of Baltimore's roughhouse elections in 1849. The circumstances are clouded, but one story relates that the poet, in poor health and possibly either drunken or drugged, was kidnaped by a gang of political hoodlums and taken from one polling place to another as a repeating voter. His health broken by the rigors of coercion, he collapsed and died soon thereafter.

During the 1850s the Know-Nothing party gained control of the city. Although it began as a reform movement the party soon became tainted with corruption. Clubs bearing such names as Plug-Uglies, Rip-Raps, and Blood-Tubs seized the polling places and beat or stabbed with shoemakers' awls anyone attempting to cast an opposition ballot. During the presidential election of 1856, there was a street battle between the Know-Nothings and the Democrats, each side using brass cannon. Reform was finally accomplished by the more responsible citizens of the town, aided by voters of the state; an assembly was elected that in 1860 made the needed changes in the election laws and put the police under direct state control.

The outbreak of the Civil War found Baltimoreans divided in their sympathies, as were the citizens of the state as a whole. One week after the outbreak of hostilities at Fort Sumter, on April 19, 1861, four soldiers and eleven citizens were killed in a riot that occurred as the Sixth Massachusetts Regiment was marching across town from one railroad station to another. News of this event moved the Baltimorean James Ryder Randall, then in New Orleans, to write the stirring song "Maryland, My Maryland."

This and other events brought military rule to the state, and throughout the war the city was subject to strict supervision under Federal officers. Some city officials were deprived of office and even of liberty, and their constitutional rights were suspended. A ring of forts encircled the city with guns trained not outward, but toward its heart.

In July, 1864, after the defeat of Gen. Lew Wallace at the Monocacy, a Confederate force under Gen. Bradley T. Johnson, composed largely of Baltimoreans and other Marylanders, passed close to the city. Bridges were burned and trains captured. Northern sympathizers in Baltimore were in terror, while Southern sympathizers prepared to greet an "army of deliverance." But Baltimore was not the objective of the movement, and the Confederates moved on toward Washington.

The war disrupted the city's normal commerce and deprived it of its extensive market in the South. But as the nearest large city to the scene of operations, Baltimore became an important military depot and profited by the traffic in army supplies. When demobilization at the end of the war put a stop to this business, Baltimore was faced with a problem of reconstruction almost as great as that of any city of the Confederacy. Among newcomers during this period were many members of leading Southern families, seeking to recoup their fortunes.

After several years of stagnation the city began to recover. New industries were established, new markets were found in Europe and elsewhere, and great improvements were made in port and railroad facilities.

The depression that began in 1873 led to cuts in the wage scale of the Baltimore & Ohio Railroad workers in 1877, with resultant strikes and riots.

Throughout the remainder of the nineteenth century Baltimore continued to grow as a trade center, but the manufacture of clothing, chemical fertilizer, and iron and steel products gained in importance. Flour milling declined because of competition from the Middle West, although the city still handled much flour and grain. Oyster packing was prominent in the city's economy; in 1880 Baltimore was the chief packing center in the world, but since then the industry has steadily declined, owing to a depletion of the beds in Chesapeake Bay.

Industrialization began to outstrip commerce as Baltimore's principal activity. Mechanization of manufacturing processes permitted large-scale operations as a national market was made available, and transportation and population increased rapidly. Capital was needed for investment in equipment and physical plants, resulting in the spread of the corporate form into combines and trusts. Consolidation was the pattern, and large concerns manufactured sugar, fertilizer, glass, and the machinery required for industrial expansion. Canneries flourished, and oil and electricity were gradually introduced as energy sources for the new machines. As business combined and its new methods displaced the skilled artisan, labor organization developed to meet corporate power. As industry grew, it moved southward and eastward along the waterfront and the railroad lines. Canton, Southwest Baltimore, Locust Point, and Curtis Bay joined Jones Falls as industrial centers. Bonding and banking expanded to serve the business community.

Baltimore's population continued to grow. Much of the increase was from native stock; urbanization and medical advances led to a decrease in infant mortality, and the shift away from agriculture brought many rural Marylanders and some Virginians and Pennsylvanians to the big city. Although more than 600,000 foreign immigrants landed in Baltimore in the period 1870–1900, only about 12,000 remained; most moved into the opening lands of the West.

Horse-drawn omnibuses served the transportation needs of the public until the late 1890s. Although the omnibuses had moved on tracks since their inauguration in 1859, the conservative gentry had consented to the installation only on condition that the tracks be the precise width of their own carriage wheels. In 1885 experimental electrified trolleys had been abandoned when people and horses kept being shocked by the third rail. Overhead electrification proceeded in other cities and was introduced to Baltimore after its merits had been demonstrated elsewhere.

On February 7, 1904, a fire that started in a warehouse, near what is now the southeast corner of Liberty and Redwood streets, was soon out of control. Embers were blown from block to block by a strong southwest wind until even the buildings of the civic center were endangered. Fire companies came from as far away as New York City and Richmond, and buildings were dynamited, but the flames were not checked until the wind shifted and drove the fire to the waterfront. The area over which the flames swept was almost the same as the arrowhead tract upon which the town was laid out in 1730—plus what was once Harrison's Marsh and a filled-in section between Water Street and the Basin. More than a thousand buildings were destroyed and the damage was estimated at $125,000,000, of which only $50,000,000 was covered by insurance. One of the many oddities of the fire was the sight among the smoking ruins of a huge pile of ice. Cut blocks of ice piled near the dock for storage and distribution in those prerefrigerator days had been fused together by the heat, and their bulk had resisted the flames.

The city was faced with an enormous task of rehabilitation. A Burnt District Commission was appointed and reconstruction began at once. Some changes were made in the city plan but, unfortunately, the automobile era was not far enough advanced for the commission to understand how imperative it would soon be to have wider streets. Baltimore's economic vitality was such that recovery was rapid, and within a few years the "great fire" was little more than a chronological marker in the community memory—a point in time before which or after which recent events had occurred.

Baltimore continued to grow, perhaps even stimulated by the civic energy mobilized to rebuild after the fire. As its manufacturing base widened, exports of industrial products increased, while agricultural products tended more and more to be consumed in the area rather than exported. Raw materials, especially petroleum and ores for the metal refineries, displaced manufactured goods in the import category. Change was accelerated by World War I, when the city's long-established shipbuilders, who had crafted sleek privateers and the swift Baltimore clippers in the days of sail, moved into full-scale production of modern metal steamships. Steel and chemicals, grains and military apparel—all were rapidly expanded during the war. From eleventh place in manufacturing in 1914, the city rose to seventh by 1919 and held that position for several years. The twenties were not a time of unqualified prosperity for Baltimore, however, and by 1929, the city had sunk to twelfth place. In 1922 a large sugar refinery was constructed, in line with the long association of Baltimore with the Caribbean trade. Fertilizer has also remained one of Baltimore's important products. Yet some industries have risen and fallen with the vagaries of time. During the depression years, for example, Baltimore, with its long South American connection, was the center of the panama hat industry.

During the fifteen years from 1930 to 1945, the face of Baltimore showed little change. Physical development was retarded, first by the depression and then by the demands of World War II. The manufacture of aircraft, begun in the thirties, was a natural outgrowth of the steel, shipbuilding, and machinery industries already established. Hundreds of Liberty ships were turned out by Baltimore's shipyards for the war effort, and munitions manufacturing was resumed on an even larger scale than in World War I. This was a far more sophisticated process than the old method of dropping lead down the Shot Tower but again was a continuation of a traditional activity, made easier by the conjunction of chemical and metals plants in Baltimore.

The lack of new investment in housing and physical plants in the downtown area was complicated by wartime prosperity and its aftermath as suburban areas began to compete, not only for middle-class residents but also for industrial plants. Roads built to serve the outlying areas, culminating in the beltway completed in the late 1950s, enticed investment from the inner city. When a major downtown department store was compelled to

close in the early fifties, choked by shopping-center encircle-
ment, downtown businessmen were appalled, and they organized around a new partnership of private capital and government to revitalize the city's core. Office towers, stores, cultural
attractions, and open spaces were planned to make an attractive
and appealing new image for Baltimore. Among the pioneering
projects was Charles Center, which has been followed by the
Inner Harbor development.

Another of the more visible transformations in Baltimore in
recent years has been population change. Blacks, hampered by
both social and economic discrimination, were not proportion-
ately represented in the sprawl to the suburbs. Suburban resistance, based on economic interest and racial prejudice, prevented any further annexation after 1918 that would consolidate
the government of the Baltimore metropolitan area. Baltimore's
total population in the decade 1960–70 decreased by about
33,000, but there was a striking difference in the impact of that
movement. White population decreased by more than 130,000,
while black population increased by almost 100,000 to make the
city 47 percent black. Yet in other respects, the change has
been far less marked. Urbanization, education, and economic
strength have been the same factors working among all segments of the population, gradually raising the standard of living
and the quality of life. The transition of the black workers into
the middle class is documented by census figures. In 1940,
blacks were 26 percent of laborers, 30 percent of domestics,
3 percent of white-collar employees, and 3 percent of the professional group. In 1970, blacks were only 10 percent of laborers
and 6 percent of domestics, while they were 19 percent of white-
collar workers and 9 percent of professionals. The figures, when
compared to overall population, still show a disproportionately
small number of blacks in the middle-class categories. One significant adjustment, however, must be made. Most of the whites
who left the city were in the young-family category, leaving the
older, more established whites in the city. Conversely, much of
the black population is still of school age and not represented
in the labor force. Even with the demographic adjustment, it is
clear that inequities based on class, race, and educational level
persist. Baltimore's future will be defined by the resolution of
its racial problem as much as by its economic development,
which is both a cause and a result of the social mosaic.

Transportation remains the lifeline of Baltimore. Port development has modernized rapidly, with the proliferation of modern
containerized freight depots for more delicate cargo and LASH
(lighters [barges]—aboard ship) facilities for bulk cargo. Automobiles are imported by the thousands through specialized piers.
The changing patterns of transportation, symbolized by the auto-
mobile-age imports, have required the construction of express-
ways to serve both the commercial centers of downtown and
the trucking needs of the port. Perhaps the most spirited clashes
in Baltimore's modern urban development have been between
the highwaymen and the aroused populace protecting its neighborhoods from the changes inevitably associated with a transformed transportation scheme. Planning and citizen activism
have combined in an attempt to shape long-term change for

Baltimore, bringing new factors to bear upon the face the city will show in the future.

DOWNTOWN BALTIMORE TOUR

The tour of downtown Baltimore is bounded roughly by the Pratt Street Waterfront on the south, the Jones Falls and Fallsway on the east, Mt. Royal Avenue on the north, and Greene and Howard streets on the west. Parking in the central area is difficult, and the traveler will probably have to pay for space in a public lot or garage, particularly during rush hours. The underground garage at Charles Center is the largest and most centrally located. On the fringes of the area parking is less difficult, with metered spaces often available on Light Street by the Basin just south of Pratt Street, the housing project area on Lombard Street across the Jones Falls, and the State Office Building area just west of Howard Street at Preston Street (*see* Northwest Baltimore). The most likely central area for street parking is near the City Hall and War Memorial. From here it is four blocks to the waterfront, four blocks to Charles Center, and six blocks to Mt. Vernon Place; the State Office Building at Preston and Eutaw streets is about a mile away, and the University of Maryland at Greene and Lombard streets about three-quarters of a mile. The tour begins at the waterfront and moves to the City Hall area and then west to Charles Center. From there it continues west to the University of Maryland and then moves north of Charles Center to Mt. Vernon Place, ending at Preston Street near the Mount Royal area.

The north side of the Inner Harbor, or "Bason," as it was labeled on a map of 1801, was the focus of activity in early Baltimore, but the area was destroyed in the fire of 1904 (*see* Baltimore). All the pre-Revolutionary city is gone, as well as much that was built in the nineteenth century. The buildings by the **Pratt Street Waterfront** (1), which include three- and four-story brick structures, were erected immediately after the fire. The structures included house cafes, ship chandlers' stores, wholesale coffee houses, rooming houses, and other stores and residential buildings. Tugboats, pleasure boats, and an occasional freighter dock at the piers on the opposite side of Pratt Street. The piers, which run from Jones Falls to Light Street, were acquired and rebuilt by the city after the fire. Before World War II, Bay craft of all kinds brought fish and produce to the piers near the markets by Jones Falls, but this traffic has disappeared. The last regular Bay steamboat service ended in 1960, and poor railroad and truck access into the narrow slips has caused cargo ships to move to other areas of the harbor. Renewal plans for the Inner Harbor include developing a small-boat marina and "boatel," converting the municipal piers along Pratt Street to other uses, and landscaping the waterfront. Other proposed redevelopment plans include the construction of apartments and town houses, to attract residents back to the downtown area, and office buildings, including a thirty-story international trade mart, for maritime-related businesses. Other new construction in the Basin area includes the Harbor Campus of the Community College of Baltimore and a new home for the Maryland Academy of Science, the Maryland Science Center designed by Edward Durrell Stone.

These sections of Pratt and Light streets were once marsh and water. Beginning in the 1780s the city dredged the Basin and used the mud to fill the marshes, gradually creating new solid land. Pratt Street, which was in existence to the west of the Basin by 1780, was named to honor Charles Pratt, first earl of Camden, an English statesman who had supported the American cause during the Revolution.

Along the Pratt Street Waterfront, tied up to Pier 1, is the **U.S.F. *Constellation*** (2) (open Mon.–Fri., 10–4; Sat.–Sun., 2–5; admission fee), the first frigate built by the fledgling United States and launched

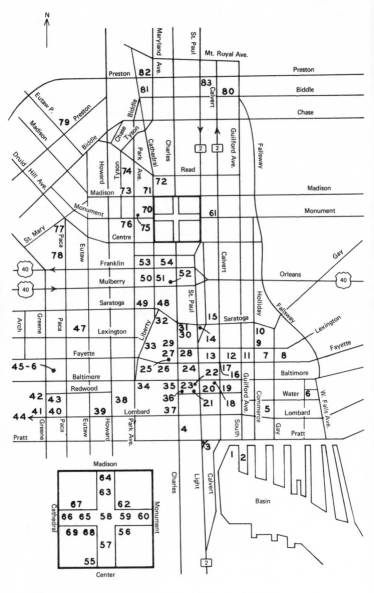

KEY

1. Pratt Street Waterfront
2. U.S.F. *Constellation*
3. Gen. Samuel Smith Park
4. U.S. Fidelity and Guarantee
5. United States Customs House
6. Marsh Market
7. Memorial Plaza
8. War Memorial
9. Zion Lutheran Church
10. Municipal Museum of the City of
    Baltimore (Peale Museum)
11. City Hall

12. Federal Courthouse
13. Baltimore City Courthouse
14. Preston Gardens
15. Mercy Hospital
16. Battle Monument
17. Site of Barnum's City Hotel
18. Alexander Brown and Sons
19. Mercantile Safe Deposit and Trust
    Building
20. Site of the Lovely Lane Meeting
    House
21. Site of the Fountain Inn

DOWNTOWN BALTIMORE TOUR

in 1797 in Harris Creek. Josiah Humphrey, a Philadelphia Quaker, designed the ship, but the builder, David Stodder, apparently altered the plans to conform more closely to those of the then-developing Baltimore clippers, a change that made the frigate unusually fast. While on her maiden trip in 1798, the United States was unofficially at war with France. In 1799 she captured the *L'Insurgente*—the first prize ship won by a U.S. vessel. The *Constellation* was renovated in 1812–13, and in 1852–53 she was lengthened twelve feet and redesigned as a sloop of war. The navy received a considerable shock when it was discovered that the mold of the ship did not follow Humphrey's plans, and the discrepancy, when rediscovered later, led to a theory that in 1852 the navy got around a congressional prohibition against new naval craft by building a new ship under the guise of remodeling an old one. During the Civil War, the *Constellation* served on the Union side, though as a sailing vessel she was rapidly becoming obsolete. She is the last remaining sailing ship to have served in the U.S. Navy during wartime, and thereafter she was used exclusively as a training vessel. In 1955, the *Constellation* was brought down from Newport, Rhode Island. Since then, the Constellation Committee of the Star-Spangled Banner Flag House has raised the necessary money to restore her as a sloop of war.

At Light and Pratt streets, the **Gen. Samuel Smith Park** (3) is a green island in the sea of automobiles created by parking and traffic arteries. The statue of General Smith (1752–1839), distinguished Revolutionary soldier who helped organize the defense of Baltimore in 1814, was unveiled July 4, 1918, on its original site at Charles and 29th streets.

Pratt Street was the scene of a mob attack on the Sixth Massachusetts Regiment on April 19, 1861. The regiment—the first fully organized

22. Maryland National Bank Building
23. Savings Bank of Baltimore
24. Blaustein Building
25. Hamburgers
26. Vermont Federal Savings and Loan
27. One Charles Center
28. Central Savings Bank
29. Fidelity Building
30. Masonic Temple
31. St. Paul's Protestant Episcopal Church
32. Two Charles Center
33. Baltimore Gas and Electric Company Building
34. Mercantile Safe Deposit and Trust Company Building
35. Morris Mechanic Theater
36. Hansa Haus
37. Sun Life Building
38. Baltimore Civic Center
39. Emerson Building
40. Davidge Hall
41. School of Dentistry
42. University of Maryland Hospital
43. Frank C. Bressler Research Laboratory
44. St. Paul's Cemetery
45. Westminster Presbyterian Church
46. Grave of Edgar Allan Poe
47. Lexington Market
48. St. Paul's Rectory
49. St. Alphonsus Roman Catholic Church
50. Enoch Pratt Free Library
51. Basilica of the Assumption of the Blessed Virgin Mary
52. Archbishop's House
53. Franklin Street Presbyterian Church
54. First Unitarian Church
55. Walters Art Gallery
56. Peabody Institute
57. Lafayette Monument
58. Washington Monument
59. Statue of George Peabody
60. Statue of Severn Teackle Wallis
61. Center Stage
62. Mount Vernon Place Methodist Church
63. Statue of Chief Justice Roger Brooke Taney
64. Statue of John Eager Howard
65. Lion
66. Military Courage
67. Tiffany-Fisher House
68. Thomas-Jencks-Gladding House
69. Garrett-Jacobs House
70. Miller House
71. 800-806 Cathedral Street
72. Emmanuel Protestant Episcopal Church
73. First Presbyterian Church
74. Tyson Street
75. Grace and St. Peter's Protestant Episcopal Church
76. Maryland Historical Society
77. St. Mary's Seminary Chapel
78. Mother Seton's House
79. State Office Building Center
80. Home of Wallis Warfield
81. Medical and Chirurgical Faculty of Maryland
82. Annunciation Greek Orthodox Church
83. Winans House

and equipped unit to respond to Lincoln's call for troops on April 15, 1861—had arrived at the President Street Station of the Philadelphia, Wilmington, and Baltimore Railroad and marched along Pratt Street to the Camden Station of the Baltimore & Ohio Railroad. Many, and perhaps most, Baltimoreans favored secession. The soldiers had been ordered to load their muskets but not to fire despite any provocation. At approximately the same time that half the troops arrived at Camden Station, crowds of Baltimoreans started throwing stones and soon blocked the railroad tracks. The remaining soldiers, about 220 in number, were formed into companies to march the distance of about a mile to Camden Station. A group of Southern sympathizers paraded defiantly in front of the Massachusetts men with a Confederate flag, which Northern partisans then attempted to seize. This incited an attack by the mob on the soldiers and also the civilian supporters of the Union. When the soldiers reached the Pratt Street bridge over Jones Falls they opened fire, whether by order or at will has never been ascertained. A running fight ensued from the bridge to Light Street; four soldiers and eleven citizens were killed and thirty-six soldiers and a great many citizens were wounded. Just west of the bridge, George William Brown, mayor of Baltimore, took charge of the troops at great personal risk, but at Light Street, where he saw the futility of his efforts, he retired. Fortunately for the soldiers, just beyond Light Street George P. Kane, marshal of the police, and forty men arrived from the Camden Station and formed a line to the rear of the troops, thus enabling the remainder of the men to reach the station in safety to board a Washington train.

Just beyond the park on Pratt Street is **U.S. Fidelity and Guarantee** (U.S.F.&G.) (4), the highest building in Baltimore City. There are entrances on each side of the building, which is bounded by Pratt, Charles, Light, and Lombard streets. A sculpture by Henry Moore is exhibited in the courtyard.

At Lombard and Gay streets is the **United States Customs House** (5) (1900–1908), a four-story neoclassic building, part of which stands on the site of the first offices occupied by the Customs when it was established here in 1786. The building was dedicated as a National Historic Landmark in 1972. Murals in the Call Room, on the first floor, include a sixty-eight-by-thirty-foot painting of a fleet of sailing vessels, ranging from schooner to frigate, with various riggings. The mural was painted by Francis D. Millet, who lost his life in the *Titanic* disaster.

The area just to the west of Jones Falls and north of Baltimore Street was known as Harrison's Marsh until after the Revolution. The city had drained the marsh by 1785 and established a market (moved from Baltimore and Gay streets) on the site. Officially called the Centre Market, it was known to all as the **Marsh** (or M'ash) **Market** (6), Market Place at Water Street. The market was rebuilt shortly after the fire of 1904, but along with other buildings in the area it is slated for demolition to make space for the extension of the Jones Falls Expressway and a new Municipal Center.

Just beyond the "Burnt District" (but only four blocks north of the Pratt Street Waterfront) and between the Fallsway and Holliday Street is a complex of public and historic buildings centered on the City Hall, the War Memorial, and the surrounding landscaped plaza bounded by Fayette and Lexington streets. From the steps of the Memorial, on Gay Street, between Fayette and Lexington, one can look across **Memorial Plaza** (7) to the massive marble facade of *City Hall*. To the left can be seen the towers of the twentieth-century office buildings that arose from the ashes of the fire. To the right is the twelve-story, limestone-faced **Municipal Building** (1927). In front of the Municipal Building, the parish house tower (1912–13) of *Zion Lutheran Church* (1807) provides a deep red accent. The brick **Headquarters of the City**

Fire Department (1922) immediately adjoins the parish house and church. Next to the parish house, but out of sight on Holliday Street, is the *Peale Museum* (1814). The waters of Jones Falls flow under the Fallsway—the stream was bricked over after the fire as a flood control project—and just across it on Front at Fayette Street, the tapered brick cylinder of the Shot Tower (1828) (*see* East and Northeast Baltimore [3]) stands in gaunt contrast to the Greek-Revival St. Vincent de Paul Roman Catholic Church (1841) (*see* East and Northeast Baltimore [4]), with its graceful white spire, half a block up Front Street.

Plans for beautifying the area around City Hall were developed after the fire of 1904, but little was accomplished until the **War Memorial** (8) (open Mon.–Fri., 10–4; Sat., 8–12) was constructed. Occupying three entire blocks, ground for the memorial was broken in 1921 by Marshal Ferdinand Foch, followed by the dedication in 1925. The neo-classic white marble hall, designed by Laurence Hall Fowler, is approached by a flight of steps that leads to a portico of Doric columns. The grand entrance opens into the main hall, which occupies the whole second floor. On the marble walls are carved the names of Marylanders who died in World War I. At the head of the stairs leading down to the first floor are two urns of black Belgian marble engraved with the names of all previous battles in which Maryland soldiers took part. On the wall over-the stairs is a mural by R. MacGill Mackall of Baltimore showing Victory standing over the tomb of the Unknown Soldier. The first floor has meeting rooms and offices for local veterans' organizations.

The brick walls of **Zion Lutheran Church** (9) (George Rohrbach and Johann Mackenheimer), on the corner of Holliday and Lexington streets, were raised in 1807, and after the fire in 1840 the church was rebuilt within them. The Gothic taste of the 1840s is reflected in the combination of the pedimented gable of the earlier church with the tiny crenellated turrets at the front corners of the roof, and a false crenellated tower front has replaced the earlier square tower with a pyramidic roof that better suited the proportions of the walls. The pale gray interior of the church is lit by a double tier of stained-glass windows, and a balcony runs along three sides. The pews of varnished oak retain the nameplates of their first owners. In the vestibule hang portraits of former pastors, beginning with Johann Daniel Kurtz (1763–1856), pastor (1785–1833) when the church was built and first president of the General Synod of Lutherans in America.

The Hofmann Library, a valuable collection of rare Bibles and church histories, is in the brick parish house, designed in 1912 by Theodore Wells Pietsch in the German-Hanseatic style. Off one side of the parish house, which fronts on Holliday Street, a brick arcade containing an old tile mosaic leads to a small parsonage built in the same style after World War I. A sculpture exhibit is held every spring in the walled garden flanked by these buildings.

German Lutherans founded Zion Church in 1755, making it one of the oldest church organizations in Baltimore. Services were conducted in German only until after World War II, and Pastor Kurtz has been Zion's only American-born pastor. During the Know-Nothing riots of the 1850s, Pastor Heinrich Scheib (1808–97) was responsible for pointing out the contributions that Maryland Germans had made in America, and because of him the church was a center of German-American life in Baltimore for half a century. Scheib, although he considered himself a Lutheran, was theologically close to the Unitarians, and during his exceptionally long pastorate (1835–96) Zion Church broke entirely with local and national Lutheran groups, a breach since repaired. He replaced the parochial school, long part of the church, with the famous nondenominational and progressive Scheib School, which in the 1860s reached an enrollment of 802 children. The establishment of the public

German-American schools after the Civil War finally led to the closing of the Scheib School in 1895. The school bell still hangs in the garden on the Gay Street side of the church.

Next to the Zion Lutheran parish house, at 225 Holliday Street, is the **Municipal Museum of the City of Baltimore** (10) (open Tues.–Fri., 10:30–4:30; Sat.–Sun., 1–5), which from 1830 to 1875 served as City Hall. Originally constructed to house "Peale's Museum and Gallery of Fine Arts," the building is still popularly known as the **Peale Museum.** Its builder, Rembrandt Peale (1778–1860), was a son of Charles Willson Peale (1741–1827), a well-known portrait painter of George Washington and founder in 1786 of the first museum in America. Rembrandt Peale was himself a talented painter, and both father and son were men of wide and varied interests. In 1796, Rembrandt and his brother Rubens opened a gallery of their paintings in Baltimore, accompanied by a "cabinet of natural history." In 1813, Rembrandt decided to establish a "Scientific Institution, such as the population and wealth of this city demands." Robert Cary Long, Sr. (1770–1833), a self-trained but prominent architect of the Classic Revival in Baltimore, designed the building, the first in America specifically planned as a museum. With no precedent to guide him, Long designed a typical town house—central hallway with two rooms on each side downstairs and a large drawing room on the second floor—to which he added a square wing at the rear. The wing consisted of two rooms, the ground floor lighted by windows, the second floor by a skylight. In August, 1814, Peale opened the doors of this "Institution intended as an elegant *Rendezvous* for taste, curiosity and leisure." He exhibited "Birds, Beasts, Fishes, Snakes, Antiquities, Indian Dresses, and War Instruments, Shells and Miscellaneous Curiosities," mastodon bones he and his father had dug up on a farm in New York State in 1801, and paintings, among them the "Court of Death, an Original Painting by Rembrandt Peale (24 feet long—13 feet high—the figures larger than life)." In 1816, Peale introduced lighting by "Carburetted Hydrogen Gas" into the museum. Peale's brother Rubens had been experimenting with this type of artificial light in Philadelphia, and installation of the system in the museum was the first practical use of gaslight in Baltimore. The same year, with Long and others, Peale formed the first gaslight company in the country, which obtained a contract for lighting the streets of the city.

The museum was not a financial success, and in the belief that he could do better with his paintings, Rembrandt turned it over to his brother Rubens in 1822. In 1830, Rubens sold the building to the City of Baltimore for use as a City Hall and moved his collection to a building that burned in 1833. The original museum building continued in use as a City Hall until 1875. Thereafter it was used first as a school, later by the city Water Board, and then it was rented as factory space until, in 1928, it was condemned as unsafe. The city was then persuaded to restore the building, although little but the shell of the original could be retained. All of the floors, woodwork, locks, mantels, and other interior features have been removed from other houses of nearly the same period.

The present museum, which opened in 1931, houses the bones of the mastodon originally exhibited by Rembrandt Peale and some of his gas illuminating equipment. Also on exhibit is a portrait of Charles Calvert, fifth proprietor, painted by Van Der Rhyn and brought to Maryland by Calvert himself in 1732, and also Charles Willson Peale's painting *Exhuming the First American Mastodon.* Among other paintings in the gallery are six portraits of heroes of the War of 1812, commissioned by the City of Baltimore in 1817–18 and painted by Rembrandt Peale in his studio on the third floor of this building. Among the museum's holdings of Baltimoreana is an exceedingly valuable collection of prints and photographs of Baltimore, some of which are on exhibit.

West of the Memorial Plaza, from Holliday to St. Paul streets, the three city blocks between Fayette and Lexington streets are occupied by three government buildings: the **City Hall** (11) (1867–75), designed in the Empire style by George Frederick, between Holliday and South streets; the **Federal Courthouse** (formerly the U.S. Post Office) (12) (1930); and the marble **Baltimore City Courthouse** (13) (1894–99) between Calvert and St. Paul streets. The City Courthouse, designed by J. B. Noel Wyatt and William G. Nolting, is in the French-Renaissance style and contains a number of murals by American painters of the late nineteenth century. Inside the St. Paul Street entrance is the *Lawgivers* by John La Farge, depicting Justinian, Moses, Mohammed, Lycurgus, and Confucius. Edwin Blashfield is represented by *Religious Toleration* (Lord Baltimore recommending Wisdom, Justice, and Mercy to the colonists) on the walls of the Court of Equity, and by *Washington Surrendering His Commission* in the Court of Common Pleas. The *Burning of the Peggy Stewart* and *Barter with the Indians for Land in Southern Maryland in 1634,* by Charles Yardley Turner, decorate the vestibule of the Criminal Court and the corridor nearby. In the Orphans' Court are four panels by the French artist Jean Paul Lauiens showing the *Surrender of Cornwallis at Yorktown.* The City Courthouse, the Federal Courthouse, and the City Hall survived the fire because the wind changed, sending the flames toward the water.

On the St. Paul Street side of the City Courthouse is **St. Paul Place.** Landscaping around a handsome fountain was finished in 1964 as a continuation of **Preston Gardens** (14), a five-block strip of greenery brilliant with tulips in May and always a pleasant greenspace in the crowded downtown area. Preston Gardens was a major downtown renewal project during World War I, named after the mayor who supported the project. At St. Paul and Saratoga streets, one block north of the City Courthouse in the Preston Gardens area, is the twenty-one-story main building of the $8,000,000 **Mercy Hospital** (15) (1963, D. K. Este Fisher and Warren Bowersock). The building is one of the most striking of the new skyscrapers built in the early 1960s as part of efforts, both municipal and private, to rehabilitate the center of the city. A fifteen-story block overhangs a smaller six-story block on all sides, creating the effect of a giant peg.

Between the courthouses, in the middle of Calvert Street, is the **Battle Monument** (16) (1815–27), raised under the auspices of the Committee of Vigilance and Safety to commemorate the Battle of Baltimore, September 12–14, 1814. The monument is the first substantial war memorial built in the United States; its cornerstone was laid on September 12, 1815, the first anniversary of the battle. The monument was designed by Maximilian Godefroy (ca. 1765–ca. 1845), an officer of the French Revolutionary army who came to Baltimore in 1805 to teach architecture and fine arts at St. Mary's College (*see below* [77]). Rising from the tapered rectangular base, apparently modeled after an Egyptian monument described in a book written after Napoleon's Egyptian campaign, is a Roman fascia, its fillets bearing the names of Americans killed in the battle. Topping the monument is a classical statue of Victory carved by Antonio Capellano, an Italian sculptor who worked in the United States from 1816 to 1828 and who came from New York to Baltimore at Godefroy's invitation. In 1964, the city planted and landscaped the square to provide an attractive setting for the monument, which for years had been lost among the large buildings and parked automobiles of the busy downtown street.

The monument is on the **Site of the Baltimore County Courthouse** built in 1768 and razed in 1809. From 1784 until its demolition, the courthouse presented a unique appearance, because Calvert Street ran under it. The tunnel was underpinned by a great stone arch twenty feet high, which gave it, in the words of one traveler, "as bad an appearance as a Man on Stilts."

On the southwest corner of Fayette and Calvert streets (on the Equitable Building side) is the **Site of Barnum's City Hotel** (17), a famous nineteenth-century hostelry that opened in 1826. In his *American Notes* Charles Dickens wrote: "The most comfortable of all the hotels of which I had any experience in the United States, and they were not a few, is Barnum's in that city [Baltimore]; where the English traveler will find curtains to his bed, for the first and probably the last time, in America; and where he will be likely to have enough water for washing himself, which is not at all a common case."

South of the City Courthouse, in the Calvert—St. Paul—Light Street area, is Baltimore's financial district, which was virtually destroyed by the fire. **Alexander Brown and Sons** (18) (1900, Parker and Thomas), at the corner of Calvert and Baltimore streets, is the only building that was not gutted by the fire. At Calvert and Redwood streets, the dark brick exterior of the **Mercantile Safe Deposit and Trust Building** (19) (1885, J. B. Noel Wyatt and Joseph E. Sperry), with its handsome Romanesque-Revival detail, is another lucky survivor of the fire. A number of tall office buildings were built or rebuilt in this area after the fire and before World War II.

Number 206 E. Redwood Street is on the **Site of the Lovely Lane Meeting House** (20) (built in 1774 and burned in 1796), where in December, 1784, representatives of Methodist societies met and organized the Methodist Episcopal Church of the United States of America. At this meeting, and at the suggestion of John Wesley, the English leader of the Methodists, Francis Asbury was chosen superintendent of the church in America. Henceforth Asbury called himself bishop, a title accepted by later Conferences (*see* West Baltimore [7]).

The **Site of the Fountain Inn** (21) is across the street from the site of the Methodist meeting house. The inn, probably built during the Revolution, enjoyed a wide reputation among travelers for more than half a century. George Washington stayed there in September of 1781 and again on April 11, 1789, while on his way to New York to take the oath as the first president of the United States.

Another building in the financial district is the thiry-four-story **Maryland National Bank Building** (originally the Baltimore Trust Building) (22) (1929) at Light and Baltimore streets.

Charles Center occupies thirty-three acres bounded by Lombard, Charles, Saratoga, and Liberty streets and Hopkins Place. All but five of the buildings standing in 1959 have been demolished, the property having been acquired by the urban renewal agency of the city and then resold to developers. The site, a blighted area between the retail center to the west along Howard Street and the financial and government centers to the east, was selected to serve as a stimulus for improvement in all areas of the city. All but two streets, Baltimore and Fayette, have been closed off to create three superblocks within which pedestrians can move freely. Three public parks create open space in the area, and the tall new buildings that have been constructed are devoted to retail and office space, a new hotel, and a theater. Because the land drops sixty-six feet from Saratoga to Lombard Street, the pedestrian walkway that begins at street level in the top superblock becomes a second-floor walkway crossing Fayette and Baltimore streets. The walkway provides pedestrian access to all of Charles Center, entering the various buildings of the lower area at the second floor. All automobile parking is underground.

Planners for Charles Center establish the size of parcels to be sold to developers, the height of buildings to be erected, and the amount of floor space that each can contain. When developers bid for parcels of land, they must submit detailed plans for the structures they propose to build, which are then examined by an Architectural Review Board to insure quality of construction and design. The whole Charles

Center development is unified by the exterior design of walkways, public parks, and landscaping, all closely controlled by city planners.

The **Savings Bank of Baltimore** (23) (1905–7, Parker, Thomas, and Rice), Baltimore and Charles streets, is designed after the Erechtheum in Athens. The two-story building has a pedimented front, supported by four Ionic columns. On the side there are six similar columns. The second floor was added in 1953.

Even before One Charles Center was completed, the **Blaustein Building** (24) (1 N. Charles Street), a thirty-story tower designed by Vincent Kling, was being constructed across the street.

From the plaza of *One Charles Center*, the pedestrian walkway crosses Fayette Street on either side of the second floor of **Hamburgers** (25) (1963, Styler, Ketcham, and Myers), which bridges the street. This clothing store is two stories in its airspace—the glassed-in second story actually hangs from third-story trusses sheaved in buff-colored brick—and three stories at the south corner of Charles and Fayette. Next to it on Fayette Street is the small seven-story glass and aluminum tower of **Vermont Federal Savings and Loan** (26) (1964, Edward Q. Rogers), which, like Hamburgers, can be reached from the second-level walkway as well as from the street. Both Hamburgers and Vermont Federal were formerly located within the redevelopment area, and their decision to buy lots helped scale down some of the plans for Charles Center, since such small enterprises could not afford the great towers originally planned.

The first new building constructed in Charles Center was **One Charles Center** (27), at Charles and Fayette streets, a twenty-four-story, dark glass and aluminum T-shaped tower completed in 1962 (Metropolitan Structures Inc., of Chicago, designed by Mies van der Rohe). Architects consider the proportions of the building perfect and admire its severe lines. Part of the first floor lobby is a glassed-in rectangle surrounding the two elevator shafts, which are faced with handsome green marble. The remainder of the lobby is open and thus becomes part of the plaza in front of the building. The plaza itself is one of the outstanding features of the whole design, for the architect used it to give the building a pleasant setting. Because of the steep drop of the land at this point, ground-floor shops are located under the plaza, and the adjacent public park is reached by handsomely designed steps that form part of the open lobby of One Charles Center.

On the southeast corner of Charles and Lexington streets is the **Central Savings Bank** (28) (1890), one of the five remaining original buildings in the area. The northward progress of the fire of 1904 was supposedly checked by this building.

The **Fidelity Building** (29) (1894, Baldwin and Pennington), on the northwest corner of Charles and Lexington streets, stands in sharp contrast to the nearby One Charles Center building.

At 223–25 N. Charles Street (opposite Charles Center) is the **Masonic Temple** (30) (1866, 1910). Washington Lodge #3 was chartered in Baltimore by the Grand Lodge of Pennsylvania on June 28, 1770, and came under the jurisdiction of the Grand Lodge of A. F. and A. M. of Maryland, which was organized on April 17, 1787. Edmund A. Lind designed the first two stories of the Second Empire facade in 1866, but fires in 1890 and 1908 led to extensive rebuilding. Among the treasures housed in a museum of Masoniana on the second floor is the desk said to be from the Old Senate Chamber in the Maryland State House in Annapolis and beside which Washington stood on December 23, 1783, when he handed his resignation as commander in chief of the American armies to Thomas Mifflin, President of the United States in Congress Assembled.

Next to the Masonic Temple, at Saratoga and Charles streets, is the lot purchased by St. Paul's Parish in 1730. The present red brick **St.**

Paul's Protestant Episcopal Church (31) (1854–56) (open weekdays, 7:20–5; Sun., 7:30–4), designed by Richard Upjohn of New York shortly after his return from Italy, adapts the walls of the previous church (built 1814–17 by Robert Cary Long, Sr., and burned in 1854) to the basilica form of twelfth-century Lombardy. The original plans called for a campanile of seven stories, but only two were built. The reliefs on the entrance front of the church were carved by Antonio Capellano (*see above* [16]). Once almost crowded out by neighboring office buildings, the church is now set off by a small brick plaza in Charles Center on the opposite corner of Charles and Saratoga streets.

On Charles and Saratoga streets is **Two Charles Center** (32) (1965–69, Conklin and Rossant). Standing on 1.9 acres, the apartment towers and adjacent buildings are constructed of reinforced concrete faced with dark brown brick. The complex contains offices, stores, restaurants, and a movie theater. From the plaza on the eastern end there is a view of old *St. Paul's Protestant Episcopal Church.*

The **Baltimore Gas and Electric Company Building** (33) (1916, Parker and Thomas) stands on Lexington and Liberty streets. On the fourth-floor level is a row of eight-foot figures that represent "knowledge, light, heat, and power." An addition was built in 1966.

The new office of the **Mercantile Safe Deposit and Trust Company Building** (34) (1969, Peterson and Brickbauer of Baltimore and Emery, Roth, and Sons of New York) is situated at Baltimore Street and Hopkins Place. It is a twenty-four-story tower with three levels below the lobby.

The **Morris Mechanic Theater** (35) (1967, John M. Johansen), Baltimore and Charles streets, is categorized as "Functional Expressionism" by its architect. From the outside, it resembles a small horizontal sculptural form when compared to the surrounding perpendicular edifices. The theater itself rests on a platform beneath which stores and restaurants are housed. The concrete of the exterior was poured so as to give the appearance of sawn oak boards.

Inside, the seating capacity of the theater is 1,800. The stage can support over thirty tons of scenery, and no view from the balcony is obstructed in any way.

At 2 E. Redwood Street stands the **Hansa Haus** (36) (1907, Parker, Thomas, and Rice), an English half-timbered cottage. At one time the North German Lloyd Steamship Company was located here. The building, now owned by the Savings Bank of Baltimore, houses the downtown branch of the Baltimore Museum of Art.

At S. Charles Street and Hopkins Place is the **Sun Life Building** (37) (1966, Peterson and Brickbauer of Baltimore, and Emery, Roth, and Sons of New York), a twelve-story building of black Canadian granite. The first-floor plaza contains an open terrace and a lobby in which a Dimitri Hadzi sculpture hangs from the ceiling.

Adjacent to Charles Center, but not a part of it, is the **Baltimore Civic Center** (38) (1962, A. G. Odell, Jr., and Assoc.), a municipally owned exhibition hall and sports arena that occupies about four acres and seats over 10,000 persons; it was built here to take advantage of the Charles Center renewal effort and to contribute to the area's growth. Many Baltimoreans criticize the design of the Civic Center, which is a barnlike rectangle with a bizarre roof line created by a series of long boxes resting on edge with tapered ends and triangular faces. The jagged profile of the roof line has suggested to some viewers the backbone of a prehistoric monster.

A plaque on the Civic Center notes that the land here includes the **Site of Congress Hall,** which stood at the corner of Liberty and Baltimore streets. This was headquarters for the Continental Congress from December, 1776, to February, 1777, and here on December 27, Washington was voted full military command. A few yards away at Baltimore and Hanover streets in the middle of Charles Center is the

Site of the Indian Queen Inn. Francis Scott Key is believed to have come here on the morning of September 14, 1814, with a draft of "The Star-Spangled Banner," which he then revised and completed, in his pocket.

The 357-foot clock tower of the **Emerson Building** or the **Bromo Seltzer Tower** (39) (1910–11, Baltimore Arts Tower), at Lombard and Eutaw streets, dominates the approach to the University of Maryland at the western edge of the downtown area. The tower, designed by Joseph E. Sperry and constructed for Capt. Isaac Edward Emerson, manufacturer of Bromo Seltzer, resembles that of the early-fourteenth-century Palazzo Vecchio in Florence, except that the numerals on the clock faces are marked by letters spelling out the name of the acid-neutralizing product. Until 1937 the tower was surmounted by a huge Bromo Seltzer bottle with a gilded crown.

The **University of Maryland Schools of Medicine, Pharmacy, Dentistry, Law, and Social Work** cluster on Greene Street at its intersections with Lombard and Redwood streets. **Davidge Hall** (40) (1812–13) (open Mon.–Fri., 9–4), the original building of the medical school, still stands on the corner of Greene and Lombard. There was little earlier precedent in America for the Roman Pantheon scheme of this building, which was designed by Robert Cary Long, Sr. (*see above* [10]), for the College of Medicine of Maryland. The building is named after John B. Davidge, a founder and member of the first faculty of the College of Medicine, who, like several other local European-trained physicians, had delivered lectures to medical students and supervised dissection of human cadavers before the college was established. A "dissection mob" destroyed his private "anatomical laboratory" on Liberty Street in November, 1807, an event that precipitated application to the legislature for the medical college charter that was granted in December of the same year. Late in 1812, the legislature authorized the College of Medicine to annex the faculties of law, divinity, and arts and sciences, the whole to be called the University of Maryland.

Across Greene Street from Davidge Hall, the **School of Dentistry** (41) houses a collection of old dental instruments and other relics of dental history, including one of George Washington's sets of teeth. Since 1923, the School of Dentistry has included the Baltimore College of Dental Surgery, established in 1840 and the oldest school of dentistry in the United States.

The brick **University of Maryland Hospital** (42) (1933–34), built in the form of a Greek cross at Greene and Redwood streets, is a teaching hospital connected with the medical school. Across Greene Street is the **Frank C. Bressler Research Laboratory** (43), founded for medical research by bequest of a local physician.

From Redwood Street to Fayette Street and from Paca Street to Arch Street, an area covering about four city blocks, everything except a church was demolished in one of the great clearance projects of the city's renewal agency. Additions to the Schools of Law and Dentistry have been built. Adjoining the university grounds to the west is **St. Paul's Cemetery** (44) (closed), at Lombard Street and Fremont Avenue, which was opened by St. Paul's Protestant Episcopal Parish about 1804. The bodies previously interred in the cemetery at Charles and Saratoga streets, where the present church stands, were moved here about 1817. Among those who repose in the cemetery are Lt. Col. Tench Tilghman (1744–86) (*see* Tour 17, Plinhimmon); Daniel Dulany the younger (1722–97); Supreme Court Justice Samuel Chase (1741–1811); John Eager Howard (1752–1827) (*see below* [64]); and Col. George Armistead (1780–1818).

The rugged brick **Westminster Presbyterian Church** (45) (1852, Thomas Dixon, Thomas Balbirnie, and James M. Dixon), at Greene and Fayette streets (churchyard open), is of early Gothic-Revival style. The churchyard gates on Paca Street, designed by Maximilian Godefroy (*see* *above* [16]), reflect the architect's interest in ancient Egyptian styles. Here is the **Grave of Edgar Allan Poe** (46) (*see* West Baltimore [2]), marked by a large stone. On the cemetery wall behind it is a bronze plaque, which was presented in 1921 by French admirers of Poe under the sponsorship of the French Literary Society. Poe died mysteriously and obscurely in Baltimore while on a visit in 1849. One of the many stories concerning his death is that, either drunken or drugged, he was kidnapped by a gang of political hoodlums and taken from one polling place to another as a repeat voter, an exhausting experience which, in his poor state of health, led to his collapse. He was originally buried in the rear of the church, but in 1875 Baltimore schoolteachers, aroused by the neglect of the grave, collected pennies from their pupils and used the money to move the body to the present spot near the entrance. Also buried here is Poe's grandfather, David Poe (1743–1816), a cabinetmaker who served in the Revolution, as well as Col. James McHenry (1755–1816), Washington's secretary of war, James Calhoun (1743–1816), first mayor of Baltimore (1797–1804), and Gen. Samuel Smith (1752–1839), defender of Baltimore in 1814.

One block north of Westminster Church, Lexington Street leads eastward through the business center of Baltimore back to Charles Center, four blocks away. At Lexington and Eutaw streets is the **Lexington Market** (47), established by John Eager Howard on the present site in 1782 and still one of the chief retail food markets of the city. Lexington Street recently became a pedestrian mall in the blocks nearest Charles Center as part of a redevelopment program for the downtown retail area.

Immediately north of Charles Center (which may be reached from Lexington Market by walking two blocks east) is one of the most delightful sections of the city. First developed in the early and mid-nineteenth century, many of the churches and houses then erected still stand.

Saratoga Street was the northernmost limit of the town as first laid out, and **St. Paul's Rectory** (48) (1789–91), 24 W. Saratoga at Cathedral Street, sits opposite the giants of Charles Center as the only eighteenth-century building left standing in the downtown area. John Eager Howard conveyed the land to the parish with the stipulation that it should always be the site of the rectory. Originally located at the very edge of the town, the rectory is a handsome example of a late-Georgian country house, one room deep with a pedimented projecting central bay that gives prominence to the handsome doorway and the Palladian window above it. Of interest is the polygonal bay at the rear of the house containing the stair.

One block west of St. Paul's Rectory is the Gothic-Revival **St. Alphonsus Roman Catholic Church** (49) (1841–45) (open weekdays, 7–4 or 6; Sun., 7–12:30), at Saratoga Street and Park Avenue, designed by Robert Cary Long, Jr. (1810–49). Like his father, Long was one of the outstanding native-born architects of nineteenth-century Baltimore. The brick walls of the church are lightly buttressed and battlemented, dominated by a spire that rises in tiers of pointed arch windows and crenellations. Sandblasting, which converted the church from gray to salmon, recently set off an uproar about esthetics and the architect's intentions.

One block north of St. Paul's Rectory, on Cathedral Street between Mulberry and Franklin streets, is the **Enoch Pratt Free Library** (50) (1933, Tilton and Githens, New York, and Clyde N. Friz) (open Mon.–Thurs., 9–9; Fri.–Sat., 9–5; Sun., 1–5), a three-story neoclassic limestone building whose entrance and twelve large display windows face on Cathedral Street. The great two-story central room of the library contains the catalogs and loan desks. Two murals by George Novikoff show Gutenberg and his press and Caxton presenting his first book to his patroness, the Duchess Marguerite. Behind the loan desks hang

Lexington Market

portraits of the six Lords Baltimore and of Gov. Benedict Leonard Calvert, which were bequeathed to the library by Dr. Hugh Hampton Young. Until Dr. Young bought the portraits in 1933, they had been in the family of Gov. Robert Eden, brother-in-law of Frederick, sixth Lord Baltimore, who died in 1771 without legitimate heirs. *George Calvert* (1580–1632) was painted by Daniel Mytens (1590–1642), court painter to the early Stuarts; *Cecilius Calvert* (1606–75), by Gerard Zoest (copy by Florence Mackubin); *Charles Calvert* (1630–1715), by Sir Godfrey Kneller (1646–1723); *Benedict Leonard Calvert* (1677–1715), by an unknown artist; *Charles Calvert* (1699–1751), by an unknown artist; and *Frederick Calvert* (1731–71), by Johann Ludwig Tietz, a German painter who followed the Hanoverian court to England. The portrait of the second *Benedict Leonard Calvert* (1700–1732), governor of Maryland from 1728 to 1732, was painted by Francis Brerewood, whose brother Thomas was married to the governor's sister Charlotte.

The rooms off the central hall house hundreds of thousands of books that circulate to the public for reading in or out of the library.

On the second floor, the **Maryland Department** houses books, pamphlets, and pictures, many exceedingly rare, that particularly relate to Maryland, including the George Cator Collection of pictures and engravings and the Hester Dorsey Richardson collection of Maryland coats of arms. The walls are decorated with murals by the Baltimore artist Lee Woodward Zeigler, showing scenes from Edmund Spenser's *Faerie Queen.* Poe manuscripts and letters are preserved in the **Edgar Allan Poe Room,** where the Edgar Allan Poe Society meets and where the library sponsors poetry readings and lectures. The **Music and Fine Arts Room** houses books and periodicals and loans phonograph records; turntables for playing records in the library are supplied.

In the **H. L. Mencken Room** on the third floor, serious students may study the collection of papers and books left to the library by H. L. Mencken (1880–1956), famous journalist, debunker, and linguistic scholar. Mencken, who lived all his life in Baltimore, began his career as a journalist in 1898 and worked for the *Sunpapers* from 1906 until a stroke terminated his literary activities in 1948. In 1908 he became literary editor of the monthly *Smart Set,* and from 1914 to 1923 he co-edited the journal with drama critic George Jean Nathan. During these years he acquired fame for his battle against provincial puritanism and smugness, which he argued were a strangling influence upon American culture. He continued his literary crusade as editor (1924–33) of the *American Mercury,* which he and Nathan founded with Alfred A. Knopf. Nietzschean philosophy of the "aristocrat" led him to attack the democratic tradition; nevertheless, he defended and practiced "free speech up to the last limits of the unendurable." He published thirty books, including several collections of his newspaper articles under the title of *Prejudices. The American Language,* first published in 1918 and later revised and supplemented, is a serious linguistic study of the American vernacular that continues to command the respect of scholars. His three volumes of memoirs, *Happy Days, Newspaper Days,* and *Heathen Days,* are generally rated the top writings turned out by any Maryland autobiographer to date.

The Pratt Library was built by one of the great philanthropists of nineteenth-century America. Enoch Pratt (1808–96) came to Baltimore from Massachusetts in 1831, and founded a wholesale ironware business at 23 S. Charles Street. He prospered, becoming a financier as well, and in 1882 he offered to build on a lot that he owned on Mulberry Street a library from which books would circulate free to the public. Pratt offered not only the land and building but also an endowment of $833,333.33, provided the city would establish a $50,000 annuity to be paid to a board of trustees named by Pratt. The city accepted Pratt's proposal, and the library and four branches, containing a total of 32,000 volumes, were opened in 1884.

Across Cathedral Street from the library is the **Basilica of the Assumption of the Blessed Virgin Mary** (51) (1806–21) (open 7–6), first Roman Catholic cathedral in the United States and one of the most handsome edifices built in the early Republic. Baltimore was named the first episcopal see in the United States on November 6, 1789, becoming the first archiepiscopal see in 1808. Bishop John Carroll laid the cornerstone of the church in 1806, and since then ten provincial councils and three plenary councils have been held here. On September 1, 1937, Pope Pius XI honored the cathedral with the rank of minor basilica, a title bestowed on historically notable churches.

The basilica's architect was Benjamin Henry Latrobe (1762–1820), an English engineer who came to the United States in 1796 and who also served as architect for the Capitol of the United States from 1803 to 1811 and again from 1815 to 1818. The War of 1812 delayed construction of the cathedral and Archbishop Ambrose Marechal did not dedicate it until 1821, a year after Latrobe's death. The building is cross-shaped with short transepts and has a great dome over the intersection of transepts and nave; the proportions of the dome in relation to the rest of the building are one of Latrobe's greatest triumphs. Windows are judiciously placed, recessed to retain the effect of strength and enclosure created by the massive and unornamented granite-faced walls. In 1890, a forty-foot extension of the church to the east successfully maintained the building's excellent geometric design. The Ionic portico (1860–63) and towers (1832) are quite acceptable modifications of the original design. The bells in the south tower, cast at Lyons in 1830 and installed in 1831, are operated by a clock made by the French clockmaker M. Collin and installed in 1866.

The pale grey interior of the basilica with its three domes creates a sense of cool, quiet space. Interior decoration is largely confined to shades of grey and blue and to small gold rosettes in the coffered ceilings. Especially effective is the treatment of the rotunda, with its inscription in Roman letters on the frieze and the delicate blue-grey-white ovaled figures of the evangelists on the pendentives. The stained-glass windows were installed in a renovation of 1943–47. The two paintings on either side of the west entrance were described by Mrs. Frances Trollope about 1830 as "abominably bad" and "incontestable indications of the state of art in the country." The one by Baron Charles von Steuben showing Louis IX burying one of his plague-stricken soldiers before the walls of Tunis in 1270 was presented to the cathedral by Louis XVIII; the other, by Baron Pierre Narcisse Guerin depicting the descent from the cross, was commissioned by Louis XVIII and presented by his successor, Charles X. Suspended from the arch above Our Lady's altar to the left at the front of the sanctuary is the biretta of James Cardinal Gibbons, which by custom must hang until it crumbles. The brightly colored umbrella and bell, set on either side of the sanctuary, are the insignia of a basilica. The bell rings at the approach of a papal procession and the umbrella shields the pope from heat and symbolizes his royal powers.

Twelve prelates have presided over the See of Baltimore: John Carroll, 1790–1815; Leonard Neale, 1815–17; Ambrose Marechal, 1817–29; James Whitfield, 1828–34; Samuel Eccleston, 1834–51; Francis Patrick Kendrick, 1851–63; John Spaulding, 1864–72; James Roosevelt Bayley, 1872–77; James Cardinal Gibbons, 1877–1921; Michael Curley, 1921–47; Francis Keough, 1947–61; Lawrence Cardinal Shehan, 1961–1974; and William D. Borders, 1974–

John Carroll (1735–1815), first Roman Catholic archbishop of the United States, was born in Upper Marlboro (*see* Tour 26a). After a year of study at the Jesuit school at Bohemia Manor (*see* Tour 24, Old Bohemia Church), he completed his education at the English Jesuit college at St. Omer's in Flanders and then passed to the novitiate at Watten. He was ordained a Jesuit priest in 1769, but in 1773 the pope suppressed the Jesuit order. In 1774 Carroll returned to Maryland, where he was an ardent supporter of the Revolution. In 1784–85 Carroll was made prefect apostolic of the American church, which by then had been removed from the jurisdiction of the bishop at London, and on August 15, 1790, he was consecrated bishop at Lulworth Castle in England, with his diocese encompassing the entire United States. When he became archbishop on April 8, 1808, the country was divided into four dioceses, each with a suffragan bishop. Carroll founded Georgetown University in 1789 and sponsored the first Catholic seminary, established by the Sulpicians in 1791 (*see below* [77]). Carmelites (*see* Tour 26b, Mount Carmel), Trappists, and Visitation nuns were among the Catholic orders he welcomed, and he aided in the founding of the Sisters of Charity by Saint Elizabeth Ann Seton (*see below* and Tour 3, St. Joseph's College).

James Gibbons (1834–1921), born in Baltimore of Irish parents and educated at St. Charles College and St. Mary's Seminary (*see below* [77]), was ordained to the priesthood on June 30, 1861. After only five years as a priest, he was chosen bishop of the new vicariate apostolic of North Carolina and was consecrated two years later, on August 16, 1868. In 1872 Gibbons was made bishop of Richmond, but he was not relieved of his former see. Chosen as coadjutor by Archbishop Bayley in 1877, he succeeded to the archbishopric upon the latter's death a few months later. Pope Leo XIII selected him to preside over the Third Plenary Council of Baltimore (1884) and named him cardinal in 1886.

Cardinal Gibbons was an equally vigorous defender of the doctrines of his church and of the principles of American democracy. While in Rome awaiting consecration as cardinal, he prevented the condemnation of the Knights of Labor, an early American labor union organized as a secret order, and kept Henry George's *Progress and Poverty* off the index of forbidden books, although he was opposed to the theories espoused in it. Gibbons's long advocacy of a Catholic university met with success when the Catholic University of America was established in Washington, D.C., and he became its chancellor and president of the board of trustees. A voluminous writer, Gibbons is best known for his books *The Faith of Our Fathers* (over 100 editions in many languages), *Our Christian Heritage,* and *The Ambassador of Christ.*

The **Archbishop's House** (52) (1830) (private), connected with the cathedral by a sheltered walkway facing on Charles Street, is a five-part building designed by William Small. Its neoclassic dignity is somewhat obscured by bay windows added at a later date. The garden was a source of joy to Cardinal Gibbons, who is said to have planted some of the crocuses that herald the coming of spring. The large elm at the corner of the lot is the last tree standing of what once was Howard's Park, the site where the Comte de Rochambeau camped on his return from Yorktown in August of 1782.

Across Franklin Street from the basilica are two other churches of interest. At the corner of Franklin and Cathedral is the brick **Franklin Street Presbyterian Church** (53) (1844), now part of the First and Franklin Street Presbyterian Church complex. Designed by Robert Cary Long, Jr., with battlemented and buttressed Tudor-Gothic walls and a great double-towered facade reminiscent of Anne Boleyn's gate at Hampton Court, the church is one of the earliest full-fledged Gothic-Revival buildings in the city. One block east, at Franklin and Charles streets, the **First Unitarian Church** (54) (1817–18) (apply at office, 1 W. Hamilton Street, Mon.–Fri., 8:30–4:30) is Maximilian Godefroy's (*see above* [16]) major architectural achievement in Baltimore. Like La-trobe's cathedral across the street, this church is distinguished for its geometric relationship of dome to block. The chief ornamentation is in the pediment above the recessed Tuscan portico, where a reddish terra-cotta relief figure of the Angel of Truth is shown surrounded by rays. The present angel (Henry Berge, 1954) is an exact copy of the one designed by Simon Willard and executed by Antonio Capellano (*see above* [16]) in 1818. Unfortunately, Godefroy's beautiful interior ornamented by Capellano carvings proved acoustically unsatisfactory, and in 1893 a barrel ceiling was put under the dome and the interior was redesigned by Joseph E. Sperry. On May 5, 1819, William Ellery Channing delivered the ordination sermon for the church's first minister, Jared Sparks. This was Channing's famous Baltimore sermon, entitled "Unitarian Christianity," which was later translated into seven languages and which is said to have been the most widely sold non-political writing of the time. No one in back of the first three rows could hear the sermon, however, and according to legend the minister of a nearby church commented from his pulpit, "There has been a new Church erected in our city for the dissemination of pernicious doctrines, but by the grace of God, nobody can hear what the minister has to say."

Mt. Vernon Place, on Monument Street between Cathedral and St. Paul streets, and **Washington Place,** on Charles Street between Center and Madison streets, form a cross radiating from the Washington Monument two blocks north of the cathedral. In 1815, when John Eager Howard gave the land for the monument, the site was the top of a hill well beyond the city limits—to ensure, some said, that no one would be in the way if the monument collapsed. After Howard's death in 1827 his heirs laid out the property in lots facing four rectangular parks with the site for the monument in the center. When the city expanded to this area in the 1850s, the plan fitted perfectly with the grid of the city streets.

For more than half a century, Mt. Vernon Place (few Baltimoreans know that part of it carries the name Washington Place) was a highly desirable residential area. Most of the houses were built between 1850 and 1900 and nearly all show a break with the earlier and more severe classical style, especially by the addition of ornamentation such as wrought-iron balconies. Many of the houses reflect the Italian-Renaissance style, with the flat brick or brownstone fronts trimmed with elaborate stone cornices, stone balconies, and thick balusters at the first floor. The four parks adjoining these houses are planted with grass, shrubs, and flowering trees, and there are fountains in all but the north square.

Baltimoreans treasure Mount Vernon Place as an island of nineteenth-century dignity and graciousness amid a city that has become increasingly modern and commercialized. They want to preserve the area both from decay and from the threat of "progress" in the form of parking lots, high-rise office buildings, and neon signs. Over the past forty years, some of the magnificent houses have been converted to apartments and others have been occupied by clubs or other organizations that have had varying success maintaining the buildings. In the spring of 1964, the city council designated Mt. Vernon Place and its environs a Historic Preservation District, establishing a commission to administer the area. From Centre to Read streets and between Howard and St. Paul streets, encompassing approximately twelve blocks, existing buildings will be rehabilitated wherever possible and all changes and new construction must be approved by the commission to ensure the integrity of the area. Thus, only four blocks from Charles Center, the essence of mid-twentieth-century design, Baltimore seeks to preserve an enclave of its nineteenth-century heritage.

The *Lafayette Monument* overlooks S. Washington Place (Charles Street) toward the **Walters Art Gallery** (55) (1905–8) (open Mon., 1–5; Tues.–Sat., 11–5; Sun. and holidays, 2–5), Washington Place and Centre Street. The original structure is a marble building of Italian Renaissance design (Delano and Aldrich, New York) built by Henry Walters (1848–1931) to house art treasures that he and his father, William Thompson Walters (1820–94), had collected over a period of ninety years.

William Thompson Walters, born in Pennsylvania of Scotch-Irish ancestry, was educated as a mining engineer. In 1841 he came to Baltimore, where he amassed a fortune in railroads while still a young man. Walters invested a portion of his first year's earnings in paintings, the beginning of the collection he was to expand throughout his life. At his death, Walters owned an excellent collection of nineteenth-century paintings, as well as an assemblage of Far Eastern porcelains that initiated the first serious interest in the subject in this country. His son, educated as a civil engineer, followed his father both as a railroad magnate and as a patron of the arts. At his father's death, Henry Walters began expanding the collection to include all forms of art in which men had accomplished significant work. A few years after he purchased the Don Marcello Massaranti collection of Italian art in 1902 (appraised at $450,000), Walters built the present gallery. In 1909 Walters opened the gallery to the public, charging a small admission fee that he donated to charity. Henry Walters died in 1931, leaving to the city his museum, its contents, and the house his father had built at 5 Mt. Vernon Place.

The Walters Museum now contains four levels. The entrance level in the new wing is used for special exhibits. An auditorium is also located here, as well as the museum store and an exhibit of arms and armor.

On the second level in the new wing are treasures of ancient civilizations. The items include early Greek bronzes, Egyptian art, Roman sarcophagi, Roman art, and Greek sculpture and vases. In the old building, coins, Sèvres porcelains, Renaissance sculpture, jewelry, and bronzes, and Limoges enamels are displayed. French art from the seventeenth and eighteenth centuries, as well as German art from the sixteenth and seventeenth centuries, is on exhibit.

The third level in the new wing houses Medieval, Romanesque,

Islamic, Byzantine, Coptic, Gothic, and late-Gothic art. Stained glass, tapestries, and manuscripts are some of the items on display. In the old building the displays cover English, Flemish, and Dutch paintings. Italian bronzes and garden sculpture are also exhibited. Art work representing different styles is shown: Italian (eighteenth-century), Italian Baroque, Mannerist, Italian Renaissance, Renaissance, Italian Medieval, and Eighteenth Century.

The fourth level in the new wing contains Oriental art (China, Japan, India), nineteenth-century paintings, drawings, Barye sculpture, and Aztec art.

In all there are over 25,000 *objets d'art* in the Walters Gallery, which is considered one of the half-dozen most comprehensive art museums in America. The gallery was expanded along Centre Street in 1974 as part of the rehabilitation and renewal effort of the Mount Vernon area. The addition (Shepley, Bulfinch, Richardson, and Abbott, of Boston) is contemporary in design, with glass on all floors but the entrance level. This new wing contains gallery space for approximately one-half of the museum's collection.

At the intersection of S. Washington and E. Mt. Vernon places is the **Peabody Institute** (56) (1861–78). Designed by Edmund G. Lind to house the Peabody library, conservatory, and art gallery (no longer maintained), the institute was established by the philanthropist George Peabody (1795–1869). The two-story marble building, which shows the influence of the academic French Renaissance, was extended along Monument Street in 1875–78. Of particular interest is the interior of the library (now a department of the Enoch Pratt Free Library), whose reading room is lighted by a skylight surrounded by five tiers of cast-iron balconies.

George Peabody, born in South Danvers, Massachusetts, came to Baltimore in 1815 and made a fortune in dry goods. While in England on business in 1835, Peabody successfully negotiated an $8,000,000 loan for the State of Maryland, which was then virtually bankrupt. In 1837, Peabody moved to London, becoming an international banker. Twenty years later he began a series of major philanthropies, among them the establishment of the Peabody Institute for the cultural enrichment of Baltimore, to which he ultimately gave $1,400,000. Although the original building was completed in 1861, the Civil War delayed the opening of the library until 1866 and the conservatory until 1868. Because the library, which now contains nearly 300,000 volumes, was established as a research library for scholars, it was criticized by those who favored a general circulating library, a need later met by the benefactions of Enoch Pratt (*see above* [50]). The Conservatory of Music and Preparatory School (in an adjacent building) are open all year, offering over 3,000 students training in all branches of musical art. To the rear, dormitories (1969, Edward Durrell Stone) have been built around a landscaped plaza, distinguished by an arcade. The architectural style (Romantic Classicism) and the materials blend with the traditional style of the buildings in the area.

At the head of S. Washington Place is the **Lafayette Monument** (57) (1924), an unusually animated bronze equestrian figure executed by Andrew O'Connor, Jr., which stands on a base designed by Thomas Hastings. Ground for the monument was broken in 1917 by Field Marshal Joseph Joffre, and it was unveiled with President Calvin Coolidge in attendance on September 6, 1924, in commemoration of the American troops sent to France in 1917 as well as of the French troops sent to America in 1778.

The **Washington Monument** (58) (open Fri.–Tues., 10–4; closed Wed., Thurs.), Mt. Vernon and Washington places, was the first monument begun in honor of George Washington, and except for the rough stone tower near Boonsboro (*see* Tour 2c), it was the first such monument completed. Planning for the monument was begun in 1809, with the site of the old courthouse chosen as its location. The War of 1812 delayed the project, and when Robert Mills's design for a giant shaft was selected, the citizens of the city decided to place the smaller *Battle Monument* within the city, accepting John Eager Howard's offer of the present site for the Washington Monument. Nearly $178,000 was raised for the project, first by a private lottery and then by funds from the state lotteries, in return for which the state took title to the site.

Robert Mills (1781–1855), the most eminent American-born professional architect of his time, designed a 164-foot unfluted Doric column on a base 50 feet square and 28 feet high. Surmounting the cap of the column, which serves as a small observation deck, is a stepped dome that is surmounted by a 16-foot statue of Washington carved by the Italian sculptor Enrico Causici. On July 4, 1815, the cornerstone of the monument was laid, and the last piece of the statue was laid on November 25, 1829. The base of the monument houses a small museum. The marble bust on exhibit is believed to be one of three made by Giuseppe Ceracchi (1751–1801), an Italian sculptor.

In E. Mt. Vernon Place, in front of the Peabody Institute, is a replica of the **Statue of George Peabody** (59) by the American sculptor William Wetmore Story. The original was unveiled by the Prince of Wales in London shortly before Peabody's death, with Robert Garrett presenting this copy to the city in 1890. At the bottom of the park facing on St. Paul Street is a **Statue of Severn Teackle Wallis** (60) (1906), the work of Laurent Marqueste. Wallis (1816–94), a noted lawyer, poet, and wit, was imprisoned for fourteen months during the Civil War for his criticism of arbitrary orders issued by the Federal government. Later he was a leader of the movement for civil service reform.

One block east (L), at 700 N. Calvert Street, is **Center Stage** (61), which was burned out of its North Avenue home in 1974. The group continued its performances at the College of Notre Dame until a site for its new theater was found. In December, 1975, the theater opened in old St. Ignatius High School. Information for show times can be obtained by calling (301) 332–0033.

Along the north side of E. Mt. Vernon Place, the brick and brownstone houses date from the 1850s. On the corner of E. Mt. Vernon Place and N. Washington Place (i.e., Monument and Charles streets) is **Mount Vernon Place Methodist Church** (62) (1870–72, Dixon and Charles L. Carson), an outstanding example of Victorian-Gothic architecture.

In N. Washington Place the bronze **Statue of Chief Justice Roger Brooke Taney** (63) (1887), given by William T. Walters, is a replica of the statue by William Henry Rinehart (1825–74) unveiled in 1872 in front of the State House in Annapolis. Rinehart, who was born in Carroll County and trained as a stonecutter, attracted the attention of the elder Walters, who enabled him to pursue the study of art. At his death Rinehart directed that his estate be used to further the study of art in America. Eventually, Rinehart's trustees founded the Rinehart School of Sculpture at the Maryland Institute (*see* Northwest Baltimore [6]), providing scholarships to promising sculptors for study in Rome. At the north end of the park, a bronze equestrian **Statue of John Eager Howard** (64) (1904) (*see above* [44]), by Emmanuel Fremiet, faces Madison Street. A copy of the medal given to Howard at the order of Congress for valor at the Battle of Cowpens is shown on the granite pedestal, together with a panel showing a Continental officer attacking a British soldier. Howard led the bayonet charge at Cowpens that is credited with bringing victory to the Americans.

A bronze **Lion** (65) (1885) by Antoine Barye (1796–1875), presented to the city by William T. Walters, sits at the east end of W. Mt. Vernon Place, and a bronze figure of **Military Courage** (66) (1885), by P. Dubois, is situated at the Cathedral Street end. Overlooking the park is one of the finest surviving Baltimore town houses in the manner of Latrobe, the **Tiffany-Fisher House** (67) (ca. 1842), 8 W. Mt. Vernon Place (private). Above the stone-faced English basement entered through a small Doric portico, the plain brick walls rise two stories higher to a dentiled cornice under a low roof balustrade. There are headings only over the middle tier of windows. The architectural trend away from the severity of the classical style is seen on the **Thomas-Jencks-Gladding House** (68) (1849–51), on the other side of the park at 1 W. Mt. Vernon Place (private). This handsome house of Georgian proportions with a Corinthian entrance portico is ornamented with floral cresting on the window headings and along the roof over the bracketed cornice, and with iron balconies at the windows. John Rudolph Niernsee, an architect born in Vienna who came to Baltimore about 1845, and his Baltimore-born partner, J. Crawford Neilson, probably designed this house and its neighbors on the south side of W. Mt. Vernon Place. In 1884, two of these houses were remodeled by Stanford White (of the famous New York firm McKim, Mead, and White) into the **Garrett-Jacobs House** (69), 7–11 W. Mt. Vernon Place (private), a grand Renaissance mansion faced with brownstone, which was extended to incorporate a third house in 1905. This house now belongs to the Engineering Society.

At Cathedral and Monument streets, facing W. Mt. Vernon Place, the **Miller House** (70) (private) (ca. 1855, John Rudolph Niernsee and J. Crawford Neilson), 700 Cathedral Street, and the **Graham House** (private) (ca. 1860, Joseph Kemp), number 704, are interesting examples of mid-century brownstones. At **800–806 Cathedral Street** (71) (private) are handsome examples of brick residences with brownstone basements and connected second-story iron balconies.

The **Emmanuel Protestant Episcopal Church** (72) (designed by Niernsee and Neilson) is a rugged granite structure located at Cathedral and Read streets (tower and addition, 1920, Waldemar N. Ritter of Boston). This is one of three Gothic churches built in the 1850s that reflect the northward expansion of the city.

The second Gothic church built in the 1850s is the **First Presbyterian Church** (73) (1854–74), Madison Street and Park Avenue, designed by Nathan Starkweather. The unusual needle-sharp spire of the church, which rests on a great cast-iron frame, was not erected until 1874. Architects consider the spire as one of the finest pieces of Victorian-Gothic architecture in the city. This church, along with the Franklin Street Presbyterian Church, forms the First and Franklin Street Presbyterian Church complex, formed in 1973 when the two churches merged.

Tyson Street (74), a short street between Read and Madison just west of Park Avenue, is lined with 2½-story pre–Civil War houses reclaimed from slums in the late 1940s. The renovations, including exteriors in assorted pastel shades, have made Tyson Street a highly desirable section of the city.

Niernsee and Neilsen also used brownstone for the third Gothic church of the area, **Grace and St. Peter's Protestant Episcopal Church** (75) (1851–52), Monument Street and Park Avenue. The structure was an early departure from the traditional rectangular building, with its projecting vestibule and transepts and semidetached sacristy reflecting the influence of rural English parish churches.

Across Monument Street from the church and one block west of Mt. Vernon Place is the original building of the **Maryland Historical Society** (76) (open Tues.–Sat., 11–4; Sun., 1–5), 201 W. Monument Street. The three-story brick house was built for Enoch Pratt in 1846; the fourth floor and mansard roof, designed by Edmund G. Lind, were added in 1871. In 1916, Mrs. H. Irvine Keyser bought the house, added the library and main gallery (designed by J. B. Noel Wyatt and William G. Nolting), and presented the building to the Historical Society as a memorial to her husband. During the 1960s, the Historical Society extended its headquarters with the addition of the Thomas-Hugg Memorial Building.

The Maryland Historical Society was founded in 1844 by an act of the state legislature. In 1846, the society became the repository for the original records of the provincial government of colonial Maryland, a responsibility it retained until the establishment in 1934 of the Hall of Records in Annapolis. In 1882, the society began publishing the most important colonial records in the series *Archives of Maryland,* and in 1906 it began issuing the *Maryland Historical Magazine.* Over the years, by gift and through endowment, the society has acquired a valuable collection of books, manuscripts, early newspapers, paintings, furniture, and Marylandia of all kinds. Among the outstanding collections of private papers are the Calvert Papers, the Carroll (both Protestant and Catholic) Papers, the Daniel Dulany Papers, the Scharf Papers, the Lloyd Papers, the Benjamin H. Latrobe Papers and the colonization papers relating to the Liberian movement. Rare books include the Eliot *Indian Bible.* The society's best-known treasure is the original manuscript of ''The Star-Spangled Banner,'' written in Francis Scott Key's own hand immediately after the British bombardment of Fort McHenry (*see* South Baltimore [8]).

The rooms on the second floor of the Historical Society contain special collections of furniture and clothing that represent various periods and styles. Of special interest is the **Bonaparte Room,** which contains furniture and other belongings of Mme Jerome Bonaparte, the former Elizabeth Patterson (1785–1879), who was briefly married to Napoleon's youngest brother, Jerome. Betsy's father, William Patterson, was one of the wealthiest men in Baltimore, and on Christmas Eve, 1803, not long after Betsy had met nineteen-year-old Jerome, the pair was married by Bishop John Carroll. Napoleon directed the French consul in New York to suspend his brother's allowance, and he ordered Jerome to come home alone at once. After several unsuccessful attempts to gain passage for France, Betsy and Jerome sailed for Portugal aboard the *Erin.* At Lisbon, Jerome landed and went to France to plead with his brother. Betsy found Napoleon's influence sufficiently pervasive to prevent her from landing anywhere in Europe, and she finally disembarked in England, where she learned a short time later that Napoleon had prevailed upon Jerome to abandon her. Betsy's son, Jerome Napoleon, was born in 1805 in Camberwell, England. Pope Pius VII refused Napoleon's demand to dissolve the marriage, but the Maryland General Assembly, urged by Betsy's relatives, declared the marriage annulled. Betsy refused Napoleon's offer of $12,000 to refrain from signing her name as Madame Bonaparte, and for a time she declined the pension offered in Jerome's name. Eventually, however, Betsy accepted an annual pension of 60,000 francs. She returned to Baltimore in 1834, spending the last years of her life in a miserly fashion, saving her money in the belief that her descendants would one day occupy the throne of France. Betsy died at the age of ninety-four in a Cathedral Street rooming house.

The **Eleanor S. Cohen Collection** at the Maryland Historical Society contains Baltimore furniture dating from the period 1790–1810.

The Baltimore double parlor is one of the most handsome museum rooms in the country. The furniture displayed here is in the French Empire style.

Enoch Pratt's study in the Pratt house retains the original furniture, all of which is in the Victorian-Gothic or Cathedral-Gothic style.

Also on display at the society is the largest Peale collection in the country. All the paintings (mostly portraits) were done by members of the Peale family. The collection is especially noted for its full-length portraits, which are rare for the period.

The **Young People's Museum of Maryland History,** donated by Richard

Bennett Darnall (1873–1957), is devoted to enlightening children about Maryland's role in history. This museum combines period rooms and dioramic displays. Beginning with the founding of Maryland, the exhibits cover the colonial and Revolutionary periods, the Civil War, the War of 1812, and the Mexican War. Other periods of Maryland history are also displayed.

The basement of the museum houses a collection of ships (models and photographs), ship apparatus, and a collection of waterfowl decoys.

Four blocks west of the Historical Society—and outside the Mt. Vernon district—stands one of the earliest Gothic-Revival buildings in Baltimore, **St. Mary's Seminary Chapel** (77) (1806–8), on the **Site of St. Mary's Seminary**, Paca Street and Druid Hill Avenue. Maximilian Godefroy (*see above* [16]) used what was considered a radical design for the building. He apparently adapted an existing brick building, adding a battlemented brick sanctuary at the rear and a brick facade, supported from behind by flying buttresses, that towers above the roof line. A limestone cornice decorated with trefoils separates the Gothic doorway from a rose window, which is flanked on either side by six niches intended for carved figures of the twelve apostles. The tower planned by Godefroy was never built, and one designed by Robert Cary Long, Jr., added in 1840, was removed in 1916 when the chapel was renovated. The interior of the church remains virtually unchanged, with the side aisles marked off from the nave by Gothic arches supported by columns with acanthus leaf capitals. The Sulpician order founded the seminary in 1791 as a training school for priests, and it was the first Roman Catholic seminary established in the United States. Because the number of students at the seminary was small, the Sulpicians also opened St. Mary's College (1799), which offered a liberal education to boys. The school was incorporated as a university in 1805, and it was here that Godefroy came to be the first professional teacher of architecture in Baltimore, and possibly in the country. The buildings of both schools have been razed to accommodate city plans.

On Paca Street stands **Mother Seton's House** (78) (open by appointment), a small 2½-story brick building in which Mother (Mrs. Elizabeth Bayley) Seton (1774–1821) conducted a school for girls during 1808–9. Mother Seton, a widow with five children and a convert to Catholicism, came to Baltimore at the invitation of Father Dubois, director of St. Mary's Seminary, who wanted to establish a Catholic school for girls. In addition to the school, Mother Seton founded an American branch of the French order of St. Vincent de Paul, aided by a gift from a student at the seminary, Samuel Cooper. Called the Sisters of Charity, the order was established in 1809 with Mother Seton serving as mother superior. At Cooper's insistence, the new order moved to Emmitsburg (*see* Tour 3), and there Mother Seton founded her school for girls, St. Joseph's College, later the same year. Although the Sisters of Charity did not officially become part of the order of St. Vincent de Paul until 1849, they followed its rule from the beginning. The first sisters, along with Mother Seton, took their vows in *St. Mary's Seminary Chapel.* Mother Seton became the first American-born Roman Catholic saint when she was canonized by Pope Paul VI in 1975.

From the site of St. Mary's Seminary, it is two short blocks along Paca and St. Mary streets to the corner of Eutaw Street and Madison Avenue, and from here it is two long blocks on Eutaw Street to the **State Office Building Center** (79) (*see* Northwest Baltimore [2]). To the east, Madison Avenue returns to N. Washington Place, passing *Tyson Street* and the *First Presbyterian Church.*

The region north of the Mount Vernon Historic District, from Read Street to Mt. Royal Avenue, was developed after the Civil War, and the nineteenth-century houses along Calvert, St. Paul, Chase, Biddle, and Preston streets were once fashionable residences. At the intersection of Eutaw Place and Biddle Street, turn left. At the intersection of Biddle and Chase streets, turn left and then right, crossing Cathedral Street. Number 212 E. Biddle Street is the childhood **Home of Wallis Warfield** (80) (private), the central figure of the modern world's most dramatic romance. Bessie Wallis Warfield, daughter of Teackle Wallis Warfield and Alys Montague Warfield, was brought as an infant to Baltimore from Monterey, Pennsylvania, where she was born on July 19, 1896. She was enrolled as a pupil of Madame Le Fevre, instructor for children of the city's most prominent families, and later was a student at the fashionable Oldfields School outside Baltimore. Presented to Baltimore society at the Bachelors Cotillon in 1914, she was married in Christ Church two years later to Lt. Earl Winfield Spencer, U.S.N. In 1928, after having divorced Spencer, she married Col. Ernest Simpson, whom she divorced to marry the former Edward VIII, King of England, in 1937. Edward abdicated his throne to marry her because the Anglican Church, which he headed as king, did not recognize divorce at that time. He was later named Duke of Windsor. For a short time after the marriage, this house was opened as a museum, with tourists paying to see the room in which the duchess had slept.

At the intersection of Biddle and Cathedral streets, turn right.

The **Medical and Chirurgical Faculty of Maryland** (81), 1211 Cathedral Street, has a collection of antique medical instruments and items of historical-medical interest on display in its halls. The faculty, founded in 1799, is the state medical society, and one of its treasures is the medicine chest of Dr. Upton Scott (1722–1814) of Annapolis (*see* Annapolis Tour [52]). It also has what purports to be Napoleon's medicine chest, stolen, according to an attached label, from Napoleon's tent by the father of Baron Munchausen, and later presented to Dr. George Keidel of Baltimore by the baron.

Along Preston Street, at Maryland Avenue, the **Annunciation Greek Orthodox Church** (82) (1889), designed by Charles Cassell, is an interesting granite structure, with a semicircular front and a cone-shaped roof. The entrance is through a curved portico supported on coupled marble columns flanked by two massive curved bays. Elements of its design can be found among the churches of fifteenth-century Milan. The church was originally built for the Congregationalist Church, which held services in the building until 1934.

Continue on Preston Street to St. Paul Street. Along St. Paul Street from Preston to Biddle streets is a row of houses built largely between 1877 and 1882. Of major interest to architects is the **Winans House** (83) (1887) (private), St. Paul and Preston streets, designed by Stanford White of New York, which is reminiscent of an early French chateau. The house is constructed of brownstone and brick with panels of carved relief, especially over windows and dormers, and a steeply pitched roof with a picturesque round tower.

St. Paul and Preston streets border the Mount Royal area and Northwest Baltimore.

NORTH BALTIMORE TOUR

For the purposes of this tour, North Baltimore is bounded on the south and west by the north side of the Jones Falls and on the east by York Road (Md. 45). Extensions of Howard, Charles, St. Paul, and Calvert streets and Guilford Avenue north to 33rd Street were developed mostly in row houses between 1870 and 1917. North of this point, what were once great suburban estates were gradually broken up into garden suburbs of sizable lots with large, freestanding houses. In 1891 an English syndicate bought 800 acres of land in the hills near the Jones Falls and employed the landscape architect Frederick Law Olmsted, Jr., of Boston to lay out Roland Park, which is today one of the choice residential areas of the city. Olmsted laid his roads around the contours of the hills and planned the lots with an eye to the vistas created;

KEY

1. Greenmount Cemetery
2. First, or Lovely Lane, Methodist Church
3. Goucher Hall
4. Poe Monument
5. Lee-Jackson Monument
6. Baltimore Museum of Art
7. Oakland Spring House
8. United States Public Health Service Hospital
9. The Johns Hopkins University
10. Gilman Hall
11. Milton S. Eisenhower Library
12. Alfred Jenkins Shriver Hall
13. Homewood
14. Johns Hopkins Memorial Monument
15. Confederate Women's Monument
16. Scottish Rite Temple
17. Sherwood Gardens
18. Loyola College
19. Evergreen House
20. College of Notre Dame of Maryland
21. Stony Run Friends Meeting
22. Friends School
23. Cathedral of Mary Our Queen
24. Church of the Redeemer

NORTH BALTIMORE TOUR

as a result Roland Park houses—many of them the large comfortable shingle-style or Tudor half-timbered houses of the 1890s and early 1900s—are still part of a romantic landscape.

This tour must be taken by automobile, but parking will not be difficult above 29th Street.

Greenmount Cemetery (1), a sixty-acre tract bounded by Greenmount and North avenues and Ensor and Hoffman streets, was founded on the estate of Robert Oliver in 1838 as a public cemetery, not connected with any church or denomination. At the time it was just within the city limits and well beyond any urban development. Among the prominent Marylanders buried here are Betsy Patterson Bonaparte (1785–1873) (*see* Downtown Baltimore [76]); Johns Hopkins (1795–1873) (*see below* [9]); the poet Sidney Lanier (1842–81); and Albert Cabell Ritchie (1876–1936), four-time governor of Maryland (1920–34).

The cemetery **Gateway** (1847–55, Robert Cary Long, Jr.), Greenmount Avenue at Oliver Street, is a battlemented one-story building of the same dark gray stone that forms the high boundary wall. A Gothic stained-glass window on each side of the gateway softens the military rigor of the general design. Just inside the grounds the brownstone **Mortuary Chapel** (1851–56, Niernsee and Neilson) is far more flamboyantly Gothic, with freestanding pinnacles, flying buttresses, and a traceried spire 102 feet high. Architectural historians have noted its resemblance to the imaginative structures in paintings by Thomas Cole.

Further west, on St. Paul Street, is one of the outstanding examples of church architecture in the city, the **First,** or **Lovely Lane, Methodist Church** (2) (1882–87), corner of 22nd and St. Paul streets. Stanford White of New York, fresh from a study of little-known medieval buildings, built this monumental Romanesque church in granite. The rugged corner bell tower tapers in nine tiers of stone to a height of 186 feet; it is modeled after the tower on the twelfth-century brick church of Santa Maria in Pomposa, near Ravenna. On either side of the tower is a deep arcaded portico framing the entrance to the church; except for the small windows of the apse and clerestory these are the only openings in the massive walls. The interior is oval-shaped and the windows in the frieze under the elliptical dome of the ceiling are reproductions in stained glass of mosaics from the Ravenna mausoleum of Galla Placidia. The ceiling dome is painted to represent the appearance of the sky over Baltimore at 3:00 A.M. on November 6, 1887, the day the church was dedicated. Simon Newcomb of the Johns Hopkins University plotted the stars. Originally the church was lit by 340 gas jets that made a circle of fire just below the frieze.

The church also houses the **Lovely Lane Museum** (open on request at parish office adjoining church, weekdays 9–4; tour every Sunday after 11 A.M. service), which contains records and treasures of the Baltimore Conference Methodist Historical Society. Among the items on view are a portrait of Francis Asbury painted by Charles Peale Polk in 1794, some of Asbury's papers and books, and the desk and chair he used on his frequent visits to Alexander Warfield. There is also an oak pulpit, believed to have been made by Robert Strawbridge, that is probably the first pulpit ever used by a Methodist preacher in America (*see* Tour 3). It long stood in the house of John Evans.

Immediately adjacent to the First Methodist Church is the granite Romanesque **Goucher Hall** (3) (1886–88, Charles L. Carson), built for the Woman's College of Baltimore, a Methodist-supported school opened in 1888, which in 1910 became Goucher College. Dr. John F. Goucher, pastor of the First Methodist Church, and from 1890 to 1907 president of the college, gave the land, and the architect designed the building to blend with the church. Between 1938 and 1952 the college moved to Towson (*see* Tour 32), and the Baltimore Regional Chapter of the Red Cross occupied Goucher Hall. According to the 1975–80 Baltimore Development Program, the state hopes to buy the building and use it for the Speech Agency of Metropolitan Baltimore.

Several blocks north and west of Goucher Hall, most of the area between Charles Street (Md. 139) on the east, Keswick Road on the west, 29th Street on the south, and University Parkway on the north is taken up either by the Johns Hopkins University (*see below* [9]) or by Wyman Park. Where Wyman Park Drive ends at 29th Street (one block west of Charles Street) is the **Poe Monument** (4) (1921), a bronze figure of Edgar Allan Poe clad in a dressing gown listening to the muses; it was designed by Moses J. Ezekiel. Inscribed on the monument is a quotation from "The Raven," which originally and incorrectly read "Dreaming Dreams no Mortals Ever Dared to Dream Before." In 1930 Edmund Fontaine, a Poe enthusiast, demanded that the Park Board remove the *s* from "Mortals," and when the board ignored his demand, he announced that on June 1 he would remove the offending letter himself. Police prepared to guard the monument on the first, but Fontaine accomplished the deed on the night of the twenty-ninth. He was arrested, admirers defended him, and the case was dropped.

At the Poe Monument begins Art Museum Drive, which runs through the bottom of the park from Wyman Park Drive and intersects Charles Street around 31st Street. Almost across from the Poe Monument is the **Lee-Jackson Monument** (5) (1948), two great bronze equestrian figures of Robert E. Lee and Stonewall Jackson conferring on the eve of Chancellorsville, where Jackson was killed; the sculptor was Laura Gardin Frazer.

Across Art Museum Drive and to the east is the **Baltimore Museum of Art** (6) (open Tues.–Sat., 11–5; Sun., 1–5; closed Mon.; free admission), which opened April 18, 1929. The building, designed by John Russell Pope and Howard Sill, is an impressive neoclassic structure of Indiana limestone with a six-columned Ionic portico. In the interior the exhibit rooms are grouped about the colonnaded atrium and the Antioch Court beyond it, an arcaded quadrangle with a formally landscaped open-air garden in the center. The museum, municipally owned, holds current loan exhibitions and has a permanent collection of great interest.

The **Horse,** a bronze sculpture by Raymond Duchamp-Villion, stands on the pedestal in front of the museum. This work is part of the Wurtzburger Collection (*see below*).

The Jacob Epstein Collection, in the **Old Masters' Wing,** contains paintings by Raphael, Titian, Tintoretto, Veronese, Rubens, Botticelli, Romano, Van Dyck, Rembrandt, Halls, Reynolds, Gainsborough, Goya, and Susterman. Bronzes in the collection include examples by Rodin, Barye, Isenstein, and Jacob Epstein, the English sculptor.

The Jacobs Collection is also housed within the Old Masters' Wing. The collection, a gift of Mary Frick Jacobs, includes paintings, tapestries, and other *objets d'art.* The English, Flemish-Dutch, French, and Italian schools are represented. The Abram Eisenberg Collection is also housed within this wing.

Antioch Court contains examples of Ancient, Byzantine, and Middle Eastern art. The Antioch Mosaics are the most notable feature. The mosaics range from the first to the sixth centuries A.D. The most popular themes are taken from Roman mythology, but naturalistic animals and plants are also used in some of the designs.

The **Saidie A. May Wing** (1950) is the center of the museum's art education program, with a lecture hall, studios, and an exhibition room. The May collection focuses on twentieth-century masters, including Kandinsky, Chagall, Gris, and others. It also includes ceramics, furniture, textiles, and art objects of many periods and countries.

In the **Woodward Wing** is the Woodward Collection of "Cherished Portraits of Thoroughbred Horses." William Woodward, owner and breeder of race horses at Belair Stables (*see Tour 27*), collected portraits of horses by British artists of the late eighteenth and nineteenth centuries. Also in this collection are trophies that represent the achievements of Belair Stables.

The **Cone Wing** houses a magnificent collection of nineteenth- and twentieth-century paintings. The paintings, collected by Dr. Claribel and Miss Etta Cone, include works by Braque, Picasso, Matisse (the most extensive collection in any public gallery), Roualt, and others. Works of Corot, Delacroix, Manet, Degas, Gauguin, and Cézanne are also represented. Three major paintings of importance are *The Blue Nude (Souvenir of Biskra)* by Matisse, *Mont Ste. Victoire Seen from Bibemus Quarry* by Cézanne, and *The Coiffure* by Picasso. The Cone Collection also includes Near Eastern and European textiles, jewelry, and furniture.

In the **American Wing** is a mid-eighteenth century room from Eltonhead Manor in Calvert County. The Oval Room from Willow Brook, which was built by Thorowgood Smith in 1799, is also here. The plaster ceiling ornamentation may have been the work of Baltimore craftsmen. The backs of the furniture, made in Baltimore in 1805 by John and Hugh Finlay, have views of Baltimore houses and public buildings.

On the second floor are architectural elements from Waterloo Row, an early-nineteenth-century row of town houses designed and built by Robert Mills. The elements include a double parlor, an entrance hall, and a staircase.

The **American Textile Room** opened in 1973. American textiles, including quilts, coverlets, and other items, are on display.

On the ground floor is the **Julius Levy Memorial Room,** which houses a collection of Far Eastern art. Chinese ceramics, ranging in date from the Neolithic era through the Ch'ing dynasty, the bronze sculpture of Kuan Yin, scrolls by Japanese and Chinese artists of the fifteenth through the nineteenth centuries, and Indian and Southeast Asian sculptures are on display.

Art of the Americas, Africa, and the Pacific are displayed in the **Wurtzburger Gallery.** Most of this collection was donated by Mr. and Mrs. Alan Wurtzburger. In 1954 Mr. Wurtzburger donated an African art collection, and in 1955 the museum was given an Oceanic collection. From 1960 until his death in 1964, Mr. Wurtzburger donated pre-Columbian and American Indian art.

In 1974 the museum acquired the Alan and Janet Wurtzburger collection of twentieth-century sculpture. A proposed sculpture garden will be used to display this internationally renowned collection.

The museum also has a **Photography Gallery.** Among the photographers that are represented are Stieglitz, Bourke-White, Curtis, Johnston, Kasebier, Steichen, and Weston. There is also a changing exhibit of works by living photographers.

The **Print and Drawing Collection** covers the period from the fifteenth century to the twentieth century. Included with original prints by Dürer, Schongauer, Mantegna, Matisse, Picasso, and German Expressionists of the early twentieth century is the Thomas Edward Benesch Memorial Collection, consisting of contemporary European and American drawings. On permanent loan from the Maryland Institute, College of Art, is the George A. Lucas Collection. Breton, Constable, Carot, Daumier, Greuze, and Millet are among those represented.

Temporary exhibitions are also maintained by the museum.

The **Oakland Spring House** (7), adjoining the garden of the museum, was formerly the dairy house on Oakland, the country estate of Gen. Robert Goodloe Harper, a leading Baltimore lawyer. Benjamin Henry Latrobe (1764–1820), architect of the Catholic Basilica (*see* Downtown Baltimore [51]), designed this graceful little Greek temple with four Ionic columns and a frieze decorated with oak leaves and flowers, bearing the inscription "Pour Elle." Robert Gilmor, a *bon vivant* of the 1820s, greatly admired the Spring House. In his diary Gilmor gives a charming picture of a garden party at Oakland: "For an hour or two carriages of all kinds were arriving, filled with well-dressed ladies and gentlemen. I hardly ever saw so much beauty assembled together as appeared on the grassy turf under the shade of the trees, dancing and promenading. About five o'clock the ladies all sat down at a long table under the trees and regaled themselves with strawberries and cream, cherries and ices, (and) with other refreshments. The dancing continued till after sunset on the grass and then was resumed in the house, where we all repaired to take our coffee." The Spring House is now being refurbished.

Just north of the museum on Wyman Park Drive is the entrance to the **United States Public Health Service Hospital** (8) (1936, Ernest R. E. Litzan), a seven-story modified Georgian structure of stone and brick, which cares for members of the merchant marine, coast guard, and lighthouse service, and civil employees of these services injured in the line of duty.

Adjoining the grounds of the hospital and museum, the campus of **The Johns Hopkins University** (9), Charles and 34th streets, consists of over a hundred acres of lawn, woodland, and park with over twenty buildings of Georgian design.

In 1867, Johns Hopkins (1795–1873), a Maryland Quaker merchant (*see* Tour 26a), promised to set aside from his estate $7,000,000 for the establishment of a university and a hospital, the largest grant made for educational and scientific purposes in this country up to that time. In 1874, after Hopkins's death, the trustees selected Daniel Coit Gilman (1831–1901), then president of the University of California, to be president of the new Johns Hopkins University. The choice was fortunate, for Gilman had a true conception of the proper scope and function of a university. The school was established primarily as a postgraduate institution, emphasizing mature scholarship and academic freedom and using seminar methods, new in America at that time. Two dwellings on Howard near Centre Street were purchased and remodeled and the university opened on October 3, 1876, with a faculty that included James Joseph Sylvester, mathematics; Ira Remsen, chemistry; Henry Augustus Rowland, physics; Henry Newell Martin, biology; Basil L. Gildersleeve, Greek; and Charles D. Morris, Latin. The poet Sidney Lanier was a lecturer in English literature from 1879 until shortly before his death in 1881. The medical school, now one of the world's most widely known, was established in 1893, and the School of Hygiene and Public Health in 1918. Innovations adopted early by "The Hopkins" were summer courses in 1911 and evening courses in 1916, both for undergraduates. The School of Business Economics conferring the degree of Bachelor of Science in Economics was established in 1922.

In 1902, a group headed by William Wyman donated Homewood tract to the University, but removal to the new site was not completed until 1916.

Gilman Hall (10) (1904, J. Harleston Parker and Douglas H. Thomas, Jr.), which contains classrooms, offices, and an undergraduate library, is the central building of the campus as originally laid out. The Gilman Memorial Room at the main entrance (on the second floor) exhibits the manuscripts, books, medals, degrees, and other personal possessions of the late Dr. Daniel Coit Gilman, first president of the university (1876–1901). On the first floor, the Archaeological Collection (open Mon.–Fri., 11–3) is of considerable interest. The collection was begun by Mendes Cohen (1796–1879), a Baltimore merchant who, having made his fortune by the time he was thirty-one, took a grand tour of Europe that led him into Egypt just as the French were beginning their excavations. Cohen's Egyptian artifacts, donated to the university in 1884, have been augmented by other donations, and the collection now contains several thousand Greek, Etruscan, and Roman items dating from 3500 B.C. to 500 A.D. Particularly noteworthy are eight exceptionally fine pieces of Attic pottery dating from the sixth and fifth centuries B.C.

Opposite Gilman Hall, and dominating the 34th Street entrance to the university, is the **Milton S. Eisenhower Library** (11) (1964), largely subterranean and with capacity for 1,500,000 volumes. In the athletic building is the **Lacrosse Hall of Fame** (open Mon.–Fri., 9–4), with pictures and trophies of great lacrosse players. In the Baltimore area, lacrosse has carried the prestige accorded to football in other parts of the country.

In the lobby of the **Alfred Jenkins Shriver Hall** (12) (1957, Buckler, Fenhagen, Myers, and Ayers), to the south of the original layout of buildings, are a series of murals of major local interest, which were **required** by the bequest that gave this auditorium to the university.

Homewood

The will of Alfred Jenkins Shriver (1867–1939) names 120 people who were to appear, among them the original faculties and boards of trustees of the schools of philosophy and medicine, the entire class of 1891 (of which he was a member), various nineteenth-century philanthropists, and—most unusual of all—ten women of his time in Baltimore, considered by him to be the most beautiful, who were to be painted in a group, each at the peak of her beauty. Shriver also required that various famous Baltimore clipper ships appear in the murals. James Owen Mahoney was commissioned to paint the ships, and Leon Kroll, the various figures. Sixty-three of the figures are life-size, with the murals covering ninety feet of wall space.

The generally Georgian character of the university buildings is designed to blend with **Homewood** (13) (1801–3) at the 34th Street entrance to the campus (not open), which was erected by Charles Carroll of Carrollton for his son Charles, Jr., on part of a tract surveyed in 1670 for John Homewood. In 1932 the house was carefully restored with funds supplied by Mr. and Mrs. Francis P. Garvan of New York.

Homewood was the source of much concern to Carroll, for his son was a self-indulgent spendthrift. Carroll ended a letter to him by saying that the "total amount of disbursements for building at Homewood will not fall short of $40,000, a most improvident waste of money, and one which you will have reason, as long as you live to look back upon with painful regret." Charles Carroll, Jr., died in 1825, and his son Charles sold Homewood to Samuel Wyman in 1840 for $25,000. Wyman lived here for some years until he built an Italianate villa nearby. The Country School for Boys, later known as the Gilman School, occupied the building until 1902, when Wyman and others gave the property to The Johns Hopkins University.

The square, 1½-story central section of Homewood is flanked by low one-story wings and outbuildings. The outer brick walls, laid in Flemish bond, are trimmed with white-painted wood and brick and decorated with plaster panels and facings. A low-pitched hip roof rises above a thin modillioned cornice, which on the main block is pierced by tiny barrel dormers.

The building throughout shows the popular taste for the Louis XVI and contemporary Adam styles typical of the period of construction. The delicately transomed entrance, approached by a broad flight of stone steps, is protected by a deep, four-columned portico that has a window draped with scrolls and ribbon swags in the pediment. Two elliptical engaged fluted columns frame the arched, eight panel door. In the high-ceilinged interior, a wide central passage is crossed by a narrow transverse corridor leading to the wings, which are at a slightly lower level. The large transomed doorway at the other end of the entrance hall opens onto a Doric portico. The interior decorations are executed with delicacy, variety, and sophistication—plain plaster walls painted in light shades; thin-molded trim with delicate flutings, leaves, beads, and interlaces; and doorways framed with engaged elliptical columns and paneled pilasters. Perhaps the most notable features of the interior are the impressive arch that divides the front and rear entrance hall and the ribbed, vaulted ceilings in the transverse corridors, which provide an early trace of Gothic Revival.

On the campus at Charles and 33rd streets is the **Johns Hopkins Memorial Monument** (14) (1934), erected by the Municipal Art Society. Hans Schuler, a Baltimorean, was the sculptor and William Gordon Beecher was the architect. A long block further north at Charles Street and University Parkway is the **Confederate Women's Monument** (15) (1913), designed by J. Maxwell Miller.

The **Scottish Rite Temple** (16) (1930–33, Clyde N. Friz and John R. Pope), Charles and 39th streets, is an imposing neoclassic structure in the form of a Greek cross with a Corinthian entrance portico fronting a wide terraced lawn.

Two blocks further north on Charles Street, in the Guilford area developed by the Roland Park Company (*see above*), Highfield Road branches right and leads three blocks east to **Sherwood Gardens** (17), 204 E. Highfield Road (open daily to the public all year round), originally the private estate of John W. Sherwood but now owned by the Guilford Association, Inc. The display of blooms draws large crowds each spring, when the dogwood, azaleas (10,000 plants), and tulips (150,000 bulbs) make a brilliant display over the seven acres of garden and lawns. The gardens also contain old boxwood from various Southern Maryland estates and many varieties of trees, and in the evergreen rock gardens are plants from practically every country in the world. This monument to one man's appreciation of the beauties of nature has been preserved and expanded by the Guilford Association in cooperation with the City of Baltimore, which plants the tulip bulbs and shares in maintenance costs.

North of Cold Spring Lane, Charles Street passes by large estates, many of which are now occupied by institutions.

Loyola College (18), 4501 N. Charles Street, a liberal arts college founded by the Society of Jesus in 1852, moved to this campus in 1921.

Immediately adjacent is **Evergreen House** (19), 4545 N. Charles Street (open Mon.–Fri., 2–5), formerly the home of the Garrett family, and bequeathed to the Johns Hopkins University by Mr. and Mrs. John Work Garrett in 1942. It is maintained by the Evergreen House Foundation as a research library and museum. The house, a Classic-Revival building, was built in the 1850s. The archway and north wing, added in 1885, house the little theater decorated by Leon Bakst, Russian ballet designer, in 1921; the Far East Room with its Oriental collection; and the Billiard Room with its collection of Blue and White Chinese porcelain.

The John Work Garrett Library of rare books is housed in the great library added to the rear of the house in 1928 (Laurence Hall Fowler). This magnificent two-story room overlooks the formal garden and the gracious lawns and trees that form part of the estate. Of special interest is the collection of natural history and bird books (Audubon elephant folio, Gould, Elliott, etc.), American and Maryland imprints published before 1800, an exceptional coin collection and an outstanding collection of early maps and atlases of the sixteenth and seventeenth centuries.

The house also contains a small collection of French Impressionistic paintings. The panel over the doors of the reading room by Miguel Covarrubias, painted in 1931, represents the various diplomatic posts held by Mr. Garrett.

The **College of Notre Dame of Maryland** (20), Charles Street and Homeland Avenue, operated by the School Sisters of Notre Dame, opened as an academy in 1847 and began offering college courses beginning in 1895. The school was the first Catholic college for women established in the United States.

The **Stony Run Friends Meeting** (21) (1949–50), 5116 N. Charles Street, is a traditional 1½-story stone rectangle that houses the meeting room and offices. The building is on the grounds of the **Friends School** (22), 5114 N. Charles Street, in existence in 1784 and established here since 1943.

Next to the Friends Meeting and overpowering in relation to it is the new **Cathedral of Mary Our Queen** (23) (1954–59, Maginnis and Walsh), Charles Street at Belvedere Avenue (open 6:45 A.M.–7 P.M.). This massive stone block—it contains no structural steel—with twin towers and almost unnoticeable transepts represents an effort to combine the contemporary with the Gothic. In the interior, tapered stone piers set off the nave from the side aisles, rising to almost flat slightly pointed arches over the nave ceiling. The arches over the side aisles are low and square with squared carvings in relief over each, giving an Egyptian rather than a Gothic effect. The decorations—the coffered ceilings, stained-glass windows, stations of the cross carved into the arches—are beautiful in detail, though the overall effect has been criticized as being too eclectic and unfocused. The cathedral was made possible through a bequest of Thomas J. O'Neill (1849–1919), an Irish-born Baltimore dry-goods merchant who left a fortune to the archdiocese on the condition that it be used to build a second cathedral.

Further up Charles Street, the Protestant Episcopal **Church of the Redeemer** (24) (1955–58, Pietro Belluschi of Cambridge, Massachusetts, and Rogers, Taliaferro, and Lamb), Charles Street and Melrose Avenue (apply at office Mon.–Fri., 9–5; Sun. morning for services), is a wood and stone T-shaped building with a great shingled roof that manages to complement rather than suppress the little Gothic-Revival stone chapel (1856–?, R. Snowden Andrews) that still stands adjacent. The interior is dominated by great wooden Gothic arches, each made of twenty-seven layers of laminated Douglas fir, which rise from the floor to the ridge of the great roof. The stained-glass altar screen was designed by Gregory Kepes of M.I.T. and made in Chartres, France. From the rear of the church the brilliance of the altar screen obscures the nickel and silver cross, designed by Ronald Pearson of Rochester, New York, that hangs over the altar in front of it. Apart from the altar screen, which is lighted by a window behind, the colors of the church's interior are muted, giving the effect of clean quiet space afire at the center.

In the landscaped courtyard is an outdoor baptismal font of rough stone used during good weather.

Charles Street (Md. 139) continues to the **Baltimore City Line** about a half mile farther, where it becomes Charles Street Avenue.

NORTHWEST BALTIMORE TOUR

Northwest Baltimore encompasses the area between the northwest curve of the Jones Falls above Preston Street and the nearly parallel course of Pennsylvania Avenue–Reisterstown Road. When the city's

KEY

1. Fifth Regiment Armory
2. State Office Building; State Highway Administration Building and Employment Security Building
3. Herbert O'Coner Building
4. Mount Royal Railroad Station
5. Maryland Line Monument
6. Maryland Institute
7. Confederate Monument
8. Bolton Hill
9. Francis Scott Key Monument
10. Eutaw Place Temple
11. Eutaw Place Baptist Church
12. Etting Cemetery
13. Druid Hill Park
14. Repeal Statue
15. Statue of George Washington
16. Conservatory
17. Statue of Columbus
18. William Wallace Monument
19. Mansion House
20. Children's Zoo
21. Maryland House
22. Grove of Remembrance
23. Reptile House
24. Cylburn Park
25. Mansion
26. Pimlico Race Track
27. Baltimore Hebrew College
28. Synagogue of the Baltimore Hebrew Congregation

NORTHWEST BALTIMORE TOUR

boundaries were extended to North Avenue in 1816, the commissioners appointed to lay out the new streets had to accommodate themselves to the area's geography. Beginning at the corner of Greene and Franklin streets, the street grid was shifted 45° so that between Pennsylvania Avenue (the downtown extension of Reisterstown Road, which ends at Greene Street) and the falls, the streets run northwest to southwest and northeast to southeast. The skewed street pattern ends at *Druid Hill Park,* and much of the area beyond remained outside the city limits until 1918. On the edge of the city by the Jones Falls is Mount Washington, a small village with a cotton mill in 1810, which became a fashionable suburb and summer resort after the Civil War. The Jones Falls Expressway, a limited-access highway, enables residents of northwest Baltimore to reach downtown within a few minutes by automobile. The expressway follows the rocky valley of Jones Falls and passes by numerous pockets of commercial and industrial development. Many of the buildings are stone or brick mills that date from the nineteenth century. Plans to create a park down the whole length of the stream are under consideration.

Except during rush hours the tourist can sometimes find metered parking space in the Eutaw–Preston Street area by the State Office buildings. If possible, the early part of the tour should be taken on foot. The latter part must be taken by automobile.

The tour begins at the **Fifth Regiment Armory** (1), which occupies a block bounded by Preston, Howard, Hoffman, and Bolton streets, with a main entrance on Hoffman Street. The exterior stone bastions (Frank E. and Henry R. Davis) were finished in 1903, but the interior was rebuilt following a fire in 1933 (J. B. Noel Wyatt and William G. Nolting). In 1912, the armory was the scene of the Democratic Convention that nominated Woodrow Wilson as the party's presidential candidate on the forty-sixth ballot. The armory is headquarters for the 175th Regiment of the Maryland National Guard, a direct descendant of Mordecai Gist's Baltimore Independent Cadets, organized in 1774, and of the valiant units of the Maryland Line during the Revolutionary War. Organized as the Fifth Regiment of militia in 1794, members of the unit fought at the battles of Bladensburg and North Point in 1814. During the Civil War, most of its members served in the First Maryland Regiment of the Confederacy, and the regiment today is permitted to display the colors of this unit. In 1867, the Fifth Regiment was reorganized, the handsome uniform it adopted at that time earning it the affectionate title in Maryland of "The Dandy Fifth." During World War I, the Fifth Regiment was merged with the First and the Fourth regiments to form the 115th Infantry Regiment. Its designation was changed to the 175th Infantry Regiment in 1940.

The armory is one of the few structures in a seventy-four-acre area bounded by Cathedral, Madison, Biddle, and Dolphin streets that was not demolished in the Mount Royal Plaza urban renewal project. The State of Maryland led in the redevelopment of the area, completing in 1960 an eighteen-acre State Office Building Center at Preston Street and Eutaw Place, immediately adjacent to the armory. The center comprises the **State Office Building** (2) (Fisher, Nes, and Campbell and Assoc.), a seventeen-story tower, the six-story **State Highway Administration Building** (2), and the **Employment Security Building** (2). Other redevelopment projects include additional office buildings and a luxury apartment tower (completed). On the corner of Howard and Preston streets stands the new **Herbert O'Coner Building** (3), a state office building that opened in 1975.

North of the armory across Howard and Preston streets, the granite **Mount Royal Railroad Station** (4) (1896, E. Francis Baldwin and Josias Pennington) (open Mon.–Sat., 9–4:30) sits in a hollow at the entrance to the tunnel that carries the Baltimore & Ohio Railroad tracks beneath the downtown area. The great central clock tower dominates the long two-story building, each end of which terminates in a rectangular hip-roofed wing. The prisonlike appearance of the structure is mitigated by the elegance of the design created by the arches and circles of the second story windows. The waiting room was famous for its rich oak paneling and polished marble, and for its rocking chairs, fireplace, and other features intended to lend comfort to a departure or a return. The grillwork and structural detail of the train sheds and staircases are also notable. The building was sold to the *Maryland Institute* in 1964. A panoramic view of these and other major buildings erected between the 1890s and 1960s may be had from a point on the rim of the hollow on Preston Street just south of Park Avenue. The Venetian arches of the heavy gray Mount Royal Station are repeated in the white marble of the Maryland Institute (1905–8), which rises above other buildings just to the north. Immediately ahead is a sixteen-story apartment house (1963) overlooking the armory.

Across the street, at 128 W. Mt. Royal Avenue, is the **Lyric Theater,** whose unfinished façade belies its attractive interior. It is the home of the Baltimore Symphony Orchestra.

The **Maryland Line Monument** (5) (1901), in the plaza formed by the intersection of Mt. Royal Avenue and Cathedral Street in front of the railroad station, was erected by the Maryland Society of the Sons of the Revolution in honor of Maryland troops who fought in the Revo-

lutionary War. The figure of Liberty atop the shaft is the work of
A. L. van der Bergen.

From the station, Mt. Royal Avenue climbs two blocks to Lanvale
Street and the **Maryland Institute** (6) (1905–8, Pell and Corbett, New
York), a notable structure of Roman classical design. Above the monumental arched windows of the first floor, the arcade of second floor
windows—each arch enclosing a pair of roundheaded openings divided
by a column and crowned with a small bull's-eye—complements the
rich elegance of the carved frieze and cornice. The building was made
possible by the generosity of Andrew Carnegie, who donated $263,000
after the fire of 1904 had destroyed an earlier building (*see* Downtown
Baltimore [6]) over the Marsh Market. The first charter of the "Maryland Institute for the Promotion of the Mechanic Arts" was granted in
1826. A new charter granted in 1849 added to the industrial curriculum
"a school of design, adapted to mechanical and manufacturing purposes" from which a well-known school of fine arts has evolved. The
present College of Art, which grants bachelor's and master's degrees
in Fine Arts, occupies several nearby buildings as well as this one
and is the home of the Rinehart School of Sculpture, established in
1896. Its **George A. Lucas Collection,** most of which is now on loan
to the Baltimore Museum of Art, contains nearly 600 bronzes by
Antoine Barye, etchings by James McNeil Whistler, rare oriental porcelains, and thousands of engravings, prints, photographs, and paintings.
Some of the porcelains and Barye figures may be seen on the second-
floor gallery of the marble entrance court.

On Mt. Royal Avenue just north of the Maryland Institute is the
Confederate Monument (7) (1903), designed by J. Wellington Ruchstuhl.

A walk along Lanvale Street from the Maryland Institute to Eutaw
Place takes one through the lower part of **Bolton Hill** (8), named for a
mansion that once stood on the site of the present Fifth Regiment
Armory. Much of the area, from the edge of the Mount Royal redevelopment area at Dolphin Street to North Avenue and from Mt.
Royal Avenue to Eutaw Place, is residential housing built shortly after
the Civil War. Now Bolton Hill is a fashionable residential section of
the city, designated as a historic and architectural preservation district.

At the intersection of Eutaw Place and Lanvale Street, in the break
of the green park strip (1853) that has helped to keep Eutaw Place one
of the most handsome streets in Baltimore, is the **Francis Scott Key
Monument** (9) (1911), an elaborate statuary group by Jean Marius
Antonin Mercie showing Key (in bronze) seated in a boat (stone)
offering the manuscript of "The Star-Spangled Banner" to a bronze Columbia standing on a marble pedestal. Before construction of the state
office buildings, the whole area was dominated by the orange-tiled
dome and twin arcaded domed towers of the granite **Eutaw Place Temple**
(10) (1893, Joseph E. Sperry), Eutaw Place and Lanvale Street, built
for the Oheb Sholem Congregation. It was bought by the Prince Hall
Masons in 1961 and is used for meetings and concerts. Some of this
first block of Eutaw Place dates from the 1850s, and the fine Gothic
Eutaw Place Baptist Church (11) at Dolphin Street was built in 1869;
its architect, Thomas U. Walter of New York, designed the dome and
wings of the U.S. Capitol. Along the upper blocks are some excellent
examples of late-nineteenth- and early-twentieth-century houses—for
instance, Number 1739 (1905, Charles M. Anderson) and Number 1801
(1890, Thomas Kennedy), both on the corner of Laurens Street.

Three blocks above Laurens Street, Eutaw Place crosses North
Avenue (U.S. 1), the Baltimore City line from 1818 to 1888. About one-
half mile to the west on North Avenue, near Pennsylvania Avenue, the
Etting Cemetery (12) lies behind commercial buildings. A brick wall and
locked gate, through which one can see some of the graves, protect
the headstones from vandals; a plaque on the wall gives 1799 as the

date of the first burial. Solomon Etting and Levi Solomon bought the plot in 1832, and it served for years as their families' burying ground, although other Jews are also interred here. Etting (1764–1847), a wealthy merchant and a founder of the Baltimore & Ohio Railroad, was elected to the City Council in 1826, a year after the passage of the "Jew Bill" that finally allowed Jews to hold office in Maryland. At the time, there were about 200 Jews in the state. Zalma Rehine is also buried here (d. 1842). The group of Jews that formed the first Baltimore Hebrew Congregation in 1829 met at his house (*see* East and Northeast Baltimore [8]).

Eutaw Place continues to **Druid Hill Park** (13), a wooded, hilly tract, part of which the city purchased in 1860 from Lloyd N. Rogers. He and his father, Nicholas Rogers (1753–1822), an aide-de-camp of Baron de Kalb during the Revolution, were responsible for much of the landscaping—which was modeled after English private parks—that makes Druid Hill a place of beauty today. The city has gradually added lakes—at present there are six, including Druid Lake (1864–70), built as a city reservoir with a 1½-mile circumference—and has provided baseball, football, and cricket fields, tennis, volleyball, and basketball courts, an archery area, playgrounds, a swimming pool, and picnic groves. The Jones Falls Expressway passes along the edge of the park, the interchange with Mt. Royal and Park avenues and 29th Street at the southeast corner of the park (reached from the Eutaw Place entrance to the park by turning right on Druid Park Lake Drive) being a twentieth-century fantasy of ramps and bridges that take one abruptly into the valley of Jones Falls. The dramatic shapes and vistas of this interchange are an attraction to photographers.

Just inside the Madison Avenue entrance of the park (at the Eutaw Place entrance turn left on Druid Park Lake Drive one block) is the **Repeal Statue** (14), believed to be the only monument in the country that commemorates the repeal of the Eighteenth Amendment. Fashioned of rough stone, the monument shows cherubs operating a distillery with corn and grapes in the background. John Monroe, an English sculptor who worked on the Albert Memorial, carved the stone for the doorway of the old Post Office. When the building was razed in 1932, William H. Parker bought the stone and presented it to the Park Board. According to the Baltimore *Sun,* April 6, 1933, the stone was brought here on that day "as a memorial to the return of beer at 12:01 tomorrow."

Following Madison Avenue into the park, one comes to the **Statue of George Washington** (15), presented to the park in 1892 by the family of Noah Walker. Of unknown origin, the statue had graced the entrance to Walker's clothing store on E. Baltimore Street for years. At the statue the road divides. A left turn leads to the **Conservatory** (16), a delightful Victorian glass cage built in 1886 that houses a botanical garden of tropical plants (open daily, 11–3:30). Beside the Conservatory are a rose garden and greenhouses. A right turn leads to the marble **Statue of Columbus** (17) (1892) in the intersection at the northwestern corner of Druid Lake. A copy by Albert Weinert of Achille Canessa's statue in Genoa, the monument was given to the city by Baltimore Italians on Columbus Day, October 12, 1892. To the right, overlooking the lake, is the **William Wallace Monument** (18) (1892), a replica of D. W. Stevenson's statue of the Scottish hero at Abbey Craig, Scotland. It was presented to the city by William Wallace Spence, one of Wallace's descendants.

A left turn at the Columbus statue leads to the zoo in the middle of the park. Here the **Mansion House** (19) includes a lunch counter, park police headquarters, zoo headquarters, and a collection of tropical birds. Col. Nicholas Rogers, considered an architect of some talent by his contemporaries, built the house in 1801, but all traces of its Federal appearance disappeared in remodelings begun in the 1860s. The mammal houses and outdoor exhibits and the **Children's Zoo** (20) (open daily, 10–4:30) are in the valley north and west of the Mansion House. Nearly 700 specimens of various mammals and birds are on exhibit. The **Maryland House** (21) (open mid-Apr. to mid-Sept.), adjacent to the Mansion House, was built for the Maryland exhibit at the Philadelphia Centennial Exposition in 1876 and afterward reconstructed here. It now contains a museum of Maryland natural history, with one wing devoted to Indian relics. The exhibits include the skeleton of a baby whale washed ashore at Oxford, Maryland, in the 1860s. A large part of the collection belongs to the Natural History Society of Maryland.

North of the zoo is the **Grove of Remembrance** (22) (R), oak trees planted by the National Service Star Legion and dedicated October 8, 1919, to the memory of the World War I dead. There is a tree for each state, a tree for Baltimore, one for the Allies, and one for President Woodrow Wilson. Still farther north (follow signs) in an old pumping station is the **Reptile House** (23) (open Tues.–Sun., 10–4:30; closed Mon.) where about 130 native and foreign lizards and snakes, including a giant python, are on exhibit.

The Reptile House is on Greenspring Avenue as it crosses Druid Hill Park. This one-time country road now winds through the city out to the Greenspring Valley. About a mile and a half from Druid Hill Park at the intersection with Cylburn Avenue is the entrance to **Cylburn Park** (24) (also reached from the Jones Falls Expressway via the interchange with Northern Parkway). Once the country estate of Jesse Tyson, this heavily wooded area has belonged to the city since 1942. Until 1959, the **Mansion** (25) (ca. 1889, George Frederick) (certain parts of the house open weekdays, 7:30–4; otherwise by appointment) was an orphanage operated by the Welfare Department. In 1954 the Cylburn Wild Flower Preserve and Garden Center Organization, a volunteer citizens' group sponsored by the Department of Recreation and Parks, began the process of identifying the various trees and plants, blazing nature trails, and making the estate into a public nature preserve. Bird walks, nature walks, star-gazing evenings, and lectures are among the activities offered. The mansion, a great stone house with a central entrance tower, has elaborately tapestried walls and exquisitely parqueted floors laid in elaborate patterns with a variety of woods. A horticultural library is housed on the second floor, and a Nature Museum on the third floor contains examples of Maryland flora and fauna. The Fessenden Herbarium (not open to the public) offers materials for the study of Maryland plants.

Pimlico Race Track (26) may be reached via the Jones Falls Expressway at the Northern Parkway–Belvedere interchange, via Greenspring Avenue and Belvedere Avenue, or via Park Heights Avenue (Md. 129), which turns off the Reisterstown Road (U.S. 140) at the northwestern tip of Druid Hill Park (reached from the Reptile House by going south on Greenspring Avenue to Auchentoroly Terrace, which is Md. 129). The Maryland Jockey Club, founded in 1830, has held races at Pimlico since 1870 and presently operates the racing plant, which includes a glass-enclosed heated grandstand. Among the major races each year are the Preakness, Dixie, Pimlico Cup, Riggs, and Futurity.

The Preakness, the second race of the Triple Crown for three-year-olds, has drawn crowds as large as 60,000 and is named for the horse that won the Dinner Party Stakes, run the first day of racing at Pimlico, October 26, 1870. According to legend, the Dinner Party Stakes was proposed at a dinner at Saratoga Springs in 1868 or 1869. As a result, the Maryland Jockey Club, dormant since the war, was revived, and racing at the Pimlico Track was inaugurated. The Preakness was first run in 1873; from 1894 to 1908 it was run at the Gravesend Course of the Brooklyn Jockey Club, but it returned to Pimlico in 1909. The Preakness is run each May at a mile and three-sixteenths.

In 1877, the U.S. Senate adjourned so that its members might come

Pimlico Race Track

here to witness the "Great Sweepstakes," advertised as a test of speed between the horses of East and West. Ten Broeck of Kentucky had broken records in the West; Parole and Tom Ochiltree had been raced successfully in the East, but neither was considered a match for the Kentucky horse. The Pimlico race was for two and one-half miles, and Parole finished first, with Ten Broeck second, and Tom Ochiltree third. A contemporary newspaper reported that "the grandstand bloomed with the fair daughters of Baltimore and the field in front was brilliant with gay equipages and rich costumes and handsome women."

Pimlico was one of the first tracks to adopt the pari-mutuel system of betting, the totalisator, and the starting gate. Under the pari-mutuel plan, the money wagered on horses to take first, second, and third is deposited in three separate pools. State tax and the track's "take," or percentage of the play, is deducted from each pool, with the remainder being divided among the holders of winning tickets. The totalisator records each bet the moment it is placed, calculating the odds each horse in the race will pay if he wins. The totalisator is placed in front of the grandstand so that bettors do not have to depend upon approximate odds in making their betting calculations. The starting gate is a metal framework of padded stalls, which prevents jostling and crowding, resulting in frequent perfect starts.

The **Baltimore Hebrew College** (27), 5800 Park Heights Avenue, was founded in 1919 as a center for "higher Hebrew and Semitic learning" by the poet and author Dr. Israel Efros. In 1958 the college built its present quarters, a handsome two-story brick building set off by a recessed two-story stone entrance. The **Joseph Meyerhoff Library,** established in 1960, contains about 25,000 volumes of Judaica, including many rare books and Bibles. A collection of modern Jewish paintings hangs on the walls of the auditorium and library reading room, and a small museum off the entrance hall holds the **Henry Sonneborn Col-**

lection of Jewish Ceremonial Objects in silver and brass, presented to The Johns Hopkins University about 1900 and on permanent loan to the college. Also on exhibit is a collection of miniature sculptures by Louis Rosenthal.

The present **Synagogue of the Baltimore Hebrew Congregation** (28) (1951, Percival Goodman, New York), 7401 Park Heights Avenue at the Baltimore City line, is one of several synagogues built in the northwest area of the city since World War II. A great rectangular triple-stone arch over the entrance dominates the facade of the brick building. Above each door are highly stylized sculptured panels of Hebrew symbols and scenes from the Old Testament. The Baltimore Hebrew Congregation was formed in 1829 (*see* East and Northeast Baltimore [8]).

At the Baltimore City Line and Park Heights Avenue, one can join Tour 33 by turning left on Slade Avenue.

SOUTH BALTIMORE TOUR

The tour of South Baltimore is bounded roughly by Pratt Street, Russell Street, and the Patapsco River, and the area covered consists mostly of the peninsula created by the river's Northwest and Middle branches. Among the earliest settlers in the area were Acadian refugees who came to Baltimore in 1755, first building huts and later houses along S. Charles Street. As late as 1824 the sections of Charles and Hanover streets near the Basin were called French Town. Some very old houses can still be seen in the area, which is now mainly devoted to industrial and commercial use. By 1800, development had reached further south, and a few eighteenth-century houses still remain on Montgomery Street. The interior of the peninsula south of Montgomery Street and east of Hanover Street is built up with row houses, simple three- and four-story brick structures built between the 1860s and World War I. The peninsula waterfront is one of the busiest and most interesting parts of the harbor.

The tour begins at the Camden Station and ends at Fort McHenry. The first four stops are within walking distance of one another, and an energetic pedestrian can go as far as Federal Hill. Fort McHenry, however, is best reached by automobile.

The **Camden Station** (1) (1851, Niernsee and Neilson), Howard and Camden streets, was the principal passenger and freight depot of the Baltimore & Ohio Railroad. When it was built, the station was intended to rival contemporary railroad stations in London. Camden was a transfer point for Abraham Lincoln on his trip from Philadelphia to Washington for his inaugural in February, 1861. Lincoln had intended to reach Baltimore from Harrisburg, Pennsylvania, by the North Central Railroad and then transfer to the Camden Station by carriage. Allan Pinkerton, a detective employed by the Philadelphia, Wilmington, and Baltimore Railroad, persuaded Lincoln's advisors that there was a plot to assassinate the president-elect in Baltimore. Pinkerton recommended that Lincoln travel to Philadelphia where he could board the Philadelphia, Wilmington, and Baltimore line to the President Street Station in Baltimore. From there, his sleeping car could be pulled by horses to Camden Station, removing all opportunity for attack. Although unconvinced of the danger, Lincoln accepted Pinkerton's advice and passed through Baltimore at 3:30 A.M. without leaving his railway car. The secrecy of Lincoln's Baltimore transfer was derided in the press, and he later regarded the event as a political error. Historians still disagree as to whether Lincoln's life was actually threatened in Baltimore. Pinkerton may simply have exaggerated the problem to promote business for the railroad. About two months later, however, the men of the Sixth Massachusetts Regiment reached the safety of Camden Station after a running battle with Southern sympathizers who attacked them as they marched from the President Street Station.

Camden Station was also a focal point of riots during the Baltimore & Ohio Railroad strike, July 20–23, 1877. The strike began on July 11 when the B & O cut the wages of employees. Governor Carroll ordered the Fifth and Sixth Maryland National Guard Regiments to Cumberland to control disorders resulting from the railroad's use of strikebreakers. On July 20, members of the Fifth Regiment were stoned as they left the armory at Fayette and Front streets, but with bayonets fixed they were able to reach the station. Here, the regiment was beseiged by a mob of thousands that disabled the train and then set fire to several railroad cars, the train dispatcher's office, and part of the station itself. The Sixth Regiment faced even stiffer resistance, killing ten of the protesters and wounding thirteen others during the confrontation. Only about half of the men in the Sixth Regiment ever reached Camden Station, and most of them quickly deserted. Regular troops from Fort McHenry relieved the militia the following day, and the crowd eventually dispersed.

A block east and south from the Camden Station is the **Otterbein Evangelical United Brethren Church** (2) (1785–86, Jacob Small, Sr.), 124 W. Conway Street (Sunday services, 11 A.M.; otherwise by appointment), a simple mellowed brick structure with two tiers of round-headed windows and a low square tower topped by an octagonal belfry. The bells in the tower were imported from Germany in 1789. After the merger of the Methodist and United Brethren denominations in 1968, it became the Old Otterbein United Methodist Church.

In the parsonage, which was built in 1811, hangs a portrait of Philip William Otterbein, pastor of the congregation from 1774 until his death in 1813. Otterbein was the second pastor of the congregation first formed in 1771. Born in 1726 at Dillenburg in Nassau, Otterbein came to Pennsylvania in 1762 with Michael Schlatter. From 1760 to 1764 Otterbein served in Frederick County, Maryland, and was responsible for the establishment of the reform church in Frederick (see Frederick Tour [12]). As pastor of the Baltimore church, Otterbein was noted for his cooperation with Methodist and Mennonite groups, especially with the Mennonite preacher Martin Boehm (1725–1812). Boehm was expelled from the Mennonites because of his evangelistic zeal and enthusiasm. In 1800, when the United Brethren denomination was formally founded at a conference held near Frederick, Otterbein and Boehm were elected bishops. The congregation of the Otterbein church is the mother church of the United Brethren in Christ.

Continue on Conway Street to Light Street.

Several blocks south on Light Street, turn left (east) on Warren Avenue two blocks to **Federal Hill Park** (3), bounded by Key Highway, Covington Street, Battery Avenue, and Warren Avenue. From this hill, just south of the Basin, is a magnificent view of downtown Baltimore and the nearby harbor. At the foot of the hill is the shipbuilding division of the Bethlehem Steel Company.

Federal Hill is thought to have acquired its name in May, 1788, when a great parade celebrating Maryland's ratification of the Constitution ended here. One of the high points of the procession was a float carrying a fifteen-foot model of a fully rigged ship called the *Federalist*, commanded by the Revolutionary hero, Com. Joshua Barney (see Tour 25b, Spout Farm), who, with the members of his "crew," entertained the crowd by pulling the sails up and down. Barney later sailed the model to Mount Vernon as a present for George Washington.

In 1796, David Porter, Sr., who had formerly sailed on a privateer and then in the U.S. Revenue Cutter Service, settled on Montgomery Street. In 1797, Porter advertised that he would build an observatory and flagstaff on Federal Hill so that "early information [might] be obtained of ships coming up the bay." Ship owners subscribing to the lookout service would have special flags flown when their ships were sighted, and telescopes were to be provided. Among the fifty-eight

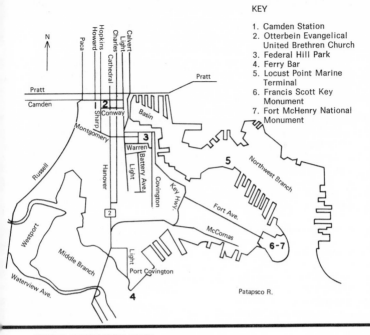

KEY

1. Camden Station
2. Otterbein Evangelical United Brethren Church
3. Federal Hill Park
4. Ferry Bar
5. Locust Point Marine Terminal
6. Francis Scott Key Monument
7. Fort McHenry National Monument

SOUTH BALTIMORE TOUR

original subscribers were the German cities of Bremen and Hamburg. The lookout service lapsed during the Civil War but was resumed thereafter, continuing until 1899 when more modern communication methods rendered flag signals obsolete.

On May 13, 1861, soon after an unsuccessful attempt by Southern sympathizers to raise a Confederate flag on Federal Hill, Maj. Gen. Benjamin Butler of the Union army occupied the site, fortifying it with guns, which he trained on the city. Butler called this move the "capture of Baltimore."

In 1875, the city developed a small lot on the hill into a park, cutting down Butler's fortification and replacing them with walks and drives. Today the city maintains a playground and courts for tennis and quoits on Federal Hill, but the primary attraction is still the magnificent view. Across from the park on Warren Avenue are several handsome mid-nineteenth-century brick houses.

At the foot of Light Street, jutting into Middle Branch at the Patapsco River, is a sand bar called **Ferry Bar** (4), now included within the Port Covington Yard of the Western Maryland Railway. The "cigar ship," designed by Ross Winans (1796–1877) and his brother Thomas, was launched from here in 1859. The long, thin iron ship was steam-powered, propelled by a huge iron wheel around its middle. The ship was supposed to cross the ocean in four days, but it did not live up to expectations. Winans is better known for his journal boxes, trucks, and other devices that enabled railroad cars to move readily around curves, making railroad locomotives more practical.

On December 16, 1897, Simon Lake (1866–1945) and ten passengers (all news reporters and public officials) set out from Ferry Bar on the maiden voyage of the *Argonaut*, an early submarine he had built. The *Argonaut* skimmed along the river's bottom while the passengers ate lunch. Although Lake made no technical contributions toward the improvement of submarine design, he was an excellent publicist for the new type of marine craft.

At the foot of Light Street, turn left on Key Highway to Fort Avenue.

This street leads to Fort McHenry at the tip of the peninsula. Just before the gate to the fort is the entrance to the **Locust Point Marine Terminal** (5). Formerly part of the Baltimore & Ohio Railroad system but now owned and operated by the Maryland Port Authority, the terminal is one of the largest facilities in the harbor. Just inside the fort's gate is the **Francis Scott Key Monument** (6) (1922, Charles Neihaus), a heroic bronze figure of Orpheus, the legendary Thracian musician. **Fort McHenry National Monument** (7) (open daily, 9–5; June– Labor Day, 8–8; free admission) is a star-shaped fort that played a crucial role in the defense of Baltimore when the British attacked on September 13–14, 1814. Located on Whetstone Point at the confluence of the Northwest and Middle branches of the Patapsco River, the fort was built to protect the entrance to the Baltimore harbor. Construction of the fort was begun in 1794 near the site of the earlier (1776) eighteen-gun Fort Whetstone, with both the citizens of Baltimore and the federal government contributing funds. Maj. John Jacob Ulrich Rivardi, who later taught at West Point, planned the outer batteries. The star-shaped fort behind these, a Vauban-type design disapproved by Rivardi, was completed by different engineers. The fort was finished about 1803, with major alterations to the structure being made between 1824 and 1837. The fort was named for James McHenry (1755–1816), a Marylander who served as secretary to George Washington during the Revolution and as secretary of war from 1796 to 1800.

Entering the fort, the visitor passes through an arched sally port and by two dungeons, which were constructed as bomb shelters shortly after the Battle of Baltimore (*see below*). During the Civil War, when the Union government kept political prisoners at Fort McHenry, unruly inmates were incarcerated in the dungeons. On the parade ground in the middle of the fort are three cannons used in the defense of Baltimore. One bearing the seal of King George III of England possibly dates back to the Revolutionary War. The parade ground is also the site of the wooden staff from which the fifteen star–fifteen stripe American flag flew during the bombardment.

At the time of the battle, the buildings within the fort were one and one-half stories tall. The present shed roofs were added in 1829 when the buildings were remodeled. The first building to the right of the sally port served as quarters for the commanding officer, and it has been restored as post headquarters. Next to this building is the powder magazine, which was hit by a 186-pound bomb during the bombardment. The building beyond once housed junior officers and is now the office of the superintendent. Enlisted men were quartered in the next two buildings. The E. Berkley Bowie Collection of Fire Arms used in America from the eighteenth century to World War I is on exhibit in the first of the two barracks. On the upper floor of the building are displays that trace the evolution of the American flag and the history of "The Star-Spangled Banner." In the second barracks, an electric map illustrates the British attack on Baltimore, and an elaborate model reconstructs the harbor and its defenses at the time. From the ramparts of the fort, the visitor has an unparalleled view of the Baltimore Harbor and of the procession of freighters that passes daily into the Northwest and Middle branches of the river. To the right of the sally port as one leaves the fort, a brick walk leads to the outer batteries, which were constructed between 1850 and 1877 as replacements for a water battery built in 1794.

The Battle of Baltimore was part of a British plan to achieve victory in the War of 1812 by capturing the capital of Washington, D.C., and the nearby major port of Baltimore. During the preceding year, Adm. George Cockburn had effectively blockaded the Chesapeake Bay, harassing and burning adjoining settlements. Following Napoleon's defeat at Waterloo in the spring of 1814, veteran British troops were freed for service in America, and about 5,000 soldiers and sailors were immediately dispatched to join the Chesapeake Bay fleet. The British attack on Washington (*see* Tours 26a, 27, and 29) succeeded, and they could easily have captured Baltimore if they had marched overland from Washington. After the poor showing of the American militia at Bladensburg, however, the British believed that the fortified eastern defenses of Baltimore could be taken without difficulty. According to the plan of attack that was adopted, Baltimore would be captured by a combined land and sea assault from the east. On September 12, about 4,000 British soldiers landed at North Point and marched toward Baltimore. About 3,200 American militia prepared to defend the city. Early in the day, the British Gen. Robert Ross was killed, and ultimately the British found opposition so stiff that they did not pursue the attack, determining to wait for the bombardment of the fort and the arrival of the fleet in the Northwest Branch where it could support the land attack (*see* Tour 2a, and East and Northeast Baltimore [24]). At dawn on September 13, sixteen British warships dropped anchor in the river about two miles below Fort McHenry. From here the fort was within range of their bombs and congreve rockets, but the thirty-six-pound guns of the fort could not reach the ships. Although the fort's guns could not hit the British ships, they did prevent the fleet from coming nearer, and at two miles the British guns could not be aimed with accuracy. Two of the buildings within the fort were damaged during the bombardment, but there were few casualties and the heavy guns of the outer battery were never silenced. Shortly after midnight on the fourteenth, the British sent a landing force up the Ferry (now Middle) Branch of the Patapsco to attack Baltimore from the south. Eleven of the twenty boats mistakenly started up the Northwest Branch, however, and were forced to retreat when they were discovered by a battery on the shore opposite Fort McHenry. The other nine boats continued up the Ferry Branch but were forced to withdraw when attacked by the guns of Fort Covington, which was located about one and one-half miles west of Fort McHenry. The failure of the naval attack up the Ferry Branch, combined with Fort McHenry's resistance to bombardment, signaled the defeat of British land and sea forces and insured that Baltimore would not fall to the enemy.

Francis Scott Key, Lt. Frederick Skinner, and Dr. William Beanes of Upper Marlboro (*see* Tour 26a) witnessed the Battle of Baltimore from the vantage point of the British fleet. Beanes was being held as a prisoner of war, and Key and Skinner had been dispatched to arrange for his release. The three men were detained on a vessel located at the rear of the British fleet until the battle was over. The three could observe the action during the day of the thirteenth, but after darkness fell they could only hope that the continued bombardment meant that the Americans were holding out. When dawn came, a heavy mist obstructed the view, but eventually the sun broke through and showed that the American flag was still flying. Later in the morning the three Americans were put ashore. Key went to an inn, probably the Indian Queen at Hanover and Baltimore streets, where he revised the notes he had made during the night into a poem entitled, "The Star-Spangled Banner." Key read the poem to his brother-in-law, Judge Joseph H. Nicholson, who suggested that the words could be sung to the music of a popular drinking song "Anacreon in Heaven," composed by Joseph Stafford Smith. That same day, Key and Nicholson had the poem printed on handbills for distribution to the crowds. Although the song was performed on numerous occasions during the nineteenth century, the first attempt to make it the national anthem came in 1904, when Admiral Dewey ordered the song played by all naval bands at colors. In 1931, Congress designated "The Star-Spangled Banner" the country's national anthem, and the music to "Anacreon in Heaven" was made the official melody of the song in 1963.

By the Civil War, Fort McHenry was obsolete as a defense facility,

Fort McHenry

so the Federal government used it as a prisoner of war camp, especially for political prisoners. On September 14, 1861, Mayor George Brown of Baltimore, his chief of police, Marshal George Kane, and several members of the General Assembly were among those arrested and imprisoned here as secessionists. From 1867 to 1900, the fort was used as an infantry post, and then the site was abandoned by the government. In 1915, the City of Baltimore leased the grounds of the fort for a park, but during World War I the government reclaimed the fort and converted it into a hospital. In 1925, Congress designated the fort and the acreage surrounding it a National Park, and in 1939 the site was named a National Monument and Historic Shrine.

On July 4, 1958, the forty-nine-star flag was unfurled here for the first time after Alaska was admitted to the union. Again, on July 4, 1959, the fifty-star flag was first flown here when Hawaii was admitted.

WEST BALTIMORE TOUR

West Baltimore may be roughly defined as the area west of Russell Street, Fremont Avenue, and the Reisterstown Road. In the easternmost sections close to the downtown area many pre–Civil War row houses still stand; blight is prevalent and public housing has replaced some slums. The southern section is heavily industrial and commercial. The residential areas north and west of Gwynn Falls Park were largely developed in the twentieth century and have little interest for the tourist. The tour begins on Lanvale Street just east of Fremont Street at Upton and moves south and west to Wilkens Avenue and Frederick Avenue; it then travels through Gwynn Falls Park to the old mill site at Dickeyville. The distances require an automobile, but parking should not be a problem.

Upton (1) (1838), 811 W. Lanvale Street (almost at Fremont Avenue), is now a public school for trainable retarded children. Its unknown architect designed this brick 2½-story house in the severe Greek-Revival mode, with nearly flat roof, flat wall surfaces broken only by balconies on the first floor windows, a deep plain white frieze, and small, square-columned portico.

The **Edgar Allan Poe House** (2), 203 N. Amity Street (open Sat., 1–4; admission charge), is in a public housing project between Saratoga and

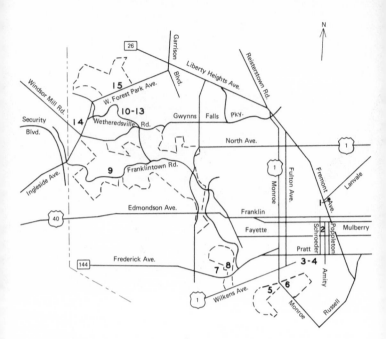

KEY

1. Upton
2. Edgar Allan Poe House
3. Baltimore & Ohio Transportation Museum
4. Round House
5. Carroll Park
6. Mount Clare
7. Mount Olivet Cemetery
8. Gwynn Falls Park
9. Leakin Park
10. Dickeyville
11. Ballymena Woolen Mill
12. Hillsdale United Methodist Church
13. Dickey Memorial Presbyterian Church
14. James Lawrence Kernan Hospital for Crippled Children
15. Forest Park

WEST BALTIMORE TOUR

Lexington streets one block east of Schroeder Street. In this narrow, steeply gabled two-story house Poe lived from 1832 to 1835. Here he wrote his only play, *Politian*, and here he courted his cousin Virginia Clemm, who later became his wife.

If one goes south on Schroeder Street several blocks to Pratt Street, a left turn on Pratt one block to Poppleton Street leads to the **Baltimore & Ohio Transportation Museum** (3) (open Wed.–Sun., 10–4; admission charge). The entrance to the museum is through the **Mount Clare Station** (1830), the first railroad station built in the United States and probably the first in the world. Immediately adjoining the station is an annex building (1891, E. F. Baldwin), once a Baltimore & Ohio printing shop, which houses working models of the earliest locomotives, including the *Tom Thumb* (*see below*), displays of equipment showing its development through time, and several elaborate HO-gauge model trainyard and rail systems, which operate either by push button or at scheduled intervals. Off this building is the **Round House** (4) (1883, E. F. Baldwin), an experiment in brick and iron fireproof construction of twenty-two sides with a slate roof dome supported by twenty-two iron columns and radial trusses. Here are full-scale models and actual examples of locomotives and passenger and freight cars used by the B & O and of earlier experimental engines. Maj. Joseph G. Pangborn created the basic collection for the Chicago Exposition of 1893, and it was shown again at the Fair of the Iron Horse, which celebrated the founding of the Baltimore & Ohio Railroad held at Halethorpe just outside the city limits (see Tour 1b) in 1927. One of the most recent items on exhibit is the first streamlined diesel locomotive, put into use in 1937.

The first stone of the Baltimore & Ohio Railroad was laid on July 4, 1828, by Charles Carroll of Carrollton, one of the railroad's promoters; it is now one of the exhibits in the museum. Early in 1829 the first mile and a half of track was laid as far as the Carrollton Viaduct, across Gwynn Falls, and the directors, including Carroll, took their first trip along this stretch in a horse car. Beginning January 7, 1830, the public was permitted to ride the same distance at nine cents a trip. The track was finally finished to Ellicotts' Mills in May, 1830, and on May 24, tickets for the first regularly scheduled railroad trip in the United States were sold to the public here at the Mount Clare Station. The passenger car *Pioneer* was horse drawn; it covered the thirteen miles in one hour and five minutes. On the same day the "official annunciation" of regular passenger service was published. "A brigade or train of coaches," said this first American timetable, "will leave the Company's Depot on Pratt Street, and return, making three trips each day. . . . The price for the 26 miles will be 75 cents for each person. Tickets to be had at the Depot. Should the demand be found to exceed the present means of accommodation, passengers will be under the necessity of going and returning in the same coach until a sufficient additional number of coaches can be furnished. . . ."

Steam was soon to supplant horse power in railroading; it was already being tried in England. On August 25, 1830, Peter Cooper, a New York inventor, industrialist, and philanthropist who had founded an iron works at Canton, now in southeast Baltimore, demonstrated the *Tom Thumb,* which he made in a shop near the station using an old engine from his New York glue factory and gun barrels for tubing. On August 28 he made the trip to Ellicotts' Mills, but it took an hour and fifteen minutes, ten minutes longer than the horse. Returning, he did better, making the downgrade trip in sixty-one minutes, including a four-minute stop for water. On this trip the famous race between the *Tom Thumb* and the horse-drawn car is supposed to have occurred. The engine was about to overtake the horses when a belt slipped, and by the time Cooper had replaced it, the horses' lead was too great to overcome. In the museum is a working model and a replica of the *Tom Thumb.* The earliest actual example of a locomotive is the *Atlantic,* the first "grasshopper" locomotive, which was built in 1832 by Phineas Davis of New Hampshire and York, Pennsylvania, and used for sixty years.

On May 24, 1844, the world's first official telegraph message passed through the Mount Clare Station to the nearby Pratt Street Station (now destroyed), when Samuel F. B. Morse sent the words "What hath God wrought?" from the chambers of the old Supreme Court in the Capitol.

Two blocks farther along Pratt Street is the intersection with Monroe Street, which here is U.S. 1 S. About a quarter of a mile south on Monroe Street, U.S. 1 turns west (R) on Wilkens Avenue; straight ahead on Monroe Street another quarter mile is an entrance to **Carroll Park** (5), the estate of Charles Carroll, chirurgeon, and his better-known son Charles Carroll, the Barrister, which the city acquired in 1890. In the middle of the park is **Mount Clare** (6) (open Tues.–Sat., 11–4; Sun., 1–4; closed Mon.), the only pre-Revolutionary building still standing in the city. It may have been started about 1754 by the Barrister's brother, who died a year later, but it was finished by the Barrister and his wife, Margaret Tilghman, whom he married in 1763. The original house was in five parts, but the present wings are conjectural restorations made about 1910. On the garden front, great brick pilasters at the corners of the main block are repeated at the corners of a three-bay central pedimented pavilion. Bands of lighter brick running down the centers of these pilasters create an effect of narrow quoins on the edges. The entrance front is simpler, with a portico that carries a pedimented porch chamber above it lit by Palladian windows. The main rooms have plaster-paneled walls and plaster cornices, but the door frames and Adam-style mantels are of wood; the mantels may be post-Revolutionary additions. Many pieces of the original furniture have been restored and placed in appropriate rooms. The gardens were originally laid out in a series of terraces, and the walks stretched from the house to the river a mile away. The Carrolls experimented with a variety of new trees and grasses; they even ordered broccoli seeds. Most of what is left of the grounds (163 acres) is laid out in playing fields of various sorts and a nine-hole golf course.

Charles Carroll, Barrister, a distant cousin of Charles Carroll of Carrollton, played an important role in Maryland during the Revolution. He is considered primarily responsible for drawing up the Maryland Declaration of Rights and much of the state constitution of 1776. He declined to be chief judge of the General Court in Maryland under the new constitution but served in the state Senate until his death on March 23, 1783. In 1970, Mount Clare was designated a National Historic Landmark by the National Park Service. The house is maintained as a museum by the National Society of Colonial Dames of America.

Leaving Carroll Park on Monroe Street (north) and turning left (west) on Wilkens Avenue (U.S. 1), one passes some of the seemingly endless blocks of row houses with white marble steps that were a visitor's impression of Baltimore for a generation while U.S. 1 was the main route through the city. These particular houses were built early in the twentieth century.

It is a half-mile or so up the Gwynn Falls to **Mount Olivet Cemetery** (7) (2500 block of Frederick Avenue, reached by crossing Wilkens Avenue on Dukeland Street), on a steep hillside above the falls, dedicated in 1849. In the **Bishop's Lot** on the north side is buried Francis Asbury (1745–1816), "Father of American Methodism," who, with Thomas Coke, was first bishop of the Methodist Episcopal Church in America. As a circuit rider he traveled more than forty years. A few months before his death he gave his address to an English correspondent as "America," saying that any postmaster would know that in due time he would pass that way. The ministry on horseback that he organized carried Methodism to the backwoods and the frontier, where it was an important civilizing influence. After Asbury's death in Virginia in 1816, his body was kept in a vault at the Eutaw Street Methodist Church in Baltimore; on June 16, 1851, he was buried in Mount Olivet. Beside him lie Robert Strawbridge (d. 1781), founder in 1764 of the first Methodist Church in Maryland, and other famous individuals in Methodist annals.

The cemetery borders on a portion of **Gwynn Falls Park** (8), mostly wooded, along the deep narrow valley of the Gwynn Falls. Automobile access is gained by crossing to the east side of the falls on Frederick Avenue and turning north (left, coming from the cemetery) on Ellicott Drive. In a four-mile drive up the valley, the road is intersected only three times by arteries. Other streets cross on viaducts high overhead, and the surrounding city seems miles away. After a mile and a half, the road joins Franklintown Road, which after another mile leaves the valley of the falls and follows Dead Run across **Leakin Park** (9)— mostly in its natural state except for bridle paths and picnic groves, but threatened by an expressway—to Franklintown on the city line. Wetheredsville Road continues up the Gwynn Falls for another mile and a half to **Dickeyville** (10), an old mill town just within the city limits.

The Gwynn Falls valley, like that of the Patapsco (*see* Tour 1b) and the Jones Falls (*see* Baltimore), was one of the early industrial

Mount Clare Mansion

centers of Maryland. About 1723 an iron furnace was established near its mouth, and after the Revolution the Ellicott brothers built a grist mill where the stream crossed their road (now Frederick Avenue) to Ellicotts' Mills (*see* Tour 2b). An old stone building still stands where Windsor Mill Road crosses the falls a little more than three miles from Frederick Road. At Dickeyville, the **Ballymena Woolen Mill** (11) (R), picturesquely situated by the falls, is located on the site of the paper mill established about 1812 by the Franklin Company, which the Wethereds bought and converted to a woolen mill in 1829. The town that developed around this and other factory operations was called Wetheredsville until sometime after William J. Dickey bought the woolen mills in 1871. Just beyond the mill, the town stretches along Wetheredsville and Pickwick roads. Beginning about 1934, there began a restoration, remodeling, and rebuilding of old stone houses and other structures built for the community of factory hands that had long lived here. The result after thirty years is a delightful village along the stream that is insulated by parks and the grounds of a hospital (*see below*) from the surrounding areas that are mostly developed in tract houses. The **Hillsdale United Methodist Church** (12), a Greek-Revival structure of stone with a wooden Doric portico, was built in 1849. The **Dickey Memorial Presbyterian Church** (13), organized in 1877, is a picturesque frame rectangle, gable-roofed with little hooded dormers and a side entrance crowned by an octagonal shingled belfry.

Across Forest Park Avenue, which borders Dickeyville on the west and north, is the **James Lawrence Kernan Hospital for Crippled Children** (14), established in 1895 as the Hospital for Deformed and Crippled Children. Beginning in 1910, it was endowed by Kernan, a Baltimore magnate of the hotel and theater business, who purchased the sixty-five-acre estate on which it still stands.

From Dickeyville, Forest Park Avenue traveling northeast passes **Forest Park** (15) (eighteen-hole golf course) and ends at Garrison Boulevard two blocks south of Liberty Heights Avenue (Md. 26), about 1.7 m from the Baltimore City line. Traveling southwest, Forest Park Avenue crosses Security Boulevard just beyond the city line (about 0.8 m. from Dickeyville). Here one may turn left to a junction with U.S. 40 and Tour 2a within the city limits (approx. 1.0 m.); turn right to a junction with Interstate 695 (the Baltimore Beltway) and Tour S 2 (approx. 2.0 m.); or continue straight ahead on Ingleside Avenue to a junction with U.S. 40 and Tour 2b near Catonsville (approx. 1.5 m.).

EAST AND NORTHEAST BALTIMORE TOUR

The tour of East and Northeast Baltimore covers all points of interest on the eastern side of the Patapsco River and east of the Jones Falls and Greenmount Avenue—York Road. The waterfront area south of the Basin includes Fells Point, one of the earliest settlements within the present city limits. Up the Jones Falls from the Basin is the site of Jonestown, established in 1732 and consolidated with Baltimore in 1745. No pre-Revolutionary buildings remain in East Baltimore so far as we know, but there are still a few late-eighteenth- and early-nineteenth-century houses and many pre—Civil War row houses in the area. Beginning in the 1830s and 1840s, Broadway developed north of Eastern Avenue as a handsome residential street. Intensive development of Baltimore east of Patterson Park came with the great tide of immigration which began in the 1880s. The Germans, who settled in large numbers in this area, joined building and loan associations, paid $200 or so down, and took out long-term mortgages on $800 to $1,000 row houses. This pattern of home ownership, which was established throughout the city even in poor neighborhoods, has spared Baltimore some of the tenement problems faced by other large eastern cities. The primarily residential northeast section of the city has developed largely in the twentieth century, especially since World War I. The southeast section of the city is heavily industrialized (see Tour S 1).

The tour begins at the Flag House by Jones Falls. The buildings in this area, which is slated to become a historic park, and those just to the east of it, are within reasonable walking distance of one another. Metered parking is usually available on Lombard Street by the public housing project just across Jones Falls, and parking spaces will eventually be provided within the park. The tour moves north of Orleans Street and then east to the Johns Hopkins Hospital. Next it moves down Broadway to the waterfront that was once Fells Point and then follows Eastern Avenue to Patterson Park. From here it moves north to scattered points of interest in northeast Baltimore.

In the **Star-Spangled Banner Flag House and Museum** (1), 822 E. Pratt at Albemarle Street (open Tues.–Sat., 10–4; Sun., 2–4:30), Mrs. Mary Pickersgill, maker of "ships banners and flags," made the huge star-spangled banner that inspired Francis Scott Key on the morning of September 14, 1814. This "American Ensign 30 by 42 feet first quality bunting" with fifteen stars and fifteen stripes, was too large to finish in the small brick house (1793), so its maker found more adequate working quarters in a nearby brewery. Mrs. Pickersgill's mother, Rebecca Young, had made the Grand Union Flag of 1775. The original star-spangled banner is now on display in the National Museum of History and Technology in Washington, D.C. By act of Congress, the Flag House may fly, day and night, both the present American flag and the star-spangled banner flag of 1814.

The house is furnished as it might have been in 1814, and a few family pieces are on display. In the museum that has been built behind the house is the receipt for the flag, giving its size and cost, $405.90. There are also family papers, mementoes of Francis Scott Key, and relics of the War of 1812.

About a block away on the corner of Lombard and Front streets is the **Caton-Carroll House** (2) (open Wed.–Fri., 10:30–4:30; Sat.–Sun., 1–5), bought in 1818 by Richard and Mary Carroll Caton (daughter of Charles Carroll of Carrollton). In 1824, Charles Carroll purchased Caton's interest in the house. Essentially an enlarged version of a town house of the 1790s, the dwelling is a three-story gable-roofed brick structure with paneled recesses instead of a stringcourse under the windows of the third floor and a lunette window in the peak of each gable. The lunette windows are among the few characteristics of the building's exterior that suggest its actual date. The conservatism of the design lends credence to the tradition that Charles Carroll had a hand in the plan. Lafayette was a guest in this house in 1824, and Carroll spent most of his last years in the house and died here in 1832. The city, which has owned the house since 1915, restored the building in the 1960s.

Three blocks north of the Carroll House on Front at Fayette Street, the tapered brick cylinder of the **Shot Tower** (3) (1828) rises 234 feet to dominate the whole area. Charles Carroll of Carrollton laid the cornerstone for this structure, which was built for the manufacture of shot advertised as "not excelled in the world." Molten lead poured through a sieve from platforms part way up the tower formed into round pellets that were hardened in a tank of water at the bottom. The tower foundation, seventeen feet deep, rests on solid rock; the walls taper from four and one-half to one and three-quarters feet in thickness and were built without scaffolding, from the inside out. This method of construction gave the tower the freedom from vibration necessary to form perfect shot. The city has cleared deteriorated buildings from Pratt Street to Fayette Street along the Jones Falls and hopes to create a historic park featuring the Shot Tower, the Carroll House, and the Flag House.

On the edge of the proposed park, one-half block further up Front Street, is the white-painted brick **St. Vincent De Paul Roman Catholic Church** (4) (1841), 120 N. Front Street (open Mon.–Fri., 8–5.30; open Sat. for midnight mass; open Sun. for services). The design is Classic-Revival church architecture with four pairs of pilasters on the pedimented entrance facade setting off the three entrances; but the three-tiered octagonal spire, which rises 150 feet, is more Georgian in style. The simple interior of the church is highlighted by four pairs of engaged columns in the sanctuary which repeat the design of the facade. Except for the church, nearly all the structures that once stood on the twenty-four acres bounded by Fayette Street, the Fallsway, Orleans Street, and Calvin Street have been demolished as part of the city's renewal effort; a regional post office was built to replace them.

The **United States Post Office** (5) (1971, Cochran, Stephenson, and Donkervoet; Tatar and Kelly), 800 E. Fayette at Front Street, is a massive six-story concrete building. The strong horizontal lines of the building, designed to complement its surroundings, make it one of the most architecturally successful federal buildings of a generally undistinguished period.

Between Fayette and Lombard streets east of the historic park area is another group of notable structures. The **Friends Meeting House** (6) (1781), Fayette and Aisquith streets, is a plain two-story brick rectangle of traditional meeting-house design. This was the first Quaker meeting house built within the city. As its membership grew, the meeting divided (1807), and another meeting house was built on Lombard Street. Dissension then beset the Friends, who could not agree over rights in the burying ground next to the Aisquith Street meeting house. The controversy was finally resolved in 1819 with the demotion of the mother meeting into a branch of its offspring at Lombard Street. Religious observances continued to be held at Aisquith Street, but by 1891 the property had been sold and the bodies in the cemetery removed to other burying grounds. The building was restored by the city in 1967.

Behind the meeting house, but facing on Baltimore Street, is the granite Doric temple built in 1822 to house the **McKim Free School** (7). The school, made possible by an endowment of $600 a year from the estate of John McKim, was founded in 1822 by his son Isaac McKim for the education of poor youths. The building, considered to be the most architecturally accurate of any in Baltimore, was designed by William Howard and William Small, who had available to them recently published measured drawings of ancient Athenean buildings. The

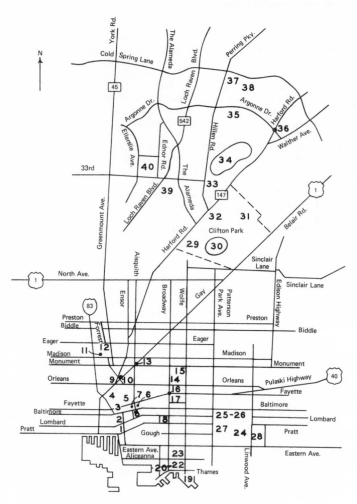

KEY

1. Star-Spangled Banner Flag House and Museum
2. Caton-Carroll House
3. Shot Tower
4. St. Vincent De Paul Roman Catholic Church
5. United States Post Office
6. Friends Meeting House
7. McKim Free School
8. Lloyd Street Synagogue
9. Number 6 Fire Engine House
10. Bel Air Market
11. City Jail
12. State Penitentiary
13. Wells-McComas Monument
14. The Johns Hopkins Hospital
15. Welch Library
16. Wildey Monument
17. Church Home and Hospital
18. 118-28 S. Broadway
19. Fells Point
20. The Cottage
21. 1600 Shakespeare Street
22. Fell Grave
23. St. Stanislaus Kosta Roman Catholic Church
24. Patterson Park
25. Pagoda
26. Star-Spangled Banner Monument
27. Conrad Kreutzer Bust
28. Pulaski Monument
29. Clifton Park
30. Lake Clifton
31. Clifton Mansion
32. Martin Luther Statue
33. Herring Run Park
34. Lake Montebello
35. Montebello State Hospital
36. Columbus Monument
37. Morgan State University
38. Carl Murphy Auditorium and Fine Arts Building
39. Baltimore City College
40. Memorial Stadium

EAST AND NORTHEAST BALTIMORE TOUR

facade, with its six heavy tapered columns, was copied from the temple of Hephaestus in Athens; the flanks were derived from the north wing of the Propylaea on the Acropolis. The interior space is one large room, similar to the cella of Greek temples and suitable for use as a schoolroom. Public schools in Baltimore built in succeeding years used a modified version of the same design.

A short distance to the right (west) on Baltimore Street, Lloyd Street branches left (south). A few feet down Lloyd Street at the corner of Watson Street is the **Lloyd Street Synagogue** (8) (1845), the first synagogue built in Baltimore by the first Hebrew congregation organized in Maryland (1829). The architect, Robert Cary Long, Jr., used a Greek-Revival design that may have been the one rejected by the session of the Franklin Street Presbyterian Church, which accepted his Gothic plan for their church that same year (see Downtown Baltimore [53]). The building is a plain brick rectangle with a heavy Doric portico of four white stuccoed and fluted columns. The simple interior features fluted columns supporting a gallery that runs along three sides. On the fourth side of the building are pillared recesses for the tablets, and in the middle of the room is a railed-in platform for the bema. The pews are made of dark-stained pine. Two great crystal chandeliers hang from the ceiling. The Jewish Historical Society of Maryland has restored the building and has opened it as a Jewish historical museum (open Oct.–May, 1:30–4:30).

From the synagogue it is a very short walk along Lloyd Street to Lombard Street and then two blocks west to the historic park area.

Just to the north of this enclave of old buildings, and within walking distance for the energetic, is the **Number 6 Fire Engine House** (9) at the junction of Gay, Ensor, and Orleans streets (reached from the Friends Meeting House by going north one long block on Aisquith Street and west two blocks along Orleans Street; reached from the historic park area by going north on Albemarle and Front streets to Gay Street). The Venetian-Gothic bell tower, 103 feet high, was added to an older building in 1853–54 by William H. Reasin and Samuel B. Wetherald for the Independent Fire Company. The company, organized in 1799 as the Federal Fire Company, was renamed in 1810. When a paid fire department was established in 1858, the city took over this building. Like other fire companies, the independents wielded considerable influence in their day as a source of grass-roots political organization and power. As the city grew, however, the volunteer fire companies provided inadequate protection, and rivalries between companies were the source of growing public dissatisfaction. Householders subscribed to particular fire companies, and if another company arrived at the scene of the fire, its fire fighters might stand by and let the building burn. If they started to put the fire out, they might be attacked by the company supposed to be in charge. Occasionally, companies were accused of setting fires in order to make business.

Two blocks up Gay Street at Forrest Street is the **Bel Air Market** (10), where on election day, November 4, 1856, the worst violence occurred between rival Democrats and Know-Nothings on a day that was characterized by disturbances throughout the city. The Know-Nothings won the election by over 9,000 votes. In the city election of 1858, most Democrats boycotted the polls, and their candidate, Col. A. E. Shutt, withdrew at noon on election day to prevent further violent demonstrations. In 1860 the state legislature intervened, refusing to seat the delegates from Baltimore City and putting control of the city police of Baltimore in the hands of a commission appointed by the governor. Protected by the new police force, voters at the following election chose a reform government, ending the reign of terror in the city. Until 1976, the Baltimore Police Commissioner was appointed by the state governor.

Four blocks to the north along Forrest Street are two buildings of interest to architects. The first is the Tudor-Gothic city jail and the second the medieval-looking state penitentiary. The granite **City Jail** (11) (1855–59, Thomas Dixon and James M. Dixon), 801 Van Buren Street (at Madison Street one block west of Forrest Street), is on the site of the first city jail built in 1768. Though now only the gate house remains, the jail was well constructed for its time, with maximum light and air as well as security. Two long cell blocks flanked a central square and were lighted by great lancet windows. The central block is defined by crenellated watch towers, and a central cupola with Gothic, traceried openings.

North of the jail is the **State Penitentiary** (12) (1893–99, Jackson C. Gott), Forrest and Eager streets, an impressive fortress of dark granite. A large square tower with a high pyramidic roof and narrow round turrets at each corner is flanked by two long lower wings that follow the oblique angle made by Forrest and Eager streets. Four-story, round-headed windows with bars are divided into groups of three by narrow turrets that repeat the design of the turrets on the main tower and on the lower towers that terminate each wing.

The penitentiary, authorized by a resolution of the General Assembly in 1804 and opened in 1811, was the second state prison established in the United States, as well as the second to introduce various kinds of manufacturing to occupy prisoners and help pay for their care. Maryland's State Use Industries, as they are now called, have been noted for their efficiency and profitability from the very beginning of the program.

Two blocks up Gay Street from Forrest Street is the intersection of Aisquith, Gay, and Monument streets at Ashland Place. Here is the **Wells-McComas Monument** (13), a plain obelisk over the grave of Daniel Wells and Henry McComas, long believed to be the two young riflemen who shot the British general Robert Ross on September 12, 1814, during the Battle of North Point (*see* Tour 2a). Both boys were killed by British fire shortly afterwards. In 1854, the Wells and McComas Riflemen, a volunteer company in the Baltimore militia, started a movement to honor them. In 1858, their bodies were removed from Greenmount Cemetery and placed in state at the Maryland Institute. On September 12, the anniversary of their death, the two were reinterred in Ashland Square. The cornerstone of the obelisk was laid in 1871.

Nearly every street in this area is lined with row houses, many of which have the attractive lines of buildings constructed before 1850, although some owners are now covering the facades with formstone. Rehabilitation and redevelopment is planned for the whole area between the Fallsway, Orleans Street, and Biddle Street nearly to Broadway.

Gay Street intersects Madison Street one block above Ashland Square. Madison Street is an eastward artery (Monument Street moves west). Gay Street crosses Broadway about a quarter of a mile further east. A right turn on Broadway for one block leads to **The Johns Hopkins Hospital** (14), which occupies more than four city blocks between Monument Street, Broadway, Jefferson Street, and Wolfe Street. The hospital, endowed in the will of Johns Hopkins who died in 1873, opened in 1889. The medical school, of which the hospital was to be an adjunct, opened in 1893 after an additional endowment had been procured. The medical school established new teaching practices, emphasizing practical demonstration in laboratories and in the hospital. Both the medical school and the hospital have achieved a worldwide reputation for work in the medical sciences.

In the **Welch Library** (15), 1900 E. Monument Street (open Mon.–Thurs., 8–10; Fri., 8–8; Sat., 9–5; Sun., 1–7), is the well-known oil painting by John Singer Sargent, *Four Doctors,* depicting Drs. William Osler, William S. Halsted, William H. Welch, and Howard A. Kelly. The Big Four, as these physicians were known, were entrusted with

Fells Point

the task of carrying out Hopkins's desire that the hospital advance the cause of medicine. William Osler (1849–1919), Canadian-born, was Professor of the Principles and Practice of Medicine at the university from 1889 to 1900, when he resigned to become Regius Professor of Medicine at Oxford. In 1911 he was made a baronet. William Halsted (1852–1922) was surgeon in chief at the hospital and Professor of Surgery at the university from 1889 until his death. William H. Welch (1850–1934) was Professor of Pathology and Hospital Pathologist from 1889 until 1930. Dr. Howard A. Kelly (1858–1943), Professor of Gynecology from 1888 until 1919, was a pioneer in experimenting with radium therapy for cancer. He invented the cystoscope, which introduces light into the human body, disclosing the diseased parts.

Two associates of the Big Four gave their lives attempting to advance the cause of medicine. Dr. Jesse Lazear died while seeking the cause of yellow fever, and Dr. Frederick H. Baetjer lost his life as a result of experiments with the X-ray.

South of the hospital, Broadway becomes a wide boulevard with a grass median strip. Nineteenth-century brick row houses, some of which date from the 1830s to the 1850s, line the street. At Fayette and Broadway is the plain shaft of the **Wildey Monument** (16) crowned by a statue of Charity. Raised in 1865, the monument commemorates Thomas Wildey (1783–1861), who in 1819 founded the fraternal order of Odd Fellows in America. On the left a block further south is the **Church Home and Hospital** (17), Broadway and Fairmount Street, where Edgar Allan Poe died in 1849 (*see* Downtown Baltimore [45]).

On the right between Lombard and Pratt streets three blocks further south stands **118–28 S. Broadway** (18), a group of six three-story row houses built about 1840. Following the Baltimore style, the outside wall of the house at each end of the row rises above the roof to make a stepped roof parapet.

At Eastern Avenue, Broadway forks on either side of the Market House to become two narrow streets that lead to the waterfront. To the left of Broadway, in the 1700 block of Thames Street, is the Recreation Pier, built in 1913. Here is the section called **Fells Point** (19), where a shipyard was active in the 1760s and many merchants built houses before and after the Revolution.

Shakespeare Street turns right off Broadway near its terminal point. On the corner of Bond and Shakespeare streets stands **The Cottage** (20), a double brick house. One section, 1608 Shakespeare Street, was built by John Smith (ca. 1781–98). It was joined with **1600 Shakespeare Street** (21), which dates from the 1790s, to form a house of two and one-half stories with a heavy stringcourse. Across the street at 1607 Shakespeare Street is the **Fell Grave** (22), where a stone records that Edward Fell came to Maryland in 1726 from Lancaster, England. His nephew, Col. Edward Fell, and his grandnephew, William Fell, are also buried here. It is known that by 1732 Edward Fell was operating a store along the east side of Jones Falls and that his brother William, a ship carpenter (not buried here), owned land on and near Fells Point, where he built a house in the 1730s. William's son Edward (the nephew of Edward Fell) laid out Fells Point in 1763; it was annexed to Baltimore in 1773.

Some of the houses on Shakespeare Street have screens painted with landscape scenes, a decoration to be seen on many houses in East and South Baltimore during the summer.

St. Stanislaus Kostka Roman Catholic Church (23) (1806), Aliceanna and Ann Streets (ask at rectory for church to be opened), two blocks north and two blocks east of Shakespeare Street, is a center of Polish life in Baltimore. Here on Easter morning can be seen a colorful procession of uniformed members of the sixteen Polish societies and of gaily clad boys and girls.

Returning by any northbound street to Eastern Avenue, continue east about half a mile to **Patterson Park** (24). The area was a pasture owned by William Patterson, father of Betsy Patterson (*see* Downtown Baltimore [76]), when the British attacked Baltimore, September 12–14, 1814. What is now the northwesternmost section of the park was Hampstead Hill, center of the eastern defense line that ran from the Northwest Branch to what is now Belair Road. The fortifications here are known as Rodgers's Bastion, named after Com. John Rodgers, who commanded the auxiliary naval forces that in part manned the hill (*see* Tour 2a, Sion Hill). About 120 cannon, supported by trenches and redoubts, and 12,000 men controlled the approaches to the hills, which were bare of any cover. On the morning of September 13, the British moved to a point about a mile away. They planned to attack the hills that night during the bombardment but withdrew instead when it became clear that the line was adequately defended and that the British navy had failed to force the abandonment of Fort McHenry (*see* South Baltimore [8]).

In 1827, William Patterson gave five acres of the pasture to the city, and following further land acquisitions, the park was formally opened in 1853. The park was the scene of military operations once more in August, 1861, when the Seventh Maine Regiment established Camp Washburn, which by October was occupied by Col. George I. Beal and the Tenth Maine Regiment. Throughout the Civil War Federal troops occupied the camp, and for a time a government hospital was maintained here. The park has extensive recreation facilities, including tennis courts, baseball diamonds, football fields, a roller skating rink, a swimming pool, and a soccer field.

Near the Lombard Street entrance on Patterson Park Avenue on the highest point in the park is the **Pagoda** (25) (1891, C. H. Latrobe) (open Sat.–Sun., 8:30–4:30), an octagonal sixty-foot iron structure wrapped in wood and glass that resembles a Chinese sacred tower. From its balconies there is a magnificent view of the city, especially of the harbor. The Pagoda stands on Rodgers's Bastion, which is marked by a line of cannon and the bronze **Star-Spangled Banner Monument** (26) (1914, A. Maxwell Miller), a monument of two children holding a scroll; Baltimore school children contributed to the fund for this statue to commemorate the centennial of the writing of "The Star-Spangled

Banner." A plaque on a cannon to the right of the monument describes the role of the bastion in the Battle of Baltimore. One block south at the Gough Street entrance is the **Conrad Kreutzer Bust** (27), won by the United Singers of Baltimore at the twenty-fourth National Saengerfest in Brooklyn, New York, in 1915.

In the park near Eastern and Linwood avenues (a half-mile or so from Patterson Park Avenue) is the **Pulaski Monument** (28) (1951), a great bronze plaque by Hans Schuler commemorating the services of the Polish count Casimir Pulaski (1748–79), a hero of the American Revolution, who raised part of his special detachment of volunteers, the "Pulaski Legion," in Baltimore and uniformed them here. Pulaski was killed the following year at the Battle of Savannah. The monument, planned since the sesquicentennial of Pulaski's death, was first delayed by the collapse during the depression of the bank in which city and private funds for the project had been placed and then by a shortage of bronze during World War II.

From Patterson Park, Northeast Baltimore can best be reached by returning west to Washington Street or Broadway. Washington Street leads directly into **Clifton Park** (29) via St. Lo Drive two miles north of Eastern Avenue. This park was acquired by the city in 1895 from the estate of Johns Hopkins. **Lake Clifton** (30) is part of the city reservoir system (*see below* [33]). **Clifton Mansion** (31), originally a farmhouse built about 1800, was expanded by Hopkins in 1852 into an Italian-style villa with a six-story square tower. It is now used for park offices, a golf clubhouse, and a tennis shop. The park maintains tennis courts and playing fields, an eighteen-hole golf course, and a swimming pool.

Harford Road (Md. 147), a main artery leading out of the city, runs along the northwest edge of Clifton Park. At its intersection with Hillen Road is the **Martin Luther Statue** (32), an eighteen-foot bronze figure of Luther by Hans Schuler that was moved here in 1962 from its original site in Druid Hill Park. The gift of Arthur Wallenhorst, a Baltimore jeweler, the statue was unveiled on Reformation Day, October 31, 1936.

At Hillen Road and 33rd Street is one of several entrances to **Herring Run Park** (33), an area of meadow and woodland in which are located the city filtration plant and **Lake Montebello** (34), a retaining reservoir in the system built between 1874 and 1881 to enable Baltimore to tap water from the Great Gunpowder River. Along with Mount Pleasant Park to the north, Herring Run Park includes almost the entire course of the Herring Run within the city. Portions of the park are suitable for picnicking and camping, and there are bridle paths as well as playing fields. On Argonne Drive, which runs through the northern portion of the park, is the **Montebello State Hospital** (35), which opened in 1953 as a state hospital for persons with chronic diseases. At the junction of Argonne Drive with Harford Road at the east side of the park is the **Columbus Monument** (36) (1792), a plain stuccoed brick shaft that was the first monument to honor Columbus, so far as is known, in the New World. The monument was erected by Charles François Adrian de Paulmier, Chevalier d'Anmour, the French consul in Baltimore both during and after the Revolution. The cornerstone was laid August 3, 1792, the 300th anniversary of the date Columbus sailed, on a site that is now at North Avenue opposite Bond Street, then part of de Paulmier's estate, Villa Belmont. Dedicated October 12, 1792, the monument was moved to this site in 1913 to make way for a building on the original location.

On Hillen Road just north of Herring Run Park is the campus of **Morgan State University** (37), Hillen Road and Cold Spring Lane, a state liberal arts university whose student body is primarily black. Founded in 1867 as the Centenary Bible Institute under the auspices of the Methodist Episcopal Church, the school's name was changed in 1890 to honor Dr. Lyttleton Morgan, whose endowment enabled the school to offer college courses. In 1917, the university moved to the present site. The school continued under Methodist control until it was purchased by the State of Maryland in 1939. In 1941, the state began a construction program that by 1964 had produced eighteen new buildings, mostly natural stone structures that blend well with the surrounding landscape.

The **Carl Murphy Auditorium and Fine Arts Building** (38) (1950, Gaudreau and Gaudreau) is a striking three-story black and grey brick oval with one-story additions for music practice rooms and studios.

Three blocks west of Hillen Road on 33rd Street is **Baltimore City College** (39) (1924–28, Riggin Buckler and George Corner Fenhagen), a collegiate Gothic building that houses the oldest high school in Baltimore. Opened in 1839 as the Male High School with a student body of seven, the school took the name Baltimore City College in 1866.

Across 33rd Street from City College is **Memorial Stadium** (40) (1950–54), between Ellerslie Avenue and Ednor Road, home of the Baltimore Colts (football) and Baltimore Orioles (baseball). Built of reinforced concrete and faced with brick, it honors those who died in the two world wars. The structure supplanted an earthwork stadium constructed in 1922.

Cambridge (11,595 pop.), seat of Dorchester County since 1686, is one of the oldest towns in Maryland, but much of its pre–Civil War appearance has disappeared. The modern traveler might still use the plat drawn in 1799 to find his way about downtown Cambridge, but fire and time have removed most of the old buildings. For more than sixty years, Cambridge has been a canning and fish-packing center for a large area, and in consequence has suffered the hardships as well as the booms of these industries. In 1961 its biggest packer, Coastal Foods— the Eastern Division of Consolidated Foods and formerly the locally based Phillips Packing Company—closed down almost completely, putting 1,200 people, nearly a third of all those employed within the city, out of work. The effect was more than local, for the company held contracts with farmers all over the Eastern Shore and in New Jersey as well, and these producers were deprived of a major market (*see* Tour 12c, Harrington Bridge). Competition in both quality and price from California growers and packers using mass production methods both on farm and in factory undoubtedly played a part. The effect on Cambridge was necessarily severe, but three years later about half the number of jobs lost had been replaced with new jobs in a printing plant (for school yearbooks), a second electronics firm, and a tuna-packing branch of a major fish-packing firm.

Future hopes appear to depend on further diversification. As a depressed area the city and county were granted $500,000 by the Area Development Administration and loaned another $600,000 by the Maryland Port Authority to build a marine terminal and to dredge a twenty-five-foot channel from the deep waters of the Choptank River. The terminal opened in January, 1964, and was put to immediate use by the deep-sea vessels that bring the frozen tuna for processing. In 1973–74, $2,000,000 was expended by the Maryland Port Authority for new port facilities at Cambridge and Crisfield.

The city has a wire cloth plant, a tin can factory, clothing factories, a fertilizer plant, and a food container plant. But the single largest industry of the town is still vegetables and shellfish processing. Eight such firms employ more than 1,500 people. A railroad and several trucking companies move the fresh and processed food to Eastern markets. At one time, thousands of muskrat skins were also shipped, but muskrats, which populate the marshes that cover a large part of Dorchester County, are a declining resource.

Two newspapers serve the Cambridge area, one a daily, and there is a radio station, a county library, and a county hospital. Municipal services include a sewage treatment plant, a police department, and an unusually well-equipped volunteer fire department—a response to several disastrous fires. One fire in 1910 destroyed $250,000 worth of property in the business section. A mayor and council constitute the city government. Special events include a regatta sponsored by the Cambridge Yacht Club each July or August and the Outdoor Show early in February, which draws fur trappers from all over the United States and includes a muskrat-skinning contest.

The economic crisis of the early 1960s was undoubtedly partly responsible for events that drew nationwide attention to Cambridge in the summer of 1963. On June 14, disorders in the city triggered by demonstrations against restaurants that refused to serve blacks caused the governor to send in the National Guard to preserve order, and except for four and one-half days (July 8–12), the guard remained here for a year. Finally, the efforts of a governor's committee and the passage by Congress of the Civil Rights Act in the summer of 1964 eased local tension and made possible reduction to a token force of one man. Among the steps that contributed to this result was a federal job-retraining program.

Cambridge is one of the very earliest settlements in Maryland. The General Assembly in 1684, in an act supplementary to the Act for the Advancement of Trade of 1683, authorized a town "in Dorchester County Att Daniell Joansis plantation on the south side of Great Choptancke." One purpose of this attempt to legislate towns into existence in a plantation economy was to provide centers for the collection of the royal customs and the proprietary taxes on tobacco. "Noe merchant Factor or Mariner or other person whatsoever tradeing into this province" was to trade at any but the "Towns Ports and places here in this act before appointed" on pain of "forfeiting all such goods & merchandizes." The site at Daniel Jones's was one of the few ever to materialize into a real town, perhaps because the courthouse was moved here. The contract for the "Erecting and building a Courthouse att the town of Cambridge" is the earliest reference to Cambridge by its name. By 1706, however, there evidently were few, if any, buildings other than the courthouse and the Anglican church (built in 1696). Proceedings for laying out the town anew in 1706 indicate that these buildings stood on High Street near their present sites and that the land between was designated as a market. The elaborate procedures required by law for the assessment of town lands by juries and for the purchase of lots from the owners of tracts preempted for town purposes were carried out in Cambridge and recorded in detail. Buyers were required to improve their lots with houses twenty feet square before the end of one year or lose their claims. Any lot not improved by anyone after seven years was to revert to the original owner of the tract, and many in Cambridge did, to the later enrichment of their owner, John Kirke, and his children.

By 1745, Cambridge was large enough to make wandering swine and geese a nuisance, so the inhabitants petitioned the General Assembly for a law requiring that such livestock be enclosed. In 1771, population was not yet dense, because Henry Murray advertised a house for rent near the courthouse, suitable for a tavern, with fifteen acres of "Pasture ground on the opposite side of the Street." In the same year, Michael Burke advertised a consignment of European, West Indies, and country goods for which he would take "Cash, Wheat, Flaxseed, Corn, Pork, Staves, Plank, and Feathers"—mostly goods carried in the West Indies trade. Tobacco is noticeably absent, for the Eastern Shore had largely shifted to grain agriculture by this time.

Like other eighteenth-century towns, Cambridge must have lost its trade to Baltimore after the Revolution. Oystering became a major activity after the Civil War, and in 1900 Cambridge was second only to Baltimore in the oyster trade. As grain gave way to truck crops on local farms, canning became an even more important source of income. In 1899 a Dorchester historian described Cambridge as "a charming city of flower-gardens, shaded streets and modern buildings that collectively decorate a well selected town location." With a substitution of "Victorian" or "Edwardian" for "modern," this describes the older parts of Cambridge today.

CAMBRIDGE TOUR

U.S. 50 runs through the eastern outskirts of Cambridge. Coming south, the first intersection after crossing the Choptank River is Maryland Avenue. To the left, at the end of Maryland Avenue, is **Meredith House** (1). This three-story brick house built about 1800 is both the headquarters of the **Dorchester County Historical Society** and a museum. Among the materials on exhibit are an Indian collection of considerable variety and interest and a display of old fishing tools, models of Bay craft, and relics from the War of 1812 in a Marine History Room (open Sun., 1–5, and by appointment).

To the right, Maryland Avenue crosses Cambridge Creek, which is lined with fishwharves, crab plants, canneries, and warehouses, and ends at Gay Street. At the intersection is the **Municipal Building** (2), a Georgian structure of the 1930s that houses the local fire department. Adjacent is the Dorchester Public Library. To the right on Gay Street a short distance is the intersection with Spring Street. Here is the **Wallace Mansion** (3), now occupied by the County Health Department and for many years before that part of a hotel. Once this was a standard 2½-story brick house, but it has been much extended and changed. In the yard are the graves of John and Margaret Woolford (1773 and 1772); the Woolfords may have built the original house. About 1838, it was acquired by Col. James Wallace, owner of an early cannery and in 1874, the first to open an oyster shucking and steaming plant in Cambridge. Spring Street, which borders the courthouse lot, is named for the spring that feeds the fountain on the courthouse lawn.

The **Dorchester County Courthouse** (4), High Street and Court Lane, built in 1853, retains its handsome Italianate facade despite later remodeling and additions. Its predecessor of 1771–72, which stood on the same site, burned in 1851. The first courthouse in Cambridge, built in 1686, may have stood on the other side of High Street to the south of the Anglican Church (open Mon.–Fri.).

The new County Office Building is adjacent to the courthouse and overlooks Cambridge Creek.

In the southern section of the city on Appleby Street, off Race Street Extended (Md. 16, which becomes Tour 19) stands **Appleby** (5) (private), a Victorian frame house that was the home of Thomas Holliday Hicks (1798–1865). As governor of Maryland from 1858 to 1862, Hicks kept Maryland in the Union during the early and crucial days of the Civil War, despite strong pressures for secession.

Across High Street from the courthouse is **Christ Protestant Episcopal Church** (6) (open continuously), built after fire destroyed the eighteenth-century church in 1882. It stands on land that has belonged to Great Choptank Parish since the 1690s. Buried in the graveyard are five governors of Maryland: John Henry (1797–98), Charles Goldsborough (1819), Henry Lloyd (1885–88), Phillips Lee Goldsborough (1912–16), and Emerson C. Harrington (1916–20).

South along High Street from the courthouse, **405 High Street** (7) (private), on the corner of Glasgow Street, is an old frame house with many additions. Its beautiful box garden may be seen from Glasgow Street. On the grounds is an outbuilding of hewn logs and shingled roof that is believed to be the oldest structure in the city.

Sycamore House (8) (private), 417 High Street, is a small gambrel-roofed frame house moved here from another site, restored, and used by the Cambridge Women's Club. Daniel and Mary Maynadier are supposed to have built it in the eighteenth century. Daniel was the son of the French Huguenot Daniel Maynadier, who was rector of St. Peter's Parish in Talbot County (see Tour 12c, White Marsh Church); his wife's grandfather was Dr. William Murray (see below).

The shade trees and greensward that line High Street create a pleasing vista toward the Choptank River. In these blocks north of the church and the courthouse about half the lots in Cambridge were laid out in 1706. No early eighteenth-century houses remain, and on most of the land there may never have been any. In 1739, when Dr. William Murray leased the area on the west side of High Street between the church and the river, the twenty-five acres was described as "the Pasture." Tradition dates **205** and **207 High Street** (9) (private) from the mid-eighteenth century, when they would have been owned by John Caille, a merchant and clerk of the Dorchester County Court. Number 207, a weatherboarded frame house, is supposed to have been transported by boat from Annapolis and rebuilt on this ground, which Caille leased from Great Choptank Parish in 1750. Its brick chimney fulfilled the requirement written into the contract that "no Fire shall be kept or made in any wooden chimney." The first floor of 205 High Street is believed to be the brick house required by the terms of the lease Caille had from David Murray in 1762. About 1884 the present strange-looking roof was put on, but the interior of the house retains corner fireplaces and paneled chimney pieces.

Across the street from these houses is **200 High Street** (10), or **Goldsborough House** (private), which must have been standing when Charles Goldsborough sold the property to Henry Dickinson for $4,000 in 1800. This 2½-story brick house with its wooden keystone lintels

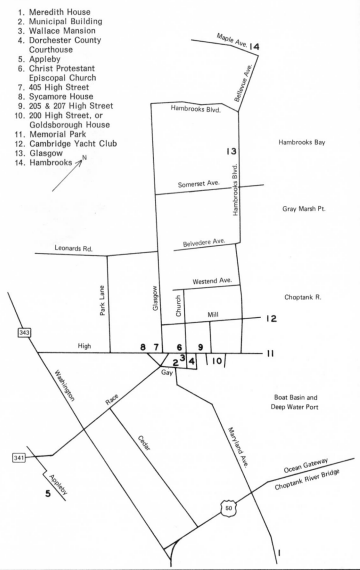

KEY

1. Meredith House
2. Municipal Building
3. Wallace Mansion
4. Dorchester County Courthouse
5. Appleby
6. Christ Protestant Episcopal Church
7. 405 High Street
8. Sycamore House
9. 205 & 207 High Street
10. 200 High Street, or Goldsborough House
11. Memorial Park
12. Cambridge Yacht Club
13. Glasgow
14. Hambrooks

CAMBRIDGE TOUR

over the windows and its fanlight over the door is one of the handsomest houses in Cambridge proper. In the late nineteenth century it housed the first yacht club in Cambridge.

The great Victorian and Edwardian structures that line the northern part of High Street as it nears the river testify to the prosperity that oystering and canning brought to Cambridge before World War I. High Street ends at **Memorial Park** (11) on the Choptank, three long blocks of waterfront that have been cleared and planted to commemorate veterans of the two world wars. Bordering the park between High and Mill streets is a large marina for both pleasure and work boats, and at the foot of Mill Street the **Cambridge Yacht Club** (12) (members only) resembles the deck and bridge of a large modern yacht. From the park hundreds can watch the regattas sponsored by the club each summer.

Two well-known old mansions, **Glasgow** (13) (private) and **Hambrooks** (14) (private, but visible from the road), stand just outside the western city limits. To reach them, follow Water Street, which runs past Memorial Park to Choptank Avenue. Turn left on Choptank Avenue, then right almost immediately onto Hambrooks Boulevard. At the city line is Glasgow, a large white brick house set back on a great lawn. William Vans Murray, minister to Holland from 1797 to 1801 and a negotiator of the Treaty of Morfontaine in 1800, was born here about 1765. His grandfather Dr. William Murray, "Chirurjeon," had fled Scotland after the failure of the Pretender's cause in the rebellion of 1715 and made a fortune that he invested in land, including a considerable part of Cambridge.

Glasgow and its grounds are an enclave of several green acres in a rapidly developing suburb along the water. At the far side of the grounds Hambrooks Boulevard turns left, and Bellevue Avenue continues along the Choptank past a row of new houses to the iron fence that encloses Hambrooks on the two sides not protected by the river. A large beautifully designed garden is visible through the fence, but trees partly conceal the house (ca. 1803), which is set back some distance, and great porches obscure its lines.

CUMBERLAND

Cumberland (641' alt., 29,724 pop.), seat of Allegany County, is located at the junction of Will's Creek and the North Fork of the Potomac River, the southern boundary of Maryland. The bowl-shaped valley carved out by the waterways is surrounded by mountains towering more than 1,000 feet above the city; clockwise from the east, they are Iron Mountain, Knobly Mountain (across the river in West Virginia), Haystack Mountain, Will's Mountain, Shriver Ridge, and Evitts Mountain. The Potomac at this point makes one of its great bends to the north, passing within six miles of the Pennsylvania border. At the top of the bend the river makes a narrow loop to the mouth of Will's Creek, so that a finger of West Virginia reaches into the center of Cumberland. Just to the west of the point where Will's Creek flows into the Potomac, a small hill now topped by the Gothic spire of Emmanuel Episcopal Church is the site of Fort Cumberland, an eighteenth-century frontier outpost around which the city developed.

The first known inhabitants of the valley were Shawnee (Shawanese) Indians, whose favorite route over the mountains to the Ohio River passed through here. Caiuctucuc, their village on the lowlands along the Potomac west of Will's Creek, was abandoned in the early eighteenth century when the Indians withdrew to the west. The British in 1744 persuaded their tribal leaders to enter into a treaty giving the Crown a claim to the Ohio territory. The Ohio Company of Virginia was then chartered to settle that land and trade with its Indian inhabitants. During the winter of 1749–50 the company built a storehouse on the south bank of the Potomac across from Will's Creek in what is now Ridgely, West Virginia. Trade flourished and a larger building was added in 1752.

France sent troops down from Canada into the Ohio territory in 1753 to protect its interests in the fur trade and in Ohio lands, which it claimed by virtue of La Salle's explorations, against the Ohio Company's increasing settlement and trading activity on behalf of the British claim. Later that year George Washington, then a young man of twenty-one, was sent by Governor Dinwiddie of Virginia to carry a warning letter to the French commandant, asserting British sovereignty in the territory. Washington stopped at Will's Creek, as the trading post was called, to hire guides and interpreters for his journey. His head guide was Christopher Gist (1705–59), a Maryland explorer and surveyor for the Ohio Company who was the first settler west of the Alleghenies. Although the French refused to withdraw, Washington learned valuable information about their positions, strength, and intentions, and met influential Indian leaders who held the balance of power in the disputed territory.

Because of his experience, the youthful Washington was appointed second in command in the Virginia regiment sent out in 1754 to meet the French. He led an expedition out of Will's Creek and succeeded in overcoming the first French party they encountered. Shortly thereafter word was received of the accidental death of the regiment's colonel, and Washington assumed command. He ordered a small fort built near Gist's farm in what is now southwestern Pennsylvania, which was grimly named Fort Necessity. The post was so isolated that delays in receiving supplies and reinforcements over the brutal track through the mountains resulted. Washington's Indian allies, alarmed at the dwindling food supply of the fort, left to forage on their own. When the French attacked, the battle lasted only a day before Washington was forced to surrender. After signing terms with the French officer in charge, Washington led his sadly depleted force back to Will's Creek, where they met Col. James Innes, leader of the North Carolina troops sent to aid the expedition. Under Innes's command, fortifications were begun on the high land across the Potomac on the Maryland side. Maryland's Gov. Horatio Sharpe visited the strategic outpost and ordered the expansion of the stronghold, including the construction of a fort that could be defended by the military. This was done to secure the passage over the Allegheny Mountains and to provide a staging point for operations against the French.

To meet the challenge of France, the British general, Edward Braddock, with more than 1,400 trained British regular troops, arrived in America in 1755 to lead the colonial forces. Braddock's plan had been drafted in England, chiefly by the Duke of Cumberland, third son of King George II. The plan emphasized the necessity for strengthening the Will's Creek outpost, which was named Fort Cumberland to honor the duke. Braddock ordered the combined force of regulars and about 800 colonial troops to gather at Fort Cumberland, and he himself rode there in his "Chariot." From the beginning Braddock was hindered by his ignorance of wilderness conditions. The unanticipated scarcity of supplies, wagons, and draft horses on the frontier was further complicated by poor roads, which were virtually impassable in the mud of early spring. Braddock was disdainful of the motley colonial militia and declined the assistance of experienced Indian scouts, having absolute faith in British discipline and firepower.

After weeks of waiting for supplies and transport for artillery to be assembled, Braddock's vanguard left Fort Cumberland at the end of May, 1755, cutting a road for the supply wagons. The heavily equipped expedition moved slowly over the mountains, giving the French ample opportunity to choose the battleground. In an attempt to increase the speed of the advance, the force was split, with about one-third of the troops left behind with the heavy equipment, to follow as fast as possible. Less than seven miles from Fort Duquesne, the French headquarters at the forks of the Ohio (now Pittsburgh), the British expedition was ambushed. Fighting from cover, behind trees and from ravines in the Indian fashion, the French and their Indian allies totally routed the invading force, which was vulnerably exposed on the road. Braddock himself was fatally wounded, and of his force of 1,459 men, 977 were killed or wounded. The survivors fled back to Fort Cumberland, abandoning their supply wagons and artillery pieces. The disaster made it impossible to consider another expedition against the French that year. Not until 1758, when troops under General Forbes marched across Pennsylvania to capture Fort Duquesne, was the frontier secured.

The pace of western settlement was retarded in the years following the French and Indian War by British policy, which forbade the granting of land west of the mountains in order to improve relations with the Indians. Thus blocked in its principal purpose, the Ohio Company folded; its planned development of a town around Fort Cumberland to serve projected western trade failed as well. The mountainous part of Maryland remained thinly populated, and the proprietor of the colony refused to grant lands in the plateau region west of Fort Cumberland until a survey, completed in 1774, allowed the reservation of extensive acres of prime land for himself. A brief land rush followed the release of Maryland's western territory, but settlement again slowed during the Revolution.

A town around Fort Cumberland was again laid out in 1785, as energetic expansion was stimulated by independence. Designated Washington Town under the original survey, it was soon officially named Cumberland when it was formally erected during the November session of the General Assembly in 1786. Interest revived in improving navigation on the Potomac River, especially in Virginia, where leaders had both economic and political reasons to encourage uniting the new country with a major trade and communications route to the West. The Potomac Company, headed by George Washington, undertook the project in 1785. Canals were dug around the falls above Harpers Ferry and at Seneca Falls, and locks were constructed around the Great Falls up the river from Alexandria. Small-keeled boats could be laboriously hauled upstream against the current as far as Cumberland. Flatboats were used to carry coal down from Cumberland during the spring floods but were broken up for

Site of Fort Cumberland

lumber at their destination. The river route, together with the improvement of wagon roads, established Cumberland as a trading community.

Promises of abundance in the land beyond the mountains led many to struggle over the mountain barriers. As western population increased, the U.S. Congress was persuaded to allow federal funds to be spent for internal improvements. The first such federal public project, authorized in 1806, was the National Road, to be built westward from Cumberland. Construction was begun in 1811, and by 1818 the road reached the Ohio Valley. To take advantage of the road and to counter Virginia's control of the feeder routes to Cumberland, Maryland determined to construct a turnpike entirely within the state connecting Baltimore to the National Road. The state added a stipulation to charters issued to banks. This stipulation allowed them to do business in Baltimore and the western counties on the banks' compulsory subscription to stock in the turnpike. It was a sound investment, for heavy traffic on the overland route quickly developed. The route stimulated the commerce of Cumberland as well as Baltimore as the National Road was extended year by year across Ohio, Indiana, and Illinois toward St. Louis.

When the Erie Canal across New York State reached the Great Lakes in 1825, a new era in transportation was initiated. The canal had been a commercial success even before completion, and tolls along its first segments were a significant factor in financing the final lengths. The canal posed an immediate and serious danger to Baltimore's advantage in the western trade derived from the National Road. Transport by horse and wagon over roadbeds constantly deteriorating from the traffic and the weather was far less efficient than water carriage. Pennsylvania had begun building an extensive canal network that also threatened Baltimore's position. In response, the merchants of Baltimore undertook the construction of the Baltimore & Ohio Railroad, the first important railroad in the United States. Maryland also cooperated with Virginia and the federal government in beginning the Chesapeake & Ohio Canal to make possible slack water navigation up the Potomac valley. The condition for Maryland's participation, essential because of the route contemplated, was a spur canal joining Baltimore to the Potomac Canal. Both the canal and the railroad officially commenced construction on July 4, 1828. Ingenious engineering solutions had to be devised as the two projects cut through the narrow, steep gorge of the Potomac in what became a race to the West. Cost overruns and financing difficulties multiplied in terrain more craggy and precipitous than any that had been crossed before by either mode of transport. The railroad won the race, reaching Cumberland in 1842 to link with the National Road. The canal was completed to Cumberland in 1850, and ended here. Ambitious early plans had called for its extension over the mountains and ultimately to the Great Lakes, but the railroad had already proved cheaper to construct over rough country. Engine, wheel, and rail design and technology had improved the speeds attainable by railroads to well beyond the slow pace of the mule-towed canal boat, which had to pause at locks. Carrying capacity had also been expanded, so that rail transportation, already flexible in its ability to run spurs to connect cities and coal regions off its main lines, was competitive with the canal even in bulk freight.

Cumberland thrived as a transfer point between the road, the railroad, and the canal. The railroad was opened through the mountains to the Ohio in 1851 and soon made the National Road obsolete. The canal, plagued by spring floods and droughts, never successfully competed with the railroad, although the coal trade supported it as a supplementary carrier until it was finally abandoned after sustaining serious flood damage in 1924. The B & O became the backbone of Cumberland's economy, establishing shops and repair facilities here. Later, the town was made a division point, where one route to Chicago and another to St. Louis united to run along the trunk line to Baltimore. Commerce was stimulated by the transportation facilities that made possible the full exploitation of the coal banks just west of the city.

Early in the Civil War the strategic importance of Cumberland, with its transportation network on the border with the South, was recognized. Consequently, the town was occupied by Union troops. A regiment of Zouaves under Gen. Lew Wallace (who later wrote *Ben Hur*) arrived in the city in June, 1861. When Benjamin F. Kelley, commanding general of a cavalry unit, was assigned to guard the railroad from Confederate raids, he made Cumberland his headquarters. Units under future Presidents McKinley and Hays were also stationed here during the latter part of the war. Despite General Kelley's efforts, the railroad service was frequently interrupted as Southern raiders blew up bridges and destroyed tracks. Snipers slowed traffic on the C & O Canal as well. Cumberland itself came through the war relatively unscathed. Although the military command was criticized for concentrating troops in the city rather than undertaking the almost impossible task of guarding the length of the railroad, the presence of the troops undoubtedly discouraged the temporary occupations and ransomings that other Western Maryland towns experienced. During 1863, when the Union troops had withdrawn temporarily, about 300 men in Imboden's Confederate cavalry swept into Cumberland on a nonviolent raid. They took horses and made purchases at the city's stores, cheerfully paying for them with Confederate money, and then departed.

The only other direct action involving Cumberland during the war was a daring mission by about sixty of McNeill's Rangers. On an icy February night in 1865 the Rangers rode across the snowy mountains of West Virginia and entered Cumberland secretly while more than 6,000 Union troops camped here. Small details entered the hotels where Union generals Kelley and Crook slept, and succeeded in capturing them quietly. When challenged as they rode out of town, one of their officers, Lieutenant Vandiver, pulled rank on the sentinel and in the early morning dark was able to pass the troop as Union cavalry. With the headstart gained by this scheme, the Rangers were able to carry the captives back to the Confederate camp deep in West Virginia, returning almost twenty-four hours after their departure on the mission under bitter winter conditions. The generals were sent to Richmond and were subsequently exchanged. Military censorship kept the episode out of Northern newspapers, but when the war ended later that year, tales of the exploit circulated.

The decade after the war was a period of great prosperity for Cumberland. The railroad built a rolling mill to manufacture steel rails and other railroad necessaries, employing nearly 1,000 men in its construction and hiring hundreds of skilled workers at high wages thereafter to run the operation. When a national depression hit hard in 1875, Cumberland particularly suffered because of its reliance on the railroad. As bankruptcies and a consequent shortage of credit cut back commerce, the transportation industry sustained grave losses, and the economic interdependence fostered by transportation spread hardship throughout the land. The rolling mill closed down in 1876. In July of 1877 the B & O announced system-wide wage cuts, and a great railroad strike ensued. Wages were not the sole issue. The railroad's procedures and reductions in service kept many of its workers waiting on the line, at their own expense, until they could catch work on a train taking them home. Among other grievances were the lack of security and safety. As the strike spread from Baltimore to Martinsburg and Pittsburgh, a gathering at Cumberland of railroad strikers, together with miners and other workers made idle due to the strike, was reported by Allan Pinkerton to his employers in the Baltimore headquarters of the B & O. Food supplies were growing short; Cumberland was an industrial, not an agricultural, center. As a net food importer the town depended on the railroad. The first serious property damage in the strike occurred in the Cumberland yards, where the mob broke into boxcars loaded with perishable foods. Although no one was hurt in that incident, the mob action spurred the state and federal governments to comply with the railroad management's request for troops to restore order. Within two weeks of the first walkouts, the trains were running again, guarded by federal troops.

The winter of 1877–78 was the lowest point of the depression. Foreclosures forced many of Cumberland's unemployed residents out of their homes, and public soup kitchens were set up. A slow recovery commenced during 1878 when the rolling mill reopened, increasing its employment until full operations were resumed in 1879. Cumberland never again experienced the rapid growth of the postwar decade, but the town gradually diversified its industry and maintained relatively stable, slow growth until the depression of the 1930s. Coal production in the George's Creek basin west of Cumberland peaked in 1907 and continued strongly into the twenties. A ruinous miners' strike in 1922–23 marked the beginning of the decline of the mining industry; the Maryland coal veins became increasingly uneconomical to work as coal lost ground to other energy sources. The age of the automobile and the truck was well underway, putting the rugged contours of Appalachia at a severe disadvantage. Significantly, the one large industry to be established in Cumberland during the twenties was a tire manufacturing company. Cumberland's fortunes were too closely associated with coal and the railroads to survive unscathed during the decline of those industries.

The population drain begun in the thirties that cost the city more than 20 percent of its people has been reversed, and new industry has been attracted. Federal programs have assisted the industrial development of the Appalachian region. Concrete levees and floodways enclose the North Fork of the Potomac River and Will's Creek as they pass through the city. They were part of the extensive network that had been built to control the raging spring floods that devastated Cumberland on several occasions, notably in 1889, coinciding with the Johnstown, Pennsylvania, flood, and in 1936, when water covered nearly five square miles of the city.

The tire plant remains the largest employer within the city. Another industry established in the twenties, several miles south of Cumberland, employs thousands to make plastics and acetate fibers. A large glass factory on the southern fringe of the city, a paper mill at Luke, and a research and development laboratory for solid rocket propellant also employ many area workers. Smaller plants, producing breads, clothing, and various other products, help to give Cumberland a strong industrial base, supplemented by continuing railroad employment. A community college serves the county, as does nearby Frostburg State College. Cumberland also supports a civic orchestra and a ballet company. Rail passenger service has been restored, and a superhighway system now links Cumberland once again to the dominant national transportation network.

CUMBERLAND TOUR

Riverside Park (1), Greene Street, is a small, grassy point on the west bank of Will's Creek where it flows into the Potomac River in the center of Cumberland. A log cabin, extensively restored, that was moved to the park in 1921, was the **Headquarters of George Washington** when he commanded the Virginia militia stationed here during the French and Indian War. The cabin was originally built within the walls

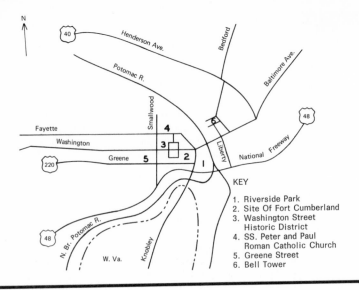

KEY

1. Riverside Park
2. Site Of Fort Cumberland
3. Washington Street Historic District
4. SS. Peter and Paul Roman Catholic Church
5. Greene Street
6. Bell Tower

CUMBERLAND TOUR

of Fort Cumberland on the hill above the park; the Allegany County Courthouse now stands on the approximate site.

Near the cabin a granite monument has been erected to the memory of Thomas Cresap, the most prominent frontiersman in Maryland (*see* Tour 8). In 1741, Cresap built a fortified home and established an Indian trading post at Oldtown down the Potomac from Cumberland. In the course of a long and vigorous life, he explored the mountains and the West, laying out trails for future settlers, traded in furs and land, and played a prominent role in public and military affairs. His descendants also distinguished themselves in political and military service.

The **Site of Fort Cumberland** (2), on the hill rising from the intersection of Washington and Greene streets, is now occupied by Emmanuel Episcopal Church. The log fort, its walls strengthened by mud and stone, was a square with star bastions projecting from its corners in which cannons were placed. The fort proper contained storehouses for provisions, command headquarters, and the powder magazine. A log stockade, running from the east wall of the fort almost down to Will's Creek, enclosed the barracks and a small parade ground. The grand parade ground west of the fort, now Prospect Square, was not enclosed.

The fort was built in 1754 after the French and their Indian allies had driven colonial troops out of the Ohio territory in the first armed conflict of the French and Indian War. At that time it became the westernmost position held under the British flag. Isolated in the mountains, the fort had grave flaws as a military installation; a British officer noted: "It covers no country, nor has it the communication behind it either by land or water." The nearest Maryland settlements were more than forty miles to the east on the Conococheague, connected only by rough mountain paths. Although a road linked the substantial Virginia town of Winchester to the fort, it was more than twice as far away, and the dirt road was frequently impassable in bad weather. Supply difficulties crippled military activity throughout the war. Potentially even more serious in the event of French attack were the high slopes within artillery range that overlooked the fort. Still, the strategic importance of securing the pass over the mountains, both against French invasion and in support of British advances, required the establishment of a stronghold.

General Braddock gathered his army here in 1755 to launch his unsuccessful attack against the French (*see above*, Cumberland). George Washington led Virginia troops garrisoned at the fort in 1756. The last military function of the fort was held in 1794, when Washington, then commander in chief as president of the United States, reviewed troops summoned here to suppress the Whiskey Rebellion. Whiskey was an important commodity in the western counties of Maryland, Pennsylvania, and Virginia. The considerable expense of transporting bulk grains by horse and wagon over rough roads to eastern markets made it far more efficient to distill spirits from corn and rye, thus vastly increasing value relative to bulk. When Congress imposed a tax on whiskey in 1791, and revenue collectors went into the hills, the mountain men rose in protest. After negotiations had failed, it was reported that an armed band was gathering in the mountains between Cumberland and Pittsburgh. When President Washington summoned the army to Cumberland, the insurgents soon disbanded.

The **Washington Street Historic District** (3), from the western property line of 630 Washington Street to the eastern bank of Will's Creek, and from the rear property lines of Washington Street, Prospect Square, the block of Baltimore Street east of Will's Creek, and 8–18 Greene Street, was the elite residential street when Cumberland and the county were at their economic peaks. The architectural styles cover the Federal period through Georgian Revival. Walking tours are available from the Allegany County Tourism Division, Baltimore at Greene Street.

Among the better-known buildings in **Prospect Square,** now bisected by Washington Street, are the Allegany County Courthouse (1894), 30 Washington Street, and the Allegany County Public Library (1850), 31 Washington Street, which have been built on the area of the grand parade ground of Fort Cumberland where Braddock and Washington drilled their troops during the French and Indian War. The library building was originally the Allegany County Academy, which was established early in the nineteenth century. Behind the library facing the square are well-preserved nineteenth-century brick town houses. On the opposite side of the square, by the jail, another row of town houses has survived. The intricate brickwork of their facade is an interesting example of early Victorian ornamentation.

Emmanuel Episcopal Church, Washington and Greene streets, is a stone building in the Gothic-Revival style, completed in 1851. Its cruciform floor plan sets off a deep chancel. A graceful spire rises above the buttressed square bell tower.

The **Gephart House,** 104 Washington Street, is a 2½-story brick house with a gable roof and brick cornice, graced by a recessed Doric portico. It was built about 1840 by Thomas Perry, a prominent lawyer, judge, and politician of the mid-nineteenth century who served one term as a U.S. Congressman in 1845–47. The house was later the residence of John Gephart, organizer of the First Methodist Protestant Church.

History House, 218 Washington Street, is a three-story brick house in the Second Empire style built in 1867 by Josiah H. Gordon, a lawyer, judge, and politician who became president of the C & O Canal in 1869. It now houses the museum and headquarters of the **Allegany County Historical Society** (open May–Oct., Sun., 1:30–4:30; group tour arrangements available).

SS. Peter and Paul Roman Catholic Church (4), Fayette Street between Johnson and Smallwood streets, is adjacent to the **Monastery** built in 1848 by the German Redemptorist Fathers. The order was established here in response to the demand for a separate parish for Catholics of German origin, who were becoming increasingly numerous as the railroad and the canal brought in as workers many of the refugees from the 1848 European political turmoil.

The first buildings in Cumberland were concentrated along **Greene**

Street (5), which at that time was the beginning of the Braddock Road into the West. None of the buildings survived the floods and fires that have swept through the city. As settlement spread to the east bank of Will's Creek, a certain rivalry between the newcomers and the western settlement was evidenced by a provision in the laws of 1815 for taxes to be expended for maintenance and improvements on the side of the creek from which they were collected.

The **Bell Tower** (6), Liberty and Bedford streets, is a small, square, solid two-story painted brick building with tall double windows. A square wooden belfry is elevated above the center of its roof. It was built in the last quarter of the nineteenth century and used as a police station until 1936. It is now owned by the Western Maryland Chamber of Commerce.

As an Urban Renewal Project, four **City Parks** have been constructed: **Hospitality Park, Heritage Park, Gateway Park,** and **The Maze.** Gateway Park faces the narrows; The Maze contains sculpture; Heritage Park and Hospitality Park have exhibits. All of the parks have been landscaped with flowers, trees, and fountains (open to the public).

FREDERICK (296′ alt., 23,641 pop.) is a small manufacturing town and a center of retail and wholesale trade for the prosperous farmers and dairymen of the fertile countryside. The town has developed gradually over the past two hundred years. In that time, Frederick has had no spectacular bursts of prosperity and no severe depressions; the moderate growth rate is reflected in the appearance of the central part of the city. Numerous buildings still in daily use are over 100 years old.

Many of the first settlers in the area were German immigrants who moved down from Pennsylvania along an old Indian trail across the Monocacy River valley toward the Shenandoah Valley and the Carolina backlands. While most settlers came inland from the already settled southern and eastern parts of Maryland, a substantial number of the holders of western lands, including Lord Baltimore, at first offered liberal terms to potential settlers. The holders realized that the more populous and developed the area, the more valuable the remaining land would be. The fertile soil of Western Maryland, available at bargain rates, was rapidly settled.

Frederick Town was laid out in 1745 at the order of Daniel Dulany, the elder, an enterprising Annapolis lawyer and provincial official who engaged in land speculation. By 1748, when Frederick County was erected, the prominence of the town (and of Dulany) was sufficient to have it named the county seat. Churches, a school, and a flourishing marketplace had been established, and several taverns were serving home-brewed "Monocacy Ale" and other refreshment to an increasing number of travelers on the route between Pennsylvania and Virginia. Water transportation was not available, so farmers did not follow the pattern of Tidewater Maryland in cultivating tobacco almost exclusively as an export crop. They raised cereal grains and basic food crops. The loamy soil was fertile, and the farmers of Frederick generally prospered.

During the French and Indian War, Frederick, by that time well behind the western edge of settlement, was a supply and rendezvous point for the British regulars and colonial militia under Gen. Edward Braddock. In 1755 Braddock stopped in Frederick on his way to Cumberland, where he was to join the main body of his troops and march on Fort Duquesne. Angry over delays in carrying out orders he had given in ignorance of frontier conditions, he "showered curses upon the colonies and especially upon Maryland." Benjamin Franklin hurried down to Frederick to assist Braddock in procuring horses and wagons to transport the equipment of his regulars. He attempted to explain to the general the difficulties of fighting in the wilderness, but Braddock maintained that though the untrained colonials may have been overcome, his drilled and disciplined British regulars would easily defeat the savages.

The arrogance displayed by the British general no doubt alienated many of the colonists, and the rout of Braddock's forces by the French and Indians did nothing to increase the respect and loyalty of the Americans to Great Britain. When the British Parliament imposed the Stamp Act upon the colonies in 1765, the Frederick County Court was the first to repudiate it. Popular approval of the nullification was shown by a celebration and town parade. The Anglican Church also was widely resented, for all citizens had to contribute to its support even though many county residents disagreed with its views. This feeling reached a peak in Frederick in 1768, when a group of citizens tried to lock a newly appointed clergyman out of his church (*see below*). When the Revolution began, there was no doubt of the devotion of the town to the American cause. A company from Frederick was the first group from the south to reach Boston at the outbreak of hostilities; their excellent marksmanship was admired and appreciated by the embattled New Englanders. After this enthusiastic beginning, Frederick and Frederick County continued to furnish a generous proportion of men and supplies to the war effort.

Loyalists in the Frederick area during the war were a small and hated minority. Seven Tories were caught and convicted of high treason after evidence of their having recruited men to fight for Great Britain had been introduced. They were sentenced to be "drawn to the Gallows of Frederick Town, and be hanged thereon; that they be cut down to the earth alive, that their Entrails be taken out and burned while they are yet alive, that their Heads be cut off and their Bodies divided into four Parts, and that their heads and quarters shall be placed where his excellency the Governor shall appoint." This grisly sentence was later commuted to death by hanging. A contemporary newspaper article indicates that three of the men were thus executed. The others presumably were pardoned.

After the war the town continued to grow and prosper, both as an important supply point on the new road to the West and as the principal town in a prosperous county. In 1791, Frederick County had "over eighty grist-mills busily employed in the manufacture of flour, two glass-works, two iron-furnaces, two forges, two paper-mills and four hundred stills."

The War of 1812 was generally regarded as unnecessary in

Frederick, as it was in much of the country. However, when it finally was declared, over considerable opposition, Frederick men volunteered readily for military service. Enthusiasm mounted as the war lengthened, reaching a peak at the perilous time when Washington was captured and Baltimore threatened. The town was not deeply affected by the war, and it continued its slow growth thereafter. The waves of immigrants arriving from Europe during this period generally either stayed in the port cities where they landed or went to the edge of settlement on the frontier; few moved to the Frederick area. Because both the Chesapeake & Ohio Canal and the main line of the Baltimore & Ohio Railroad passed considerably to the south of Frederick, the economy of the town was only slightly affected. When the Civil War began, Frederick was a small city serving the farmers, whose principal crop was wheat, and it was dominated by wealthy planters and their families.

During the Civil War, Frederick was in the path of the armies of both sides as they advanced and retreated. The town was extensively involved in providing supplies and in caring for the wounded of several important battles fought near the city, including the bloodiest day of the war at Antietam (Sharpsburg), September 17, 1862. In July, 1864, Gen. Jubal Early's army crossed into Maryland to threaten Washington. There was a skirmish on the outskirts of Frederick as Union troops under Gen. Lew Wallace (who later wrote *Ben Hur*) resisted the Confederate advance. The townsmen astonished Wallace by climbing on fences and housetops to watch the conflict. Wallace wrote afterward that even battle had apparently ceased to have horrors for the people of Frederick. The Confederate forces, victorious at the Battle of the Monocacy a few miles away, proceeded to occupy Frederick briefly, and General Early levied a $200,000 ransom on the city, threatening to destroy the town if the ransom was not paid. Town officials raised the money through local banks, which was financed by a bond issue on which an estimated $600,000 in interest was paid before the last bond was redeemed in 1951. Periodically, Maryland politicians have sought reimbursement for the ransom from the U.S. Treasury, thus far unsuccessfully.

In the last part of the nineteenth century, Frederick gradually acquired some small manufacturing enterprises, although it still was principally supported by agriculture. The first industries introduced, a canning factory and a fertilizer plant, were based on the agricultural economy. By 1890, knit goods were being manufactured; other clothing companies followed, and today men's clothing and sportswear are produced here. Electrical and electronic equipment, eyeglass frames, dairy products, aluminum products, and iron and steel products are also made. The abundant limestone underlying the region is processed here to be marketed as lime, cement, and crushed rock.

Only since World War II has the value of manufactured goods in the county outstripped that of agricultural products, which still comprise a substantial portion of local production. However, the character of agriculture has changed to meet the new competition and to take advantage of new opportunities created by improved transportation and the growth of nearby metropolitan areas. Commercial grain production has generally been abandoned; the principal crops are hay and corn to feed the livestock that are now the chief interest of the farmer. Dairy farming has become the dominant agricultural activity, and a large milk producers' cooperative has headquarters in Frederick. Fruit orchards and fish hatcheries are also numerous in the county. Local products are exhibited each year at a large county fair during the first week of October.

The Biological Warfare Laboratory in the U.S. government installation at Fort Detrick, adjoining the city limits, has influenced both the economy and the culture of Frederick. Established by the U.S. Army Chemical Corps in 1943, the laboratory was operated for the government by a private chemical company from 1953 until 1973. It was the largest single employer in the county, and its employees were primarily highly paid, college-trained chemists, engineers, and technicians from other parts of the country. During World War II the work of the laboratory—experimentation with highly infectious micro-organisms—was a well-kept secret, although two townsmen are said to have heard enough about the base to have become alarmed. They tapped the Detrick sewer line as it entered the city sewage system and took samples for laboratory examination. After this considerable labor, their doubts were allayed; wastes from the laboratory had been extensively processed, and the sewage proved to be sterile.

In 1972–73, biological warfare research ceased at Fort Detrick. A branch of the National Institutes of Health (NIH) moved out from Bethesda, and cancer research is now being conducted. The army is still maintained here, as well as a Walter Reed Hospital unit.

Frederick today has thus developed and diversified its economy sufficiently to sustain the character of a living city, while the pace of the change has been gentle enough for it to retain an unusually clear connection with its long history. Frederick's well-preserved buildings and narrow streets strongly suggest the atmosphere in which previous generations lived and worked.

FREDERICK TOUR

Mount Olivet Cemetery (1) (open), at the south end of Market Street, was chartered in 1852. Near the entrance is the **Francis Scott Key Monument,** which includes a 9'5" bronze statue of the author of "The Star-Spangled Banner." At the base is a group of three figures representing Patriotism, War, and Music; the seal of Maryland is on the pedestal. This is one of the few places where the United States flag is never lowered. Key (1779–1843), who was born in a part of Frederick County that is now Carroll County, practiced law in Frederick and elsewhere for several years before moving to the District of Columbia in 1805. Citizens organized as the Key Monument Association had the bodies of Key and his wife brought from Baltimore for burial here, and they erected the monument, which was designed by Alexander Doyle, in 1898.

In the southern part of the cemetery is the **Barbara Fritchie Monument,** marking the grave of the heroine of John Greenleaf Whittier's popular poem. Nearby is the grave of Thomas Johnson (1732–1819), first governor of the State of Maryland (1777–79) and associate justice of the U.S. Supreme Court (1791–93). Along the west border are

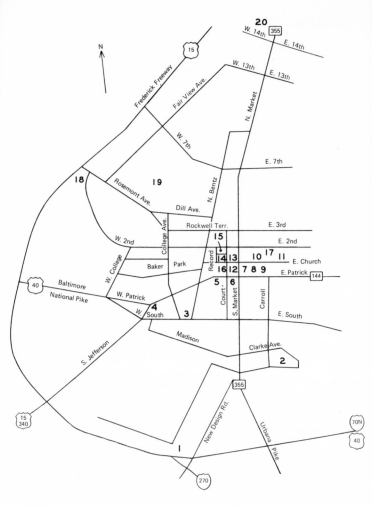

KEY

1. Mount Olivet Cemetery
2. Maryland School for the Deaf
3. Roger Brooke Taney Home and
   Francis Scott Key Museum
4. Steiner House
5. Barbara Fritchie House and
   Museum
6. John Hanson House
7. Kemp Hall
8. Winchester Hall
9. Headquarters of the Historical
   Society of Frederick County
10. Evangelical Lutheran Church
11. Frederick Academy of the
    Visitation
12. Trinity Chapel
13. Evangelical Reformed Church
14. Frederick County Courthouse
15. Courthouse Square
16. All Saints' Parish House
17. St. John's Roman Catholic Church
18. Schifferstadt
19. Hood College
20. Rose Hill Manor

FREDERICK TOUR

buried a number of Confederates killed in the Civil War battles of
Monocacy and Antietam.

At the **Maryland School for the Deaf** (2), corner of Market and Clarke
streets, children receive an academic education similar to that offered
by the public school and also thorough instruction in speech reading,
speech, auditory training, and the use of individual hearing aids. The
four-story main building was constructed in 1870 of red brick in the
Victorian style. The **Hessian Barracks** (open by appointment with the

school), on the school grounds, were begun in the spring of 1778 on land belonging to Daniel Dulany. During the Revolution the barracks were used as prisons. Among the captives were Hessian mercenaries, who found much in common with the German-speaking people of this region. Relations between the prisoners and the townsmen were generally friendly, with the Hessians making fireworks for the American victory celebration in 1783. A number of the prisoners settled here after the war. Prior to May 23, 1786, Dulany reclaimed the land and the barracks. In 1797, Benjamin (son of Daniel) and Rebecca Dulany inherited the land. The state received the official deed on June 21, 1799.

From 1801 to 1861 the barracks were used principally as a public arsenal for the state. U.S. troops were quartered at the barracks in 1812. From August 17 to September 1, 1861, the barracks were used as a general hospital for the Union. In December of 1861, the barracks became a division hospital for the Army of the Potomac. By March 1, 1862, the building became a general hospital once again. It finally closed in September, 1865. In 1867 the state established the Maryland Institution for the Deaf and Dumb.

The **Roger Brooke Taney Home and Francis Scott Key Museum** (3) (open Tues.–Sun., 10–4; Oct. 15–May 15, by request), 123 S. Bentz Street, is the two-story brick house where Taney lived from 1815 to 1823, when he moved to Baltimore. In it are articles and portraits that belonged to the Taneys, including the table on which Taney wrote the Dred Scott decision and the robe he wore as chief justice of the U.S. Supreme Court. One room contains belongings of Francis Scott Key, Taney's friend and brother-in-law.

Born in Calvert County in 1777, Taney was admitted to the bar in 1799. He came to Frederick to practice law with Key in 1801 and in 1806 married Key's sister, Anne. His practice prospered, his legal reputation grew, and he became influential in politics. Elected to the state senate in 1816, Taney was appointed attorney general of Maryland in 1827. After Andrew Jackson had been elected president in 1828, Taney, who had supported him effectively for years, was put in charge of federal appointments in Baltimore. In 1831 President Jackson appointed Taney attorney general of the United States and in 1835 selected him to fill the vacancy on the Supreme Court created by the death of Chief Justice John Marshall.

Under Taney, the court began to favor the common man and the public welfare in cases raising legal points not previously determined, thus changing its character considerably from that at the time of Marshall, who scrupulously upheld the rights and privileges of property. Many opinions written by Taney protected "human rights" when they conflicted with powerful interests in business and government. However, Taney is best known for his decision in the Dred Scott case, which aroused bitter resentment in the North because it failed to protect the Negro. Ironically, Taney had long maintained that slavery was evil and had manumitted his own slaves. He died in 1864 and is buried next to his mother in St. John's Roman Catholic Cemetery, E. Third and East streets.

The **Steiner House** (4) (open Tues.–Sun., 10–4; Oct. 15–May 15, by appointment only), 368 W. Patrick Street, a two-story brick house, was built in 1807 by Col. Stephen Steiner, architect and prominent citizen of Frederick. The wide doorway is a particularly striking feature of this well-proportioned building, which is operated by the Frederick Civic Club.

The **Barbara Fritchie House and Museum** (5) (open daily; admission fee), 156 W. Patrick Street, is a 1½-story brick house with dormers and a steeply pitched gable roof. It is a supposed reproduction of the home and glove shop of Barbara Fritchie and her husband, John, a glovemaker; the original house was torn down about 1867. The house contains some clothing and other articles said to have belonged to the heroine of Whittier's poem "Barbara Fritchie."

The authenticity of the incident related in the poem has never been established. In the debate over whether Barbara Fritchie actually defied Gen. Stonewall Jackson and his "rebel horde" by flying the Stars and Stripes, Whittier remained noncommittal. He once wrote: "There has been a great deal of dispute about my poem, but if there is any mistake in the details, there was none in my estimate of her noble character, her loyalty and her patriotism." Generations of Americans have treasured Stonewall's gallant response to Barbara's courageous defiance: " 'Who touches a hair of yon gray head / Dies like a dog! March on!' he said."

During World War II, Sir Winston Churchill accompanied President Roosevelt on a drive to the presidential retreat of Shangri-la in the mountains north of Frederick. In response to Churchill's inquiries about the Barbara Fritchie House signs along the highway, Roosevelt explained that Fritchie was the heroine of a poem about a Civil War incident. All he could remember was the couplet, " 'Shoot, if you must, this old gray head, But spare your country's flag,' she said." Churchill, with some assistance, proceeded to recite the entire poem, saying afterward that he had not thought of it for at least thirty years.

The **John Hanson House** (6), 108 W. Patrick Street, a three-story brick structure, has been altered extensively since John Hanson (1721–83), the "first President" of the United States, lived in it for ten years (1773–83). Hanson, one of Maryland's representatives at the Philadelphia Convention, was elected to preside over the delegates in 1781 with the title "President of the United States in Congress Assembled" under the Articles of Confederation. Hanson's son-in-law, Dr. Philip Thomas, owned the house at 110 W. Patrick Street. Both homes are private.

Kemp Hall (7), N. Market and E. Church streets, a three-story brick structure built in 1860, housed meetings of the Maryland General Assembly during a critical session in 1861. Gov. Thomas Holliday Hicks, who opposed secession, ordered the legislators to meet at the courthouse in Frederick because Annapolis was occupied by Federal troops. Because the courthouse proved inadequate the General Assembly moved to Kemp Hall. Incidental to the governor's decision, it may be noted that public sentiment was more pro-Union in the Frederick area than in Eastern and Southern Maryland. The legislators never had the opportunity to vote a clear "yes or no" on secession, for the antisecession minority, by adroitly absenting themselves to thwart quorum counts and through other parliamentary maneuvers, managed to hold up a vote for several months. As secessionist fervor increased, the possibility of its success so alarmed the Federal government that its troops intervened, arresting and detaining secessionist legislators. Thus Maryland remained in the Union.

Winchester Hall (8), 14 E. Church Street, consists of two large red brick buildings of Greek-Revival design connected by a corridor. This impressive structure was erected in 1843–44 for the Frederick Female Seminary and was named for its president, Hiram Winchester. Like most other large buildings in Frederick, it was used as a hospital during the Civil War. Later, a women's college, which is now Hood College, occupied the hall, which now houses a number of county departments and other offices.

The **Headquarters of the Historical Society of Frederick County** (9) (open Thurs., Fri., and Sat., 10–4; and by appointment) is a large four-story brick house built about 1830. The annex now housing a gift shop was probably added after 1854, for it does not appear on a Frederick map of that date in the society's collection. Originally a residence, it was established as a home for female orphans by the terms of the

Hessian Barracks

will of the last owner, who died in 1879. The orphanage was closed in 1958, and the house was purchased by the society. The spacious rooms with exceptionally high ceilings are an attractive setting for the society's collections of early Frederick printing, paintings, furniture, silver, and glass, including a green glass Amelung goblet and other objects of historical interest.

The **Evangelical Lutheran Church** (10), E. Church Street between Market Street and Middle Alley, is a two-story building in the Norman-Gothic style. To a structure built about 1753, the present front with twin spires was added in 1854. During the Civil War a false floor was built over the pews so that sick and wounded soldiers could be hospitalized here.

The **Frederick Academy of the Visitation Convent** (11), E. Church Street and Chapel Alley, was established in 1824 by the Sisters of Charity. In 1845, the Sisters of the Visitation replaced them. The south wing of the building was added in 1847. The east wing, containing the chapel and the monastery proper, was built in 1851.

Trinity Chapel (Evangelical Reformed) (12), W. Church Street near Market Street, is a two-story building with a square stone tower carrying a high octagonal spire. The site was reserved for the Reformed congregation by Daniel Dulany in 1745, although the legal transfer was not completed until 1764. First a schoolhouse was built on the lot, then a wooden church in 1747–48. In 1764, a stone church was built, and the congregation soon boasted, "Our church is the only one in the province that has got a steeple." In 1807 the tower clock was installed and the old steeple was replaced by the present spire. The stonework visible today beneath the spire is part of the 1764 building.

The **Evangelical Reformed Church** (13), 9–12 W. Church Street, built in 1848, is a red brick structure trimmed with granite, with an Ionic portico in the Greek-Revival style and two open towers. While in Frederick in September, 1862, Gen. Thomas J. "Stonewall" Jackson came to a Sunday evening service, reportedly to prevent a possible disturbance by his soldiers, for the minister had announced his intention to pray for the success of the Union forces. However ardent the cleric's intercession may have been, it did not arouse any reaction from Jackson, who slept soundly through the service.

The **Frederick County Courthouse** (14), on Court Street between Record and Church streets, built during the Civil War, is a two-story, red brick structure surmounted by a wooden cupola.

Construction of the first courthouse on this site was begun in 1750 but not completed until 1756. The delay is attributed to the conscription of some of the workmen by General Braddock during the French and Indian War, but there is no evidence of this. However, it seems that the construction period was not extended in order to improve the quality of the building, for within a few years it had begun to deteriorate.

A second courthouse was erected in 1787. In this building on April 26, 1861, the Maryland General Assembly met in a special session, held in Frederick because Annapolis was then occupied by Federal troops. The courthouse proved inadequate, so the next day the legislators moved to *Kemp Hall,* where they proceeded to consider the question of secession. A few days after the move, the courthouse burned. Construction of the present building began at once.

Courthouse Square (15) is lined by a number of distinguished homes of the Federal period. The **Potts House** (private), 100 N. Court Street, a three-story brick house, was designed by Robert Mills, who was later appointed architect for public buildings by President Andrew Jackson. Mills also designed the First Baptist Church, Waterloo Row, and the Washington Monument in Baltimore. The third story of the house is a later addition. A principal feature is the wide front entrance with double doors ornamented with small oval panels, bordered by beautifully leaded fanlight and sidelights.

The **Ross and Mathias Houses** (private), 103 and 105 Council Street, are adjoining brick houses built in 1817 by Col. John MacPherson and his son-in-law, John Brien, on the site of the old jail. On a visit to Frederick in 1824, Lafayette was entertained here by Colonel Mac-Pherson. Both houses had a number of outbuildings—smokehouse, slave quarters, icehouse, and stables; those of the Ross house have survived intact.

The house at **111 Record Street** (private) is the birthplace of William Tyler Page, author of "The American's Creed." Page was an administrative official of the United States House of Representatives for many years, and he also wrote *Page's Congressional Handbook.*

The **Spite House** (private), 112 W. Church Street, was originally a two-story brick Georgian house built in 1814 by Dr. John Tyler, one of the first eye specialists in America. A third story and a two-story wing were added in 1857. The house is said to have received its name because it was hurriedly constructed to serve as a barrier preventing a proposed extension of Record Street.

The **C. Burr Artz Free Library,** Record and Council streets, a one-story red brick building erected in 1936, has documents bearing the signatures of George Washington, Thomas Jefferson, John Hanson, and John Jay. It is on the site of the Frederick Academy building, constructed in 1796. When Roger Brooke Taney was a member of the governing board of the academy, Salmon P. Chase applied for a teaching position but was refused appointment. Chase later succeeded Taney as chief justice of the U.S. Supreme Court.

C. Burr Artz owned a farm in Frederick County. He died in 1874, followed by his wife, Catherine Thomas Artz, in 1887. When she died, she stipulated in her will that if her daughter died without issue, her estate was to be placed in the hands of three trustees. The money was to be used for a library, which was to be named after her husband.

All Saints' Parish House (16), 21–25 N. Court Street, a small well-proportioned building with white-stuccoed brick walls, was erected in 1812 as the church of All Saints' Parish, with funds raised by a lottery and by subscription. The building has been used as a parish house for the present Gothic-style church on W. Church Street since 1892. In the colonial period, All Saints' Parish comprised all of Western Maryland; since the population of the parish determined the income of the rector, it was also the richest parish. Thomas Bacon, noted for his work in compiling the laws of Maryland and for his pioneering efforts to establish charity schools for poor children of all races, was in charge of All Saints' from 1758 until his death in 1768. He was succeeded by the dandy and duelist Bennett Allen, who was reputed to be an illegitimate son of Lord Baltimore. Although the men of All Saints' attempted to lock Allen out of the church in protest against his character and against the failure of the government to split the parish into smaller, more effective units, Allen, with the aid of a pistol, managed to install himself legally in the church. Promptly thereafter he hired a curate to hold services and he then left for Pennsylvania, where he continued to receive the income as rector of All Saints' until the Revolution disestablished the Church. From 1847 to 1853, Rev. William Pendleton was rector of All Saints' Parish. A Virginian and a graduate of West Point, he became a brigadier general in the Confederate army and served as chief of artillery in the Army of Northern Virginia.

St. John's Roman Catholic Church (17), Second Street and Middle Alley, is a cruciform building of stuccoed masonry ornamented with quoins and Ionic pilasters. The cornerstone of this structure was laid in 1833. The steeple was not completed until 1845, but the building as it now stands was finished and consecrated in 1837.

Schifferstadt (18), W. Second Street and Rosemont Avenue, is an early German farmhouse (ca. 1736), and an example of the architecture and construction of that era (open Tues.–Sun., 10–4; also by appointment). The Visitors' Information Center is open seven days a week, 9–9.

Hood College (19), Dill Avenue and College Parkway, is a small liberal arts college for women, offering B.A. and B.S. degrees. Students attend classes in the college's Georgian-Colonial-style buildings. Founded in 1893 as The Woman's College of Frederick, Maryland, its name was changed to Hood College in 1913 in recognition of Mrs. Margaret E. S. Hood, a generous benefactor.

Rose Hill Manor (20), 1600 block of N. Market Street, was the home of John C. and Ann Johnson Grahame. Gov. Thomas Johnson resided here several years prior to his death in 1819. The colonial house was built in 1767. The building and grounds are part of the Frederick County Park system. The house contains a Children's Historical Museum (open 9–4 during the school year and Sat., 9–12; also by appointment).

HAGERSTOWN (560′ alt., 35,862 pop.), the county seat of Washington County, lies in a fertile valley of the Blue Ridge Mountains at the intersection of two important trunk routes, I-81 and I-70. These roads follow respectively the historic north-south pathway through the Cumberland and Shenandoah valleys and the old National Pike, over which pioneers for decades traveled to settle in the country beyond the Appalachians.

The architecture of the city reflects its solid, prosperous growth through the years. Many modern structures line the downtown streets, although buildings of earlier design predominate. In the older residential sections, rambling Victorian frame houses are mixed with tall, squared-off buildings in the styles of the first few decades of the twentieth century. Newer dwellings, concentrated in the outlying districts, are generally of the popular postwar ranch house type. The branches of aged trees arch over many of the streets, and in the newer developments builders have made efforts to preserve the trees. The appearance of the city is also enhanced by well-tended parks; the City Park, with its wooded slopes and gemlike lake, has received national recognition for its beauty. The pleasant residential character of Hagerstown has not been destroyed by its factories, which produce organs, furniture, clothing, airplanes, chemicals, truck parts, concrete products, and a variety of industrial equipment. The complex technology involved in the manufacture of such products requires trained professionals and highly skilled craftsmen, who form a valuable sector of the city's population.

Equally important as manufacturing to the local economy are banking, shipping, retailing and other services for the city's residents and businesses, and for the farmers, dairymen, and orchardists of the surrounding countryside. Hagerstown's relationship with the countryside is unusually close; officials endeavor to make many of the public services available to the rural area as well as to the town, and there are many economic ties. The bookmobile, a traveling library service, originated here in 1905. The community pioneered in the use of closed-circuit television in the schools. An active, large, and well-patronized farmers' market for local produce is advantageous for both agriculturalists and city dwellers and provides yet another link between them.

The area was a sparsely settled wilderness in 1737 when Jonathan Hager, a Westphalian German, arrived and patented several tracts of land. Here he built a house with an arched stone cellar over a natural spring. "Capt. Hager," writes a historian, "was frequently assailed by the savages, and his family found the cellar a most useful asylum." Gradually other settlers arrived, many of them Germans or of German descent, and in 1762 Hager laid out a town on his land. He named it "Elizabeth Town" after his wife, but it was popularly termed "Hager's Town." Eventually custom prevailed and in 1813 the name was changed officially. Within a decade of its founding, the city contained a hundred dwellings and was an important trading point.

When Washington County, formerly part of Frederick County, was erected in 1776, Hagerstown was named the county seat. The increase in population of the area, which led to the separate establishment of the county, stimulated the growth of the town as merchants and craftsmen came to manufacture and sell goods needed by the settlers. The rigors of frontier life did not daunt the spirit of these early pioneers, as is evidenced by the names they chose when patenting tracts of land. Among the farms of Hager's neighbors were "Love in a Village," "The Widow's Last

Shift," "All That's Left," "Scared from Home," "Near the Navel," and "I Am Glad It Is No Worse." Amusements were often boisterous, and sometimes cruel, especially cockfighting and bullbaiting. Trials of strength were popular, and at one time almost everyone played "Long Bullet," a competitive sport which involved hurling an iron shot weighing about five pounds. Players, absorbed in the game and often under the influence of the liquid produced in the distilleries that were a fixture of all well-equipped farms, had little regard for whatever or whoever happened to be in the line of fire. The sport was so dangerous that it was eventually prohibited by legislative act. The best-attended form of entertainment was the public execution. Hangings, open to all free of charge and considered a powerful improving force upon the morals of the people, were accompanied by blood-curdling, soul-searing sermons delivered from the gallows by impassioned preachers of the hellfire-and-brimstone school.

In 1795, a young printer from Pennsylvania, John Gruber, came to Hagerstown to establish a German-language newspaper. The *Washington Spy,* an English-language paper, had flourished in the town since 1790. As part of his printing business, Gruber in 1797 published the first issue of the *Hagers-Town Town and Country Almanack,* in German. The *Almanack* has been published every year since, and currently has a circulation of about 225,000 copies. An English edition of the *Almanack* was added in 1822, but the German edition was not discontinued until 1918. The style and general format of the almanac has changed little over the years. Replicas of Gruber's original woodcuts are still used for illustration; there is always a "Large Multiplication Table" and a rhyme, started by Gruber, listing the presidents of the United States. Its "conjectures of the weather," which have proved about 60 percent accurate, have been consulted by generations of farmers.

By 1814, the population of Hagerstown had reached about 2,500. Articles manufactured in the town at the time included cards and brushes for making wool cloth, shoes, hats, nails, rope, linseed oil and flour, guns, and whiskey-distilling equipment. One prominent citizen of the town was Nathaniel Rochester, who was involved in several of these enterprises and who helped to form the town's first bank. In 1810, he moved to upstate New York, where the city of Rochester was named for him.

Following the first settlement in Washington County, the population of the area grew, both through natural increase and by internal migration. The waves of new Americans who arrived from Europe in the nineteenth century usually remained in the large Atlantic ports of entry or went through Hagerstown or other settlements to the virgin lands farther west. Still, the town steadily prospered because of the thriving agricultural economy of the region, even though it remained an unsophisticated village compared to the rapidly developing cities on the seaboard. One traveler, Mrs. Anne Royall, reported in 1827 that "Hagerstown is principally settled by Germans and their descendants, and, of course, retains many of their customs. The women are short and ill-shaped and have a vacancy of countenance which too evidently shows the want of proper schools." In 1829, Mrs.

Royall's habit of waspish commentary resulted in her being tried and convicted in a Washington, D.C., court on the charge of being a common scold.

In the late 1850s, a strange and arresting figure appeared on the streets of Hagerstown. Tall and gaunt, with a fanatically intense stare, "I. Smith" bought provisions and farming implements for a tract of land he had rented nearby and concluded his transactions with a prayer. Gossips whispered that "Smith" had an uncanny power over animals. A year later, hundreds of Hagerstown people crossed the Potomac River to Charles Town to watch this strange man, now known as John Brown, walk with his fixed, brilliant eyes to the scaffold after his raid on Harpers Ferry.

The small farmers in the Hagerstown district owned few slaves and in 1861 local sentiment generally opposed secession. The first year of the war brought an economic boom to the area because of the demand for foodstuffs. As the war continued, the city was frequently imperiled because of its location near the border of the Confederacy. Both Southern and Northern armies often occupied the town, disrupting its commerce. The bloody Battle of Antietam (Sharpsburg) on September 17, 1862, took place just south of the city. Many of the wounded, including the younger Oliver Wendell Holmes, were hospitalized in Hagerstown. In July, 1864, Gen. John McCausland arrived with 1,500 Confederate troops, threatening to burn the city unless he received a ransom of $20,000 in cash and a large amount of clothing. The money and enough of the clothing were raised to satisfy McCausland, who soon rode away to join the main body of Gen. Jubal Early's force for his march toward Washington, D.C.

At the close of the Civil War, both Hagerstown and the surrounding countryside were impoverished, but business soon revived, especially after completion in 1867 of the spur connecting Hagerstown to the main line of the Baltimore & Ohio Railroad. In 1872, the first train of the Western Maryland Railroad reached Hagerstown from Baltimore, cutting still further the traveling time and hauling distance to the port of Baltimore. As the line was extended west, the officials of the Western Maryland Railroad made the city a division point and established offices here. Rail transportation to the South was developed by 1880 over the Shenandoah Valley Railroad. These railroads were vital to the economic growth of Hagerstown in the era of rapid industrialization that began after the Civil War.

In 1880, Mathias Peter Möller (1855–1937) opened a factory in Hagerstown for the manufacture of pipe organs. Emigrating from Denmark in 1872, Möller had constructed an organ for the Philadelphia Centennial Exposition of 1876. He developed a new kind of wind chest that improved the tonal quality of the instrument. Möller's experimental work and his philanthropic activities won him wide recognition, and in 1926, his native Denmark made him a Knight of the Ancient Order of Dannebrog. The M. P. Möller Organ Works, greatly expanded from its original plant and still operated by Möller's descendants, is today one of the world's largest pipe organ builders. Thousands of organs constructed here are now in use in churches, halls, schools, undertakers' chapels, and homes all over the world.

In an effort to stimulate economic growth, as early as 1905 Hagerstown officials offered tax concessions to industries willing to build plants in the area. The initiative and skills of the town's natives also aided its development. In the early 1920s two local men still in their teens, Lewis and Henry Reisner, began experimenting with aircraft, constructing new designs in an old shack in back of their house on Salem Avenue. They expanded their work in 1926, with financial assistance from their father and a new partner, Ammon Kreider. Soon they had a completely equipped shop for servicing planes. The first airplane built in the new shop was a low-winged racer, with which they won the air meet at the Philadelphia Susquicentennial celebration. The firm, organized as the Kreider-Reisner Airplane Company, opened a larger plant in 1928. After the death of Ammon Kreider at the Detroit Air Meet in 1929, the company was sold to the Fairchild Corporation, which expanded the plant and built the famous "Flying Boxcars" here during World War II. Electronic components for space vehicles as well as aircraft and helicopters are now produced at the plant. Hagerstown also has a manufacturer of blast-cleaning and dust-collecting equipment, which, with the increasing efforts to control air pollution, is a future source of growth and diversification.

The cultural activity in Hagerstown is unusual for a city of its size. The community supports a small but excellent art museum, and its large new library building was constructed with funds raised exclusively by voluntary gifts and subscriptions. An annual concert series is well patronized and a local dramatic group presents live theater. Other important facets of community life are the churches and the numerous fraternal and civic clubs. These and other organizations participate in the Mummers' Parade on Halloween. Originally intended to divert youngsters from pranks, the parade has developed into an evening spectacle with elaborate floats and costumes. Other popular annual events include Fair Week, when the best examples of local animals, crafts, and agricultural products are exhibited, and the horse races, with pari-mutuel betting, held for two weeks each year at Hagerstown's 5/8-mile track.

HAGERSTOWN TOUR

Zion Reformed Church (1), Potomac and Church streets, was built in 1774 as the German Reformed Church; successive alterations have greatly changed its appearance. While dressing logs for the church, Jonathan Hager, founder of Hagerstown, was accidentally killed at his sawmill. The present gray limestone building has tall narrow windows and a square tower with an open belfry. One day during the Civil War, Gen. George Custer climbed the bell tower to take observations. Realizing that he had become a mark for sharpshooters, Custer abandoned his position with more haste than dignity. In the graveyard back of the church are buried Jonathan Hager (1719–75); John Gruber (1768–1857), founder of The *Hagers-Town Town and Country Almanack;* and Peter Humrichhouse, who, by his timely dash from Philadelphia, supplied Washington's troops with much-needed ammunition for the siege of Yorktown.

In the **Park** (2), on the corner of Potomac Street and North Avenue, stands a weathered bronze cannon made for the army of Louis XV in 1757 at Douai, France, by Beranger, the leading French ordnance manu-

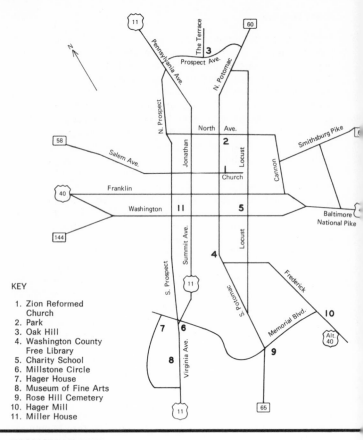

KEY

1. Zion Reformed Church
2. Park
3. Oak Hill
4. Washington County Free Library
5. Charity School
6. Millstone Circle
7. Hager House
8. Museum of Fine Arts
9. Rose Hill Cemetery
10. Hager Mill
11. Miller House

HAGERSTOWN TOUR

facturer. Used by Napoleon's forces during the Peninsular War, the cannon was later captured by the Spanish at Cordova, and eventually sent to Fort Morro, Cuba. After American forces captured this stronghold during the Battle of Santiago (1898), the cannon was presented to Hagerstown, in recognition of the fact that Washington County supplied more volunteers for service than any other county in the state. Near the cannon is a pyramid of cannonballs, manufactured to replace the originals carried off by souvenir collectors before the wire net was installed to protect them.

Oak Hill (3) (private), 921 The Terrace, a rambling three-story frame house in the ornate Victorian-Gothic style, was the home of William T. Hamilton, a former governor of Maryland (1880–84). It is said that he always consulted the *Hagers-Town Town and Country Almanack* before setting a date for public executions, in an effort to insure fair weather for such a popular event.

Embedded in the driveway is the old slave block that formerly stood at the Antietam Street entrance to the Hotel Hamilton. Planters bid for slaves exhibited on the block, and politicians sought support of the electorate from the same stone. Both Andrew Jackson and Henry Clay spoke from the slave block in 1830.

From The Terrace, return to Potomac Street.

The **Washington County Free Library** (4), 100 S. Potomac Street, is a modern glass, concrete, and white stone structure with predominating horizontal lines. The library was founded in 1901 through the efforts of a clergyman, a banker, a papermaker, two lawyers, a farmer, and a

Hagerstown Park

storekeeper. The sound and progressive development of the institution was largely due to the dedication of the first librarian, Mary L. Titcomb, who devoted half a lifetime to the library and its services. One of the first county libraries in the country and antedating the Carnegie program, it opened in an area where there was only one small private high school, where bookstores were unknown, and where reading was regarded as the privilege of the idle and the rich. The library was an immediate success, as is evident from the enthusiastic comments of two of its first patrons. A country woman, her first book wrapped in a starched apron, remarked as she left the building: "It's a great day when poor folks like us can take home such handsome books." And a rural boy, who happened to select one of Shakespeare's plays on the opening day, returned it with the request: "Give me another by that same man; I think he's a right good writer."

The library sought to provide services to outlying districts, at first by placing cases of books in general stores, schools, and private homes. After a few years, Miss Titcomb established the first "bookmobile": a two-horse wagon equipped with bookshelves. The bookmobile and its successors have regularly visited even the most remote county districts except for a temporary interruption in 1912 when the library truck stalled on a railroad track and was destroyed by a train. The idea spread rapidly, and bookmobiles are now a familiar institution all over the country and in many foreign lands.

The library, with its six permanent branches, houses more than 200,-000 volumes, including a special local history collection. Library services include summer programs, children's programs, films, a reading club, and orientation tours arranged through the local school system.

At the corner of Potomac and Baltimore streets, turn left and walk to Locust Street. Proceed up Locust Street to Washington Street.

The building on the corner of Washington and Locust streets is a two-story brick structure erected in 1842. The **Charity School** (5) was established in 1815 by a group of young women as a free school for poor children. Formally incorporated in 1818, the institution educated thousands of young people until free schools were established by the state government. In 1907 the school became the Hagerstown Day Nursery and Kindergarten, providing nursing care and kindergarten instruction for preschool-age children whose mothers were employed.

At the corner of Locust and Washington streets, turn left. Proceed to Prospect Street and turn left.

Millstone Circle (6), the junction of Prospect Street, Summit Avenue, and Memorial Boulevard at the entrance to the City Park, is named for the historic stones set into the sidewalk around it. Some of these millstones, removed from old water-powered grist mills throughout Washington County, date back to the eighteenth century. The millstones are of two types: those cut from a single piece of stone, and segmented stones held together with an iron band.

The **Hager House** (7) (open May–Oct., Tues.–Sat., 10–12 and 2–4; Sun., 2–5; closed Mon.), in the north end of the City Park, is an extensively restored 2½-story gray stone building. The house, built by the founder of Hagerstown, is typical of prosperous early settlers' homes in the area. Many household objects of the late eighteenth and early nineteenth centuries were discovered in the excavations during the restoration of the house. These, with other period furnishings, are on display in the interior.

The Museum of Fine Arts (8) in the City Park on S. Prospect Street is a handsome, classically simple brick building facing the lake. It houses a varied collection of over 3,000 objects and an excellent art library. Opened in 1931, the museum was given to the community by Anna Brugh Singer, a former resident of Hagerstown and wife of the American painter William H. Singer, Jr. Works by Benjamin West, Veronese, Rodin, Titian, Rembrandt, Viti, LeNain, Thomas Moran, and other noted artists have been exhibited here. There are special exhibits and activities each month (open Tues.–Sat., 10–5; Sun., 1–6).

From *Millstone Circle,* take Memorial Boulevard to **Rose Hill Cemetery** (9), S. Potomac Street. Near the entrance is Washington Cemetery, where 2,468 Confederate soldiers killed in the battles of Antietam and South Mountain are buried. The bodies, over 2,000 of which are unidentified, were reinterred here after removal from rough battlefield graves. The speaker at the original dedication shortly after the Civil War was Maj. Gen. Fitzhugh Lee, C.S.A., and when the cemetery was rededicated in 1961, those assembled were addressed by former President Dwight D. Eisenhower. Standing among the graves is a marble figure representing Hope leaning on an anchor.

In the southeastern part of the cemetery is the **Kennedy Monument,** a gray granite shaft erected in 1918 by Jewish citizens to honor Thomas Kennedy. Kennedy spent years fighting for the legislation that granted Jews full civil rights in the state, finally achieving his goal in 1826. Hagerstown lawyer, merchant, and poet of Scottish birth, Kennedy is buried near the monument.

Continue on Memorial Boulevard to the **Hager Mill** (10), at the rear of Hager Park on Frederick Street. The mill is a three-story stone structure built about 1790 by the brother of the town's founder. Now used as a furniture warehouse, the building looks much as it did in the early days. The water wheel, preserved until the 1950s, had to be dismantled as a safety hazard after a caretaker damaged its structure by removing part of it for firewood.

Turn left on Frederick Street to Locust Street, then right on Locust to Franklin Street. Turn left on Franklin to Prospect Street. Turn left off Prospect and walk one block to Washington Street. Turn left and proceed down Washington Street.

The **Miller House** (11), 135 W. Washington Street, a restored Federal period town house, houses the Washington County Historical Society. On display are dolls, antique clocks, and items of historical interest (open year-round Tues.–Sun., 1–4).

SALISBURY

SALISBURY (23′ alt., 15,252 pop.) is an industrial and shipping point at the head of the Wicomico River and has been the county seat since Wicomico County was erected from Somerset and Worcester counties in 1867. The town until then lay in both of the older jurisdictions, Division Street being the boundary. Salisbury was founded in 1732, but fires in 1860 and 1886 destroyed all the material reminders of earlier history, and within the town limits only one pre-Victorian house remains; most buildings belong to the twentieth century. Main Street, with its eight-story hotel, metal facades, and neon signs, is in spirit and appearance the main street of any modern small city.

Since 1930 the population of the city and its immediate environs has more than doubled. Even during the depression years the town prospered, and it is now the major commercial center of the Lower Eastern Shore. Its central location on the Delmarva Peninsula only partly accounts for its growth. Salisbury promotes itself; for instance, it sponsors the Delmarva Chicken Festival, which receives state and even nationwide publicity for chicken recipe contests with $1,000 prizes.

Most industries in and near Salisbury depend on local agriculture. Wicomico County produced $30,801,000 worth of poultry and poultry products in 1969. By 1975, over 2,200 people were employed in industries that process poultry and poultry products in Salisbury. Packing and marketing of vegetables and fruits are of equal importance. In 1975 two plants in Salisbury supplied ice for refrigeration of fresh vegetables, and packers in the city employed over 700 people, depending on the season. Lumber mills in the county manufacture barrels and crates for farm produce as well as construction woodwork sawed from the timber of peninsular forests. Fertilizer and feed plants supply poultry and truck farms over a large area. In addition, light industries take advantage of local labor willing to work for a minimum wage. Over 1,200 people were employed in six clothing factories during 1975, of which the largest was a nationally known shirt company. Over 500 more persons worked for a pump company.

Eleven truck lines, three with terminal facilities in Salisbury, and the Penn-Central Railroad supply transportation, and the city is a distribution point for oil, gasoline, and coal that small freighters and barges bring up the Wicomico River. There is also an airport that is owned and maintained by Wicomico County and the City of Salisbury.

Equally important to the city is its role as a shopping center that draws customers from three states. This form of commercial growth began to slow down in Salisbury during the 1950s, and in 1956 the community paid $35,000 for an economic survey to find a cure. Among the study's many recommendations was redevelopment of the central business district. A twenty-year, federally assisted project is now being planned to widen streets in order to provide parking, landscape the now blighted river front, and otherwise revitalize the downtown area, which from 1956 to 1961 showed no increase in business income. Today Salisbury has one of the best downtown malls in the East. The opening of the bridge-tunnel at the mouth of the Chesapeake Bay, which has made U.S. 13 a major north-south interstate route, may or may not assist the downtown, although it will surely provide a general economic lift to the area. The study also recommended drastic political reorganization. Salisbury has been governed by a mayor and council since 1888, but its suburbs have developed so rapidly in recent years that the county government must participate increasingly in making plans and administering services. As in other growing urban areas, more integrated political organization is recognized as essential to orderly growth.

Two state-operated hospitals, a large private general hospital, nursing home and convalescent home facilities, and a large concentration of practicing physicians make Salisbury the medical center of the Lower Peninsula. The city is also known for its many churches. In 1969, there were forty churches in Salisbury, most of which are of Protestant denominations. One of four state colleges is located here, as well as the county library, two newspapers (one a daily), four radio stations, and two TV stations. There is a small zoo in the Municipal Park.

The General Assembly authorized the laying out of Salisbury Town at Handy's Landing in 1732. Fifteen acres of Pemberton's Good-Will were purchased from William Winder and twenty lots laid out, but the "well-bound book" in which the assembly had ordered the proceedings to be kept has been lost, and thus we have no records to tell us how many there were of original "takers-up" of lots. Several travel routes along the peninsula converged at Salisbury, and a survey of 1817 shows three taverns. In these early days, the Salisbury street fair held at Whitsuntide attracted the whole countryside. Baltimore merchants brought goods to sell, and dancing bears and trained monkeys provided an exotic note. Improved transportation eventually made it possible for Salisbury merchants to stock the goods formerly brought here only once a year at fair time, and the importance of the fair declined.

During the nineteenth century, the town's growth was steady but not rapid. Before the Civil War the river was the main commercial highway. Although by mid-century it had ceased to be navigable to Salisbury proper, the development of steam navigation was a help nevertheless. In 1852, the *Wilson Small* began running twice a week between Baltimore and the "Cotton Patch," a landing two miles below Salisbury. At each high tide after the arrival of the steamer the river between the town and the patch would be full of flat-bottomed scows taxiing cargo; at low tide a loaded scow could not maneuver. In the 1890s, with the help of the federal government, a channel was dredged to the town landing. By 1906 additional dredging had created a small harbor.

Although these efforts have made Salisbury into a port, its prosperity has been dependent on railroad and motor highways, not waterways. If the Eastern Shore Railroad, killed by the Panic of 1837, had been built, Salisbury would likely have stayed a village, and Sharptown and Nanticoke on the Nanticoke River, where railroad stops were planned, would have become the centers of commerce for the Lower Shore. When in 1858 a railroad through Delaware reached the state line at what is now Delmar, Salisbury businessmen were leaders in the project to continue the line to Crisfield and Pocomoke City. Before the Civil War put a stop to construction, the road had reached East Salisbury, and the town immediately became a center for freight and passenger traffic. The introduction of refrigerator-car service in 1901 was a great stimulus to the development of Peninsula truck crops, and Salisbury became a chief mart for the auctioning and shipping of fresh produce.

The city's rapid advance since World War I has been the result, not of railroads, but of highways and motor vehicles. As farmers began to own cars, they started to drive to Salisbury to buy supplies they had formerly ordered from mail-order houses or bought in the crossroads stores. Trade in consumer goods became big business, and Salisbury businessmen have made the most of it. The city now derives trade from the whole peninsula.

Although the town is modern in appearance and outlook, it has its legends and has played its role in history. The marshes and creeks of the Lower Shore were Tory havens during the Revolution. Tories and riffraff masking as Tories made piratical raids on plantations along the river. By January of 1777, citizens were petitioning the Continental Congress for military forces to foil supposed Tory designs, and Gen. William Smallwood (*see* Tours 25a and 31) took a company of militia to Salisbury and Princess Anne in February. A legendary Tory pirate was Ben Allen, an illiterate giant of great strength and recklessness who lived in a cave in what is now the Municipal Park and eventually died before a firing squad. Bones of a giant dug up a century later, when excavations were being dug for St. Peter's Episcopal Church, are believed to be his. Salisbury's Revolutionary hero is Alexander Roxburgh, a Scot who served with General Smallwood, who was promoted to captain for conspicuous gallantry in the Battle of Long Island and ended the war as a major. After the war he eloped with Frances Handy, granddaughter of Col. Isaac Handy of Pemberton Hall (*see* Tour 12c) and a half-sister of William Stone (1779–1838), later Protestant Episcopal bishop of Maryland.

During the Civil War, Union soldiers—Maryland and Delaware volunteers—were stationed in the town, which was a central point from which to suppress Confederate activities in divided Delaware and the secessionist Eastern Shore of Virginia, as well as Maryland shore counties. The soldiers made occasional forays through the peninsula, disarming secessionists, but there was no actual fighting. At elections, troops were posted at the polls to "preserve order," but the accusation that their presence was intended to keep Democrats away from the polls may have some foundation.

SALISBURY TOUR

Poplar Hill Mansion (1), in the northern part of town, at 117 Elizabeth Street one block west of Division Street, is an attractive frame house built in 1795 for Maj. Levin Handy. The builder failed to center the

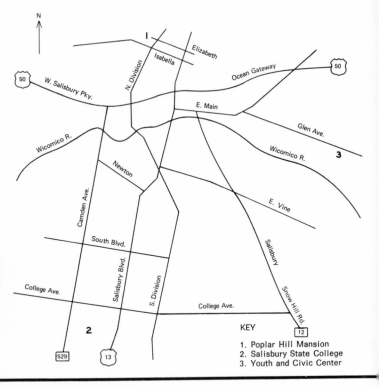

SALISBURY TOUR

doorway and the Palladian window above it, but the joiner who decorated the interior was a master of woodcarving in the Adam style. The house is undergoing restoration and is not open to the public.

Salisbury State College (2), in the southern part of town between U.S. 13 and Md. 529 at College Avenue, occupies an imposing building of Georgian-Colonial design that was finished in 1932. The college started as a two-year state normal school in 1925. It now offers a two-year junior college course and a four-year course that includes two years of intensive teacher training and leads to the degree of Bachelor of Science.

In one wing of Holloway Hall is the **Wildfowl Museum.** Made possible by the Ward Foundation, the museum opened in April, 1976. The foundation is named in honor of Lem and Steve Ward of Crisfield, two of the best-known carvers in the country. By purchase and loan, the museum has established a collection valued at more than $100,000, ranging from simple duck decoys to elaborate prairie falcons and doves. Salisbury hosts an annual wildfowl carving competition each spring.

The **Youth and Civic Center** (3), on Glen Avenue (which branches off Main Street east of its intersections with U.S. 13 and Md. 12), was constructed in 1959 as a War Memorial. Each year the National Indoor Tennis Tournament is held here.

INDEX

The Johns Hopkins University Press

This book was composed in Linotype Permanent text and Prisma display type by the Maryland Linotype Composition Co., Inc., from a design by Susan Bishop. It was printed on Warren 50-lb. Olde Style paper and bound in Joanna Arrestox cloth by Universal Lithographers, Inc.

Library of Congress Cataloging in Publication Data
Main entry under title:
Maryland: a new guide to the Old Line State.

 (Studies in Maryland history and culture)
 Based on the 1940 ed. of Maryland, a guide to the Old Line State, compiled
by the Writers' Program of the Work Projects Administration in the State of
Maryland.
 Includes index.
 1. Maryland—Description and travel—1951- —Tours. I. Papenfuse, Ed-
ward C. II. Writers' Program. Maryland. Maryland, a guide to the Old Line
State. III. Series.
F179.3.M37   917.52′04′4   76-17224
ISBN 0-8018-1874-5
ISBN 0-8018-1871-0 pbk.